slow wine

A YEAR IN THE LIFE OF ITALY'S VINEYARDS AND WINES

Slow Food®Editore

slow wine 2013
A YEAR IN THE LIFE OF ITALY'S VINEYARDS AND WINES

Editors: Giancarlo Gariglio, Fabio Giavedoni

Assistant editors: Paolo Camozzi, Dario Ferro, Jonathan Gebser, Davide Panzieri, Fabio Pracchia

Chief contributors: Francesco Abate, Davide Acerra, Duccio Armenio, Vittorio Barbieri, Alessia Benini, Francesca Bidasio degli Imberti, Gian Paolo Ciancabilla, Sara Contu, Alessandra Etzo, Andrea Fontana, Stefano Ferrari, Fausto Ferroni, Karin Huber, Vito Lacerenza, Maria Grazia Melegari, Francesco Muci, Luciano Pignataro, Mario Plazio, Max Plett, Francesco Quercetti, Diego Soracco, Fabio Turchetti, Simone Zoli

Contributors: Marina Alaimo, Andrea Aldrighetti, Alberto Alfano, Licia Altilia, Paolo Ambrosoni, Maurizio Amoroso, Francesco Anastasi, Adriano Anglani, Tommaso Aronov, Stefano Asaro, Marie Eve Asselin, Artemio Assiri, Cecilia Auxilia, Bruno Bacci, Emidio Bachetti, Antonio Balassone, Alessandro Barletta, Simone Baroni, Gabriele Bartalena, Mario Basco, Salvatore Basta, Paolo Battimelli, Richard Baudains, Claudia Beccato, Marco Bechi, Annarita Beltrame, Nino Bentivegna, Anna Berghella, Lorenzo Berlendis, Maurizio Bertolo, Riccardo Binda, Margherita Bisoglio, Carla Bocchio, Federica Bolla, Giulia Bonetti, Francesco Bonini, Matteo Bonvicini, Valerio Borgianelli Spina, Nicola Bove, Marco Braganti, Filippo Bregonzo, Massimo Brucato, Ilaria Bruzzesi, Michela Bunino, Sara Cabrele, Marco Cagnetta, Marco Callegari, Mara Campo, Alberto Capasso, Tommaso Caporale, Giorgio Cariaggi, Pasquale Carlo, Giulio Carli, Sara Carnati, Daniele Castronovo, Carlo Catani, Paolo Cesarini, Felix Chamorro, Roberto Checchetto, Valter Chiabolotti, Marco Cipolla, Graziano Cipriano, Carlo Cleri, Maria Cobo, Pierluigi Cocchini, Enzo Codogno, Filippo Colombo, Lorenzo Colombo, Francesco Costa, Tonia Credentino, Corinne Cremonini, Giovanni Cucchiara, Barbara D'Agapiti, Mario D'Alesio, Anna Dall'Ara, Silvana Dal Maso, Silvia Dal Molin, Savio Del Bianco, Marco Dell'Era, Annamaria D'Eusanio, Massimo Di Cintio, Gianni Di Mattia, Serena Di Nucci, Giulio Di Sabato, Anete Dinne, Sonia Donati, Florian Ehn, Peter Engelmayer, Alberto Farinasso, Luigi Fenoglio, Lapo Ferrini, Piero Fiorentini, Alessandro Foggi, Fabio Fusina, Andrea Gaggero, Marcello Gallotti, Sonia Gambini, Valerie Ganio Vecchiolino, Pietro Garibbo, Roberto Gazzola, Francesco Ghiglione, Marianna Giancola, Mariasole Giannelli, Federico Giovannone, Francesca Gori, Danilo Gramegna, Paolo Granchi, Renato Grando, Davide Grimaldi, Matteo Guidorizzi, Shota Hayashi, Kelly Hau, Günther Hölzl, Sandra Ianni, Marcello Ingrassia, Chiara Ingui, Francesco Paolo Lauriola, Gianpiero Laviano, Francesca Litta, Cristiana Locci, Pierangelo Lodolo, Lorenzo Maini, Carmelo Maiorca, Michele Marangio, Filippo Marchi, Matteo Marenghi, Sara Marte, Franco Martino, Mino Martucci, Mirco Masera, Daniele Massa, Patrizio Mastrocola, Giulia Mattalia, Silvano Mattedi, Lorenzo Marziali, Giacomo Mazzavillani, Tommaso Mazzocca, Paolo Mazzola, Ermanno Mecozzi, Marco Meistro, Lanfranco Meritotti, Teresa Mincione, Marco Minetto, Andrea Monico, Andrea Montanari, Doris Moser, Monica Mostino, Franco Motta, Gaia Muci,

Pierfrancesco Multari, Nicola Nebbia, Nicole Nigro, Giovanni Norese, Gabriel Olivieri, Carmen Ordiz, Elisa Padoin, Edoardo Paggi, Maria Josè Parra, Daniele Parri, Elena Pasero, Carlotta Passuello, Giovanni Pastorino, Gaspare Pellecchia, Marco Peluso, Gianluca Pepe, Anna Perini, Peppino Placentino, Giorgio Picco, Adriana Pieroni, Myriam Pinkas, Alessandra Piubello, Ivan Pizzoni, Giuseppe Pollio, Pier Paolo Porcu, Antonio Previdi, Salvatore Pulimeno, Paolo Ricci, Sara Rigamonti, Lara Rocchietti, Giancarlo Rolandi, Claudio Romano, Francesco Rossi, Andrea Russo, Susan Russo, Giancarlo Russo, Anna Sacchetto, Alice Saglia, Luisa Sala, Alessandra Saponara, Flora Saponari, Maria Teresa Scarpato, Marco Schiavello, Isabelle Schoebi, Gregorio Sergi, Eugenio Signoroni, Maurizio Silvestri, Francesca Solarino, Riccardo Soncini, Benedetto Squicciarini, Maurizio Stagnitto, Enrico Tacchi, Riccardo Taliano, Giada Talpo, Valentina Tamborini, Salvatore Taronno, Camilla Tomao, Stefano Tonanni, Lello Tornatore, Oto Tortorella, Franco Utili, Andrea Vannelli, Federico Varazi, Laura Vescul, Riccardo Vendrame, Irene Vianello, Teodoro Viola, Alessandra Virno, Luisa Vismara, Massimo Volpari, Andrea Zucchetti, Chiara Zucchetti

Italian editing: Antonio Attorre, Clarissa Monnati

Translation editor: John Irving

Art director: Fabio Cremonesi

Information sistems, automation and graphics: Maurizio Burdese

Maps: Touring Editore

Printed November 2012
by G. Canale & C. S.p.A., Borgaro Torinese (Turin) ITALY

Slow Food® Editore srl © 2012
All rights reserved under copyright law

Slow Food® Editore srl
Via della Mendicità Istruita, 14 - 12042 Bra (Cn)
Tel. 0172 419611 - Fax 0172 411218

Website: www.slowine.it - www.slowfood.it

Editor in chief: Marco Bolasco

Managing editors: Olivia Reviglio

ISBN 978-888499-324-3

SWITZERLAND

AUSTRIA

SLOVENIA

FRANCE

AOSTA VALLEY

PIEDMONT

LOMBARDY

ALTO ADIGE

TRENTINO

FRIULI VENEZIA GIULIA

VENETO

LIGURIA

EMILIA-ROMAGNA

TUSCANY

MARCHE

UMBRIA

LAZIO

ABRUZZO

MOLISE

SARDINIA

CAMPANIA

PUGLIA

BASILICATA

CALABRIA

SICILY

Contents

Introduction

The English-language edition of Slow Wine, now in its second year, is richer than ever. Ours is more than a wine guide; it's a a project that addresses new challenges and embraces different concepts. Recent climate changes, for example, are certainly affecting wine. August 2011, which came to an end with scorching "African" heat, left its mark. The white wines of Central and Northern Italy are over-alcoholic and largely devoid of their usual suite of aromas, all of which prevents them from realizing their true potential. Barbaresco 2009 and Brunello di Montalcino 2007 also suffered the "crazy" temperatures, thus demonstrating that heat and drought aren't good for the nebbiolo and sangiovese grapes. In the years to come it will be possible to investigate the consequences of global warming on wine. In the meantime, in the pages that follow, we explain how agronomists and winemakers are preparing the right countermeasures, experimenting new techniques with good old-fashioned common sense and wisdom.

Slow Wine is the only guide to set aside so much space for the leading actors in Italian wine, viewed and profiled in their roles as wine men and women. More than 200 collaborators travelled the length and breadth of Italy to review the 1,909 wineries in the Italian guide, and the 400 in the English-language edition (the editors' selection of the best wineries for Slow Food) that you will find in these pages. It was a gigantic effort that required more than 8,000 hours of work. We believe that effort was crucially important. Visiting the wineries in person before expressing an opinion is, we think, a gesture of honesty towards our readers.

Now, two years on, we have decided to define the meaning and substance of the Snail and Slow Wine recognitions more clearly. Which is why they have both been supplemented by a concept very dear to us: namely, value for money. With the 2013 edition, a Slow Wine is not only good, it is also fruit of attentive, sustainable agriculture, anchored to its terroir and reasonably priced in relation to when and how it was produced.

In an effort to be innovative and keep in step with the times, the guide has thus undergone changes and set itself new objectives. Our beacon continues to be the philosophy of "good, clean and fair" and helping to make Italian viticulture more sustainable from an environmental point of view continues to be one of our goals. The adoption of natural practices among the vine rows and in the vineyard is increasingly a criterion that influences our choice when we buy wine. We are thus proud to acknowledge this widely felt new demand, which makes Slow Wine all the more a benchmark for the most attentive, informed and conscious enthusiasts.

Giancarlo Gariglio and Fabio Giavedoni
Editors, Slow Wine 2012

How to read the guide

Winery:

 snail

symbol awarded to a winery that we particularly like for the way it interprets Slow Food values (sensory perceptions, territory, environment, identity) and also offers good value for money.

▌ bottle

symbol awarded to wineries whose bottles presented excellent average quality at our tastings.

€ coin

symbol awarded to wineries whose bottles are good value for money.

Wines:

slow wine SLOW WINE

bottles of outstanding sensory quality, capable of condensing in the glass territory-related values such as history and identity, as well as offering good value for money.

Great Wine

the finest bottles from the sensory point of view.

Everyday Wine

bottles that offer excellent value for money with a retail price of €10 or under.

Promotion:

10% discount

this symbol denotes wineries that offer a 10% discount on purchases to customers who present a copy of Slow Wine 2013. The promotion is valid for one year from January 2013 to January 2014.

Editing was completed on November 20 2012.

ha
hectares of land, owned or leased, managed and cultivated directly
by the winery.

bt
total number of bottles produced by the winery.

○ white wine

◉ rosé wine

● red wine

General abbreviations:
Cl. ....Classico (Classic)
Et. ....Etichetta (Label)
M. ....Method
　　　　　(e.g., M. Cl. = Metodo Classico/Classic Method)
P.R. ....Peduncolo Rosso (Red Bunchstem)
Rip. ....Ripasso
Ris. ....Riserva (Reserve)
Sel. ....Selezione (Selection)
Sup. ......Superiore (Superior)
V.T. ....Vendemmia Tardiva (Late Harvest)

Geographical abbreviations
(names of DOCs and DOCGs):
A.A. ....Alto Adige
C.B. ....Colli Bolognesi
COF ....Colli Orientali del Friuli
C.P. ....Colli Piacentini
O.P. ....Oltrepò Pavese

FERTILIZERS
PLANT PROTECTION
WEED CONTROL
YEASTS
GRAPES
CERTIFICATION

The data in the box on viticultural and enological practices were
supplied directly by the wineries during our visits.

Glossary

FERTILIZERS

Organic-minerals
Obtained from the blending or reaction of one or more organic fertilizers with one or more parts of simple mineral fertilizer or compound, organo-minerals are halfway between organic fertilizers, with respect to which they have more nutritional elements, and mineral fertilizers, with respect to which they are more efficient. Nitrogen and phosphorus must come at least in part from organic fertilizers, while potassium and the remaining parts of nitrogen and phosphorus must derive from the mineral part.

Minerals
Fertilizers obtained from mineral compounds. Most of these products are made by the extractive and chemical industries, hence mineral fertilizers are largely known as chemical fertilizers. Since they do not contain carbon, they are defined by their principal component. Hence, phosphorus, nitrogen, potassium fertilizers and so on.

Manure
Manure is fundamental in any type of agriculture. It is an organic fertilizer which permits improvements to the physical and chemical characteristics of the soil. From the physical point of view, it acts as a soil improver, enriching the mechanical properties of the soil. From the chemical point of view, it provides precious substances for the fertility of the soil. The characteristics of a manure vary according to the animal it comes from.

Compost
Compost is made from the decomposition of a mixture of organic substances, residues from pruning, left-over food, manure and sewage. Fundamental agents are oxygen and the balance between the chemical agents present in the matter as it transforms. The action of micro and macro-organisms takes place in special conditions and tends to form a dark, damp mass of matter that is valuable for agriculture. Its use with the addition of organic substance improves the structure of the soil and the availability of nutritional elements. As an organic activator, compost also improves the biodiversity of micro-flora in the soil.

Biodynamic preparations
Agricultural actions designed to improve the physical and chemical peculiarities of the soil and vegetation in biodynamic vineyard management. There are basically two types of preparation: sprays and composts, both used in precisely defined quantities. The two main sprays are: 500, or horn manure, which develops the humus in the soil, and 501, or horn silica, which aids photosynthesis. Compost preparations are used to enrich the organic substances to be spread over the soil. Compost made with precisely defined vegetable and animal elements is a precious fertilizer.

Green manure
An agronomic practice whereby specific crops are ploughed under the soil to maintain and improve its fertility. Its many results include: increase in the amount of organic matter in the soil; suppression of soil erosion; preservation of the soil's nitrogen component. Especially important are leguminous green manures, which fix atmospheric nitrogen into the soil.

PLANT PROTECTION

Used to protect plants from the attack of parasites and pathogens, to control the development of weeds and ensure high quality standards for agricultural produce. They may be natural or synthetic and may be marketed only in sealed, tamper-proof wrappers or packages with labels authorized by the Italian Health Ministry bearing the name of the commercial formula and trademark, if any. Other compulsory information includes the primary activity or action performed by the active substance, denominated according to ISO classification, on the target (insecticide, fungicide, weed killer) and the type of formulation (dilutable, powder, emulsionable) with which the product is presented.

Chemicals
This group comprises all products made synthetically.

Copper and sulphur
The most common fungicides, copper against downy mildew, sulphur against powdery mildew. Sulphur presents risks of phytotoxicity in young shoots, especially with high summer temperatures. It may interfere with the fermentation process, especially in the case of early-ripening white grapes. The prolonged use of copper determines a sizeable increase in its levels in the soil, creating ecotoxicological problems for the environment.

Organics
Organic substances, such as milk, infusions and tisanes, are used in organic and biodynamic farming. Their action must be coordinated with a series of other interventions, mostly preventive, disciplined by the agricultural management system adopted.

WEED CONTROL

Weed control is an integral part of vineyard soil management and is designed to prevent weeds from entering into competition with the vine and jeopardizing its development. Chemical weeding is carried out with synthetic products which act by contact (on the visible part of the plant), by transfer (systemic products which attack root and plant) or by residual action (over time they prevent the seed from germinating). Although it damages organic substances in the soil, chemical weeding is now becoming simpler and more effective, safer for the plant and more respectful of the environment. Mechanical weeding uses mechanical actions, such as mowing, to remove weeds. This practice ensures total respect for the environment and is part of organic and biodynamic vineyard management.

YEASTS

Yeasts are responsible for fermentation, the process by which sugar in must is transformed into alcohol (ethanol) and carbon dioxide. Yeasts, known as native or wild or ambient yeasts, are to be found in the bloom of the skins of grapes. Improvements in cellar techniques have made it possible to select strains of yeast capable of responding to the special needs of each producer or to aid native yeasts if they encounter obstacles in this delicate and fundamental phase in the vinification process. On the basis of these requirements, each producer may choose to carry on the fermentation with native yeasts, hence only those of his or her own grapes, or with selected yeasts, when fermentation is performed with yeast strains brought in from the outside. Activating yeasts also exist. These are used with particularly lazy musts or in the case of a stuck fermentation.

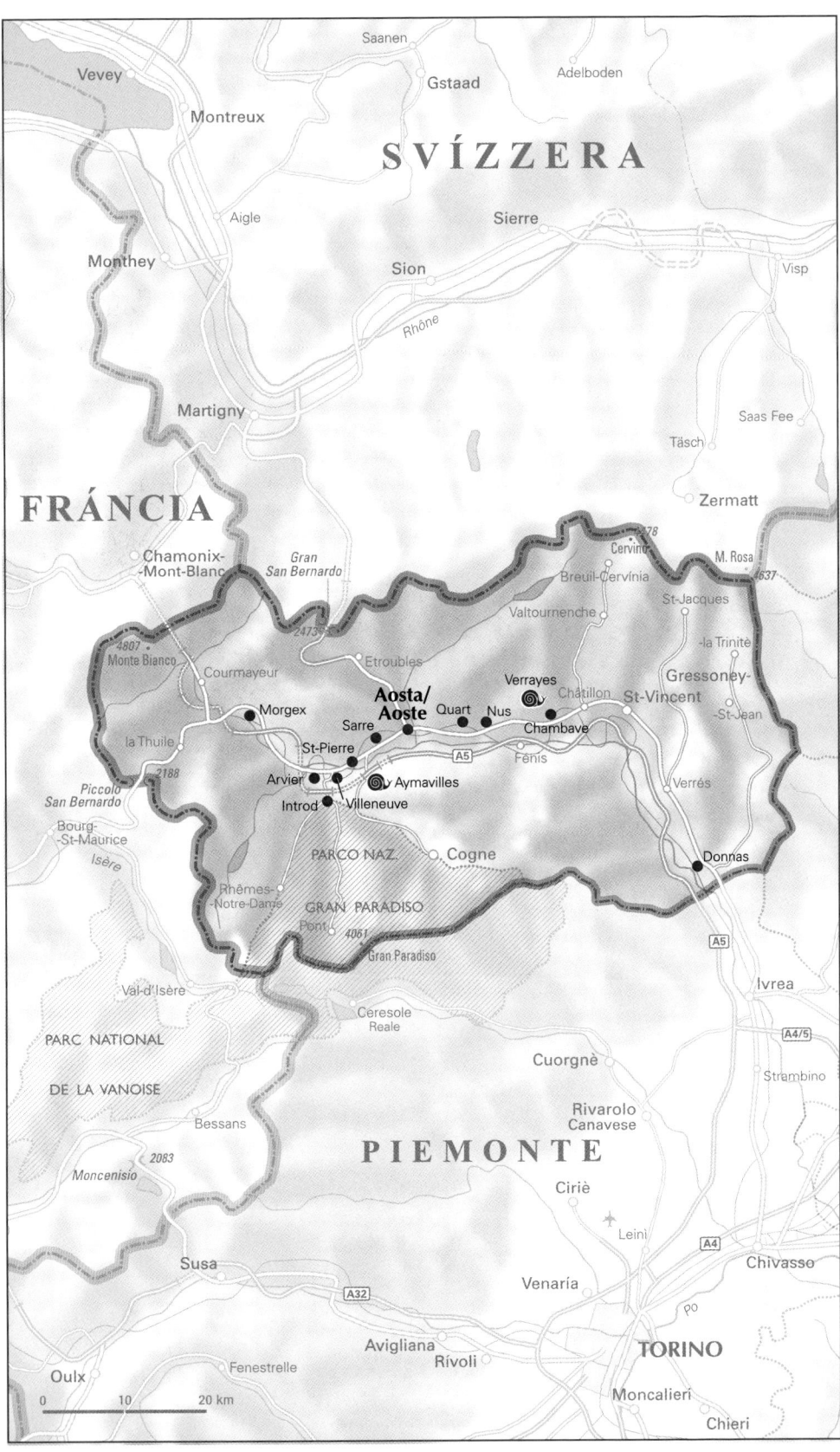

VAL D'AOSTA

From the vine-growing point of view, the Val d'Aosta is the smallest region in Italy. With fewer than 350 hectares of vineyards, it's a dwarf among giants. The same area could easily be that of a large-scale Italian wine company, but in the valley it is subdivided among hundreds of *vignerons*, who nonetheless accept their condition of inferiority intelligently. Many of them are elderly and continue to cultivate their vines and sell their grapes to one of the region's six cooperatives We have to be grateful to these cooperatives for saving viticulture in a region in which climate and steep slopes make it a complicated business. It was thanks to them, for example, that the sector managed to soldier through the 1970s and 1980s, when a great many hectares were uprooted and abandoned. Then in the 1990s, at least ten years after Piedmont, the valley enjoyed a wine renaissance. Over the last 15 years, thanks to the efforts of small winemakers under the aegis of the Viticulteurs Encaveurs association, quality has improved tremendously. Today a connoisseur has no qualms about saying that some of the best whites in Italy come from the Val d'Aosta without being considered crazy — because he or she is telling the truth! This year the quality came out again in the course of our tastings — it's great fun to drink Val d'Aosta wines. The region gives life to some of the most enjoyable, intriguing Pinot Grigios, Chardonnays, dry Moscatos and Petite Arvines in Italy. In our opinion, the last named are the wines with the greatest potential for quality improvement and are already admired nationally and internationally.

snails 🐌

16	LES CRÊTES
17	LA VRILLE

bottles 🍾

16	LO TRIOLET
17	ANSELMET

AYMAVILLES (AO)

Les Crêtes

Località Villetos, 50
tel. 0165 902274
www.lescretes.it
info@lescretes.it

INTROD (AO)

Lo Triolet

Frazione Junod, 4
tel. 0165 95437
www.lotriolet.vievini.it
lotriolet@vievini.it

---

25 ha - 220,000 bt   **10% discount**

5 ha - 40,000 bt

❝ It is partly thanks to Costantino Charrère that the wine of the Val d'Aosta is now known all over the world. His wines, bound indissolubly to their terroir, are veritable icons. But despite all the fame he has gained, Costantino still goes on experimenting, in the vineyard and in the cellar. *Chapeau*! ❞

PEOPLE - We were accompanied on our tour of the winery by sisters Eleonora and Elena Charrère. They were two memorable hours thanks to their professional expertise and training, which promise great things in the future for all concerned.

VINEYARDS - In some vineyards they are experimenting with organics and biodynamics, and in general the use of weed killers is decreasing constantly. We saw this during our walk among the vine rows of the Coteau La Tour vineyard in Aymavilles, traditionally the symbol of Les Crêtes, a cliff dominated by a splendid medieval tower.

WINES - We had a long chat with Charrère about the range of wines presented this year because those aged in oak seemed to us to be somewhat compressed. Costantino reassured us that the aim was to increase their longevity. Aged for 10 months on yeasts, **M. Cl. Brut Neblù 2009** (○ 15,000 bt) has an elegant perlage. The best of the bunch is **Valle d'Aosta Petit Arvine 2011** (○ 16,000 bt), which has sinew and tanginess in the mouth, supported by pleasant fruity notes. The enjoyable **Valle d'Aosta Chardonnay 2011** (○ 30,000 bt) is readier than **Valle d'Aosta Chardonnay Cuvée Bois 2011** (○ 18,000 bt), which still has to assimilate the wood of the barrique. **Valle d'Aosta Pinot Nero 2011** (● 14,000 bt) has ripe fruit with spicy nuances. **Valle d'Aosta Fumin 2010** (● 16,000 bt) is worth watching as it evolves.

PEOPLE - Marco Martin is the man who runs this winery, one of the finest in the Val d'Aosta. Before resuming a family tradition and launching the business in 1993, he had worked as a vine-dressing technician. His decision, taken 20 years ago, to replace petit rouge in an old vineyard at an altitude too high for the grape with pinot grigio proved to be the right one. The upshot is that the winery is now famous precisely for pinot grigio, but actually the whole range is of the highest quality.

VINEYARDS - Marco manages his vineyards at Introd, Villeneuve and Nus intelligently, banking on high-density plantings and short pruning to lighten the load on the single vines. The white grapes are grown at altitudes up to 900 meters, the red up to 600 meters. In between grows pinot nero. Thanks to the favorable climate, treatments are limited and Marco is experimenting with alternatives to chemical weeding with relatively uncompetitive plantings.

WINES - Acid-crisp with a silky body, **Valle d'Aosta Pinot Gris élevé en Barriques 2010** (○ 2,000 bt) has all the finesse of the vintage, and benefited from an extra year in the bottle. Congratulations! The stylishly aromatic **Valle d'Aosta Muscat Petit Grain 2011** (○ 1,500 bt) is assertive and long. **Valle d'Aosta Gewürztraminer 2011** (○ 4,000 bt) has classic spicy notes and a rich palate. Partly aged in wood **Valle d'Aosta Rouge Coteau Barrage 2010** (● syrah, fumin; 5,000 bt) is a well-structured, spicy red. The fruity **Valle d'Aosta Nus 2011** (● vien de Nus, cornalain, petit rouge; 4,000 bt) is light but surefooted.

> **slow wine** **VALLE D'AOSTA PINOT GRIS 2011** (○ 10,500 bt) A white with a strong sense of place, good flesh and a lively, racy finish. True, the grape isn't native, but Marco has nonetheless turned it into a terroir classic.

FERTILIZERS natural manure	FERTILIZERS none
PLANT PROTECTION copper and sulphur	PLANT PROTECTION chemical, copper and sulphur
WEED CONTROL chemical, mechanical	WEED CONTROL chemical, mechanical
YEASTS selected	YEASTS selected
GRAPES 30% bought in	GRAPES 20% bought in
CERTIFICATION none	CERTIFICATION none

La Vrille

Hameau du Grandzon, 1
tel. 0166 543018
www.lavrille-agritourisme.com
lavrille@gmail.com

1.5 ha - 12,000 bt

❝ Hervé's disarming simplicity and modesty are reflected in his wines. This year he is going to try his hand with organics, in the meantime limiting the use of copper ❞

PEOPLE - Hervé has taken time off from work for once. He contemplates the postcard panorama as he waits for us. It's rare for him to take time off, seeing how he and his wife Luciana Neyroz run the business, which includes an agriturismo with bedrooms and restaurant, all on their own.

VINEYARDS - The vineyards surround the agriturismo, apart from one situated at the bottom of the valley. They are fertilized with cow's manure provided by a livestock breeder friend of Hervé's, while drip irrigation is necessary in the torrid summer heat to help the vines on the leaner soil.

WINES - Hervé opened a new cellar, partly hewn into the rock, in 2005. The excellent **Valle d'Aosta Chambave Muscat Flétri 2010** (○ 1,000 bt) is made with grapes dried there. The palate amazes for its perfect marriage of tangy freshness and sweetness. **Valle d'Aosta Gamay 2010** (● 700 bt) caresses the nose, while **Valle d'Aosta Cornalin 2010** (● 21,300 bt) is immediate and immensely enjoyable, more complex and fuller-bodied yet very drinkable.

> **slow wine** VALLE D'AOSTA CHAMBAVE MUSCAT 2010 (○ 3,300 bt) A great white to write home about on account of its hugely elegant, alluringly soft bouquet and its racy, sinuous, well-paced, long mouthfeel. It consistently expresses the characteristics of the grape and the terroir.

Anselmet

Frazione Vereytaz, 30
tel. 0165 95419
www.maisonanselmet.vievini.it
renato.anselmet@alice.it

8.5 ha - 70,000 bt | **10% discount**

PEOPLE - Our visit to Giorgio Anselmet's cellar was true eye-opener. We went through the door, sat down in front of Giorgio and the huge fireplace that dominates the tasting room and listened in respectful silence. He spoke of viticulture in the Val d'Aosta and of his own wines with infectious energy. He is helped in his work by his father Renato, son Henry in the vineyard and wife Bruna, who plays an all-rounder role.

VINEYARDS - This year the company began to rent a one-hectare petite arvine vineyard. At Saint-Pierre Giorgio cultivates plots of chardonnay, at Aymavilles and Champanole of petite arvine, merlot and fumin. The vines are trained low using the Guyot and cordon systems. The spectacular Torrette vineyard, also at Saint-Pierre, has dry-stone walls and very steep slopes.

WINES - Valle d'Aosta Petite Arvine 2011 (○ 1,300 bt) has brilliant flavor, tanginess to spare and a nice wave of acidity, plus lingering minerality. The acid component interplays perfectly with the sweet — a Great Wine! The first-rate **Valle d'Aosta Chardonnay Élevé en Fût de Chêne 2011** (○ 4,500 bt) offers the palate almost chewy creaminess and a body of great structure and power. **Valle d'Aosta Pinot Gris 2011** (○ 1,500 bt) is finely mineral with marked notes of white fruit, while **Valle d'Aosta Chardonnay 2011** (○ 1,300 bt) offers more floral aromas. The red stable also reaches dizzy heights. **Valle d'Aosta Fumin 2011** (● 2,200 bt) has balsamic nuances in which licorice stands out distinctly, while **Le Prisonnier** (● petit rouge, mayolet, fumin, cornalin; 1,300 bt), for which the grapes are dried slightly, is a feast of red fruits, especially sour cherry.

FERTILIZERS natural manure	FERTILIZERS manure pellets
PLANT PROTECTION copper and sulphur	PLANT PROTECTION chemical, copper and sulphur
WEED CONTROL mechanical	WEED CONTROL chemical, mechanical
YEASTS selected, native	YEASTS selected
GRAPES 100% estate-grown	GRAPES 15% bought in
CERTIFICATION none	CERTIFICATION none

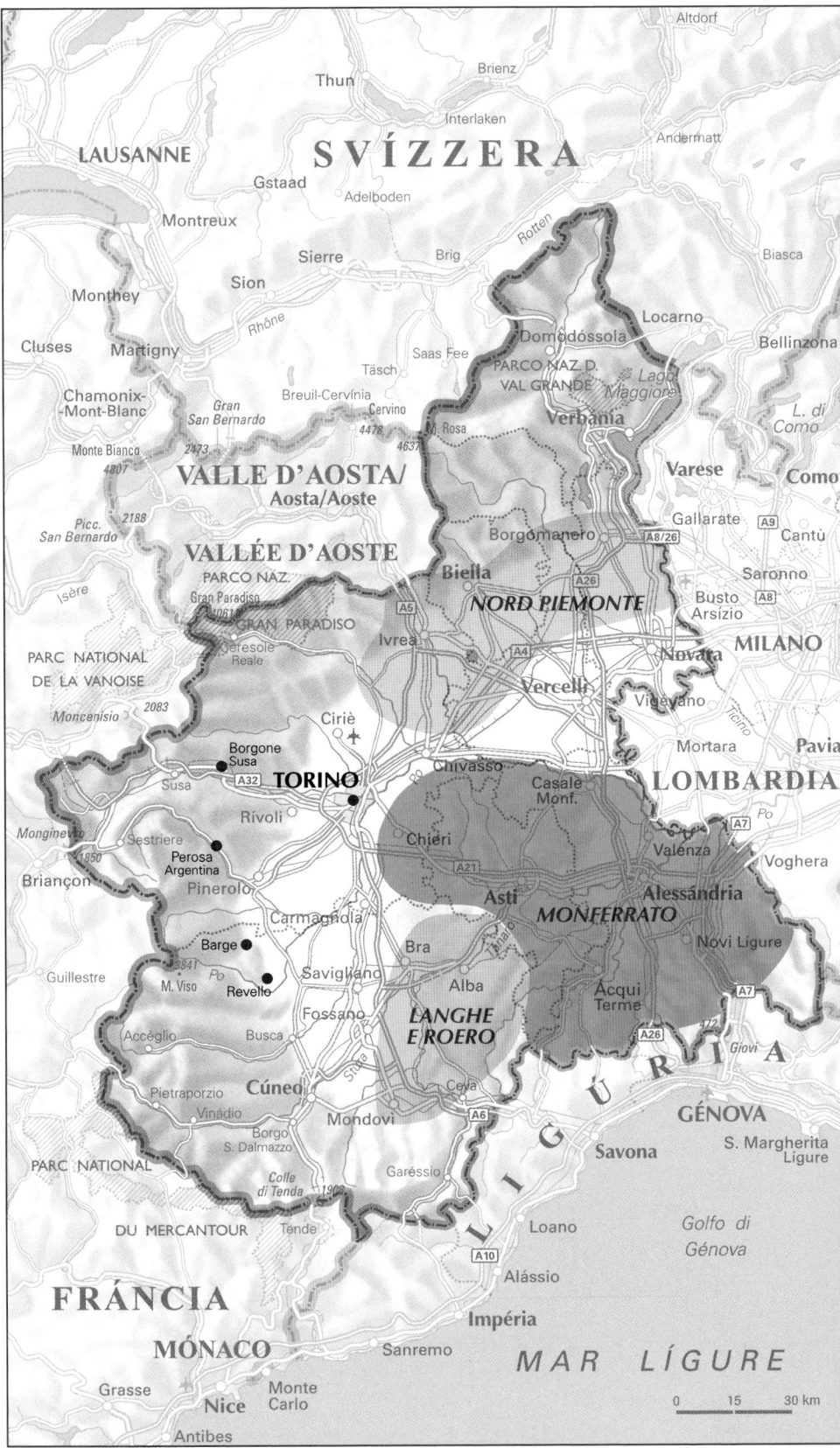

PIEDMONT

In Piedmont an area of 52,000 hectares is planted with vines producing more than 3,500,000 hectoliters of wine. The most significant data concern the quality of the wines, mostly high, which has been favored by a series of growing years positive either in general or specifically for this or that grape variety. Which is precisely why we have more than one perplexity about the new zoning of Barolo, regarded by many as the "king" of Piedmontese wines and, to a lesser degree, of Barbaresco. Vested interests, shortsightedness and, to be honest, the egoism of individuals have ended up extending magnificent vineyard terrain beyond all reasonable boundaries.

All this was happening in a year that was virtually perfect for Barolo. For us, in fact, 2008 was a special vintage, arguably unique, which yielded deep, rich, creamy wines, already ready to drink.

We agree, finally, with the application to call "Nizza" Barberas from the area long delimited round Nizza Monferrato and regarded as particularly conducive to production of the typology.

snails 🐌

21	LE PIANE
23	ANTICHI VIGNETI DI CANTALUPO
23	BIANCHI
28	TEOBALDO RIVELLA
28	ROAGNA - I PAGLIERI
31	GIUSEPPE RINALDI
31	G.D. VAJRA
32	CASCINA CA' ROSSA
34	BROVIA
35	CAVALLOTTO FRATELLI
37	CASCINA CORTE
38	PECCHENINO
39	ANNA MARIA ABBONA
41	ELIO ALTARE - CASCINA NUOVA
43	CONTERNO FANTINO
44	ELIO GRASSO
46	PIERO BUSSO
46	SOTTIMANO
47	ELVIO COGNO
47	HILBERG - PASQUERO
50	CA' DEL BAIO
51	FIORENZO NADA
51	ALESSANDRIA FRATELLI
53	DACAPO
54	IULI
55	LUIGI SPERTINO
56	VIGNETI MASSA
58	CARUSSIN
58	CASTELLO DI TASSAROLO

bottles 🍾

21	ANTONIOLO
22	NERVI
26	GAJA
27	MARCHESI DI GRÉSY
29	BORGOGNO & FIGLI
30	BARTOLO MASCARELLO
33	MALVIRÀ
33	MONCHIERO CARBONE
35	PAOLO SCAVINO
36	VIETTI
36	MARZIANO ABBONA
37	CA' VIOLA
38	QUINTO CHIONETTI
39	SAN FEREOLO
40	LA SPINETTA
42	CORDERO DI MONTEZEMOLO - MONFALLETTO
42	GIUSEPPE MASCARELLO E FIGLIO
43	GIACOMO CONTERNO
48	CASA DI E. MIRAFIORE
49	ETTORE GERMANO
49	MASSOLINO
50	GIOVANNI ROSSO
57	MARCHESI ALFIERI
59	LA COLOMBERA

coins €

22	GIANCARLO TRAVAGLINI
25	MARCO E VITTORIO ADRIANO
25	GIGI BIANCO
26	GIUSEPPE CORTESE
27	PRODUTTORI DEL BARBARESCO
29	GIACOMO BREZZA & FIGLI
41	BRANDINI
44	GIACOMO FENOCCHIO
48	MOSSIO FRATELLI
54	PAOLO AVEZZA
55	BORGO MARAGLIANO
56	EREDE DI ARMANDO CHIAPPONE
57	LA GIRONDA

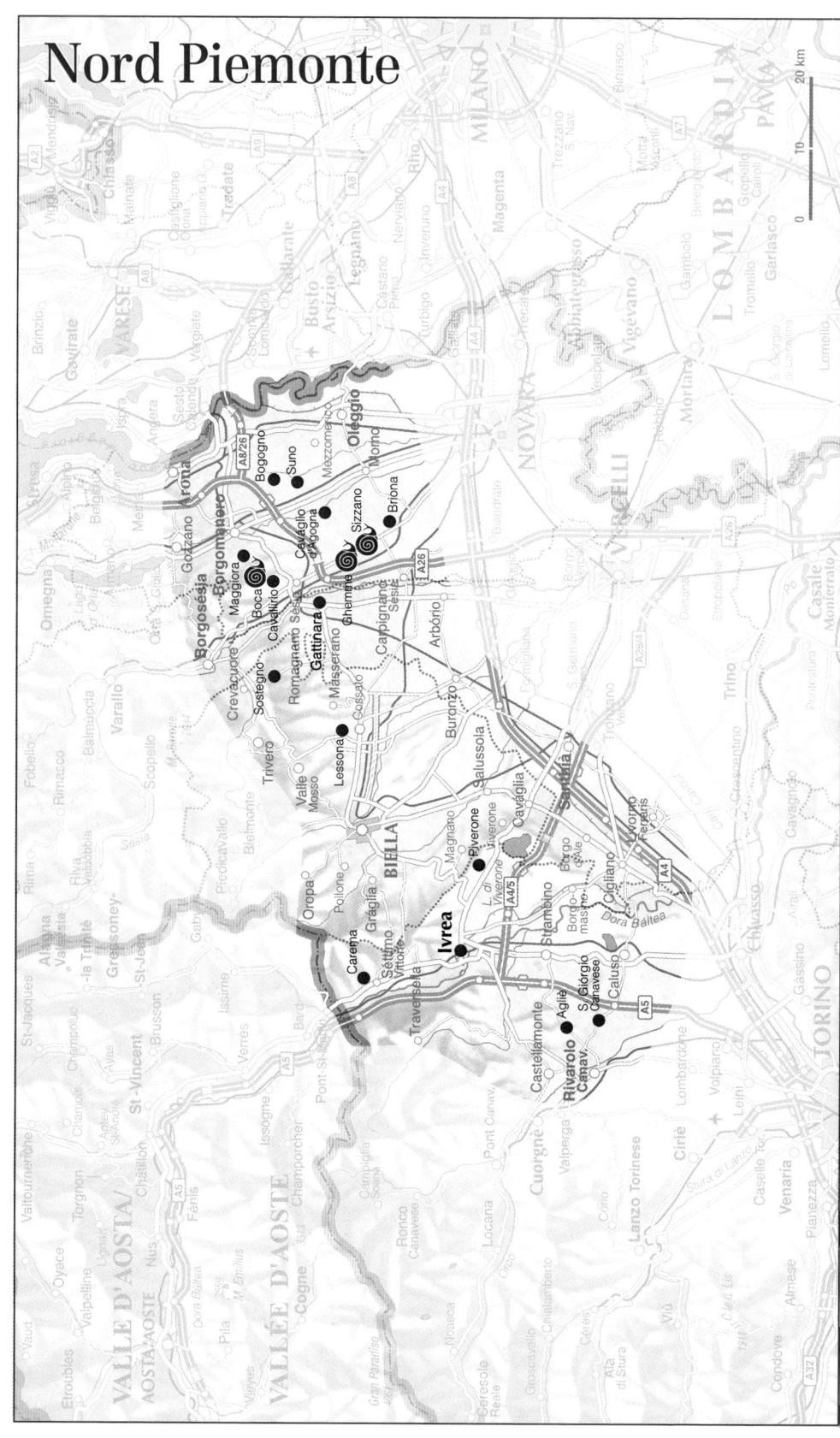

Nord Piemonte

BOCA (NO)

Le Piane

Località Le Piane
tel. 348 3354185
www.bocapiane.com
info@bocapiane.com

8 ha - 35,000 bt

66 Every year we turn up at this cellar thinking we know everything about the place. But we couldn't be more wrong. Looking up Christoph Künzli is always a reminder of how a winemaker's progress is never-ending 99

PEOPLE - Christoph captains the well-knit, talented team of Nicola del Boca, who tends the vineyards, and Sergej Zhukov the cellarman. The only outside consultancy is provided by Stefano Zaninotti, an enologist of great sensibility.

VINEYARDS - The cellar has taken over another four lovely vineyards trained with the traditional *maggiorina* system, which otherwise would have been left in a state of neglect. The level of care it devotes to its vines — testing to reduce the use of products (systemic, endotherapeutic, copper, sulfur) by 50 per cent and experimentation with Irish algae to stimulate defense mechanisms — is hard to find elsewhere.

WINES - In the cellar Christoph interprets the wine aging in the various barrels (selections divided by vineyard or grape variety) with amazing sensitivity, developing them according to their natural inclination. Boca 2008 (● nebbiolo, vespolina; 10,000 bt) shakes off all the potential limits of a year that started badly with a distinctly intense, almost pungent, fine nose of crisp fruit and a firm, compact palate of elegant depth and rhythm — a Great Wine with a sense of place. **Colline Novaresi Le Piane 2009** (● croatina, nebbiolo; 5,000 bt) is warm and enveloping, brimming over with tannins, yet tempting and fluent thanks to just the right acid counterpoint. From the older vineyards comes **Maggiorina 2011** (● croatina, vespolina, uva rara, nebbiolo; 15,000 bt), which this year displays a new-found maturity and racy flavor that make it an ideal accompaniment to food.

FERTILIZERS natural manure, green manure	
PLANT PROTECTION chemical, copper and sulphur, organic	
WEED CONTROL mechanical	
YEASTS native	
GRAPES 10% bought in	
CERTIFICATION none	

GATTINARA (VC)

Antoniolo

Corso Valsesia, 277
tel. 0163 833612
antoniolovini@bmm.it

12 ha - 60,000 bt

PEOPLE - Formed in 1948 by Mario Antoniolo, this company is now a synonym of great Northern Piedmontese Nebbiolos. Rosanna, Mario's daughter, ran the business with a sure hand, and now it is overseen by her son Alberto, the production manager, and daughter Lorella Zoppis Antoniolo, the sales manager and also president of the High Piedmont Nebbiolo Protection Consortium.

VINEYARDS - In the 1970s, the Antoniolos were the first to promote single crus with separate bottling. They own vineyards in some of the most sought after zones of Gattinara, on acid terrains of volcanic origin, rich in porphyry, granite and quartz, at altitudes of 300-400 meters: a hectare at Castelle, a hill dominated by an old 11th-century tower, four hectares in the San Francesco district and another five and a half — the highest, steepest vineyard, with very compact soil — in the Osso zone.

WINES - Fermented in cement and mostly aged in large barrels, the wines stand out for their soundness and expressive purity. The excellent **Gattinara San Francesco 2008** (● 4,000 bt) is elegant, racy and zippy with impressive overall harmony. **Gattinara Castelle 2008** (● 3,200 bt) is fine and floral, more approachable and full-textured, lively and long. The beefy but still stiff **Gattinara Osso San Grato 2008** (● 5,500 bt) has riper, deeper fruit and well-knit tannins. The drinkable, never dull **Coste della Sesia Nebbiolo Juvenia 2010** (● 8,000 bt) is flowery and fruity.

> **slow wine** **GATTINARA 2008** (● 16,000 bt) Expressive and fine with a sense of place, a great version of the wine at an affordable price. The bouquet is sound and earthy, the palate racy, elegant and compact with great zip and a long tannin trail behind it. If you want to find out what Gattinara is, this is the wine for you.

FERTILIZERS organic-mineral, natural manure	
PLANT PROTECTION chemical, copper and sulphur	
WEED CONTROL chemical, mechanical	
YEASTS native	
GRAPES 100% estate-grown	
CERTIFICATION none	

Nervi

Corso Vercelli, 117
tel. 0163 833228
www.gattinara-nervi.it
nervi@gattinara-nervi.it

Giancarlo Travaglini

Via delle Vigne, 36
tel. 0163 833588
www.travaglini.com
info@travaglinigattinara.it

---

25 ha - 100,000 bt

PEOPLE - Nervi, the historic Gattinara winery, was set up at the start of the 20th century and from last year has been under new ownership: four new Norwegian partners plus, at the helm, Daniele Di Noia, who over the last two years has demonstrated his unbounded love for the terroir. Daniele is intent upon restoring to Nervi its old, his main aim being to produce wines that totally identify with the local area. His consultants in the vineyard and wine cellar are Luca De Marchi and agronomist Stefano Zaninotti.

VINEYARDS - The Molsino vineyard with vines with an average age of about 20 is as magnificent as ever. A terrace overlooking the Vercelli area, it covers an area of five hectares and plans are underway to expand it. Also underway are a project to map all the vineyards with analysis of the soil and the vines and another, in collaboration with local old-timers, to recover their toponomy. The soil between the vine rows is fertilized with barley-based green manure. No less spectacular are vineyards such as those in the Valferana (1.5 hectares) and at Garavoglie (4.5 hectares). The lean and rocky soil is of volcanic origin.

WINES - The new management began vinifying for the first time in 2011. **Gattinara Valferana 2005** (● 7,000 bt) has a profound, mineral bouquet which enjoys a reprise on the palate, stupendous for its sinew, dynamic elegance and follow-through. It's a Great Wine. Molsino 2005 went into the base wine, **Gattinara 2005** (● 18,000 bt) which has a better developed bouquet and less weight. **Coste della Sesia Rosa 2011** (⊙ nebbiolo; 15,000 bt) is juicy and succulent with a lingering palate. **Coste della Sesia Nebbiolo Spanna dei Ginepri 2009** (● nebbiolo, vespolina; 18,000 bt) offers a tempting, nicely mature suite of aromas, very fine tannins. We were lucky enough to taste it just a day after it was uncorked.

PEOPLE - This historic Gattinara winery is one of the largest in the area, consolidated over the years by its late founder Giancarlo Travaglini with the onus on quality. Today his daughter carries on the good work in her role as administrative and sales manager. In charge of the vineyard and cellar is her husband, assisted by agronomist Flavio Bera and enologist Sergio Molino.

VINEYARDS - The company boasts a wealth of vineyards, including a recently acquired plot of two hectares alongside the previously owned hectare in the so-called Alice zone. The others ate situated in the Molsino, Ronchi, Permolone, Lurghe, Valferana, Ucineglio and Sas dei Mariani crus. The splendid parcel in the latter zone was planted in 2000 after literally snatching the land out of the stone. The lean and mineral soils are of rocky origin.

WINES - **Gattinara Ris. 2007** (● 47,500 bt) captures the early, warm vintage with remarkable intactness. It has a suave, nuanced bouquet with a sedately elegant palate and a well-developed tannic structure. Fruity, sinewy and caressing, **Coste della Sesia 2010** (● nebbiolo; 15,000 bt) is wonderfully expressive. The unusual **Altro Sogno 2007** (● 2,400 bt) is made with dried nebbiolo grapes with residual sugar of eight grams per liter. Gattinara Tre Vigne 2007, erroneously reviewed last year in place of the 2006, wasn't released and went into the base Gattinara 2007 instead.

> **slow wine** **GATTINARA 2008** (● 190,000 bt) Notwithstanding the sheer number of bottles produced, this wine displays impeccable classicism. It offers cut-glass, crunchy fruit and strikes a deft balance between acidity and richness of flavor. Another plus is that the price is very reasonable indeed.

| FERTILIZERS green manure, humus |
| PLANT PROTECTION chemical, copper and sulphur |
| WEED CONTROL mechanical |
| YEASTS selected |
| GRAPES 100% estate-grown |
| CERTIFICATION none |

| FERTILIZERS mineral, natural manure |
| PLANT PROTECTION chemical, copper and sulphur |
| WEED CONTROL chemical, mechanical |
| YEASTS selected |
| GRAPES 100% estate-grown |
| CERTIFICATION none |

GHEMME (NO)

Antichi Vigneti di Cantalupo

Via Michelangelo Buonarroti, 5
tel. 0163 840041
www.cantalupo.net
info@cantalupo.net

35 ha - 200,000 bt   **10% discount**

66 The history of the Cantalupo winery spans that of Ghemme. The company deserves thanks for the way they held quality high in the DOC's darkest periods. Its wines from the 1980s are still magnificent 99

PEOPLE - The top dog at the cellar is Alberto Arlunno, the historical memory of Ghemme, who has been running the business since the early 1980s. Enologist Donato Lanati acts as a consultant.

VINEYARDS - The vineyards are on the first and second hills of Ghemme, both of fluvioglacial origin (moraines created by the Monte Rosa glacier and flooding of the River Sesia), where the silty, clayey soil has an acid pH. The 2.5-hectare Roccolo del Tordo vineyard is immersed in woodland in the Basin district on the second hill. Alberto told us that, "It took 30 years to bring the properties together into a single plot because of the high number of people who owned parts of it and refused to sell!"

WINES - An inimitably classic style for very elegant, fine wines. Alberto likes his bottles to be fully mature so he sometimes waits before releasing them. We had another taste of Ghemme Cantalupo 2006, fruit of the bottling of a second batch of grapes. Longer time in the bottles has made the wine deeper, more complex and tauter. **Ghemme Signore di Bayard 2005** (● 2,000 bt) has a slightly underdeveloped nose with subtle hints of oak and a richly textured palate. It's a masterpiece, hence a Great Wine. **Colline Novaresi Primigenia 2009** (● nebbiolo, uva rara; 14,000 bt) has a nicely crisp, spicy nose and a leisurely, buttery palate. Albeit light and fresh, the fruity **Colline Novaresi Nebbiolo Il Mimo 2011** (◉ 84,000 bt) has nicely tangy follow-through.

FERTILIZERS organic-mineral, natural manure
PLANT PROTECTION chemical, copper and sulphur
WEED CONTROL chemical, mechanical
YEASTS selected
GRAPES 8% bought in
CERTIFICATION none

SIZZANO (NO)

Bianchi

Via Roma, 37
tel. 0321 810004
www.cantinabianchi.it
info@cantinabianchi.it

21 ha - 130,000 bt

66 The Bianchi cellar was one of the first in Piedmont to believe in organic production, releasing top quality labels and keeping the Sizzano denomination alive 99

PEOPLE - Today it is run by Paolo Tealdi Bianchi, who converted it to organics before anyone else had even thought about such a move. The cellar is worth a visit for its small wine museum and agriturismo facility where, in a warm, welcoming environment, you can enjoy dishes of the local tradition.

VINEYARDS - The vineyards, a few of which are rented, are scattered across different districts. Most of them are around Sizzano on acid, clayey, pebbly soils of morainal origin. Similar soils are to be found in the vineyards on a plateau in the Baraggiole district near Ghemme where Paolo cultivates a few plots of land, but in Gattinara the soil changes. Here it is still acid but of volcanic origin, reddish in color and rich in minerals, porphyry, granite, quartz and iron.

WINES - In his traditional-style vinification, Paolo can count on the help of the enologist Donato Lanati. **Colline Novaresi Nebbiolo 2011** (● 20,000 bt), very floral, lively and full of brio, is as enjoyable as ever. Excellent too is **Colline Novaresi Sanclemente 2011** (● nebbiolo, vespolina, uva rara; 13,000 bt), deeper, juicier and longer. **Colline Novaresi Passione Rosa 2011** (◉ 7,000 bt) is a fresher and lighter summer version of the Nebbiolo. The racy, gusty, vibrant **Gattinara 2007** (● 9,000 bt) is already rich in aroma. **Sizzano 2007** (● 7,000 bt) is an unusual wine with spicy notes, redolent almost of roots. We tasted Ghemme 2008 again; it proved earthy, full-bodied and well textured, eminently quaffable like all Paolo's wines.

FERTILIZERS organic-mineral
PLANT PROTECTION copper and sulphur
WEED CONTROL mechanical
YEASTS selected
GRAPES 100% estate-grown
CERTIFICATION organic

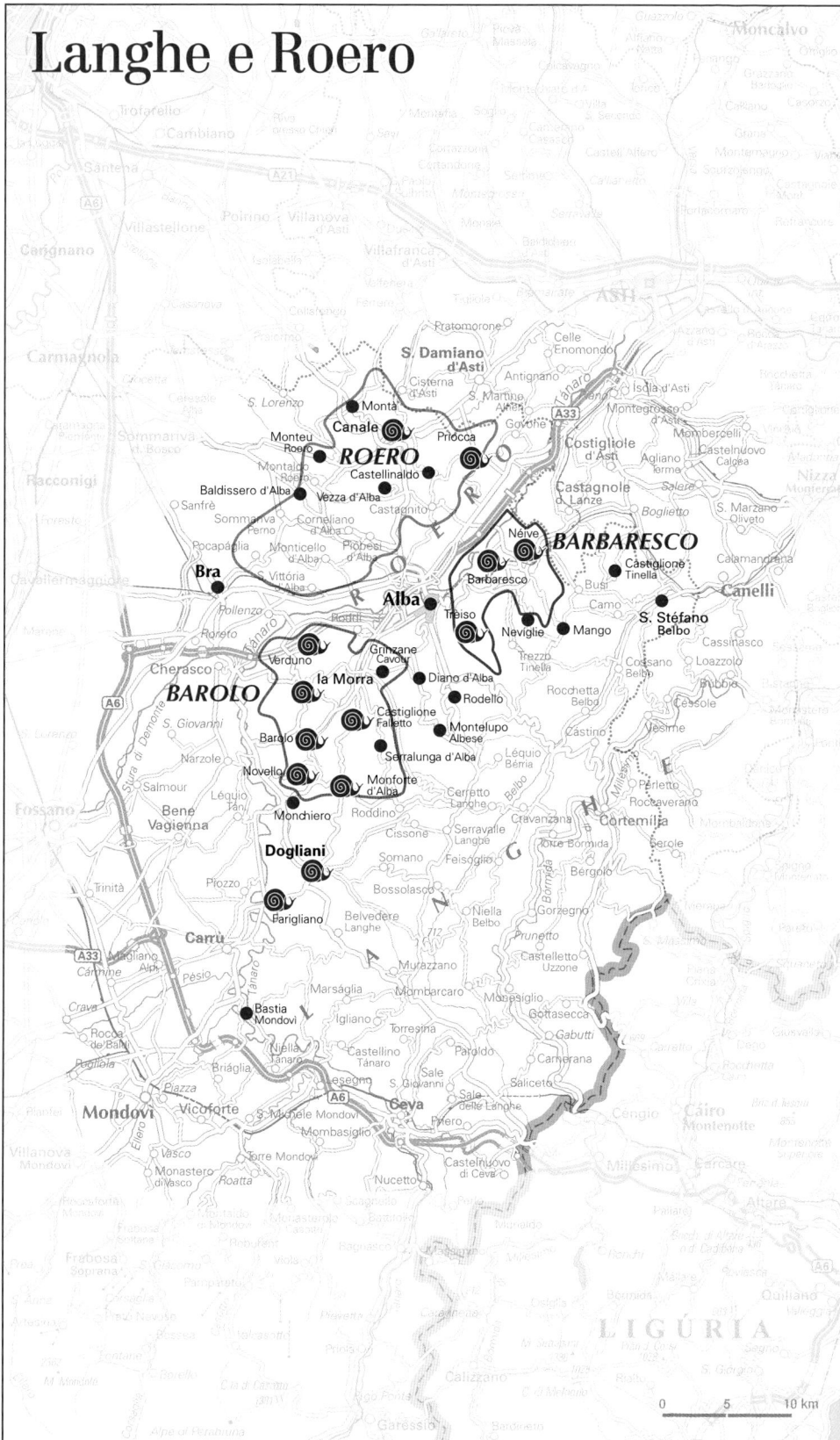

Langhe e Roero

Marco e Vittorio Adriano €

Frazione San Rocco Seno d'Elvio, 13 A
tel. 0173 362294
www.adrianovini.it
info@adrianovini.it

---

22 ha - 130,000 bt   **10% discount**

PEOPLE - 1994 was a turning point for this farm just outside Alba. Previously it had raised livestock and bottled wine, but in that year it bought up land in bordering districts and nearby communes and put its money on winegrowing. Today Marco Adriano oversees the vineyards and Vittorio the cellar. Their wives Luciana Garabello and Maria Grazia Sordo take care of the administrative side.

VINEYARDS - The vineyards are situated on the sandy soil round the cellar and grow dolcetto, barbera, moscato and sauvignon grapes. Some vines date from the 1970s, others are more than 80 years old. The Basarin vineyard is situated at an altitude of 280-350 meters on the steep hill of the same name in Neive, where the soil is siltier. A hectare of freisa vines was planted here recently.

WINES - The excellent **Barbaresco Basarin 2009** (● 30,000 bt), aged in large barrels, has a spicy, fruity bouquet and a nicely tart palate with hints of vanilla. **Barbaresco Sanadaive 2009** (● 10,000 bt) has lighter, balsamic aromas. The well-crafted **Langhe Nebbiolo 2010** (● 5,000 bt) offers pervasive nuances of soil and red berries. **Barbera d'Alba Sup. 2010** (● 12,000 bt) is complex with a taut, satisfying palate. **Dolcetto d'Alba 2011** (● 20,000 bt) is succulent and rich in fruity flesh, notably sour cherry and strawberry. **Langhe Sauvignon Basaricò 2011** (○ 13,000 bt) has pleasant notes of sweet fruit that make for a supple palate.

Gigi Bianco €

Via Torino, 63
tel. 0173 635137
www.gigibianco.it
aziendagigibianco@libero.it

2.7 ha - 18,000 bt

PEOPLE - Small is beautiful — that's how we'd define this winery, managed simply and professionally by Susanna Bianco and her mother Maria Vittoria with the contribution of Salvatore Angelica, Susanna's companion, and Angelo and Sergio Lembo for the agronomic side. The beautiful old cellar, complete with brick barrel vaults houses small (used) and medium sized casks. A trapdoor leads to a cavern where the old Bianco bottles are kept.

VINEYARDS - The winery's neatly kept vineyards (including a small newly acquired plot of nebbiolo vines) are situated in historic red wine crus: Ovello, planted with nebbiolo, dolcetto and barbera grapes, and Pora, which adds power and solidity to the Barbaresco. Chemical weed control is taboo and integrated management and mating disruption strategies are adopted to control pests.

WINES - The Bianco family's value-for-money wines are enjoyable and approachable with all the impeccable cleanness and subterranean energy of the Langhe hills. **Barbaresco Ovello 2009** (● 3,000 bt) has beautifully fine floral notes with an irresistibly juicy, graceful palate. The wonderfully quaffable **Langhe Nebbiolo 2010** (● 2,400 bt), a Barbaresco in miniature, is not to be missed. With its juicy, perky palate, balance and typicality, **Barbera d'Alba 2010** (● 4,500 bt) is practically perfect. **Dolcetto d'Alba 2011** (● 1,900 bt) has the same drinkable quality and sense of place.

---

slow wine **BARBARESCO PORA 2009** (● 2,200 bt) A wine that excels for typicality — notes of blossom and damp soil — at a competitive price. It's complex, it's solid, it's packed with personality — a joy to drink.

	Marco e Vittorio Adriano	Gigi Bianco
FERTILIZERS	manure pellets	none
PLANT PROTECTION	chemical, copper and sulphur	chemical, copper and sulphur
WEED CONTROL	chemical, mechanical	mechanical
YEASTS	selected	native
GRAPES	100% estate-grown	100% estate-grown
CERTIFICATION	none	none

Giuseppe Cortese €

Strada Rabajà, 80
tel. 0173 635131
www.cortesegiuseppe.it
info@cortesegiuseppe.it

Gaja

Via Torino, 36
tel. 0173 635158

---

8 ha - 50,000 bt

PEOPLE - This family-run winery in the heart of Barbaresco's Rabajà district, was founded in the 1970s by Giuseppe and his wife Rosella. Their children Piercarlo and Tiziana, who also work in the business, recently opened a swish bed and breakfast among the vineyards.

VINEYARDS - The company's eight hectares of vines are all situated near the cellar: four are in the Trifolera district on clay soil with a west-northwestern exposure at an altitude of 260 meters and are given over to dolcetto, barbera, chardonnay and nebbiolo grapes. The other four are all in the famous Rabajà vineyard — one of the great crus of Barbaresco — on calcareous soil with white marls and south-southwestern exposure at the same altitude. Here only nebbiolo grapes are grown on vines over 60 years old.

WINES - The Nebbiolos age in 16-25 hectoliter Slavonian oak barrels, the Barberas in French barriques. We tasted an enjoyable refreshing, leisurely **Langhe Chardonnay 2011** (○ 4,000 bt), a very good fragrant, rough **Dolcetto d'Alba Trifolera 2011** (● 10,000 bt), and a decent balanced, fruity **Barbera d'Alba 2011** (● 6,000 bt). Moving on to the Nebbiolos, **Langhe Nebbiolo 2010** (● 10,000 bt) is for all the world like a Barbaresco Rabajà in miniature, with a bouquet of tobacco and chocolate, a young palate amply endowed with freshness, fruit and acidity and a very pleasant finish indeed. The Riserva wasn't produced in 2009.

> **slow wine** BARBARESCO RABAJÀ 2009 (● 17,000 bt) Floral, mineral, potent, deep and irresistible — the quintessence of this unbeatable cru. A superlative wine at an affordable price. Not to ne missed!

100 ha - 350,000 bt

PEOPLE - It's possible to say without fear of contradiction that Angelo Gaja's winery is the most prestigious in Piedmont and the best known abroad. Angelo's success is the fruit of a life lived with irrepressible enthusiasm, a great spirit of sacrifice and obsessive attention to detail. Today he is also lucky enough to be flanked by his two daughters, Gaia and Rossana, and his wife Lucia, of whom he is justly proud

VINEYARDS - Without trumpeting the fact or shouting it from the rooftops, the company is one of most sensitive to environmental and social sustainability in Piedmont. For years it has exploited slagheaps to produce humus and now boasts a modern phytodepuration plant. No chemical weed control is performed under the vines, botrycides are banned and pesticides are only used when the harvest is at risk. The old farm buildings are currently being restored to provide accommodation for employees.

WINES - Though it fails to achieve the *état de grace* of 2008, we can safely say that 2009 gave a good account of itself. True, it was a warm vintage, but not as warm as 2003 or 2007. All the Langhe wines are made with 95% nebbiolo grapes plus 5% barbera. **Langhe Nebbiolo Sorì San Lorenzo 2009** (● 12,000 bt) certainly strutted its stuff. Like all the other Langhes, it was aged for 12 months in barriques and for as many again in large wooden casks. **Langhe Nebbiolo Sorì Tildin 2009** (● 12,000 bt) is superb and . Langhe Nebbiolo Costa Russi 2009 (● 12,000 bt), our favorite is complex and deep — a Great Wine. Not that **Barbaresco 2009** (● 50,000 bt) isn't very good too. The two Barolos come from a great year and they behave accordingly. **Langhe Nebbiolo Conteisa 2008** (● 15,000 bt) is warmer and readier, while **Langhe Nebbiolo Sperss 2008** (● 24,000 bt) has Serralunga-style tannins and goodness.

| FERTILIZERS none |
| PLANT PROTECTION copper and sulphur |
| WEED CONTROL mechanical |
| YEASTS selected |
| GRAPES 100% estate-grown |
| CERTIFICATION none |

| FERTILIZERS humus |
| PLANT PROTECTION chemical, copper and sulphur |
| WEED CONTROL mechanical |
| YEASTS selected |
| GRAPES 100% estate-grown |
| CERTIFICATION none |

BARBARESCO (CN)

Marchesi di Grésy

Strada della Stazione, 21
tel. 0173 635221
www.marchesidigresy.com
wine@marchesidigresy.com

35 ha - 200,000 bt

BARBARESCO (CN)

Produttori del Barbaresco

(€)

Via Torino, 54
tel. 0173 635139
www.produttoridelbarbaresco.com
a.vacca@produttoridelbarbaresco.com

110 ha - 550,000 bt

PEOPLE - The thriving Marchesi winery owns four properties: two — La Serra and Monte Colombo — at Cassine in the Monferrato hills, Monte Aribaldo at Treiso and Martinenga, the largest and most prestigious, at Barbaresco. The latter covers 11 hectares and is given over to nebbiolo for Barbaresco. It was Alberto di Grésy, adamant about the potential of ths noble wine, who decided to give up selling grapes and other crops to specialize in winemaking in the early 1970s.

VINEYARDS - Our tour of the Martinenga cru, in which grapes from the Camp Gros and Gaiun vineyards are selected, was an education. We were impressed by the differences in soil, age of vines and exposure. Increasing atttempts are being made to avoid altering the natural balance of the vine with a reduced use of weed killers and the introduction of new tools for working the soil under the vines. Matteo Sasso manages work in the various holdings with the assistance of consultant agronomist Gian Piero Romana.

WINES - All the wines are clean, elegant and recognizable thanks to rational vinification and aging in the versatile cellar — stainless steel and cement tubs, large barrels and barriques — supervised by enologist Piero Ballario. **Barbaresco Camp Gros 2008** (● 6,200 bt) and **Barbaresco Gaiun 2008** (● 6,200 bt) are both young and both excellent, with extrovert personallity and stratospheric typicality. We favored the first and elected it a Great Wine. **Barbaresco Martinenga 2009** (● 23,000 bt), a fine specimen for its category, has fine tannins, fruit and succulence. We enjoyed the simpler **Dolcetto d'Alba Monte Aribaldo 2011** (● 23,000 bt) and **Barbera d'Asti Monte Colombo 2008** (● 4,900 bt) and **Langhe Chardonnay 2011** (○ 9,300 bt) deserves a round of applause too.

PEOPLE - A bundle of bottles of Barbaresco have been served at the tables all over the world since 1958, when the very first were vinified with a few quintals of grapes in the village of the same name. Today the cooperative has 52 members and production is thriving under the impeccable technical management with quality as the priority objective. Work on the cellar under the old tower of Barbaresco was completed this year.

VINEYARDS - In the vineyards, members have to comply with strict rules with regard to treatments and soil management, and special attention is paid to leaf removal to obtain perfect grapes. The grapes from nine crus are vinified separately.

WINES - In the cellar we noted a large number of containers, older cement ones and new stainless steel ones. After long macerations the wines are aged in large wooden barrels. **Langhe Nebbiolo 2010** (● 190,000 bt) was as good as ever with ripe, crispy fruit and plenty of raciness and balance. **Barbaresco 2008** (● 225,000 bt) has a wonderfully spunky, sweet bouquet of fruit with hints of rose and a nice juicy finish. Moving on to the company's crus, we were impressed by the finesse and quaffability of the consummately elegant **Barbaresco Pora Ris. 2007** (● 16,500 bt). **Barbaresco Montefico Ris. 2007** (● 13,000 bt) is solid and compact with gutsy sweet tannins — a wine built to last. **Barbaresco Asili Ris. 2007** (● 13,000 bt) offers delectable floral, balsamic notes and a palate with sweetish tannins.

| slow wine | BARBARESCO MONTESTEFANO RIS. 2007 (● 14,000 bt) Solid and mineral, long and leisurely — a great ageworthy Barbaresco that mirrors the cooperative's philosophy. And has an unbeatable price with it. |

FERTILIZERS manure pellets
PLANT PROTECTION chemical, copper and sulphur
WEED CONTROL chemical, mechanical
YEASTS selected
GRAPES 100% estate-grown
CERTIFICATION none

FERTILIZERS natural manure
PLANT PROTECTION chemical, copper and sulphur
WEED CONTROL chemical, mechanical
YEASTS selected
GRAPES 100% estate-grown
CERTIFICATION none

Teobaldo Rivella

Località Montestefano, 6
tel. 0173 635182

2 ha - 11,000 bt

" A "wedding cake" of a cellar with a laid-back approach and a single aim: to make wines with a sense of place and sell them only when they are really ready. This is the philosophy and the lifestyle of Teobaldo Rivella, one of the leading winemakers in Piedmont's Langa hills "

PEOPLE - Teobaldo Rivella is a farmer who runs his small winery with his wife Maria Musso. Rigorously but silently, out of the spotlight. Extremism and autarky are not for him; all he wants to do is produce simple, family wines.

VINEYARDS - Montestefano is one of the finest Barbaresco crus. Here on his two-hectare property, Teobaldo grows mainly nebbiolo grapes and, true to peasant tradition, some dolcetto at the top of the hill. This 50-year-old vineyard stands as an extraordinary testimony to the district's suitability for winegrowing. Teobaldo develops all its potential through careful management, without the use of chemicals but with plenty of common sense and insight.

WINES - Coming as it does from such an ideal vineyard, the deeply textured **Dolcetto d'Alba 2010** (● 2,000 bt) is a wine that combines drinkability and character, body and sense of place. More than a range filler, this is a label of rank that adds value to the denomination. **Barbaresco Montestefano 2008** (● 8,500 bt) is on a par with previous vintages; the product of a good year, it starts out shy and diffident, but then opens out with a grin, very much like the man who produces it. It's a wine that speaks of the artisan Langa we are so fond of.

FERTILIZERS	manure pellets, natural manure
PLANT PROTECTION	copper and sulphur
WEED CONTROL	mechanical
YEASTS	selected
GRAPES	100% estate-grown
CERTIFICATION	none

Roagna - I Paglieri

Località Paglieri, 9
tel. 0173 635109
www.roagna.com
info@roagna.com

12 ha - 60,000 bt

" 'The wild men' — that's how father and son Alfredo and Luca Roagna like to describe themselves. Theirs is a winery you won't forget in a hurry. Their clear, precise philosophy is based on naturalness and their approach is uncompromising, some would say stubborn. We prefer to call it coherent "

PEOPLE - Besides four hectares at Barbaresco (in the Montefico, Asili and Pajé crus), the Roagnas also own another eight hectares at Castiglione Falletto, where they monopolize the Pira cru.

VINEYARDS - On our tour of the vineyards with Luca, we had to clamber over the tall grass, which is neither weeded nor cut but simply stamped down by foot. Seen from a distance, their Asili vineyard is like a splash of green in a sea of brown. The Roagnas devote religious care and attention to the age of their vineyards, into which they invest time, resources and commitment.

WINES - Luca has chosen to vinify the grapes of Montefico and Asili separately. If our opinion is anything to go by, it's the right choice. **Barbaresco Montefico 2007** (● 1,200 bt) is the most elegant, subtle, delicate and graceful. **Barbaresco Asili 2007** (● 1,200 bt) is deeper and more potent, the Asili soil being richer in clay. This is the one we have chosen as a Great Wine. **Barbaresco Pajé 2007** (● 5,000 bt) has silky tannins and huge depth. With its powerful, full-bodied, nicely acid palate, **Barolo La Pira 2007** (● 15,000 bt) is a massive wine too. Considering the vintage, **Langhe Rosso 2006** (● nebbiolo; 5,000 bt) is a wonderful wine at a very reasonable price. **Dolcetto d'Alba 2011** (● 10,000 bt) is packed with character and aroma. Pira and Pajé 2006 will be released in a year or two, when the Roagnas deem them ready.

FERTILIZERS	none
PLANT PROTECTION	copper and sulphur
WEED CONTROL	mechanical
YEASTS	native
GRAPES	100% estate-grown
CERTIFICATION	none

Borgogno & Figli

Via Gioberti, 1
tel. 0173 56108
www.borgogno.com
info@borgogno.com

16 ha - 100,000 bt | **10% discount**

PEOPLE - Andrea Farinetti, 22, is the dedicated, enthusiastic captain of the team of Beppe Caviola, Alberto Grasso and Beppe Valletti in a historic winery as bound to tradition as it is dynamically projected into the future. In the company's historic underground cellars in Barolo rest thousands of old vintages and large barrels, while from the scenic terrace of its new facility it's possible to admire virtually all the commune's great vineyards.

VINEYARDS - The names of the Borgogno crus, all in Barolo, are familiar to enthusiasts: Liste, the winery's first vineyard, planted in 1947 on unusual soil formed by the erosion of the hillside, a hectare at Cannubi, rich in sand, Fossati and Paiagallo. Weed control is carried out mechanically and the use of systemic products has been reduced with the introduction of new technologies.

WINES - The wines are classical in style, the fruit of long macerations at low temperatures and aging in large barrels. Ba**rolo Ris. 2005** (● 20,000 bt) has a fine, floral bouquet and a gentle palate with a hint of menthol. **Barolo Liste 2007** (● 3,500 bt) has notes of rose and violet on the nose and sweetness on the palate with well-controlled tannins. **Barolo 2007** (● 37,000 bt) is well-developed and generous with hints of spices. **Langhe Nebbiolo No Name 2008** (● 12,000 bt), a "polemical" wine made in protest against elaborious red-tape, comes from a good vintage and works well. **Dolcetto d'Alba 2011** (● 10,000 bt) is also good.

> **slow wine** BARBERA D'ALBA SUP **2010** (● 8,000 bt) 2010 was the first "true" vintage produced by the new management. What this wine tells us is that the future of Borgogno is going to be exciting: native yeasts, great sense of place and juicy drinkability.

FERTILIZERS natural manure
PLANT PROTECTION chemical, copper and sulphur
WEED CONTROL mechanical
YEASTS native
GRAPES 100% estate-grown
CERTIFICATION none

Giacomo Brezza & Figli

Via Lomondo, 4
tel. 0173 560921
www.brezza.it
brezza@brezza.it

16.5 ha - 80,000 bt

PEOPLE - Still flanked by his father Giacomo, Enzo Brezza runs this farm — of whose 23.5 hectares, 16.5 are given over to vine growing (the rest are occupied by hazelnut groves and woodland) — with a combination of knowhow and disarming simplicity. For generations they've been producing topnotch classic wines, the result of long macerations and aging in large barrels, respecting tradition with an eye to innovation (the use of glass caps for the base wines, for example). Worth stressing is the fairness of their prices.

VINEYARDS - The big news this year was the decision to convert to organic cultivation of the vineyards. This is a company of great prestige, so we certainly welcomed the move. The vineyards of nebbiolo grapes for Barolo are at Cannubi. Thanks to climate change, its eastern exposure produces increasingly successful results, adding elegance and longevity to the wines. Other vineyards are in the Sarmassa, a closed, sheltered, hence warmer valley, where the soil contains more clay.

WINES - The first-rate **Barolo Bricco Sarmassa 2008** (● 5,400 bt) is intense and balsamic, well-developed and fresh with a long finish and clear-cut fruity notes. **Barolo Sarmassa 2008** (● 8,300 bt) is more reticent for the time being, but displays raciness on the palate with fine tannins and a finish redolent of cocoa. With its nuances of red fruit and lively, refreshing mouthfeel, **Barbera d'Alba 2010** (● 17,000 bt) is a classic. Though it has lost nothing of the noble grape it's made with, **Langhe Nebbiolo 2010** (● 7,000 bt) is zippy and ready to drink. **Dolcetto d'Alba 2011** (● 14,000 bt) has marked fruit accompanied by just the right freshness.

> **slow wine** BAROLO CANNUBI **2008** (● 7,000 bt) Unabashed classicism, incomparable finesse and all the energy of the cru — all at price that couldn't be more honest price.

FERTILIZERS natural manure
PLANT PROTECTION copper and sulphur
WEED CONTROL mechanical
YEASTS selected
GRAPES 100% estate-grown
CERTIFICATION converting to organics

BAROLO (CN)
Damilano
Via Roma, 31
tel. 0173 56105
www.cantinedamilano.it
info@damilanog.com

BAROLO (CN)
Bartolo Mascarello
Via Roma, 15
tel. 0173 56125

58 ha - 450,000 bt

5.5 ha - 33,000 bt

PEOPLE - Many changes have been made at this cellar, which dates from 1890 and has always been managed by the descendants of founder Giuseppe Borgogno. A key moment in its recent history was the two-year period 1996-1997, when the fourth generation of the Damilano family joined the company. It is thanks to their hefty investment in vineyard and cellar — overseen by their cousin —that the quality of the wines has improved considerably.

VINEYARDS - The company boasts a vast number of vineyards, cultivated with the consultancy of Gian Piero Romana. They fan out over a number of plots in renowned crus such as Liste, Brunate, Cerequio and Cannubi. It is precisely in Cannubi that the Damilanos have decided to invest, cultivating 10 hectares of a total 15 for the production of what they have earmarked as their benchmark Barolo.

WINES - The wines, made with the consultancy of Beppe Caviola, are precise and well-crafted. **Barolo Liste 2008** (● 8,000 bt) has aromas of undergrowth, roots and macerated flowers, a zippy palate and a rigorous tannic structure. It's a wine worthy of applause. **Barolo Brunate 2008** (● 3,500 bt) is fine with aromas of spice and vanilla with good supporting acidity. The full-bodied **Barolo Cannubi 2008** (● 38,000 bt;) has highly complex nuances, a plump, well-rounded palate and a top-notch finish — a Great Wine. **Barolo Lecinquevigne 2008** (● 100,000 bt) is ideal as a wine to start from for anybody approaching this denomination for the first time. The beautifully made **Barbera d'Alba Lablù 2010** (● 20,000 bt) is fruity and meaty with a caress of a finish. **Langhe Arneis 2011** (○ 45,000 bt) is an agreeable white.

PEOPLE - At Maria Teresa Mascarello's cellar you breathe in an atmosphere of rigor and professionalism. And you also note great ability in communicating the value of the wines and the Langa hills. It's easy, almost inevitable, to meet visitors, mostly foreigners, in the cellar tasting its classic wines, which have acquired impeccable cleanness without losing any of the personality — comparabel to Maria Teresa's! — that made them famous in the first place.

VINEYARDS - The company's five hectares or so of vines are to be found mostly in the commune of Barolo — San Lorenzo and Cannubi have vines 50 years old, the others vines about 30 years old — plus a parcel at Torriglione di La Morra. The vineyards are managed without chemical weed control and without the use of systemic products. Work in the fields as in the cellar is based on simplicity and common sense without too much bunch thinning or other pointless interventions. What counts is good-old fashioned know-how, hence the preservation of the health and the natural fertility of the soil.

WINES - With its clean aromas of cherry and elegant bittersweet finish, **Dolcetto d'Alba 2011** (● 5,500 bt) is truly excellent. **Barbera d'Alba 2010** (● 5,500 bt) is irresistibly traditional in character with distinct acidity and plenty of flesh. **Langhe Nebbiolo 2010** (● 2,500 bt) seduces with notes of violet and a dynamic, juicy palate. The sumptuous **Barolo 2008** (● 19,000 bt) is classic dull garnet red in color with fine, deep notes of earth and wild rose, hints of spice, almost of pine needles, a beautifully sweet palate, the irresistible freshness of the vintage and a long, lingering, fruity, tangy finish with tannins that are never aggressive — a Great Wine! **Langhe Freisa Monrobiolo 2010** (● 2,000 bt), a true speciality of the Mascarello house is solid and succulent.

FERTILIZERS manure pellets
PLANT PROTECTION chemical, copper and sulphur
WEED CONTROL chemical, mechanical
YEASTS selected, native
GRAPES 3% bought in
CERTIFICATION none

FERTILIZERS organic-mineral
PLANT PROTECTION copper and sulphur
WEED CONTROL mechanical
YEASTS selected
GRAPES 100% estate-grown
CERTIFICATION none

Giuseppe Rinaldi

Via Monforte, 3
tel. 0173 56156

G.D. Vajra

Via delle Viole, 25
tel. 0173 56257
www.gdvajra.it
info@gdvajra.it

6.5 ha - 38,000 bt

❝ Over the years, cultured, curious Beppe Rinaldi has regaled Barolo fans with wines of great typicality and quality, the result of painstaking work in the vineyards and respect for the environment ❞

PEOPLE - Beppe Rinaldi, assisted by his daughter Marta, is a wine connoisseur and a strenuous defender of the Barolo area. His knowledge translates into profound, classic wines that age magnificently and tell the full story of the land of their birth.

VINEYARDS - The Beppe and Marta Rinaldi duo tend the vineyards in prestigious Barolo crus — Cannubi San Lorenzo and Ravera (whose eastern exposure signifies hefty tannins), Brunate and Le Coste — with the utmost naturalness and rigorous respect for the environment. Their approach stems from a close bond with the land and its traditions, hence awareness of the fundamental importance of peasant culture.

WINES - This grapey **Dolcetto d'Alba 2011** (● 4,000 bt) is typical and supple with bundles of fruity flesh and freshness. **Barbera d'Alba 2011** (● 6,500 bt) bears all the classic features of the grape, hence plenty of flesh and a good acid back-up. **Langhe Nebbiolo 2010** (● 8,000 bt) is shot with a nice balsamic vein and offers the palate solidity and freshness followed by a retrotaste with floral notes. **Barolo Cannubi San Lorenzo-Ravera 2008** (● 6,000 bt) has as yet subdued aromas against a balsamic background and a wonderfully youthful palate in which fruit, tannins and acidity are nicely balanced.

slow wine **BAROLO BRUNATE - LE COSTE 2008** (● 10,000 bt) A wine that faithfully captures the characteristics of its cru of origin. An irresistible mixture of succulence, depth and drinkability that hides great thrust and aging capacity.

FERTILIZERS natural manure
PLANT PROTECTION copper and sulphur
WEED CONTROL mechanical
YEASTS native
GRAPES 100% estate-grown
CERTIFICATION none

---

50 ha - 350,000 bt

❝ Milena, her husband Aldo Vaira and their three children Francesca, Giuseppe and Isidoro have created a model winery with agricultural practices respectful of the environment, reasonable prices and top quality. Besides rediscovering the freisa grape, they have *discovered* riesling as a grape for growing in the Langa hills ❞

PEOPLE - The Vaira family cellar is evolving all the time, its ultimate objective being to make wines that are a fuel for the soul. Which is why their products capture the very essence of the spirit of the Langa hills.

VINEYARDS - It was a real pleasure to hear Aldo talking about his vineyards when we visited one splendid day in May. Every parcel of land on this impressive estate is tended with care. With the aim of lengthening the lives of the vines, treatments with chemicals are reduced to a bare minimum. Under-vine mowing is mainly carried out mechanically, only partly through flame weeding and rarely using desiccants.

WINES - We love these wines, whose strong points are mouthfeel and sense of place. **Barolo Bricco delle Viole 2008** (● 10,000 bt) has spectacularly intact fruit, great juice and amazing depth. It's a *vin de garde* and a Great Wine. With its scent of violets and savory, tannic palate, the magnificent **Barolo Albe 2008** (● 60,000), offers enviable value for money. The intense, sweet **Barbera d'Alba Sup. 2009** (● 10,000 bt) comes from a vintage tailor-made for the grape, while **Langhe Nebbiolo 2010** (● 30,000 bt) is an elegant wine. Many of the vineyards are at Sinio. One real treat is **Langhe Bianco Petracine 2011** (○ riesling; 9,400 bt), acid and supple with a powerful finish. **Barbera d'Alba 2010** (● 50,000 bt) seduces the palate before closing on a spirited, flavorsome note.

FERTILIZERS natural manure
PLANT PROTECTION copper and sulphur
WEED CONTROL chemical, mechanical
YEASTS selected
GRAPES 100% estate-grown
CERTIFICATION none

CANALE (CN)

Cascina Ca' Rossa

Località Cascina Ca' Rossa, 56
tel. 0173 98348
www.cascinacarossa.com
angelo.ferrio@gmail.com

13 ha - 70,000 bt

66 Slowly but surely this winery has developed an eco-awareness for the environment that is now the leitmotiv of its high quality production 99

PEOPLE - In the cellar, situated in a pretty red farmhouse, the enthusiastic, untiring Angelo Ferrio will treat you to wines of great naturalness and simplicity that reflect the characteristics of the vineyards they are born in.

VINEYARDS - This year Angelo, always a great fan of organic vine growing, received the appropriate certification. Besides arneis, barbera and nebbiolo grapes, his meticulously tended vineyards are also home to herbs, insects and flowers. The chalky Mompissano vineyard is a spectacular place, where caves have been hewn by hand out of the overhanging crag to provide shelter for workers in the event of rain. No less beautiful is the sandy, steep Audinaggio, in which all the work is manual.

WINES - Roero Mompissano Ris. 2009 (● 6,000 bt) is well-developed and potent, full of sweet tannins and capable of lingering on the palate. **Roero Audinaggio 2010** (● 4,000 bt) combines finesse and elegance with deft tannins and a nice juicy finish with hints of menthol. Aged in stainless steel, **Langhe Nebbiolo 2010** (● 20,000 bt) is pleasantly quaffable. **Barbera d'Alba Mulassa 2010** (● 5,000 bt) ages in barriques and has a nuanced nose, a fleshy, juicy palate and a clean finish. **Barbera d'Alba 2010** (● 15,000 bt) is simpler, with ripish fruit and just the right degree of vivacity on the palate. Roero Arneis Merica 2011 (○ 20,000 bt) is beautifully blossomy with a classic fruity note and a generous palate with a sweet, fruity finish. An excellent Everyday Wine.

CANALE (CN)

Matteo Correggia

Località Garbinetto
Case Sparse, 124
tel. 0173 978009
www.matteocorreggia.com
cantina@matteocorreggia.com

20 ha - 135,000 bt

PEOPLE - The memory of Matteo Correggia will always be with us. It's him we have to thank for deciding to produce high quality wines in the Roero district. He was the first to begin selecting the finest vineyards in Canale and Santo Stefano Roero, and it was thanks to him that this small winery is now famous worldwide, a success sealed by the amazing Barbera d'Alba Marun 1990. After his early death, the place was taken over by his widow Ornella, who has been helped for years now by technician Luca Rostagno.

VINEYARDS - In the last few years, two vineyards, one of barbera and one of arneis, have been developed a stone's throw from the cellar. The splendid Marun vineyard is situated on dizzy slopes at an altitude of 280 meters. Given the steepness, the land is cover cropped to avoid wash-out. Even higher up in Canale, the Roche d'Ampsèy cru is given over to nebbiolo and barbera.

WINES - Roero Ròche d'Ampsèj Ris. 2008 (● 2,700 bt) conveys a magnificent sense of place with mineral, earthy notes and toasty nuances from brief aging in new barriques. **Roero 2010** (● 24,000 bt) offers balsamic notes. **Barbera d'Alba Marun 2010** (● 11,200 bt) is juicy and fleshy, while **Barbera d'Alba 2010** (● 23,000 bt), made with grapes from the Podio vineyard, is slightly tarter. **Roero Arneis 2011** (○ 45,000 bt) is mineral with notes of exotic fruit.

> **slow wine** **ROERO VAL DEI PRETI 2010** (● 10,700 bt) Ornella has made this wine, previously a simple Nebbiolo d'Alba, climb up a rung, and never was a decision more fortunate. We liked it very much indeed, especially its incredible land-rootedness and graceful body. It's fresh and juicy and the price is more than reasonable.

FERTILIZERS natural manure	FERTILIZERS green manure
PLANT PROTECTION copper and sulphur	PLANT PROTECTION chemical, copper and sulphur
WEED CONTROL mechanical	WEED CONTROL chemical, mechanical
YEASTS selected	YEASTS selected
GRAPES 100% estate-grown	GRAPES 100% estate-grown
CERTIFICATION organic	CERTIFICATION none

CANALE (CN)

Malvirà

LocalitàCanova
Case Sparse, 144
tel. 0173 978145
www.malvira.com
malvira@malvira.com

CANALE (CN)

Monchiero Carbone

Via Santo Stefano Roero, 2
tel. 0173 95568
www.monchierocarbone.com
info@monchierocarbone.com

42 ha - 350,000 bt   **10% discount**

17 ha - 150,000 bt

PEOPLE - There can be no doubting the importance of this copmay on the Roero wine scene. For many years now Massimo and Roberto Damonte have been putting passion and total dedication into the promotion not only of wine, but also of the whole Roero area, its history (they have restored Villa Tiboldi) and traditions. Their aim is to protect a land that is as beautiful and, at times, as rugged as it is fragile. Now that they have completed the building of their new cellar, they'll be able to delight us all the more with their wines.

VINEYARDS - The vineyards, equally divided between red and white grapes, are managed with respect for the environment. The plant in which manure is transformed into humus will stimulate the life of the soil without straining it excessively. The vineyards have different soil compositions — from sand to limestone — and ages — from 60 years downwards — and the principal grapes are arneis and nebbiolo.

WINES - **Roero Renesio Ris. 2008** (● 8,000 bt) possesses the classic characteristics of pronounced, plump fruit and a finish full of verve. **Roero Trinità Ris. 2008** (● 25,000 bt) is fine and spicy with perky fruit and a lingering finish. An important novelty is **Roero 2009** (● 20,000 bt), a drinkable, fruity base wine at a very affordable price. The Arneis table features **Roero Arneis Saglietto 2010** (○ 10,000 bt), half-aged in wooden barrels, stands out for its minerality and an intriguing oaky note. **Roero Arneis Trinità 2010** (○ 20,000 bt), born from sandier soil, is stylish with notes of herbs, nice length and a finish of fruit and menthol.

slow wine ROERO ARNEIS RENESIO 2010 (○ 20,000 bt) For some years now, Malvirà has been releasing more aged Arneis than previously, all top-notch labels. This floral, fleshy, lively, typical version from the Renesio vineyard proves the point.

PEOPLE - Francesco Monchiero runs this impressive winery just outside Canale with his wife Lucrezia Scarsi and his mother Lucia Carbone. With its pursuit of quality without compromise and wines true to the terroir, in the last few years the company has become an institution in the Roero district. The modern part, designed to process arneis grapes with the utmost delicacy (by gravity and reduction) is situated below the old farmyard alongside the historic cellar.

VINEYARDS - The strong, structured Barbera is made with grapes from a three-hectare vineyard with clay and limestone soil and an east-west exposure in the Mombirone cru. Cecu d'la Biunda is made with grapes from the Renesio wine hill and from the ultra-sandy Tanone di Vezza vineyard, where the arneis grape acquires mineral aromas. Printi is a long, west-facing hillside with clay and limestone soil, while the Srü vineyard, a few hundred meters away, has sandier soil.

WINES - "Complete and unfussy" — Francesco is adamant that arneis is one of Italy's great white grapes. Tasting the excellent **Roero Arneis Cecu D'la Biunda 2011** (○ 20,000 bt), vibrant and flowery with hints of citrus fruit, elegant, mineral — well, you can't say he's wrong. **Roero Arneis Recit 2011** (○ 80,000 bt), which captures the quintessence of the grape, is great value for money. Delicate and floral with notes of grass on the nose, it has a juicy, refreshing mouth with a hint of bitterness to lengthen the finish. It's an excellent Everyday Wine. **Barbera d'Alba Monbirone 2010** (● 8,000 bt) lives up to expectations, combining depth, beef and elegance thanks to its vivacious, long mouthfeel. Fascinating too is **Barbera d'Alba Pelisa 2011** (● 25,000 bt), aged only for a third part in oak and modulated with fresh and fruity notes. The release of Roero Srü 2010 and Roero Printi Ris. 2009 ha been postponed.

FERTILIZERS humus
PLANT PROTECTION chemical, copper and sulphur
WEED CONTROL chemical, mechanical
YEASTS selected
GRAPES 3% bought in
CERTIFICATION none

FERTILIZERS natural manure
PLANT PROTECTION copper and sulphur
WEED CONTROL chemical, mechanical
YEASTS selected
GRAPES 15% bought in
CERTIFICATION none

Marsaglia

Via Madama Mussone, 2
tel. 0173 213048
www.cantinamarsaglia.it
cantina@cantinamarsaglia.it

15 ha - 90,000 bt   **10% discount**

PEOPLE - This company, run by young-sters Enrico and Monica Marsaglia, abetted by their mother Marina Mortara, is situat-ed in the small town of Castellinaldo. In the newly restructured cellar — alongside which stands an old brick building that used to serve as an icehouse — stainless steel tanks have almost completely replaced the old ce-ment vats. Large and medium-sized barrels are used for the Nebbiolos, small casks, only a few of which new, for the Barberas.

VINEYARDS - Enrico studied at enolo-gy school but he also tends the vineyards, which are divided equally between arneis, barbera and nebbiolo. He uses weed killers just once in the early spring, after which he reverts to mechanical interventions. In the clayier soil of the Bric d'America vineyard, we noted lots of shells, while the sandier Serramiana resembles a vertical rock face. Here Enrico avoids using copper "so as not to burn the scents of arneis".

WINES - Roero Arneis Serramiana 2011 (○ 30,000 bt) has marked notes of white peach, is full and agreeably sweet on the palate and has a tangy finish. La **Barbera d'Alba Castellinaldo 2008** (● 8,000 bt) has ripe cherry on the nose and nice tanginess in the mouth with classic notes of soil in the finish. The floral, nicely textured **Nebbiolo d'Alba 2008** (● 8,000 bt) has ripe fruit and a sapid finish. **Barbera d'Alba San Cristoforo 2010** (● 15,000 bt) is compact on the nose and palate with a lovely quaffable finish. The unusual **Monferrato Rosso Complotto 2010** (● nebbiolo, barbera, syrah; 2,500 bt) has solid structure.

| slow wine | **ROERO BRIC D'AMERICA 2008** (● 8,000 bt) An excellent red characterized by the classic rich, sweet fruit of the area, beautiful-ly refreshing with a tangy, lingering finish. |

FERTILIZERS mineral, natural manure
PLANT PROTECTION chemical, copper and sulphur
WEED CONTROL chemical, mechanical
YEASTS selected
GRAPES 100% estate-grown
CERTIFICATION none

Brovia

Frazione Garbelletto
Via Alba-Barolo, 54
tel. 0173 62852
www.brovia.net
info@brovia.net

16.5 ha - 60,000 bt

❝ We visited the Brovia family winery on a wet spring day. What we found there — namely, top quality wines with a strong sense of the land and impeccably workmanlike vineyard management — provided full confirmation of its potential ❞

PEOPLE - The winery is run by two sisters, Cristina, who takes care of all matters agro-nomic, Elena, who works in the cellar, and Elena's Catalan husband, Alex Sanchez So-lana, who looks after the commercial side of the business. The trio can also count on the advice of Giacinto Brovia, a doyen of Barolo.

VINEYARDS - In 2010 we visited the Rocche di Castiglione Falletto cru, last year the Villero cru. This year, despite the rain, we couldn't miss the chance to take in the fantastic, scenic view of the Ca' Mia di Ser-ralunga vineyard, better known as Brea. The place is perfectly located with vines over 50 years old. It is here in the best years that Dol-cetto Solatio is produced with grapes from the old vines. Since 2010 the cellar has been experimenting with organic agriculture.

WINES - Cellar practices are tradition-al without frills or fuss. The results are ex-ceptional. The star wine is Barolo Ca' Mia 2008 (● 5,000 bt), whose nose is a hymn to the classicism of the nebbiolo grape, with se-ductive violet notes and a long, lingering tart palate. Worth buying now and opening no earlier than 2016, it's a Great Wine. Fresh, seductive **Barolo Rocche 2008** (● 5,000 bt) is more delicate. **Barolo Villero 2008** (● 5,000 bt) also hits dizzy, likely unrepeatable, heights. **Barolo Garblèt Suè 2008** (● 3,600 bt), which comes from the Altenasso cru, is more rustic and tannic. **Barbera d'Alba Sorì del Drago 2010** (● 4,500 bt) is inviting and **Dolcetto d'Alba Vignavillej 2011** (● 8.000 bt) does not disappoint either.

FERTILIZERS manure pellets, natural manure
PLANT PROTECTION copper and sulphur
WEED CONTROL mechanical
YEASTS native
GRAPES 8% bought in
CERTIFICATION converting to organics

Cavallotto Fratelli

Località Bricco Boschis
Strada Alba-Monforte, 40
tel. 0173 62814
www.cavallotto.com
info@cavallotto.com

23 ha - 100,000 bt **10% discount**

❝ Bottles cloaked in the myth of the Cavallotto family that reserve us great emotions thanks to their sense of place and ability to challenge the passing of time. Organic management of the vineyards translates into tradition and innovation all rolled into one ❞

PEOPLE - This cellar has been run by brothers and sisters for three generations. The first were Giuseppe, grandfather of the present owners, and Marcello, then came Olivio, their father, and his brother Gildo. Today it's the turn of Alfio and Laura.

VINEYARDS - What can we say about the great Langa cru, Bricco Boschis? We visited it on April 12 and, braving the rain, had a walk among the vine rows, which stand in grass on soil that is sandier than many other Langa vineyards. From this hilltop holding — well ventilated and cultivated organically, albeit without certification as yet — it is possible to admire virtually all the communes of the Barolo denomination.

WINES - The two Barolo Reserves are monumental — inevitably so, given the excellent 2006 harvest. As is often the case, with its stupendous, super-elegant floral notes, **Barolo Vignolo Ris. 2006** (● 7,000 bt) is the readier of the two, while the magnificent **Barolo Bricco Boschis Vigna San Giuseppe Ris. 2006** (● 13,300 bt) is richer, fleshier and more complex — a Great Wine. The dry, tonic, elegant, gutsy **Barolo Bricco Boschis 2008** (● 26,000 bt) was also produced after a vintage that will be remembered for a long time in the Langa district and is much more than just a base wine. **Langhe Freisa 2010** (● 3,200 bt) is a real treat for lovers of the genre. The beautifully juicy **Barbera d'Alba Vigna del Cuculo 2009** (● 12,000 bt) is aged in 30-hectoliter barrels. Last but not least, **Dolcetto d'Alba Vigna Scot 2011** (● 16,000 bt) is nicely fragrant.

FERTILIZERS green manure
PLANT PROTECTION copper and sulphur
WEED CONTROL mechanical
YEASTS native
GRAPES 100% estate-grown
CERTIFICATION none

Paolo Scavino

Strada Alba-Barolo, 59
tel. 0173 62850
www.paoloscavino.com
info@paoloscavino.com

24 ha - 150,000 bt

PEOPLE - Enrico Scavino is an innovator, not so much on account of the old story of his use of barriques, but because of his constant quest for quality by experimenting with new tecniques in the cellar and in the vineyards. Our visit and our chat with Enrico gave us the chance to appreciate his clear, confident ideas about enology and agronomy. Scavino boasts five crus of absolute prestige and he has been sharing his tough but exciting work with his two daughters, Enrica and Elisa, for years.

VINEYARDS - During our visit, Enrico took us to see Cannubi, a jewel of a vineyard. He showed us how he works the soil under the vines, with a disk and at least once a year — usually in May when the grass grows prolifically — with weed killer. The other vineyards are Monvigliero in Verduno, Prapò in Serralunga (the wines from which have yet to be marketed), Fiasco in Castiglione Falletto, Rocche dell'Annunziata in La Morra and Bricco Ambrogio in Roddi.

WINES - One of Enrico Scavino's innovations was the introduction of the rotor macerator to the Langa hills. Now he and his daughters are about to experiment with Barolo in large wooden barrels. **Barolo Rocche dell'Annunziata Ris. 2006** (● 2,700 bt), the fruit of a memorable vintage, was on top form. As superlative as ever was **Barolo Bric dël Fiasc 2008** (● 8,000 bt), first produced in 1978. The 2008 is sublime, a Great Wine. **Barolo Cannubi 2008** (● 3,000 bt) is blossomy and headily scented. **Barolo Monvigliero 2008** (● 5,000 bt) is nice and spicy. The base wines are also very good indeed. **Barbera d'Alba 2011** (● 10,000 bt) is fresh and juicy with luscious fruit to the fore. **Dolcetto d'Alba 2011** (● 10,000 bt) has a typical tone and a flavorsome, winy finish.

FERTILIZERS natural manure
PLANT PROTECTION chemical, copper and sulphur
WEED CONTROL chemical, mechanical
YEASTS selected
GRAPES 100% estate-grown
CERTIFICATION none

Vietti

Piazza Vittorio Veneto, 5
tel. 0173 62825
www.vietti.com
info@vietti.com

Marziano Abbona

Borgata San Luigi, 40
tel. 0173 721317
www.abbona.com
abbona@abbona.com

---

40 ha - 180,000 bt   **10% discount**

50 ha - nd bt

PEOPLE - Vietti is one of the most prestigious wineries in the Langhe hills. Capably managed by Mario Cordero and Luca Currado, it has achieved its success through painstaking selection of crus. With years of history under its belt, the company treats us to wines of staggering longevity.

VINEYARDS - The technician and consultant Gian Piero Romana offers advice on the management of the family's massive properties. The rest is charged to the experience of Mario, Luca and their staff, who have the job and honor of bringing out all the distinctive features of vineyards such as Lazzarito, Rocche, Brunate, Villero and Scarrone. Besides this inestimable patrimony in the Langa hills, the company also boasts vineyards in the Asti area. The most prestigious crus are managed using organic methods, while the steepest vineyards are cultivated according to the principles of integrated pest management.

WINES - "Fashion lasts five seconds. At the sixth you're not fashionable any more." Here, *in nuce*, is the company's philosophy, which places the onus on the Langa winemaking tradition. The range of excellent wines is too broad for us to review all of them. We had no qualms about naming Barolo Lazzarito 2008 (● 6,000 bt) a Great Wine. It has an outstanding bouquet and a sensational palate — no more, no less. The great vintage also delivered a **Barolo Castiglione 2008** (● 43,000 bt) of ample finesse, made with grapes from a selection of different crus, and a **Barolo Brunate 2008** (● 3,800 bt) that epitomizes the elegance of this great La Morra cru. **Langhe Nebbiolo Perbacco 2010** (● 18,000 bt), a Barolo in miniature combining depth and great value for money, is up to standard as always. **Barbera d'Asti Tre Vigne 2010** (● 60,000 bt) is succulent and lively.

PEOPLE - Over the years, Marziano Abbona has built up a first-rate winery by promoting Dolcetto di Dogliani and the other classic Langa wines, at once dabbling with non-native grapes. His helpfulness towards others, his interest in the outside world and his commitment to his own work as a winemaker are tied to his profound respect for his land and his roots. Today he can count on the help of his two daughters, Chiara and Mara.

VINEYARDS - The cellar, round which Marziano has replanted the trees that were growing there in his grandfather's day, is situated in the enchanting Valle dell'Olmo, encircled by the company's vineyards. No chemical weedkillers are used here and the same is true of the ones in Monforte, Novello and other communes. In Dogliani dolcetto grapes predominate, alongside pinot nero, used for spumante, and viognier. The Pressenda cru at Monforte nestles on a dizzy slope and the Terlo Ravera cru is near Novello.

WINES - The blossomy and balsamic **Barolo Pressenda 2008** (● 16,000 bt) has fantastic structure, just the right maturity and all the length of the very best vintages. **Barolo Terlo Ravera 2008** (● 15,000 bt) has distinct notes of wild rose, a fleshy palate and a lingering, racy finish. The nicely drinkable **Dolcetto di Dogliani San Luigi 2011** (● 65,000 bt) has notes of fresh grass and a lively finish. After maturing for a year in wood, **Barbera d'Alba Rinaldi 2010** (● 35,000 bt) has clear notes of cherry, crunchy, juicy fruit on the palate and a refreshing finish. **Langhe Bianco Cinerino 2011** (○ viognier; 16,000 bt) has a bouquet of apricots.

> **slow wine** **DOGLIANI PAPÀ CELSO 2010** (● 36,000 bt) A wine that sees the light in a 70-year-old vineyard. It has a fruity bouquet with plenty of flesh and juice and fantastic length. In other words, it speaks the language of its terroir.

FERTILIZERS natural manure	FERTILIZERS natural manure
PLANT PROTECTION chemical, copper and sulphur	PLANT PROTECTION chemical, copper and sulphur
WEED CONTROL chemical, mechanical	WEED CONTROL mechanical
YEASTS native	YEASTS native
GRAPES 100% estate-grown	GRAPES 100% estate-grown
CERTIFICATION none	CERTIFICATION none

DOGLIANI (CN)

Cascina Corte

Borgata Valdiberti, 33
tel. 0173 743539
www.cascinacorte.it
info@cascinacorte.it

5.5 ha - 25,000 bt **10% discount**

" Sandro Barosi and Amalia Battaglia bought their old farmhouse eleven years ago. Since then they have restored it magnificently, opened a bed and breakfast, and started to produce wonderful wines using organic methods — a fact that adds luster to their achievements "

PEOPLE - Slowly but surely, Sandro Barosi and Amalia Battaglia have turned their property into a little corner of paradise and continue to tend to it as serenely and imperturbably as ever.

VINEYARDS - Sandro was quick to realize that conventional agriculture wasn't his cup of tea and with the help of agronomist Gian Piero Romana decided to go over to organics. The vineyards, mostly 60 years old, surround the farmhouse on chalky soil, though further up, where the barbera grapes grow at an altitude of 450 meters, it also contains clay. The steep Pirochetta vineyard changes soil halfway down and yields a wine of notable depth and character.

WINES - These wines are at once earnest with a sense of place, but also easy to drink and exceptionally absorbing. The two Dolcettos are aged only in stainless steel: fresh, fruity **Dolcetto di Dogliani 2011** (● 9,000 bt) has the most classic aromas and a lean, robust, assertive palate with plenty of earthiness and a gutsy finish. With its dark, elegant character, perkiness and length, **Dogliani Pirochetta Vecchie Vigne 2010** (● 6,500 bt) is much more structured. **Piemonte Barbera 2010** (● 6.000 bt) is racy and juicy, cocky and tangy. Aged in large barrels, **Langhe Nebbiolo 2010** (● 5,000 bt) has finely floral, spicy notes and a solid, refined palate. **Barnedòl** (● 4,500 bt) is a tasty blend of barbera, dolcetto and nebbiolo.

DOGLIANI (CN)

Ca' Viola

Borgata San Luigi, 11
tel. 0173 70547
www.caviola.com
caviola@caviola.com

10 ha - 50,000 bt

PEOPLE - You always expect nothing but the best from an enologist as talented as Beppe Caviola, who, regular as clockwork, harvest by harvest, comes up with the goods in the form of wines that combine typicity, elegance and depth. Some of the credit for all this has to go to his team of business partner Maurizio Anselmo, wife Simonetta, and young collaborator Alessandro Scarrone. Following recent restructuring work, the company now boasts a photovoltaic plant and an elegant b&b.

VINEYARDS - Save for a two-hectare nebbiolo plot in the commune of Novello, all the company's vineyards are at Montelupo Albese, where they are given over to barbera and dolcetto. The steep marl and limestone terrains have south and southwest exposures. Guyot-pruned and thinned with almost obsessive care, they have all it takes to produce top quality grapes — and wines.

WINES - Aged in casks and 50-hectoliter barrels, **Barolo Sottocastello 2007** (● 6,500 bt) is typical with flowery aromas, ripe fruit and hints of undergrowth. It's a well-balanced wine with fine tannins, ready now but also with great development prospects. Its "younger brother" is the deep **Langhe Nebbiolo Sottocastello 2010** (● 2,000 bt). The house specialty is the Vera dolcetto grape. The excellent **Dolcetto d'Alba Vilot 2011** (● 5,000 bt) is refreshing and full of flavor, while the alluring **Dolcetto d'Alba Barturot 2011** (● 8,000 bt) is more complex and potent. The spicy, complex **Barbera d'Alba Bric du Luv 2010** (● 6,000 bt) is made with grapes from a vineyard with vines 60 years old. It's so good it's the only Barbera d'Alba to win the Great Wine accolade. **Barbera d'Alba Brichet 2011** (● 13,000 bt) is rich in flavor.

FERTILIZERS natural manure
PLANT PROTECTION copper and sulphur
WEED CONTROL mechanical
YEASTS native
GRAPES 100% estate-grown
CERTIFICATION organic

FERTILIZERS manure pellets, natural manure
PLANT PROTECTION chemical, copper and sulphur
WEED CONTROL chemical, mechanical
YEASTS native
GRAPES 100% estate-grown
CERTIFICATION none

Quinto Chionetti

Borgata Valdiberti, 44
tel. 0173 71179
www.chionettiquinto.com
chionettiquinto@chionettiquinto.com

---

15 ha - 80,000 bt

PEOPLE - Quinto Chionetti is a symbol of the Langa district and a synonym of Dolcetto di Dogliani, of which it is one of the loftiest, purest expressions. Quinto himself, 85 and still the heart and soul of the company, epitomizes the figure of the working winemaker, true to tradition and respectful of the land. His grandfather Giuseppe and his father Andrea had been making wine in Dogliani since the start of the 20th century, their name enjoying a great reputation among bottlers for their quality, the end-result of low yields and rigorous selections.

VINEYARDS - The vineyards encircle the Briccolero farm, the cellar's headquarters, which gives its name to the most important wine. The dolcetto grapes are planted on two different terrains: San Luigi, where the hygroscopic red earth and southwest exposure yield readier, more aromatic wines; and the more structured Briccolero cru with a southeast exposure, where the white soil is poorer and the climate warmer. A new vineyard in a nearby valley with a special microclimate and soil more similar to that of the Alba area, is to be planted with nebbiolo grapes.

WINES - Obsessive care and attention for the vines and limited use of chemicals translate into the healthiest of grapes. Marco Devalle, at Chionetti since 1989, turns into crystal-clear, clean precise wines that capture the essence of the Dogliani terroir. Fine and fruity, **Dolcetto di Dogliani San Luigi 2011** (● 48,000 bt) is a joy to drink. **Langhe Nebbiolo 2010** (● 1,700 bt), made with grapes from the Roero hills, is forthright and elegant.

> **slow wine** **DOLCETTO DI DOGLIANI BRICCOLERO 2011** (● 36,000 bt) A thoroughbred wine with a bouquet of raspberry and bramble followed up by a long, rich palate and just the right tannins. It is vinified in steel tanks and left unfiltered (only being slightly clarified). Last but not least, sulfur is added only sparingly.

FERTILIZERS	natural manure
PLANT PROTECTION	copper and sulphur
WEED CONTROL	mechanical
YEASTS	native
GRAPES	100% estate-grown
CERTIFICATION	converting to organics

Pecchenino

Borgata Valdiberti, 59
tel. 0173 70686
www.pecchenino.com
pecchenino@pecchenino.it

---

24 ha - 110,000 bt   **10% discount**

66 The Pecchenino winery was a leading player in the Dolcetto renaissance and continues to be at the cutting edge in the Dogliani zone, a champion in battles in support of the Denomination 99

PEOPLE - It only takes one word to sum up the work of Orlando and Attilio Pecchenino, and that word is professionalism. Their Dolcetto, or rather Dogliani — the result of hard work in the vineyards — has become a model of enological credibility on the international scene.

VINEYARDS - The vineyards are the be all and end all for this company and winegrowing area and visiting them is a moral obligation. Those of Siri d'Jermu and Bricco Botti at Valdiberti, a hamlet on the outskirts of Dogliani, are situated near the cellar itself and managed in compliance with good agricultural practice, based on common sense and a modern, pragmatic Vision.

WINES - The Barolo zone borders on that of Dogliani. This overlapping of landscape and culture has led the Pecchenino brothers to invest in two small vineyards in the Le Coste district near Monforte. The results of their gamble are **Barolo San Giuseppe 2008** (● 6,000 bt) and **Barolo Le Coste 2008** (● 6,000 bt). The first has a nose of great expressive finesse and a long palate, whereas the second is spicier and less immediate but with great aging potential. The unmissable **Dogliani Sirì d'Jermu 2010** (● 20,000 bt) was fruitier and sweeter than previous vintages. **Dogliani San Luigi 2011** (● 45,000 bt), a juicy expression of both grape variety and terroir, is juicy and drinkable, well worthy of recognition as an Everyday Wine. **Langhe Nebbiolo Vigna Botti 2011** (● 7,800 bt) is very good too.

FERTILIZERS	manure pellets
PLANT PROTECTION	chemical, copper and sulphur
WEED CONTROL	mechanical
YEASTS	native
GRAPES	100% estate-grown
CERTIFICATION	none

DOGLIANI (CN)

San Fereolo

Borgata Valdibà, 59
tel. 0173 742075
www.sanfereolo.com
info@sanfereolo.com

FARIGLIANO (CN)

Anna Maria Abbona

Frazione Moncucco, 21
tel. 0173 797228
www.annamariaabbona.it
info@annamariaabbona.it

---

13 ha - 40,000 bt

11 ha - 75,000 bt   `10% discount`

PEOPLE - Anyone with a smidgeon of curiosity should go visit Nicoletta Bocca, the owner of this great winery, and hear her speak about biodynamics. With regard not so much to viticulture, the part never addressed directly by the father of the theory, Rudolf Steiner, father, as to the basic ideas that motivate winemakers who, like Nicoletta, believe in the philosophy. At any rate, her wines speak a new, truly interesting language.

VINEYARDS - It's a real pleasure to walk through vineyards in which balance reigns among all forms of life. The herbs and flowers between the vine rows are changing all the time, and you have the impression that the vines enjoy excellent health. Planted with dolcetto, barbera and nebbiolo grapes, plus two non-native varieties, riesling and gewürztraminer, the various parcels are scattered around the hills of the Dogliani area. They are managed using organic and biodynamic methods with a limited use of copper and sulfur.

WINES - **Langhe Bianco Coste di Riavolo 2008** (○ riesling, gewürztraminer; 3,000 bt) has subtle scents of mint and sage accompanied by notes of exotic fruit. On the palate it is lively and well-textured with a final marked by bitterish notes of rhubarb and gentian. **Langhe Nebbiolo Il Provinciale 2007** (● 2,500 bt) offers the nose floral aromas with a hint of soil and a whiff of metal. Acidity in the mouth sets off the ripe fruit, which follows through into well-crafted tannins and a lingering finish. **Dolcetto di Dogliani Valdibà 2010** (● 13,000 bt) won us over for the umpteenth time with its fine aromas of flowers and cherries, its huge drinkability, fleshiness, raciness and a flavorful finish in which an intriguing licoricey note peeps through. It's a truly excellent Everyday Wine.

66 Every time we taste Anna Maria Abbona's wines we are amazed by the way they encapsulate the soul of the land — at honest, competitive prices too 99

PEOPLE - The most important novelties this year were the advent of Federico, 22, Anna Maria Abbona and Franco Schellino's son, and the production of a white wine with nascetta grapes.

VINEYARDS - Situated at an altitude of more than 500 meters, vineyards are managed with rigorous respect for the environment without the use of chemicals. Flavescence dorée is fought largely by keeping the woods and other potential hotbeds of infection clean. "Some jobs have to be done irrespective of the costs and work they involve," Franco told us. Altitude and day-night temperature swings explain why the wines are so fresh and full of aroma.

WINES - **Langhe Bianco Netta 2011** (○ nascetta; 1,800 bt) is full-bodied and buttery with well-defined aromas. The floral, forceful **Langhe Bianco L'Alman 2011** (○ riesling; 3,300 bt), full of freshness and unmistakable aroma, is expansive on the palate. **Dogliani Sorì dij But 2011** (● 30,000 bt) is as packed with intact fruit and brio as ever, fleshy and leisurely. **Dogliani San Bernardo 2009** (● 3,500 bt), which is aged in large wooden barrels, has structure and complexity with sweet tannins and a long finish — a powerful, richly extracted red of commendable harmony. **Langhe Nebbiolo 2009** (● 6,000 bt) has typical floral notes and sweet tannins.

> **slow wine** **DOGLIANI MAIOLI 2010** (● 7,000 bt) Made with grapes from a vineyard planted in 1936, a wine that is mineral, earthy and intense, well-balanced, long and leisurely.

FERTILIZERS biodynamic preparations, green manure	
PLANT PROTECTION copper and sulphur	
WEED CONTROL mechanical	
YEASTS native	
GRAPES 100% estate-grown	
CERTIFICATION organic	

FERTILIZERS none	
PLANT PROTECTION copper and sulphur	
WEED CONTROL mechanical	
YEASTS native	
GRAPES 100% estate-grown	
CERTIFICATION none	

FARIGLIANO (CN)

Giovanni Battista Gillardi

Cascina Corsaletto, 69
tel. 0173 76306
www.gillardi.it
gillardi@gillardi.it

8 ha - 35,000 bt

PEOPLE - "Our Dolcettos will never see wood." So spoke the ever drastic Giacolino Gillardi, who often seems to enjoy going against the tide with his highly personal ideas and methods. He manages his winery with his father Giovanni Battista and his mother. His attractive, efficient cellar houses many-colored cement tanks alongside the stainless steel ones, and the second-hand barrique area is particularly suggestive.

VINEYARDS - The vineyards fan out round a 17th-century farmhouse at an altitude of about 500 meters. They form a natural amphitheater, where the stiff ventilation slows down the ripening of the grapes and ensures their wholesomeness. The Cursalet vineyard was planted at least 80 years ago and still enjoys excellent health. A lot of work had to be carried out to improve drainage in the steep Vigna Maestra holding nearby. Weeding control is only performed below the vine rows and no systemic products are used.

WINES - **Dogliani Cursalet 2011** (● 12,000 bt) is vibrant on the nose with a palate on which the classic fruit typical of the typology gradually emerges. **Dogliani Vigna Maestra 2011** (● 20,000 bt) is distinctly redolent of cherry and almond with a racy, typical palate and a scrumptiously juicy finish — a successful Everyday Wine. **Langhe Rosso Harys 2010** (● syrah; 2,000 bt), spicy yet at once fine and potent, is a modern-style red that translates the grape's characteristics with precision. **Langhe Rosso Fiore di Harys 2010** (● dolcetto, syrah, merlot, cabernet sauvignon; 3,800 bt) is a rather unorthodox assemblage of grapes of very different characteristics that nonetheless achieve a certain harmony. **Langhe Rosso Merlò 2009** (● merlot; 800 bt) has pronounced notes of graphite and tobacco.

FERTILIZERS	organic-mineral, natural manure
PLANT PROTECTION	copper and sulphur
WEED CONTROL	chemical, mechanical
YEASTS	native
GRAPES	100% estate-grown
CERTIFICATION	none

GRINZANE CAVOUR (CN)

La Spinetta

Località Campé
Via Carzello, 1
tel. 0141 877396
www.la-spinetta.com
info@la-spinetta.com

100 ha - 440,000 bt

PEOPLE - The Rivetti siblings — Giorgio, Bruno, Carlo and Giovanna — run a company that is unique on the Piedmontese wine scene. Fully-fledged, dynamic entrepreneurs all four of them, over the years they have increased the number of their properties and the range of their wines. So much so that today they offer every typology of regional wine, from spumantes — last year they took over the celebrated Contratto maison — to important reds, to the sweet Moscato d'Asti, a family classic.

VINEYARDS - The company owns 100 hectares of vineyard, scattered over numerous zones of Piedmont. The nebbiolo and barbera vineyards are neither treated with herbicides nor with systemic products. This is a big decision to make for a company of this size and deserves a round of applause. Radical bunch thinning explains the richness of the wines. The Barbaresco crus bear the prestigious names of Gallina, Starderi and Valeirano, while the Barolos come from the commune of Grinzane Cavour.

WINES - **Langhe Sauvignon 2009** (○ 3,000 bt) is wonderfully refreshing, tangy and drinkable. **Barbera d'Asti Sup. Bionzo 2010** (● 27,000 bt) is as convincing as ever with its great fruity flesh, balance and brio, though it lacks a touch of length on account of the poor harvest. **Barolo Garetti 2008** (● 6,000 bt) is very good indeed: floral, solid and zippy on the palate, it has a long, lingering finish enhanced by hints of wild rose. It's a Great Wine. The nicely textured **Barbaresco Bordini 2009** (● 12,000 bt) strikes a balance between oak and fruit and decent acidity on the palate. **Barbaresco Gallina 2009** (● 11,000 bt) is rich, powerful and concentrated with evident signs of aging in wooden cask. The classic **Monferrato Rosso Pin 2010** (● 18.000 bt) is again a successful modern blend of nebbiolo and barbera.

FERTILIZERS	natural manure
PLANT PROTECTION	chemical, copper and sulphur
WEED CONTROL	mechanical
YEASTS	selected, native
GRAPES	100% estate-grown
CERTIFICATION	none

LA MORRA (CN)

Elio Altare
Cascina Nuova

Frazione Annunziata, 51
tel. 0173 50835
www.elioaltare.com
elioaltare@elioaltare.com

10.5 ha - 60,000 bt

❝ Silvia Altare is still very young but she has inherited an important, daunting legacy. With seriousness and dedication she makes wines of the highest quality and works the vineyards conscientiously without using weedkillers and chemical fertilizers ❞

PEOPLE - Working alongside her father Elio, Silvia Altare isn't afraid to get her hands dirty in the vineyards and the cellar. Completing the team is their trusted Japanese assistant Tesu Cyo.

VINEYARDS - Responsible for work in the countryside is the indestructible Edoardo Cassinelli, who at the ripe old age of 76 never misses a day among the vine rows. The Altares don't stress the vines with chemical agents. Their Arborina cru surrounds the cellar and represents Elio's trademark. For some years now they have also rented a magnificent property in the Cerretta cru in Serralunga.

WINES - Here they respect tradition, but it's not just any old tradition. No, it's the tradition of Elio Altare: meaning five-day macerations and aging in barriques. **Barolo 2008** (● 12,000 bt) has a nose of violets and wild strawberries. **Barolo Arborina 2008** (● 8,000 bt) is harsher and more potent, rich with a precise, juicy finish and plenty of tannins. **Barolo Vigna Bricco Cerretta 2006** (● 6,000 bt) is floral and fruity with notes of violet, strawberry and cherry. It has an intense palate with pleasant tannins on the finish. The wine that impressed us most was **Langhe Rosso La Villa 2010** (● nebbiolo, barbera; 2,300 bt) in which the two grape varieties fuse to perfection. Very interesting too is **Langhe Rosso Arborina 2010** (● nebbiolo; 2,300 bt), which has aromas of violet and sweet tannins. **Langhe Rosso Larigi 2010** (● barbera; 2,300 bt) feels the effects of a vintage that wasn't exceptional for the barbera grape.

FERTILIZERS	natural manure
PLANT PROTECTION	copper and sulphur
WEED CONTROL	mechanical
YEASTS	native
GRAPES	100% estate-grown
CERTIFICATION	none

LA MORRA (CN)

Brandini   €

Frazione Brandini, 16
tel. 0173 50266
www.agricolabrandini.it
info@agricolabrandini.it

9.5 ha - 65,000 bt

PEOPLE - For many years Carlo Cavagnero did a different job but in 1995, converted on the road to La Morra, he decided to buy a small piece of farmland, where he began to cultivate vines and sell the grapes. The real turnaround came in 2007 when members of the Eataly group bought a stake in the enterprise. Carlo has stayed on as technical manager.

VINEYARDS - It's a pleasure to walk round the vineyards of Brandini, one of the few organic wineries in La Morra. You can tell the difference — lush grass between the vine rows, mating disruption for insects, education with a special learning trail among the vineyards. The Brandini isn't the most celebrated winery in the Barolo denomination, but it has great growth potential with wines that owe their elegance to the white soil of the area.

WINES - Consultant enologist Beppe Caviola vinifies the grapes with an eye to naturalness: hence native yeasts, no filtration and only large wooden barrels for the nebbiolo grapes. Another strong point is the wines' excellent value for money. The intriguing **Dolcetto d'Alba Sant'Anna 2011** (● 8,000 bt) has aromas of freshly squeezed red fruit with sweet, fragrant tannins. Langhe Rosso 2011 (● nebbiolo, barbera; 4,000 bt) is complex and refreshing on the palate — a perfect Everyday Wine. **Langhe Nebbiolo Filari Corti 2010** (● 8,000 bt) is very pleasant and floral. **Barbera d'Alba Sup. Rocche del Santo 2010** (● 8,000 bt), made with grapes from a Cherasco vineyard is rich in flesh and packed with energy. **Barolo 2008** (● 25,000 bt) is so elegant as to be almost aristocratic. The hefty **Barolo Brandini 2008** (● 8,000 bt) is a welcome new addition to the stable.

FERTILIZERS	manure pellets
PLANT PROTECTION	copper and sulphur
WEED CONTROL	mechanical
YEASTS	native
GRAPES	100% estate-grown
CERTIFICATION	organic

LA MORRA (CN)
Cordero di Montezemolo Monfalletto

Frazione Annunziata, 67 Bis
tel. 0173 50344
www.corderodimontezemolo.it
info@corderodimontezemolo.com

---

35 ha - 230,000 bt

PEOPLE - The winery managed by Alberto Cordero and his sister Elena — members of the latest generation of one of Piedmont's oldest families — is one of the finest in the Langa hills. On the hill of Monfalletto, alongside the property, towers the company symbol: a cedar of Lebanon planted over 150 years ago. The spectacular cellar combines modernity and tradition perfectly.

VINEYARDS - The vineyards all surround the cellar, apart from two hectares at Castiglione Falletto (Villero cru), were the nebbiolo grapes that go into Enrico VI are grown. The average age of the vines ranges from 20 to 70 years, and exposures vary too. The use of synthetic products was abolished years ago and the onus is placed on total naturalness all along the production chain. The company draws water from a storage tank and an artesian well and is thus independent from the municipal supply network.

WINES - Barolo Enrico VI 2008 (● 9,000 bt) is austere and potent with aromas redolent of spices and ripe fruit and a thrilling palate. A Great Wine and an essay in elegance. **Barolo Bricco Gattera 2008** (● 5,000 bt) offers nuances of violet and jam with a soft, enfolding finish. **Barolo Monfalletto 2008** (● 45,000 bt) is an assemblage of grapes from various vineyards and has floral, fruity aromas. **Barbera d'Alba Sup. Funtanì 2009** (● 8,000 bt) comes from an old vineyard, hence its intensity and freshness and well-balanced finish. **Dolcetto d'Alba 2011** (● 50,000 bt) is fresh and fruity. **Langhe Chardonnay Elioro 2010** (○ 8,000 bt) has tropical, toasty notes with a full-bodied, very intense finish. The wines are aged in barriques, casks and barrels of various ages.

FERTILIZERS organic-mineral, natural manure	
PLANT PROTECTION copper and sulphur	
WEED CONTROL mechanical	
YEASTS selected	
GRAPES 100% estate-grown	
CERTIFICATION none	

MONCHIERO (CN)
Giuseppe Mascarello e Figlio

Strada del Grosso, 1
tel. 0173 792126
www.mascarello1881.com
mauromascarello@mascarello1881.com

12.5 ha - 60,000 bt

PEOPLE - "When I was a kid, I never started primary school before All Saints' Day. Even though I was just little, I had the job of stemming the grapes during pressing." These are the words of Mauro Mascarello, who in 1967 took over the running of the company from his father Giuseppe. His massive experience of vineyards and wine is pretty well unique in the Langa districts. His own son Giuseppe has lent him a hand over the last few years.

VINEYARDS - The feather in the cellar's cap is the Monprivato vineyard which, after never-ending arguments with his father, he vinified separately for the first time in 1970. A portion of the vineyard is given over to the nebbiolo michet clone, whose vines give life to the monumental Riserva Ca' d'Morissio. The other jewels in the crown are Villero and Santo Stefano di Perno in Monforte. If you're looking for classicism and tradition in unique vineyards, this is the place for you.

WINES - Mauro says that, "The limestone soil makes the wines mature later, and michet accentuates this sensation". Which is why his Barolo Monprivato Ca' d' Morissio Ris. 2004 (● 3,500 bt) is seemingly very young and very refreshing, juicy and deep. It's a hymn to the nebbiolo grape and a Great Wine. **Barolo Monprivato 2007** (● 22,000 bt) is elegant, scented and very enjoyable despite the poor vintage. **Barolo Villero 2007** (● 3,500 bt) is warmer with delicate blossomy notes and soft tannins. **Barolo Santo Stefano di Perno 2007** (● 3,700 bt) has notes of soil and fruit and gutsy tannins. **Langhe Nebbiolo 2010** (● 4,000 bt) is enjoyable, recherché and austere. Last but not least, **Langhe Freisa Toetto 2006** (● 4,500 bt) is Mascarello's tribute to a grape that deserves greater consideration in view of the results achieved when vinified properly.

FERTILIZERS natural manure	
PLANT PROTECTION chemical, copper and sulphur	
WEED CONTROL chemical, mechanical	
YEASTS selected	
GRAPES 100% estate-grown	
CERTIFICATION none	

MONFORTE D'ALBA (CN)

Conterno Fantino

Via Ginestra, 1
tel. 0173 78204
www.conternofantino.it
info@conternofantino.it

25 ha - 150,000 bt

66 A winery that wages war against cliché. Modernists? Traditionalists? Who cares? The cellar exploits geothermics and photovoltaics, the vineyards are converting to organics and the wines reflect the terroir 99

PEOPLE - In the three hours we spent together in his vineyards and cellar, we were won over by Claudio Conterno's energy. It made us realize how the company is at the cutting-edge of Langhe winegrowing.

VINEYARDS - Walking through the vineyards of the Ginestra and Mosconi crus in the company of Claudio Conterno was a privilege for us. His clear, precise words allowed us to understand the philosophy that moves the company in pursuit of a by no means simple balance between the will to gather perfect fruits and the desire not to harm the quality of the surrounding environment. Interesting practices here include cover cropping, the creation of humus and the organic fight against pests.

WINES - The cellar is the domain of Guido Fantino and his son Fabio. **Barolo Sorì Ginestra 2008** (● 16,000 bt) reaches great levels of excellence. It is made from grapes grown with a southern exposure in tufaceous, clayey soil, both factors which add power, richness and longevity. **Barolo Mosconi 2008** (● 5,000 bt) is more perfumed and less powerful. It was our favorite and we have chosen it as a Great Wine. **Barolo Vigna del Gris 2008** (● 10,000 bt) is also from the Ginestra vineyard, but from sandier soil. It is floral and satisfying on the nose. **Langhe Rosso Monprà 2009** (● nebbiolo, barbera, cabernet; 10,000 bt) is a historical label that will be produced without cabernet in the future. **Langhe Nebbiolo Ginestrino 2010** (● 20,000 bt) offers good value for money and **Barbera d'Alba Vignota 2010** (● 25,000 bt) is succulent and juicy.

FERTILIZERS green manure, humus
PLANT PROTECTION copper and sulphur
WEED CONTROL mechanical
YEASTS native
GRAPES 100% estate-grown
CERTIFICATION converting to organics

MONFORTE D'ALBA (CN)

Giacomo Conterno

Località Ornati, 2
tel. 0173 78221
www.conterno.it

17 ha - 60,000 bt

PEOPLE - A company that's famous all over the world despite its limited production. Or maybe because of it, insofar as it has created a halo almost of legend that surrounds not only Barolo Monfortino, but all the wines of this historic Langa cellar. Roberto Conterno runs it with exceptional expertise, without losing sight of the final goal — namely to produce wines that talk of the land of their birth. Hence austere, deep and outstandingly expressive.

VINEYARDS - The decision not to use the grapes from the prized Cerretta vineyard for Barolo, because the vines, planted 20 years ago, are considered too young, just goes to show the rigor with which the cellar addresses every aspect of the production chain. The vineyard grows nebbiolo and barbera grapes, the cellar's only varieties, as does the splendid Cascina Francia vineyard, another Serralunga cru, worth a visit to get an idea of the care it devotes to viticulture, the cornerstone of wine quality.

WINES - By virtue of its vintage an exceptionally drinkable wine, **Barolo Cascina Francia 2008** (● 18,000 bt) is deep and very, very long — a breathtaking Great Wine, likely one of the finest versions ever tasted. **Barolo Monfortino Ris. 2005** (● 10,000 bt) came through with flying colours, *ça va sans dire*, once more firing the myth of this austere, eternal red. **Langhe Nebbiolo Cerretta 2010** (● 6,500 bt) has a magnificent palate with a mixture of earthy and floral sensation and a long, succulent finish. The excellent **Barbera d'Alba Cascina Francia 2010** (● 18,000 bt) is tangy and vivacious on the palate.

> **slow wine** **BARBERA D'ALBA CERRETTA 2010** (● 4,000 bt) A Slow Wine that has a great impact on nose and palate, with flesh as juicy as it is rich in mineral aromas and a long, lingering finish.

FERTILIZERS natural manure
PLANT PROTECTION chemical, copper and sulphur
WEED CONTROL mechanical
YEASTS selected
GRAPES 100% estate-grown
CERTIFICATION none

MONFORTE D'ALBA (CN)

Giacomo Fenocchio €

Località Bussia, 72
tel. 0173 78675
www.giacomofenocchio.com
claudio@giacomofenocchio.com

MONFORTE D'ALBA (CN)

Elio Grasso

Località Ginestra, 40
tel. 0173 78491
www.eliograsso.it
info@eliograsso.it

---

14 ha - 90,000 bt   **10% discount**

PEOPLE - Claudio Fenocchio's story is exemplary. After inheriting this small farm from his father Giacomo, he has perseveringly turned it into a pearl of a place. Not for him the fashionable wine world. Keeping a low profile, he has continued to make traditional wines with and accomplished, clear-cut style. He exports most of his bottles and his direct sales prices are exceptional. From him you can buy great Barolos at just 20 euros.

VINEYARDS - Most of the vineyards encircle the production facility itself in Bussia Sottana, a major cru. The best positions — five hectares in all — are given over to nebbiolo, barbera and dolcetto being grown in those with southern exposures. Besides Bussia, Claudio owns another two truly excellent vineyards: Cannubi di Barolo, a few hundred meters from the cellar, and Villero di Castiglione Falletto.

WINES - The company range is dominated by Barolo. The subtle **Barolo Cannubi 2008** (● 4,000 bt), produced with grapes that grow on soil sandier than that of the other two crus, is sheer class. **Barolo Villero 2008** (● 6,000 bt) is hefty and complex, while **Barolo Bussia Ris. 2006** (● 6,000 bt) is the fruit of a selection of the finest grapes in the cellar, hence a wine of immense character and traditional flavor. **Dolcetto d'Alba 2011** (● 15,000 bt) is vinous and fruity. **Roero Arneis 2011** (○ 5,000 bt) was vinified for the first time by Claudio with grapes from a vineyard at Monteu Roero

> **slow wine** **BAROLO BUSSIA 2008** (● 32,000 bt) Thanks to a magnificent vintage, a floral, ultra-scented wine with distinct notes of violet. The palate is tannic yet, at the same time, supple. Great value for money with perfect sense of place.

18 ha - 85,000 bt

❝ There are many things we like about this model cellar: careful management of the agricultural side under the supervision of doyen Elio Grasso, wines with a rare sense of place, the decision to hew a cellar out of the tufa rock, the purchase of a whole wood to avoid future speculation ... ❞

PEOPLE - Elio Grasso, born in1943, was a teetotaler until the age of 36. Then, following the death of his father in 1979, he left his job to take over the family estate. Since 1995 his son Gianluca has been running the business successfully.

VINEYARDS - My father did everything he could to stop me doing this job," says Elio. It's a good job he didn't listen. This cellar can count upon some of the most interesting vineyards in the Langa district, especially Gavarini in the Ginestra cru, which surrounds the cellar. The part in which the Casa Maté selection is produced has clayier soil which makes for an earlier harvest, while the vine rows below the farmhouse are given over to Runcot.

WINES - **Barolo Ginestra Casa Maté 2008** (● 14,000 bt) is an excellent wine: it has notes of red berries with almost lactic nuances and a fine, juicy, deep, racy palate. It is almost matched by **Barolo Gavarini Chiniera 2008** (● 14,000 bt), from a very nearby cru with lighter soil, a wine that is less rich and more elegant. Like all the nebbiolo wines of the vintage **Barolo Runcot Ris. 2006** (● 6,000 bt) is still not fully developed and has no-nonsense tannins. Aged for 15 years in barriques, **Barbera d'Alba Vigna Martina 2009** (● 20,000 bt) is interesting and linear. **Langhe Nebbiolo Gavarini 2011** (● 15,000 bt) is headily scented and floral. **Dolcetto d'Alba Dei Grassi 2011** (● 20,000 bt) is juicy and easy to drink.

FERTILIZERS humus	FERTILIZERS natural manure
PLANT PROTECTION chemical, copper and sulphur	PLANT PROTECTION chemical, copper and sulphur
WEED CONTROL chemical, mechanical	WEED CONTROL mechanical
YEASTS selected	YEASTS selected, native
GRAPES 100% estate-grown	GRAPES 100% estate-grown
CERTIFICATION none	CERTIFICATION none

MONTÀ D'ALBA (CN)

Giovanni Almondo

Via San Rocco, 26
tel. 0173 975256
www.giovannialmondo.com
almondo@giovannialmondo.com

MONTEU ROERO (CN)

Angelo Negro & Figli

Frazione Sant'Anna, 1
tel. 0173 90252
www.negroangelo.it
negro@negroangelo.it

---

15 ha - 80,000 bt   **10% discount**

PEOPLE - Domenico always transmits great passion whenever we go to seem him. As soon as we arrived, he took us up onto Bricco delle Ciliegie, the hill he's so fond of overlooking the house in which he was born and the first vineyard to be owned by his father Giovanni, who set up the winery. Today, offering a helping hand in the cellar are Domenico's sons Stefano and Federico, an enologist.

VINEYARDS - What can we say about Bricco delle Ciliegie, literally Cherry Hill, other than that it's a wonderful place. The location of the top, kissed by sunlight all day long, is ideal, while lower down the slopes are so steep it's impossible to work the soil mechanically. Bric Valdiana, bought in 1990 — it used to be rented — has a due south exposure and calcareous soil. 20-year-old arneis vines grow at the bottom, nebbiolo at the top.

WINES - Domenico' passion comes out in his wines. The two whites are very rich in aroma. **Roero Arneis Bricco delle Ciliegie 2011** (○ 38,000 bt) offers tangy mineral notes and a nice bouquet of white-fleshed fruit. Roero Arneis Vigne Sparse 2011 (○ 40,000 bt) has nuances of tropical fruits and plenty of length. It's one of the best whites in the Roero district, hence, for us, an Everyday Wine. Aged 24 months in barriques, **Roero Giovanni Almondo Ris. 2008** (● 1.500 bt) is a wine of character that blends potency and tannic weave. **Roero Bric Valdiana 2009** (● 5,000 bt) has fresh notes of red berries. Still young and exuberant, it's a red for aging. **Barbera d'Alba Valbianchera 2010** (2 5,000 bt) is spicy, while **Langhe Bianco Sassi e Sabbia 2011** (○ riesling; 2.500 bt), with its typical notes of petrol, is a joy to drink.

---

54 ha - 300,000 bt

PEOPLE - This family winery, now one of the largest in the Roero district, laid down its roots way back in 1670 at least — and the documents are there to prove it — but it is very much projected into the future. Ever since he started bottling his wine, Giovanni Negro, abetted first by his wife Maria Elisa Gatti, now by his kids, Angelo, Gabriele, Emanuela and Giuseppe, has been one of the leading players in the growth of the local area. The company's large modern landscaped cellar epitomizes its dedication to absolute quality.

VINEYARDS - Most of the vineyards are in Monteu Roero on the sandy, calcareous hills that encircle the company buildings. The rest are in Canale, Santo Stefano, Montaldo and Neive. In the young San Giorgio vineyards, experiments are proceeding with organic methods, while the management of the other vineyards is totally virtuous, with weed control only in the steepest parcels and the use of humus to stimulate soil vitality, water capacity and stability.

WINES - **Roero Arneis Serra Lupini 2011** (○ 80,000 bt) has typical fruity and herbaceous notes, plenty of juice and optimal freshness and minerality. Made with grapes from a vineyard planted in 1982, sandy and rich in marine fossils, **Roero Arneis Perdaudin 2011** (○ 20,000 bt) is deeper and tangier. The excellent **Roero Pracchiosso 2009** (● 10,000 bt) is fine, floral and spicy with a very elegant palate. **Barbaresco Basarin Ris. 2007** (● 4,000 bt), made with grapes from a vineyard planted in 1951, combines thrust and refinement. The three Barberas are all super. We recommend **Barbera d'Alba Nicolon 2010** (● 14,000 bt) is aged in wooden casks and barrels.

| slow wine | **ROERO SAN BERNARDO 2009** (● 5,000 bt) A true Slow Wine for its sense of place, impeccable execution and optimally dynamic flavor. |

FERTILIZERS organic-mineral, natural manure
PLANT PROTECTION chemical, copper and sulphur
WEED CONTROL mechanical
YEASTS selected
GRAPES 100% estate-grown
CERTIFICATION none

FERTILIZERS natural manure, green manure, humus
PLANT PROTECTION copper and sulphur
WEED CONTROL chemical, mechanical
YEASTS selected
GRAPES 100% estate-grown
CERTIFICATION none

NEIVE (CN)

Piero Busso

Via Albesani, 8
tel. 0173 67156
www.bussopiero.com
bussopiero@bussopiero.com

10 ha - 40,000 bt

66 We visited the dizzyingly steep San Stefanetto vineyard, 56 vine rows near the small town of Neive. Here all work is carried out by hand and the decision not to use any weed killers stands as proof of a precise philosophy 99

PEOPLE - The stars of the cast are: Ada, the grandmother with 60 harvests behind her, as get-up-and go as ever; Piero, the son, a tenacious and capable player in the local wine renaissance; Pier, the grandson, symbol of an effective generational turnover. If you want to get to know the Langa district, head for the Borgese area in the Neive hills. Here the Busso family, especially the women, Emanuela and Lucia, will give you a right rural welcome.

VINEYARDS - The Busso property is sensational. Take the old vines of the michet clone, for example, an added value in the move to exalt the genetic diversity of the Barbaresco hills.

WINES - Piero and Pier have created a model family business of great balance. **Langhe Nebbiolo 2010** (● 3,000 bt) is a perfect example of a base wine with a strong sense of place. **Barbaresco Albesani Borgese 2009** (● 5,000 bt) is spicy and immediate. After long aging in the bottle, **Barbaresco Gallina 2008** (● 2,000 bt) is already ready. It's even educational in the way it tells the story of the historical Neive vineyard. There's no space here to describe the rest, though the very enjoyable Barbera deserves a mention.

> slow wine **BARBARESCO SAN STUNET 2009** (● 7,000 bt) A splendid wine from the rugged vineyard of the same name in Treiso. Potent, seductive with a strong sense of place, just put it in the cellar and leave it there!

FERTILIZERS natural manure	
PLANT PROTECTION copper and sulphur	
WEED CONTROL mechanical	
YEASTS native	
GRAPES 100% estate-grown	
CERTIFICATION none	

NEIVE (CN)

Sottimano

Località Cottà, 21
tel. 0173 635186
www.sottimano.it
info@sottimano.it

18 ha - 85,000 bt | 10% discount

66 Sottimano's vineyard work is exemplary. The cellar seeks to raise the terroris' profile, as its decision to produce four Barbarescos from as many single curs proves 99

PEOPLE - Rino Sottimano's knowledge of the Barbaresco zone is encyclopedic, to say the least! A tour of his vineyards and cellar and a chat over a glass of wine — these are the keys to understanding of the local area and the winery, a family affair run carefully and competently by Rino, his daughter and son Elena and Andrea and his wife Anna.

VINEYARDS - Grapes from the prolific Basarin hilltop vineyard could go into another Barbaresco. The agronomic management is carried on with care and experiments have begun in collaboration with the University of Turin to produce wines with zero residues.

WINES - Andrea and Rino have a recognizable style in which minimum intervention in the cellar favors wines of character and authenticity. **Barbaresco Fausoni 2009** (● 3,500 bt), an example of the finesse of the nebbiolo grape, is the label that best expresses the vintage and the Sottimano touch. **Barbaresco Pajoré 2009** (● 5,000 bt) is richer and more potent, whereas **Barbaresco Cottà 2009** (● 10,000 bt;) is balsamic with hefty tannins. After due aging in the bottle, **Barbaresco Currà 2008** (● 2,500 bt), our favorite, displays all the elegance of the vintage with plenty of spiciness and fruit. The cellar's seriousness shines through even in its simplest wines, which include the very enjoyable **Dolcetto d'Alba Bric del Salto 2011** (● 20,000 bt).

FERTILIZERS natural manure, none	
PLANT PROTECTION chemical, copper and sulphur	
WEED CONTROL mechanical	
YEASTS native	
GRAPES 100% estate-grown	
CERTIFICATION none	

NOVELLO (CN)

Elvio Cogno

Via Ravera, 2
tel. 0173 744006
www.elviocogno.com
elviocogno@elviocogno.com

11 ha - 68,000 bt `10% discount`

❝ In fewer than 20 years, this magnificently restructured cellar at the heart of the Ravera cru has become one of the talked about among Barolo connoisseurs. Its success is the result of a policy of one step at a time and attention to detail in the vineyard and in the cellar ❞

PEOPLE - It takes talent to have success with Barolo in the Langa district. And talent is what Valter Fissore and his wife Nadia Cogno, daughter of Elvio, who "wrote the history" of Marcarini, have got. They are assisted in their work by the accomplished team of Daniele Gaia and Szymon Jachimowicz.

VINEYARDS - Strolling through the vineyards round the cellar we were able to observe the care with which Valter tends the vine rows. No chemicals are used in weeding and for some years the sexual confusion technique has been used against pests. The winery deserves credit for two considerable achievements: first, it has made Novello famous internationally; secondly, it has rediscovered the special nascetta grape variety.

WINES - Valter's grandiose suite of wines starts with the magnificent Barolo Ravera 2008 (● 15,000 bt), aged in large wooden barrels, Burgundy in style with an austere, rich finish — a Great Wine that is sure to age well. **Barolo Bricco Pernice 2007** (● 3,300 bt) is warmer and solar with fruit at the forefront. The granitic, balsamic **Barolo Vigna Elena Ris. 2006** (● 3,300 bt) is a red wine with great aging potential. **Langhe Nascetta del Comune di Novello 2011** (○ 10,500 bt) is one of the finest versions of this wine so far. Powerful and drinkable thanks to scything, refreshing acidity. **Barbera d'Alba Bricco dei Merli 2010** (● 10,000 bt) is very good indeed and **Langhe Rosso Montegrilli 2010** (● nebbiolo, barbera; 4,000 bt) is a pleasant drink.

FERTILIZERS	natural manure, green manure
PLANT PROTECTION	chemical, copper and sulphur
WEED CONTROL	mechanical
YEASTS	native
GRAPES	100% estate-grown
CERTIFICATION	none

PRIOCCA (CN)

Hilberg - Pasquero

Via Bricco Gatti, 16
tel. 0173 616197
www.hilberg-pasquero.com
hilberg@libero.it

5.5 ha - 24,000 bt `10% discount`

❝ Miclo lives virtually in symbiosis with the vine and practices agriculture with a capital A. He has lived his life at the service of the land and environmental sustainability ❞

PEOPLE - Here you will be welcomed by Michelangelo (Miclo) Pasquero and Annette Hilberg, two people with whom you can spend whole days talking about life and wine. About real life, the one that ties them to the land and sees them as leading players in a viticulture that respects the environment.

VINEYARDS - The main plot surrounds the winery buildings. The soil is white and rich in clay, but there are also other redder terrains on which nebbiolo and barbera are grown. Nebbiolo and barbera are also trained in the Monteforche district, the second being used in the Superiore blend. The grapes from the Bricco Stella district are earmarked for the production of the base Barbera. Algae-based products are used instead of copper.

WINES - Maison Hilberg-Pasquero grows no white grapes, devoting itself solely to nebbiolo and barbera and a small portion of brachetto. **Langhe Nebbiolo 2010** (● 2,500 bt), spicy with plenty of fruit, is the only wine aged in large wooden barrels. **Nebbiolo d'Alba 2010** (● 5,500 bt) was successful again. It offers clear-cut floral sensations with a racy palate and a rich, almost creamy body. **Nebbiolo d'Alba Pinìn 2008** (● 400 magnums), which matures three years in the barrel, is well structured with a very long finish. **Barbera d'Alba Sup. 2010** (● 4,000 bt) has crisp red fruit with balsamic notes, whereas **Barbera d'Alba 2011** (● 8,000 bt) contains a vein of acidity that enhances its drinkability. **Vareij 2011** (● barbera, brachetto; 5,000 bt) is pleasant and enjoyable.

FERTILIZERS	compost, biodynamic preparations, green manure
PLANT PROTECTION	copper and sulphur
WEED CONTROL	mechanical
YEASTS	native
GRAPES	100% estate-grown
CERTIFICATION	organic

RODELLO (CN)

Mossio Fratelli €

Via Montà, 12
tel. 0173 617149 - 338 4002835
www.mossio.com
mossio@mossio.com

SERRALUNGA D'ALBA (CN)

Casa di E. Mirafiore

Via Alba, 15
tel. 0173 626117
www.mirafiore.it
info@mirafiore.it

---

10 ha - 45,000 bt   **10% discount**

PEOPLE - Despite the difficult economic situation, this small, highly reliable company is managing to sail a steady course on the market thanks mainly to the quality of its wines — plus their good value for money — and the all-round commitment of Remo and Valerio Mossio with their contagious optimism and level-headedness. Like the rest of the farmhouse, the small cellar in which they vinify and age their wines dates back to 1528 at least, as a recently recovered stone tablet testifies.

VINEYARDS - The Bricco Caramelli vineyard at an altitude of 480 meters is situated next to the cellar. It is characterized by calcareous soil, good ventilation and considerable day to night temperature swings — ideal conditions for viticulture and for the health of the grapes in wet years. Only one under-row weed control intervention is done at the start of spring and, thanks to the favorable climate, treatments are reduced to a minimum.

WINES - The Dolcettos are only aged in stainless steel. **Dolcetto d'Alba Piano delli Perdoni 2011** (● 25,000 bt) has pronounced, zippy notes of almond and cherry, a fruity, refreshing palate and a clear-cut juicy finish. As always, it's an exemplary Everyday Wine. **Dolcetto d'Alba Bricco Caramelli 2011** (● 5,000 bt) remains faithful to the wine's fleshy, drinkable fame and is sure to age well. Thanks to a favorable vintage for the grape, the potent **Barbera d'Alba 2009** (● 4,000 bt) is good, fragrant and juicy **Langhe Rosso 2009** (● barbera, nebbiolo, dolcetto; 2,500 bt) manages to combine the qualities of its three grape varieties into a cut-glass whole. **Langhe Nebbiolo 2008** (● 5,000 bt) has seductive notes of violet and a nicely juicy, textured palate with an assertive finish and sweet, unaggressive tannins.

---

40 ha - 120,000 bt

PEOPLE - The company was set up by Emanuele Alberto di Mirafiore, son of Rosa Vercellana and Vittorio Emanuele II, the first king of Italy, in 1878. In the last century the trademark enjoyed spells of exceptional prestige, but was then overshadowed for 77 years by that of Fontanafredda, now to all intents and purposes the mother company. In 2009 the decision was taken to create a company within the company to bottle wines made with grapes exclusively from its own vineyards.

VINEYARDS - Casa di E. Mirafiore boasts vineyards of indisputable worth, including crus such as Lazzarito and La Rosa in Serralunga and Paiagallo in Barolo. The cultivation systems implemented by agronomist Alberto Grasso seek to reduce impact on the environment. Chemical manures, under-vine weed killers, and botrycides are all banned. The agronomic experience gained at Fontanafredda has certainly come in handy.

WINES - The enologist Danilo Drocco has had *carte blanche* in designing the wines of Mirafiore. The style is traditional with very long macerations and aging in large wooden barrels. The result is particular wines that take time to open out in the glass. This year we tasted a version of the wonderful **Barolo Paiagallo 2008** (● 10,000 bt). The bouquet and palate are balanced with notes of iodine and algae and sweet, long tannins. It's a Great Wine. With its aromas of violet and cherry, its "younger brother" **Langhe Nebbiolo Mirafiore 2010** (● 20,000 bt) rates highly too. **Barolo Ris. 2005** (● 20,000 bt) is a major classic with aromas of truffle and anchovy. **Dolcetto d'Alba 2011** (● 20,000 bt) is alluring and **Barbera d'Alba Sup. 2009** (● 20,000 bt) has pervasive juiciness.

FERTILIZERS organic-mineral, manure pellets	
PLANT PROTECTION chemical, copper and sulphur	
WEED CONTROL chemical, mechanical	
YEASTS native	
GRAPES 100% estate-grown	
CERTIFICATION none	

FERTILIZERS manure pellets	
PLANT PROTECTION chemical, copper and sulphur	
WEED CONTROL mechanical	
YEASTS selected, native	
GRAPES 100% estate-grown	
CERTIFICATION none	

SERRALUNGA D'ALBA (CN)

Ettore Germano

Località Cerretta, 1
tel. 0173 613528
www.germanoettore.com
germanoettore@germanoettore.com

SERRALUNGA D'ALBA (CN)

Massolino

Piazza Cappellano, 8
tel. 0173 613138
www.massolino.it
massolino@massolino.it

15 ha - 80,000 bt

PEOPLE - We met Sergio Germano, who runs this solid company with his wife Elena, while he was lovingly preparing the yeasts for the *liqueur de tirage* for his excellent Alta Langa. The cellar houses barrels of various sizes with a preference for larger ones, ideal for the maturation of the robust local Barolos, most of which are sold abroad. This is a company that combines tradition and innovation with excellent results.

VINEYARDS - Sergio owns parcels in some of the best vineyards of the whole Barolo denomination. They include Lazzarito, where the vines are 80 years old, as well as the recently acquired and legendary Vigna Rionda, a small freshly replanted holding with wood poles at the ends of the vine rows. At La Cerretta, atop a dizzyingly steep hillside, especially in the lower portion, the Germanos run a small b&b. It stands at an altitude of 400 meters and offers a magnificent view of the surrounding countryside.

WINES - The range Sergio delivered this year was staggeringly vast. Blossomy and very fine on the nose, **Langhe Bianco Hérzu 2010** (○ riesling; 13,500 bt) teases the palate with a perfect blend of ripe fruit and acidity. **Alta Langa Brut 2009** (○ pinot nero, chardonnay; 6,000 bt) has fine perlage and a racy palate without any lazy softness. The lively, fleshy **Barbera d'Alba Sup. Vigna della Madre 2010** (● 10,000 bt) is a joy to drink. **Barolo Cerretta 2008** (● 12,000 bt), the only wine aged in small wooden casks, has balsamic notes, zippy tannins and good length — one to wait for and, in our opinion, a Great Wine. **Barolo Prapò 2008** (● 6,000 bt) has heady, clear-cut florality, juicy tannins and just the right sweetness. **Barolo Lazzarito Ris. 2006** (● 3,000 bt) enchants with its notes of rose, deep palate, tannic without bitterness.

26 ha - 130,000 bt

PEOPLE - The restructuring work has now been completed. The Massolino brothers, Roberto and Franco, have treated themselves to a spectacular cellar with a breathtaking view from the terrace. Plus, it turns out wines of absolute stylistic rigor and sense of place. It is situated in the center of Serralunga, where the Massolinos are an institution. Their labels from the 1970s and 1980s are memorable but their latest aren't to be sniffed at either.

VINEYARDS - It's always a great pleasure to visit the winery in the company of Roberto, whose passion for his job is infectious. The vineyards he took us round are of the highest level with names that thrill every enthusiast: Vigna Rionda, in a southern exposure with old plantings; Parafada on a dizzy slope with vines planted in 1957; and the almost humpbacked Margheria and Parussi in the commune of Castiglione Falletto.

WINES - On of the most interesting stables in the Langa hills. Tangy, austere and deep **Barolo Vigna Rionda Ris. 2006** (● 9,000 bt) should be uncorked in 10 years' time or more. Exceptional too is **Barolo Parafada 2008** (● 4,000 bt), which has fantastic fruity, licorocey nuances. **Barolo Margheria 2008** (● 4.000 bt) has inviting aromas of seawater with sweet tannins. It was our favorite and we rate it a Great Wine. **Barolo Parussi 2008** (● 4,000 bt) is edgier, more balsamic and floral, while **Barbera d'Alba 2011** (● 20,000 bt) is juicy and refreshing, a hymn to the grape.

> **slow wine** **BAROLO 2008** (● 40,000 bt) Finding a label of this caliber (typically Langa-style with heady scents of violets, a succulent palate, just the right tannins and a finish to write home about) is a rare occurrence. A wine that vouches for the seriousness of the company.

FERTILIZERS natural manure
PLANT PROTECTION chemical, copper and sulphur
WEED CONTROL chemical, mechanical
YEASTS selected
GRAPES 100% estate-grown
CERTIFICATION none

FERTILIZERS natural manure
PLANT PROTECTION chemical, copper and sulphur
WEED CONTROL chemical, mechanical
YEASTS selected
GRAPES 100% estate-grown
CERTIFICATION none

SERRALUNGA D'ALBA (CN)

Giovanni Rosso

Località Baudana, 6
tel. 0173 613142
www.giovannirosso.com
info@giovannirosso.com

TREISO (CN)

Ca' del Baio

Via Ferrere, 33
tel. 0173 638219
www.cadelbaio.com
cadelbaio@cadelbaio.com

---

15 ha - 90,000 bt · **10% discount**

PEOPLE - "Over the last few years too much money has come to the Langhe district — and not enough books." These words sum up Davide Rosso, the founder. With stubbornness and dedication, in just over 10 years he has made the cellar famous in more than 30 countries round the world. He is a man with clear ideas, always ready to listen to and respect other people's opinions. The latest news is that he is building a new cellar.

VINEYARDS - Davide Rosso has maintained part of the Vigna Rionda parcel, the exceptional Langhe cru planted in 1946, which he inherited recently. After careful drainage and rearrangement of the vine rows, he has replanted the other part. It was a thrill to see the first leaves on the new vines. None of the company's vineyards, all in excellent winegrowing districts, sees any chemical weed control.

WINES - This year Davide Rosso surpassed himself by delivering what is probably the finest set of Barolos in the whole Langa district. **Barbera d'Alba Donna Margherita 2010** (● 30,000 bt) offers a combination of lovely fruity flesh and refreshing acidity. The well-made, precise **Langhe Nebbiolo 2010** (● 15,000 bt) is dense, flowery and very vibrant. **Barolo Cerretta 2008** (● 8,000 bt) has fine floral notes, tanginess and assertiveness. **Barolo Vigna Rionda Tommaso Canale 2008** (● 1,000 bt) displays all the fantastic depth and assertiveness of this great cru. **Barolo La Serra 2008** (● 4,800 bt) is a Great Wine with enticing notes of dried flowers, followed by a wonderfully creamy, leisurely palate.

slow wine **BAROLO SERRALUNGA 2008** (● 50,000 bt) Rosso isn't just magnificent crus. It's also this base wine that stands out for sense of place and outright quality. Bravo, Davide.

---

20 ha - 100,000 bt

❝ A winery characterized by scrupulously hard work and great wines with a sense of place at attractive prices. It's hard in the Langa hills to find a more winning combination ❞

PEOPLE - Giulio Grasso and his wife Luciana run the business with their daughters Paola and Valentina and turn to Beppe Caviola for enological consultancy. The cellar is essential and functional with medium-sized barrels.

VINEYARDS - The company's crus are divided between Treiso (the relatively young Marcarini and Valgrande with classic marl soil of the Langa hills) and Barbaresco (Pora, home to special clones, and Asili, a great vineyard that yields wines of notable elegance, are both very old with chalky soil). The vineyards are managed with the utmost care, from pruning to bunch thinning, and the viticulture is conventional with as little outside intervention as possible.

WINES - With its mature nose and brio-filled palate, **Barbaresco Valgrande 2009** (● 15,000 bt) is a convincing interpretation of the vintage. **Barbaresco Asili 2009** (● 12,000 bt) displays all the elegance of the cru, with a ripeness and richness of fruit that are out of the ordinary. Racy, juicy and still young, **Langhe Nebbiolo Bric del Baio 2010** (● 20,000 bt) is the delicious fruit of a wonderful harvest. **Langhe Nebbiolo 2011** (● 20.000 bt; 9 €) is immediate, fresh and balanced. The well-crafted **Dolcetto d'Alba 2011** (● 15,000 bt) has notes of cherry with an almondy finish.

slow wine **BARBARESCO PORA 2008** (● 3,000 bt) A great show of strength from this classic Barbaresco. Nuanced and ultra-fine on the nose, extremely elegant on the palate with an irresistible floral vein and a long, juicy, full-flavored finish. An impeccable take on the cru.

FERTILIZERS natural manure	FERTILIZERS organic-mineral, manure pellets
PLANT PROTECTION chemical, copper and sulphur	PLANT PROTECTION chemical, copper and sulphur
WEED CONTROL mechanical	WEED CONTROL chemical, mechanical
YEASTS native	YEASTS selected
GRAPES 100% estate-grown	GRAPES 100% estate-grown
CERTIFICATION none	CERTIFICATION none

TREISO (CN)

Fiorenzo Nada

Località Rombone
Via Ausario, 12-C
tel. 0173 638254
www.nada.it
nadafiorenzo@nada.it

7 ha - 45,000 bt   **10% discount**

❝ Bruno Nada's passion and competence are immense. During our visit we saw in his eyes the burning desire to produce great wines capable of evoking the flavor of Treiso in the glass ❞

PEOPLE - "Life is full of meetings," says Bruno Nada as he thinks back to the encounters that determined his decision to become a winemaker. Visiting Italian and French cellars when he was still working as a teacher, he realized that the wine world was changing and opted to join it to produce top quality bottles.

VINEYARDS - The two Barbaresco selections are made with grapes from the two main vineyards, Rombone and Manzola, which form a sort of natural amphitheater below the cellar on soils that are, respectively, chalky and sandy. Seifile is made with barbera grapes from vines replanted following floods in 1948 and nebbiolo grapes from the Rombone hill. All the vineyards stand in grass and enjoy optimal exposures.

WINES - It was Bruno's son Danilo who accompanied us on our visit and presented the cellar's wines. After 18 months' aging in casks, **Langhe Rosso Seifile 2008** (● barbera, nebbiolo; 3,000 bt) is charged with floral notes, but it is in the mouth that it comes out in all its splendor with strong hints of red berries and a perfect marriage of acidity and tannins. Aged in barrels, **Barbaresco Manzola 2008** (● 6,600 bt) is fine and elegant with nuances of damp soil and spices. **Barbaresco Rombone 2008** (● 4,000 bt) is even more enthralling thanks to notes of menthol on the nose and palate and a long, spirited finish. **Langhe Nebbiolo 2010** (● 10,000 bt) is mineral and fresh, while **Dolcetto d'Alba 2011** (● 10,000 bt) is fruity and fleshy. **Barbera d'Alba 2010** (● 5,000 bt), finally, is at once soft and taut.

FERTILIZERS natural manure
PLANT PROTECTION chemical, copper and sulphur
WEED CONTROL mechanical
YEASTS native
GRAPES 100% estate-grown
CERTIFICATION none

VERDUNO (CN)

Alessandria Fratelli

Via Beato Valfrè, 59
tel. 0172 470113
www.fratellialessandria.it
info@fratellialessandria.it

14 ha - 75,000 bt   **10% discount**

❝ The family that runs the cellar is firmly rooted in Verduno. That bond translates into a love of the land, respect for tradition and willingness to herald in the new — whenever it signifies real medium- and long-term benefits, that is ❞

PEOPLE - With the assistance of his father Gian Battista and his uncle Alessandro, Vittore Alessandria is pushing ahead with this splendid cellar, closely bound up in the history and wines of the village of Verduno. Cellar extension work has now terminated, with the old part still housing large classic, oval barrels.

VINEYARDS - It was Vittore who took us on a stroll among the vine rows that stand in grass in the steep Riva Rocca vineyard, where the soil is silty. The other crus are the magnificent Monvigliero and Gramolere di Monforte, where the soil is very sandy. They are managed with common sense adopting all-mechanical weeding.

WINES - Classic clear-cut wines made with consummate confidence. **Verduno Pelaverga Speziale 2011** (● 14,000 bt), the house specialty, is precise and captivating, as excellent as ever. **Barbera d'Alba 2011** (● 7,000 bt) has the fruit and flesh and brio typical of a good vintage. **Langhe Nebbiolo 2010** (● 10,000 bt), which comes from young vineyards, is floral and fine, gutsy and elegant. The delectable **Barolo San Lorenzo 2008** (● 5,000 bt) is marked by notes of aromatic herbs, beautiful, lingering sweetness on the palate. **Barolo Gramolere 2008** (● 6,000 bt) is minty with well-defined aromas, compact and juicy.

> **slow wine** **BAROLO MONVIGLIERO 2008** (● 6,500 bt) All the juiciness, zest and unmistakable notes of aromatic herbs of the Barolos of Verduno. A great classic which you can either drink today or age in the cellar.

FERTILIZERS mineral, manure pellets
PLANT PROTECTION chemical, copper and sulphur
WEED CONTROL mechanical
YEASTS native
GRAPES 100% estate-grown
CERTIFICATION none

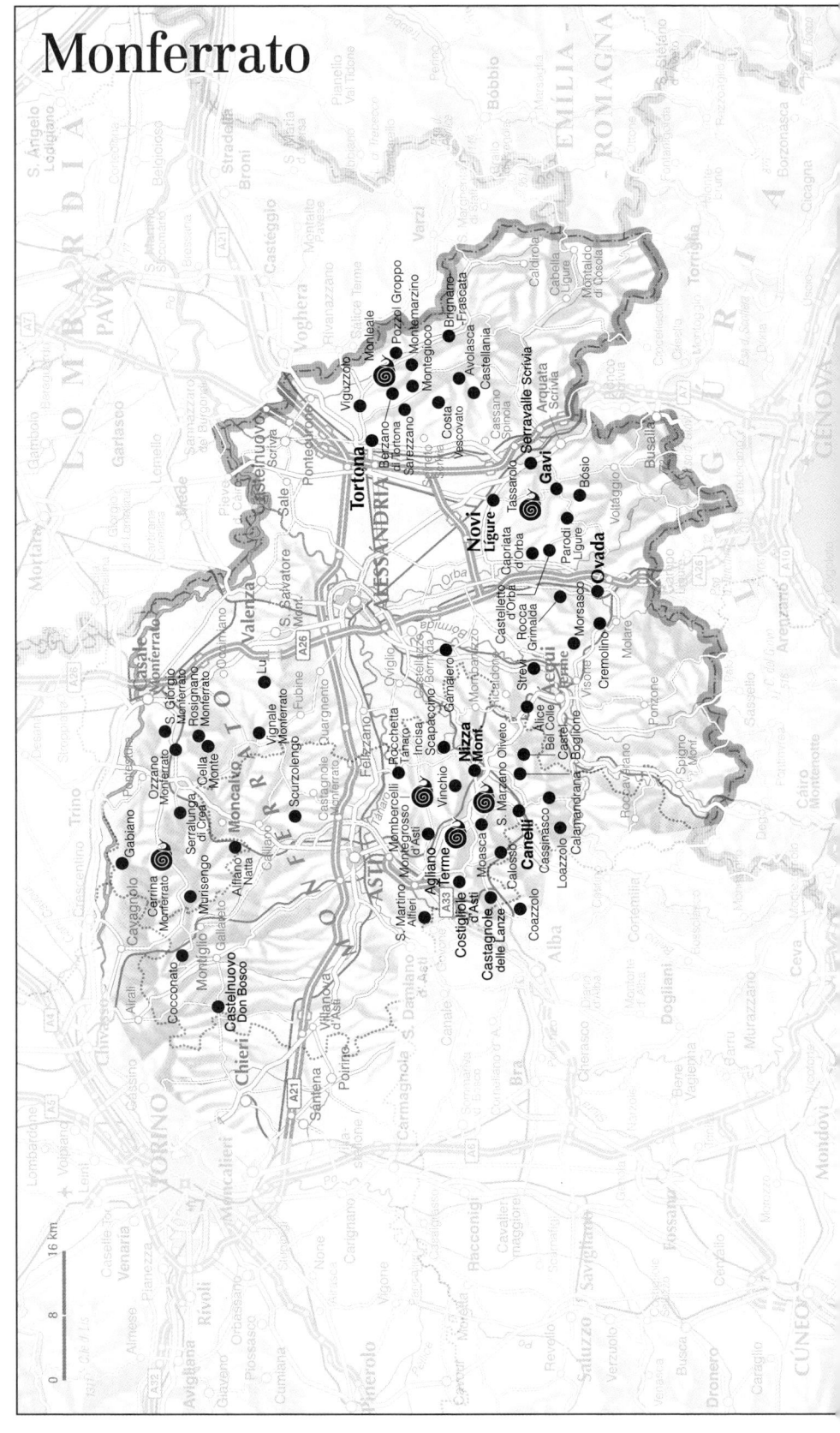

Monferrato

Dacapo

Strada Asti-Mare, 4
tel. 0141 964921
www.dacapo.it
info@dacapo.it

7.5 ha - 50,000 bt

❝ Lovely vineyards, exhilarating wines with a sense of place, organic methods, fair prices. It can't get better than this! ❞

PEOPLE - This is the story of a friendship and a passion. It was in 1997 that, fed up with their jobs, old buddies and wine freaks Paolo Dania and Dino Riccomagno decided to set up their winery. They called it Dacapo (which means "from scratch") to stress the big change it was bringing not only to their work but also to their lives.

VINEYARDS - In our stroll through the vineyards with Dino, we were able to appreciate the love and care he puts into managing them. He explained to us some of the problems involved in organic vine growing. In 2010, for example, an attack of peronospora destroyed the harvest for almost two hectares of barbera grapes. Besides the vineyards round the cellar, Paolo and Dino also own a property in Castagnole Monferrato where they grow ruchè, pinot nero and nebbiolo grapes.

WINES - Barbera d'Asti Sanbastiàn 2010 (● 25,000 bt) is one of those fresh, nicely acid wines that gives of its best at the table. The cellar has now bought a 25-hectoliter barrel to make more use of wood in the future. A standout label is the acid, inviting and enjoyable **M. Cl. Brut Rosé 2008 (⊙** pinot nero, chardonnay; 3,500 bt), while the floral, spicy **Ruchè di Castagnole Monferrato Majoli 2011 (**● 4,000 bt) came as a pleasant surprise.

slow wine | **BARBERA D'ASTI SUP. NIZZA VIGNA DACAPO 2009 (**● 6,500 bt). Barbera's earthy, mineral character is well interpreted in this favorable vintage against a background of great balance.

Crealto

Località Cardona
Strada Crealto 6
tel. 345 5686278
www.crealto.it
info@crealto.it

4.5 ha - 15,000 bt

PEOPLE - Though they had degrees in their pockets and the prospect of certain jobs, in 2008, Luigi Armanino and Eleonora Costa went crazy and made what's termed a life choice: they decided to go into agriculture. They were then lucky enough to meet Carlo Quarello, a famous "maestro" of Grignolino, who was prepared to sell them his business and spend two years teaching them how to manage it. Elisa Armanino, Luigi's sister and her partner Andrea Piano help them run the agriturismo.

VINEYARDS - Situated in the hills inside the Crè Alto nature park, partly surrounded by woodland and looking out over the vast Moferrato landscape, the vineyard with 60-year-old grignolino and barbera vines couldn't enjoy a more spectacular position. Attentive to the lessons of their "maestro" as they are, the new owners manage the winery with ideas of their own. One such is the decision to convert it to organics.

WINES - We found the couple's first bottles convincing enough and, what with Luigi busily engaged in his enology studies, they are bound to improve in the future. The typical, spicy **Grignolino del Monferrato Casalese 2010 (**● 3,500 bt) has an assertive, tart palate with fine, juicy tannins. The classic **Barbera d'Asti Agricolae 2010 (**● 3,500 bt) is racy and succulent with impressive, laid-back drinkability. The intriguing **Barbera d'Asti Sup. La Svolta 2010 (**● 2,800 bt), aged in barrels and barriques, is less explosive but offers dark earthy notes. On the palate it has texture and depth with a long, tangy finish — an excellent Everyday Wine. Aged in amphorae, **Barbera d'Asti Vis 2010 (**● 350 bt) is complex and less approachable, textured with an assertive mineral finish. **Monferrato Rosso Pionda 2010 (**● nebbiolo; 1,900 bt) plays on notes of red fruit.

FERTILIZERS green manure
PLANT PROTECTION copper and sulphur
WEED CONTROL mechanical
YEASTS selected
GRAPES 100% estate-grown
CERTIFICATION converting to organics

FERTILIZERS green manure
PLANT PROTECTION copper and sulphur
WEED CONTROL mechanical
YEASTS native
GRAPES 100% estate-grown
CERTIFICATION converting to organics

CANELLI (AT)

Paolo Avezza

Regione Monforte, 62
tel. 0141 822296
www.paoloavezza.com
contatti@paoloavezza.com

CERRINA MONFERRATO (AL)

Iuli

Via Centrale, 27
tel. 0142 946657
www.iuli.it
cavimon@iuli.it

---

7 ha - 22,000 bt   **10% discount**

PEOPLE - The adventure of the Avezza family began in 1956, when grandfather Natale bought this farm in the hills near Canelli. Since 1987 Paolo Avezza, helped by his dad Armando, his wife Daniela and consultant enologist Beppe Rattazzo, has been running the winery with passion and commitment, so much so that the place is now an institution for enthusiasts. The company produces only a few labels, though since the 2011 vintage they include a "classic method" rosé with nebbiolo grapes.

VINEYARDS - With the agronomic consultancy of Piero Roseo, Paolo Avezza manages a seven-hectare vineyard divided into two separate plots with different soil compositions, and does so with impressive care and passion. The first is near the cellar and is characterized by marly calcareous soil. The second is situated in the nearby commune of Nizza, where the soil has a high percentage of sand, which gives the wines greater finesse and elegance.

WINES - The wines resemble Paolo Avezza: meaning that they are sincere, direct and great fun. **Barbera d'Asti Sup. Sotto la Muda 2009** (● 3,000 bt) offers fruity, meaty aromas with pleasurable notes of sweet spice released by 12 months' resting in small casks. It's a full-bodied, well-crafted wine whose finish has nice soft-acid contrasts. The racy **Barbera d'Asti 2011** (● 6,000 bt) is vinous and crisp with floral, fruity aromas. Pleasantly refreshing, it's a worthy Everyday Wine. **Moscato d'Asti 2011** (○ 5.000 bt) is a rich wine that reflects its vintage: on the nose it's complex with aromas of honey and ripe yellow fruit, in the mouth its full flavor makes it deliciously drinkable. **Alta Langa Brut 2009** (○ pinot nero, chardonnay; 2,700 bt) is drier, fruity and mineral.

8.5 ha - 45,000 bt

66 If the organic approach means keeping things basic without taking shortcuts, then, deep-down, Fabrizio Iuli has always been an organic producer. His clear, uncomplicated vision is a rare gift in the wine world 99

PEOPLE - In this winery, five minds think alike. Meaning that Fabrizio Iuli, his sister Cristina and Dan, Gad and Umberta Lerner all want their wines to bring out the soul of the Monferrato hills with a productive philosophy — no selected yeasts, no filtration and no clarifying — that couldn't be simpler.

VINEYARDS - The vineyards are deliberately situated in areas that are a long way from each other to allow their differences to emerge. A common feature is the composition of the soil, which, as is the case all over the Val Cerrina, is chalky, clayey and white. This year Fabrizio's father Renzo, the true agricultural brains behind the winery. We all miss him deeply.

WINES - Fabrizio Iuli's talent emerges even when he works with grape varieties not native to the Monferrato district, somehow giving them a mixture of typicality and sense of place. A really successful wine this year is the juicy, pleasant **Monferrato Rosso Nino 2010** (● pinot nero; 2,500 bt). The accomplished palate is set off by tangy, acid hints that lead into precise, notable length. **Barbera del Monferrato Sup. Rossore 2009** (● 10,000 bt) has strong hints of macerated red berries and is ready for drinking. **Monferrato Rosso Malidea 2009** (● barbera, nebbiolo; 2,000 bt) is more straitlaced with a less expressive nose, good body and well-knit tannins.

FERTILIZERS manure pellets	FERTILIZERS none
PLANT PROTECTION chemical, copper and sulphur	PLANT PROTECTION copper and sulphur
WEED CONTROL chemical, mechanical	WEED CONTROL mechanical
YEASTS selected	YEASTS native
GRAPES 100% estate-grown	GRAPES 100% estate-grown
CERTIFICATION none	CERTIFICATION organic

LOAZZOLO (AT)

Borgo Maragliano €

Regione San Sebastiano, 2
tel. 0144 87132
www.borgomaragliano.com
info@borgomaragliano.com

MOMBERCELLI (AT)

Luigi Spertino

Strada Lea, 505
tel. 0141 959098
www.luigispertino.it
luigi.spertino@libero.it

19 ha - 310,000 bt   **10% discount**

9 ha - 45,000 bt   **10% discount**

PEOPLE - Borgo Maragliano is a winery with a very long history. Today it's run by Carlo Galliano, whose grandfather was already making Moscato passito — the forerunner of Loazzolo — way back in 1890. After gradually buying up new properties, in 1987 the company decided to stop selling grapes and to put its money on classic method sparkling wines. The view of the hills from the courtyard is breathtaking and the cellar — a veritable grotto — is lovely too.

VINEYARDS - The pinot nero and chardonnay vineyards, planted in 1984, are situated opposite the cellar at an altitude of 450 meters. In 2011 other vineyards were bedded, one of riesling for classic method production and one —spectacularly located overlooking a small lake — of pinot nero. On the steep slopes of the splendid moscato vineyard — a single plot in a due south exposure —agricultural machinery is nowhere to be seen.

WINES - The range of sweet wines was very impressive indeed. The elegance of **Moscato d'Asti La Caliera 2011** (○ 138,000 bt) derives from a combination of balsamic and white fruit notes – an excellent Everyday Wine. **Loazzolo 2009** (○ 3,300 bt) is dominated by nuances of honey with pronounced notes of aromatic herbs. A standout in the classic method range is **M. Cl. Brut Giuseppe Galliano 2008** (○ pinot nero, chardonnay; 13,000 bt) on account of its heavyweight yet elegant structure and, even more so, of its edgy acidity. **M. Cl. Brut Blanc de Blancs Francesco Galliano 2009** (○ chardonnay; 8,200 bt) is supple and deep with racy notes, while **M. Cl. Brut Rosé Giovanni Galliano 2008** (○ pinot nero; 4,200 bt) is more flowery. **Spumante Brut Chardonnay 2010** (○ 72,000 bt) is a classic method Charmat with an expressive bouquet and a palate redolent of tropical fruit.

66 Wines of great depth with next to no stabilization. Mauro doesn't consider himself to be natural, but the reality speaks of a *non-interventiste* enology and a viticulture that achieves exciting results 99

PEOPLE - We like the earnestness with which father and son Luigi and Mauro go about everything they do at the winery. Luigi, born in 1928, is a little less active than he used to be, but talking to him is like being treated to a lesson in viticulture that would be a useful experience for any wine enthusiast.

VINEYARDS - Bush cutters are used under the vines on the steepest slopes. It's from details like this that you can appreciate Mauro Spertino's caliber as a winemaker. Varieties have been planted according to a lucid calculation of positions so that the pinot nero faces east, the barbera west. If the soil in the vineyards is soft, it's partly because the tractor is used only rarely. Worth of mention is the cortese vineyard, which has vines of over 70 years of age.

WINES - Spertino's wines express massive personality. Sometimes the choice to intervene as little as possible creates problems, especially in the case of the richer wines. That is why Mauro has decided to age Barbera La Mandorla 2010 in wood for an extra year. We took comfort with the ultra-elegant **Barbera d'Asti 2010** (● 11,000 bt), which is juicy, fresh and a delight to drink. The Burgundy-style **Monferrato Rosso La Mandorla 2009** (● pinot nero; 2,600 bt) is fine, while **Piedmont Cortese Vilèt 2010** (○ 1,850 bt), macerated on the skins for 50 days, is more acid and quaffable than last year.

> **slow wine** **GRIGNOLINO D'ASTI 2011** (● 13,500 bt) Classicism, juice, impeccable measure, great drinkability, balance — in a word, perfection. Professor Spertino strikes again!

FERTILIZERS manure pellets, natural manure	
PLANT PROTECTION chemical, copper and sulphur	
WEED CONTROL chemical, mechanical	
YEASTS selected	
GRAPES 30% bought in	
CERTIFICATION none	

FERTILIZERS none	
PLANT PROTECTION chemical, copper and sulphur	
WEED CONTROL mechanical	
YEASTS native	
GRAPES 100% estate-grown	
CERTIFICATION none	

Vigneti Massa

Piazza Capsoni, 10
tel. 0131 80302
vignetimassa@libero.it

23 ha - 110,000 bt | 10% discount

❝ Walter Massa is a big-hearted, gifted winemaker. We'll never tire of repeating that if Timorasso has become what it is today, much of the credit belongs to him. Always in pursuit of the very best, Walter is a great experimenter and pays out of his own pocket whenever things, inevitably, go wrong ❞

PEOPLE - Walter Massa has worked incessantly in the cellar, investing time and sweat to promote the Tortona area. In 1987 he began to vinify the first bottles of Timorasso and has enjoyed success ever since.

VINEYARDS - The cellar's 23 hectares are all in the commune of Monleale, at an altitude of about 300 meters on soil which varies from chalk-clay to shingle with marl and streaks of silica. The oldest vineyards are on the hills of Cerreta and Bigolla in the Boscogrosso property. The most recent are those of the Valverta property. Ten hectares are planted with timorasso grapes, the others with barbera, croatina, freisa and moscato bianco.

WINES - For some years now, the winery has shunned DOCs for table wines. We enjoyed **Terra 2011** (● 15,000 bt), a fresh, balanced base Barbera redolent of fruit and earth. **Pertichetta 2007** (● croatina; 7,000 bt) starts off hard and mineral, then improves and amazes with the power and fullness of its body. **Derthona 2010** (○ timorasso; 4,000 bt) is tangy and mineral, so dry it conjures up the Loire. Balanced and typical, herby and fruity, **Sterpi 2010** (○ timorasso; 6,000 bt) is a wonderful wine. **Costa del Vento 2010** (○ timorasso; 7,000 bt) is opulent and rich with very ripe grapes and hints of candied fruit and resin. **Anarchia Costituzionale 2011** (○ moscato bianco; 4,500 bt), finally, has antique color and is balsamic, fruity, sweet and more balanced than usual.

FERTILIZERS natural manure, green manure
PLANT PROTECTION chemical, copper and sulphur
WEED CONTROL chemical, mechanical
YEASTS selected, native
GRAPES 100% estate-grown
CERTIFICATION none

Erede di Armando Chiappone

€

Strada San Michele, 51
tel. 0141 721424
www.eredechiappone.com
erededi@virgilio.it

10.5 ha - 35,000 bt | 10% discount

PEOPLE - This solid little country winery is run by the young but accomplished Daniele Chiappone. Full of energy, he devotes heart and soul not only to the business, but also to the promotion of the local area as a whole. Hence his willingness to take up and argue the cases of fellow winemakers. He is abetted by his sister Michela and his folks Franco and Liliana.

VINEYARDS - The vineyards, managed with care and attention, are concentrated round the hamlet of San Michele di Nizza, a stone's throw from the company headquarters, the oldest below the cellar itself. Recently a great deal of time and effort went into the choice of the rootstock for one splendid property where, in the space of just a few hundred meters, the soil changes from clay to silt and chalk to sand, thus adding great complexity to its wines. Daniele's mother recently inherited a four-hectare vineyard near Acqui Terme.

WINES - The wines are traditional in style and stand out for their character, richness of flavor and technical precision. **Barbera d'Asti Sup. Nizza Ru 2009** (● 3,000 bt) was the fruit of a great vintage. Complex and balsamic, racy, succulent and mouthfilling, it's a delight for the palate. The excellent **Barbera d'Asti Brentura 2010** (● 5,000 bt) has explosive fruit: it impressed us for its nice acidity and flavorful finish — an amazing Everyday Wine. We were fascinated by **Freisa d'Asti Sanpedra 2008** (● 4,000 bt) too. It's earthy and spicy, solid and robust, animated by punchy acidity. **Angel 2011** (○ 3,000 bt), the fruit of fermentation of favorita, cortese and chardonnay, is scented, heady, fresh and gutsy on the palate. The wonderfully drinkable **Dolcetto d'Asti Mandola 2009** (● 3,000 bt) is light with faint hints of herbs and the classic, palate-lengthening, bitterish tannic touch.

FERTILIZERS none
PLANT PROTECTION chemical, copper and sulphur
WEED CONTROL chemical, mechanical
YEASTS selected
GRAPES 100% estate-grown
CERTIFICATION none

NIZZA MONFERRATO (AT)

La Gironda €

Strada Bricco,12
tel. 0141 701013
www.lagironda.com
info@lagironda.com

SAN MARTINO ALFIERI (AT)

Marchesi Alfieri

Piazza Alfieri, 28
tel. 0141 976015
www.marchesialfieri.it
alfieri@marchesialfieri.it

8.5 ha - 40,000 bt   **10% discount**

21 ha - 100,000 bt

PEOPLE - Susanna Galandrino and her husband Alberto Adamo manage this young winery in the Bricco district of Nizza with the expert help of enologists Giuliano Noé and Beppe Rattazzo. In the cellar it is possible to admire the inventions of Susanna's father, who used to produce winemaking machinery. They include a cask cleaner and an contraption to facilitate work on small barrels. Fermentations and macerations are brief and take place in horizontal tanks.

PEOPLE - Giovanna, Antonella and Emanuela San Martino are the owners of this splendid Monferrato winery, which boasts strong bonds with the local farming world and culture. The competent, passionate Mario Olivero manages the vine dressing and winemaking with the capable assistance of enologist Christian Carlevero and agronomist Piero Roseo. The historic cellars of the castle, still used to age the wines, are a sight to see.

VINEYARDS - The vineyards are divided into various parcels, all round Nizza, save for one with a fortunate exposure and good ventilation on a steep slope in Calamandrana, where five grape varieties, including brachetto, are grown. The vineyards are managed with attention to the environment without the use of weed killers and with treatments reduced to a minimum. The soil in both communes is very pale and rich in limestone and gray marl. A great deal of attention is devoted to the foliage.

VINEYARDS - The lion's share is claimed, rightly enough, by barbera, which yields great results here. Agronomic practices are conventional and respectful of the environment. The old Alfiera vineyard, for example, enjoys optimal exposure and drainage and is left without weed control. We believe that the same methods will soon be adopted in the other vineyards. Attention to detail with an eye to quality is evident in both vineyards and cellar.

WINES - Barbera d'Asti La Lippa 2011 (● 10,000 bt) is typical, refreshing and wonderfully quaffable. **Barbera d'Asti La Gena 2010 (●** 8,000 bt), which comes from an old vineyard, is tangy, fruity and racy. **Monferrato Rosso Chiesavecchia 2009 (●** cabernet, nebbiolo, barbera, merlot; 6,000 bt) is well-crafted, while the intriguing **Monferrato Nebbiolo Soul 2008 (●** 600 bt) is floral and earthy with plenty of juice a sweet, fine tannins. The lively, sweet **Brachetto d'Acqui 2011 (●** 6,000 bt) has notes of strawberry and dried herbs.

WINES - Barbera d'Asti La Tota 2010 (● 72,000 bt) matures in used wooden casks and large barrels. The bouquet is elegant with clean fruit and the juicy, lively palate has, as always, overwhelming progression and typicality. **Monferrato Rosso Sostegno 2010 (●** barbera, pinot nero; 13,000 bt) has intense aromas and luscious flesh. The floral, spicy **Piemonte Grignolino Sansoero 2011 (●** 4,200 bt) is warm and textured on the palate with measured tannins.

> **slow wine** **BARBERA D'ASTI SUP. NIZZA LE NICCHIE 2009** (● 6,000 bt) A true Slow Wine on account of its character and earthiness, its vibrant acidity and fruity flesh, its mineral finish and nice juice. A fine interpretation of the vintage.

> **slow wine** **BARBERA D'ASTI SUP. ALFIERA 2009** (● 13,000 bt) An exemplary modern yet profoundly terroir-based Barbera with classic notes of fruit and autumn leaves accompanied by fleshiness and the acidity typical of this, the main grape in the Asti area. We were impressed by its drinkability.

FERTILIZERS natural manure
PLANT PROTECTION chemical, copper and sulphur
WEED CONTROL mechanical
YEASTS selected
GRAPES 100% estate-grown
CERTIFICATION none

FERTILIZERS organic-mineral, compost
PLANT PROTECTION chemical, copper and sulphur
WEED CONTROL chemical, mechanical
YEASTS selected
GRAPES 100% estate-grown
CERTIFICATION none

Carussin

Regione Mariano, 27
tel. 0141 831358
www.carussin.it
ferrobruna@inwind.it

15 ha - 90,000 bt	**10% discount**

66 Naturalness is the watchword at this winery both in the vineyard, where organics have been in place for some years now, and in the cellar. The results are as enthralling as they are convincing 99

PEOPLE - The Ferros are a solar farming family. The four of them run this multi-faceted business which combines wine production, Luigi's responsibility, with an educational farm, featuring donkeys, Bruna's abiding passion, an *agri-bar*, the Grappolo Contro Luppolo, organized by their son Matteo, and a microbrewery to be opened soon by their other son Luca (who already makes beer under the Clan!Destino trademark).

VINEYARDS - The man responsible for the vineyards is Luigi: he doesn't trim the vines but bundles them onto wires. The vine rows stand in grass, the under rows are worked by hand and the land undergoes periodic soft plowing and cover cropping to strengthen the soil. Luigi still grows plots with ancient grape varieties such as carica l'asino and ancellotta.

WINES - The winery pursues purity and naturalness both in the vineyard and in the cellar. Luigi uses no sulfur (apart from the odd small dose at bottling) and no selected yeasts. **Barbera d'Asti Asinoi 2011** (● 40,000 bt), an assemblage of grapes from vineyards up to 50 years old, is fresh and drinkable. **Barbera d'Asti Lia Vì 2011** (● 16,000 bt), from a single vineyard and aged in steel, has body, plenty of fruit and a juicy finish — an excellent Everyday Wine. Soft and round with notes of cherry and red berries, **Barbera d'Asti Tranquilla 2011** (● 15,000 bt) comes from a vineyard of almost an hectare and is aged for 10 months in large barrels. **Barbera d'Asti Sup. Nizza Ferro Carlo 2008** (● 1,500 bt) is lean, long and elegant. Also worthy of mention is the mineral, tangy, earthy **Carica l'Asino 2011** (○ carica l'asino, cortese; 2,500 bt).

FERTILIZERS biodynamic preparations, green manure
PLANT PROTECTION copper and sulphur
WEED CONTROL mechanical
YEASTS native
GRAPES 100% estate-grown
CERTIFICATION organic

Castello di Tassarolo

Via Alborina, 1
tel. 0143 342248
www.castelloditassarolo.it
info@castelloditassarolo.it

17 ha - 120,000 bt	**10% discount**

66 Talking to Henry, you realize that concepts such as the central role of horses and looking ahead with an eye to the past are more than mere nostalgia. No, they represent a bond with the land and one's roots 99

PEOPLE - Winemaking is a life choice for Henry Finzi Costantine and Massimiliana Spinola, who have made naturalness a cornerstone of their existence. Organics and biodynamics combine to make the vineyards of Castello di Tassarolo a place of more than just wine production.

VINEYARDS - The vineyard where the grapes are grown for Titouan, the Gavi Henry has dedicated to his beloved horse, are a thrill to see. Here he is experimenting with cultivation systems in which mechanization is replaced by horse power. The property, which has a flat conformation, has an area of an hectare and is situated at an altitude of about 300 meters.

WINES - The linear, rich, racy white **Gavi del Comune di Tassarolo Titouan 2011** (○ 15,000 bt) is exceptional. The result of a slightly late harvest, **Gavi del Comune di Tassarolo Il Castello 2011** (○ 25,000 bt) is complex and juicy with a precise mineral vein and lots of freshness; it is an excellent Everyday Wine. **Gavi del Comune di Tassarolo Alborina 2009** (○ 12,000 bt) comes from a 70-year-old vineyard: it is unctuous and structured with a slightly oaky finish. **Gavi del Comune di Tassarolo Frizzante Spinola 2011** (○ 18,000 bt) is tangy, dry and nicely fresh. **Gavi del Comune di Tassarolo Spinola 2011** (○ 30,000 bt) has slightly vegetable notes. The sulphite-free **Monferrato Rosso 2011** (● barbera, cabernet; 12.000 bt) is winey and spicy.

FERTILIZERS biodynamic preparations, green manure
PLANT PROTECTION copper and sulphur
WEED CONTROL mechanical
YEASTS selected
GRAPES 100% estate-grown
CERTIFICATION organic

La Colombera

Frazione Vho
Strada Comunale per Vho, 7
tel. 0131 867795
www.lacolomberavini.it
info@lacolomberavini.it

20 ha - 60,000 bt

PEOPLE - Grapes plus … peaches, potatoes, chickpeas, meadows and orchards. In other words, an old-fashioned farm and an institution for the locals, travellers and tourists who want to pop in for a glass of wine. Elisa and her dad Piercarlo Semino are the heart and soul of this attractive winery, which plays a central role in redeveloping the entire area in the hills a few kilometers outside Tortona. It's worth the journey.

VINEYARDS - Piercarlo and Elisa are in love with the timorasso grape. But though they faun over it, they never forget the Tortona tradition of which they're also fond. They manage their 14-hectare plot a few meters from the cellar with common sense and an eye to organics, and it's no coincidence that, besides barbera, cortese and croatina, they also grow the celebrated nibiò, the local dolcetto.

WINES - We are pleased to say that, locally, the company runs a thriving business selling well-produced, unbottled wine. As for the bottled, it is always of the highest quality. **Colli Tortonesi Timorasso Derthona 2010** (○ 15,000 bt) stands out for its elegance, drinkability and depth. Colli Tortonesi Timorasso Il Montino 2010 (○ 4,500 bt) was exceptional. The nose strikes a perfect balance between flint and butter and the palate has class to spare with measured acidity and unique depth. It's a Great Wine, Piedmont's only white to win the accolade — some achievement! **Colli Tortonesi Bianco Bricco Bartolomeo 2011** (○ cortese; 10,000 bt) has thrust and character. The reds — **Colli Tortonesi Rosso Elisa 2009** (● barbera; 4,000 bt) and **Colli Tortonesi Croatina Arché 2009** (● croatina; 7,000 bt) are good too, and we also found the experimental vinification of the nibiò grape interesting.

FERTILIZERS natural manure	
PLANT PROTECTION chemical, copper and sulphur	
WEED CONTROL mechanical	
YEASTS selected	
GRAPES 100% estate-grown	
CERTIFICATION none	

Claudio Mariotto

Località Vho
Strada per Sarezzano, 29
tel. 0131 868500
www.claudiomariotto.it
info@claudiomariotto.it

30 ha - 80,000 bt

PEOPLE - Claudio Mariotto one of the first Colli Tortonesi producers to believe in the timorasso renaissance, is now a great advocate of the grape. Self-effacing but also sociable and volcanic, he is also a champion of the local area. He is helped in his work by his companion Rossana and brother Mauro.

VINEYARDS - The sprawling Mariotto vineyards are split up into a vast number of parcels. Claudio interprets them all intelligently to achieve greater complexity in his wines. A great many hectares are devoted to timorasso but, true to local tradition, there's no shortage of croatina, barbera and freisa either. Claudio adopts a conventional agronomic approach and is planning to introduce rational eco-compatible systems, such as alga extracts as an alternative to chemicals.

WINES - Pitasso 2002 and Derthona 2001, fresh with magnificent aging capacity are two fine examples of Claudio's brilliant take on timorasso. Even the new vintages, with clear-cut notes of sulfur and petrol and huge drinkability — the feather in the company's cap — reveal great potential. **Colli Tortonesi Timorasso Pitasso 2010** (○ 10,000 bt) is top class too. All the reds are very good, stating with the croatina-based **Colli Tortonesi Montemirano 2010** (● 6,500 bt). The Barberas — the well-structured, beefy **Colli Tortonesi Rosso Poggio del Rosso 2007** (● 5,500 bt) and its everyday version il **Colli Tortonesi Rosso Territorio 2010** (● barbera; 15,000 bt) — are both well-crafted.

> **slow wine** **COLLI TORTONESI TIMORASSO DERTHONA 2010** (○ 13,000 bt) A white with huge personality and 100% typicity, capable of melding the potency of the grape and good drinkability within a beautifully clean taste profile. We're gluttons for this Timorasso with a "leaner" feel.

FERTILIZERS organic-mineral	
PLANT PROTECTION chemical, copper and sulphur, organic	
WEED CONTROL chemical, mechanical	
YEASTS selected	
GRAPES 100% estate-grown	
CERTIFICATION none	

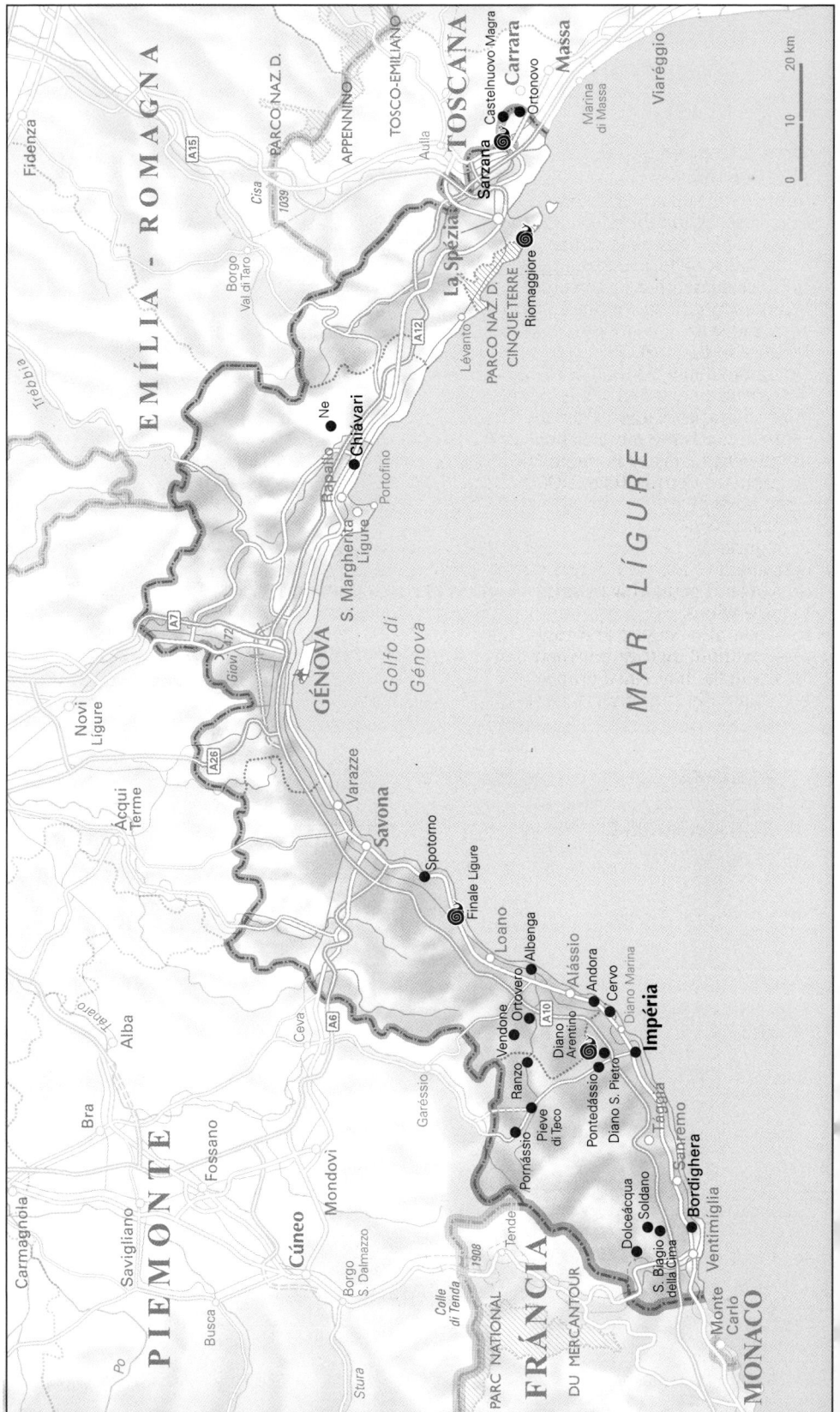

LIGURIA

1972 was the year of the first Ligurian DOC. Since then the number of producers focused on making quality wine and raising the profile of their terroirs has increased, but there is still room for further growth. We are referring here to Rossese di Dolceacqua, Dolceacqua for short. Calling the wine with the name of a single village may be annoying for others in which it is produced (the discipline lists 14 altogether), but the habit has a historical explanation since it was the Marquisate of the Dorias, centered in Dolceacqua, that first promoted cultivation of the grape.

What cannot be questioned is the quality of the wine: warm, dry and well-structured — a red with typical Ligurian pride, docile yet at once rebellious. Also in Western Liguria, in the Valle Arroscia, they produce Ormeasco, protected by the Ormeasco di Pornassio denomination, and, courageously and commendably, are striving to recover other varieties, granaccia in particular. On the eastern Riviera, the ciliegiolo and sangiovese grapes come under the Colli di Luni and Colline di Levanto denominations. Vermentino is the most common white grape variety (and wine) and is to be found in the Riviera Ligure di Ponente, Val Polcevera, Golfo del Tigullio, Colline di Levanto, Colli di Luni and Cinque Terre DOCs, in the latter with albarola and the revaluated bosco. The native pigato, common from Savona to Imperia, is another leading player on the Ligurian scene.

In Liguria 1,700 companies, mostly small, produce about 100,000 hectoliters, the equivalent of four and a half million bottles. The sector boasts an area of 1,477 hectares of land planted with vines, of which 777 given over to DOCs, 103 to GTIs and 597 to table wines.

Between mid-August and mid-September, the 2011 vintage recorded high temperatures without swings between day and night and this caused a loss of aromas and acidity in the harvested grapes. The phenomenon varied in intensity according to area but, generally speaking, the level of the wines was good, in a few cases exceptional.

snails 🐌

62	MARIA DONATA BIANCHI
63	CASCINA DELLE TERRE ROSSE
64	WALTER DE BATTÉ
65	SANTA CATERINA

bottles 🍾

62	TERRE BIANCHE
65	MACCARIO DRINGENBERG

DIANO ARENTINO (IM)

Maria Donata Bianchi 🐌

Località Valcrosa
Via Merea
tel. 0183 498233
www.aziendaagricolabianchi.it
info@aziendaagricolabianchi.com

4 ha - 30,000 bt

66 The director and star of the enterprise is Emanuele Trevia, whose commitment and dedication are a guarantee of wines of indisputable quality. His are wines bound to the *terroir*, packed with personality thanks to impeccably managed vineyards 99

PEOPLE - Emanuele Trevia shares his success with his daughter Marta, an apprentice enologist currently working under the wing of the expert Valter Bonetti, and resolute wife Donatella Bianchi, who runs the family *agriturismo*.

VINEYARDS - The main vineyard covers three hectares and is part of a larger ten-hectare plot near the main farmhouse. Situated halfway up a hill, it faces eastward, its clayey, pebbly soil is planted with 13-year-old plants. The other three vineyards have chalky soil and are situated in the commune of Diano Castello: two are given over to white grapes with 50-year-old vines, the other to red grapes with vines planted 15 years ago.

WINES - Trevia intelligently combines grape varieties to achieve fresh, crisp, full-bodied wines. Conscientious work in the vineyards and cellar do the rest. **Riviera Ligure di Ponente Pigato 2011** (○ 10,000 bt) supplements sensations of balsam and aromatic herbs on the nose with clear-cut fruit, saltiness and good progression on the palate. La Mattana is produced only in the best years, which wasn't the case this time round. But **Bormano 2010** (● granaccia, syrah; 2,000 bt) caught the eye, or rather the palate, for its freshness, quaffability and balance, not to mention its fruity, spicy nose.

slow wine RIVIERA LIGURE DI PONENTE VERMENTINO **2011** (○ 20,000 bt) Great finesse, nice floral, fruity tones that spread out and linger on the palate with consummate elegance — a hymn to the *terroir* of origin.

FERTILIZERS	organic-mineral
PLANT PROTECTION	copper and sulphur
WEED CONTROL	mechanical
YEASTS	selected
GRAPES	100% estate-grown
CERTIFICATION	none

DOLCEACQUA (IM)

Terre Bianche

Località Arcagna
tel. 0184 31426
www.terrebianche.com
terrebianche@terrebianche.com

8.5 ha - 65,000 bt

PEOPLE - Filippo Rondelli and Franco Laconi run their company with passion, assisted by consultant agronomist Diego Passaniti and enologist Mario Ronco. A combination of enterprise and determination has allowed them to achieve high levels right across their wine range. Worth stressing is their commitment to reducing the environmental impact of their work in the countryside.

VINEYARDS - The vineyards are all situated on terraced hillsides on three plots in the areas of Dolceacqua and Camporosso. The Arcagna vineyard, which has plants 20-50 years old, looks over the Val Nervia, while Terre Bianche, given over to vines of 15 years of age, affords a breathtaking view over white clay gullies, and Scartozzoni grows vines of an average age of 10 years. Their exposure ensures an ideal ripening curve for the grapes.

WINES - The wines are all clean-tasting with a strong sense of place. Their style is to preserve the particularities of the vines, bringing out their personality, finesse and aging capacity. **Riviera Ligure di Ponente Vermentino 2011** (○ 16,500 bt) has well-defined floral and fruity aromas with a vertical, harmonious palate. Fruity and balsamic, blending freshness, body and balance, **Rossese di Dolceacqua 2011** (● 16,000 bt) evokes the production zone perfectly. Better still is **Rossese di Dolceacqua Bricco Arcagna 2010** (● 3,200 bt) with its intriguing aromas of fruit, flowers and spices and juicy, assertive palate.

slow wine RIVIERA LIGURE DI PONENTE PIGATO **2011** (○ 19,600 bt) Beautiful and complex on the nose, elegant, solid and long on the palate with drink-inducing acid thrust — this wine's bond with the land is as clear as its price is tempting.

FERTILIZERS	manure pellets, green manure
PLANT PROTECTION	copper and sulphur
WEED CONTROL	mechanical
YEASTS	selected
GRAPES	10% bought in
CERTIFICATION	none

Cascina delle Terre Rosse

Via Manie, 3
tel. 0196 98782

4.5 ha - 25,000 bt

---

66 Vladi sets great store by his land, which he loves and respects profoundly. You can tell that by the way his vineyards fit perfectly into the breathtaking landscape 99

PEOPLE - With the assistance of his wife Paola and consultancy of agronomist Gianni Forte and enologist Giuliano Noè, Gianni Vladimiro Galluzzo has raised the work commenced by his father to levels of winemaking excellence.

VINEYARDS - In the three vineyards, two on the plateau of Le Manie, at an altitude of 200-300 meters, and one in the hills overlooking Pietra Ligure, the soil changes from chalk and clay to white clay. The age of the vines changes too, varying from five to 40 years. The land looks from south to southwest and on the terraces, some very narrow with just two vine rows, others wider, the vines are Guyot- and spur-pruned. The vineyards are managed with respect for the environment.

WINES - Galluzzo looks for elegance and aging potential in his wines. **Apogeo 2011** (○ pigato; 3,000 bt) is particularly exciting. Rich and suave with fruity, balsamic aromas, it has a fleshy palate with great follow-through. The fine, flavorsome **Riviera Ligure di Ponente Pigato 2011** (○ 10,200 bt) has bundles of fruit. It is a wine to be reckoned with, as is **Paola 2011** (○ pigato; 450 bt) with its inviting aromas and enveloping, rich, dynamic palate. Though it still needs to age a little longer, **Le Banche 2011** (○ vermentino, pigato; 600 bt) already has plenty of fruity flesh and lingering flavor. **Riviera Ligure di Ponente Vermentino 2011** (○ 5,200 bt) is packed with freshnes, balance and verve, while the brilliantly fruity **Solitario 2010** (● granaccia, barbera, merlot; 900 bt) is inviting to the palate and full of impetus and freshness.

FERTILIZERS green manure
PLANT PROTECTION copper and sulphur
WEED CONTROL mechanical
YEASTS selected
GRAPES 100% estate-grown
CERTIFICATION none

VisAmoris

Strada Privata Molino Javè, 23
tel. 348 3959569
visamoris@libero.it

3.5 ha - 25,000 bt   `10% discount`

PEOPLE - Ten or so years ago, mixing passion with energy, Roberto Tozzi and Rossana Zappa set up this winery devoted to the production of Pigato. Their commitment in the vineyard, a well-equipped cellar and the accomplished technical assistance of Piero Roseo and Giuliano Noè have allowed them to make quantum leaps forward at every harvest. In fact they are now making experiments to widen their productive horizon and discover the versatility of their wines.

VINEYARDS - The largest vineyard — a couple of hectares of very steep terraces of varying breadth on calcareous, pebbly soil with a south-southwest exposure — is situated halfway up a well-ventilated hill looking onto the sea and Porto Maurizio. The property is completed by another two plots further down, where the breeze from the Vasia valley increases the night-to-day temperature swing. The Guyot-pruned vines are eight to 15 years old.

WINES - The wines show balance, a personal aromatic tone and originality. The top-level **Riviera Ligure di Ponente Pigato Sogno 2010** (○ 2,500 bt) has sweet fruit, an enfolding palate and great dynamism. **Regis 2009** (○ pigato; 1,000 bt) is temptingly expressive, while the fruity fragrance, balance and suppleness of **Riviera Ligure di Ponente Pigato Domè 2011** (○ 15,000 bt) make it hugely quaffable. **Vis Amoris Brut Millesimato 2009** (○ pigato; 1,000 bt) is pleasurable and the interesting **Dulcis in Fundo 2010** (○ pigato; 800 bt) is made with grapes dried on the vine.

---

slow wine **RIVIERA LIGURE DI PONENTE PIGATO VERUM 2011** (○ 2,500 bt) The fruit of fermentation on the skins, a wine that is complex, full-bodied and fleshy with good acidity and a variegated suite of aromas. It conjures up Mediterranean scrub and a nuanced sense of place.

FERTILIZERS green manure
PLANT PROTECTION copper and sulphur
WEED CONTROL mechanical
YEASTS selected
GRAPES 100% estate-grown
CERTIFICATION none

RIOMAGGIORE (SP)

Luciano Capellini

Via Montello, 240 B
tel. 0187 920632
www.vinbun.it
capellini@vinbun.it

RIOMAGGIORE (SP)

Walter De Batté

Via Trarcantu, 25
tel. 0187 920127

1.5 ha - 6,500 bt   **10% discount**

5 ha - 13,000 bt

PEOPLE - The Capellini cellar is one of the oldest — seven generations! — in the Cinque Terre. In 2004 Luciano Capellini took it over and, in next to no time, won consensus and important accolades. Of fundamental importance is the experience of enologist Giorgio Baccigalupi, Carlo Canali Chiavelli and Luciano's mother Giulia.

VINEYARDS - The vineyards are situated in Riomaggiore and in the Volastra district: 60 or so *cian*, the famous terraces, divided into about 40 parcels, a myriad of small strips of land supported by millenary dry-stone walls. They stand at altitudes of 150-350 meters and are arbor-trained. Plans are underway to raise the vines by at least a meter and a half from the ground to avoid workers the effort of bending over.

WINES - **Cinque Terre 2011** (○ bosco, albarola, vermentino), vinified in stainless steel tanks, is a complex wine with a bouquet ranges from notes of Mediterranean maquis and citrusy nuances and a nice salty finish. A novelty this year is **Cinque Terre Vin de Damisana 2011** (○ bosco, albarola, vermentino; 300 bt), which is aged in demijohns after long maceration on the skins. A wine of great acidity with unusual balsamic notes and hints of resin, it's not easy to approach but will certainly fascinate the curious taster.

> **slow wine** CINQUE TERRE SCIACCHETRÀ RIS. 2008 (○ bosco, albarola, vermentino; 800 bt) A wine with a generous palate that captivates with distinct hints of walnut and candied citron and an interesting note of licorice. Unique of its kind, it has to be tasted at least once in a lifetime — sense of place in liquid form.

66 This company is the flag-bearer of a great farming revolution at the service of a *terroir* of great fragility but of rare beauty 99

PEOPLE - When we think back to the terrible flooding that hit the Cinque Terre last autumn our thoughts inevitable turn to to ta people like Walter who, with his colleagues, showed just how important viticulture is in this corner of Liguria.

VINEYARDS - Walter's vineyards sit on the terraces of Vernazza and Riomaggiore and also in the nearby Val di Magra. He manages them with commitment and application. "Working among the vines here," he explains, "means not only taking home the grapes, but above all reclaiming and cleaning public pathways the surrounding woodland, keeping wild animals at bay and protecting the land from the effects of human negligence, such as fires."

WINES - Walter replicates the determination with which he does his work as a viticulturist in the cellar, where he produces wines of massive personality using vinifications that enhance the quality of the grapes. The wines are made with grapes both from the company's vineyards and from those of the Prima Terra group. The excellent **Altrove 2010** (○ 1,500 bt), a white made with a number of rare grapes, is the rich, balanced result of fermentative maceration. **Carlaz 2010** (○ 1,800 bt) is Walter's personal take of vermentino grapes from a vineyard in the hills inland from Carrara. **Tonos 2009** (● 2.000 bt) is made from local and other grapes from a vineyard over 70 years old, whereas the rich, well textured **Bozolo 2009** (● dolcetto, merlot; 800 bt) comes from a vineyard near Brugnato.

FERTILIZERS organic-mineral, compost
PLANT PROTECTION copper and sulphur
WEED CONTROL mechanical
YEASTS selected
GRAPES 100% estate-grown
CERTIFICATION none

FERTILIZERS organic-mineral
PLANT PROTECTION chemical, copper and sulphur
WEED CONTROL mechanical
YEASTS selected, native
GRAPES 100% estate-grown
CERTIFICATION none

SAN BIAGIO DELLA CIMA (IM)

Maccario Dringenberg

Via Torre, 3
tel. 0184 289947
maccariodringenberg@yahoo.it

SARZANA (SP)

Santa Caterina

Via Santa Caterina, 6
tel. 0187 629429
andrea.kihlgren@alice.it

---

4 ha - 23,000 bt

PEOPLE - The dynamic Giovanna Maccario and her husband Goetz Dringenberg have been producing Rossese for well nigh 20 years. With another 13 producers they have formed an Association of Historic Vineyards with the aim of defining and raising the profile of the best crus for this great Italian red, which has hit the Italian and international limelight only recently. Giovanna's pledge is to promote and protect a local area that is as fragile as it is beautiful.

VINEYARDS - The company recently bought the historic Curli cru — a 3,000-hectare steep terraced parcel with very old bush-trained vines —, once lauded by the renowned Italian wine critic Veronelli. The same pruning system is adopted for the Luvaira vineyard, less impracticable but just as old, which yields spicy, refreshing wines. The Posaù vineyard, finally, is an enchanting spot, again steep but a little warmer. Here they grow massarda, an endangered native grape.

WINES - The wines are matured exclusively in stainless steel and, in the case of the crus, clearly express the diverse characteristics of their *terroirs* of origin. An assemblage of grapes from different parcels, **Rossese di Dolceacqua 2011** (● 11,000 bt) is nicely precise with cut-glass notes of aromatic herbs and great elegance. **Rossese di Dolceacqua Sup. Luvaira 2010** (● 6,000 bt) is still very young and undeveloped, but already exhibits all the spiciness of this magnificent cru with a hint of white pepper and a pacey, long, juicy, racy finish.

> **slow wine** ROSSESE DI DOLCEACQUA SUP. POSAÙ 2010 (● 6,000 bt) More pervasive and fruity than the other wines and arguably a little less vertical, but nonetheless the one that has the best balance at the moment. It has a leisurely, flowery aftertaste with distinct hints of Mediterranean *maquis*. A hymn to its *terroir*.

7.7 ha - 40,000 bt

❝ A model farm on Liguria's Eastern Riviera, with vineyards as tidy as gardens thanks to the great agricultural sensitivity of Andrea Kihlgren. Its albeit excellent wines need time to express themselves to the full ❞

PEOPLE - Andrea Kihlgren, who has been running the place for more than 20 years with the help of his wife Alessandra, cultivates the vineyard naturally using biodynamic methods.

VINEYARDS - Santa Caterina is a small round-topped hill with mainly clay soil. On it the cellar, offices and farmhouse form a cluster that merges perfectly into the landscape. Round about you can admire a garden with flowers, fruit trees and vermentino, albarola and merla vines. In the Ghiaretolo district, on sandy soil, are the merlot and cabernet sauvignon vineyards with vines over 20 years old.

WINES - Andrea has changed his system for vinifying **Colli di Luni Vermentino Poggi Alti 2011** (○ 4,500 bt) by reducing the maceration time on the skins. The resulting wine is more drinkable and exhibits its minerality more distinctly. **Colli di Luni Vermentino 2011** (○ 18,000 bt) is lean and pleasurable thanks to its citrusy freshness. It's an excellent Everyday Wine. Born of the union of sauvignon and tocai, **Giuncàro 2011** (○ 4,000 bt) has fruitier, tangier notes than the other wines. The excellent debut wine, **Colli di Luni Albarola 2011** (○ 600 bt) is refreshing and fruity and won us over, partly on account of its low alcohol content. The fruity, winy **Colli di Luni Rosso 2009** (● sangiovese, merla; 2,600 bt) and the vegetal **Ghiaretolo 2009** (● merlot, cabernet; 3,200 bt) were both good too.

FERTILIZERS none
PLANT PROTECTION copper and sulphur
WEED CONTROL mechanical
YEASTS native
GRAPES 100% estate-grown
CERTIFICATION none

FERTILIZERS compost, biodynamic preparations, green manure
PLANT PROTECTION copper and sulphur
WEED CONTROL mechanical
YEASTS native
GRAPES 100% estate-grown
CERTIFICATION none

LOMBARDY

Lombardy, the driving force of the national economy, is home to veritable agricultural "presidia", unique areas that help diversify and enhance the national wine panorama. It is precisely this diversity, made up of culture, history, landscape and ideas that create the added value of Lombard wine. A huge number of DOC wines are concentrated in the region, from Sondrio to the Oltrepò, and production accounts for about 7 per cent of the national total. But, especially in this moment of crisis in which production is necessarily contained, it is not mere figures that give Lombardy impetus.

With the new *Slow Wine* guide, we are pleased to see the main winegrowing zones asserting the quality of their products and promoting their individual identities. We welcome, for example, the recent initiative in the **Garda** zone, where the Valtènesi DOC has been introduced to "tidy up" all the miscellaneous names, denominations and appellatives that used to generate confusion and sketchiness. The same applies to the Cruasé project in the **Oltrepò**, which — though not everyone agrees with it yet — uses improved quality to reinforce the terroir's image as a major classic method pinot nero district. From **Franciacorta** there's nothing noteworthy to report on the enological front, only the consolidation of a general style that places the onus on linearity and minerality. In this important terroir, home to an array of excellence, what we really expect to see is a growth in the level of the base Franciacortas, hence of the concept of value for money. Where we did note new developments was in the field of agriculture with the introduction of virtuous models geared to the sustainability and prolongation of the life-span of vineyards.

In early July 2012, the heroic viticulture of the **Valtellina** suffered the setback of a violent hailstorm. Despite the usual problems of management and lack of support, it nonetheless continues in its uphill struggle to strengthen this unique nebbiolo growing zone, where consolidated and virtuous major wine companies are being supplemented by the growth of small artisan ones. More good news comes from the **Lugana** zone, where the wineries work as a team to convey an image of local cohesion, and from "minor" ones such as **Botticino**, **Capriano del Colle** and the recently instituted **Terre Lariane** district, all keen to promote their identities and quality. A more critical situation was recorded in the province of **Bergamo**, especially in the Valcalepio, where stylistic confusion generates reds that are too often top-heavy and over-opulent. We believe in the potential of this terroir, as evidenced by Moscato di Scanzo, and we sincerely hope that collaboration with the two local consortia will prompt the reorganization that is needed.

snails ◉

69	TOGNI REBAIOLI
71	IL PENDIO
73	AR.PE.PE.
73	FAY
75	PODERE IL SANTO
75	AGNES

bottles ▮

69	BELLAVISTA
70	CA' DEL BOSCO
70	CAVALLERI

coins €

71	MARANGONA

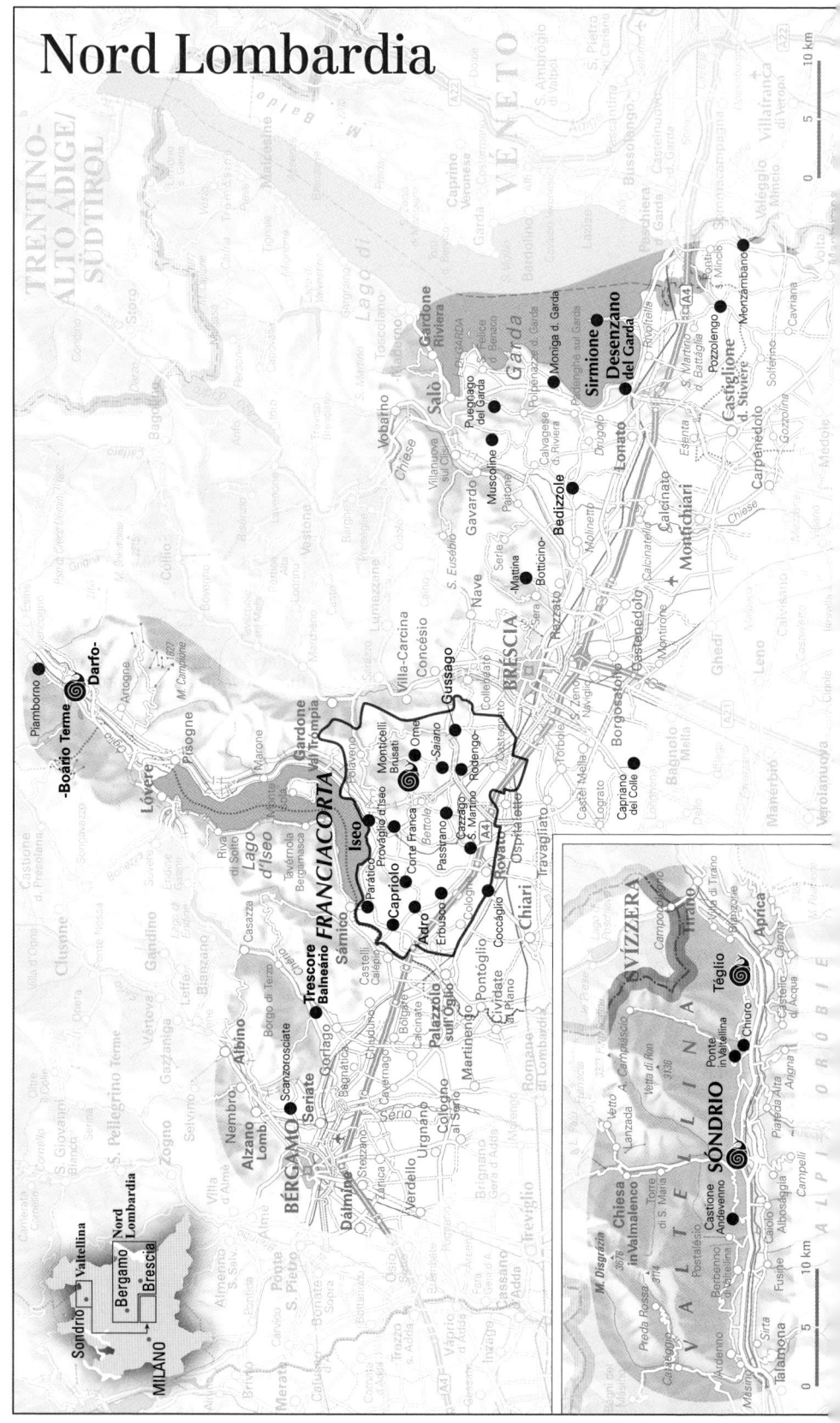

Nord Lombardia

DARFO BOARIO TERME (BS)

Togni Rebaioli

Frazione Erbanno
Via Rossini, 19
tel. 0364 529706
www.togni-rebaioli.it
info@togni-rebaioli.it

ERBUSCO (BS)

Bellavista

Via Bellavista, 5
tel. 030 7762000
www.bellavistasrl.it
info@bellavistasrl.it

4 ha - 15,000 bt — 10% discount

187 ha - 1,300,000 bt

66 Belief in a virtually abandoned terroir mistreated by many —this is the social, economic and symbolic contribution of a winery that's an emblem of a renaissance in agriculture 99

PEOPLE - The unpredictable Enrico Togni is a young winemaker with farming in his DNA, a fascinating figure for any wine lover. A trip up into the Valcamonica to meet and talk with him is a moral duty if you want to understand the significance of his labors, which have positive fallouts on the redevelopment of the land and a profession at risk.

VINEYARDS - Enrico follows his vineyards with total respect for the local farming tradition. He shows particular sensitivity to the work done by his grandfather, including the use of traditional training methods such as the pergola technique. He is also keen to maintain dry-stone walls, a symbol of the "heroic" viticulture of the past, and encourage other local farmers to continue to make wine.

WINES - The range of wines has grown as a result of experimentation and a desire to understand the real potential of the area. It is worth mentioning here the efforts made to raise the profile of erbanno, a mysterious local grape variety we find in the curious, simple and nicely spicy **San Valentino 2010** (● 500 bt). We were also impressed by **Barbera Vidur 2009** (● 900 bt), a potent, balanced wine, while **Lambrù 2009** (● marzemino, barbera, merlot; 5,000 bt) was as reliable as ever. The intriguing nebbiolo monovarietal **1793 2009** (● 900 bt) conserves typicality, spiciness and tannin. Opol, the "social" wine, has yet to develop and all the wines have low measures of sulfur.

PEOPLE - Bellavista *is* Franciacorta! Formed with an innovative and visionary spirit by the Moretti family in 1977, since then the company has become one of the benchmark names in Italian enology. Under the technical guidance of the illustrious Mattia Vezzola Bellavista, it proves once again to be at the cutting-edge, capable of perceiving changes and interpreting them in a modern, purposeful way

VINEYARDS - Agronomically speaking, Bellavista can be seen as a dynamic work in progress, open to experiment and innovation. It's no coincidence that, for a few years now, it has been official home to the Simonit & Sirch method School of Pruning, at the service not only of its own vineyards, but of the whole district and beyond. Some of the quality development decisions, especially those that move in an eco-compatible direction, are fruit of the expertise of Fabio Sorgiacomo.

WINES - The whole local area is very much indebted to the Mattia Vezzola's all-round professional skills. With his Bellavista wines, Vezzola shows off a style of great consistency and precision that rarely disappoints. Of the wines presented this year, the one that stood out most was **Franciacorta Pas Operé Gran Cuvée 2006** (○ 25,000 bt): profound, plump and textured, it's a Great Wine. On a par with it is **Franciacorta Brut Gran Cuvée 2007** (○ 150,000 bt), which banks on verticality. Given how it effectively "tells the tale" of the typology, **Franciacorta Satèn Gran Cuvée** (○ 75,000 bt) might be defined a "narrative" wine. **Franciacorta Brut Rosé Gran Cuvée 2007** (⊙ 45,000 bt) is juicy with a nice streak of tartness. **Franciacorta Brut** (○ 850,000 bt) is as good as ever, a testimony to the company's consistency.

FERTILIZERS organic-mineral
PLANT PROTECTION copper and sulphur
WEED CONTROL chemical, mechanical
YEASTS selected
GRAPES 100% estate-grown
CERTIFICATION none

FERTILIZERS natural manure
PLANT PROTECTION chemical, copper and sulphur, organic
WEED CONTROL mechanical
YEASTS selected
GRAPES 100% estate-grown
CERTIFICATION none

ERBUSCO (BS)
Ca' del Bosco
Via Albano Zanella, 13
tel. 030 7766111
www.cadelbosco.com
cadelbosco@cadelbosco.com

ERBUSCO (BS)
Cavalleri
Via Provinciale, 96
tel. 030 7760217
www.cavalleri.it
cavalleri@cavalleri.it

160 ha - 1,400,000 bt

47 ha - 250,000 bt

PEOPLE - Sometimes it's hard to find new ways of describing this monumental winery. With consistently high standards of quality, it has helped keep the Italian flag flying round the world for four decades. Maurizio Zanella is the brains behind the company's success. He is a visionary and a leading promoter of the identity of Franciacorta wine, not only inside the company, but also as president of the local consortium.

VINEYARDS - Surrounded as he is by very experienced collaborators such as the agronomist Luigi Reghenzi, Maurizio Zanella has had clear ideas right ever since he started buying up the vineyards in the best local areas. Many of these are cordon-trained very low down, a system unusual for Franciacorta. For some years now, the company has managed its vast properties with low impact on the environment and has also experimented with organic methods.

WINES - Ca' del Bosco has a consistent, recognizable style from its excellent base wines upwards. Witness the approachable, fragrant, drinkable **Franciacorta Brut Cuvée Prestige** (O nd). **Franciacora Brut 2007** (O nd) is very elegant with a palate that walks the tightrope between fruit and acidity with ease. The real masterpiece is, as always, Franciacorta Dosaggio Zero 2007 (O nd), a wine that combines softness with deep minerality. A Great Wine, no doubt about it. **Franciacorta Satèn 2007** (O nd) is pleasant and consistent with the typology. Franciacorta **Extra Brut Rosé Anna Maria Clementi 2004** (☉ nd), finally, is a blend of structure, sweetness, impact and pervasive fruitiness.

PEOPLE - A visit to the Cavalleri winery always leaves a lasting impression. Meeting this Franciacorta winery and its experienced staff means coming into contact with exemplary levels of seriousness, competence, style and personality. Among the most accomplished interpreters of the terroir, the Cavalleris stand out for their impeccable winemaking and pragmatic, cutting-edge agronomy.

VINEYARDS - Extreme variability is the common denominator of the Cavalleri family vast properties. The vineyards are split up into small plots, some 30 years old, and cover the best winegrowing districts in Franciacorta. Under the guidance of the experienced Gian Paolo Turra, now with 10 years' experience running the vineyards under his belt, the company is increasingly oriented towards eco-compatibility. The hectare managed using organic methods is proof of the fact.

WINES - The Cavalleri style is as impressive as ever and the decision to quote the amount of sulfur added on the label is a significant, widely appreciated one — a sign of openness and seriousness. The exemplary **Franciacorta Pas Dosé 2007** (O 11,000) is a very deep, weight that lingers on the palate. No less delightful is the astonishingly vertical **Franciacorta Satèn 2008** (O 17,000 bt). Franciacorta Brut Grandi Cru Collezione 2007 (O 11,000 bt) is a masterpiece of elegance. A Great Wine and deservedly so. **Franciacorta Brut Selezione Esclusiva Giovanni Cavalleri 2004** (O 2,800 bt) has more restrained structure and depth but also plenty of finesse. We also enjoyed **Franciacorta Brut Blanc de Blancs** (O 120,000 bt).

FERTILIZERS organic-mineral, natural manure
PLANT PROTECTION chemical, copper and sulphur
WEED CONTROL mechanical
YEASTS selected
GRAPES 20% bought in
CERTIFICATION none

FERTILIZERS natural manure
PLANT PROTECTION chemical, copper and sulphur
WEED CONTROL chemical, mechanical
YEASTS selected
GRAPES 100% estate-grown
CERTIFICATION none

MONTICELLI BRUSATI (BS)

Il Pendio

Via Panoramica, 50
tel. 030 6852570
www.ilpendio.com
info@ilpendio.com

4 ha - 25,000 bt

66 Il Pendio is something else compared to the ferment of Franciacorta. This small winery used to be a wine cooperative for local farmers and its still preserves a precise artisan identity that makes it unusual and original 99

PEOPLE - Founded in the late 1980s by Gianluigi Balestra, the winery is now run with renewed energy and skill by Michele Loda, who has innovated without changing the essence of the place.

VINEYARDS - Many distinctive features make the winery unique: vineyards at an altitude of 450 meters (the highest for the denomination), a rural landscape in which traces of urbanization are few and far between, vast expanses of woodland in the proximity (ask the wild boars!), constant ventilation ... These and Michele's careful management (he makes the most of the local biodiversity and white rock soil without using chemicals) are all premisses for high quality wines.

WINES - The wine repertoire is by no means monotonous and, true to local tradition, includes red and still white wines. The reason for this is a matter of altimetry, which gives the right level of grape ripeness while preserving finesse and elegance. Proof of the fact is **Pinot Nero La Valletta 2008** (● 1,200 bt), varietal and rich in fruit. **Terre di Franciacorta Rosso Etichetta Rossa 2007** (● 2,000 bt) is up to its customary standard, a model that lends credibility to the Bordeaux character of Franciacorta. We also liked **Curtefranca Bianca Etichetta Nera 2008** (○ 2,000 bt), a chardonnay with plenty of acidity and depth. The much awaited **M. Cl. Rosé Brusato** (⊙ 1,800 bt) is slightly rustic and **Franciacorta Pas Dosé Il Contestatore 2008** (○ 5,000 bt; 28 €) has minerality by the bundle.

FERTILIZERS	natural manure
PLANT PROTECTION	copper and sulphur
WEED CONTROL	mechanical
YEASTS	selected
GRAPES	100% estate-grown
CERTIFICATION	none

POZZOLENGO (BS)

Marangona €

Località Marangona
tel. 030 919379
www.marangona.com
info@marangona.com

27 ha - 35,000 bt   **10% discount**

PEOPLE - The Lugana wine undoubtedly owes much of its success to the capacity of local wineries to work as a team and convey a precise, authentic sense of identity. One of the stars of the side is Alessandro Cutolo, a young enthusiast who develops an artisan idea of Lugana, critically but with an unfailing desire to improve.

VINEYARDS - When he inherited the company in 2007, Alessandro embarked upon a new adventure based on autonomous management with the aim of clear quality improvement. He owns vines of different ages, from eight to 40 years old. Experience in the field is convincing Alessandro of the need to adopt increasingly eco-compatible techniques.

WINES - Only a small portion of the grapes — production figures are increasing every year — is earmarked for vinification. This enables Alessandro and his consultant friend to develop gradually, testing and experimenting as they go. Judging by the wines, which are improving all the time, their approach is the right one. We liked **Lugana Marangona 2011** (○ 15,000 bt), an enjoyably savory base wine. **Lugana Tre Campane 2011** (○ 8,000 bt) is a selection that impresses for its greater depth. It's worth mentioning that Alessandro also produces a brut version.

slow wine LUGANA SUP. IL RINTOCCO **2009** (○ 3,000 bt) The nice thing about this typology is that it adds credibility to the terroir. We recommend this wine for the way it aims at linearity and flavor as opposed to opulence and structure. It's a good advert for the denomination's potential to evolve.

FERTILIZERS	organic-mineral
PLANT PROTECTION	chemical, copper and sulphur
WEED CONTROL	mechanical
YEASTS	selected, native
GRAPES	100% estate-grown
CERTIFICATION	none

POZZOLENGO (BS)

Tenuta Roveglia

Località Roveglia, 1
tel. 030 918663
www.tenutaroveglia.it
info@tenutaroveglia.it

PROVAGLIO D'ISEO (BS)

Barone Pizzini

Via Brescia, 3 A
tel. 030 9848311
www.baronepizzini.it
info@baronepizzini.it

70 ha - 500,000 bt	10% discount

PEOPLE - Founded over ten years ago and owned by the Zweifel-Azzone family, Tenuta Roveglia is one of the historic Lugana wineries. Since it began bottling its wine, it has been managed by Paolo Fabiani — for years president of the Lugana Protection Consortium — with the help of 11 collaborators in vineyard and cellar. The historic cellar, situated in the 15th-century farmhouse, and the tasting room, built into the old stables, are both very evocative.

VINEYARDS - Seventy hectares of vineyards are situated round the company buildings in the heart of the Lugana area. All stand in grass and the soil below the vine rows is worked mechanically. The soil is clayey and rich in minerals. Besides trebbiano di Lugana, the main grape, cabernet sauvignon is also grown for the company's two red wines. The grapes for the production of Chiaretto are bought-in.

WINES - The company produces three Luganas, one spumante and a table white, all made with trebbiano di Lugana grapes. **Lugana Vigne di Catullo 2010** (○ 35,000 bt), matured only in stainless steel, has freshness, elegance and vibrant minerality. **Lugana Filo d'Arianna 2009** (○ 8,000 bt) is softer and more structured, fruit of a late harvest and vinification in 30-quintal barrels. It has a bouquet of ripe and candied citrus fruit with a faint note of vanilla. Lugana Limne 2011 (○ 360,000 bt) is tangy, almost salty with a nice wave of acidity. Since 2011 this latter wine has been bottled under screw cap. **Garda Cabernet Sauvignon Cà d'Oro 2008** (● 9.000 bt) is well structured and alcoholic, vaguely reminiscent of Amarone.

47 ha - 340,000 bt	10% discount

PEOPLE - Barone Pizzini, set up in 1993 and now run by Silvano Brescianini, is one of the most cutting-edge wineries in the area. Not only because it was the first, in 1998, to go down the avenue of organic agriculture, but also because, with the pragmatism typical of these parts, it has successfully combined environmental sustainability with business ambition.

VINEYARDS - The team captained by Pierluigi Donna and Leonardo Valenti maintains a close contact between vineyard and cellar, managing the 47 hectares of vines with the utmost care and attention. Practices such as cover cropping and the decision not to harvest grapes from vine rows that border with non-organic vineyards aim not only to respect organic protocol — though this is obviously of central importance — but also and above all to achieve the finest quality possible.

WINES - The wines, made from chardonnay and pinot nero grapes are authentic, clean, vertical and invariably well-structured. One such is **Franciacorta Brut** (○ 120,000 bt). **Franciacorta Brut Nature 2008** (○ 20,000 bt), is deep with a lively acid vein, while **Franciacorta Extra Brut** (○ 10,000 bt) has mature notes, partly thanks to assemblage with reserve wines. **Franciacorta Brut Rosé 2008** (⊙ 20.000 bt; 24 €) amazes for its capacity to combine varietal aromas and freshness and its lovely color foreshadows a rich, broad palate.

> **slow wine** FRANCIACORTA SATÈN 2008 (○ 30,000 bt) A wine that rewards the company's original and brilliant idea to go not so much for softness as for minerality and the enhancement of chardonnay, without losing the character typical of Satèn. It's a model that impressed us a lot.

FERTILIZERS organic-mineral, manure pellets, natural manure
PLANT PROTECTION copper and sulphur
WEED CONTROL mechanical
YEASTS selected
GRAPES 5% bought in
CERTIFICATION none

FERTILIZERS biodynamic preparations, green manure
PLANT PROTECTION copper and sulphur
WEED CONTROL mechanical
YEASTS selected
GRAPES 100% estate-grown
CERTIFICATION organic

SONDRIO

Ar.Pe.Pe.

Via del Buon Consiglio, 4
tel. 0342 214120
www.arpepe.com
info@arpepe.com

11 ha - 60,000 bt   **10% discount**

❝❝ Year after year, Isabella and Emanuele Pellizzati Perego add new pieces to their exciting and personal enological journey which, thanks to their visionary and modern genius, has made them a model of new viticulture ❞❞

PEOPLE - The most noteworthy new developments of the last year were the inauguration of a welcoming tasting room and the activation of a geothermal plant.

VINEYARDS - The company has a complex system of vineyards. Emanuele takes care of the agronomic side with a reasoned approach and increasing attention to sustainability. In the old vineyards, which are situated in the main Valtellina districts, extreme altimetric differentiation helps give force and credibility to the decisions taken in the cellar.

WINES - The wines of Ar.Pe.Pe. have a very personal touch and supreme elegance. The company never produces all its wines in the same vintage, but distinguishes between great Reserves and small according to the thickness and integrity of the grape skins during the harvest. The mature, complex **Valtellina Sup. Sassella Rocce Rosse Ris. 2001** (● 18,000 bt) is considered a great Reserve, the excellent, enveloping **Valtellina Sup. Inferno Fiamme Antiche Ris. 2007** (● 2,200 bt) a small Reserve. **Rosso di Valtellina 2010** (● 26,000 bt), finally, is balsamic and spicy, tangy and juicy.

> slow wine **VALTELLINA SUP. SASSELLA ULTIMI RAGGI 2005** (● 4,300 bt) is made with grapes that are allowed to dry slightly on the plant and picked in the late autumn (Ar.Pe.Pe. has deliberately never made a Sforzato). It is a wine that combines to perfection rich aromas, warm, lingering fruitiness and an enviably taut palate.

FERTILIZERS organic-mineral, natural manure
PLANT PROTECTION chemical, copper and sulphur, organic
WEED CONTROL mechanical
YEASTS native
GRAPES 100% estate-grown
CERTIFICATION none

TEGLIO (SO)

Fay

Località San Giacomo di Teglio
Via Pila Caselli, 1
tel. 0342 786071
www.vinifay.it
info@vinifay.it

14 ha - 50,000 bt

❝❝ Marco Fay has not only reorganized the company rationally, he has also brought a wave of youth and positive innovation for the entire Valtellina area ❞❞

PEOPLE - The historic Valtellina wine producer Sandro Fay's great merit is that he has passed on all his passion and enthusiasm to his son Marco, who manages the vineyards and the cellar, and his daughter Elena, who sees to the commercial side and the red-tape.

VINEYARDS - Progressive acquisitions of vineyards have given the winery a solid base in the best zones in the valley. Marco is convinced of the importance of the altimetric position of its holdings. The lowest suffer the excessive cold of the valley floor, the highest the mountain chill. It is thus the intermediate range that is best for the vine, and that is where the Fays went in 1998 to plant new vineyards with the broadest range of clones as possible for the purposes of complexity. The vines are tended attentively and rationally.

WINES - Clear-cut fruit and character of the grape are the features Marco seeks to bring out in his wines. The results are there for all to taste. With its well-defined, entrancing suite of aromas, **Valtellina Sup. Valgella Cà Moréi 2010** (● 9,200 bt) has recherché finesse and depth. **Valtellina Sup. Valgella Carteria 2010** (● 9,200 bt) is balsamic and fruity, fresh and soft on the palate, and also very dynamic. **Valtellina Sup. Sassella Il Glicine 2009** (● 4,200 bt) is genuine, on the rustic side, while **Valtellina Sup. Costa Bassa 2009** (● 14,000 bt) is warm and robust with ripe fruit.

FERTILIZERS natural manure
PLANT PROTECTION chemical, copper and sulphur
WEED CONTROL chemical, mechanical
YEASTS native
GRAPES 100% estate-grown
CERTIFICATION none

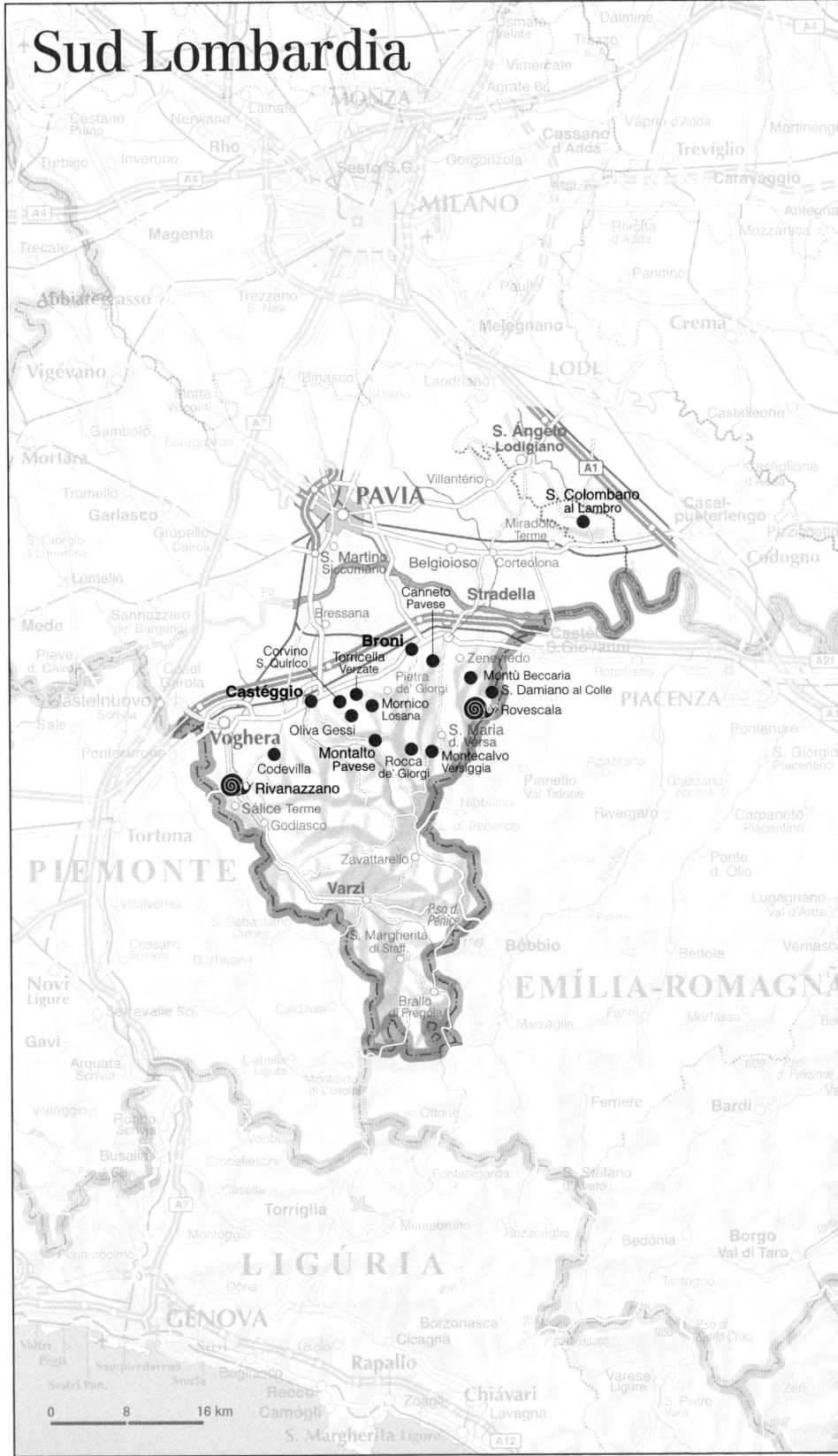

Sud Lombardia

RIVANAZZANO (PV)

Podere Il Santo

Via Kennedy, 36
tel. 0383 92244
www.ilsanto.biz
info@ilsanto.biz

5 ha - 5,500 bt

66 "Don't mention the words "wine producer" here! Podere Il Santo is a complex, multifunctional, closed-cycle farm managed by a young man with earnestness, passion, humility and competence. A rare model, alas 99

PEOPLE - On his farm Eugenio Barbieri grows native cereals and vegetables and breeds Varzese cattle, pigs and hens —everything necessary to meet his family's food requirements. And he also makes wine, incidentally.

VINEYARDS - A visit to this small farm on the south bank of the Po near the border with Piedmont transcends interest in wine alone. Here the outstanding combination of crops helps animate the variegated landscape. Without shouting from the rooftops or seeking certifications, Eugenio goes about his work with total respect for nature and naturalness. He follows his vineyards, which cover five hectares and are situated in particularly good growing zones, with rigor and spontaneity using natural methods.

WINES - True, the lack of a proper cellar — just cement tanks in a corner of the farm — may come as something of a shock. But this is a place of exciting surprises. As we have said, wine is just one — albeit followed painstakingly — of the farm's many activities. With its classic grape blend and aging capacity, the intriguing **Novecento 2004 (●** barbera, croatina; 3,500 bt) is proof of the potential of this terroir. It's a sound, succulent wine with pleasant spiciness.

> slow wine **RAIRON 2006 (●** 2,000 bt) is a rarity in the true sense of the term. Produced separately with long-macerated uva rara grapes, it's a wine that thrills and breaks rules and offers a fresh, personal image of the Oltrepò zone.

FERTILIZERS manure pellets
PLANT PROTECTION copper and sulphur
WEED CONTROL mechanical
YEASTS native
GRAPES 100% estate-grown
CERTIFICATION none

ROVESCALA (PV)

Agnes

Via Campo del Monte, 1
tel. 0385 75206
www.fratelliagnes.it
info@fratelliagnes.it

21 ha - 100,000 bt

66 Moving against the trend towards industrialized viticulture, the Agnes brothers are among the few standard bearers of a "wise" agriculture aimed at protecting old vineyards 99

PEOPLE - History and innovation go hand in hand at the winery the Agnes brothers, Cristiano and Sergio, have been running for the last 20 years. In their extraordinary everyday work, respect for the past translates into a small revolution at the service of the company and the whole surrounding area.

VINEYARDS - The Loghetto vineyard has existed since 1906! There is no shortage of failed areas, but these have been duly replaced with new plants based on the old ones. The others were added, decade by decade, throughout the 20th century. Cristiano and Sergio are assisted in their work by their father Luigi. He sometimes has complaints to make, but not about the company project, which is based on methods that respect the environment.

WINES - The Agnes' wines might be defined as simply complex. The simplicity lies in the original decision, consistent with the area, to favor vintage fizzy wines without aiming at power and structure, the complexity in the capacity to convey the richness and depth of grapes from the old vineyards. **Hence Loghetto 2011 (●** croatina; 1,400 bt), a wine from the oldest vineyard of all. All the fizzy wines are commendable, and we have chosen to recognize O.P. Bonarda Frizzante Cresta dei Ghiffi 2011 (● 13,000 bt) as an Everyday Wine. Also excellent are **O.P. Bonarda Frizzante Campo del Monte 2011 (●** 13,000 bt) and **O.P. Bonarda Possessione del Console 2010 (●** 13,000 bt). Worth a mention too is **Popolum 2009 (●** croatina, merlot; 3,000 bt).

FERTILIZERS green manure
PLANT PROTECTION copper and sulphur
WEED CONTROL mechanical
YEASTS native
GRAPES 100% estate-grown
CERTIFICATION none

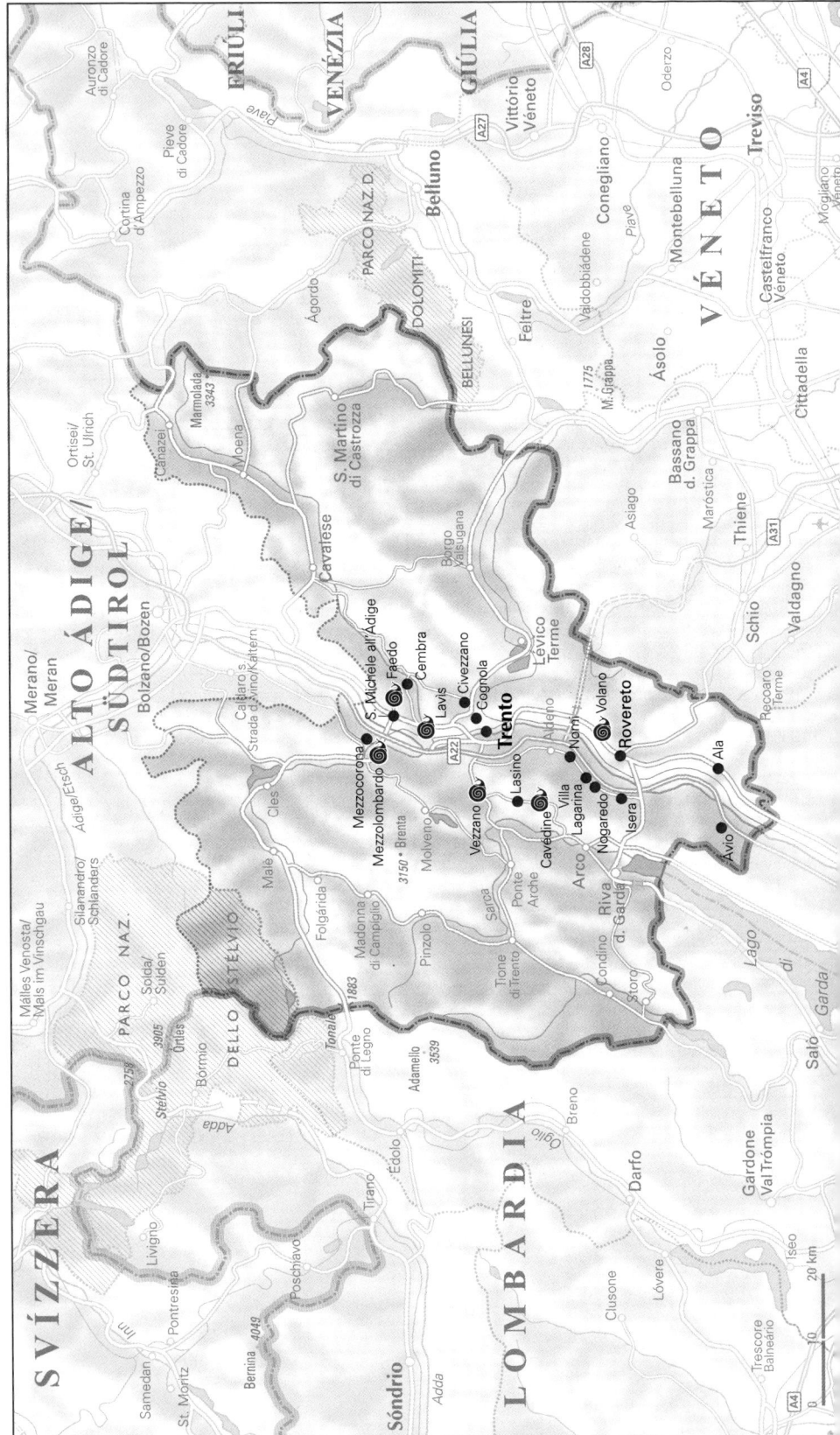

TRENTINO

To begin with, after our tours of local wineries and tastings, a few margin notes about the Trentino region and its production.

What meets the eye is the growth of Trentodoc, not so much in terms of the number of bottles produced — sizable as ever — as of its quality. Winegrowers have obviously gained more experience of cellar work, but, even more important than that, they have also worked more attentively in the vineyards with clearer ideas about the management of the ones given over to the production of classic method wines, carefully selecting parcels of land at higher altitudes. Trentodoc would make a further leap forward if a minimum altitude of 300-350 were to be established for vineyards earmarked for this typology.

Often underrated by punters and critics, white wines are improving in quality and attracting more and more interest. Nosiola, incrocio Manzoni, müller thurgau and riesling are grapes that achieve high standards in Trentino, as the virtuous producers we mention below demonstrate. It would be interesting to study the propensity of the various terroirs to grow this variety or that. The Agrarian Institute of San Michele all'Adige is already working on this., so what we need to do now is figure out how to apply its studies.

The same is true of the various red wines. In-depth studies have already been carried out on marzemino and teroldego, the two main native grape varieties (along with schiava, to which the same attention has yet to be reserved). Now it might be worth repeating the exercise with the international varieties that are so important on the Trentino wine scene.

Trentino, like other Italian regions, suffered the dry summer of 2011, yet the results achieved here were better than elsewhere. Though it wasn't an exceptional year for white wines, the high altitudes and knowhow of winemakers contained the effects of the heatwave. In the years to come, after due aging, we shall be able to judge the region's classic method and big red wines.

snails @

78	GINO PEDROTTI
79	POJER & SANDRI
80	CESCONI
80	GIUSEPPE FANTI
81	MASO FURLI
81	FORADORI
83	FRANCESCO POLI
83	EUGENIO ROSI

bottles ▮

78	TENUTA SAN LEONARDO
82	FERRARI

coins €

79	ARCANGELO SANDRI
82	ENDRIZZI

AVIO (TN)

Tenuta San Leonardo

Frazione Borghetto all'Adige
Località San Leonardo
tel. 0464 689004
www.sanleonardo.it
info@sanleonardo.it

25 ha - 180,000 bt

PEOPLE - Vines have been grown on the land of San Leonardo for more than a thousand years. In 1724, it was inherited by the Guerrieri Gonzaga family and wine production began. It is still being produced today with acumen and elegance by Marchese Carlo and his son Anselmo. The secrets behind this award-winning company's success are few and simple: care for the vineyards, vinification in cement and aging in barriques. "I don't like steel," says Guerrieri Gonzaga, "but I adore mechanical harvesting. Since I started doing it in 1999, I've been making better wines."

VINEYARDS - The vineyards border and intersect with 300 hectares of woodland inhabited by red and roe deer. At first only carmenère grapes were grown, then in the 1970s the first cabernet franc and sauvignon were planted from French clonal selections. Last but not least, merlot began to be grown, especially in the Villa Gresti vineyard. The management is mindful of environmental considerations and tends to seek harmony and balance between the vine and its surrounds.

WINES - San Leonardo 2007 (● cabernet sauvignon e franc, carmenère, merlot; 70,000 bt) is a masterpiece of finesse and measure with notes of graphite and spices on the nose and velvety flesh and elegant tanginess on the palate. It is once more a Great Wine. **Terre di San Leonardo 2009** (● 90,000 bt) is a well-crafted, austere, robust *deuxieme vin* made with the grapes earmarked for San Leonardo, which won't be released for this vintage. **Villa Gresti 2007** (● merlot, carmenère; 10,000 bt) asserts the vineyard's diversity with a dry, herbaceous timbre. **Vette di San Leonardo 2011** (○ 25,000 bt) is a white made with sauvignon grapes bought in from vineyards monitored by the company. It has notes of tropical fruit on the nose and assertive, dynamic, juicy flavor.

FERTILIZERS natural manure
PLANT PROTECTION copper and sulphur
WEED CONTROL mechanical
YEASTS selected, native
GRAPES 100% estate-grown
CERTIFICATION none

CAVEDINE (TN)

Gino Pedrotti

Frazione Pietramurata
Via Cavedine, 7
tel. 0461 564123
www.ginopedrotti.it
info@ginopedrotti.it

5 ha - 22,000 bt

66 A family that for a century has been constantly committed to keeping the land healthy and clean, good for producing simple wines and telling interesting stories 99

PEOPLE - This family company achieved an important landmark this year, with the third generation, represented by Giuseppe, Tullia and Clara, celebrating its centenary with their parents Gino and Rosanna. Besides the cellar, the family also manages the adjacent *locanda*, or inn, a popular meeting place in the Valle dei Laghi.

VINEYARDS - Assisted by his father, Giuseppe tends to the vineyards, which cover an area of five hectares and are subdivided into eight holdings. Near the cellar are the red grapes, while the white nosiola grapes are trained in the small vineyards round Lake Cavedine. Giuseppe applies biodynamic principles. Some of the vines, especially the oldest, are arbour-trained, the rest are Guyot-trained.

WINES - Pedrotti's wines have a story to tell — that of a solar family and a unique local area. Nosiola 2010 (○ 5,600 bt) is summery, inebriating and juicy, with enveloping salinity. It is a perfect Everyday Wine. An interesting blend of white grapes, **Aura 2009** (○ 1,600 bt) combines nosiola's floral hints with the fruit and structure of chardonnay to create a wine of massive personality. Last but not least, **Auro 2008** (● 2,900 bt) is made with dried cabernet franc and fresh merlot grapes. Aged 24 months in the barrel, it is well-rounded with notes of red fruits and spices.

slow wine **TRENTINO VINO SANTO 1999** (○ 3,000 bt) Made from dried nosiola grapes, a wine rich in aromas of dried fruit and spices, backed by an explosive freshness unusual in a passito aged 12 years. An experience worth living!

FERTILIZERS natural manure, biodynamic preparations, green manure
PLANT PROTECTION copper and sulphur
WEED CONTROL mechanical
YEASTS native
GRAPES 100% estate-grown
CERTIFICATION organic

Pojer & Sandri

Località Molini, 4
tel. 0461 650342
www.pojeresandri.it
info@pojeresandri.it

Arcangelo Sandri

Via Vaneggie, 4
tel. 0461 650935
www.arcangelosandri.it
info@arcangelosandri.it

---

30 ha - 250,000 bt

❝ "In continuous re-evolution" — could be the motto of two "phenomenal" characters' who enjoy seeking out innovative solutions to make wines that have a story to tell ❞

PEOPLE - The story of this winery began in 1975, when two friends, Mario Pojer and Fiorenzo Sandri, decided to join forces. The first is an enologist, the second had just inherited a small vineyard. They made their debut with the legendary Müller Thurgau Palai 1975, which was an immediate success.

VINEYARDS - Red grape varieties are grown at Faedo, at an altitude of 250 meters. Pinot nero, nosiola and other varieties are grown higher up. In the Palai district, at an altitude of 700 meters, grow chardonnay and pinot nero, used to make spumantes, and müller thurgau. The other white varieties are grown on the volcanic soil at Maso Besleri, in the Val di Cembra.

WINES - Of the numerous labels, we recommend the fresh, juicy and mineral **Besler Biank 2007** (○ sauvignon, pinot bianco, incrocio Manzoni, kerner, riesling; 3,600 bt). **Essenzia 2010** (○ chardonnay, kerner, sauvignon, traminer, riesling; 6,000 bt) once again shows a nice balance between freshness and sweetness. We also recommend **Merlino 09/95** (● 11,000 bt), a fortified red wine made with partially fermented lagrein must to which brandy produced and aged in the company distillery is added.

> **slow wine** **Filii 2011** (○ 10,500 0.5 l bt) An intriguing, complex wine made from a blend of various grape varieties: riesling and its "offspring", müller thurgau, kerner and incrocio Manzoni. It is the fruit of careful early harvesting aimed at achieving naturally low alcohol content (10°).

---

3 ha - 22,000 bt

PEOPLE - The company was formed in 1979 and is situated on the hill of Faedo, once an important mining center, now one of the best winemaking districts in Trentino. Since 2005, Arcangelo has been helped in vineyard and cellar by his daughters Nadia and Sonia, both graduates in enology at the Istituto Agrario in San Michele all'Adige. The two sisters share Arcangelo's passion and desire to make wines with a sense of place.

VINEYARDS - The Faedo zone is located on a fan of Ice Age origin characterized by three types of soil: from clay to mixed debris (especially dolostones with surface pebbles) to limestone. The Sandris own three hectares of vineyards at different altitudes on different soils. In the lower ones they grow schiava, lagrein, chardonnay and traminer, in the higher ones, at 600 meters, müller thurgau.

WINES - To their wines Nadia and Sonia seek to convey as faithfully as possible the characteristics of the local area and the distinctive features of its grapes. One successful example is **Trentino Müller Thurgau Cosler 2011** (○ 6,000 bt), characterized by fragrant citrusy and balsamic aromas. Trentino **Gewürztraminer Razer 2011** (○ 6,000 bt) impresses with its subtle, elegant aromatic notes and richness of flavor. Matured first for a year in wooden casks, then aged for another year in the bottle, **Trentino Lagrein Capòr 2009** (● 4,000 bt) is redolent of red fruit and vanilla. **Frill 2011** (● schiava gentile; 2,500 bt) is refreshing, tangy and excellent value for money.

FERTILIZERS manure pellets, natural manure
PLANT PROTECTION copper and sulphur
WEED CONTROL mechanical
YEASTS selected, native
GRAPES 100% estate-grown
CERTIFICATION none

FERTILIZERS none
PLANT PROTECTION chemical, copper and sulphur
WEED CONTROL mechanical
YEASTS selected
GRAPES 100% estate-grown
CERTIFICATION none

Cesconi

Frazione Pressano
Via Marconi, 39
tel. 0461 240355
www.cesconi.it
info@cesconi.it

20 ha - 120,000 bt

❝ Respecting the environment and letting nature follow its own course and find its own remedies, helping it only when necessary with good old-fashioned common sense — this is what the Cesconi winemaking family believes in ❞

PEOPLE - The four Cesconi brothers run their family winery with great dynamism. Though, as often happens, all are capable of doing everything, they share out their tasks, with Alessandro and his father taking care of work in the vineyards, Lorenzo and Roberto of production and Franco of administrative matters.

VINEYARDS - The main plot is situated at Pressano, behind the cellar, where there is also a pretty nosiola vineyard, at an altitude of 350-500 meters, with very old vines. Another 10- hectare vineyard with red grapes was planted about ten years ago in the Arco district. The vineyards are managed organically, albeit without certification.

WINES - The Cesconi style envisages expressiveness and rotundity, always accompanied by freshness and precise mineral finish. Rich in crisp fruit, freshly aromatic and tangy, Prabi 2011 (O incrocio Manzoni, riesling, pinot bianco; 15,000 bt) is an excellent Everyday Wine. **Sauvignon 2010** (O 2.500 bt) has good varietal length, while **Nosiola 2010** (O 8.000 bt) has a nose rich in aromatic herbs, sage, and beeswax, and a full palate with a dynamic, dry finish. The two reds are really good: **Moratel 2009** (● merlot, lagrein, teroldego, cabernet; 15,000 bt), a cuvée of all the red grapes, has austere texture and plenty of fruit, while **Pivier 2009** (● merlot, cabernet franc e sauvignon; 12,000 bt) is softer and velvety.

Giuseppe Fanti

Località Pressano
Piazza G. N. della Croce, 3
tel. 0461 240809
www.vignaiolofanti.it
info@vignaiolofanti.it

4.2 ha - 17,000 bt

❝ As we strolled through his vineyards, Alessandro Fanti said, "There's only one earth. Once this one comes to an end, there won't be another. We should treasure the one we have". Simple words that clearly explain the complexity of his farm work ❞

PEOPLE - Giuseppe Fanti started making wine in 1972. In 1991 his son Alessandro took over the company and recovered old agronomic practices, decisive for producing good grapes.

VINEYARDS - The vineyards are divided into six properties, though the incrocio Manzoni grapes for Isidor come from a wonderful vineyard at the mouth of the Valle di Cembra, at an altitude of 600 meters. Alessandro has almost religious respect for his vines and the biodiversity of his land, an attitude that derives from good old-fashioned common sense.

WINES - Elegance and depth are the hallmarks of Alessandro's wines, which are at once entrancingly simple and incredibly complex. Exemplary in this sense are both **Nosiola 2010** (O 4,200 bt), delicatre and tangy, and **Manzoni Bianco 2010** (O 3,300 bt), fine and citrusy, subtle and assertive. Perfection is achieved with Isidor 2009 (O incrocio Manzoni; 2.400 bt), a masterpiece of elegance and pleasantness in which a profound palate is rounded off by a finish with a sharp citrusy component and infinite minerality. Truly a Great Wine. **Chardonnay 2010** (O 1,200 bt) is characterized by finesse and balance, while **Pritianum 2010** (O chardonnay, incrocio Manzoni; 2,000 bt) is more exuberant and rich, full-bodied and soft on the palate.

FERTILIZERS	manure pellets, biodynamic preparations, green manure
PLANT PROTECTION	copper and sulphur
WEED CONTROL	mechanical
YEASTS	selected, native
GRAPES	100% estate-grown
CERTIFICATION	converting to biodynamics

FERTILIZERS	biodynamic preparations
PLANT PROTECTION	copper and sulphur
WEED CONTROL	mechanical
YEASTS	selected, native
GRAPES	100% estate-grown
CERTIFICATION	organic

Maso Furli

Località Furli
Via Furli, 32
tel. 0461 240667
www.masofurli.it
masofurli@alice.it

4 ha - 16,000 bt   **10% discount**

❝ Observation of natural cycles to avoid intervening in the vineyard and artisan ingeniousness in inventing machines and remedies to reduce the impact on the plants — that in a nutshell is the daily work of Marco Zanoni, a rigorous and gifted winemaker ❞

PEOPLE - The once isolated late-17th-century *maso*, or farmhouse, has now been swallowed up by the town. Bought by his father, a sharecropper there, in the 1950s, it is now run by Marco Zanoni.

VINEYARDS - Less than a hectare of vineyard is situated in the Martignano district, while the central plot is alongside the farmhouse. Interventions among the vine rows — total grassing, cover cropping without trimming or systemic treatments — are kept to a bare minimum. Marco's aim is to let the vineyard regulate itself, helping it with hour upon hour of manual labor.

WINES - The expressive rotundity of Maso Furli's wines sometimes jeopardizes their formal perfection, but this is a positive. **Chardonnay 2010** (○ 2,600 bt) is fresh, fruity and racy with an enjoyable finish. **Gewürztraminer 2010** (○ 4,600 bt) offers the nose the distinctive features of the variety, while its palate is full-bodied and dry with a tangy almost salty palate, which lengthens its follwthrough. **Sauvignon 2010** (○ 4,600 bt) offers balsamic notes and a very dry, assertive palate. With its oxidative style, **Manzoni Bianco 2009** (○ 1,100 bt), finally, conserves great elegance and depth, with faint sensations of citrus fruit.

> **slow wine**   **ROSSO 2008** (● cabernet sauvignon, merlot; 1,100 bt). A very austere, typical take on the classic Bordeaux grape blend. A wine that is forthright and robust with well ripened fruit. The palate is smooth and enjoyable.

FERTILIZERS biodynamic preparations, green manure
PLANT PROTECTION copper and sulphur, organic
WEED CONTROL mechanical
YEASTS selected, native
GRAPES 100% estate-grown
CERTIFICATION organic

Foradori

Via Damiano Chiesa, 1
tel. 0461 601046
www.elisabettaforadori.com
info@elisabettaforadori.com

23 ha - 150,000 bt

❝ A woman of contagious enthusiasm curious enough to change her relationship with the vine and with life in order to renew agriculture ❞

PEOPLE - When her father died in 1984, Elisabetta Foradori took over the reins of the family winery. She then grew only teroldego, but with the passing of time her desire to expand has driven her to diversify.

VINEYARDS - In her various vineyards on the Piana Rotaliana, where the soil is of alluvial origin, Elisabetta grows only teroldego grapes. In 1985, in her 13-hectare property she began massal selection work to single out the most interesting varieties. The experiment subsequently gave rise to a vine seedling project. At Cognola, overlooking Trento, she grows nosiola, the fruit of selections from the Val dei Laghi, and incrocio Manzoni grapes.

WINES - Research isn't confined to the vineyards, but also continues in the cellar in an attempt to find vinification techniques capable of maintaining the characteristics of the grapes intact. One example is the use of amphorae, handmade in Spain, for the vinification of the grapes. Made in this way is **Nosiola Fontanasanta 2010** (○ 8,000 bt), a wine which has achieved balance and elegance in the bottle. Soon to be released are the two teroldego crus: Sgarzon, made with grapes from sandy soils that add freshness and salinity, and Morei, an austere, powerful wine, that comes from pebbly soils. Looking forward to Granato 2009, we had the chance to taste again and compare old vintages of this incredible, historic wine, which captures the very essence of teroldego.

FERTILIZERS compost, biodynamic preparations
PLANT PROTECTION copper and sulphur
WEED CONTROL mechanical
YEASTS native
GRAPES 100% estate-grown
CERTIFICATION biodynamic, organic

SAN MICHELE ALL'ADIGE (TN)

Endrizzi €

Via Masetto, 2
tel. 0461 650129
www.endrizzi.it
info@endrizzi.it

TRENTO

Ferrari

Via del Ponte di Ravina, 15
tel. 0461 972 311
www.cantineferrari.it
info@ferrarispumante.it

17 ha - 600,000 bt   **10% discount**

PEOPLE - The interest for viticulture of the Endrici family (Endrizzi in Trentino dialect) goes back a long way. They have been producing wine on the historic San Michele all'Adige estate for more than a century. Today Paolo, a member of the fourth generation, and his German wife Christine are carrying on the business with style, level-headedness and commitment. The talented enologist Vito Piffer is charged with the technical management.

VINEYARDS - The company's vineyards are split into three main plots where soil and weather conditions differ considerably. The vine rows round the cellar rest on calcareous-dolomitic soil. The soil of the Masetto estate is gravelly with calcareous pebbles, that in the Kinderleit vineyard has a substratum rich in mineral elements. Strict agronomic standards are maintained to preserve the terrains and reduce environmental impact both in the company's vineyards and in those of historic grape suppliers.

WINES - The wines replicate the style with which the owners run the company; meaning unfussy, familiar, forthright and pleasant. Exemplary in this sense is **Teroldego Rotaliano 2010** (● 65,000 bt), an excellent Everyday Wine that combines the typical huskiness of the grape with great fruity freshness, juicy flesh and great drinkability. Then come three good whites: the fruity and linear **Trentino Chardonnay 2011** (○ 34,000 bt), Trentino Nosiola 2011 (○ 6,000 bt), a soft, richly flavored take on the grape, and the warm, enfolding **Trentino Gewürztraminer 2011** (○ 24,000 bt), which has full, well-rounded flavor. Last but not least, a red of big structure, **Masetto Nero 2009** (● merlot, cabernet sauvignon, lagrein, teroldego; 18,000 bt), velvety with stylish fruitiness and a properly dry finish.

120 ha - 4,960,000 bt

PEOPLE - Established more than a century ago by the legendary Giulio Ferrari, this cellar has written the history of the "classic method" in Italy. In 1952 it was taken over by 1952 Bruno Lunelli and, thanks to sound family management, has become a respected international brand. Today the new generation has taken charge with cousins Camilla, Marcello and Matteo managing, respectively, communications, production and sales.

VINEYARDS - The company's hillside vineyards — eight in all, one of which, the famous Maso Pianizza, has grown the chardonnay grapes that go into Riserva del Fondatore since 1972 – are overseen by Diego Trainotti and Luca Pedron, agronomists who show they believe in viticulture with a low impact on the environment — virtually organic, in fact. Local growers who supply grapes to the cellar are obliged to observe a strict protocol drawn up and controlled by its technicians.

WINES - The cellar is managed by the experienced enologist Ruben Larentis, who has given Ferrari wines a clear-cut style of their own. It only takes the simple, subtle, fragrant **Trento Brut** (○ 2,940,000 bt) to prove the fact. Bearing in mind the company's huge output, **Trento Brut Perlé 2007** (○ 575,000 bt) is excellent too; it offers refreshing, open aromas of flowers and fruit and a well-developed, flavorful palate. **Trento Brut Perlé Nero 2006** (○ 20,000 bt) is a wine of great weight and substance. **Trento Brut Riserva Lunelli 2005** (○ 37,000 bt) is complex but rounder and mouthfilling. We have left the cellar's true masterpiece — a Great Wine — for last. **Trento Brut Giulio Ferrari Riserva del Fondatore 2002** (○ 35,000 bt) is as capable as ever of bewitching with an apparent simplicity that actually conceals complexity and unmatchable elegance.

FERTILIZERS organic-mineral, natural manure
PLANT PROTECTION chemical, copper and sulphur, organic
WEED CONTROL mechanical
YEASTS selected
GRAPES 60% bought in
CERTIFICATION none

FERTILIZERS manure pellets, natural manure, biodynamic preparations, green manure
PLANT PROTECTION chemical, copper and sulphur
WEED CONTROL mechanical
YEASTS selected
GRAPES 70% bought in
CERTIFICATION none

VEZZANO (TN)

Francesco Poli

Frazione Santa Massenza
Via del Lago, 13
tel. 0461 340090
www.distilleriafrancesco.it
info@francescopoli.it

6.5 ha - 28,000 bt | **10% discount**

66 With the great respect for the land and its traditions he has inherited from his father, Alessandro has become Italy's benchmark producer of Vino Santo Trentino 99

PEOPLE - The winery of Francesco Poli, a modest farmer and a great winemaker and distiller, is situated in the small village of Santa Massenza, in the Valle dei Laghi. Over the last few years his son Alessandro has taken over the reins, working the vineyards in an increasingly natural manner.

VINEYARDS - Alessandro's decision to eliminate all chemical treatments is based on the fortunate locations of his vineyards, which cover just over six hectares in an unspoilt environment ventilated by the Ora breeze from Lake Garda in the hills surrounding the lakes of Santa Massenza and Toblino. Since 2006 he has been using biodynamic preparations to give the soil greater vitality.

WINES - The simplest wine is **Nosiola Sottovi 2011** (○ 6,500 bt), though it is by no means banal. In the mouth it has structure and weight, which develop into a typical almondy finish. The complex and soft **Maiano Bianco 2010** (○ 2,500 bt) is made with nosiola grapes vinified in acacia barriques: on the nose it combines notes of buttery and dried fruit, which do not cover the fine aromas typical of the grape variety.

slow wine | **TRENTINO VINO SANTO 2001** (○ 3,650 bt; 36 €) An icon of the Valle dei Laghi and a mirror of its maker's soul, this wine is the tangible result of meticulous attention to detail. It's a wine that reveals itself slowly but finishes off thrillingly. This version has splendid juiciness thanks to the sweet softness of the sugars, which are set off by a tangy finish.

FERTILIZERS natural manure, biodynamic preparations, green manure
PLANT PROTECTION copper and sulphur
WEED CONTROL mechanical
YEASTS selected, native
GRAPES 100% estate-grown
CERTIFICATION organic

VOLANO (TN)

Eugenio Rosi

Via Tavernelle, 3 B
tel. 0464 461375
tamaramar@virgilio.it

5 ha - 21,000 bt

66 He's an errant winemaker, roving from cellar to vineyard and travelling around in pursuit of abandoned winegrowing areas where he can restore the vine… and People 99

PEOPLE - Eugenio Rosi used to enjoy walking and running round the vineyards when he was a kid. That passion was one of the reasons why he chose to become an enologist. After learning the ropes in a series of wine cooperatives, in 1999 he decided to make his own idea of wine materialize.

VINEYARDS - Rosi works five hectares of land — of which he owns just over one — between Volano, where marzemino grapes are arbour-trained to let them have as much light as possible, and Noriglio, where pinot bianco and nosiola are grown ungrafted. In Noriglio he also has a new terraced vineyard. In Rovereto, he grows cabernet franc and at Villarsa, at an altitude of 750 meters, the wonderful chardonnay vineyard resembles a small garden in the woods.

WINES - The aim in the cellar is to give wines the distinctive features of the terroir and the grape varieties used through skillful used of wood. A successful example of this approach is **Anisos 2009** (○ pinot bianco, nosiola, chardonnay; 3,200 bt), macerated on the skins and aged in the barrel. This is a wine with complex scents of flowers and tropical fruits accompanied by seductive salinity. **Doron 2008** (● 1,600 bt), made with dried marzemino grapes, is a sweet wine with powerful notes of cherry, elegant tannins and perfectly balanced sugars. Also worth a mention is **Esegesi 2008** (● merlot, cabernet sauvignon; 6,800 bt).

slow wine | **POIEMA 2009** (● 7,000 bt) Complex and elegant, Poiema 2009 is an intriguing wine in which the typicality of the marzemino grape is exalted by aging in cherry wood barrels.

FERTILIZERS natural manure, green manure
PLANT PROTECTION copper and sulphur
WEED CONTROL mechanical
YEASTS native
GRAPES 100% estate-grown
CERTIFICATION organic

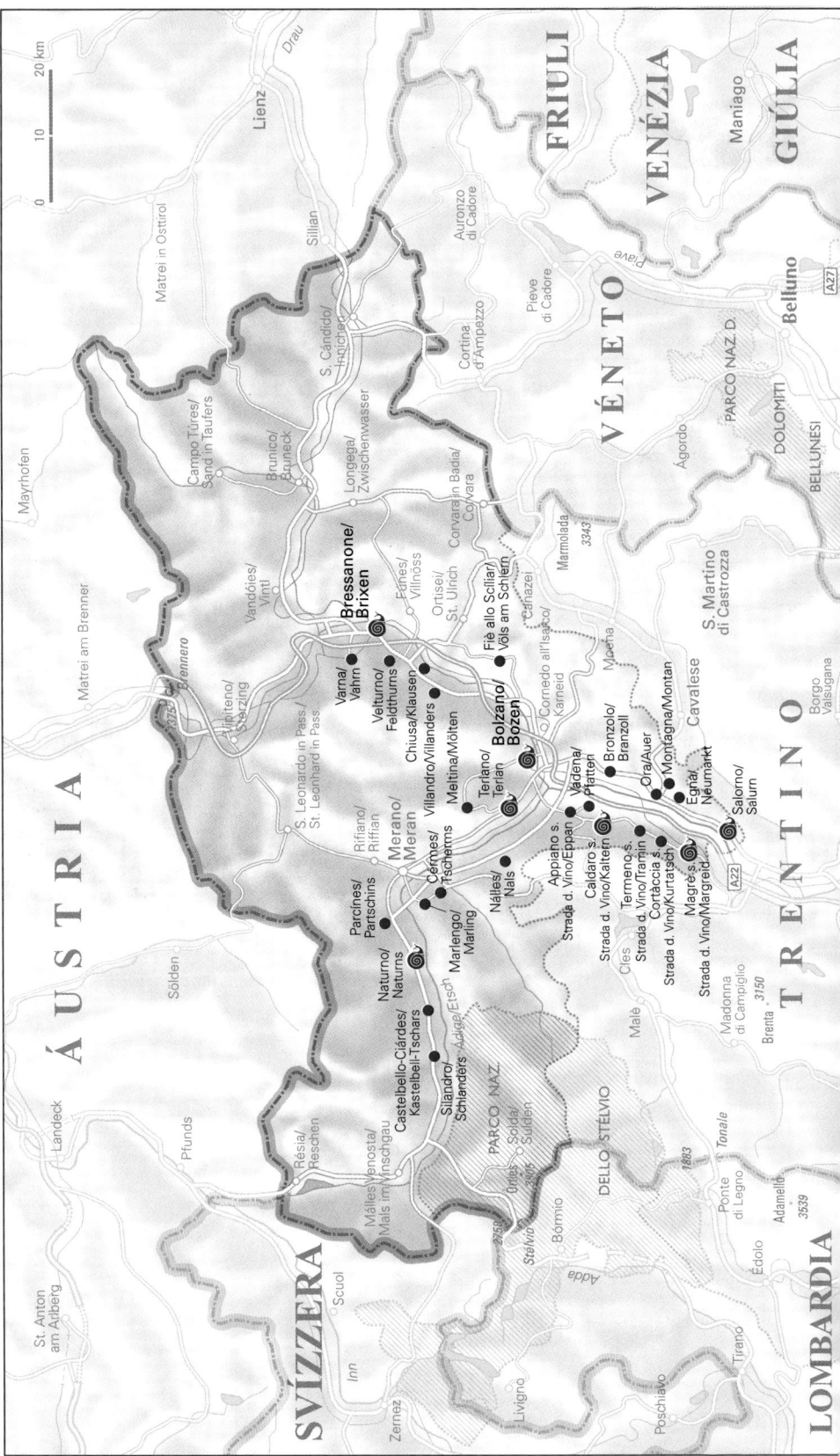

ALTO ADIGE

To realize just how popular the wines of the region are among Italian consumers, you only have to see the crowds flocking to its pavilion at the Vinitaly event in Verona or at any of the many local wine events. It's not just a passing trend, it's a phenomenon built on solid foundations: namely, variety of grapes, terrains, location and climate of the Alto Adige, a sort of permanent laboratory with wines for every taste.

Foresight and the ability to interpret market and taste trends are an important tool. Suffice it to think how, over the last 20 years, the region has moved from being a supplier of unbottled red wine to being a producer of excellent whites without losing its bond with tradition. At the same time, it has revitalized the native grape par excellence, schiava, regaling it with a fresh, new image. Success is also the result of teamwork and the capacity to appear to the outside world as an organic, unitary whole, notwithstanding the complexities of the production world. On the one hand are the *vignerons*, a symbol of artisan excellence, who account for just 5 per cent of total production; on the other are the large cooperatives, which produce about two thirds of Alto Adige wines, and a number of large family maisons.

It's worthy pausing for a moment's reflection on the region's cooperatives, which have long been an example to follow for all other Italian regions and which are now undergoing new developments. Having reached excellent standards of quality, they are now encouraging their members to improve the sustainability of their viticulture, teaching them practices with lower environmental impact and performing significant experiments with organic management. Which is why we decided to assign the first Snail precisely to a cooperative, the one in Terlano, a virtuous example of a new approach to associative viticulture.

In 2011 the late-summer heatwave had negative effects in Alto Adige too, forcing many growers to bring the grape harvest forward. In general, the white wines we tasted had a well-developed, mature taste profile, not always with adequate supporting acidity, and sometimes somewhat alcoholic — though there were, of course, exceptions. It wasn't a great vintage for the schiava grape either, with the sudden appearance of Drosophila suzukii obliging many producers to anticipate the harvest and depriving wines of their customary body and intensity. The 2011 vintage proved favorable instead for red grapes — especially lagrein — with nicely fleshy wines with plenty of intact fruit and juice. And once they've aged properly, wines made with merlot, cabernet and pinot nero will prove well-crafted. The reds tasted from the 2009 vintage were mature and well-structured but, at the same time, elegant and expressive.

snails 🐌

88	NUSSERHOF - HEINRICH MAYR
89	KUENHOF - PETER PLIGER
90	MANINCOR
91	TENUTAE LAGEDER
92	UNTERORTL - CASTEL JUVAL
93	HADERBURG
93	CANTINA TERLANO

bottles 🍾

86	CANTINA GIRLAN
87	STROBLHOF
88	WALDGRIES CHRISTIAN PLATTNER
89	HOANDLHOF - MANNI NÖSSING
91	PETER DIPOLI
94	J. HOFSTÄTTER
95	ABBAZIA DI NOVACELLA
95	KÖFERERHOF GÜNTHER KERSCHBAUMER

coins €

87	CANTINA CONVENTO MURI-GRIES
90	CANTINA VALLE ISARCO
92	CANTINA NALS MARGREID
94	CANTINA TRAMIN

Cantina Girlan

Località Cornaiano
Via San Martino, 24
tel. 0471 662403
www.girlan.it
info@girlan.it

220 ha - 1,000,000 bt — **10% discount**

PEOPLE - This recently restructured cooperative cellar, set up in 1923, is all set to address the challenges of the future, with its 230 members ready and willing to follow the ideas of president Helmut Meraner and director Oscar Lorandi. The quality of the wines, which has improved consistently over the last few years, is guaranteed by enologist Gerhard Kofler.

VINEYARDS - The members' vineyards are overseen by the cellar's technicians. They are mostly situated around Girlan, home also to the historic Gschleier vineyard where schiava vines of 80-100 years grow. The others are at Montiggl at an altitude of 500 meters, ideal for aromatic grapes, and at Plattenriegl at an altitude of 450-550 meters, where pinot bianco and sauvignon are grown. At Mazzon, finally, 10 hectares are given over to pinot nero grapes.

WINES - The standout red is **A.A. Pinot Nero Trattmann Ris. 2009** (● 15,000 bt), with its gutsy personality and soft, rounded tannins. **A.A. Pinot Nero Patricia 2010** (● 50,000 bt) is lighter and more approachable, with crisp, sweet fruit on the nose and an elegant, supple palate. **A.A. Schiava Fass n° 9 2011** (● 100,000 bt) was as good as ever, with well-defined fruity notes and a tangy, juicy finish. The intenser, deeply mineral **A.A. Schiava Gschleier 2010** (● 15,000 bt) is a "great classic" with intact fruit and a perfectly dry finish. The excellent **A.A. Sauvignon Flora 2010** (○ 15,000 bt) is confident and well-paced with a perfect balance between fruity juiciness and lively acidity. The star of the collection, the excellent A.A. Bianco Riserva Bianca 2009 (○ pinot bianco, chardonnay, sauvignon; 8,000 bt) is a blend that impresses with its full taste profile and commanding follow-through on the palate. A Great Wine if ever there was one.

FERTILIZERS organic-mineral, natural manure, compost, humus
PLANT PROTECTION chemical, copper and sulphur
WEED CONTROL chemical, mechanical
YEASTS selected
GRAPES 100% estate-grown
CERTIFICATION none

Ignaz Niedrist

Località Cornaiano
Via Ronco, 5
tel. 0471 664494
ignazniedrist@rolmail.net

9.5 ha - 45,000 bt

PEOPLE - Cornaiano is a natural terrace in the eastern part of the commune of Appiano, a sunny area conducive to grape growing. It is here that Ignaz Niedrist decided to lay down roots and carry on his family's winemaking tradition. Today he is considered one of the most accomplished *vignerons* in the Alto Adige, anchored to peasant culture but possessing enough knowhow to be a point of reference for friends and colleagues. Working alongside him as ever is his wife Elisabeth.

VINEYARDS - Most of the vineyards are round the family *maso*, or farmhouse, at an altitude of 500 meters, one of the highest points on the hill. Others are spread out between Caldaro, Appiano Monte and Gries. Over the years, Ignaz's unrelenting curiosity has driven him to experiment with a number of great varieties. Today he is concentrating on the most suited to the single terrains, while continuing to recover old clones of minor native grapes.

WINES - **A.A. Terlano Sauvignon 2011** (○ 10,000 bt) has good grip and seductive floral and herbaceous notes, which follow through into a long, racy palate. **Trias 2011** (○ chardonnay, petit manseng, viognier; 3,000 bt) is more earthy and fruity with a juicy, medium-textured palate and a tangy, citrusy finish. **A.A. Terlano Pinot Bianco 2011** (○ 4,500 bt) has subtle floral aromas, an elegant, soft, creamy palate and a salty finish. Solid, robust and deep, **A.A. Lagrein Gries Berger Gei 2010** (● 10.000 bt) is very typical and expressive. Albeit tight, **A.A. Pinot Nero 2010** (● 2.600 bt) has good body and perky acidity.

slow wine **A.A. RIESLING BERG 2011** (○ 2,600 bt) Great purity of expression, delicate fruity notes, a complex palate with a soft attack and a well-knit, mineral finish — a worthy take on the grape.

FERTILIZERS natural manure, compost, green manure
PLANT PROTECTION chemical, copper and sulphur
WEED CONTROL mechanical
YEASTS selected, native
GRAPES 100% estate-grown
CERTIFICATION none

APPIANO/EPPAN (BZ)

Stroblhof

Località San Michele
Via Piganò, 25
tel. 0471 662250
www.stroblhof.it
weingut@stroblhof.it

4.5 ha - 35,000 bt   **10% discount**

PEOPLE - Wine estate, hotel, health farm, restaurant all rolled into one — Andreas Nicolussi-Leck and his wife Rosi Hanny run the whole show in exemplary fashion. Though the job demands huge commitment, they manage to make everything look easy. Their sense of style is reflected in every detail. Not only in appearance — here the charm of the old *maso*, or farmhouse, lives harmoniously side by side with the modern cellar, design with functionality — but also in substance with the choice of natural materials, the use of local resources and a sustainable approach to the vineyard.

VINEYARDS - Andreas has chosen to go for "fewer varieties, but planted in the right positions". Pinot nero and pinot bianco thrive round the farmhouse on gentle slopes and calcareous, porphyric soil at the foot of the Mendola massif at an altitude of 520 meters, where they benefit from the cool mountain breezes. The chardonnay grapes grow on morainal soils, sandier and rich in pebbles at Appiano, while the sauvignon come from a vineyard at Cortaccia, where it draws character from the calcareous soil.

WINES - The wines — fine, elegant, precise — fit perfectly into this harmonious settting. The excellent **A.A. Pinot Bianco Strahler 2011** (○ 11,000 bt) has subtle fruity, floral, mineral notes with a racy, creamy palate. **A.A. Chardonnay Schwarzhaus 2011** (○ 3,500 bt) is similar in style but more laid back, elegant, of medium stature, gingered up by tangy sinew. **A.A. Sauvignon Nico 2011** (○ 3,000 bt) has fine, unobtrusive varietal notes, delicacy and length. It was a good year for the two Pinot Neros: **A.A. Pinot Nero Pigeno 2009** (● 12,000 bt) has fine, pure fruity eloquence, while the spicy, blossomy **A.A. Pinot Nero Ris. 2009** (● 7,000 bt) has a darker character. It's excellent already, but it'll give of its best in a few years' time.

FERTILIZERS none
PLANT PROTECTION chemical, copper and sulphur
WEED CONTROL mechanical
YEASTS selected, native
GRAPES 100% estate-grown
CERTIFICATION none

BOLZANO/BOZEN

Cantina Convento Muri-Gries   €

Piazza Gries, 21
tel. 0471 282287
www.muri-gries.com
info@muri-gries.com

---

30 ha - 500,000 bt

PEOPLE - If the name Gries is now a synonym of Lagrein, much of the credit must go to the Benedictine monks of the monastery of Gries. Obedient to the rule of "ora et labora" (pray and work), they came to Bolzano in 1845 and began to cultivate the vineyards in one of the best terroirs for this noble native red. For years they produced it for their own consumption and sold it unbottled. Today wine production has effectively become a business under the supervision of enologist Christian Werth, while vineyard work is overseen by agronomist Walter Bernard.

VINEYARDS - The company owns vineyards in two main zones: a number of holdings are near Bolzano on often flat land with alluvial, gravely soil rich in porphyry. One such is the Gries vineyard adjacent to the monastery. Another ten hectares are situated at Appiano Monte, at an altitude of 420-600 meters, where the calcareous, gravely soil is ideal for the cultivation of white grapes. Major mass selections have been made with the lagrein grapes from the oldest vineyards.

WINES - The wine that stood out for us was **A.A. Lagrein Abtei Muri Ris. 2009** (● 60,000 bt), which has well-developed, deep aromas and packs a punch on the palate. It may be still young but it has wonderfully fresh fruit and well-knit mineral texture. On a par was A.A. Lagrein 2011 (● 300,000 bt), which has a subtler but highly impressive taste profile — a very good Everyday Wine and a faithful interpretation of the grape. We were won over too by **A.A. Pinot Nero Abtei Muri Ris. 2009** (● 10,000 bt) whose bouquet is still slightly marked by aging on oak, while the palate is refined, racy and energy-packed. **A.A. Moscato Rosa Abtei Muri 2010** (● 4,500 bt) has a bouquet of ripe fruit and plays on the contrast between sweetness and acidity. **A.A. Terlano Pinot Bianco 2011** (○ 20,000 bt) is nicely drinkable, floral, full-bodied and flavorful.

FERTILIZERS none
PLANT PROTECTION chemical, copper and sulphur
WEED CONTROL chemical, mechanical
YEASTS selected
GRAPES 29% bought in, wine bought in
CERTIFICATION none

BOLZANO/BOZEN

Nusserhof
Heinrich Mayr

Via Josef Mayr-Nusser, 72
tel. 0471 978388

3.5 ha - 20,000 bt

66 Hemmed in between the River Isarco, industrial warehouses and the rail track, Nusserhof is a special place. A symbol of resistance to uncontrolled construction work and, more recently, to the madness of red-tape in the wine sector 99

PEOPLE - We like both the company's wines and its charismatic owners. Heinrich Mayr and his wife Elda are a splendid people of great culture and humanity, both musicians and art lovers — and keepers of a winemaking tradition that dates back to 1788.

VINEYARDS - At Nusserhof, situated in the Piani di Bolzano on alluvial soil rich in porphyry on the surface and pebbles and gravel deeper down, they have practiced healthy, commonsense agriculture — moderately but staunchly organic — since 1994. The schiava used to make Elda comes from a hillside in the Santa Maddalena zone, where old vines are supplemented by native varieties.

WINES - "Why try to make southern wines in Alto Adige?" Heinrich wonders aloud. For his part, he goes for elegance of expression through traditional vinification and long aging in wood barrels. All the wines have personality and aging capacity. Witness **A.A. Lagrein Ris. 2007** (● 5,000 bt), robust and mineral with great depth, still a little clenched perhaps but, as we discovered from older bottles, capable of relaxing and releasing soil and spices. Likewise, **T..... 2010** (● 900 bt) expresses the cold, slightly wild character of teroldego in a blunt, linear manner. **B...... 2011** (○ 1.000 bt), made from the rare native blatterle grape, is straightforward and salty. Looking forward to Elda 2010, we had another taste of the excellent 2009 version, laid back, fine and scented, with subtle, penetrating forcefulness.

FERTILIZERS green manure
PLANT PROTECTION copper and sulphur
WEED CONTROL mechanical
YEASTS native
GRAPES 100% estate-grown
CERTIFICATION organic

BOLZANO/BOZEN

Waldgries
Christian Plattner

Località Santa Giustina, 2
tel. 0471 323603
www.waldgries.it
info@waldgries.it

8.2 ha - 65,000 bt

PEOPLE - The Waldgries estate, which dates from the 12th century, is immersed in a sea of vineyards in the historic heart of Santa Maddalena Classico. It is impressive not only for its architecture, but also for the quality of its wines. Christian Plattner, a young, dynamic winemaker, has been running the show since 1994. Determined, open-minded and extremely gifted, he has added a touch of class to the wine by making them more contemporary, personal and coherent.

VINEYARDS - For Christian the concept of quality extends beyond the glass. A sensitive viticulturist, he began his career as an advocate of organics. In the meantime, a succession of plant diseases has forced him to accept a compromise and he now adopts a common sense integrated approach. An ambitious project designed to recover old varieties of schiava grafted onto an old vine is producing great results. Besides the vineyards around the *maso*, or farmhouse, there are also properties at Appiano and Ora.

WINES - Christian brings out the most essential features of his wines, all a pleasure to drink. The product of a warm vintage, A.A. Santa Maddalena Cl. 2011 (● 25,000 bt) offers dark, earthy fruit with a juicy expressive, supple palate. It's a pleasing Everyday Wine. The well-crafted **Cabernet Sauvignon Laurenz 2009** (● 4,000 bt) is rich and creamy on the nose, dense and caressing on the palate. The enthralling **A.A. Moscato Rosa 2009** (● 2,500 bt) is complex and deep with notes of dried flowers and hints of oxidation; the palate is elegant, tangy and full of contrasts. **A.A. Sauvignon 2011** (○ 8,000 bt) shows off an assertive, long finish.

slow wine **A.A. SANTA MADDALENA CL. ANTHEOS 2011** (● 4,000 bt) Made with old schiava clones, a wine with spicy notes on the nose and a stong, deep, charismatic palate. A modern archetype.

FERTILIZERS natural manure
PLANT PROTECTION chemical, copper and sulphur, organic
WEED CONTROL mechanical
YEASTS selected, native
GRAPES 100% estate-grown
CERTIFICATION none

Hoandlhof
Manni Nössing

Frazione Kranebih
Via dei Vigneti, 66
tel. 0472 832672
www.manni-noessing.com
manni.vino@tiscali.it

6 ha - 45,000 bt

PEOPLE - Manfred "Manni" Nössing is an extrovert, volcanic character. He began to make wine at a very young age in 1997 with the few vine rows available to him. He then persuaded his father to dig up the family orchards and plant vineyards in their place. He is one of the undisputed champions of the improved image of the Valle Isarco. He's a man of great creative ferment, always on the move; the only way to pin him down is to go and seek him out among his vineyards.

VINEYARDS - The present six hectares of vineyard are situated on the hills behind Bressanone. Manni works them personally following the rules of agronomics and old-fashioned common sense. He seeks to limit the use of chemicals on his vines and to contain the sugar ripeness of the grapes, hence the alcohol content of the wines.

WINES - All the wines, the result of simple vinification in stainless steel tanks, have well-defined character and are impeccably crafted. **A.A. Valle Isarco Müller Thurgau Sass Rigais 2011** (O 5,000 bt) is subtle and brash with notes of citrus fruit that make for a racy, pleasant mouthfeel. **A.A. Valle Isarco Kerner 2011** (O 20,000 bt) is delicately aromatic with a finely balanced taste profile and a lingering palate. The charismatic **A.A. Valle Isarco Sylvaner 2011** (O 5,000 bt), finally, is juicy, racy and complex with floral notes and a long, solid palate.

> **slow wine** **A.A. Valle Isarco Veltliner 2011** (O 12,000 bt) A pure, cut-glass take on the variety. The first impact on the palate is on the sweet side, but the sensation appears immediately to be swept away by a domineering acid-mineral vein. Beautifully balanced flavors and a varied suite of aromas.

Kuenhof
Peter Pliger

Località Mara, 110
tel. 0472 850546
pliger.kuenhof@rolmail.net

6 ha - 35,000 bt

" Harmony and dedication are the best words to describe this company's work. The owners have a serene, intense rapport with the vineyard and the world around them. And this comes out in their wines "

PEOPLE - Peter decided to tend his family's vineyards 25 years ago. Since then, applying the results of his experiments with curiosity and single-mindedness, he has turned Kuenhof into one of the finest wineries in the Alto Adige. He has always acknowledged his own limits, however, cultivating only the hectares he can manage firsthand. "Only I can look after my vines because I know them one by one," he quips.

VINEYARDS - The way in which Pliger manages his vineyards has served as an example for many of his colleagues: plenty of manual labor, no chemicals, natural remedies in the event of disease. The old vineyards round the *maso*, or farmhouse, and the new Lahner vineyard (which Pliger shares with his buddy, Peter Wachtler of Taschlerhof) enjoy enviable exposures: old steep terraces recovered after long, tiring rebuilding of the containment walls.

WINES - Four wines of unmistakable style which, as usual, only need time to develop and express themselves to the full. **A.A. Valle Isarco Riesling Kaiton 2011** (O 11,000 bt) is rounder in the mouth than usual and plump with fruit. **A.A. Valle Isarco Veltliner 2011** (O 6,000 bt) has notes of fresh flowers and yeast on the nose and a soft bouquet that lingers with flavor and fullness. The nicely soft, intensely fruity **A.A. Valle Isarco Sylvaner 2011** (O 7,000 bt) is a benchmark for the typology. **A.A. Valle Isarco Gewürztraminer 2011** (O 2,000 bt) is simple, contained and subtly aromatic.

FERTILIZERS organic-mineral, natural manure, humus
PLANT PROTECTION copper and sulphur
WEED CONTROL chemical, mechanical
YEASTS selected
GRAPES 100% estate-grown
CERTIFICATION none

FERTILIZERS natural manure
PLANT PROTECTION copper and sulphur, organic
WEED CONTROL mechanical
YEASTS native
GRAPES 100% estate-grown
CERTIFICATION none

CALDARO/KALTERN (BZ)

Manincor

San Giuseppe al Lago, 4
tel. 0471 960230
www.manincor.com
info@manincor.com

50 ha - 280,000 bt

66 With calm determination, Michael von Goëss-Enzenberg, the owner of Manincor, has built up a company in which biodynamics is a complex philosophy that pervades every aspect of daily life 99

PEOPLE - Since 2008 Helmut Zozin has managed the company with great seriousness, adamant that biodynamic practices are the best, and capable of transmitting his values to the people around him.

VINEYARDS - The vineyards are clustered in two main areas: on the land that descends from the cellar to the shores of the lake at Caldaro, where red grapes prevail, and two parcels at Mazon and Campan; at Terlano on the splendid Lieben Aich property, where white grapes reign. The vineyards are managed with manic care and attention to detail to make sure the vines grow naturally.

WINES - Manincor's wines are recognizable for their incisive, elegant, perfectly refined style. **A.A. Terlano Réserve della Contessa 2011** (○ pinot bianco, chardonnay, sauvignon; 32,000 bt) is intensely fruity, rich in acidity and zesty. **A.A. Terlano Sauvignon Tannenberg 2011** (○ 13,600 bt) caresses the nose with tropical fruit, then follows up with full, racy flavor and a distinctly mineral finish. **A.A. Terlano Chardonnay Sophie 2011** (○ 13,600 bt) has well-defined ripe fruit and a beautifully fresh, even, compact bouquet. The elegant, spicy, juicy **Cassiano 2009** (● merlot, cabernet franc, other red grapes; 17,000 bt) is nicely developed.

slow wine **A.A. Terlano Pinot Bianco Eichorn 2011** (○ 10,000 bt) The wine that best represents the philosophy of its makers. Notes of apricot pervade the palate — confidently, dynamically and creamily.

FERTILIZERS compost, biodynamic preparations, green manure
PLANT PROTECTION copper and sulphur
WEED CONTROL mechanical
YEASTS native
GRAPES 100% estate-grown
CERTIFICATION biodynamic, organic

CHIUSA/KLAUSEN (BZ)

Cantina Valle Isarco €

Via Coste, 50
tel. 0472 847553
www.cantinavalleisarco.it
info@cantinavalleisarco.it

140 ha - 700,000 bt

PEOPLE - The cooperative was founded in 1961 and based at the historic Reinthalerhof farm, ten kilometers or so from Bressanone, next to the freeway exit. The 24 founders subsequently decided to buy the farm. Today the grapes are bought in from 135 members in 11 communes, from Varna to Renon. The enologist is Thomas Dorfmann, who has also been production manager since 1991.

VINEYARDS - The many hours of sunshine and the winds that blow up the valley help sylvaner, a grape with amazing aging potential, to ripen. Long underrated, the variety is now being rediscovered. The morainal soils in the central part of the Valle Isarco vary from pebbly to sandy. Some of the vineyards sit on terraces supported by spectacular drystone walls.

WINES - The excellent **A.A. Valle Isarco Sylvaner Sabiona 2010** (○ 2.000 bt), made with grapes from the oldest vines on the plot near the monastery of the same name, is crystalline, juicy and notably savory. No less impressive is **A.A. Valle Isarco Kerner Sabiona 2010** (○ 1,200 bt), which has remarkable structure and depth. Then come three very good wines in the Aristos line: the subtle and elegant **A.A. Valle Isarco Riesling Aristos 2011** (○ 10,000 bt) is citrusy, forthright and taut. **A.A. Sauvignon Aristos 2011** (○ 4,000 bt) stands out for its overall harmony: it's precise and delicate on both nose and palate. l'**A.A. Valle Isarco Sylvaner Aristos 2011** (○ 12,000 bt) is full-flavored, full-bodied and complex.

slow wine **A.A. Valle Isarco Veltliner Aristos 2011** (○ 9,000 bt) A faithful, crystalline expression of the valley terroir at a very reasonable price. Rich, contained and elegant, it has plump fruit and a very mineral finish.

FERTILIZERS mineral, natural manure
PLANT PROTECTION chemical, copper and sulphur
WEED CONTROL chemical, mechanical
YEASTS selected
GRAPES wine bought in
CERTIFICATION none

Peter Dipoli

Via Villa, 5-I
tel. 0471 813400
www.peterdipoli.com
vino@finewines.it

4.7 ha - 40,000 bt

PEOPLE - Peter Dipoli is a combative, blunt character, who has the courage of his own convictions. He has experienced the wine world at every level, working first as a restaurateur, then as a distributor, then as a consultant for other companies and, finally, as a producer in his own right. He started out 20 years ago when he planted his first hectare of sauvignon on the *maso*, or farm, his family had just bought. The land is situated on the steep slopes of Penon, above Cortaccia, where he had to first uproot the old rows of schiava. In the course of time he has bought more small parcels and his vineyards now cover an area of three hectares. The red grapes come from the remaining vineyards in the Magrè district.

VINEYARDS - The sauvignon vines are clustered in three main holdings at an altitude of 550-600 meters on sandy soil rich in gravel of Dolomitic origin in an area where night-to-day temperature swings are sharp. Bordeaux varieties are grown on the ideal calcareous-clayey soil of Magrè, lower down at an altitude of about 300 meters. The viticulture Dipoli and his collaborators adopt is conventional.

WINES - Of the three wines Dipoli usually produces we only got to taste Sauvignon Voglar, vinified as usual in 20- to 90-hectoliter acacia barrels. We'll still have to wait a while before tasting the new Merlot Fihl and Merlot-Cabernet Iugum vintages.

slow wine **A.A. SAUVIGNON VOGLAR 2010** (○ 26,000 bt) An anomalous Sauvignon on the Alto Adige scene insofar as it interprets the grape by concentrating more on roundness and complexity as opposed to its exceptional suite of aromas. As a result, notes of tropical fruit overwhelm any vegetal nuances, while the palate is gratifying and complete with thick texture and an ultra-tangy finish.

FERTILIZERS none
PLANT PROTECTION chemical, copper and sulphur
WEED CONTROL chemical, mechanical
YEASTS selected
GRAPES 100% estate-grown
CERTIFICATION none

Tenutae Lageder

Vicolo dei Conti, 9
tel. 0471 809 500
www.aloislageder.eu
info@aloislageder.eu

50 ha - 280,000 bt

❝ Alois Lageder started off in the wine world as a merchant. Then, without repudiating his past, he followed his heart and his head to become a champion of clean viticulture. He thus applies the principles of biodynamics to make wines that respect the environment and the consumer ❞

PEOPLE - Tenutae Lageder is the trademark that identifies the wines produced from the company's vineyards using organic and biodynamic methods. The Alois Lageder logo appears on wines made from bought-in grapes.

VINEYARDS - Lageder's vineyards are scattered across the best growing areas in the region. On the historic Löwengang property in Magrè, which his family bought in 1934, prosper chardonnay (in the vineyards close to the park of Hirschprunn) and the Bordeax red varieties. Here there is also a pergola over a century old. The vineyards are managed by the agronomist Johann Ranzi.

WINES - The company's two flagship labels are pure class: **A.A. Chardonnay Löwengang 2009** (○ 41,000 bt) is leisurely and elegant with a taut, tangy, gutsy bouquet, while **A.A. Cabernet Löwengang 2008** (● 13,000 bt) gets over its initial shyness to become ethereal and balsamic. It's fascinating to compare the two Pinot Neros: the historic **A.A. Pinot Nero Krafuss 2009** (● 16,500 bt) is dry, on the husky side, with plenty of fruit, whereas the new **A.A. Pinot Nero Apollonia 2009** (● 18,000 bt), made with grapes bought in from a biodynamic grower, has fresh, crisp fruit and a dynamic, satisfying bouquet. **A.A. Pinot Grigio Porer 2011** (○ 50,000 bt) and **A.A. Chardonnay Gaun 2011** (○ 26,000 bt) are both interesting. The first is soft and full-bodied, the second caresses the palate with ripe fruit.

FERTILIZERS compost, biodynamic preparations, green manure
PLANT PROTECTION copper and sulphur, organic
WEED CONTROL mechanical
YEASTS native
GRAPES 100% estate-grown
CERTIFICATION biodynamic, organic

NALLES/NALS (BZ)

Cantina Nals Margreid €

Via Heiligenberg, 2
tel. 0471 678626
www.kellerei.it
info@kellerei.it

150 ha - 950,000 bt

PEOPLE - Born in 1985 of the fusion of the Nalles cellar with that of Magrè, this cooperative is now one of the most dynamic on the Alto Adige winemaking scene. The cellar — functional, modern design with low impact on the environment — is a good reflection of the progressive, forward-looking spirit that animates this great family of 140 hard-working viticulturists, efficiently coordinated by president Walter Schwarz and the young and highly talented *kellermeister* Harald Schraffl.

VINEYARDS - Precise demands are made of the members with protocols requiring integrated viticulture without the use of weed killers and plant protection with mainly contact products. Varieties are spread out all along the Valdadige, intelligently clustered in the most suitable zones. The feather in the cooperative's cap is the Baron Salvadori estate in Magrè, where the most prestigious selections are made, ever in the vanguard when it comes to experimenting with sustainable cultivation methods.

WINES - Production is again excellent in every line: Classic, Cru and Baron Salvadori. We were especially impressed by **A.A. Sauvignon Mantele 2011** (○ 35,000 bt), elegant and floral with a linear, taut palate and plenty of texture — a splendid Great Wine. Impressive too was **A.A. Chardonnay Baron Salvadori 2010** (○ 13,000 bt), aged in small casks, with its nuanced bouquet of ripe fruit, textured palate and length. **A.A. Schiava Galea 2011** (● 35,000 bt), headily scented, dense and racy, was as delicious as ever. The elegant, deep **A.A. Lagrein Ris. Gries 2009** (● 12,500) is still young with slight balsamic, spicy notes. **A.A. Pinot Bianco Sirmian 2011** (○ 40,000 bt) has well-concentrated ripe fruit and good grip. **A.A. Pinot Bianco Penon 2011** (○ 80,000 bt) is simpler but tangy on the palate.

FERTILIZERS manure pellets, compost, humus
PLANT PROTECTION copper and sulphur, organic
WEED CONTROL mechanical
YEASTS selected, native
GRAPES 100% estate-grown
CERTIFICATION none

NATURNO/NATURNS (BZ)

Unterortl Castel Juval

Località Stava/Staben
Juval 1 B
tel. 0473 667580
www.unterortl.it
familie.aurich@dnet.it

4 ha - 32,000 bt

66 Martin Aurich and his wife Gisela run this splendid winery — a Garden of Eden in miniature that clings to the hill of Juval — with deep love for the land and their work, virtuously with exemplary attention to detail 99

PEOPLE - The property belongs to mountaineer Reinhold Messner, but it's the Aurichs who have been the soul of the company since it opened in 1992.

VINEYARDS - The steep vineyards — some terraced, others planted *a ritocchino*, that is to say according to height — climb up the hill of Juval from an altitude of 600 meters to one of 850 meters. The wines suck minerality from the gneiss rock and the constant *föhn* wind creates a dry climate with sharp temperature swings between night and day which help to preserve the acidity and aroma of the grapes. An average of 900 hours of all-manual labor is devoted to each hectare every year. Talk about heroic viticulture!

WINES - We were very impressed by **A.A. Valle Venosta Müller Thurgau Spielerei 2010** (○ 1,000 bt), made with late-harvested, mostly botrytized grapes, which walks the tightrope between residual sweetness and acidity. **A.A. Valle Venosta Pinot Bianco 2011** (○ 6,500 bt) is pure and rocky, dry and taut. As reliable as ever, **A.A. Valle Venosta Riesling 2011** (○ 6,000 bt) is well-knit and mineral, a crystalline expression of the grape. **A.A. Valle Venosta Pinot Nero 2010** (● 6,500 bt) is fine and racy. Fruity **Gneiss 2011** (● pinot nero, zweigelt; 2,600 bt) is as jagged as the mountain it originates from.

slow wine **A.A. VALLE VENOSTA RIESLING WINDBICHL 2010** (○ 2,100 bt) A grandiose, elegant wine with a fine, récherché bouquet and a long, juicy palate. It's again one of the most effective takes on a grape that thrives in the Val Venosta.

FERTILIZERS organic-mineral, natural manure
PLANT PROTECTION chemical, copper and sulphur, organic
WEED CONTROL mechanical
YEASTS selected
GRAPES 100% estate-grown
CERTIFICATION none

Haderburg

Località Pochi, 30
tel. 0471 889097
www.haderburg.it
info@haderburg.it

11.5 ha - 95,000 bt

66 The Ochsenreiter family's company is an example of harmony and integrity. The family all move in one direction: that of common sense, transparency, open-mindedness and quality 99

PEOPLE - Alois Ochsenreiter, a man of many talents, bought the Hausmannhof farm in 1985 and went to live there with his wife Christine. Now they are helped by their daughter Erika, who works in the vineyards, and son Hannes, an enologist like his father, who works in the cellar. In 1977 Alois rented a cellar under Haderburg castle and began to produce spumante there.

VINEYARDS - The *maso*, or farmhouse, stands on the steep slopes of Chiusa di Salorno. Some of the vineyards are situated round the *maso*, but the company also owns properties in Salorno, Cortaccia and Buchholz, plus 2.2 hectares at Obermairlhof, in the Valle Isarco. They have all been managed using biodynamic methods since 2002. The composition of the soil varies from vineyard to vineyard, but is generally heavy and clayey. The vineyards stand at altitudes of 300-700 meters.

WINES - **A.A. M. Cl. Pas Dosé Haderburg 2008** (O chardonnay, pinot nero; 11,000 bt) is characterized by scents of flowers, elegance and complexity. Seductive, rounded and creamy, **A.A. M. Cl. Brut Haderburg** (O chardonnay, pinot nero; 20,000 bt) is as good as ever. The most "playful" wine is **A.A. Gewürztraminer Hausmannhof 2011** (O 1,900 bt), close-focused, tangy and harmonious, with no over-the-top aromas. **A.A. Chardonnay Hausmannhof Ris. 2003** (O 2,500 bt) is soft and rich. **A.A. Pinot Nero Hausmannhof Ris. 2009** (● 2.500 bt) has a structured body and fine spices and is ready to drink. **A.A. Pinot Nero Hausmannhof 2010** (● 10,000 bt) is fruity and, given the vintage, shows good aging potential.

FERTILIZERS natural manure, biodynamic preparations
PLANT PROTECTION copper and sulphur, organic
WEED CONTROL mechanical
YEASTS native
GRAPES 100% estate-grown
CERTIFICATION biodynamic

Cantina Terlano

Via Colli d'Argento, 7
tel. 0471 257135
www.cantina-terlano.com
office@cantina-terlano.com

150 ha - 1,200,000 bt

66 This cooperative stands out for its top quality and sustainable viticulture. But its biggest merit is the way in which it has raised pride among its members, who are now all model farmers 99

PEOPLE - The cellar is managed by Rudi Kofler, who has taken over from enologist Sebastian Stocker, a legend in the history of Alto Adige winemaking, following the same approach and improving the quality of the wines.

VINEYARDS - The vineyards are spread out over seven large areas: from warm, sunny Winkl to the steep slopes of Vorberg with gradients of up to 60 per cent, eight hectares split into pinot bianco vineyards. For some years, Norbert Spitaler has managed the vineyards with significant results. Weeding with chemicals is banned and plans are underway to convert to substantially organic methods.

WINES - The pick of a very high quality crop is **A.A. Terlano Chardonnay 1999** (O 3,340 bt), a masterpiece of integrity and freshness. With its perky fruit, extreme elegance and length, it's a Great Wine. The excellent **A.A. Terlano Sauvignon Quarz 2010** (O 55,000 bt) is delicate and pervasive with a plump, fine, tangy bouquet. Excellent too are cheaper wines such as the nicely fresh and racy **A.A. Terlaner Cl. 2011** (O pinot bianco, chardonnay, sauvignon; 200,000 bt) and **A.A. Pinot Bianco 2011** (O 100,000 bt), very taut and deep with crisp fruit. **A.A. Lagrein Porphyr Ris. 2009** (● 20,000 bt) is powerful and well-rounded.

slow wine **A.A. TERLANO PINOT BIANCO VORBERG RIS. 2009** (O 70,000 bt) Juicy, full-bodied and creamy, but also wonderfully fresh with a long fruity finish. A symbol of the cellar and the whole Alto Adige.

FERTILIZERS mineral, compost, biodynamic preparations
PLANT PROTECTION chemical, copper and sulphur
WEED CONTROL mechanical
YEASTS selected
GRAPES 100% estate-grown
CERTIFICATION none

Cantina Tramin €

Strada del Vino, 144
tel. 0471 096633
www.cantinatramin.it
info@cantinatramin.it

J. Hofstätter

Piazza Municipio, 5
tel. 0471 860161
www.hofstatter.it
info@hofstatter.com

---

245 ha - 1,500,000 bt

PEOPLE - This cooperative has been impeccably managed for the last 20 years by the enologist Willi Stürz. In that time it has become the symbol of an entire village. Modernization work has now been completed on the cellar, now not only a perfect place to work in but also an attractive reception area.

VINEYARDS - Keeping up with 290 members growing 245 hectares of vines is a complicated, stressful business. The cellar technicians, supervised by Stürz himself and agronomist Erwin Haas, couldn't do the job better — as results prove. The highest vineyards and the ones in optimal exposures produce the best grapes, but a lot has been done to raise the quality of all the vineyards, including extensive experiments with organics which will be augmented in future.

WINES - Let's start with two assemblages: T Bianco 2011 (O chardonnay, pinot bianco, sauvignon, riesling; 150,000 bt) is once again a lovely Everyday Wine with a juicy, satisfying palate, and **A.A. Bianco Stoan 2011** (O chardonnay, sauvignon, pinot bianco, gewürztraminer; 40,000 bt), rich in aromas of ripe fruit, enhanced by the vegetal notes of the sauvignon which follow through into a well-rounded palate. The excellent **A.A. Sauvignon 2011** (O 110,000 bt) is plumply fruity and nicely rounded with a precious exotic touch. **A.A. Pinot Grigio Unterebner 2011** (O 170,000 bt) is beautifully refreshing and lean, while **A.A. Gewürztraminer Nussbaumer 2011** (O 70,000 bt) is the opulent version of the variety, capable of acquiring elegance and finesse in the course of time.

> **slow wine** **A.A. GEWÜRZTRAMINER 2011** (O 300,000 bt) Not only the symbol of the cellar, but also the benchmark of the typology in the region. It's elegant, suave and light yet deep, without over-the-top aromas but hugely terroir-typical.

FERTILIZERS natural and green manure, compost
PLANT PROTECTION chemical, copper and sulphur, organic
WEED CONTROL chemical, mechanical
YEASTS selected, native
GRAPES 100% estate-grown
CERTIFICATION converting to organics, none

---

54 ha - 800,000 bt

PEOPLE - Behind the Hofstätter trademark is a long, glorious history of winemaking. It was given a new lease of life years ago when Martin Foradori took over the reins of the company from his father Paolo. Young and dynamic, Martin has always worked with great skill, dedication and respect for the local area, thus raising even further the already high profile of the cellar, situated on the main piazza in Termeno.

VINEYARDS - It's interesting to discover the location and characteristics of the company's vineyards on its beautifully designed website. The feathers in its cap are the Kolbenhof estate, in the high part of Termeno, where the gewürztraminer grape is preponderant, and the Barthenau and Yngram vineyards in Mazzon, given over to pinot nero and pinot bianco. The grapes for S. Urbano come from the two oldest parcels, planted in 1942 and 1962. The viticultural methods adopted are attentive and complex and respect every site and every variety.

WINES - True to habit, Hofstätter delivered a range of impeccable, clean, direct wines. The quaffable A.A. Pinot Bianco Joseph 2011 (O 50,000 bt) has fresh, crisp fruit. It's a perfect Everyday Wine. **A.A. Pinot Bianco Barthenau Vigna S. Michele 2010** (O 11,000 bt) is more complex with riper fruit. Aged in large barrels, it is deeply mineral. **A.A. Gewürztraminer Kolbenhof 2011** (O 50,000 bt) has its usual typical and elegant taste and fine tanginess on the finish. Two wines come from the historic Mazzon vineyard: the solid, sumptuous **A.A. Pinot Nero Barthenau Vigna S. Urbano 2009** (● 18,000 bt), which has a finer, more elegant style than usual, and **A.A. Pinot Nero Mazon Ris. 2009** (● 35,000 bt), which replicates the same impeccable tone but with less power and profundity. Last but not least, **A.A. Lagrein Steinraffler 2009** (● 10,000 bt) is consistent and typically husky.

FERTILIZERS organic-mineral, natural manure, green manure, humus
PLANT PROTECTION chemical, copper and sulphur
WEED CONTROL mechanical
YEASTS selected, native
GRAPES 100% estate-grown
CERTIFICATION none

Abbazia di Novacella

Frazione Novacella
Via dell'Abbazia, 1
tel. 0472 836189
www.abbazianovacella.it
info@abbazianovacella.it

24 ha - 700,000 bt

PEOPLE - The Abbey of Novacella, an important historical landmark, in the valley, has produced wine for hundreds of years. Today the cellar is overseen by enologist Celestino Lucin and manager Urban von Klebelsberg. This year it celebrates the Klimaneutralität's 25th birthday. Since 1987, in fact, it has generated its own energy from a small hydroelectric power plant. On top of that, for two decades now it has heated all its offices with a wood chip system.

VINEYARDS - One half of the grapes vinified comes from the company's vineyards, the other is supplied by about 400 farmers, whose vine-dressing work is constantly monitored. Most of the company vineyards are to be found on the hill of Cornaiano at an altitude of 430 meters, ten kilometers or so from Bolzano, where the Abbey owns the historic Marklhof estate, rich in pebbly, morainal soil.

WINES - The truly A.A. Valle Isarco Riesling Praepositus 2010 (○ 8,000 bt) is well-rounded and floral with good texture. Its follow-through on the palate is taut and vibrant and the finish is mineral to just the right degree. It's an elegant, assertive Great Wine. **A.A. Pinot Nero Praepositus Ris. 2009 (●** 15,000 bt) is finely fruity, floral and very complex, a combination of power and elegance. Lean and juicy, **A.A. Valle Isarco Kerner Praepositus 2011** (○ 35,000 bt) is fresher and crisper. **A.A. Valle Isarco Sylvaner Praepositus 2011** (○ 15,000 bt) is aromatic. **A.A. Valle Isarco Gewürztraminer 2011** (○ 20,000 bt) is varietal with a plush structure. **A.A. Valle Isarco Sylvaner Free Wine 2011** (○ 7,000 bt) is vinified without sulfites.

FERTILIZERS natural manure, green manure	
PLANT PROTECTION chemical, copper and sulphur	
WEED CONTROL chemical, mechanical	
YEASTS selected	
GRAPES wine bought in	
CERTIFICATION none	

Köfererhof
Günther Kerschbaumer

Frazione Novacella
Via Pusteria, 3
tel. 0472 836649
www.koefererhof.it
info@koefererhof.it

5.5 ha - 70,000 bt

PEOPLE - Since 1995 Günther Kerschbaumer has been vinifying his own grapes, assisted by agronomist Florian Sinn. It has to be said that if the wines of the Valle Isarco have achieved their present quality, part of the credit has to go to Köfererhof and the excellent work he's done in his vineyards, the northernmost in Italy. With his companion Gaby Tauber, Günther also runs a traditional osteria in his millenary *maso*, or farmhouse.

VINEYARDS - Günther is putting a lot of his money on the kerner grape. The vineyards fan out round the *maso* at an altitude of 600-800 meters and descend to the Abbey of Novacella on the valley floor. Exposure and altitude are ideal for whites, which benefit enormously from the mixed soil, which is sandy and morainal in some places, but contains slate and granite in others. In the vineyard and in the new cellar, Günther does everything on his own and devotes special care to the choice of the grapes to grow on the various plots.

WINES - All the wines reflect Günther's fine, pure, sinewy personal style. Especially successful are A.A. Valle Isarco Veltliner 2011 (○ 4,000 bt), subtle yet assertive, flavorsome and sharp, and **A.A. Valle Isarco Riesling 2011** (○ 10,000 bt), taut and crisp, well-structured with a nice sweet-acid contrast. The first of the two is the more pleasurable and, for us, a Great Wine. The excellent **A.A. Valle Isarco Gewürztraminer 2011** (○ 6,000 bt), is stylish and lively with well-rounded fruit. We liked the plumpness and richness of **A.A. Valle Isarco Sylvaner 2011** (○ 8,000 bt), and the typicality, juiciness and zest of **A.A. Valle Isarco Pinot Grigio 2011** (○ 6,000 bt). **A.A. Valle Isarco Kerner 2011** (25,000 bt) is fresh, tangy and taut and needs to spend time in the glass to express itself.

FERTILIZERS natural manure	
PLANT PROTECTION chemical, copper and sulphur	
WEED CONTROL chemical, mechanical	
YEASTS selected, native	
GRAPES 30% bought in	
CERTIFICATION none	

VENETO

With the 2011 harvest, Veneto proved once more to the Italian region that produces the most wine. Here 72,000 hectares of land are planted with vines and produce almost eight million hectoliters of wine in terroirs growing different grapes in a variety of soil and climate conditions. Our observation of trends in the various districts, and of their history and our tasting of their wines allows us to take stock of the situation and offer a few morsels of food for thought.

The westernmost part of the region seems to be enjoying a happy spell: the whites of Custoza are well-defined, Bardolino is making a name for itself as a light but satisfying wine for everyday drinking and Chiaretto — especially the fizzy versions — are very popular at the moment. The situation in the Valpolicella is complex. Amarone is recording impressive production and sales figures, though it's hard to figure out what this prized wine's average retail prices are. We are skeptical about the ongoing Ripasso "phenomenon" — a mass of labels with completely different styles but no precise identity. Which is why we recommended only a few of them. The base Valpolicellas — light, fruity, ideal for easy everyday drinking — have virtually disappeared. It's a pity because the ones left are very good indeed.

The Soave and Gambellara felt the weather in the summer of 2011. The scorching heat on the second half of August and consequent early harvests brought about generally alcoholic wines, poor aromatic focus, somewhat grassy without much complexity on the palate. There were a number of welcome exceptions, of course. The Colli Berici suffer from a certain lack of identity, which we feel should be based on the tai rosso grape and not on other varieties, whereas the Breganze and Colli Euganei — together with Bolgheri one of the finest terroirs in Italy for Bordeaux grapes — is suffering the drop in sales that is currently affecting this kind of wine. On the other hand, increased sales are arousing great excitement in the vast Prosecco area, which extends throughout the east of the region, with its heart in the Conegliano-Valdobbiadene area. Luckily, the situation is being handled with great intelligence. The fact that we recommend only Proseccos from companies in the two DOCGs was an editorial decision.

snails 🐌

99	LE FRAGHE
100	MONTE DEI RAGNI
101	CORTE SANT'ALDA
103	MONTE DALL'ORA
104	VILLA BELLINI
107	LA BIANCARA
108	PRÀ
108	FONGARO
109	LEONILDO PIEROPAN
111	CA' OROLOGIO
113	VIGNETO DUE SANTI
115	TESSÈRE
116	CASA COSTE PIANE
117	SILVANO FOLLADOR
117	SORELLE BRONCA

bottles 🍾

99	ALLEGRINI
100	CAV. G.B. BERTANI
102	GIUSEPPE QUINTARELLI
104	ANGELO NICOLIS E FIGLI
107	CA' RUGATE
111	VIGNALTA
112	IL FILÒ DELLE VIGNE
113	LA MONTECCHIA CONTE EMO CAPODILISTA
115	ANDREOLA

coins €

102	LE MORETTE - VALERIO ZENATO
103	BRIGALDARA
105	CAVALCHINA
109	MONTE TONDO
112	IL MOTTOLO
116	MALIBRAN

Valpolicella e Veneto occidentale

Le Fraghe

Località Colombare, 3
tel. 045 7236832
www.fraghe.it
info@fraghe.it

Allegrini

Via Giare, 5
tel. 045 6832011
www.allegrini.it
info@allegrini.it

---

30 ha - 90,000 bt `10% discount`

❝ Long live dailyness! That could be the slogan for Matilde Poggi's outstanding and incessant work on developing and promoting her simple, drinkable wines with a strong sense of place. Hers is an example of sobriety and of a new, reborn viticulture ❞

PEOPLE - The progress Le Fraghe has made under Matilde over almost 30 years is admirable to say the least. Every agronomic and enological decision is well pondered with critical acumen and rationality. Matilde also runs her new agriturismo facility with a sense of genuine hospitality.

VINEYARDS - Complexity rules among Matilde's four vineyards, each with different characteristics but also a common denominator: namely greater freshness than in the southern zone of the Bardolino denomination. The soil is morainal and rich in gravel and minerals. Each property is given over to one grape variety to exalt the particularities of each selection.

WINES - "I want wines for drinking," says Matilde who sets great store by quaffability and value for money. **Bardolino Chiaretto Rodon 2011** (⊙ 12,000 bt) is immediate, linear and racy, something of a faux white with its fresh, convincing character. Spices and fruit usher in **Garganega Camporengo 2011** (○ 15,000 bt), pervaded by refreshing, pleasant acidity. The release of Cabernet Quaiare has been postponed until next year.

> **slow wine** **BARDOLINO 2011** (● 42,000 bt) A wine with a stylish, elegant demeanor. This year it exhibits a heftier structure than usual. Spices and fruit accompany gutsy tannins that are sure to develop.

90 ha - 700,000 bt `10% discount`

PEOPLE - Half a century ago, Giovanni Allegrini was instrumental in raising the profile of Valpolicella winemaking. More recently, his children Marilisa and Franco — respectively the sales manager and the production manager — have helped to spread the fame of the family brand in Italy and throughout the world.

VINEYARDS - The Allegrini vineyards are situated in the loveliest and highest points of the Valpolicella. One such is the historic ten-hectare Fieramonte holding which stands at an altitude of 400 meters. Others are the 30-hectare Grola at Sant'Ambrogio, at an altitude of 300 meters, planted in 1978 and the Poja, parcel just above it. The more recently planted Villa Cavarena, a stupendous natural amphitheater at an altitude of 500 meters, is given over solely to corvina and corvinone. Franco takes painstaking care of the vineyards and is keen to reduce their impact on the environment. Hence his patenting of a machine for working the land without the use of chemical weed killers.

WINES - The superlative **Amarone della Valpolicella Cl. 2008** (● 127,000 bt) has character and elegance to spare, satisfying the palate with its juiciness and finishing on a perfectly dry note. A Great Wine if ever there was one. We were impressed by the roundness and sweet-acid balance of **Recioto della Valpolicella Cl. Giovanni Allegrini 2009** (● 20,000 bt). The quality of the three labels that take their names from the single vineyards is improving all the time: **Palazzo della Torre 2009** (● corvina, rondinella, sangiovese; 275,000 bt) is simple, linear and well-structured; **La Grola 2009** (● corvina, syrah; 180,000 bt) is enveloping and velvety with fine, spicy aromas; **La Poja 2008** (● corvina; 13,500 bt) has stronger impact and character, supported by an elegant tannic structure and dynamism on the palate.

FERTILIZERS green manure	**FERTILIZERS** natural manure, compost
PLANT PROTECTION copper and sulphur	**PLANT PROTECTION** chemical, copper and sulphur
WEED CONTROL mechanical	**WEED CONTROL** mechanical
YEASTS selected, native	**YEASTS** selected
GRAPES 100% estate-grown	**GRAPES** 100% estate-grown
CERTIFICATION organic	**CERTIFICATION** none

FUMANE (VR)

Monte dei Ragni

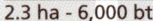

Località Marega, 3
tel. 045 6801600
www.montedeiragni.com
info@montedeiragni.com

GREZZANA (VR)

Cav. G.B. Bertani

Via Asiago, 1
tel. 045 8658444
www.bertani.net
bertani@bertani.net

2.3 ha - 6,000 bt

❝ "This is the land we possess, we haven't got another one in reserve," says Zemo. Which is why he feels it's his duty to guard that land. He thus argues the importance of implementing what he calls "deep ecology" to preserve the undersoil as well as the surface. "Winemaking is a gift you have to deserve and only when you've deserved it will you make Wine" ❞

PEOPLE - Zeno Zignoli lends his intellect and labor to the vineyards. Making wine is his way of thanking Mother Nature. A man of deep conviction and great culture, he likes telling visitors lucky enough to meet him what it means to live in harmony with respect for the Earth. When you walk into the courtyard that leads to the cellar, you have the distinct perception that here time slides to the rhythms of nature.

VINEYARDS - Two hectares of vineyard across the hill that leads to Mazzurega — an optimal dimension for a man to manage his vineyards with the care they deserve. Where possible horses are used for work in the vineyards to avoid compacting the soil. A convinced opponent of monocropping, which weakens the soil, Zeno also grows cereals and vegetables among the vines.

WINES - The utmost attention is devoted to selection of the grapes, which hang in bunches on nets in the loft to dry. Zeno looks for elegance and aging capacity in his wines. Witness **Amarone della Valpolicella Cl. 2006** (● 1,900 bt), which opens slowly, but then proceeds to release scents of spices and red berries with a hint of toast. Give it time, it's a wine to be listened to. In **Valpolicella Cl. Sup. Ripasso 2007** (● 3,800 bt) we find intriguing spiciness and balsamic notes, plus a nose-caressing, tangy bouquet.

---

220 ha - 1,600,000 bt

PEOPLE - In 1857 brothers Giovan Battista and Gaetano Bertani, *carbonari* wanted by the Austrians, were forced into an exile of four years in Burgundy. On their return to the land of their birth they brought with them the new vineyard management techniques they had picked up in France and began to produce quality wine. This long tradition makes Bertani, taken over this year by the Angelini pharmaceutical group, a sort of historic soul of Valpolicella winemaking.

VINEYARDS - The company owns 220 hectares of vineyards, some in the Soave zone and the rest, obviously, in Valpolicella, on the splendid Villa Novare estate, which the Bertani family has owned since 1957. Here you can appreciate the seriousness of the company's agronomic management, specifically planned to respect the vines and the surrounding environment.

WINES - The wine cellar is in Grezzana di Valpantena. All the wines presented were inspired by a serious, austre tradition. Refreshing, subtle and flavorful, **Valpolicella Cl. Villa Novare 2011** (● 75,000 bt) is an excellent Everyday Wine, while **Valpolicella Cl. Sup. Vigneto Ognissanti 2009** (● 25,000 bt) has more weight and depth with the same drinkability. **Amarone della Valpolicella Valpantena Villa Arvedi 2009** (● 80,000 bt) has potent, ripe fruit and a well-balanced palate. **Valpolicella Valpantena Secco Bertani 2010** (● 400,000 bt) is a classic, delicious red, while **Soave Sereole 2011** (○ 100,000 bt) is as racy and mouth-filling as ever.

slow wine **AMARONE DELLA VALPOLICELLA CL. 2005** (● 40,000 bt) An icon that holds the banner of Amarone and the Italian spirit all over the world. It reasserts its greatness with a fine, elegant style of pleasurable balance.

FERTILIZERS natural manure, green manure
PLANT PROTECTION copper and sulphur, organic
WEED CONTROL mechanical
YEASTS native
GRAPES 100% estate-grown
CERTIFICATION none

FERTILIZERS organic-mineral, manure pellets, natural manure
PLANT PROTECTION copper and sulphur
WEED CONTROL mechanical
YEASTS selected
GRAPES 100% estate-grown
CERTIFICATION none

Trabucchi

Località Monte Tenda, 3
tel. 045 7833233
www.trabucchidillasi.it
info@trabucchidillasi.it

27 ha - 100,000 bt

PEOPLE - Ninety years have gone by since the lawyer Marco Trabucchi, grandfather of Giuseppe, the present owner, bought the splendid Monte Tenda estate in the hills that act as a watershed between the Illasi and Tramigna valleys behind Soave. Today Giuseppe, with his wife Raffaella at his side, is carrying on where his father Alberto left off, and now also organizes the annual Trabucchi Award for Civil Passion.

VINEYARDS - Since 1993 the company has been certified organic and only vinifies grapes from its own vineyards or vineyards that it manages. The vineyards encircle the cellar alternating with splendid olive groves. It's interesting the small parcel at Cereolo, where the vines are still trained with the traditional *pergola veronese* system. The company's commitment towards a viticulture with low environmental impact is also demonstrated by its very limited use of copper and sulfur.

WINES - The choice to use organic methods in the field translates into great care for the grapes and the wine in the cellar. Wood is used sparingly and evenly with non-invasive results. We really enjoyed **Amarone della Valpolicella Cent'Anni Ris. 2004** (● 8,000 bt) with its characteristic aromas of morello cherry and juice, well supported by good acidity. It's one of the best versions ever, for us a Great Wine. The fine, mineral **Valpolicella Sup. Terra di San Colombano 2007** (● 25.000 bt) has a taut, juicy palate. The sweet, characteristic **Recioto della Valpolicella 2006** (● 10,000 bt) has ripe fruit, well supported by the alcohol, and balsamic notes. The only white we tasted was **Recioto di Soave 2006** (○ 6,000 bt) which has typical notes of almond and exotic fruit accompanied by pleasurable tartness.

FERTILIZERS	organic-mineral, natural manure, biodynamic preparations
PLANT PROTECTION	copper and sulphur, organic
WEED CONTROL	mechanical
YEASTS	native
GRAPES	100% estate-grown
CERTIFICATION	organic

Corte Sant'Alda

Località Fioi
Via Capovilla, 28
tel. 045 8880006
www.cortesantalda.it
info@cortesantalda.it

19 ha - 80,000 bt

❝ With a sensible one-step-at-a-time policy, this company has revolutionized its way of doing agriculture, pragmatically experimenting with biodynamics and making wines with a strong sense of place and massive aromatic quality ❞

PEOPLE - For Marinella Camerani, Corte Sant'Alda is much more than a wine company. It is, above all, a life choice that has now culminated in the decision to practice agriculture geared to respect for the land and consumers.

VINEYARDS - Observation of nature and plant cycles, communication with the vines — this is the approach Marinella has followed since 1985, making improvements all the way. Her vineyards, which she manages using biodynamic methods, are situated in the hills of Mezzano, where the views are breathtaking. For some time now, a single wine has been produced from each vineyard to highlight the specificity that rises from the soil.

WINES - Marinella's character is mirrored in her wines. Precise and personal, oblivious to fashion, they are the result of spontaneous fermentations in oak tubs. Aging is very long and perfectly in tune with the development of the wine. Beginning with a white, **Soave Vigne di Mezzane 2011** (○ 12,000 bt) stands out for the finesse of its aromas and its balanced, mineral palate. It's a fine Everyday Wine. The reds are rather undeveloped and need time to show off their body and finesse. This is true of **Amarone della Valpolicella 2008** (● 10,000 bt) and **Valpolicella Sup. Mithas 2008** (● 5,000 bt), two elegant wines of crystalline class. **Valpolicella Sup. Ripasso Campi Magri 2009** (● 20,000 bt) is full of finesse and body and **Valpolicella Ca' Fiui 2011** (● 25,000 bt) is simple but impressive.

FERTILIZERS	biodynamic preparations, green manure
PLANT PROTECTION	copper and sulphur
WEED CONTROL	mechanical
YEASTS	native
GRAPES	100% estate-grown
CERTIFICATION	biodynamic, organic

NEGRAR (VR)

Giuseppe Quintarelli

Via Cerè, 1
tel. 0457 513241
giuseppe.quintarelli@tin.it

PESCHIERA DEL GARDA (VR)

Le Morette
Valerio Zenato

€

Viale Indipendenza
tel. 045 7552774
www.lemorette.it
info@lemorette.it

12 ha - 50,000 bt

30 ha - 180,000 bt   10% discount

PEOPLE - "Bepi Quintarelli is dead, long live Bepi Quintarelli!" This grand old man of Italian wine truly was the heart and soul of Valpolicella. His idea of wine can be summed up in three words: finesse, elegance and complexity. He was a great viticulturist who strove to make great wine with the humility of a peasant. Now the baton has passed on to Bepi's daughter Fiorenza, her husband Gianpaolo, and his grandsons Francesco and Lorenzo. It's up to them to carry on where Bepi left off.

VINEYARDS - The vineyards are situated in the commune of Negrar and at Sant'Ambrogio, Montorio and Valgatara, where the hilly terrain is volcanic and calcareous. The training systems — old pergola and Guyot — mix tradition and modernity. The ground rules are care for the vineyard, respect for the grapes and patience.

WINES - **Amabile del Cerè 2003** (O garganega, trebbiano, sauvignon, chardonnay, saorin; 2,000 bt) is back after a long period away. It was released for the last time in 1990, for the first in 1947. Also known as Bandito, this passito of exceptional personality is aged for six to seven years in acacia barrels — a triumph of complexity. Produced with the same varieties, **Bianco Secco 2011** (O 9,000 bt) is fresh, buttery, rich and leisurely. Moving on to reds, **Primofiore 2008** (● cabernet, corvina, corvinone; 10,000 bt) is intense, almost austere. **Valpolicella Cl. Sup. 2003** (● 15,000 bt) is fine, elegant, juicy and long. Amarone della Valpolicella Cl. 2003 (● 11,000 bt) is invitingly refreshing despite the torrid vintage. Poetic and floral, it's once more a Great Wine. **Alzero 2001** (● cabernet sauvignon e franc, merlot; 3,000 bt) is a magnificent passito.

PEOPLE - Le Morette started up in the 1960s with the production of unbottled wine and a plant nursery business that is still thriving. Sensing the place's potential, Valerio Zenato started bottling wine in 1990, since when his sons Paolo and Fabio have joined him and helped him raise production figures. Lugana is the family passion.

VINEYARDS - Twenty-four hectares are at Peschiera, six at Sirmione. The influence of the lake obviously makes itself felt and makes for mineral, slow-developing wines, relatively unexpressive in their early years of life but with long aging potential. The vineyards contain a large quantity of yellow earth with a high percentage of clay. In the vineyard Valerio practices integrated pest control management and prefers mechanical grubbing to chemical.

WINES - The most convincing wine is **Lugana Benedictus 2011** (O 15,000 bt), made with late-harvested grapes from the old vines. It opens with mineral and citrusy notes and reveals strong character in its acid follow-through. It's a wine that's built to last. **Lugana Mandolara 2011** (O 120,000 bt) is salty and earthy with leaner texture and more direct drinkability. Rounding up the range is **Lugana Brut** (O 10,000 bt), a dry, enjoyable spumante. The quaffable **Bardolino Chiaretto Cl. 2011** (⊙ 10,000 bt) is a perfect summer wine of exemplary cleanness. Arguably not one of the most complex of wines, **Bardolino Cl. 2011** (● 10,000 bt) is nice and fruity nonetheless. **Perseo 2009** (● cabernet sauvignon, corvina; 8,000 bt), aged in large barrels to build up power and alcohol, exhibits massive tannins.

FERTILIZERS natural manure
PLANT PROTECTION chemical, copper and sulphur
WEED CONTROL mechanical
YEASTS native
GRAPES 100% estate-grown
CERTIFICATION none

FERTILIZERS natural manure
PLANT PROTECTION chemical, copper and sulphur
WEED CONTROL mechanical
YEASTS selected
GRAPES 100% estate-grown
CERTIFICATION none

Brigaldara

Frazione San Floriano
Via Brigaldara, 20
tel. 045 7701055
www.brigaldara.it
info@brigaldara.it

50 ha - 250,000 bt `10% discount`

PEOPLE - More than a quarter of a century has gone by since Stefano Cesari revolutionized this family company. Until the mid 1980s it used to sell all its grapes to other producers, but in 1986 it gradually began to bottle its own wine and, at the same time, to extend tis vineyards, even moving into the area east of Verona that is part of the Valpolicella and Soave DOCs.

VINEYARDS - Until last year, the only treatment used to fight vine moth, an insect that harms the grapes, often irremediably. Today Brigaldara and other viticulturists in the Negrar area have espoused the cause of naturalness and more sustainable management. In this way, it is possible to avoid spraying the vineyards with substances harmful for the environment and for people and thus ensure the health of the grapes.

WINES - It may seem strange to start with Soave Cl. 2011 (○ 13,000 bt), but we rated it highly for its refreshing mineral notes and its long finish of bitter almonds, typical of garganega. Valpolicella Cl. 2010 (● 100,000 bt), which we reviewed by mistake last year, proves once more to be a highly drinkable, personality-packed wine. Both deserve the accolade of Everyday Wine. **Amarone della Valpolicella Cl. Case Vece 2009** (● 13,000 bt) is a certainty as always. It has aromas of fruit and spices with an austere mouthfeel and great elegance. Traditional and plump and sweet, **Recioto della Valpolicella Cl. 2008** (● 5,000 bt) is redolent of ripe fruit. Also worth remembering are **Valpolicella Cl. Sup. Ripasso Il Vegro 2009** (● 40,000 bt) and **Amarone della Valpolicella Cl. 2009** (● 70,000 bt), pleasant and typical, though the two vintages presented are not quite up to their traditional standard of quality.

FERTILIZERS organic-mineral, natural manure
PLANT PROTECTION copper and sulphur
WEED CONTROL mechanical
YEASTS selected
GRAPES 100% estate-grown
CERTIFICATION none

Monte dall'Ora

Via Monte dall'Ora, 5
tel. 045 7704462
www.montedallora.com
info@montedallora.com

6.5 ha - 30,000 bt `10% discount`

" Alessandra Zantedeschi and Carlo Venturini, both wildly in love with nature, realized it was possible to adopt a new approach to the vineyards. Hence their creation of this virtuous, eco-sustainable model winery "

PEOPLE - The Valpolicella of Monte Dall'Ora is something else. The winery sits in a natural amphitheater protected by woodland that includes an hectare of cherry trees to avoid monocropping and favor biodiversity. In just over ten years, the company has managed to assert itself as one of the best in the area.

VINEYARDS - Castelrotto is a spur in the hills to the south of the Valpolicella Classica zone. The eccentric location creates an unusually warm, ventilated microclimate: here the breeze from Lake Garda is crucial for the natural drying of the grapes. The soil is soft and well-ventilated, and the stratum between vine and underlying rock is very thin.

WINES - Listing the wines in order of quality is a tough task, each being a jewel in its genre. We were hugely impressed by **Amarone della Valpolicella Cl. 2008** (● 6,000 bt), which is refined, mineral and deep. Dry and unsugary, the balsamic **Valpolicella Cl. Sup. Ripasso Saustò 2008** (● 5,000 bt) is a joy to drink. **Valpolicella Cl. Sup. Camporenzo 2009** (● 6,000 bt) is perky with crunchy fruit, while Valpolicella Cl. Saseti 2011 (● 5,000 bt) is at once rustic and complex, dynamic and packed with fruit — a fine Everyday Wine.

> **slow wine** RECIOTO DELLA VALPOLICELLA CL.SANT'ULDERICO 2008 (● 2,000 bt) A wine that confirms its stature with minutely gauged sweetness, calibrated concentration, superior finesse and a sumptuous palate.

FERTILIZERS compost, biodynamic preparations
PLANT PROTECTION copper and sulphur, organic
WEED CONTROL mechanical
YEASTS native
GRAPES 100% estate-grown
CERTIFICATION organic

SAN PIETRO IN CARIANO (VR)

Angelo Nicolis e Figli

Via Villa Girardi, 29
tel. 045 7701261
www.vininicolis.com
info@vininicolis.com

SAN PIETRO IN CARIANO (VR)

Villa Bellini

Località Castelrotto di Negarine
Via dei Fraccaroli, 6
tel. 0457 725630
www.villabellini.com
villabellini@villabellini.com

---

42 ha - 220,000 bt

3.5 ha - 10,000 bt   **10% discount**

PEOPLE - "The soul of our wines is our land," claims Giuseppe Nicolis, who runs the family company with his brothers Giancarlo and Massimo, following the tradition initiated by their dad Angelo in 1951. In love with their local area, the Nicolis brothers devote their lives to wine with a simple, genuine enhanced by experience acquired over the years — not to mention huge entrepreneurial efforts, insight and farsighted investment in both vineyard and cellar.

VINEYARDS - The vineyards are scattered across a number of communes in the Valpolicella Classica zone. The classic vintage wines are produced with grapes from the ones in the foothills, where the soil is fertile and of medium texture. The arbor-trained grapes that go into the most prized, cellarable wines grow on the hillside terraces, which are supported by the classic stone walls known locally as *marogne*. The crus are born in the Seccal and Ambrosan microzones, where the weather and soil conditions are particularly conducive to winemaking.

WINES - Giuseppe argues that wines should respect the fruit they originate from and come to life with as little conditioning as possible. **Amarone della Valpolicella Cl. Ambrosan 2006** (● 25,000 bt) has an elegant robustness of character harmonized by dynamic aromatic structure, while **Valpolicella Cl. Sup. Ripasso Seccal 2009** (● 50,000 bt) is opulent but well balanced by lively flavor. **Valpolicella Cl. Sup. 2009** (● 10,000 bt) has characteristic, intense aromas, and the creamy-sweet **Recioto della Valpolicella Cl. 2008** (● 5,000 bt), finally, is fresh and typical.

> **slow wine** AMARONE DELLA VALPOLICELLA CL. 2006 (● 35,000 bt) Potent and aristocratic on the nose, finely textured on the palate, simple yet, in essence, noble — a wine that epitomizes the Nicolis style.

" Identitary, elegant, original but rooted in the land and filled with nuances that transcend mere taste — a sip of Taso tells the story of this cellar better than a thousand words ever could "

PEOPLE - Villa Bellini is a cluster of 18th-century buildings in the Castelrotto hills. When she bought the place with her husband Marco in 1987, Cecilia intended to convert it into a restaurant-resort. But the desire to make wine prevailed and now the company is a unique player on the Valpolicella stage.

VINEYARDS - Perfect harmony reigns in the walled vineyard-cum-garden. Here old pergolas alternate with young bush-trained vine rows according to the rules of agronomic common sense and precise principles of style. The vineyard has been managed using organic methods for the last 20 years and recently a number of biodynamic practices were also introduced.

WINES - Taso has always been the only wine produced, together with — harvest permitting — a Recioto della Valpolicella. But this year we have an exciting debut to report. That of **Valpolicella Cl. Sotto le Fresche Frasche 2011** (● 2,000 bt), fresh and juicy with intense notes of cherry on the nose that linger on the palate too to create a soft, enfolding finish. The wine, which isn't aged in wood, is already ready for drinking — in short, a success story.

> **slow wine** VALPOLICELLA CL. SUP. TASO 2009 (● 5,000 bt) The 2009 vintage has regaled us with a great Taso, as refined as ever. It has very fine texture and alluring softness with elegant notes of chocolate and spices on the nose. An original, effective interpretation of the grapes and the terroir of Valpolicella.

FERTILIZERS natural manure	FERTILIZERS compost, biodynamic preparations
PLANT PROTECTION chemical, copper and sulphur	PLANT PROTECTION copper and sulphur
WEED CONTROL mechanical	WEED CONTROL mechanical
YEASTS native	YEASTS native
GRAPES 100% estate-grown	GRAPES 100% estate-grown
CERTIFICATION none	CERTIFICATION organic

SOMMACAMPAGNA (VR)

Cavalchina €

Frazione Custoza
Località Cavalchina
tel. 045 516002
www.cavalchina.com
cavalchina@cavalchina.com

---

28 ha - 300,000 bt

PEOPLE - Brothers Luciano and Franco Piona have been running this cellar, set up by the father Giulietto in 1962, for years now. In the course of time they have also added the Prendina estate at Monzambano, in the province of Mantua. Thanks to level-headed management and a strong sense of land-rootedness, Cavalchina is now a model for the whole area. True to local tradition, it produces no fizzy wines. Albeit unusual in the Veneto region, we judge the decision positively.

VINEYARDS - The main property fans out behind the cellar on gently rolling hills at an altitude of 100-150 meters. Another 14 hectares of vines were planted in 2000 on the Torre d'Orti estate in Valpolicella. The composition of the vineyards that grow the grapes for Custoza is a singular mix of garganega, fernanda, trebbianello and trebbiano. The management is attentive, mindful of the needs of the vines and the surrounding environment.

WINES - All the wines have a precise style characterized by cleanness, approachability and drinkability. Of this year's wines the one that impressed us most was the fresh, fruity **Bardolino 2011** (● 30,000 bt), a pleasant Everyday Wine that won't disappoint. **Bardolino Chiaretto 2011** (⊘ 30,000 bt) is soft and intense with notes of cherries. Moving on to the whites, **Custoza 2011** (○ 180,000 bt) is as reliable as ever: taut and assertive, it displays fresh, crunchy fruit. At its first vintage without the use of oak during vinification, **Custoza Sup. Amedeo 2010** (○ 10,000 bt) is more convincing than previously thanks to its full flavor and elegantly mineral finish. From Valpolicella, finally, we welcome **Amarone della Valpolicella Torre d'Orti 2008** (● 6,000 bt) elegant and quaffable with a complex, intact nose of sour cherries preserved in alcohol, chocolate and dried figs.

VERONA

Tezza

Frazione Poiano di Valpantena
Stradella Maioli, 4
tel. 045 550267
www.tezzawines.it
info@tezzawines.it

---

25 ha - 160,000 bt

PEOPLE - Flavio, Vanio and Federico Tezza love the Valpantena and its vineyards. When they took over the family company in the 1990s, their first thought was for the countryside. Hence incessant restructuring work on the vineyards, alternating classic pergonala-training with more modern Guyot-trained vineyards. Today the company has achieved balanced production.

VINEYARDS - The Tezza winery manages 25 hectares of vines almost in a single plot at the mouth of the Valpantena just outside Verona against the background of the Monti Lessini. It began to abandon the use of synthetic products a few years ago to the benefit of a more rational agriculture.

WINES - The company uses barriques of different woods — though never dominant over the wine — to achieve elegance and finesse as opposed to power. The characteristic **Recioto della Valpolicella Valpantena 2006** (● 4,000 bt) has crispy fruit and good acidity. We were struck by **Valpolicella Valpantena Sup. Ripasso Brolo delle Giare 2005** (● 3,300 bt), which has excellent notes of ripe fruit. Interesting too were **Valpolicella Valpantena Sup. Ripasso Tezza 2009** (● 6,600 bt) and the refreshing, tangy **Valpolicella Sup. Ripasso Ma Roat 2010** (● 15,000 bt), aged only in stainless steel.

 **AMARONE DELLA VALPOLICELLA VALPANTENA TEZZA 2006** (● 10,000 bt) Emblematic — that's how we define this Amarone, the product of meticulous work in the vineyard and impeccable interpretation in the cellar, plus long aging and, above all, a pricing policy that serves to promote the denomination. It has a fresh, fruity bouquet and soft, full, enfolding palate with a long balsamic finish.

FERTILIZERS organic-mineral	FERTILIZERS none
PLANT PROTECTION chemical, copper and sulphur	PLANT PROTECTION chemical, copper and sulphur
WEED CONTROL mechanical	WEED CONTROL chemical, mechanical
YEASTS selected	YEASTS selected
GRAPES 100% estate-grown	GRAPES 100% estate-grown
CERTIFICATION none	CERTIFICATION none

Terre della garganega

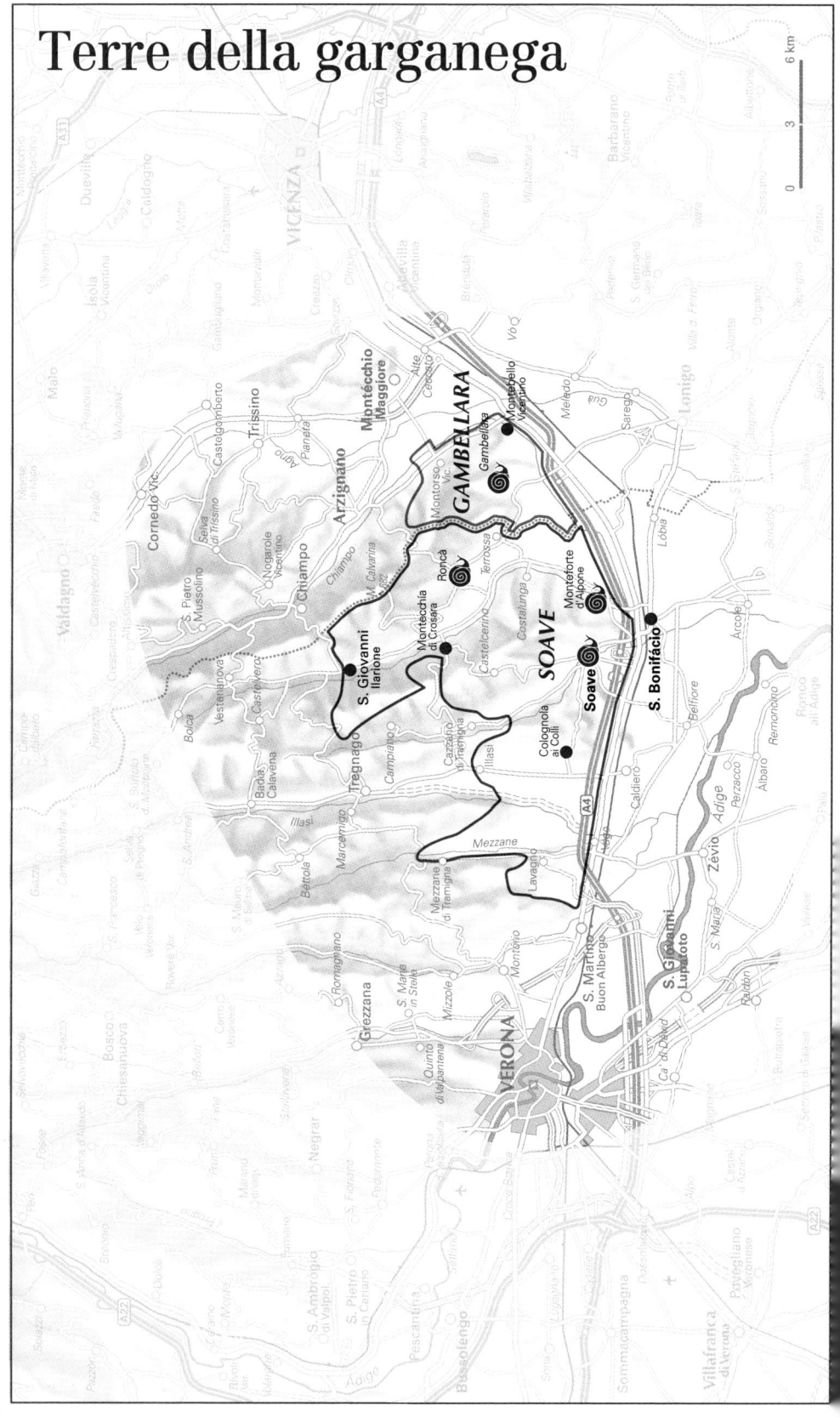

GAMBELLARA (VI)

La Biancara

Frazione Sorio
Contrada Biancara, 14
tel. 0444 444244
www.biancaravini.it
biancaravini@virgilio.it

12 ha - 60,000 bt

66 Angiolino Maule has been much talked about over the last few years. Maybe it's because of his single-mindedness and charisma, maybe it's on account of the infectious energy that has made him a leader of the natural wine movement. Whatever the reason, he has invented a revolutionary way of playing the role of the modern winemaker 99

PEOPLE - The hills of the Sorio di Gambellara zone are where Angiolino and his wife Rosa Maria chose to embark upon their brilliant winemaking adventure about 20 years ago. Over the last few years they have been joined on the job by their sons Francesco, Alessandro and Tommas. Maybe the future here has already been written.

VINEYARDS - Vineyards supplements cellar and vice versa to exalt the wine's spontaneity. No weed killers, pesticides and chemical fertilizers, reduced use of copper and sulfur, turfing between the vine rows, hand-picking of grapes, fermentations with native yeasts, no micro-oxygenation, limited use of sulfites ... It sounds like a recipe, but it's not. On the contrary, it's a gradual, undogmatic process that stems from dialogue with the vines and human sensitivity.

WINES - **Bianco Masieri 2011** (○ 25,000 bt) has heady, juicy fruitiness with a whiff of brewer's yeast. **Pico 2010** (○ 6,000 bt) has intense flowery scents and a hint of sweetness on the finish. **Recioto di Gambellara 2008** (○ 2,000 bt), finally, is as impressive as ever, nice and plump with a good sweet-acid balance.

> **slow wine** SASSAIA 2011 (○ 17,000 bt). The height of essence, equilibrium and expression. A narrative wine that tells the story of Angiolino and his idea of wine.

FERTILIZERS compost, green manure
PLANT PROTECTION copper and sulphur, organic
WEED CONTROL mechanical
YEASTS native
GRAPES 100% estate-grown
CERTIFICATION organic

MONTECCHIA DI CROSARA (VR)

Ca' Rugate

Via Pergola, 72
tel. 045 6176328
www.carugate.it
carugate@carugate.it

58 ha - 550,000 bt | **10% discount**

PEOPLE - "A country without a historical memory is like a plant without roots." The citation is a perfect reflection of the experience of the Tessaris, a family whose history is closely tied to that of Brognoligo, a small village on the outskirts of Monteforte d'Alpone. The valley which connects the place to the hamlet of Fittà, where the company has its headquarters, is known as Le Rugate. Today Michele Tessari is at the head of an impressive team that has a vision of the future while keeping a close eye on its roots.

VINEYARDS - All the attention currently directed towards the new Campo Lavei vineyard in Valpolicella doesn't mean that the company has reduced its commitment to the renewal of its properties in the Soave area. On Monte Tenda, for example, it has recovered 2.5 hectares of land planted with trebbiano di Soave. The above-mentioned Campo Lavei vineyard is immersed in a pretty, unspoiled environment on limestone soil. The natural coolness of the climate allows the grapes to ripen with plenty of acidity.

WINES - Compared to the recent past, **Soave Cl. Monte Fiorentine 2011** (○ 50,000 bt) is readier and more approachable, very good but arguably less stylish on account of the poor vintage. **Soave Cl. Monte Alto 2010** (○ 10,000) stands out for its structure and concentration — one of the best versions ever. The magnificent **Recioto della Valpolicella l'Eremita 2009** (● 5,000 bt) is spicy and well-extracted with immense class and length. Also spicy is the sumptuous, balanced **Valpolicella Sup. Campo Lavei 2010** (● 25,000 bt).

> **slow wine** STUDIO 2010 (○ trebbiano di Soave, garganega; 5.000 bt) A hymn to the essence of the trebbiano grape, a wine capable of combining sense of place, style and innovation. Subtle and deep, it amazes for its huge minerality.

FERTILIZERS organic-mineral, natural manure, green manure
PLANT PROTECTION chemical, copper and sulphur
WEED CONTROL chemical, mechanical
YEASTS native
GRAPES 100% estate-grown
CERTIFICATION none

Prà

Via della Fontana, 31
tel. 045 7612125
www.vinipra.it
info@vinipra.it

28 ha - 200,000 bt **10% discount**

66 The quest for quality is the motor that drives every move Graziano Prà makes. He is a faithful interpreter of his teroir which he exalts with wines of extraordinary elegance and endurance 99

PEOPLE - In the early 1980s, after the death of his father, Graziano Prà graduated in enology, returned to the family company and decided to take charge of the vineyards. And that's how his electrifying celebration of Soave began.

VINEYARDS - The vineyards fan out high up in the hills in the most prestigious Soave crus, among which Froscà, Foscarino, Montegrande and Ponsara. This is part of Graziano's secret. The rest consists of constantly perfecting agronomic practices. The introduction of new machinery, for example, has put a stop to chemical weeding and increased biodiversity in the vineyards. The Morandina holding, where the reds come from, is now managed using organic methods.

WINES - The class of the whites is embodied in the sumptuous version of **Soave Cl. Montegrande 2010** (○ 15,000 bt), characterized by unstoppable progression and rare aromatic precision. **Soave Cl. 2011** (○ 150,000 bt) is built rund acidity and freshness. The reds are improving all the time. **Valpolicella Sup. La Morandina 2010** (● 5,000 bt) is fragrant and brimming over with fruit. The juicy **Valpolicella Sup. Ripasso La Morandina 2010** (● 5,000 bt) is an elegant fusion of spices and cherries with much more structure and oomph.

> **slow wine** **SOAVE CL. STAFORTE 2010** (○ 6,600 bt) A visiting card for the grandiosity of Soave. Elegant and complex, it has cut-glass purity and a mineral length that can't go unnoticed.

FERTILIZERS none	
PLANT PROTECTION copper and sulphur	
WEED CONTROL mechanical	
YEASTS selected	
GRAPES 100% estate-grown	
CERTIFICATION organic	

Fongaro

Via Motto Piane, 12
tel. 045 7460240
www.fongarospumanti.it
info@fongarospumanti.it

12 ha - 100,000 bt **10% discount**

66 The Fongaros have always done their utmost to promote the identity of the Lessinia area. With their work they have shown how great results can be achieved even with an apparently commonplace grape 99

PEOPLE - Since 1975 the company has developed the lucid insight of Guerrino Fongaro. First through his son Giancarlo, now through Giancarlo's sons Matteo and Alessandro.

VINEYARDS - The durella grape is difficult and delicate, requiring soil and vineyard management systems that respect its moody character. The minerality and acidity of the wines made in the Lessinia hills have a perfect foil in the "classic method". The vineyards, managed using organic methods, fan out over the terrains of volcanic origin round the canteen at altitudes of 300-500 meters. The vines are trained with the classic Veronese pergola system.

WINES - With the introduction of new undosed spumantes, the range is now complete and offers a unique chance to taste the various versions of Durello. Only very low amounts of sulfur are added. The fruit of 60 months' resting on yeasts, **Lessini Durello M. Cl. Pas Dosé Et. Nera Ris. 2006** (○ 7,000 bt) has exceptional volume and length. The best wine of the bunch was **Lessini Durello M. Cl. Pas Dosé Et. Verde 2009** (○ 20,000 bt), very mineral, edgy and dry with burgeoning complexity. Aged for 42 months, **Lessini Durello M. Cl. Et. Nera Ris. 2007** (○ 11,000 bt) is mature, spicy and balsamic. **Lessini Durello M. Cl. Et. Viola 2009** (○ 22,000 bt) is focused and racy, but needs more time in the cellar. **Lessini Durello M. Cl. Et. Grigia 2009** (○ 17,000 bt) is a leisurely, pleasant tipple.

FERTILIZERS natural manure, green manure	
PLANT PROTECTION copper and sulphur	
WEED CONTROL mechanical	
YEASTS selected	
GRAPES 100% estate-grown	
CERTIFICATION organic	

Monte Tondo €

Via San Lorenzo, 89
tel. 045 7680347
www.montetondo.it
info@montetondo.it

Leonildo Pieropan

Via Camuzzoni, 3
tel. 045 6190171
www.pieropan.it
info@pieropan.it

---

25 ha - 200,000 bt

40 ha - 380,000 bt

PEOPLE - Gino Magnabosco is the soul of Monte Tondo. An indefatigable worker, in just a short period of time he has created a modern, efficient cellar cum tourist accommodation center. The present facility was completely renovated in 2000 with state-of-the-art technologies. Gino's daughters Stefania and Marta attend to the sales side of the business, while his son Luca helps him in the vineyards and the cellar.

VINEYARDS - In the 1980s the winery focused on the purchase and reorganization of vineyards in the best Soave winegrowing areas. More recently it has shifted its attention to red wines, planting five hectares of vines on the white calcareous soil up in the hills at Campiano. The white grapes come from Monte Tondo, where the soil is calcareous, and from the two vineyards on the volcanic Foscarino, parts of which are terraced and grow old pergolas on dizzily steep slopes.

WINES - The Soaves we tasted were full of character, well-structured and lively. **Soave Cl. Sup. Foscarin Slavinus 2010** (○ 12,000 bt) was first-rate. The fruit of a late harvest and fermentation in stainless steel and wood, it is spicy and mineral, full of thrust and acidity, with a finesse that supports it through its long finish. We were also highly impressed by Soave Cl. Monte Tondo 2011 (○ 30,000 bt), made with garganega grapes, which was approachable and charismatic — an excellent Everyday Wine. Reciotto di **Soave Nettare di Bacco 2009** (○ 3,000 bt) was racy. We also liked **Valpolicella San Pietro 2010** (● 8,000 bt) and the delightfully warm and refreshing **Amarone della Valpolicella 2008** (● 4,000 bt).

> **slow wine** **SOAVE CL. CASETTE FOSCARIN 2010** (○ 15,000 bt) A wonderful, citrusy, taut, deep wine of great minerality. A reward for the passion and respect for tradition of the people who made it.

66 A vast terroir isn't always a synonym of great wines. You also need great winemakers capable of making sensitive use of the fruits of the earth. Pieropan has never been a lover of compromise and it's thanks to his obstinacy that Soave can be described today as one of the great Italian whites 99

PEOPLE - Pieropan is universally renowned for his whites — wines whose class is crystal-clear, capable of amazing even decades on. A few years ago, Leonildo and his wife Teresita set up a new winery in Valpolicella for their sons Dario and Andrea to manage. With growing skill and sureness of touch, the two are now showing how to make elegant wines while still remaining true to tradition.

VINEYARDS - The Soave crus are all converting to organics and are subject to constant care. In the vineyard of La Rocca, for example, new garganega vines from a massal selection in situ are being plantd with vertical trellising. The aim is to increase variability within each micro-zone.

WINES - The excellent 2010 vintage treated us to Soave Cl. Calvarino 2010 (○ 46,000 bt), which has a sharp taste profile. Edgy, fine and deep, we'll remember it for a long time as one of the most dynamic versions ever. Which is why it's a Great Wine. It's fascinating to compare it with **Soave Cl. La Rocca 2010** (○ 36,000 bt), which is more opulent on the palate and solar without losing a subtle streak of acidity. **Soave Cl. 2011** (○ 320,000 bt) is a good wine but pays the price of a relatively poor vintage. **Amarone della Valpolicella Vigna Garzon 2009** (● 8,100 bt) is delicate and elegant, mineral and floral. It's still young, however, and has yet to achieve its full potential. **Valpolicella Sup. Ruberpan 2009** (● 16,000 bt) is original and balsamic — and it works.

FERTILIZERS natural manure	FERTILIZERS none
PLANT PROTECTION chemical, copper and sulphur	PLANT PROTECTION copper and sulphur
WEED CONTROL chemical, mechanical	WEED CONTROL mechanical
YEASTS selected	YEASTS selected, native
GRAPES 100% estate-grown	GRAPES 100% estate-grown
CERTIFICATION none	CERTIFICATION organic

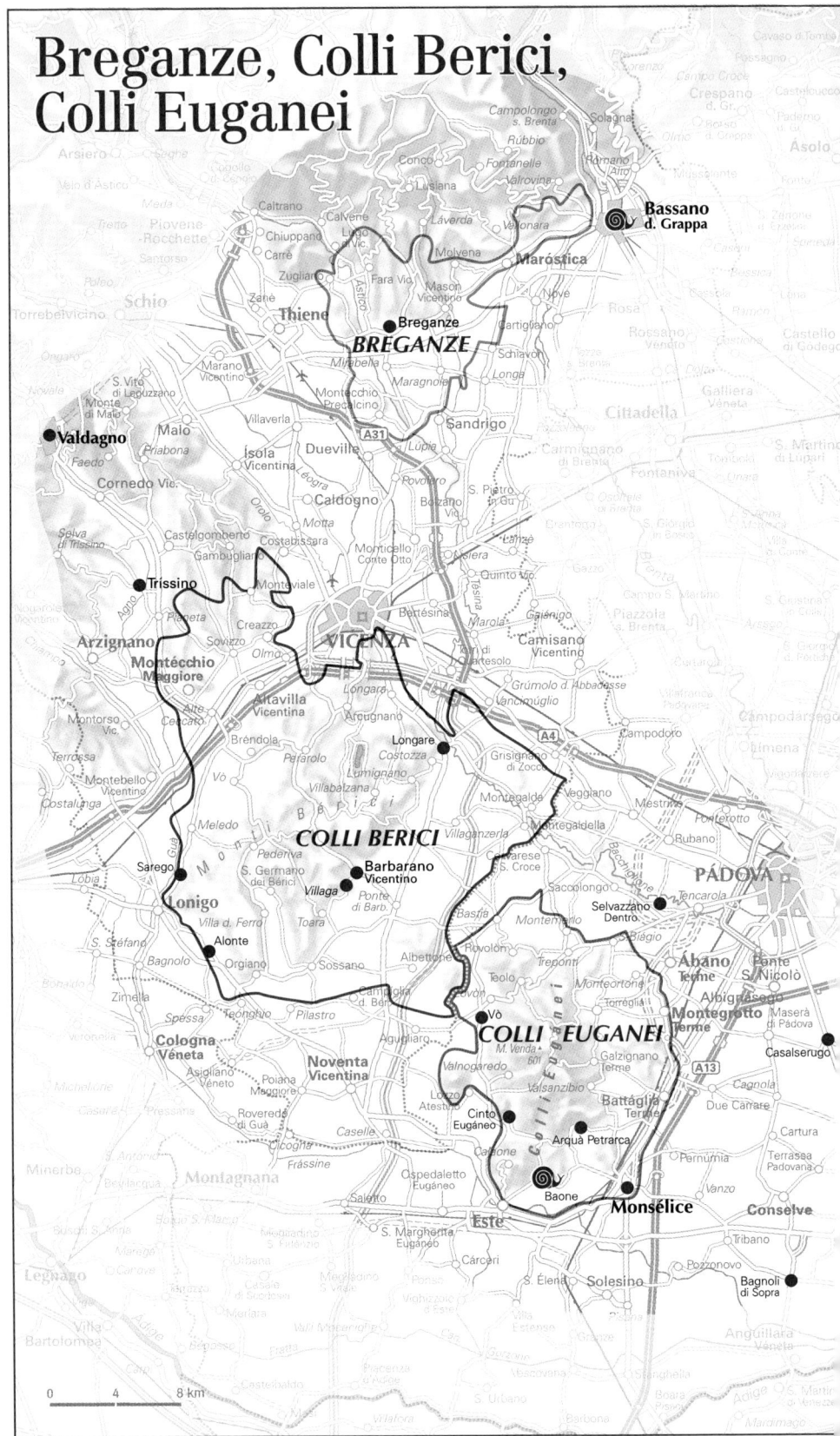

Breganze, Colli Berici, Colli Euganei

0   4   8 km

ARQUÀ PETRARCA (PD)

Vignalta

Via Scalette, 23
tel. 0429 777305
www.vignalta.it
info@vignalta.it

50 ha - 250,000 bt   **10% discount**

PEOPLE - The Euganean Hills used to be a place where wine was sold unbottled, hence remained anonymous. Luca Gomiero, the owner Vignalta was one of the first to champion quality winemaking. His cellar is hewn out of the rock in the hills of Arquà Petrarca, a lovely village dedicated to the poet Petrarch, and is managed by Michele Montecchio.

VINEYARDS - Vignalta's vineyards fan out over the exceptional surrounding terrains. From the outset every grape was recorded according to soil and climate. The various parcels differ one from another and are situated in the best winegrowing districts of the Euganean Hills. The Bordeaux blend is preferred to the varietal for the reds. The Gemola vineyard stands out for its fantastic loose volcanic soil, rich in organic substances and minerals, whereas flakey white soil dominates at Arquà, which gives the wines their potency and structure.

WINES - The company adopts a straightforward style with careful use of wood. Elegance is the main quality of Colli Euganei Gemola 2007 (● merlot, cabernet franc; 26,000 bt), silky and lingering with nuances of herbs and iodine that denote a strong sense of place. It's a classic and, in our opinion, a Great Wine. Creamy and potent, **Marrano 2007** (● cabernet sauvignon, merlot; 26,000 bt) is also a top-notch wine, as is **Colli Euganei Arquà 2009** (● 11,000 bt) with its scents of pepper and ferrous notes. We were impressed by the character of the stylish, complex **Pinot Nero 2009** (● 1,500 bt), cellarable but already irresistible — one of the best we've ever tasted in the region, in fact. **Colli Euganei Moscato Sirio 2011** (○ 10,000 bt) is dry, light and edgy, while **Colli Euganei Agno Casto 2011** (○ 3.500 bt) stands out for length and structure.

FERTILIZERS organic-mineral
PLANT PROTECTION chemical, copper and sulphur, organic
WEED CONTROL chemical, mechanical
YEASTS selected
GRAPES 100% estate-grown
CERTIFICATION none

BAONE (PD)

Ca' Orologio

Via Ca' Orologio, 7 A
tel. 0429 50099
www.caorologio.it
info@caorologio.com

12 ha - 28,000 bt   **10% discount**

❝ A city dweller in love with the countryside, Maria Gioia has reinvented herself as a winemaker with clear ideas who applies the values she firmly believes in; namely great respect for the rhythms of nature, organic management of her vineyards and hospitality towards visitors ❞

PEOPLE - Maria Gioia bought the Ca' Orologio estate in 1995, and soon picked up the ropes of the winemaking profession. Now she manages the place in partnership with Luigi Bertazzo, the old estate manager and cellarman. Besides making wine, she also runs an attractive agriturismo with rooms in her historical villa.

VINEYARDS - New vineyards have been planted round the initial two hectares of very old vineyards on the spurs of Monte Cecilia, behind the cellar on limestone soil. The older Calaone vineyard is situated in the hills on the other side of Baone on soil of volcanic origin. After being managed using organic methods, the two different holdings have now been converted to biodynamics.

WINES - Despite a difficult year with a lot of heavy rain during the harvest season, the 2010 kept the immediate, forthright tone that has always been their distinctive and original leitmotiv. Warm and caressing, **Colli Euganei Rosso Calaòne 2010** (● merlot, cabernet, barbera; 12,000 bt) has very ripe fruit and well-rounded flavor. **Relògio 2010** (● carmenère, cabernet franc; 4,000 bt) is more austere and linear with confident progression and a dry, solid finish. **Lunisole 2010** (● barbera; 2,000 bt) is lighter in structure but fresher, while the white **Salaròla 2011** (○ friulano, moscato, riesling; 3,500 bt) comes with its usual intriguing aromatic tones and a taut, tangy finish.

FERTILIZERS biodynamic preparations, green manure
PLANT PROTECTION organic, copper and sulphur
WEED CONTROL mechanical
YEASTS native
GRAPES 100% estate-grown
CERTIFICATION organic

Il Filò Delle Vigne

Via Terralba, 14
tel. 0429 56243
www.ilfilodellevigne.it
info@ilfilodellevigne.it

Il Mottolo

Via Comezzara, 13
tel. 347 9456155
www.ilmottolo.it
ilmottolo@fastwebnet.it

20 ha - 50,000 bt | 10% discount

PEOPLE - Il Filò delle Vigne embarked on its adventure in the 1990s. It is managed by Carlo Giordani and Nicolò Voltan who, guided by the steady hands of cellarman Matteo Zanaica, agronomist Filippo Giannone and enologist Andrea Boaretti, have made it one of the most important wineries in the area. The first bottles were released in 1995 and the principal grape is cabernet, cultivated in a terroir acknowledged as being of superior level.

VINEYARDS - The company is situated southeast of Monte Cecilia inside the breathtakingly beautiful Euganean Hills Park. It owns 20 hectares of vineyards and the red grapes grown range from the classic cabernet sauvignon e franc, carmenère (explosive here) and merlot to a group of old experimental varieties. The white grapes grown are tocai, garganega, moscato bianco, moscato fior d'arancio and riesling italico.

WINES - Colli Euganei Cabernet Borgo delle Casette Ris. 2008 (● 10,000 bt) captures the nature of the grape wonderfully. Made from old vines, finely aromatic, redolent of flowers and herbs, it is complex and packed with huge potential. The body is velvety, rich in flesh, juicy and permeated by lingering hints of blackcurrant and licorice — truly a Great Wine. Unlike the latter **Colli Euganei Cabernet Vigna Cecilia di Baone Ris. 2008** (● 10,000 bt) is aged on cement as opposed to wood, but it's on the same wavelength and is just as effective with its notes of ripe fruit and spicy nuances. The excellent **Calto delle Fate 2009** (○ chardonnay, tocai, riesling, moscato; 4,000 bt) has refined oaky tones. On its debut release, **Terralba di Baone 2011** (○ tocai, chardonnay, riesling, pinot bianco; 3,600 bt) proved very good too.

6 ha - 15,000 bt | 10% discount

PEOPLE - Il Mottolo is a young winery in the Euganean Hills. Since it was formed in 2003 it has rapidly reached heights of quality for the denomination. Its passionate owners Sergio Fortin and Roberto Dalla Libera weren't winemakers by profession but they've been quick to learn this challenging art. They are backed up by the invaluable assistance of enologist Flavio Prà, agronomist Filippo Giannone and cellar man Nicola Sattin, not to mention that of their wives Marisa and Renata.

VINEYARDS - The company owns 12 hectares of land of which six are vineyards, the rest woodland and olive groves. The properties are situated on calcareous-clayey land in the communes of Baone and Arquà Petrarca, southeast of the Euganean Hills, in what can be defined a fully-fledged cru. The vines are trained using the Guyot, spurred cordon and the local *casarsa* systems.

WINES - The use of sulfur is reduced to a minimum, whereas wood is used skillfully. It's worth stressing the high level of quality and value for money of the entire range. Colli Euganei Merlot Comezzara 2010 (● 4,500 bt) is very good indeed, with plump fruit, spices and body. It fully deserves to be an Everyday Wine. With its vertical floral aromas and grassiness, **Colli Euganei Cabernet Vigna Marè 2010** (● 3,500 bt) is just as good. Now a member of the local wine elite **Colli Euganei Rosso Serro 2009** (● merlot, cabernet sauvignon, carmenère; 3,500 bt) has fine, elegant aromas, great freshness and drinkability now a member of the local wine elite plus it's built to last. The superlative **Vignanima 2009** (● carmenère, merlot; 1,500 bt) is rich in fruit and toastiness. Impressive too was **Colli Euganei Moscato Fior d'Arancio Passito Vigna del Pozzo 2010** (○ 1,100 bt), a passito that knows what it's about.

FERTILIZERS natural manure	FERTILIZERS none
PLANT PROTECTION chemical	PLANT PROTECTION chemical, copper and sulphur
WEED CONTROL mechanical	WEED CONTROL mechanical
YEASTS selected	YEASTS selected
GRAPES 100% estate-grown	GRAPES 100% estate-grown
CERTIFICATION none	CERTIFICATION none

Vigneto Due Santi

Viale Asiago, 174
tel. 0424 502074
www.vignetoduesanti.it
info@vignetoduesanti.it

18 ha - 100,000 bt | **10% discount**

66 Adriano and Stefano Zonta aren't the two saints you see on the label. No, they are two charismatic winemakers who amaze for the rigor and passion they manage to pack into their excellent, reasonably priced wine 99

PEOPLE - Adriano and Stefano, consummate interpreters of the Bassano terroir, have raised the standard and reputation of its wines. At their cellar they lay on a real royal welcome, always ready to share a glass of wine with anyone who happens to be passing through.

VINEYARDS - The vineyards fan out in the area that stretches from Marsan to the mouth of the Valsugana, near Bassano. The oldest were planted 65 years ago and have not been grubbed with chemicals for a long time. All the most recent plantings were made with great effort and at considerable cost to conserve the profile of the hills intact. This type of decision signifies respect for the land.

WINES - The Zontas favor a linear, fresh style, hence drinkability. The exemplary **Breganze Merlot 2009** (● 25,000 bt) is at once complex and authoritative and easy and accessible. It's a perfect Everyday Wine. **Breganze Cabernet 2009** (● 25,000 bt) is slightly less immediate, stiffer and more austere. **Breganze Bianco Rivana 2011** (○ friulano; 10,000 bt) is stylish, while **Malvasia Campo di Fiori 2011** (○ 4,000 bt) is plump and spicy. **Breganze Torcolato 2007** (○ 1,500 bt) is powerful and sweet.

slow wine **IL BERGANZE CABERNET VIGNETO DUE SANTI 2009** (● 15,000 bt) Arguably the best version ever. Albeit still young, it stands out for its fresh aromas of flowers and fruit and its refined, forceful palate.

FERTILIZERS natural manure
PLANT PROTECTION chemical, copper and sulphur
WEED CONTROL mechanical
YEASTS selected, native
GRAPES 100% estate-grown
CERTIFICATION none

La Montecchia Conte Emo Capodilista

Via Montecchia, 16
tel. 049 637294
www.lamontecchia.it
lamontecchia@lamontecchia.it

30 ha - 130,000 bt | **10% discount**

PEOPLE - Giordano Emo Capodilista, the last representative of a noble family with a centuries-old tradition, manages his historic vineyards with passion, acumen and vitality. The vineyards are situated round the cellar and the marvelous Villa Capodilista, in Selvazzano, and in the Baone district on land acquired in 2001.

VINEYARDS - The land at Baone is dominated by calcareous white rock. For the new plantings, it has been possible to preserve the old vine rows and recover the abandoned terraces, surrounded by woodland and olive trees. The 10-hectare vineyard is given over mainly to cabernet sauvignon and carmenère, which thrive on the soil here. At Montecchia, a cooler area, the soil is made up of friable trachyte. Cabernet franc and merlot are grown on one side of the hill, moscato fior d'arancio is grown lower down on the other. The vineyards are managed using virtually organic methods with no chemical weed killers or systemic treatments.

WINES - The symbol of the company is a Great Wine, Colli Euganei Rosso Villa Capodilista 2009 (● 6,500 bt; 21). It has a gutsy, austere, fruit-rich palate with very fine texture and elegant tanginess. **Colli Euganei Cabernet Sauvignon Ireneo 2009** (● 6,000 bt) has a no-nonsense character and is full-bodied and dry on the palate, while **Baon 2008** (● cabernet sauvignon, merlot; 6,000 bt) has richer pulp, but still possesses elegance and finesse. The young **Cabernet Franc Godimondo 2011** (● 24,000 bt) is floral and slightly vegetal on the nose with great raciness and drinkability. Last but not least, **Colli Euganei Fior d'Arancio Spumante 2011** (○ 30,000 bt) is very agreeable with measured sweetness and great fragrance, while **Colli Euganei Fior d'Arancio Passito Donna Daria 2010** (○ 4,000 bt) is well-rounded and well-balanced.

FERTILIZERS none
PLANT PROTECTION chemical, copper and sulphur
WEED CONTROL mechanical
YEASTS selected, native
GRAPES 100% estate-grown
CERTIFICATION none

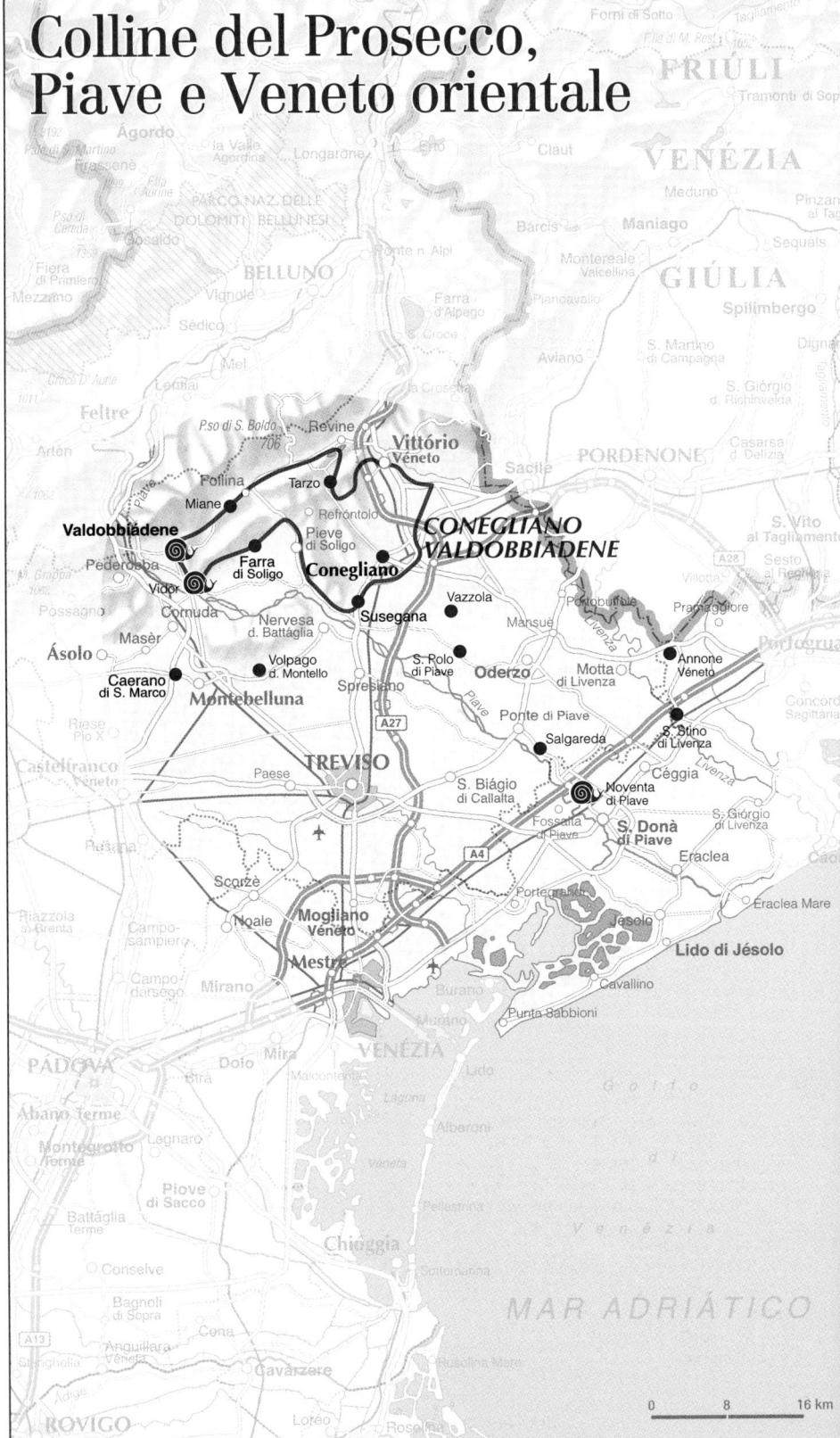

Colline del Prosecco,
Piave e Veneto orientale

FARRA DI SOLIGO (TV)

Andreola

Località Col San Martino
Via Cal Longa, 52
tel. 0438 989379
www.andreola.eu
info@andreola.eu

35 ha - 6,000,000 bt	10% discount

PEOPLE - "Ours is an agriculture with traditional bases updated to the present context. Everything nature gives you, you have to keep." Stefano Pola is the thoughtful owner of this impeccable cellar to which he dedicates his meticulous labor. His father Nazareno works in the vineyard. Stefano explained to us that the new cellar allows him to manage every single productive phase in total autonomy and thus preserve the delicate aromas of the glera grape without oxidation.

VINEYARDS - The vineyards run in a ten-kilometer line between the villages of Valdobbiadene and Farra. They are split into over 60 micro-parcels, patiently bought up over the years, all very different one form another, all kept with hard work and passion. Many, like the Dorupo selections, perch on steep hillsides. Mas de Fer is one of the highest vineyards in the zone and is situated at an altitude of 450 meters, where the gradient is sharp and temperature swings are huge.

WINES - The wines are characterized by stylistic unity and clear-cut aromas and all are at the top of their respective categories. We were particularly impressed by **Valdobbiadene Sup. di Cartizze 2011** (○ 15,000 bt), which has ripe fruit and a potent, salty palate. Then comes **Valdobbiadene Prosecco Sup. Extra Dry Mas de Fer 2011** (○ 16,000 bt), the most mineral and exotic of the series. Excellent too is **Valdobbiadene Prosecco Sup. Brut 26esimo I 2011** (○ 12,000 bt), sincere, fine, taut and vibrant. Notes of almonds and white-fleshed fruit usher in Valdobbiadene Prosecco Sup. Brut Dirupo 2011 (○ 100,000 bt), a lovely Everyday Wine, softer than the last-mentioned and very well-balanced. **Valdobbiadene Prosecco Sup. Dry Millesimato 2011** (○ 60,000 bt) is big-hearted and generous, complex and deep. **Valdobbiadene Prosecco Sup. Extra Dry Dirupo 2011** (○ 80,000 bt) has delicate aromas.

FERTILIZERS natural manure
PLANT PROTECTION chemical, copper and sulphur
WEED CONTROL mechanical
YEASTS selected
GRAPES 15% bought in
CERTIFICATION none

NOVENTA DI PIAVE (VE)

Tessère

Località Santa Teresina
Via Bassette, 51
tel. 0421 320438
www.tessereonline.it
info@tessereonline.it

15 ha - 50,000 bt	10% discount

❝ In love with raboso in every shape and form, a sensitive interpreter of the environment and an active supporter of the local culture, a promoter of "social work" to reveal the other face of agriculture — Emanuela Bincoletto is all this and more ❞

PEOPLE - Emanuela guides the company set up by her father Ilario in 1979 with passion and competence in an attempt to realize the potential of the Piave area in the province of Venice.

VINEYARDS - The vineyards differ in age and are Guyot- and rod and spur-trained. They are situated on the alluvial clay soil of the San Donà area and benefit from their vicinity to the sea. They are managed using organic methods. The grapes are produced with low yields and picked very ripe. The raboso grapes in particular are selected row by row.

WINES - "Raboso takes time," says Emanuela, and the results of her quest for expressiveness confirm the fact. This year she presented two new wines: **Piave Raboso M. Cl. Brut Sui Lieviti Rosato Redentor 2008** (⊙ 1,500 bt), pleasant and deep with notes of brackish water and standout acidity, and **Piave Raboso M. Cl. Brut Redentor 2008** (⊙ 1,500 bt), complex and elegant on the nose with a tangy, creamy bouquet. We liked **Piave Raboso Barbarigo 2007** (● 12.000 bt), aged in oak casks for two years, for its leanness and pleasant spiciness. Aged in steel, the fruity **Piave Raboso Spezier 2009** (● 15,000 bt) is simpler and fresher.

slow wine | **PIAVE RABOSO PASSITO REBECCA 2006** (● 6,000 bt) A wine that condenses Tessère's experimentation into a refined expression of the grape. Spicy and balsamic, this marvelous fusion of sweetness and acidity conjures up the ripeness of grapes and the brackishness of seawater.

FERTILIZERS green manure
PLANT PROTECTION copper and sulphur, organic
WEED CONTROL mechanical
YEASTS selected
GRAPES 100% estate-grown
CERTIFICATION organic

Malibran €

Via Barca II, 63
tel. 0438 781410
www.malibranvini.it
info@malibranvini.it

Casa Coste Piane

Frazione Santo Stefano
Via Coste Piane, 2
tel. 0423 900219
casacostepiane@libero.it

---

7 ha - 90,000 bt | 10% discount

PEOPLE - Young he may be, but Maurizio Favrel has the non-nonsense self-confidence of someone who knows his job. Malibran is to all intents and purposes his baby, the end-result of a project designed to convert the family farm into a productive company. In just a few years the dream has come true and the outfit is now enjoying success thanks to the quality of its wines. The recipe is apparently a simple one, the ingredients being clear ideas, control over the refermentation process and great sensitivity in the vineyard and cellar.

VINEYARDS - The vineyard is the domain of Maurizio's dad Momi, who tends every vine as if it were a child of his. A glera clone, balbi, has been chosen for its optimal quality and because it grows in loose bunches. This avoids rot and helps reduce treatments. Yields are low and the vigor of the vines is held back naturally. The vineyards are vinified separately to develop the distinctive features of each single parcel.

WINES - Maurizio is rigorous and painstaking in every stage in production. Long lees contact produces well-structured wines and avoids the need for invasive interventions. Dry, mineral and sharp, **Valdobbiadene Prosecco Sup. Brut Favrel Cinquegrammi 2011** (○ 3,300 bt) enhances the grape-terroir marriage without taking the shortcut of added sugar. **Valdobbiadene Prosecco Sup. Extra Dry Gorio 2011** (○ 40,000 bt) and **Valdobbiadene Prosecco Sup. Dry Millesimato 2011** (○ 6,600 bt) are measured, soft and balanced. **Valdobbiadene Prosecco Sup. Brut Ruio 2011** (○ 30,000 bt) is exotic.

> **slow wine** Valdobbiadene Prosecco Sup. ColFondo Sottoriva 2011 (○ 8,000 bt) A fruit of traditional refermentation in the bottle, the wine combines personality and aromatic complexity with a tempting, fresh, perfectly mature palate.

---

6 ha - 60,000 bt

 "Farmer? Vine dresser? Winemaker? No, I am and always will be a peasant." That's how Loris Follador defines himself. A man of great sensitivity, he talks about his work, farming, climate change and local history with discretion and irony, peppering his words with quotations from Iranian poets. A genius of culture and passion, he's a unique figure in the wine world **"**

PEOPLE - Loris's sons Adelchi and Raffaele are symbols of continuity in this farming family which, dividing its time between livestock breeding and work in the fields, carries forward an alternative vision of Prosecco.

VINEYARDS - You have to see Loris's vines — old plants, some of which planted 110 years ago, clinging to the sandy conglomerate soil typical of the area — to understand how his wines are born. The Brichet vineyard, which grows on limestone and red earth at an altitude of 450 meters, was recovered and put back in place by Piero, an elderly vine dresser. The roots sink into the soil to absorb the minerals that add zest to the wines.

WINES - Credit where credit is due. Loris Follador has always been a great believer in the bottle refermentation technique, even when everyone else was abandoning it. **Brichet Frizzante...Naturalmente 2011** (○ 5,000 bt) is introvert and moody and still needs time in the bottle. **Valdobbiadene Prosecco Sup. Extra Dry S. Venanzio 2011** (○ 3,500 bt) is designed for people who aren't enamoured of spontaneous refermentation. **Valdobbiadene Prosecco Sup. Tranquillo 2011** (○ 3.000 bt) is the company's only still wine.

> **slow wine** Valdobbiadene Prosecco Sup. Frizzante... Naturalmente 2011 (○ 38,000 bt) Born of a fortunate harvest, a paradigm of the typology with rich complexity. Aromas of pepper and citrus fruit with a mineral streak.

FERTILIZERS organic-mineral, manure pellets, compost
PLANT PROTECTION chemical, copper and sulphur
WEED CONTROL mechanical
YEASTS selected
GRAPES 100% estate-grown
CERTIFICATION none

FERTILIZERS organic-mineral, natural manure
PLANT PROTECTION copper and sulphur
WEED CONTROL chemical
YEASTS native
GRAPES 100% estate-grown
CERTIFICATION none

Silvano Follador

Frazione Santo Stefano
Via Callonga, 11
tel. 0423 900295
www.silvanofollador.it
info@silvanofollador.it

4 ha - 20,000 bt

66 Paring away to get down to the bare essentials, shunning current practices to get to the core of the grape — these bottles sum up an idea of wine that is precise and free and far removed from all forms of standardization 99

PEOPLE - After a few years in which he contented himself with "doing things like everybody else", Silvano Follador, helped by his sister Alberta and his father, figured out that he wasn't happy with the humdrum, "serial" wines he was producing and that's how the process got underway that has turned him into one of the top producers in the area.

VINEYARDS - The two main vineyards are at Cartizze and Saccol, and new ones were planted more recently at San Giovanni. The average age of the vines is very high. The agronomic management is geared, first and foremost, to the defense of biodiversity. Biodynamic practices were introduced recently to boost the cause.

WINES - Grapes are picked by hand, packed into boxes and pressed immediately, after which they undergo long fermentation on the yeasts. These are the two key phases in the life of this cellar. **Valdobbiadene Prosecco Sup. Brut Nature 2011** (○ 12,000 bt), from a vintage that digs deep into the soil, is essential yet, at once, rich in texture, fine, dry and tangy. **M. Cl. Dosaggio Zero 2010** (○ 8,000 bt) fuses the delicate nuances of the grape with the complexity of the "classic method".

slow wine VALDOBBIADENE SUP. DI CARTIZZE BRUT NATURE 2011 (○ 6, 600 bt) Splendid! A singular example of how much a terroir can give without sugars stepping in to mediate. The texture is lively, vibrant, long and mineral in the noblest meaning of the term, bereft of any elements that might mask the wine's strong character.

FERTILIZERS natural manure, biodynamic preparations
PLANT PROTECTION copper and sulphur, organic
WEED CONTROL mechanical
YEASTS selected, native
GRAPES 100% estate-grown
CERTIFICATION none

Sorelle Bronca

Frazione Colbertaldo
Via Martiri, 20
tel. 0423 987201 987009
www.sorellebronca.com
info@sorellebronca.com

20 ha - 250,000 bt   10% discount

66 A company that moves at its own pace, day by day with a business strategy based on well pondered, modern decisions — but without ever losing sight of the values of tradition 99

PEOPLE - Sisters Antonella and Ersiliana Bronca inherited their family firm 30 years ago. That's when they embarked on a journey of quality and respect for the land. A vital role in all this has been played by Antonella's husband, Piero Balcon, who follows the vineyards and the cellar firsthand in an enlightened, accomplished manner.

VINEYARDS - The main property is situated at Rua di Feletto: 13 hectares, mostly given over to red grapes and managed using substantially organic methods. Other parcels of land are cultivated on the steep slopes round Colbertaldo. One such is the historical Particella 68, a very old, south-facing vineyard that enjoys perfect ventilation.

WINES - All Proseccos are bottle-fermented with the addition of must apart from **Valdobbiadene Prosecco Sup. Brut Particella 68 2011** (○ 10,000 bt), which is made entirely from must to preserve the freshness of the grapes and their suite of aromas. It is plump with fruit and has a deep, racy, dry finish. Fragrant and taut, **Valdobbiadene Prosecco Sup. Brut 2011** (○ 100,000 bt) has a lovely dry, citrusy finish. **Valdobbiadene Prosecco Sup. Extra Dry 2011** (○ 100,000 bt) is softer and not excessively sweet, spacious and juicy on the palate. **Colli di Conegliano Bianco Delico 2011** (○ 2,400 bt) offers intense notes of citrus fruit on the nose, a progressive palate and massive minerality. **Colli di Conegliano Rosso Ser Bele 2009** (● cabernet sauvignon e franc, merlot, marzemino; 4,000 bt) is warm in style, mouthfilling with beautifully ripe fruit.

FERTILIZERS natural manure, green manure
PLANT PROTECTION copper and sulphur
WEED CONTROL mechanical
YEASTS selected, native
GRAPES 100% estate-grown
CERTIFICATION converting to organics

FRIULI VENEZIA GIULIA

The Friuli wine world prompts two considerations for the moment. On the one hand, a rapid increase in production and sales has transformed a significant portion of the regions ampelographic base, especially in the Friuli Grave, Annia, Latisana, Aquileia denominations, where large new glera vineyards have been planted for the production of Prosecco. On the other, we note a sort of indolence towards what appear to be new challenges for Italian winegrowing: climate change and, as a consequence, higher temperatures. The phenomenon manifested itself clearly, in certain respects dramatically, in August 2011 and again in summer 2012. This complex problem needs to be studied in-depth and demands effective solutions. It will no longer be enough to simply anticipate the grape harvest, since this practice usually leaves the wines with very different, often unconvincing profiles and identities.

We had proof of this tasting white wines from the 2011 vintage, which we generally found a little grassy with poorly defined aromas and lacking in the complexity of palate-lengthening flavor that lengthens the palate. There were of course plenty of exceptions to this general rule, thanks mainly to producers who devote proper time and attention to work in the field. Even faced with heatwaves worthy of the Sahara, relatively old, healthy, deep-planted, well-balanced vineyards were able to activate defense mechanisms and allow their owners to harvest successfully at the traditional time of year.

snails 🐌

123	MEROI
123	MIANI
124	I CLIVI
126	LE DUE TERRE
127	RONCO DEL GNEMIZ
127	VIGNAI DA DULINE
129	BORGO SAN DANIELE
131	EDI KEBER
134	KANTE
135	SKERK
135	ZIDARICH
136	GRAVNER
137	LA CASTELLADA
137	DAMIJAN PODVERSIC
138	RADIKON
139	SKERLJ

bottles 🍾

121	VISTORTA
125	LE VIGNE DI ZAMÒ
130	COLLE DUGA
131	ISIDORO POLENCIC
132	DORO PRINCIC
132	DARIO RACCARO
133	RONCO DEL GELSO
134	VENICA & VENICA
138	VIE DI ROMANS
139	ZUANI

coins €

121	BORTOLUSSO
124	VISINTINI
126	PIZZULIN
130	DRIUS
133	FRANCESCO VOSCA

Terre di pianura

AUSTRIA

SLOVENIA

CROAZIA

VÉNETO

Weissenbach · Kreuzen · Hermagor · Nötsch

Pso di M. Croce · Battendorf · Tropolach · Paularo · Pontebba · Malborghetto

Comèlico Sup · S. Stéfano di Cad. · Sappada · Ravascletto · Paluzza · Bevorchiàns · Valbruna · Cave d. Predil

Candide Cas. · Rigolato · foto · Tarvisio

Auronzo di Cadore · Vigo di Cad. · Comeglians · Arta Terme · Móggio Udin. · Chiusaforte

Lózzo di Cadore · Lorenzago di Cad. · Sàuris · Villa Santina · Sella Nevea (Bischl)

Calalzo di Cadore · Pso d. Mau. · Forni di Sopra · Ampezzo · Tolmezzo · Prato · Bovec (Plezzo)

Pieve di Cadore · Forni di Sotto · Tagliamento · Cavazzo Càrnico · Carnia · Resia · Pso di Tanamea

Perarolo di Cad. · Fld d. M. Rosso · Venzone · SLOVENIA

Cimolàis · Tramonti di Sopra · Gemona d. Friuli · Luséver · Kobarid (Caporetto)

Erto · Clàut · Meduno · Osoppo · Artegna · Tarcento · Platischis · Drenchia

Bàrcis · Maniago · Pinzano al Tagl. · Nimis · Adamis · Maserolis · Pulfero

Montereale Valcellina · Sequàls · Tricésimo · Faèdis · Cividale d. Friuli

Farra d'Alpago · Pancevàrio · S. Daniele d. Friuli · Fagagna · Pieve (Piçâs)

Aviano · Spilimbergo · Rive d'Arcano · Dignano · ÚDINE · Cormòns

S. Martino di Campagna · S. Giórgio d. Richinvelda · S. Martino al Tagliamento · Basiliano · A23

S. Quirino · Valvasone · Casarsa d. Delizia · Codróipo · Mortegliano · Pavia di Údine · Gradisca d'Isonzo

Vittório Veneto · Canéva · PORDENONE · Passariano · Castions di Strada · Palmanova

Sacile · Prata di Pordenone · S. Vito al Tagliamento · Rivignano · Gonàrs · Bagnária Arsa · Villa Vicentina · Rónchi dei Legionari

Conegliano · Villalta · Sesto al Régbena · A28 · Muzzana · S. Giórgio di Negaro · Cervignano d. Friuli · Monfalcone

Oderzo · Portobuffolè · Pravisdómini · Tuignano · Carlino · Aquiléia

A27 · Motta di Livenza · Portogruaro · Concordia Sagittaria · Marano Lagunare · Ausa-Corno · Grado

Ceggia · Lignano Sabbiadoro

S. Biágio di Callalta · S. Donà di Piave · S. Giórgio di Livenza · Cáorle · Bibione · Lignano Riviera

Eraclea · Eraclea Mare

VENÉZIA · Jésolo · Lido di Jésolo

Murano · Burano · Cavallino

Punta Sabbioni · CROAZIA · Umag/Umago

VENÉZIA · Lido · MAR ADRIÀTICO

Laguna · Alberoni

Venézia · Malamocco

Pellestrina

Chióggia · Sottomarina

0   8   16 km

CARLINO (UD)

Bortolusso €
Via Oltregorgo, 10
tel. 0431 67596
www.bortolusso.it
info@bortolusso.it

SACILE (PN)

Vistorta

Via Vistorta, 82
tel. 0434 71135
www.vistorta.it
vistorta@vistorta.it

40 ha - 150,000 bt

34 ha - 200,000 bt

PEOPLE - This family company, run by siblings Clara and Sergio Bortolusso, is one of the most important in Friuli in terms of output and value for money. The cellar is beautifully located in a nature reserve near Marano Lagunare. The Bortolussos are helped by enologist Luigino De Giuseppe and consultant agronomist Carlo Petrussi.

VINEYARDS - The vineyards are all situated in southern Friuli, an area of plainland rich in spring water and, in the past, of reclamation and deforestation work. The fertile alluvial soil is rich in clay, while the influence of the Adriatic and proximity, as the crow flies, of the Carso create good ventilation and sharp night-to-day temperature swings. All 40 hectares of vineyard are Guyot-trained.

WINES - The microclimate of the plain with its marine influence and temperature fluctuations helps concentrate aromas. The consistent quality of the aromatic and semi-aromatic grapes of this part of the regions is no coincidence. Proof of the fact is Friuli Annia Sauvignon 2011 (O 13,000 bt) whose elegant aromatic profile impressed us very favorably indeed. The fresh, juicy, stylish, deeply mineral palate closes the circle with excellent drinkability. It's a really good Everyday Wine. The exceptionally balanced **Friuli Annia Malvasia 2011** (O 10,000 bt) performed as well as ever. Another well-crafted wine is **Traminer Aromatico 2011** (O 10,000 bt). **Friuli Annia Friulano 2011** (O 13,000 bt) has a deliciously citrusy palate with a pleasurably bitter finish.

PEOPLE - After graduating in Agricultural Sciences and a lengthy experience in Bordeaux, where he owns Château Greysac, Brandino Brandolini d'Adda — a descendant of the family that has owned the estate for almost two centuries — took over the reins of the company and made it a model. Production manager Alec Ongaro, who can count upon the consultancy of French enologist Samuel Tinon, has also done his bit.

VINEYARDS - At Vistorta they cultivate only merlot, the most suitable variety for its poor, pebbly soil. In this single plot, plantings and clones vary substantially, hence an intelligent prolongation of the harvest and grapes with highly complex characteristics. The vines and the farm's other crops are managed using strictly organic methods.

WINES - The vineyards that the company manages in the Cordignano zone on the border with the Veneto region yield the grapes for a nice range of white wines. Friuli Grave Pinot Grigio 2011 (O 50,000 bt), simple and well-rounded with intense notes of fresh fruit and bread crust, is sapid and dry on the palate. It's a convincing Everyday Wine. **Friuli Grave Chardonnay 2011** (O 20,000 bt) has a nice flavorful, citrusy character and is fine and dynamic on the palate. Balsamic and slightly vegetal, **Friuli Grave Sauvignon 2011** (O 20,000 bt) is subtle in flavor but with thrust and bite.

> **slow wine** FRIULI GRAVE MERLOT VISTORTA 2009 (● 70,000 bt) A wine that confirms its elegant, typically Bordeaux style. Albeit undemonstrative and subtle, it boasts a long, silkily fine, satisfying palate. It's the end-result of an intelligent project, developed with far-sightedness and rigor.

FERTILIZERS organic-mineral, manure pellets, natural manure, green manure
PLANT PROTECTION chemical, copper and sulphur
WEED CONTROL chemical, mechanical
YEASTS selected, native
GRAPES 100% estate-grown
CERTIFICATION none

FERTILIZERS organic-mineral, manure pellets, natural manure
PLANT PROTECTION copper and sulphur
WEED CONTROL mechanical
YEASTS selected
GRAPES 100% estate-grown
CERTIFICATION organic

Colline orientali

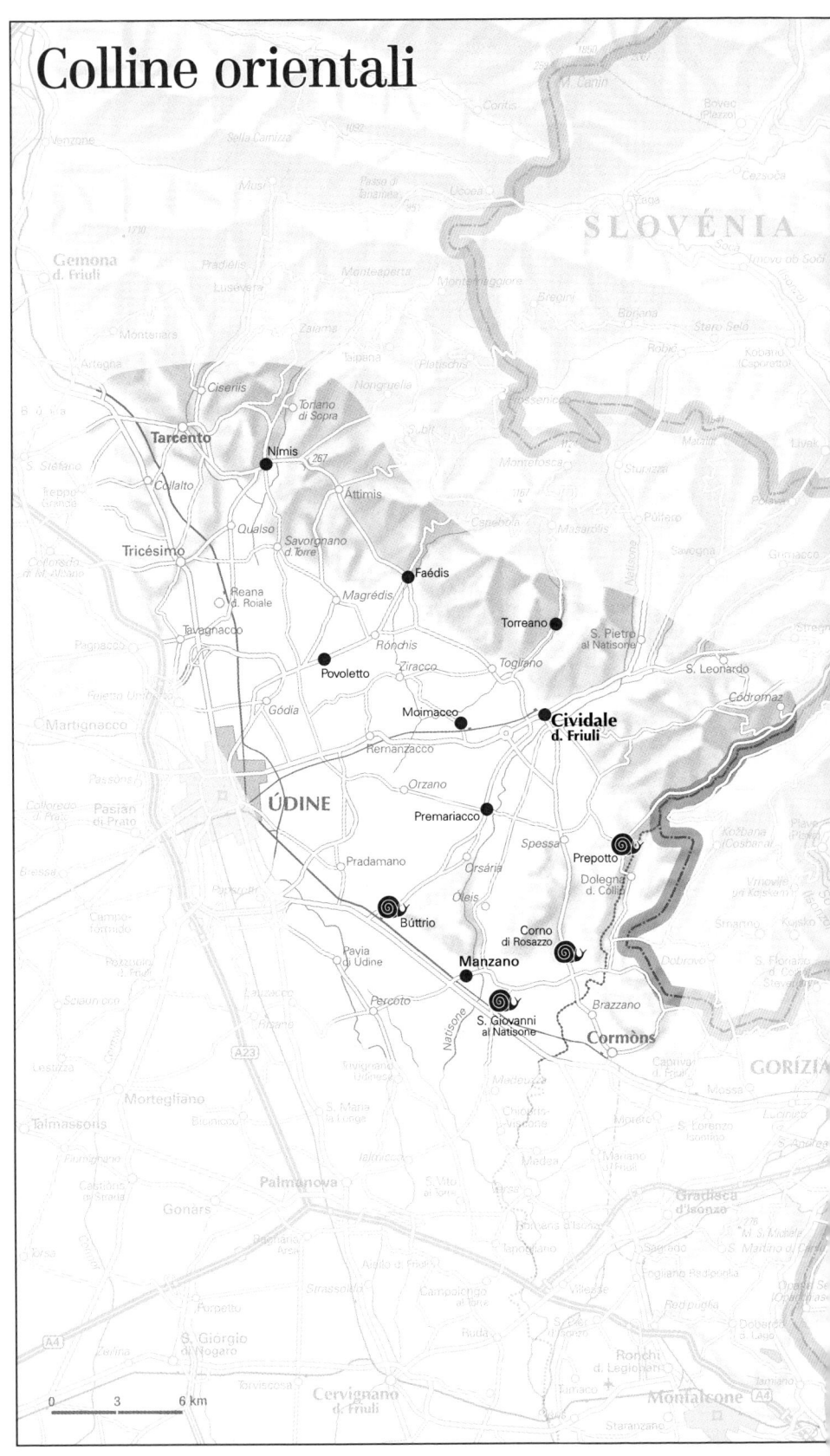

Meroi

Via Stretta, 6 B
tel. 0432 674025
www.meroidavino.com
info@meroidavino.com

12 ha - 25,000 bt   **10% discount**

❝ Paolo Meroi has two passions — good food and good wine — and he combines them to perfection. But life isn't all pleasure. Paolo also has great respect for nature, a sense of belonging and an urge to raise the profile of his land. All of which makes him a virtuous producer ❞

PEOPLE - Paolo Meroi divides his time between the Ristorante Il Parco (which he manages, also working at its huge grill) and the adjacent cellar. Today he can count on the valid collaboration of his young son Damiano.

VINEYARDS - Everything got underway with Dominin, a spectacular natural amphitheater of vines bequeathed to Paolo by his grandfather. The original vineyard has been virtually replicated on the neighboring terraces and the property now covers an area of eight hectares. The red grapes are at the top, the white at the bottom. The grapes from the Le Zitelle vineyard, planted by Paolo his friend and partner Enzo Pontoni (Miani), will soon go into production.

WINES - The dry, austere **COF Ros di Buri 2009** (● merlot; 3,000 bt) is characterized by intense spices and ripe fruit. In **COF Chardonnay 2011** (○ 2,000 bt), the aromas develop headily, with the use of wood making the wine velvety and rich in flavor. **COF Friulano 2011** (○ 2,000 bt) is fresh and creamy, while **COF Picolit 2010** (○ 800 bt) is once more a wine of great elegance.

---

slow wine **COF MERLOT VIGNA DOMININ 2009** (● 1,200 bt) "Can you taste it? This is the stuff of Buttrio, you can only get these tannins here." Paolo stresses the concept in Friulan dialect. Tasting the wine you can't help but agree with him. Pervasive balsamic, leathery notes open the way for a potent, generous, velvety balance of great harmony. A wine that rewards all the hard work carried out in this historic vineyard.

FERTILIZERS natural manure
PLANT PROTECTION copper and sulphur
WEED CONTROL mechanical
YEASTS selected
GRAPES 100% estate-grown
CERTIFICATION none

Miani

Via Peruzzi, 10
tel. 0432 674327

13 ha - 12,000 bt

❝ Obstinacy at work and farming wisdom —Enzo Pontoni elevates these two "virtues" to the highest levels. As you can see from his cellar where the human element is everywhere ❞

PEOPLE - Enzo started making wine in the 1990s, when he took care of his mother Edda Miani's vineyards. He was an *enfant prodige*, capable of producing just a few bottles of very high quality, now sought after in every corner of the world.

VINEYARDS - The main plot is at Buttrio, where the newly planted Le Zitelle is taking shape. The properties at Rosazzo have now been joined by the Gramogliano vineyard, planted in 2007. Enzo has been friendly with his colleague Paolo Meroi for some time, and now they share their work in the vineyards, which often border with each other, and both use organic methods.

WINES - Pontoni vinifies the grapes of each vineyard separately, always using wood casks. It's his way of highlighting the differences between the single zones. Witness the four versions of Friulano. Two wines come from the grapes of old vineyards: **COF Friulano Buri 2011** (○ 1,900 bt), from Buttrio, is full-bodied and fleshy, but with plenty of bite and finesse, whereas **COF Friulano Filip 2011** (○ 1,300 bt), from the vineyards of Rosazzo, is the more elegant and expressive and stands out for its depth and minerality. Two come from new plantings: **COF Friulano Gramogliano 2011** (○ 1,300 bt) has stylish fruit and tanginess, while **COF Friulano 2011** (○ 1,900 bt) has less fruit and more mineral notes with a linear, sharp bouquet. The first edition of **COF Malvasia 2011** (○ 1,000 bt), finally, is finely aromatic with lively acid-tangy tautness, which lengthens the mouthfeel. Enzo shuns awards and accolades; we respect that and have decided not to give him any — though he'd deserve some.

FERTILIZERS natural manure
PLANT PROTECTION copper and sulphur
WEED CONTROL mechanical
YEASTS selected, native
GRAPES 100% estate-grown
CERTIFICATION none

I Clivi

Località Gramogliano, 20
tel. 328 7269979
www.clivi.it
iclivi@gmail.com

10 ha - 40,000 bt | **10% discount**

66 The Zanussos are singular winemakers. They may seem wrapped up in their own business — meaning a very natural approach to viticulture with great respect for the environment and biodiversity — but actually they have a dynamic rapport with the outside, which projects them into the world to spread the words about the products of their land 99

PEOPLE - Ferdinando Zanusso made his debut as a winemaker in 1994 when, after years in Africa, he decided to devote himself to a world he had known previously as an enthusiast. Today he is carrying the story forward with his son Mario.

VINEYARDS - The organic vineyards are situated in Gramogliano, round the cellar, and in Brazzano, in the contiguous Collio area. Both are beautifully located with average ages of over 60 years for the first, Galea, and over 75 for the second, Brazan.

WINES - Mario pursues a precise idea of what wine should be: namely immediate, deep and drinkable. The exciting **Collio Malvasia 2010** (○ 2,000 bt), made with grapes from vines 80 years old, is full-bodied and, at once, gently light with a slightly lemony finish. The pleasantly typical **COF Ribolla Gialla 2011** (○ 10,000 bt) encapsulates all the acidity and zest of the grape. **COF Friulano San Pietro 2011** (○ 10,000 bt) is an engrossing wine.

> **slow wine** **COF VERDUZZO 2011** (○ 3,000 bt) A truly excellent wine that ennobles an often underrated native grape variety. Dry and elegant, it offers aromas of aromatic herbs and yellow pepper. Don't worry if you forget it in the cellar. As our tasting of this old bottle showed, you'll love it just the same in time to come.

FERTILIZERS	none
PLANT PROTECTION	copper and sulphur
WEED CONTROL	mechanical
YEASTS	native
GRAPES	100% estate-grown
CERTIFICATION	organic

Visintini

Via Gramogliano, 27
tel. 0432 755813
www.vinivisintini.com
info@vinivisintini.com

28 ha - 150,000 bt

PEOPLE - The landscape you see arriving in Gramogliano — hills dotted with splendid vineyards and a peacefulness out of this world — is like a picture postcard. Here the Visintini company buildings stand round an old medieval tower. The business is now run by Oliviero, Palmira and Cinzia who are carrying on where their father Andrea left off with great enthusiasm and tenacity. Oliviero tends the vineyards, while Cinzia and Palmira manage sales and public relations.

VINEYARDS - Most of the vineyards are concentrated round the cellar. They include wines half a century old and others planted more recently. More properties are to be found at Rosazzo and another nine hectares are rented. All vineyard are managed with total respect for the environment and Oliviero uses only green biodynamic manure. The company has converted to organics and is currently awaiting certification.

WINES - The cellar deserves a visit if only for the warm welcome and the informal family atmosphere. Plus the fact that the Visintini family's wines stand out for their exceptional value for money. A truly great Everyday Wine is **COF Bianco 2011** (○ pinot bianco, picolit, friulano, sauvignon; 4,000 bt), in which complex aromas are matched by pleasurable, full flavor. Also first-rate is **COF Sauvignon 2011** (○ 26,000 bt), which seduces with its soft pervasiveness. The excellent **COF Friulano 2011** (○ 16,000 bt) is varietal, full-bodied and long, while **COF Pinot Bianco 2011** (○ 4,000 bt) is subtle and elegant. Top of the reds is **COF Refosco P.R. 2010** (● 4,000 bt), harmonious with well-polished tannins.

FERTILIZERS	biodynamic preparations, green manure
PLANT PROTECTION	copper and sulphur
WEED CONTROL	mechanical
YEASTS	selected
GRAPES	10% bought in
CERTIFICATION	converting to organics

Le Vigne di Zamò 🍴

Località Rosazzo
Via Abate Corrado, 4
tel. 0432 759693
www.levignedizamo.com
info@levignedizamo.com

67 ha - 250,000 bt

PEOPLE - The Zamò family has always been a leading player in the enological history of Friuli. Their company, situated next to the Abbey of Rosazzo, is now managed by Pierluigi and Silvano Zamò, sons of the founder Tullio. Adriano Qualizza manages the agricultural side of things and Alberto Toso runs the cellar under the supervision of Franco Bernabei. Recently Oscar Farinetti's Eataly group bought a stake in the company.

VINEYARDS - The property is divided into three zones: there are five hectares of old vineyards of friulano and red grapes at Buttrio, while white grapes thrive in the historic Vigna del Leon vineyard between Ipplis and Rocca Bernarda. The main vineyard lies at the foot of the Abbey of Rosazzo and includes both old and newly planted vineyards. Great care is devoted to the viticulture and some hectares are managed using organic methods.

WINES - The excellent **COF Rosazzo Bianco Ronco delle Acacie 2009** (○ chardonnay, friulano; 9,800 bt) has a wonderfully elegant oxidatively matured style with a fresh palate and a dry finish. Just as flavorful is **COF Merlot Vigne Cinquant'anni 2008** (● 4,400 bt), which is solid and dry with close-knit tannins and a nice fruity reprise on the finish. **COF Friulano 2011** (○ 10,000 bt) is flavorful, simple and effective with a beautifully extended palate. **COF Ribolla Gialla 2011** (○ 30,000 bt) has fresh fruit and a nice citrusy finish. **Zamò Bianco 2011** (○ various white grapes; 13,300 bt), is a reasonably priced, lightly aromatic blend, rich in ripe fresh fruit and crisply tart on the palate. It works well.

slow wine **COF Friulano Vigne Cinquant'anni 2010** (○ 9,400 bt) Elegant and subtle on the nose with a measured palate and a refined citrusy finish. Born in 1996 to make the most of the old Rosazzo vines, this label is a symbol not only of the company, but also for the whole of Friuli.

FERTILIZERS	manure pellets, humus
PLANT PROTECTION	copper and sulphur, organic
WEED CONTROL	mechanical
YEASTS	selected
GRAPES	100% estate-grown
CERTIFICATION	none

Aquila del Torre

Frazione Savorgnano del Torre
Via Attimis, 25
tel. 0432 666428
www.aquiladeltorre.it
info@aquiladeltorre.it

18 ha - 50,000 bt

PEOPLE - In the mid 1990s Claudio Ciani, previously a businessman, made his life's dream come true when he bought the Aquila del Torre estate. Today the company is run by his two children and their families: Michele, a trained enologist and a keen advocate of the biodynamic and organic approaches, Francesca, the sales manager, and her husband Pier, who helps out in the cellar and takes care of the corporate image.

VINEYARDS - On the estate, steep slopes alternate with level ground and vine rows with woods rich in biodiversity to create a spectacle of rare beauty. The terrain is characterized by the classic flysch rocks. Since 2005 the company has been converting to organics, proof of the importance Michele and Francesca attach to the balance between humans and nature. The estate will soon be recognized as an Oasi Naturale, or nature reserve.

WINES - The location of the vineyards and the terrain combine to create notable minerality and vibrant acidity. Sweet fragrances of honey and biscuits characterize **Picolit 2009** (○ 1,200 bt). The dry version, **Oasi 2010** (○ picolit; 1,400 bt), is astonishing: fresh and minty on the nose, it has a subtly soft palate supported by slighlty lactic nuances and hints butter and *fines herbes*. It's a wine to drink without prejudice. **COF Riesling AT 2010** (○ 7,000 bt), finally, is citrusy and dry.

slow wine **COF Friulano AT 2011** (○ 8,000 bt) A fantastic wine with undemonstrative fleshiness, supported by perky acidity, characteristics that make it almost crisp. Subtle and drinkable with a tangy finish, it's a pleasure to drink. This masterful interpretation of the variety is the fruit of painstaking, sustainable viticulture.

FERTILIZERS	natural manure, compost
PLANT PROTECTION	copper and sulphur
WEED CONTROL	mechanical
YEASTS	selected
GRAPES	100% estate-grown
CERTIFICATION	converting to organics

Le Due Terre

Via Roma, 68 B
tel. 0432 713189
fortesilvana@libero.it

5 ha - 18,000 bt

66 United by their great passion for wine, Silvana Forte and Flavio Basilicata have built up a prestigious company. Recognizing their own limits, they do everything with extreme naturalness and measure and respect for the environment 99

PEOPLE - Silvana and Flavio embarked on their life project in 1984 when they bought a piece of land, planted their first vines and renovated an old farmhouse to serve as a cellar. Since then they have turned out rare pearls of enology. Today they are assisted by their daughter Cora.

VINEYARDS - The vineyards run along the slopes of the hill on which the unusual house-cum-cellar, shaped like an upturned ship, stands. The terrain is different on the two sides of the hill, hence the company's name, literally "The Two Lands". On one side, the soil is composed of dark marl, known as *ponca*, on the other of red earth. Flavio has always cultivated his vineyards with a great deal of manual labor and a limited use of chemicals (only copper and sulfur) to preserve the rich biodiversity of the surrounding environment.

WINES - The character-packed **COF Bianco Sacrisassi 2010** (○ friulano, ribolla gialla; 3,300 bt) is subtle and refined on the nose with a measured bouquet. **COF Merlot 2010** (● 2,700 bt) has austere notes of red berries. With its silky texture and gentle flavor, **COF Pinot Nero 2010** (● 3,600 bt) is one of the finest wines made with the pinot grape in Italy.

slow wine | **COF Rosso Sacrisassi 2010** (● 7,000 bt) This blend of refosco and schioppettino in equal parts combines the characteristics of the two native varieties to perfection. Peppery and fruity, the initial impact is one of great finesse, while the palate is ultra-elegant, velvety and soft. The consistency of this wine at every harvest deserves an award in its own right.

FERTILIZERS none
PLANT PROTECTION copper and sulphur
WEED CONTROL mechanical
YEASTS native
GRAPES 100% estate-grown
CERTIFICATION none

Pizzulin

Via Brolo, 43
tel. 0432 713073
www.pizzulin.com
info@pizzulin.com

11 ha - 20,000 bt

PEOPLE - As down-to-earth and blunt as his wines, Denis Pizzulin belongs to a family that has worked in the vineyard for three generations. At the helm since 2003, he has succeeded in the difficult task of adding a personal touch to a company that has been producing wine since the 1920s. Protecting grape varieties and maximum respect for the individual characteristics of the various terrains — these are the main features of the work of this young winemaker and his family.

VINEYARDS - Thanks to the care and attention of Denis and his dad, the company vineyards are thriving famously. They cover an area of 12 hectares: one in Albana with vines 45 and 80 years old; three in Prepotto, on optimally located terraces and vines 12 years old; the remaining seven fan out across bordering districts. The vines are grown at a density of 5,000 per hectare and trained with double-arched canes — choices dictated by loving respect for the natural needs of native grapes.

WINES - Denis's constant quest to capture the character of the terroir to the full comes out in his wines, always very clean and linear. The extremely typical COF Friulano 2011 (○ 3,000 bt) has an elegant bouquet and a long, tangy, refreshing, satisfying palate — a perfect Everyday Wine. **COF Bianco Rarisolchi 2011** (○ 1,000 bt) is elegant too with a tempting, sharp citrusy nose followed by a lean, racy palate. Also memorable is **COF Pinot Bianco 2011** (○ 1,500 bt), which has sweet hints of almond on the nose and a tangy palate with nicely balanced acidity. Moving on to the reds, how can we forget **COF Schioppettino 2009** (● 1,500 bt) with its scents of cherry and deep palate with marked fruit and spicy finish?

FERTILIZERS organic-mineral
PLANT PROTECTION chemical, copper and sulphur
WEED CONTROL mechanical
YEASTS selected
GRAPES 100% estate-grown
CERTIFICATION none

SAN GIOVANNI AL NATISONE (UD)

Ronco del Gnemiz

Via Ronchi, 5
tel. 0432 756238
www.roncodelgnemiz.com
serena@roncodelgnemiz.com

14 ha - 25,000 bt

❝ True to tradition, Serena Palazzolo and Christian Patat make their wine simply and grow grapes organically. They do so by applying the good, old-fashioned rules of farming based on respect for the vines and for nature. Yet their "simplicity" originates complex wines that speak for their land ❞

PEOPLE - Serena Palazzolo inherited the family business in the 1990s. Since then she has run it with her companion Christian Patat and today with her children too.

VINEYARDS - The vineyards surround the house-cum-cellar in one of the loveliest parts of Friuli, a stone's throw from the historic abbey of Rosazzo. Old vineyards, whose grapes are reserved for selections, alternate with younger ones. Their exposures vary, but all grow on soil rich in dark marl.

WINES - All wines are vinified in the classic oxidative manner, without macerations and with the use only of wood, both in fermentation and in aging. The two 2010 Sauvignon selections (Peri and Sol) are not ready yet, but we enjoyed **COF Sauvignon 2011** (○ 2,650 bt), whose taste profile has nothing vegetal about it. It is instead full of fruit with a plump, well developed bouquet of great depth. **COF Pinot Grigio 2011** (○ 1,333 bt) is subtle, refined and extremely elegant. **COF Bianco San Zuan 2011** (○ friulano; 1,640 bt) is dry on the palate with a pleasant note of bitter almonds. The only red tasted, **COF Rosso del Gnemiz 2009** (● cabernet, merlot; 2,425 bt), is austere and impeccable.

> **slow wine** **COF CHARDONNAY 2011** (○ 2,470 bt) A wine that expresses the style of the company that makes it and its terroir of provenance exceptionally well. On the nose it is light but deep with fine notes of straw. Elegant and subtle on the palate, it has an intensely citrusy, mineral finish.

FERTILIZERS natural manure, compost, biodynamic preparations
PLANT PROTECTION copper and sulphur
WEED CONTROL mechanical
YEASTS selected, native
GRAPES 100% estate-grown
CERTIFICATION biodynamic, organic

SAN GIOVANNI AL NATISONE (UD)

Vignai da Duline

Località Villanova
Via IV Novembre, 136
tel. 0432 758115
www.vignaidaduline.com
info@vignaidaduline.com

8 ha - 20,000 bt

❝ Working on the basis of studies on the correlation between soil and synergic grassing, Lorenzo now manages his vineyards without irrigation or fertilization. His vines has achieved a natural balance which reduces human intervention in the field to a minimum — all to the benefit of environmental conservation and the elegance and veracity of the wines ❞

PEOPLE - Lorenzo Mocchiutti, a self-styled "agrologist", is the cellar manager of this lovely winery, which he owns in partnership with his companion Federica Magrini.

VINEYARDS - The vineyards are divided into two distinct plots: the old vine rows in the Duline district, inherited from Lorenzo's grandfather, and the historic Ronco Pitotti property, which has always been managed using organic methods. Through ecological sustainability and maximum care for the vines, Lorenzo strives to extract the essence of the terroir. The native yeasts that have adapted to the soil are left intact. No chemicals whatsoever are used on the vines in this, one of the most respected environments in Friuli.

WINES - **Morus Alba 2010** (● 2,800 bt), a successful barrel aged blend of malvasia and "historic" sauvignon friulano — a clone devoid of intense vegetal notes but resistant to downy mildew — has aromatic impact, a full-bodied palate, raciness and style. **COF Chardonnay Ronco Pitotti 2010** (○ 2,200 bt) is well amalgamated and austere, with a sublime, still champenoise-style nose. **COF Pinot Grigio Ronco Pitotti 2011** (○ 3,200 bt) has subtle, refined texture and is sure to develop well.

> **slow wine** **MORUS NIGRA 2010** (● refosco; 1,150 bt) Yet another great interpretation of Refosco. Candid and floral on the nose, it gives of its best on the palate, where it reveals excellent grip and gutsy personality with exuberant but well-crafted tannins.

FERTILIZERS none
PLANT PROTECTION copper and sulphur
WEED CONTROL mechanical
YEASTS selected, native
GRAPES 100% estate-grown
CERTIFICATION organic

Collio, Isonzo e Carso

0   3,5   7 km

Villa Russiz

Via Russiz, 6
tel. 0481 80047
www.villarussiz.it villarussiz@villarussiz.it

Borgo San Daniele

Via San Daniele, 16
tel. 0481 60552
www.borgosandaniele.it
info@borgosandaniele.it

---

40 ha - 220,000 bt | **10% discount**

PEOPLE - The Fondazione Villa Russiz has taken on a new lease of life. Giordano Figelj, a keen and capable agronomist with more than 40 years of experience under his belt, has been charged with the management of the vineyards and general supervision of the company, while the wine cellar has been entrusted to two very young enologists: Giovanni Genio, who has already been at Villa Russiz for six years, and Marco Chestè, a native of the Alto Adige who "grew up" at the Cantina Tramin.

VINEYARDS - Villa Russiz owns 10 hectares of vineyards in the hills in the Spessa district, where a clear balance can be seen between wild vegetation and vines. The oldest, most interesting vineyards are to be found to the rear of the hill named for the French count Teodoro de La Tour, the man who launched the Villa Russiz farming and charity venture in the late 19th century. The land is increasingly managed with the preservation of the soil in mind.

WINES - Villa Russiz wines have always been characterized by great style, at once potent and elegant. **Les Enfants 2011** (○ pinot grigio, pinot bianco, ribolla gialla, sauvignon; 10,400 bt) is superlative: the bouquet is rich and elegant with notes of citrus fruits and blossom and the palate is dynamic, complex and sapid. It's truly a Great Wine. With its scents of white flowers and dense palate **Collio Pinot Bianco 2011** (○ 16,700 bt) is very good too. **Collio Friulano 2011** (○ 29,400 bt) has subtle aromas of grass and talcum powder and a juicy, potent palate, while **Collio Pinot Grigio 2011** (○ 46,300 bt) has distinct hints of ripe and sweet citrus fruit that converge in a luscious palate. **Collio Malvasia 2011** (○ 5,400 bt) is floral, expressive and eminently quaffable.

---

18 ha - 56,000 bt | **10% discount**

" Poetry should accompany the floral musicality of wine. This is Alessandra and Mauro's vision of their job. Hence simplicity, modesty and plain, unfussy labels — but charged with passion and rhythm "

PEOPLE - Sister and brother Alessandra and Mauro Mauri are friendly and kind and brim over with genuine, infectious enthusiasm. They work as a twosome: Mauro seeing to the vineyard and cellar work, Alessandra to sales and communications.

VINEYARDS - The vineyards are scattered round various plots of land in low-lying sunlit areas, mostly between Brazzano and Giassico, a splendid village suspended in time. Mauro takes care of the vineyards, which stand in grass, reducing treatments to a bare minimum and adopting many "natural" ideas. He always shows profound respect for the environment and the life that inhabits it.

WINES - For white wines, grapes are vinified and rested for a long time on the lees. The wines are then aged in the bottle prior to release. **Friuli Isonzo Pinot Grigio 2010** (○ 13,000 bt) is warm and caressing. **Arbis Blanc 2010** (○ sauvignon, chardonnay, friulano, pinot bianco; 10,000 bt) amazes for its balance of ripe fruit and meadow flowers. It is zesty and compact and, at the same time, fresh and supple.

slow wine **Friuli Isonzo Friulano 2010** (○ 13,000 bt) Expressive, fresh and elegant with a lively rich bouquet and a forthright, pleasant palate. One of the most convincing, personal wines to be made with this grape variety in the Cormons area.

FERTILIZERS organic-mineral, mineral, natural manure, green manure
PLANT PROTECTION chemical, copper and sulphur
WEED CONTROL chemical, mechanical
YEASTS selected, native
GRAPES 100% estate-grown
CERTIFICATION none

FERTILIZERS natural manure, humus
PLANT PROTECTION copper and sulphur
WEED CONTROL mechanical
YEASTS native
GRAPES 100% estate-grown
CERTIFICATION converting to organics

Colle Duga

Località Zegla, 10
tel. 0481 61177
www.colleduga.com
info@colleduga.com

Drius   €

Via Filanda, 100
tel. 0481 60998
www.driusmauro.it
info@driusmauro.it

---

9 ha - 50,000 bt

PEOPLE - Damian Princic runs this interesting winery with his father Luciano. The cellar is in Zegla di Cormons, a village on the border with Slovenia. In view of the suitability of both soil and climate for viticulture, the name of the place is a sort of hallmark, a seal of quality. Damian, level-headed but passionate, is helped not only by his father but also by Alessandro Zanutta, an experienced consultant agronomist who has attended to the vines for years.

VINEYARDS - Most of the vineyards stand in grass and fan out over three hills. Some are situated on Colle Duga, near the village, where the soil is rich in marine sedimentary rock. Others are situated at Novali, on level land and slopes with red earth rich in iron with a low pH, and in the hills of Russiz, which look towards Slovenia. These differences add to the complexity of the wines.

WINES - Vinifications without skin contact and aging without wood, just steel and cement tanks — these are Damian's favored methods. *Bâtonnages* are performed throughout the winter. In summer 2011 the Colle Duga vineyards were hit by hailstorms, but the overall quality is very high nonetheless. At the top of the range, Collio Bianco 2011 (○ 3,400 bt) is leisurely and mineral on the nose, full of flavor and fruity flesh on the palate. A happy combination of the fullness of chardonnay, the aroma of malvasia and sauvigon and the sinew and raciness of friulano, it's a Great Wine. Then comes **Collio Friulano 2011** (○ 13,000 bt) with its aromas rich in mineral nuances and yellow flowers, nice freshness and flavor. **Pinot Grigio 2011** (○ 6,500 bt) is balanced and expressive.

15 ha - 60,000 bt

PEOPLE - The unassuming Mauro Drius is one of those guys who still goes about his work with the no-nonsense approach typical of the farming world he comes from. At the start of the 20th century this was a place of cattle breeding and maize cultivation. It was only towards the end of the century that the farm decided to put its money on viticulture. Today, with the valuable support of the whole family, Mauro offers wines of great quality at very reasonable prices.

VINEYARDS - Most of the vineyards spread out near the cellar on classic alluvial soils formed by the River Isonzo. The rest are in the Collio DOC. The vines have different ages and are mostly white and the vineyards are managed using what we might define as mixed methods: hence, pest management, where possible, and minimum use of synthetic products. The soil is fertilized with certified organic cow dung.

WINES - Precise craftsmanship, elegance and good aging potential — these are the distinctive features of Mauro's wines. An excellent example is **Friuli Isonzo Pinot Bianco 2011** (○ 6,600 bt), with pronounced blossom, good texture and refreshing minerality. We also rated highly **Friuli Isonzo Pinot Grigio 2011** (○ 6,600 bt), fruity, tangy, and long, characteristics perfectly tempered by freshness, and **Collio Friulano 2011** (○ 9,950 bt), full, well-structured and, at once, racy. **Friuli Isonzo Malvasia 2011** (○ 6,600 bt) originates from three different vineyards and stands out for its fine aromas and tannic structure. The red that impressed us most was **Friuli Isonzo Merlot 2008** (● 5,850 bt), still clenched on the nose, but warm and cocky on the palate.

FERTILIZERS organic-mineral, mineral, manure pellets, natural manure, green manure
PLANT PROTECTION chemical, copper and sulphur
WEED CONTROL chemical, mechanical
YEASTS selected
GRAPES 10% bought in
CERTIFICATION none

FERTILIZERS manure pellets
PLANT PROTECTION chemical, copper and sulphur
WEED CONTROL chemical, mechanical
YEASTS selected
GRAPES 100% estate-grown
CERTIFICATION none

Edi Keber

Località Zegla, 17
tel. 0481 61184
edi.keber@virgilio.it

Isidoro Polencic

Località Plessiva, 12
tel. 0481 60655
www.polencic.com
info@polencic.com

12 ha - 25,000 bt   **10% discount**

28 ha - 120,000 bt

" Edi Keber has never stopped loving and promoting his native land by tirelessly raising the profile of the Collio trademark and its products. Not even when it does everything to make his life hard — as was the case with last year's violent hailstorm "

PEOPLE - Edi Keber's family, which hailed from Medana, in Slovenia, settled in Zegla, on the Italian side of the border by a few meters, decades ago. Edi has made this interesting cellar grow with determination and commitment. He now runs it with the valid help of his son Kristian, who has already shown he's ready to follow in his father's footsteps.

VINEYARDS - The vineyards, virtually organic, are situated on the terraces of the hill on top of which stands the farmhouse-cum-cellar. In July 2011 they were hit by a devastating hailstorm, but the Kebers not only had the spirit to react, but also the determination to get going again and partly redesign their vineyards. The move is sure to pay off in the future.

WINES - Albeit with a struggle, Edi and Kristian have managed to release 25,000 bottles from 2011 (instead of the usual 40,000) without any quality deficit. After seeing the devastation of the vineyards firsthand, one is amazed how malign nature can be, but also how it can offer unhoped for satisfactions — if you treat it right and don't betray it, that is.

slow wine **COLLIO BIANCO 2011** (○ friulano, ribolla gialla, malvasia; 25,000 bt) The fruit of the company's understandable and decisive decision to produce only one wine. Rich and satisfying, it has a well-defined, elegant aromatic framework and an enveloping finish. A pure, crystalline expression of the Zegla vineyards.

PEOPLE - The capable Polencic siblings are carrying on where the father Isidoro — one of the first producers in quality Friulan viticulture — left off. Michele, Elisabetta and Alex, in fact, work the same vineyards their father designed and tended for years. The desire to respect such an important past hasn't stopped the Polencic trio from making the innovations necessary to maintain the company's status as one of the most interesting in the Collio district.

VINEYARDS - The company is based in Plessiva, where its original vineyards are situated. In the course of time it has expanded its properties to include some of the best winegrowing districts in the Collio district. Dolegna, Ruttars and Mossa are the names — now famous for lovers of the finest Friulan wines — of the localities in which the other vineyards grow. Today the vines have an average age of about 25 years. All of the vineyards have southern exposure and after recent torrid summers, more foliage is now left on the plants to ensure optimal vegetative equilibrium.

WINES - The Polencic style never changes: hence rich, full-bodied wines, well-balanced and never over-the-top. **Collio Friulano 2011** (○ 16,000 bt) is very fine and full of flavor with a nice streak of acidity that lengthens and perks up the palate. It's truly a Great Wine. Almost as good is **Collio Pinot Grigio 2011** (○ 40,000 bt), elegant and prim with a bouquet of well-defined, fresh white-fleshed fruit and an intense but measured taste profile. Excellent too is **Collio Pinot Bianco 2011** (○ 3,000 bt), citrusy and full-bodied and dry on the palate. **Collio Friulano Fisc 2010** (○ 4,000 bt) is opulent and well-developed, rich in creamy fruit and fine flavor.

FERTILIZERS none
PLANT PROTECTION copper and sulphur
WEED CONTROL mechanical
YEASTS selected
GRAPES 100% estate-grown
CERTIFICATION converting to organics

FERTILIZERS natural manure
PLANT PROTECTION chemical, copper and sulphur
WEED CONTROL chemical, mechanical
YEASTS selected
GRAPES 100% estate-grown
CERTIFICATION none

CORMONS (GO)

Doro Princic

Località Pradis, 5
tel. 0481 60723
doroprincic@virgilio.it

CORMONS (GO)

Dario Raccaro

Via San Giovanni, 87
tel. 0481 61425
az.agr.raccaro@alice.it

---

10 ha - 55,000 bt

PEOPLE - Unconsciously maybe, but the charismatic Alessandro Princic runs one of the best tourist agencies in all the Collio district! He's lost count of the number of enthusiasts who flock to the cellar from all over the world not only to taste his wines — among Friuli's finest — but also to meet him. Cordiality, agricultural knowhow and innate *savoir faire* — a natural prerogative of bright people — are the main traits of this company that is carrying on brilliantly where Alessandro's unforgettable father Doro left off more than ten years ago.

VINEYARDS - The winery's ten hectares of vineyard are split into 30 or so terraced plots at Pradis, one of the most prestigious zones in the Collio district, but also one of the warmest. This worries Alessandro since, in the last few vintages, he had to struggle to contain sugar ripeness and maintain the proper acidity in the grapes. The average age of the vines is about 15 years and the soil is worked to refresh the roots.

WINES - The 2011 season delivered rich, concentrated wines, some with a minor lack of freshness and raciness. But Sandro has managed to limit these flaws by reasserting his classic, rigorous style. The **Collio Pinot Bianco 2011** (○ 12,000 bt) is full-bodied and rich in flavor, arguably less acid-crisp than usual. Just as rich and tangy is **Collio Friulano 2011** (○ 12,000 bt) whose taut finish is supported by lively minerality. **Collio Sauvignon 2011** (○ 8,000 bt) has good grip and attractive freshness, while **Collio Malvasia 2011** (○ 8,000 bt) evidences robust alcohol and an intact, fragrant suite of aromas. **Collio Merlot 2009** (● 9,000 bt) has a staid, austere, dry finish.

---

6 ha - 27,000 bt

PEOPLE - If the small village of Rolat di Cormons is well known in the wine world, it's thanks to one producer: Dario Raccaro. So fond of his "micro-terroir" as to feature the local church of Santa Maria on his labels, Dario has drawn on all his personality and tenacity to develop his respected, reliable winery, which he now runs with the support of his sons Luca and Paolo.

VINEYARDS - A stroll among the turfed hillside and terraced vineyards near Monte Quarin, just behind the cellar, conveys an idea of the quality and painstakingness of the work that goes into the land. Management is conventional with great care and attention being paid to the vines and the environment. A short distance away is the famous Vigna del Rolat, a sunny vineyard in an optimal location which already appears in maps dating from 1724. Dario has been managing it for years.

WINES - Raccaro's aim is to produce wines of *recherché* finesse and body. Which is why he vinifies by reduction with fermentations induced with selected yeasts and temperature control. He only adds small amounts of sulfur at the bottling stage. **Collio Bianco 2011** (○ 12,000 bt) is deep with a tempting bouquet and an agreeably refreshing palate. **Collio Malvasia 2011** (○ 3.000 bt) is opulent and fleshy.

> **slow wine** COLLIO FRIULANO VIGNA DEL ROLAT **2011** (○ 12,000 bt) The grapes come from vines at least 40 years old which ensure constant productive quality. Herbaceous and elegant on the nose, it is silky and fine on the palate. It usually achieves fullness of expression a year after the harvest.

FERTILIZERS none
PLANT PROTECTION chemical, copper and sulphur
WEED CONTROL chemical, mechanical
YEASTS selected
GRAPES 100% estate-grown
CERTIFICATION none

FERTILIZERS none
PLANT PROTECTION chemical, copper and sulphur
WEED CONTROL mechanical
YEASTS selected
GRAPES 100% estate-grown
CERTIFICATION none

CORMONS (GO)

Ronco del Gelso

Via Isonzo,117
tel. 0481 61310
www.roncodelgelso.com
info@roncodelgelso.com

CORMONS (GO)

Francesco Vosca €

Via Sottomonte, 19
tel. 0481 62135
www.voscavini.it
info@voscavini.it

---

25 ha - 150,000 bt

9 ha - 40,000 bt

PEOPLE - Starting virtually from scratch, over the last 20 years Giorgio Badin has worked with obstinacy, curiosity and perseverance to make Ronco del Gelso, one of the finest cellars in Friuli and, above all, to squeeze his own very precise idea of viticulture into the bottle. One intelligent move was to develop a cogeneration plant fueled by twigs from the vineyards. Combined with a few photovoltaic panels, it makes the cellar self-sufficient energy-wise.

VINEYARDS - Giorgio began with three hectares of land and has achieved his present scale by planting vines in every pockethandkerchief of land he could find on the Isonzo plain. He now has 22 parcels, which he knows intimately one by one and manages with careful, respectful viticultural methods. Since it tends to become compacted and dry, the soil is oxygenated by working it by alternate rows every year.

WINES - In pursuit of his own ideal wine, Giorgio experiments and innovates at every harvest, without ever betraying his characteristically rigorous, satisfying style. Fine richness of flavor makes **Friuli Isonzo Friulano Toc Bas 2011** (O 22,000 bt) linear and pervasive, flavorsome and deep, satisfying on the palate. The ultra-elegant, subtle **Friuli Isonzo Pinot Bianco 2011** (O 5,000 bt) expresses scents of blossom and straw, while **Friuli Isonzo Bianco Latimis 2011** (O 8,000 bt) is headily fruity and fleshy with a refreshing finish. A slight hint of hazelnut adds to the aromatic complexity of **Friuli Isonzo Pinot Grigio Sot Lis Rivis 2011** (O 20,000 bt), which has a spacious, well-defined palate. **Friuli Isonzo Sauvignon 2011** (O 26,000 bt) has muted vegetal and varietal notes, while the palate is full-bodied, taut and very zesty.

PEOPLE - This small family winery, situated in Brazzano di Cormons, supplements genuine, humble "peasant" sensitivity, hence respect for the land and tradition, with intelligent openness to novelty. Helped by his son Gabriele, Francesco tends the vineyards with meticulous care and without using synthetic products. Maintaining natural balance is central to his modus operandi.

VINEYARDS - Behind the cellar, in the Collio zone, a portion of the company's vineyards rises from the plain and, in a matter of meters, climb across the slopes of Monte Quarin as far as the woods. Intelligently, the Voscas have planted a number of different grapes on these steep, heterogeneous terrains. The first friulano grapes, planted by Francesco's father Mario in 1953, grow with malvasia and international varieties slightly further along in the Isonzo DOC area.

WINES - "Keep me poor and I'll make you rich!" Francesco uses the old popular saying to sum up his approach to work in the vineyard and the essence of his well-balanced, enjoyable wines. **Collio Bianco Frut Blanc 2010** (O friulano, pinot grigio; 2,000 bt), arguably the company's most representative wine, has a nicely complex bouquet that translates into impeccable structure. Good too is **Collio Malvasia 2011** (O 1,600 bt), warm and very long with a bouquet of spices and nuances of bay leaf.

> **slow wine** COLLIO FRIULANO **2011** (O 6,000 bt) Elegant and vibrant, plump and juicy, plush and cheering. Besides being a thrill to drink, it conveys values too. Namely, a family's toil, the grandiosity of a terroir and honest pricing.

FERTILIZERS organic-mineral, mineral, manure pellets, biodynamic preparations, humus
PLANT PROTECTION chemical, copper and sulphur
WEED CONTROL chemical, mechanical
YEASTS selected
GRAPES 100% estate-grown
CERTIFICATION none

FERTILIZERS mineral, humus
PLANT PROTECTION copper and sulphur, organic
WEED CONTROL mechanical
YEASTS selected
GRAPES 100% estate-grown
CERTIFICATION none

DOLEGNA DEL COLLIO (GO)

Venica & Venica

Località Cerò, 8
tel. 0481 61264
www.venica.it
venica@venica.it

DUINO AURISINA (TS)

Kante

Frazione San Pelagio
Località Prepotto, 1 A
tel. 040 200255
kante.edi@libero.it

---

37 ha - 262,000 bt

PEOPLE - One company, one family. The concept captures the essence and success of an enterprise that is now over 80 years old. It was 1930 when grandfather Daniele bought the farmhouse and vineyard, where the cellar now stands. Today the company is modern and dynamic, one to which everyone makes a contribution, each in a different way. Gianni Venica is tasked with the countryside and his brother Giorgio manages the cellar. Untiring sales manager Ornella, Giorgio's wife, has taken the company's wines all over the world.

VINEYARDS - Ably teased with different varieties and practices, varying soils and microclimates give of their best here, in one of the most prolific winegrowing zones of the Collio district. Most of the vineyards are situated in the hills, not far from the cellar, where they enjoy good ventilation and sharp temperature swings. Gianni tends the vineyards with consummate skill and technical expertise, combining traditional agricultural methods with a conscientious use of technology.

WINES - The wines are again top-notch with a common denominator of consistent quality. Capable of producing labels that bring out the distinctive varietal features of the grape, the Venicas thrilled us this year with their splendid Collio Pinot Bianco 2011 (O 15,000 bt), which has intense fruity, spicy aromas and full, lingering flavor. Ultra-elegant, it is truly a Great Wine. Hot on its trail comes **Collio Friulano Ronco delle Cime 2011** (O 20,000 bt), which is typical on the nose and tangy on the palate, with well-balanced acidity. Juicy, unctuous and pervasive, **Collio Sauvignon Ronco delle Mele 2011** (O 40,000 bt) is as convincing as ever, and **Collio Malvasia 2011** (O 6,500 bt) is pleasurable too.

---

13 ha - 45,000 bt

  ❝ Edi sees himself as a free agent and likes nothing better than to put himself to the test. "I achieve what I deserve," he says **❞**

PEOPLE - Edi Kante is a point of reference for the Carso zone. He combines exuberance and creative verve with level-headedness, maturity and common sense. He has radical ideas about his work. A dedicated pursuer of perfection, he is critical and self-critical in equal measure.

VINEYARDS - The numerous small vineyards are surrounded by woodland and were torn from "a land without soil", as the Carso is affectionately referred to. Their common denominator is low Guyot-training with vines fixed and aligned by acacia wood poles. Sparsely coated with red earth, the limestone rocks give the wines fine body and longevity and a potential that is still waiting to be explored. Edi's "heroic" viticulture shuns chemicals and embraces human labor. Lots of it!

WINES - The wines are unfiltered and unmacerated and are released only after long aging. All the base wines age a year in wooden barrels, then rest in steel tanks. The naturally low temperatures of a cellar hewn out of the rock help the wines to decant and mature. The use of wood enhances the depth and dry finish of the palatable **Vitovska Selezione 2004** (O 5,000 1 l bt). **Chardonnay 2009** (O 5,000 bt) is fresh and complete with linear, precise, refined nuances.

> slow wine **VITOVSKA 2009** (O 10,000 bt) We really enjoyed this salty, citrusy version of vitovska, a taut, beautifully measured wine in which the Carso terroir comes to the fore.

FERTILIZERS mineral, natural manure	FERTILIZERS natural manure
PLANT PROTECTION chemical, copper and sulphur	PLANT PROTECTION copper and sulphur
WEED CONTROL chemical, mechanical	WEED CONTROL mechanical
YEASTS selected	YEASTS selected, native
GRAPES 100% estate-grown	GRAPES 100% estate-grown
CERTIFICATION none	CERTIFICATION none

Skerk

Frazione San Pelagio
Località Prepotto, 20
tel. 040 200156
www.skerk.com
info@skerk.com

6 ha - 22,000 bt

66 The dynamics of wine are mysterious, says Sandi Skerk, and to understand them better he follows the advice of his grandparents. As president of the Committee for the Protection of Carso DOC Wines, he is committed to keeping the winemakers of this extreme northeast corner of Italy together 99

PEOPLE - Sandi is a friendly, humble all-rounder of a winemaker. And he's also a hospitable kind of guy, like the rest of his family who run a lovely *osmizza*, or traditional osteria, in Prepotto.

VINEYARDS - When we visited the vineyards, we saw new vines being bedded on the karstic ridge on terraces, locally known as *pastini*, of clay soil. Sandi has rebuilt the stone steps and walls to recover strips of land once planted with vines. His entrepreneurial commitment is admirable and the view of the sea from the new vineyard is breathtaking.

WINES - Skerk cellar work proceeds as follows: long maceration at natural temperature (never more than 35°C) in open top fermenters in the underground cellar, late pressing and aging of the wine on oak, assemblage and very slow decantation, and, finally, bottling without clarification and filtering and minimum addition of sulfur (about 20 milligrams). The excellent **Malvasia 2010** (○ 5,000 bt) is juicy, mature and intriguing, while **Ograde 2010** (○ vitovska, malvasia, sauvignon, pinot grigio; 6,000 bt), whose name means "courtyard", is a hefty, nicely supple, long wine.

slow wine **VITOVSKA 2010** (○ 6,000 bt) Well-layered on the nose with an elegant, satisfying taste profile, a wine that has all the finesse and complexity that only vitovska can give — when it's properly vinified, that is.

FERTILIZERS natural manure, green manure, humus
PLANT PROTECTION copper and sulphur, organic
WEED CONTROL mechanical
YEASTS native
GRAPES 100% estate-grown
CERTIFICATION organic

Zidarich

Frazione San Pelagio
Località Prepotto, 23
tel. 040 201223
www.zidarich.it
info@zidarich.it

8 ha - 25,000 bt | 10% discount

66 Benjamin Zidarich loves the Carso, and his wines are a hymn to the area. He works unflaggingly to raise its profile and generously helps his neighbors with sound advice and by example 99

PEOPLE - Benjamin, a frank, affable man, set out years ago by vinifying the grapes from his hectare and a half of vineyard in his garage. Now he is one of the most representative winemakers of this wonderful area. The cellar he recently carved out of the rock and his family's *osmizza*, or osteria, overlooking the Gulf of Trieste are both well worth a visit.

VINEYARDS - In the hope that other producers will follow his example — and that young people might take up viticulture — Benjamin plans to recover the odd *pastino*, terrace, or two on the karstic ridge. The ones on which the vineyards, now mostly abandoned, are situated are the steepest, most impracticable places in the area. The present vineyards were recovered in this way and are all managed with virtually organic methods.

WINES - Grapes are macerated on their skins without temperature control. At least two years' aging prior to bottling imparts unmistakable finesse to the whole line. The superlative **Prulke 2010** (○ sauvignon, vitovska, malvasia; 4,000 bt) is spacious and complex on the nose and zesty and racy on the palate. **Malvasia 2010** (○ 4,000 bt) opens with enticing aromas of ripe fruit, which ushers in lovely fresh juiciness on the palate. **Ruje 2006** (● merlot, terrano; 2,000 bt) is notable for its potency.

slow wine **VITOVSKA 2010** (○ 14,000 bt) A classic, deep version. Elegant and fruity on the nose, very long and tangy on the palate. An impeccable representation of the Carso and its most characteristic grape variety.

FERTILIZERS natural manure
PLANT PROTECTION copper and sulphur
WEED CONTROL mechanical
YEASTS native
GRAPES 100% estate-grown
CERTIFICATION none

Bressan Mastri Vinai

Via Conti Zoppini, 35
tel. 0481 888131
www.bressanwines.com
bressanwines@tin.it

20 ha - 35,000 bt

PEOPLE - Fulvio Bressan is somewhat impatient with the "conventional" wine world and says so in no uncertain terms. His softer side comes out when he speaks with visceral passion about forgotten local grapes, the art of the old barrel makers and wine — wine as the fruit of the vine and the vine as the fruit of the earth in a natural cycle in which the less people intervene the better.

VINEYARDS - Fulvio's father Nereo, 80, who used to be a butcher in Gorizia, is the one who gets up every morning at five o'clock to go to work in the countryside. In the luxuriant vineyards the bunches are few in number, small, healthy and beautiful. The soil is worked — weed killers have never been used here — treatments with mined sulfur and copper are kept to a bare minimum and irrigation is taboo ("Not over my dead body! Even in times of drought!" says Nereo). Fulvio isn't a great fan of the pinot grigio grape, which he's phasing out, or of merlot, also slated for uprooting. So the future's going to be all-native — save for his beloved pinot nero.

WINES - Don't be taken aback by the current vintages on the market. Fulvio lets his wines age in wooden barrels for as long as he deems necessary. They are wines of great impact and enthralling complexity, such as Schioppettino 2006 and Pignol 2000, which we have reviewed in the past. This year only two wines were presented: **Pinot Nero 2006** (● 6,000 bt) is dark and full-bodied with notes of rhubarb and subtle tannins. It's an original interpretation of the variety.

> **slow wine** **CARAT 2006** (○ friulano, malvasia, ribolla gialla; 6,600 bt) A beautifully crafted blend of macerated grapes. The nose is pervaded by pronounced notes of orange zest and dried fruit with faint balsamic nuances, while the palate is fresh and complex, packed with energy and length.

FERTILIZERS none
PLANT PROTECTION copper and sulphur
WEED CONTROL mechanical
YEASTS native
GRAPES 100% estate-grown
CERTIFICATION none

Gravner

Frazione Oslavia
Località Lenzuolo Bianco, 9
tel. 0481 30882
www.gravner.it
info@gravner.it

16 ha - 38,000 bt

❝ Josko Gravner is a star in the modern Italian wine firmament. Deeply bound to the hills of Oslavia, he has reached every corner of the world with his fascinating, innovative ideas and his unforgettable bottles, the product of clean, old-fashioned, non-standardizing viticulture ❞

PEOPLE - Josko has never been afraid to take important decisions, which he always talks over with his mother Maria. In 1982 he told Luigi Veronelli that, sooner or later, he would produce only Ribolla Gialla. Now, 30 years on, he has taken the big decision. 2012 will see the last harvest for Breg; after which the label and the grapes used to make it will disappear for good.

VINEYARDS - Some things have changed in the Gravner vineyards over the last few years. The innovative bush-trained vineyards of Oslavia are now fully productive and the sumptuous Hum vineyard, in Slovenia, is taking on shape and substance. But Iosko's profoundly organic approach to viticulture — based on manual labor and careful observation of the vines to understand their needs, prevent problems and support their natural development — is the same as ever.

WINES - In order to achieve the quality target Josko deems optimal for Ribolla Gialla and Breg 2006, the wines will only be released next year after seven years' aging in the cellar. In the meantime, we had the chance of a second taste of Breg Anfora 2005 and Ribolla Gialla Anfora 2005, which we reviewed last year. It seemed to us that their character and expression were better defined this year.

> **slow wine** **ROSSO GRAVNER RIS. 2000** (● 2,000 bt) A deep, enfolding red that opens reticently on the nose before "growing" in the glass with unstoppable dynamism and increasingly rounded, complex.

FERTILIZERS none
PLANT PROTECTION copper and sulphur
WEED CONTROL mechanical
YEASTS native
GRAPES 100% estate-grown
CERTIFICATION none

GORIZIA (GO)

La Castellada

Località Oslavia, 1
tel. 0481 33670
nicolobensa@virgilio.it

10 ha - 25,000 bt

66 At La Castellada making wine is a normal, everyday task. It signifies following a long family tradition of respect for hard work, the vineyards, for the land and for the people who drink the cellar's prestigious bottles 99

PEOPLE - The Bensa family has always lived and worked in Oslavia, an ideal area for vine growing. Nicolò, nicknamed Niko, and his brother tend the vineyards, while his sons Matteo and Stefano, the cellar manager, ensure family continuity.

VINEYARDS - The aim of preserving old clones goes hand in hand with maximum grape ripening, achieved by limiting production and adopting natural "remedies" to increase their potential. For Nicolò freshness is a key factor for a wine that has to last long, which is why he recently performed experiments to boost the acidity of the grapes.

WINES - Made with grapes macerated on their skins, the wines are an example of how it is possible to achieve great results by extracting substance, while still preserving finesse, balance and texture. **Collio Friulano 2008** (○ 1,300 bt) is especially complex with its wide range of fruity aromas and mouthwatering juiciness. **Collio Ribolla Gialla 2008** (○ 5,400 bt) is good as it is, but aging usually makes it sublime.

> **slow wine** COLLIO ROSSO DELLA CASTELLADA 2001 (● merlot, cabernet sauvignon; 3,200 bt) A wine that excites for the way in which it slowly opens out to reveal an array of rich tertiary aromas. The palate is full, tidy and satisfying with refined complexity and scope for further development.

FERTILIZERS	manure pellets, green manure, humus
PLANT PROTECTION	copper and sulphur
WEED CONTROL	mechanical
YEASTS	native
GRAPES	100% estate-grown
CERTIFICATION	none

GORIZIA (GO)

Damijan Podversic

Via Brigata Pavia, 61
tel. 0481 78217
www.damijanpodversic.com
damijan.go@virgilio.it

10 ha - 22,500 bt

66 Damijan is the typical wholehearted farmer, single-minded and proud of his work. True to tradition, he operates with great respect for nature, attentive to what is going on around him and curious about the world. A modern farmer straight out of the past — that's what he is 99

PEOPLE - Just 40, Damijan Podversic already has enviable experience under his belt. He began to take care of the family vineyards (he subsequently bought more) as a young man, learning to make wine from his "master", Josko Gravner. His wife Elena lends him a hand in the "complicated" business of managing the company, which involves a house-cum-office in Doberdò sul Lago, vineyards on Monte Calvario and a cellar in Scriò, on the border with Slovenia.

VINEYARDS - Besides a few small parcels scattered round the Collio district, the company's most important vineyards are situated on the south-facing wooded slopes of Monte Calvario, just outside Gorizia, in an unspoiled environment ideal for growing healthy, flavorful grapes. The viticulture practiced is organic, mindful of the balance and health of the vines.

WINES - Damijan has taken the understandable but by no means easy decision to age his wines in the bottle before releasing them on the market. Which is why we'll have to wait to taste the 2009 labels. In the meantime, we recommend the following two 2005 selections, wines which have aged three years more in the barrel (and bottle) than the others already released from the same vintage. **Ribolla Gialla 2005** (○ 3,000 bt) is full of texture and body, but it has also managed to maintain subtle elegance and enviable depth. **Kaplja 2005** (○ 4,800 bt) has apricots on the nose and a dynamic, dry palate, slightly clenched but rich in flavor and full of character.

FERTILIZERS	green manure, none
PLANT PROTECTION	copper and sulphur, organic
WEED CONTROL	mechanical
YEASTS	native
GRAPES	100% estate-grown
CERTIFICATION	organic

GORIZIA (GO)

Radikon

Località Tre Buchi, 4
tel. 0481 32804
www.radikon.it
info@radikon.it

12 ha - 30,000 bt

66 Stanko and Saša Radikon are a father and son team united by a strong passion for wine and an uncompromising, original idea of enology. Symbiosis in the vineyard and precise procedures in the cellar make for labels of personality and charm 99

PEOPLE - Stanislao Stanko Radikon inherited the family legacy and began making wine on his own in the 1980s. He subsequently became a leading player in the creative winegrowing movement that has invested Collio over the last few years.

VINEYARDS - Work in the vineyard is impeccable and attentive without the use of chemicals. The ribolla vineyards, some of which 60 years old, are situated in the best growing areas and are bush-trained. The rest are Guyot-trained. Constant work is carried out on the steepest slopes to maintain the hydrogeological integrity of the terrain.

WINES - In the cellar, grapes are fermented with the skins induced by solely native yeasts. The wines age in wood for at least 36 months and are bottled without the addition of sulfur. **Merlot 2002** (● 1,960 1 l bt) develops slowly into a complete, deep, mature nose. The palate doesn't disappoint and ends assertively with flavor and rich extracts. The two wines produced by the younger Radikon undergo shorter maceration (10 days) and aging (18 months): flavorful but not overdynamic, **Slatnik 2010** (○ chardonnay, friulano; 8,000 bt) has intriguing notes of aromatic herbs and thyme, while **Pinot Grigio 2010** (○ 8,000 bt) is more expressive on the nose — more aromatic herbs — with a dry, taut bouquet.

| FERTILIZERS natural manure, compost, green manure |
| PLANT PROTECTION copper and sulphur, organic |
| WEED CONTROL mechanical |
| YEASTS native |
| GRAPES 100% estate-grown |
| CERTIFICATION none |

MARIANO DEL FRIULI (GO)

Vie di Romans

Località Vie di Romans, 1
tel. 0481 69600
www.viediromans.it
viediromans@viediromans.it

50 ha - 250,000 bt `10% discount`

PEOPLE - Friulan winemaking owes a lot to the level-headed, cultured Gianfranco Gallo, a man whose style and agronomic decisions are precise and scientifically motivated, irrespective of fashions and trends. Proof of the fact that particular and universal, local and cosmopolitan don't necessarily have to enter into conflict. Gallo has interpreted the Isonzo terroir and translated it into top quality wines that have nothing to envy the world's greats.

VINEYARDS - In the Vie di Romans vineyards nothing is decided empirically. No, every single action is determined by careful analysis of the data collected. Vines, varieties and labels have precise identities that presuppose healthy, organically active soil. Thanks to an efficient irrigation plant, it is possible to gauge the water input and keep the vines in constant equilibrium. You only have to see the brightness of the leaves to understand how.

WINES - Gianfranco has given the wines of Vie di Romans a recognizable style: warm, enfolding and richly structured. Let's begin with a Great Wine, **Friuli Isonzo Chardonnay Ciampagnis Vieris 2010** (○ 27,000 bt), vinified in stainless steel tanks and characterized by freshness and vivacity, balance and flavor. Aged in wood, **Friuli Isonzo Chardonnay Vie di Romans 2010** (○ 40,000 bt) is creamy, fine with marked pastry-shop sensations. **Friuli Isonzo Sauvignon Piere 2010** (○ 46.000 bt) has a fine, elegant suite of aromas and is tangy and generous on the palate. **Friuli Isonzo Bianco Flors di Uis 2010** (○ riesling renano, malvasia istriana, friulano; 20,000 bt) has a variegated bouquet redolent mostly of white flowers and sage. The refinement of **Friuli Isonzo Malvasia Dis Cumieris 2010** (○ 9,600 bt) is exemplary.

| FERTILIZERS organic-mineral, mineral, manure pellets, humus |
| PLANT PROTECTION chemical, copper and sulphur |
| WEED CONTROL chemical, mechanical |
| YEASTS selected |
| GRAPES 100% estate-grown |
| CERTIFICATION none |

SAN FLORIANO DEL COLLIO (GO)

Zuani

Località Giasbana, 12
tel. 0481 391432
www.zuanivini.it
info@zuanivini.it

SGONICO (TS)

Skerlj

Frazione Sales, 44
tel. 040 229253
www.agriturismoskerlj.com
info@agriturismoskerlj.com

---

12 ha - 65,000 bt

2.3 ha - 3,000 bt

PEOPLE - Intelligence, experience and determination — these are the qualities Patrizia Felluga, daughter of Marco, one of the founding fathers of modern Friulan winemaking, exhibited when she chose this corner of Collio to give life to this enterprise of hers. Albeit still young, the project has already made her winery a symbol of good viticulture in the area. She is helped by her very able son and daughter Antonio and Caterina, who work full-time in the production and promotion sectors.

VINEYARDS - Patrizia and her children, abetted by the experienced enologist Donato Lanati, began by preserving the old terraced vineyards. Then they set out to duplicate them, making in-depth analysis of the terrains and micro-climatic conditions to figure out the right sites and planting patterns for each variety.

WINES - We've always admired the original idea of producing just two wines — one vinified in stainless steel tanks, the other in wooden barrels — fruit of the assemblage in equal parts of the four grapes grown. We also appreciate the intelligence of the decision to postpone the release of Collio Bianco Zuani Ris. 2010, a blend from late-harvested grapes vinified in oak that requires longer periods of maturation. Our second tasting of the 2009 version, more resolute and poised than in the past, proved the point.

66 Matej Skerlj's work is humble, precious and consistent. He runs a family farm that is at once simple and complex in which the wine, cured meats and cooking reflect the local area, while respecting the surrounding environment 99

PEOPLE - Young winemaker Matej is as hospitable as the rest of the family, helping out at the agriturismo run by his sister Kristina and his parents, which serves homemade wine, cured meats and other specialties.

VINEYARDS - The small vineyards — pocket-handkerchief plots of land clawed back from the woods and the Mediterranean scrub — grow on red earth rich in silicates. Matej tends to his vines with painstaking care to minimize the use of chemicals even in unfavorable vintages. The naturally ventilated Carso environment is conducive to salubrious grapes and permits "clean" viticulture with low impact on the environment.

WINES - All the distinctive features of the Carso area are captured in these wines, produced in compliance with a few rules and with as little intervention as possible in the vinification process. We were favorably impressed by **Vitovska 2009** (○ 1,400 bt), an eminently quaffable wine of great warmth and juiciness with a wonderfully vivacious finish. **Terrano 2009** (● 800 bt) is complete, full-bodied and taut.

slow wine **COLLIO BIANCO VIGNE 2011** (○ friulano, pinot grigio, sauvignon, chardonnay; 55,000 bt) Crispness, plump fruit, meaty flesh, dynamic flavor, depth and elegance — all the qualities that any Collio wine worth its salt should have. In other words, a hugely satisfying drink.

slow wine **MALVASIA 2009** (○ 800 bt) Very rich on the nose with hints of ripe and crisp fruit, fleshy and rich in extracts on the palate. The mouthfeel is simple, assertive and elegant. A pure, crystalline tribute to a grape variety that flourishes in the Carso area.

FERTILIZERS manure pellets, natural manure
PLANT PROTECTION chemical, copper and sulphur
WEED CONTROL mechanical
YEASTS selected
GRAPES 100% estate-grown
CERTIFICATION none

FERTILIZERS natural manure
PLANT PROTECTION copper and sulphur
WEED CONTROL mechanical
YEASTS native
GRAPES 100% estate-grown
CERTIFICATION none

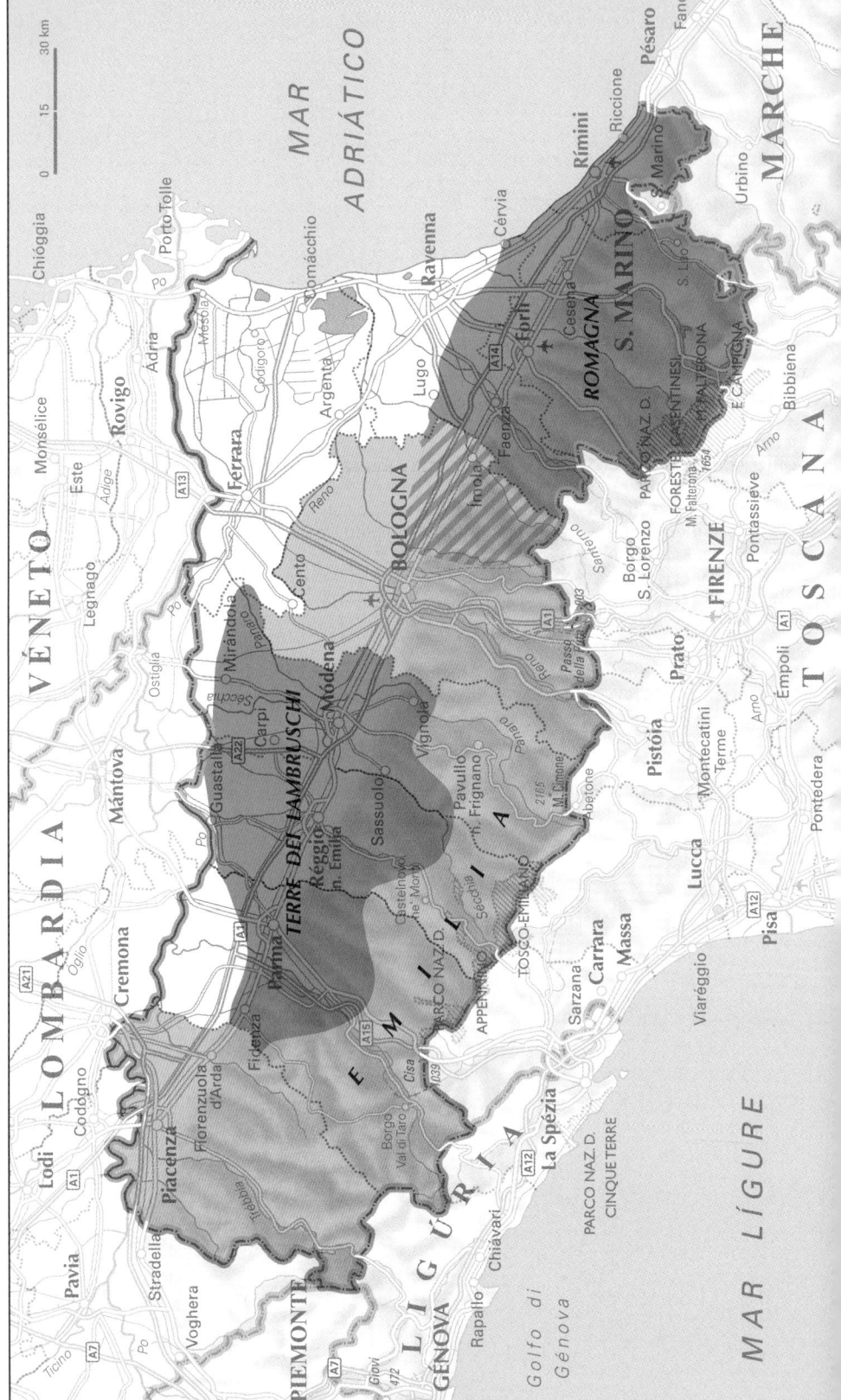

EMILIA-ROMAGNA

A lively but chaotic region which, paradoxically, insofar as it sometimes it seems to be groping in the dark, may even come across as undynamic. The fact is that it is on the move, albeit not always in a homogeneous, compact manner.

Among the giants — cooperatives and large wine companies — many small wineries sprang to the fore run by virtuoso winemakers in search of different, challenging forms of expression, and rightly so, to show how new avenues are open, even when it comes to managing the vineyard and the wine cellar.

Quantitatively speaking, fizzy wines dominate from the Colli Piacentini to Colli Bolognesi, whereas Sangiovese reigns from Imola to the Colli Riminesi. The infinity of chiaroscuros and nuances that comes in between we shall try to explain in the pages that follow.

The 2011 vintage was characterized almost everywhere by a scorching August, followed by two or three drier weeks in September which weighed down the profiles of the wines, some of which warm with over-ripe aromas and almost all with lower acidity than in 2010.

In this edition of *Slow Wine* we have slightly altered the subdivision of the subzones consolidating Colli Piacentini and Colli Bolognesi into Emilia. The Colli Piacentini yield Gutturnio, fizzy and still — we reckon the former should be the standard-bearer of Piacenza winemaking — and exceptional passitos and Vinsantos among the best sweet wines in Italy. The Colli Bolognesi offer excitingly original interpretations of local grapes such as pignoletto (still wines and other interesting versions refermented in the bottle) and the less known negretto, both capable of individualizing the zone's wine scene.

The Terre dei Lambruschi recorded an almost unthinkable growth until a few years ago. The impression is that, of the various typologies, the sorbaras may have suffered the warmth of the vintage more than others and are a little less subtle and essential than usual, though there are plenty — especially among those refermented in the bottle — that partly belie that impression.

Last but not least, Romagna. This year the 2009 Sangiovese Riservas were released along with a few "leftover" 2008s: the two vintages delivered important bottles. Moving on to Albana, we noted once more that a number of producers are emerging capable of raising the profile of the wine.

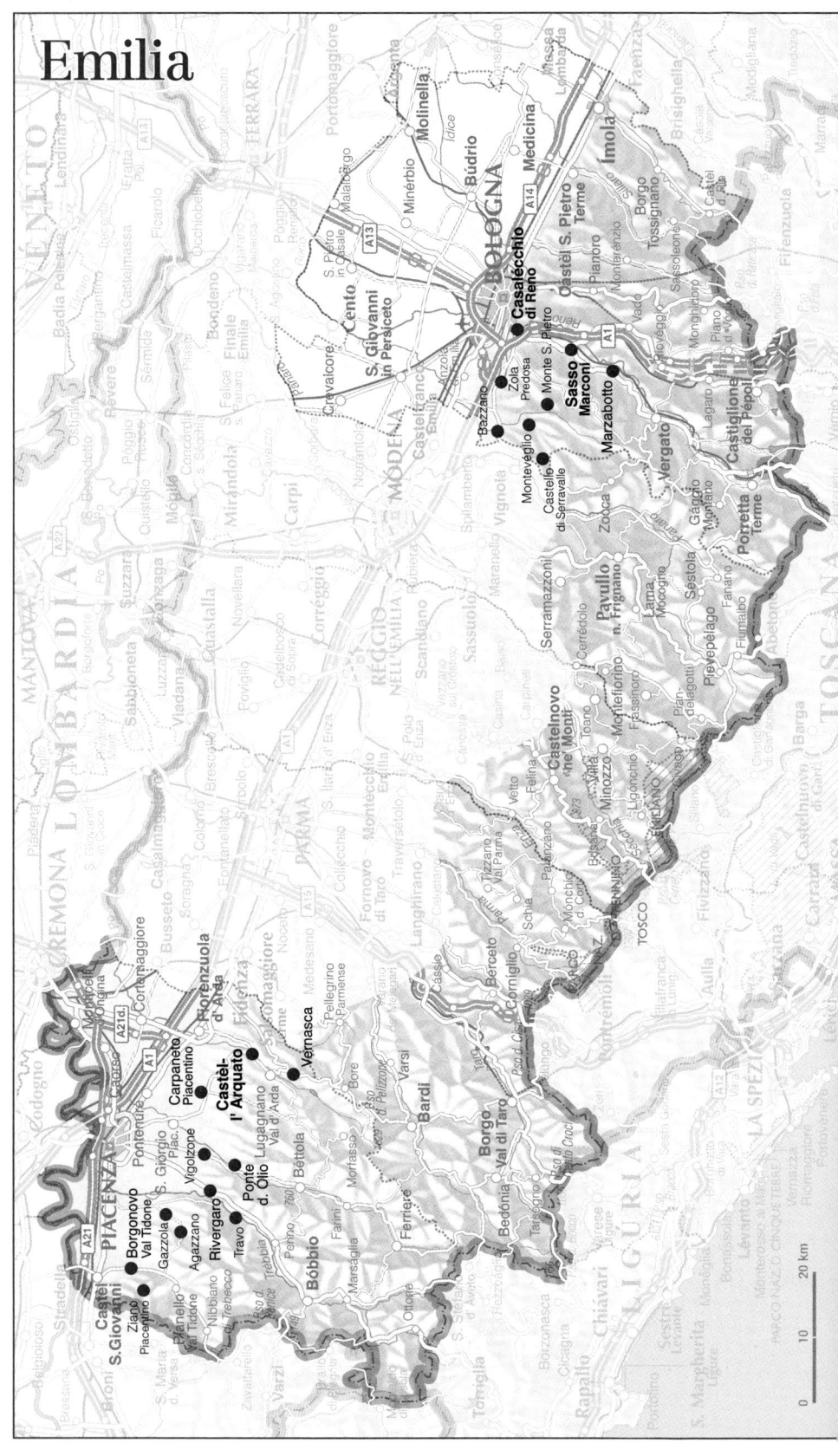

Emilia

Orsi - Vigneto San Vito

Località Oliveto
Via Monte Rodano, 8
tel. 051 964521
www.vignetosanvito.it
info@vignetosanvito.it

---

16 ha - 20,000 bt   **10% discount**

PEOPLE - Federico Orsi is an enterprising young man. He's been running this historic Colli Bolognesi winery with his companion Carola Pallavicino since 2005. Sensitive to environmental problems and an advocate of clean, healthy viticulture, Federico has converted his vineyards to biodynamics. A talented and dynamic team of technicians helps him on work in the vineyard under the supervision of agronomist Leonello Anello and enologist Federico Giotto.

VINEYARDS - The vineyards spread out through the lush hills of Monteveglio, at an altitude of about 200 meters, where the mainly clay soil has traces of limestone and sand. Natural agronomic practices such as turfing, cover cropping and the use of biodynamic preparations have restored the soil to good health, while the Guyot- and spurred cordon-trained vines live in perfect equilibrium with the environment.

WINES - Robust, assertive and full-bodied, the wines of San Vito evoke a strong sense of place thanks to natural viticultural practices. As Federico says, "We find everything that's in the soil in the grape". The fascinating **Pignoletto Frizzante Sui Lieviti 2010** (○ 7,000 bt), refermented in the bottle unracked, has delicate aromas and a creamy palate. **C.B. Barbera Martignone 2010** (● 3,000 bt) is tonic and juicy with intense aromas of ripe, fleshy red fruit. The company also produces white and red wine which it markets in attractive recyclable straw flasks.

> **slow wine** **C.B. Pignoletto Cl. Vigna del Grotto 2010** (○ 5,000 bt) Very good indeed! A wine born of clean agriculture with distinct varietal notes of dried white flowers. The palate is pervasive and stylish with a wave of acidity to add vivacity and raciness.

FERTILIZERS biodynamic preparations, green manure
PLANT PROTECTION copper and sulphur
WEED CONTROL mechanical
YEASTS native
GRAPES 100% estate-grown
CERTIFICATION biodynamic, organic

Lusenti   €

Località Casa Piccioni di Vicobarone, 57
tel. 0523 868479
www.lusentivini.it
info@lusentivini.it

---

17 ha - 120,000 bt

PEOPLE - Lodovica Lusenti has taken up the legacy of her father Gaetano, who passed away recently, and supervises vinification with the precious assistance of Anderson do Nascimento. With her husband Giuseppe Ferri, who tends the vineyards, she runs a company that is charting its course with increasing clarity, displaying great interest in eco-sustainable practices and sound, sensible vinification.

VINEYARDS - The vineyards are situated on different parcels round Ziano. One such is the five-hectare Pozzolo Piccolo, which produces the best malvasia grapes for the Bianca Regina selection as well as the croatina and barbera (from vines about 50 years old) for the reds for aging. Six hectares at Case Piccioni are being gradually rationalized to favor the grapes most suited to the coolness of the subzone, such as ortrugo, malvasia and pinot nero for refermentation.

WINES - These no-nonsense, powerful wines are the fruit of careful vinification. The finest labels have forthright, undemonstrative taste profiles. The *passiti* and wines refermented in the bottle are vinified only with native yeasts. One such is the successful **C.P. Malvasia Frizzante Emiliana 2011** (○ 3,500 bt), which combines pleasant fruity roundness with the bitterish raciness typical of the grape. An Everyday Wine and deservingly so. One of the reds we liked was the fleshy and flowery **Martin 2010** (● barbera, croatina, merlot; 2,500 bt) — a joy to drink. **C.P. Gutturnio Sup. Cresta al Sole 2008** (● 7,000 bt) is richer with notes of jam and a weighty palate. **Gutturnio Frizzante 2011** (● 35,000 bt) is mature and well-structured with a nicely complex taste profile. **C.P. Malvasia Passito Il Piriolo 2009** (○ 1,500 bt) is very dense and enfolding.

FERTILIZERS natural manure
PLANT PROTECTION copper and sulphur
WEED CONTROL mechanical
YEASTS selected
GRAPES 20% bought in
CERTIFICATION converting to organics

Terre dei Lambruschi

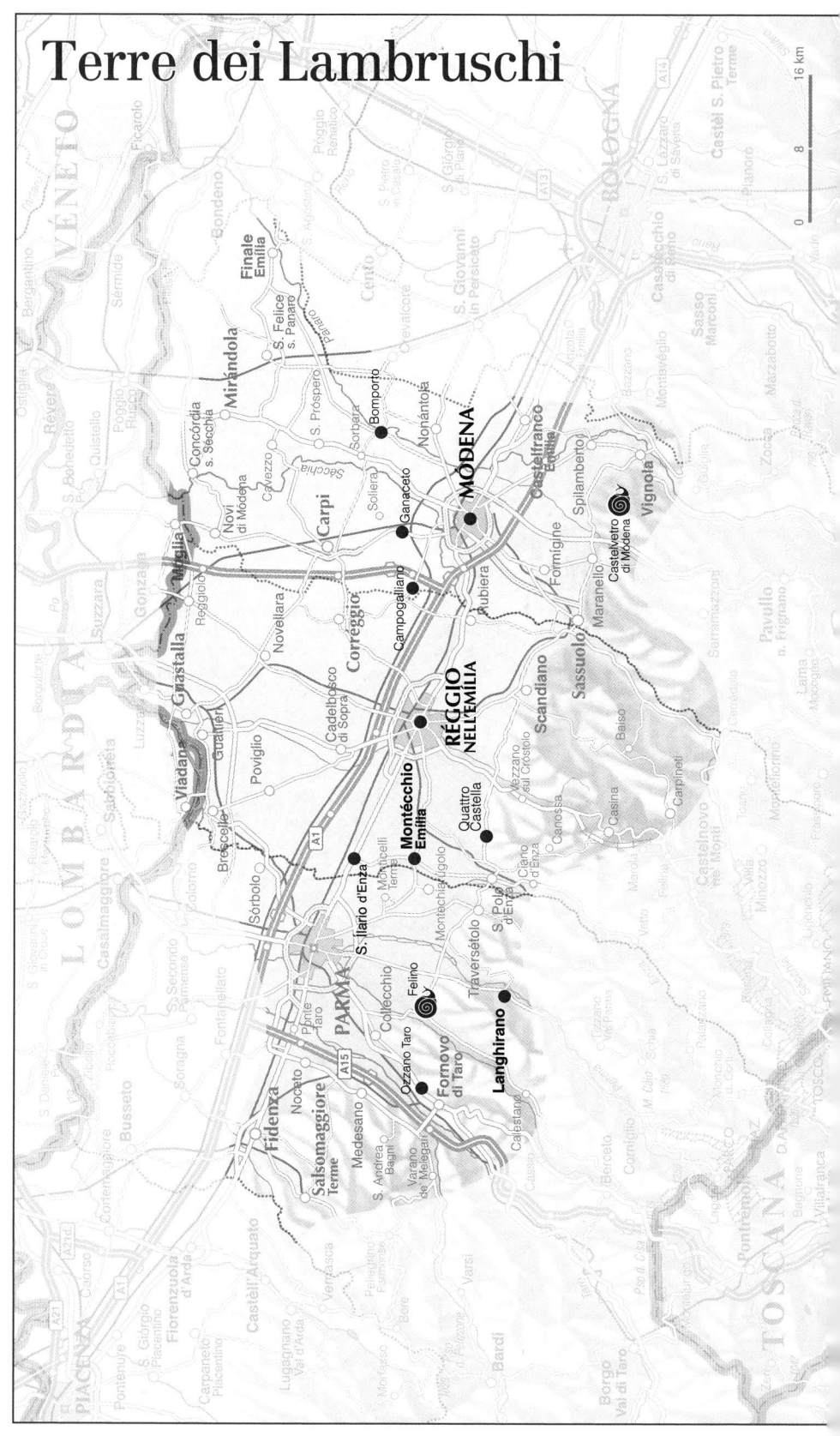

Gianfranco Paltrinieri

Frazione Sorbara
Via Cristo, 49
tel. 059 902047
www.cantinapaltrinieri.it
info@cantinapaltrinieri.it

Cleto Chiarli

Via Belvedere, 8
tel. 059 3163311
www.chiarli.it
italia@chiarli.it

---

15 ha - 90,000 bt   **10% discount**

100 ha - 900,000 bt

PEOPLE - Alberto Paltrineri, agronomist and heir to Gianfranco, who died in 2011, has been at the helm since 1996, supported in the task by his wife Barbara Galassi. Assisted by Attilio Pagli and Leonardo Conti for the enological side of the business, the twosome embody the spirit of Lambrusco di Sorbara. Their labels are better defined year by year and encapsulate all the subtlety and suppleness typical of the typology.

VINEYARDS - The flat-lying vineyards, mostly trained with the double-curtain system (though the most recent are high-trained), are situated at the heart of the denomination inside a historic subzone of the Cristo district on a narrow, fertile patch of silty, loose alluvial soil, between the rivers Secchia and Panaro. The prevalent variety is Sorbara which, insofar as it is sterile, is traditionally alternated with the salamino variety, which acts as a pollinator.

WINES - Though the warm year complicated vineyard management and vinification, we were presented with a prime range of Sorbara: educational and, above all, extremely enjoyable. The top wine was **Lambrusco di Sorbara Sant'Agata 2011** (● 20,000 bt), which offers aromas of sweet fruit to the nose with a harmonious palate. Made using the long Charmat method with grapes from vineyards 20 years old, **Lambrusco di Sorbara Leclisse 2011** (● 18,000 bt) has something of a restless nose, but displays well-rounded, full-bodied texture and a fresh, enjoyable aftertaste. **Lambrusco di Sorbara Piria 2011** (● 18,000 bt) is pleasurable, simple and winy with a back-up of salamino to soften the palate.

slow wine **LAMBRUSCO DI SORBARA RADICE 2011** (● 12,000 bt) A marvelous bottle-refermented Sorbara. Dull in color, it is fresh and confident with well-balanced acidity and good fruity flesh. A benchmark for its typology.

PEOPLE - The Chiarli family has been indissolubly linked to Lambrusco since 1860. Today the brand is in the capable hands of Anselmo and Mauro, who manage the various estates, one of which, Cleto Chiarli, dating from 2001, vinifies only the best grapes in the plant at Castelvetro. The technical side is charged to Michele Faccin in the vineyard and Franco De Biasi in the cellar, while Roberto Saletta is the sales manager.

VINEYARDS - The vineyards are split into a number of large plots, all in the best zones of the principal Lambrusco denomination. At Sozzigalli and Soliera 30 hectares of sorbara grow on the sandy, silty soil typical of the area, whereas at Castelvetro, where the soil is clayier, another 50 hectares grow at the foot of the hills on the alluvial deposits, with traces of silt and gravel, of the River Guerro. The 20-hectare Spilamberto vineyard, finally, is given over to grasparossa.

WINES - The most advanced technologies and good selection in the vineyard produce a vast and reliable range, technically exceptional, approachable and clean wine range year in, year out. The successful **Lambrusco Grasparossa di Castelvetro Vigneto Enrico Cialdini 2011** (● 50,000 bt) is a modern, crisply pleasurable, well-balanced take on Lambrusco di Castelvetro. Interesting as ever, **Lambrusco di Sorbara del Fondatore 2011** (● 12,000 bt), refermented in the bottle, is fresh, precise, supple and sexy. Subtle, soft and lushly fruity, **Lambrusco di Sorbara Vecchia Modena Premium M.H. 2011** (● 60,000 bt) is an enjoyable tipple. Last but not least, **Lambrusco Grasparossa di Castelvetro Villa Cialdini 2011** (● 80,000 bt) has soft fruit.

FERTILIZERS none	FERTILIZERS natural manure
PLANT PROTECTION chemical, organic	PLANT PROTECTION chemical, copper and sulphur
WEED CONTROL mechanical	WEED CONTROL chemical, mechanical
YEASTS selected	YEASTS selected
GRAPES 100% estate-grown	GRAPES 100% estate-grown
CERTIFICATION converting to organics	CERTIFICATION none

CASTELVETRO (MO)

Vittorio Graziano

Via Ossi, 30
tel. 059 799162

5 ha - 30,000 bt

66 Energetic, determined, loathe to accept compromises, Vittorio Graziano undertook the tough life of the winemaker in the Castelvetro hills 30 years ago. To his solitary labors he brings strong ethical and political convictions and a desire to defend old-fashioned farming values and traditions. His aim is to "defend the local area and make it speak through wine" 99

PEOPLE - Vittorio is adamant that "the only viticulture capable of raising the profile of the local area is natural viticulture with a low impact on the environment". Likewise, spontaneous refermentation in the bottle is the only way to keep the qualities nature gives the grapes intact in the wine.

VINEYARDS - The vineyards are situated at an altitude of about 250 meters and managed according to the criteria of natural viticulture to preserve the treasures of the ecosystem. The non-use of systemic treatments, insecticides and weed killers allows plants to grow robust and healthy in an environment characterized by great plant biodiversity. The composition of the soil gives the grapes extraordinary phenolics.

WINES - A fierce enemy of the use of pressure tanks, Vittorio is fighting to preserve the biodiversity of his land by unceasingly seeking out old, forgotten clones, which play a decisive part in all his wines. The vigorous phenolics of the grapes and natural refermentation make for slow maturation, which is why the wines need time to take shape and be appreciated. And also why we are postponing our review of Lambrusco Grasparossa Fontana dei Boschi 2011, richly extracted on account of the warm year, until next year. In the meantime, we enjoyed the 2010 version again, plus **Ripa di Sopravento 2011** (○ 4,000 bt), a white from various clones of trebbiano modenese, rich and plump with nice tannins.

FERTILIZERS green manure
PLANT PROTECTION copper and sulphur
WEED CONTROL mechanical
YEASTS native
GRAPES 100% estate-grown
CERTIFICATION none

FELINO (PR)

Camillo Donati

Frazione Bambiano
Via Costa, 3 A
tel. 0521 637204
www.camillodonati.it
camillo@camillodonati.it

15 ha - 90,000 bt

66 Camillo Donati is one of the most genuine, sincere people in the wine world. He runs his company with his wife Francesca and his niece Monia. All their work is pervaded by great naturalness. "I make simple wine to be drunk at the table every day. To make it well, I do things simply, without fuss." All this simplicity conceals deep awareness, refined thinking and enviable farming skills 99

PEOPLE - In the 2011 harvest, Camillo's inauguration of a new small, functional cellar near the vineyards had positive effects on the quality of his wines, all refermented in bottle with crown caps.

VINEYARDS - Going against the general trend, Donati has decided to give up some of the vineyards he leases in order to be able to concentrate on the ones he owns and control them firsthand. He began adopting organic methods in 2001, since when he has been an example for all the producers in the area.

WINES - Like all the finest wines refermented in the bottle, Camillo's are good immediately. And they get even better at least a year on from the harvest. This became clear to us when we retasted Mio Malvasia 2010 and Mio Sauvignon 2008. We thus decided taste the 2011 vintage at its best and to review it in the next edition of the guide. In the meantime, we recommend **Mio Barbera 2009** (● 7,000 bt), not overfizzy with a slight residual sweetness that softens the bouquet, in which the power and fragrance of the fruit mingle lusciously. Last but not least, the tangy, dry **Mio Malvasia Rosa 2010** (● 1,000 bt) is as curious as it is drinkable.

FERTILIZERS none
PLANT PROTECTION copper and sulphur
WEED CONTROL mechanical
YEASTS native
GRAPES 100% estate-grown
CERTIFICATION organic

Denny Bini Podere Cipolla €

Località Coviolo
Via Pomponazzi, 29
tel. 320 0229600
denny.bini@libero.it

1 ha - 7,000 bt **10% discount**

PEOPLE - Almost ten years have gone by since, as a young man, Denny Bini decided to take the small vineyard rented by his grandfather into hand. An expert of the local area and of the bottle refermentation technique, which he uses for all his wines, he is adamant that only natural viticulture and non-invasive vinification practices can raise the profile of the terroir and create identity.

VINEYARDS - Podere Cipolla is a vineyard of one hectare managed without the use of systemic and weed control treatments and with the use of copper and sulfur only in tiny amounts. It faces south on medium-texture clay soil and enjoys a cool climate thanks to the proximity of two rivers and thick vegetation, which mitigate the summer heat. Here grow the much loved native malbo, grasparossa, malvasia and barbera grapes.

WINES - Denny Bini delivers increasingly interesting wines with a strong sense of place every year. They are the fruit of hard work, passion and healthy, clean viticulture. Enjoyable with a fine acid streak, **Levante 90 2011** (○ 1,500 bt) is a delicately aromatic Malvasia with elegant sensations of dried fruit and flowers. Intense acidity makes the lightly scented rosé, **Rosa dei Venti 2011** (◉ lambrusco grasparossa; 700 bt), extremely refreshing and drinkable. Aromas of fruit in alcohol and licorice characterize **Libeccio 225 2011** (● lambrusco grasparossa; 1,000 bt).

slow wine | **PONENTE 270 2011** (● lambrusco grasparossa, malbo, barbera; 2,500 bt) An outstanding wine, refermented in the bottle and packed with phenolics and mature tannins. It offers intense notes of officinal herbs on the nose and a fleshy, fragrant palate with plenty of minerality.

FERTILIZERS natural manure, green manure	
PLANT PROTECTION copper and sulphur	
WEED CONTROL mechanical	
YEASTS native	
GRAPES 100% estate-grown	
CERTIFICATION none	

Ermete Medici & Figli €

Località Gaida
Via Newton, 13 A
tel. 0522 942135
www.medici.it
info@medici.it

75 ha - 700,000 bt

PEOPLE - This historic winery on the plain of Reggio Emilia came into being at the end of the 19th century. It still carries on a solid family tradition with Giorgio Medici managing enology and his son Alberto sales. It owns a wine cellar at Gaida and two farms — Quercioli and Rampata, which also offers accommodation and includes a vinegar house— and turns out huge number of bottles. For the last 20 years the vineyards have been capably managed by Angelo Chezzi with the help of enologist Otello Venturelli.

VINEYARDS - The vineyards are managed with an integrated system and fertilized solely with vinasse. They are situated in the old bed of the River Enza in the foothills between Parma and Reggio Emilia. The oldest vine rows are to be found on the Rampata estate and include lambrusco salamino vines grapes planted in the early 20th century whose grapes go into the Concerto selection. Last year the historic Rampata and Quercioli vineyards in the Cavriago district were joined by new acquisitions, among which a nine-hectare lambrusco vineyard at Barco.

WINES - Considering only the labels made with the company's own grapes, we have to report that the level of all the wines was as good as ever this year. The label that impressed us the most — not for the first time — was Reggiano Lambrusco Concerto 2011 (● lambrusco salamino; 150,000 bt) with its enticing fleshy fruit and measured, supple but pulpy palate. **Reggiano Rosso Assolo 2011** (● ancellotta, lambrusco salamino; 90,000 bt) has softer fruit and is highly approachable. **Reggiano Lambrusco I Quercioli 2011** (● lambrusco salamino, lambrusco Marani; 190,000 bt) has definite brambly prickle and is well-rounded with a pleasantly expressive bouquet. Last but not least, **M. Cl. Gran Concerto 2010** (● lambrusco salamino; 5,000 bt) is balanced with spicy, green varietal nuances.

FERTILIZERS natural manure	
PLANT PROTECTION copper and sulphur	
WEED CONTROL mechanical	
YEASTS selected	
GRAPES 100% estate-grown	
CERTIFICATION none	

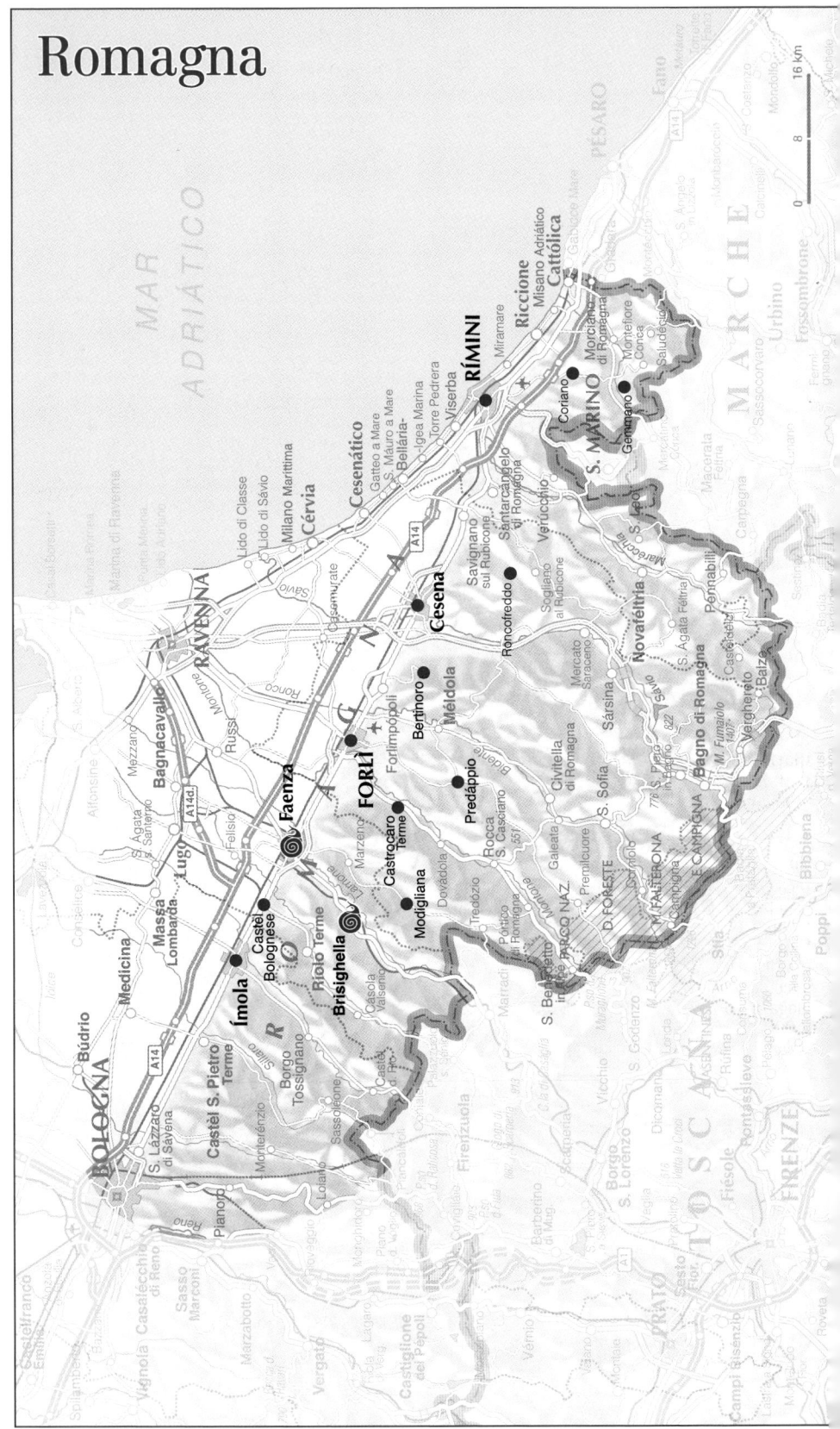

Romagna

Vigne dei Boschi 🌀

Via Tura, 7/A
tel. 0546 51648
www.vignedeiboschi.it
vignedeiboschi@alice.it

6.5 ha - 15,000 bt · 10% discount

❝ "Man is at the service of nature," is a phrase Paolo Babini and his wife Katia Alpi, owners of Vigne dei Boschi, often repeat. They have been cultivating their wines organically since 1994. Research, respect for biodiversity and natural cycles are the key principles of their daily work ❞

PEOPLE - The company came to live in Valpiana di Brisighella in 1989, but it was only in 2000 that it stopped delivering its grapes to the local wine cooperative. In 2002 interest lit up and the company carried out its first experiments with biodynamic farming.

VINEYARDS - The ecosystem, encircled by woods, matches the company's philosophy. After careful analysis, in 1989 vineyards were planted at altitudes of 300-500 meters in the locations best suited for the grape varieties. All are cordon-trained and spur-pruned, apart from the sangiovese grapes, which are head-trained in the Romagna style at high densities on soil rich in marl and sandstone. Green manure made with herbs and hour upon hour's toil in the vineyard — this is Paolo's recipe.

WINES - Paolo and Katia's wines are more than just a pleasure to drink. Behind a complex suite of aromas and the finest minerality — a prerogative of the whites — they conceal a capacity to "listen to" and respect the land. **Settepievi 2007** (● malbo; 3,000 bt) is a top quality wine with a nose of ripe fruit and a succulent, velvety bouquet. The supremely elegant **16 Anime 2010** (○ riesling renano; 2,000 bt) has mineral aromas with notes of delicate aromatic herbs, tanginess and depth.

> **slow wine** **POGGIO TURA 2008** (● sangiovese; 3,500 bt) A fantastic "mountain" Sangiovese with pervasive floral and balsamic notes. The palate is vibrant, supported by acidity and tannins, complex and full of length. Buy it immediately.

FERTILIZERS biodynamic preparations, green manure
PLANT PROTECTION copper and sulphur, organic
WEED CONTROL mechanical
YEASTS native
GRAPES 100% estate-grown
CERTIFICATION biodynamic, organic

Maria Galassi €

Frazione Paderno
Via Casetta, 688
tel. 0547 21177
www.galassimaria.it
info@galassimaria.it

18 ha - 15,000 bt · 10% discount

PEOPLE - In the early 1990s, when in Italy organic viticulture was considered the mere whim of the odd eccentric producer, Maria Galassi already had very clear ideas. After inheriting the vineyards from her father, she unhesitatingly converted them to organics. She knew the only way to produce wines with a sense of place was through sustainable agriculture respectful of the land.

VINEYARDS - The vineyards are situated round the owners' residence at an altitude of about 250 meters and are, in turn, encircled by old olive and fruit trees. Maria decided to keep the old spacing arrangement with the cordon-trained and spur-pruned vines set well apart from one another. They produce only 70 quintals of grapes per hectare. The lean, fresh soil is composed of composed of evolved yellow sand and calcareous marls. The vineyards are tended by agronomist Francesco Bordini.

WINES - A synthesis of power and elegance, these wines capture the essence of the Bertinoro terroir thanks to the natural viticulture and skill of Bordini, who also follows vinification operations. The maison's newest wine, **Sangiovese di Romagna Sup. E Be' de Smembar 2011** (● 5,000 bt) is extremely enjoyable and drinkable with marked balsamic notes, flesh and great balance. Insofar as it's a Sangiovese we'd be happy to drink every day, we've named it an Everyday Wine. The excellent **Sangiovese di Romagna Sup. NatoRe Ris. 2009** (● 3,600 bt), aged in barrels, has stylish notes of leather and delicate hints of citrus fruit, a full, tangy, lingering palate, dynamic and exceptionally refined. Plums and fruit preserved in alcohol come to the fore in the well-structured, tannic **Sangiovese di Romagna Sup. PaterNus 2010** (● 3,000 bt).

FERTILIZERS natural manure, green manure
PLANT PROTECTION copper and sulphur
WEED CONTROL mechanical
YEASTS selected
GRAPES 100% estate-grown
CERTIFICATION organic

Fattoria Zerbina

Frazione Marzeno
Via Vicchio,11
tel. 0546 40022
www.zerbina.com
info@zerbina.com

29 ha - 220,000 bt   **10% discount**

66 Maria Cristina Geminiani's aim is to constantly improve her wine and the area she works in. Her approach makes her company a benchmark for all Romagna producers 99

PEOPLE - Maria Cristina, a graduate in agriculture with a passion for experimentation, took over the company formed by her grandfather in the mid-1980s. It is one of the first to tie quality to the name of the Romagna region.

VINEYARDS - The vineyards are at Marzeno, in the hills east of Faenza at an altitude of 250 meters. The terrain is generally composed of red clay, which merges into the gully formations typical of the area. Most of the vines are bush-trained with a central pole, a traditional system in Romagna. The sangiovese grapes were selected from a rare Romagna clone

WINES - These extremely elegant, potent wines are complex, austere and full-bodied, the fruit of meticulous work in the vineyard and the cellar. The excellent **Marzieno 2008** (● sangiovese, cabernet sauvignon; 10,500 bt) has aromas of pepper and fruit preserved in alcohol. On the palate it is rich, taut and elegant. We were also impressed by **Sangiovese di Romagna Ceregio 40° Anniversario 2011** (● 122,000 bt) which is blossomy and fruity on the nose, lean and lingering in the mouth, wonderfully quaffable and complex. It's a perfect Everyday Wine. **Sangiovese di Romagna Torre di Ceparano Ris. 2009** (● 30,000 bt) is flavorsome, rich and complex with gutsy character and zest. The quality of **Albana di Romagna Passito Scaccomatto 2008** (○ 2,800 bt) comes as no surprise. Slithery and caressing on the palate, it is sweet but supported by vibrant acidity.

FERTILIZERS organic-mineral, manure pellets, green manure
PLANT PROTECTION chemical, copper and sulphur
WEED CONTROL chemical, mechanical
YEASTS selected
GRAPES 100% estate-grown
CERTIFICATION none

Paolo Francesconi

Località Sarna
Via Tuliero, 154
tel. 0546 43213
www.francesconipaolo.it
pfrancesconi@racine.ra.it

14 ha - 20,000 bt   **10% discount**

66 "My aim," says Paolo Francesconi, "is to produce wines with character of their own that reflect the terroir and the work I do. This is why I apply the principles of organic and biodynamic farming in the vineyard and in the cellar" 99

PEOPLE - Paolo has managed his family wine company, situated at the foot of the hills west of Faenza, for the last 20 years. His aim is to raise the profile of an area with no great viticultural calling, yet capable, thanks to sustainable practices and his own skill, of producing outstanding wines.

VINEYARDS - Walking among the vineyards you have the immediate sensation that you are immersed in a healthy, clean environment, where the vine has found an equilibrium of its own. Populated by worms, ladybirds, bees and butterflies, the vineyards spread out over the ancient bed of the River Lamone.

WINES - Paolo's wines are simple and direct. They embody the idea of a healthy form of agriculture, exalted by the passionate commitment of a winemaker who knows how to evoke a sense of place. Full-bodied and fleshy with complex tannins, **Sangiovese di Romagna Sup. Le Iadi Ris. 2008** (● 3,200 bt) gives off sumptuous aromas of ripe red fruit. **Sangiovese di Romagna Sup. Limbecca 2010** (● 12,000 bt) is vigorous and pervasive. **Impavido 2009** (● merlot; 2,000 bt) couldn't be more elegant, its rich body accompanied by a hefty acid component that makes it supple and tonic.

> **slow wine** **ARCAICA 2011** (○ 1,500 bt) Heady scents of dried flowers and yellow fruit, crisp tannins and lively acidity give this wine thrust and dynamism. Living proof that, used well, according to tradition, the albana grape can produce excellent results.

FERTILIZERS biodynamic preparations, green manure
PLANT PROTECTION copper and sulphur
WEED CONTROL mechanical
YEASTS native
GRAPES 100% estate-grown
CERTIFICATION organic

FORLÌ (FC)

Drei Donà
Tenuta La Palazza

Località Massa di Vecchiazzano
Via del Tesoro, 23
tel. 0543 769371
www.dreidona.it
palazza@dreidona.it

27 ha - 130,000 bt

PEOPLE - It's impossible to speak about the winemaking history of the region without mentioning Tenuta La Palazza. It was Claudio Drei Donà who bought the estate in the early 1980s, moving immediately into quality production. Today his son Enrico who carries on the business with the help of the able agronomist Monia Ravagli and enologist Franco Bernabei. The use of photovoltaic panels and precision viticulture help to make the company sustainable.

VINEYARDS - The vineyards are in the Vecchiazzano district of Predappio subzone — looking onto the Montemaggio hill near Bertinoro — where they form a single plot with a south-southeast exposure at an altitude of 160 meters. The vineyards, which are, on average, 15 years old and situated on partly sandy soil rich in clay, are being converted to rod and spur pruning. They are managed using increasingly natural methods.

WINES - Heedless to fashion and market demand, Tenuta La Palazza has the great quality of producing wine with a style all of its own — authentic, uncompromising and timeless. The elegance that defines its labels achieves a peak of expression in the first **Sangiovese di Romagna Sup. Cuvée Palazza Ris. 2009** (● sangiovese, altri vitigni; 8,000 bt), the modern version of the maison's historic 1960s reserve, aged in 15- and 15-hectoliter oak barrels. It is a wine of generous notes of fruit, spice and leather, vibrant on the palate with velvety tannins and a tangy, ever so long finish. Dark and intriguing, potent and austere, **Sangiovese di Romagna Sup. Pruno Ris. 2009** (● 20,000 bt) is as good as ever. The excellent **Magnificat 2009** (● cabernet sauvignon; 13,000 bt) is sharp and herbaceous, while **Notturno 2010** (● sangiovese; 60,000 bt) is eminently drinkable.

RONCOFREDDO (FC)

Villa Venti

Frazione Villa Venti
Via Doccia, 1442
tel. 0541 949532
www.villaventi.it
info@villaventi.it

7 ha - 26,000 bt   `10% discount`

PEOPLE - Mauro Giardini and Davide Castellucci's inexhaustible energy infects anyone arriving at Villa Venti, in the steep wine hills of Roncofreddo. The small family winery came into being in 2002, since when it has always used organic methods. It also provides accommodation and houses a traditional restaurant.

VINEYARDS - The young vineyards are candelabra-trained — a variation on bush-training — and have developed an optimal natural equilibrium with the terrain and surrounding eco-system. The grapes are robust and healthy, the red clay and sand in the soil adding extract and sugar ripeness. The climate is characterized by sharp day to night temperature swings and the sea breezes mitigate the high summer temperatures.

WINES - The wines of Villa Venti stand out for their sense of place, a feature enologist manages to coax out by evidencing their exuberant Mediteranean character. The company's latest label, **Sangiovese di Romagna Sup. Primo Segno 2010** (● 15,000 bt) is potent and full-blooded. The fruit of a cold, wet vintage, it is lean and elegant with refined vegetal notes. **Serenaro 2011** (○ 2,000 bt), made from the indigenous famoso di Cesena grape, has aromas of dried flowers and refreshing acidity. **Nanì** (● 1,000 bt), made with overripe centesimino grapes, is intensely aromatic with intriguing notes of cocoa.

slow wine	**SANGIOVESE SUP. RIS. 2009** (● 5,000 bt) The long, patient toil of Mauro and Davide, brilliant at waiting for and respecting the rhythms of nature, has rewarded by this superlative wine. The palate is well-developed and laid-back, and the bouquet exudes red fruit and spices.

FERTILIZERS natural manure	FERTILIZERS none
PLANT PROTECTION copper and sulphur	PLANT PROTECTION copper and sulphur
WEED CONTROL mechanical	WEED CONTROL mechanical
YEASTS selected	YEASTS selected
GRAPES 100% estate-grown	GRAPES 100% estate-grown
CERTIFICATION none	CERTIFICATION organic

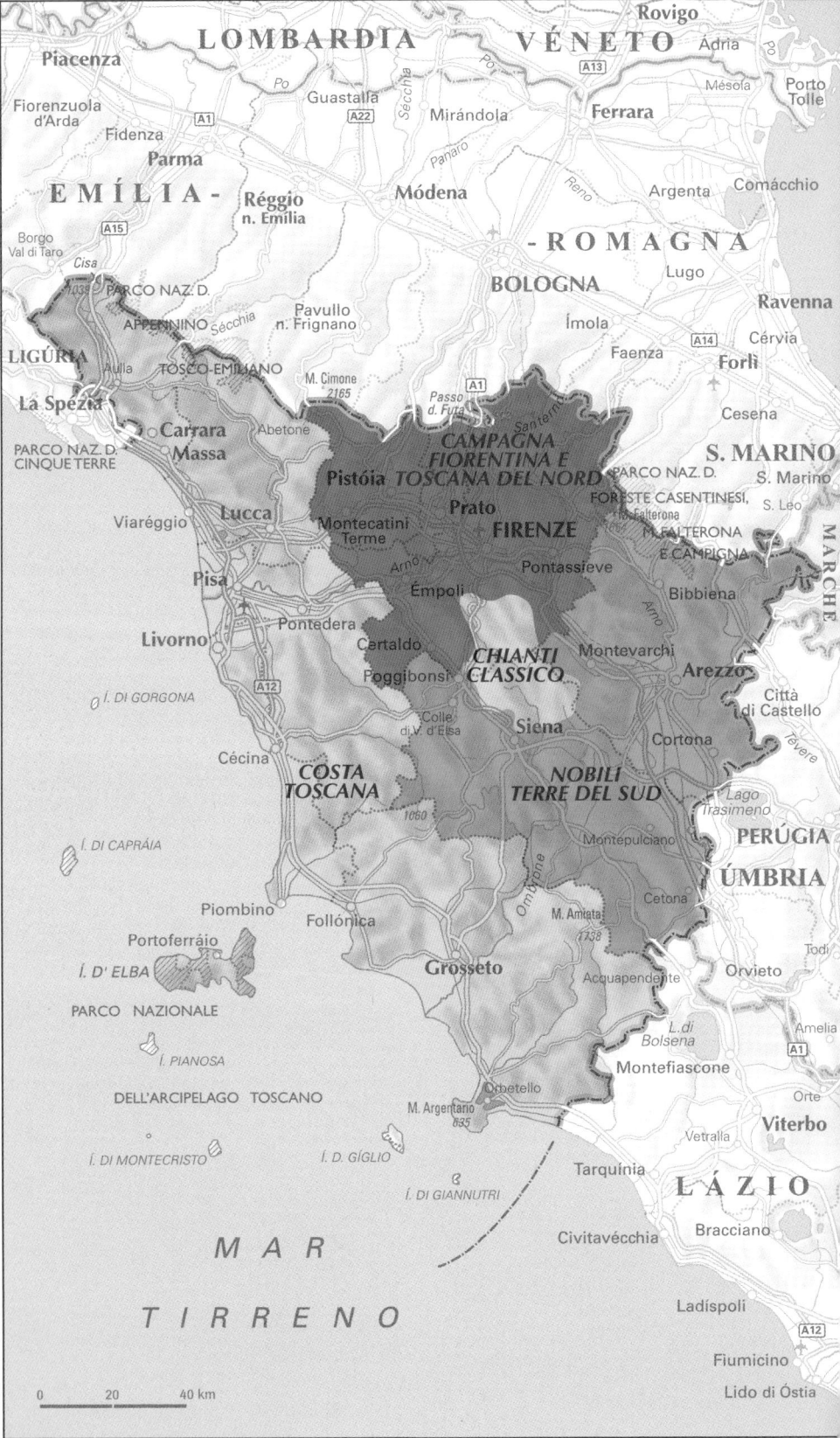

TUSCANY

With almost 65,000 hectares of vineyards, Tuscany is, quantitatively speaking, one of the most important regions on the variegated Italian wine scene. The general quality of its many, distinct winegrowing districts is also high. From its myriad of increasingly convincing wines and wineries, we have picked the ones that, for history, eco-sustainability and quality, can best represent the region to our readers. One of the objectives we set ourselves was to single out as many wineries as possible that combine virtuous viticulture with reasonable prices. So keep a close eye on our Coins, Everyday Wines and Slow Wine, which, in relation to the various denominations of origin, encapsulate our critical philosophy applied to wine. Negative per se, the economic crisis nonetheless offers a chance to find out more about the lesser know wines that constitute one of the most interesting sides of Tuscan viticulture today. In fact, wines such as Rufina, Chianti Classico, Rosso di Montalcino and Rosso di Montepulciano can be cited as examples of top quality, affordable wines that conjure up a pure sense of place.

Costa toscana

Le Macchiole

Via Bolgherese, 189 A
tel. 0565 766092
www.lemacchiole.it
info@lemacchiole.it

20 ha - 140,000 bt

PEOPLE - Still not content with all the successes she has achieved at home and abroad, Cinzia Merli is intent upon improving the quality of her wines. Though she and her staff are convinced that the route they took a few years ago to bring out the potential of the Bolgheri terroir through monovarietal production is the right one, the experiments continue. The consultant is Luca D'Attoma, the company enologist Luca Rettondini.

VINEYARDS - The old two-hectare vineyard behind the cellar where tests and experiments took place over the years has been uprooted. It will now be left to rest for 12 months, then replanted with the finest clone of cabernet franc, a grape that is giving Cinzia a lot of satisfaction. After deciding to use only organic methods, the company now wants to go one step further and is already applying biodynamic principles to four hectares of vineyard.

WINES - Now that the vineyards have matured, the company's wines are becoming increasingly consistent and complex with unique character. One that we rated very highly was **Messorio 2009** (● merlot; 10,000 bt), which combines its proverbial potency with elegant finesse and stylish tannins, plus a textbook finish. No less impressive was **Paleo 2009** (● cabernet franc; 25,000 bt), which though young and a tad underdeveloped, has a rich, dense, earthy bouquet and an enfolding, vertical palate. **Scrio 2009** (● 4,000 bt) is a monovarietal Syrah packed with power and allure. "This is my tribute to the Bolgheri terroir," says Cinzia of her **Bolgheri Le Macchiole 2010** (● merlot, cabernet franc, syrah; 95,000 bt). **Paleo Bianco 2010** (○ sauvignon blanc, chardonnay; 6,500 bt), finally, is succulent and sapid.

FERTILIZERS	natural manure, green manure
PLANT PROTECTION	copper and sulphur
WEED CONTROL	mechanical
YEASTS	selected
GRAPES	100% estate-grown
CERTIFICATION	none

Tenuta San Guido

Località Capanne, 27
tel. 0565 762003
www.sassicaia.com
info@sassicaia.com

85 ha - 660,000 bt

PEOPLE - It only takes one word to describe this monumental name in Italian winemaking and that word is professionalism! It's a concept that, without any rhetoric, you find every time you come into contact with Tenuta San Guido and the experise and competence of director Carlo Paoli, Marchese Nicolò Incisa della Rocchetta and all their skilled staff. This company has built a new identity from scratch, which now translates into the kind of image that legend is made of.

VINEYARDS - Here too, everything revolves round the vineyard. Variable exposures, the age of the vines (the oldest were planted in 1944), microclimates and altimetry make the agronomic scene at Tenuta San Guido a variegated one. Thanks to painstaking care for the vine rows, it is possible to identify different selections, exalted by the three labels in the cellar. Sensitivity towards the land and landscape is not confined to the vineyard with great efforts being made to promote the Oasi di Bolgheri nature reserve, which belongs to the Incisa della Rocchetta family.

WINES - It's no great surprise that **Bolgheri Sassicaia 2009** (● cabernet sauvignon; 200,000 bt), consistently one of the finest versions of this historic label from the Tuscan coast, is a Great Wine. We like the way it manages to combine depth, texture, complexity, elegance, drinkability and, amazingly, distinct minerality. It's a textbook wine. Convincing too is **Guidalberto 2010** (● cabernet sauvignon, merlot, petit verdot; 200,000 bt), more fruity than potent. **Le Difese 2010** (● 300,000 bt) has a precise intent: to raise the profile of Tuscan identity by striking a balance between sangiovese and cabernet sauvignon. The price offers exceptional value for money.

FERTILIZERS	natural manure
PLANT PROTECTION	chemical, copper and sulphur
WEED CONTROL	mechanical
YEASTS	native
GRAPES	20% bought in
CERTIFICATION	none

Tenuta di Valgiano

Frazione Valgiano
Via di Valgiano, 7
tel. 0583 4022710
www.valgiano.it
info@valgiano.it

21 ha - 70,000 bt

❝ Tenuta di Valgiano's natural approach to viticulture is influencing a whole new generation of winemakers ❞

PEOPLE - Valgiano functions as a closed-cycle agricultural system, in which different experiences come together. Here the key values of the farming world — protection of the landscape, environmental sustainability and encouragement of field labor — offer an alternative opportunity to the blind consumerism of the "contemporary Middle Ages".

VINEYARDS - In the company of enologist Saverio Petrilli, we visited the six-hectare vineyard that surrounds the cellar. Here an old river bed has left sandstone soil with *alberese* rock outcrops. The first plantings go back to 1994. Now three hectares have been explanted and, after three year's resting, the same mix of native grapes will be restored. The remaining part of the property is rented on three different plots.

WINES - When they bought the estate back in 1993, Moreno Petrini and Laura di Collobiano steered a clear, direct course to the production of their own ideal wines, precursors of biodynamics applied to viticulture. The wines reflect their extremely natural approach and clearly display a sense of place. **Colline Lucchesi Tenuta di Valgiano 2009** (● sangiovese, syrah, merlot; 10,000 bt) has become an institution. We enjoyed its complexity and naturalness. It's a deep and leisurely, silky and pleasurable on the palate — a Great Wine. The excellent **Colline Lucchesi Palistorti 2010** (● sangiovese, syrah, merlot; 48,000 bt) is tangy with an edgy finish. **Palistorti Bianco 2011** (○ vermentino, trebbiano, malvasia; 12,000 bt), finally, is warm, racy and mineral.

FERTILIZERS biodynamic preparations, green manure
PLANT PROTECTION copper and sulphur
WEED CONTROL mechanical
YEASTS native
GRAPES 100% estate-grown
CERTIFICATION biodynamic

Grattamacco

Località Podere Grattamacco
tel. 0565 765069
www.collemassari.it
info@collemassari.it

12 ha - 81,000 bt

PEOPLE - Grattamacco nestles in an enchanting position between the Bolgheri hills and the sea. We were welcomed there by Luca Marrone, an enologist and collaborator of owner Claudio Tipa. Since the cellar was undergoing renovation work, Luca took us round the vineyards and we were thus able to witness this company's outstanding winemaking vocation firsthand. Luca showed us the incredible variety of the soils available, capable of adding complexity to the wine produced.

VINEYARDS - The wine hills are characterized by rocky soil of marine origin. As the vine rows gradually come close to the woods, the formation turns into what's known as "sand of Donoratico". In the vineyards one notes many different nuances in the soil; one in particular is the strip of clay that cuts through it. The low vigor of the vineyards resting is at the base of grapes of exciting complexity.

WINES - Luca would never be prepared to give up the oldest vineyards, planted in the mid 1980s. "We are a young terroir," he explains, "and we have the possibility, indeed the duty, to show off the denomination's vocation." One wine from these vineyards is **Bolgheri Sup. Grattamacco 2009** (● cabernet sauvignon, sangiovese, merlot; 30,000 bt), which ages in barriques for 18 months: it offers concentrated, intact fruit and a silky palate. It's a Great Wine. The splendid **Bolgheri Vermentino Grattamacco 2010** (○ 10,000 bt) ferments half in stainless steel and half in barriques and is mineral, juicy and dynamic. The full-textured **Bolgheri Sup. L'Alberello 2009** (● cabernet sauvignon e franc; petit verdot; 6,000 bt) comes from a vineyard with bush-trained vines. **Bolgheri 2010** (● cabernet sauvignon e franc, sangiovese, merlot; 35,000 bt) brims over with fruit.

FERTILIZERS natural manure, green manure
PLANT PROTECTION copper and sulphur
WEED CONTROL mechanical
YEASTS native
GRAPES 100% estate-grown
CERTIFICATION organic

CASTAGNETO CARDUCCI (LI)

I Luoghi

Località Campo al Capriolo, 201
tel. 0565 777379
www.iluoghi.it
info@iluoghi.it

CINIGIANO (GR)

Collemassari

Località Poggio del Sasso
tel. 0564 990498
www.collemassari.it
info@collemassari.it

3.5 ha - 12,000 bt

66 Miracle in Bolgheri — flavorsome, succulent and light wines of the highest quality. Products of clean agriculture at reasonable prices 99

PEOPLE - A native of Milan, Stefano Granata went to live in the countryside near Castagneto Carducci at the age of five. There he later met his wife Paola De Fusco and since then, in the space of just a few years together, they have built up one of the most innovative wineries in Bolgheri.

VINEYARDS - The secret of their success is in their vineyards — 3.5 hectares split into two properties on flat land in the Laschi and Ritorti districts — which they tend with loving care. Since planting them in 2002, the cellar has privileged the growth cycle and the slow development of the vines to grow grapes with balanced phenolics.

WINES - The cellar work is followed by Paola. Fermentations are lengthy without added yeasts. Each single grape variety and each single parcel are vinified separately with manual *piegage* and long aging in French oak. The wines stand out for their strong personality and their balance of freshness and substance. **Bolgheri Sup. Campo Al Fico 2009** (● cabernet sauvignon e franc; 3.000 bt) ages for 24 months in mostly new wooden casks. It is elegant on the nose with notes of soil and Mediterranean scrub. In the mouth its very fine tannins are supported by almost saline tanginess.

> slow wine **BOLGHERI SUP. PODERE RITORTI 2009** (● cabernet sauvignon e franc, merlot, syrah; 9,000 bt) The result of briefer aging, a fine, velvety wine with just the right fruit and overall balance. The price is more than reasonable.

---

100 ha - 400,000 bt

PEOPLE - To visit the Castello Collemassari and Tenuta di Montecucco wineries is to enter the heart of the dynamic Tuscan denomination situated between the coast and Montalcino. These two important companies have raised the zone's profile worldwide. Responsible for all the hefty investment is the Bertarelli Tipa family who, over the last few years, has created a major private group that also owns the Poggio di Sotto and Grattamacco estates.

VINEYARDS - We can't speak about the vineyards of Cinigiano, a commune at the heart of the Montecucco commune, without stressing the Collemassari's commitment to protecting the landscape and distinctive features of the local agriculture. Collaboration with others has generated a concentration of organic wineries that adds credibility to the whole area.

WINES - The two distinct wineries are united by a single mission: to raise the profile of Montecucco and the sangiovese, currently the subject of clonal studies. Of the Collemassari line, we recommend the excellent **Montecucco Sangiovese Lombrone Ris. 2008** (● 6,000 bt), varietal with plenty of character. **Montecucco Rosso Collemassari Ris. 2009** (● 50,000 bt), which includes cabernet grapes, has sweet notes with a pleasant whiff of toast. **Montecucco Rosso Rigoleto 2010** (● 80,000 bt) is pleasant and juicy. We also liked **Montecucco Vermentino Melacce 2011** (○ 40,000 bt). We chose the very pleasant **Montecucco Rosso Passonaia 2010** (● sangiovese, ciliegiolo; 60,000 bt) from the other estate as an Everyday Wine. **Montecucco Sangiovese Rigomoro Ris. 2008** (● 5,000 bt) is more structured with a veil of huskiness.

FERTILIZERS green manure	FERTILIZERS natural manure
PLANT PROTECTION copper and sulphur, organic	PLANT PROTECTION copper and sulphur
WEED CONTROL mechanical	WEED CONTROL mechanical
YEASTS native	YEASTS native
GRAPES 100% estate-grown	GRAPES 100% estate-grown
CERTIFICATION converting to organics	CERTIFICATION organic

Salustri

Località La Cava
Frazione Poggio del Sasso
tel. 0564 990529
www.salustri.it
info@salustri.it

20 ha - 92,000 bt

66 The old vineyards are still alive and kicking, ready to tell the story of Leonardo Salustri and his ethical and aesthetic promotion of Montecucco 99

PEOPLE - Wine, oil, Cinta Senese pigs and a gorgeous agriturismo where you can stay in total peace — this is the bucolic setting of Leonardo and his son Marco's farm, where respect for biodiversity and tradition is total.

VINEYARDS - Not that Leonardo limits himself to keeping the vines and the vineyards alive. He is also carrying on a project in collaboration with the University of Pisa to recover old sangiovese clones (so far about 800 have been singled out) and protect the old vineyards. When we visited the latter, about 70 years old, Leonardo proudly showed us his technique for "rejuvenating" the various properties. It's an obsessive task that requires all his old-fashioned peasant wisdom.

WINES - The old sangiovese vineyards produce wines of character, texture and strong personality. Vinification is performed with the help of Maurizio Castelli and privileges long macerations in wooden fermenters (Leonardo's approach), though stainless steel is used for the simpler wines. The beautifully succulent **Montecucco Rosso Marleo 2010** (● 40,000 bt) is pleasant and dynamic with clear-cut fruit. A novelty this year is **Montecucco Sangiovese Terre d'Alviero 2007** (● 3,000 bt), the result of a "social" scheme to raise the profile of an old vineyard owned by an elderly peasant called Alviero. It is an important wine with very open ethereal notes, rustic hints and no lack of acidity, tanginess and progression. We also liked **Montecucco Vermentino Narà 2011** (○ 12,000 bt) a lot.

Fabbrica di San Martino

Frazione San Martino in Vignale
Via Pieve Santo Stefano, 2511
tel. 0583 394284
www.fabbricadisanmartino.it
info@fabbricadisanmartino.it

2.2 ha - 12,000 bt

PEOPLE - In the hills near Lucca, Giuseppe Ferrua and Giovanna Tronci have created a minor masterpiece. Fabbrica di San Martino today is an all-round farm, which breeds Garfagna cattle and donkeys and produces oil and wine. In 2008, Giuseppe, ever a champion of organics, converted the farm to biodynamics.

VINEYARDS - The vineyards spread out for about two hectares round the farmhouse. The soils are characterized by clay, silt and gravel. The spacing of plants is traditional as is the Guyot-training. The old vineyard boasts an interesting number of local grape varieties. The best specimens undergo massal selection.

WINES - Vinifcation is very simple and interventions on the must are kept to a bare minimum. Giuseppe is less dogmatic than he used to be and has cleaned his wines up without altering their personality. **Colline Lucchesi Arcipressi Bianco 2011** (○ malvasia, vermentino, trebbiano; 4,000 bt) is tangy and generous with a nice vein of acidity. **Colline Lucchesi Fabbrica di San Martino Rosso 2009** (● sangiovese, ciliegiolo, colorino; 5,000 bt) has stylish notes of ripe cherry, a taut mineral palate and crunchy tannins. **Colline Lucchesi Arcipressi Rosso 2011** (● 3,000 bt) is flowery and warm with a refreshing finish.

slow wine COLLINE LUCCHESI FABBRICA DI SAN MARTINO BIANCO 2010 (○ vermentino, trebbiano, malvasia; 3,000 bt) Finesse on the nose, good impact on the palate, freshness, mineral finish, wonderful harmony … here's to the laudable recovery of the old clones and strains that went into the wine's production.

FERTILIZERS natural manure, green manure
PLANT PROTECTION copper and sulphur
WEED CONTROL mechanical
YEASTS selected
GRAPES 100% estate-grown
CERTIFICATION organic

FERTILIZERS compost, biodynamic preparations, green manure
PLANT PROTECTION copper and sulphur
WEED CONTROL mechanical
YEASTS native
GRAPES 100% estate-grown
CERTIFICATION biodynamic

La Parrina   €

Frazione Albinia
Località La Parrina
tel. 0564 862626
www.parrina.it
info@parrina.it

57 ha - 150,000 bt

PEOPLE - It's said that wine has been produced in this zone since the time of the Spanish domination. Today Franca Spinola is the last descendant of her family and has been running La Parrina since the start of the century. With an area of 504 hectares and all-round agricultural production — from wine to oil, from cheese to vegetables, from cereals to honey — it is one of the most important farms in the whole Maremma area.

VINEYARDS - The vineyards cover an area of 57 hectares at the foot of the hills a few kilometers from Orbetello, where the clay soil is rich in limestone. The vines are planted at a density of no more than 5,000 per hectare and are mainly cordon-trained and spur-pruned. They are overseen by Stefano Lattanzi and the agronomist Gian Piero Romana, who have always defended them using an integrated pest management system.

WINES - Andrea Fioriello, the cellar manager, and enologist Beppe Caviola interpret the peculiarities of the grapes and the uniqueness of the land supremely well. **Radaia 2006** (● merlot; 7,000 bt) has astonishing power and elegance. **Parrina Ris. 2008** (● sangiovese, cabernet sauvignon, merlot; 9,000 bt) impresses for its concentrated suite of aromas, which opens with unobtrusive wood backed by red berries and balsamic notes. We recommend **Parrina Muraccio 2008** (● sangiovese, cabernet sauvignon; 20,000 bt) for its great value for money. Of the whites, the excellent **Poggio della Fata 2011** (○ sauvignon, vermentino; 3,000 bt) offers very pleasant aromatic notes. Worth tasting for its freshness and harmony — besides its price —is **Parrina Bianco 2011** (○ ansonica, vermentino, chardonnay, trebbiano; 9,000 bt), an excellent Everyday Wine.

Caiarossa

Località Serra all'Olio, 59
tel. 0586 699016
www.caiarossa.com
info@caiarossa.com

32.5 ha - 80,000 bt

❝ Caiarossa has become an institution for anyone practicing sustainable agriculture in Tuscany. Its success is due to a series of human and environmental factors which combine to create the "Caiarossa model" ❞

PEOPLE - Without the skilled hand of Dominique Genot, a young French enologist, who over the years has studied and coaxed the best out of the vines and wines of this corner of Tuscany, Caiarossa wouldn't be what it is today.

VINEYARDS - The company's vineyards are divided into two separate plots. The first is shaped like an amphitheater round the cellar, the second, bought recently and ready for replanting, is situated in the Nocolino district, not far from the estate buildings but in a higher position. The vines are cultivated according to biodynamic principles to exploit to the full the potential of the soils and various cultivars, whose characteristics are clearly expressed in the wines.

WINES - The common denominators of Caiarossa's wines are elegance and tanginess. These are qualities that emerge to the full in **Caiarossa Bianco 2010** (○ chardonnay, viognier; 2,300 bt). Some of the grapes for **Pergolaia 2009** (● sangiovese, cabernet, merlot; 30,000 bt) are bought in from trusted local growers. It is a juicy, concentrated wine, but highly drinkable with it. The unusual **Oro di Caiarossa 2009** (○ petit manseng; 1,000 bt) is made with late-harvested grapes and offers aromas of apricots and saffron, set off by an acidity that supplements the wine's structures. **Caiarossa 2009** (● sangiovese, cabernet, merlot, petit verdot, grenache; 46,000 bt) combines structure and elegance and shows off mature tannins, minerality and a long, lingering finish.

FERTILIZERS organic-mineral, natural manure
PLANT PROTECTION chemical, copper and sulphur
WEED CONTROL chemical, mechanical
YEASTS selected
GRAPES 100% estate-grown
CERTIFICATION none

FERTILIZERS compost, biodynamic preparations, green manure
PLANT PROTECTION copper and sulphur
WEED CONTROL mechanical
YEASTS native
GRAPES 30% bought in
CERTIFICATION biodynamic

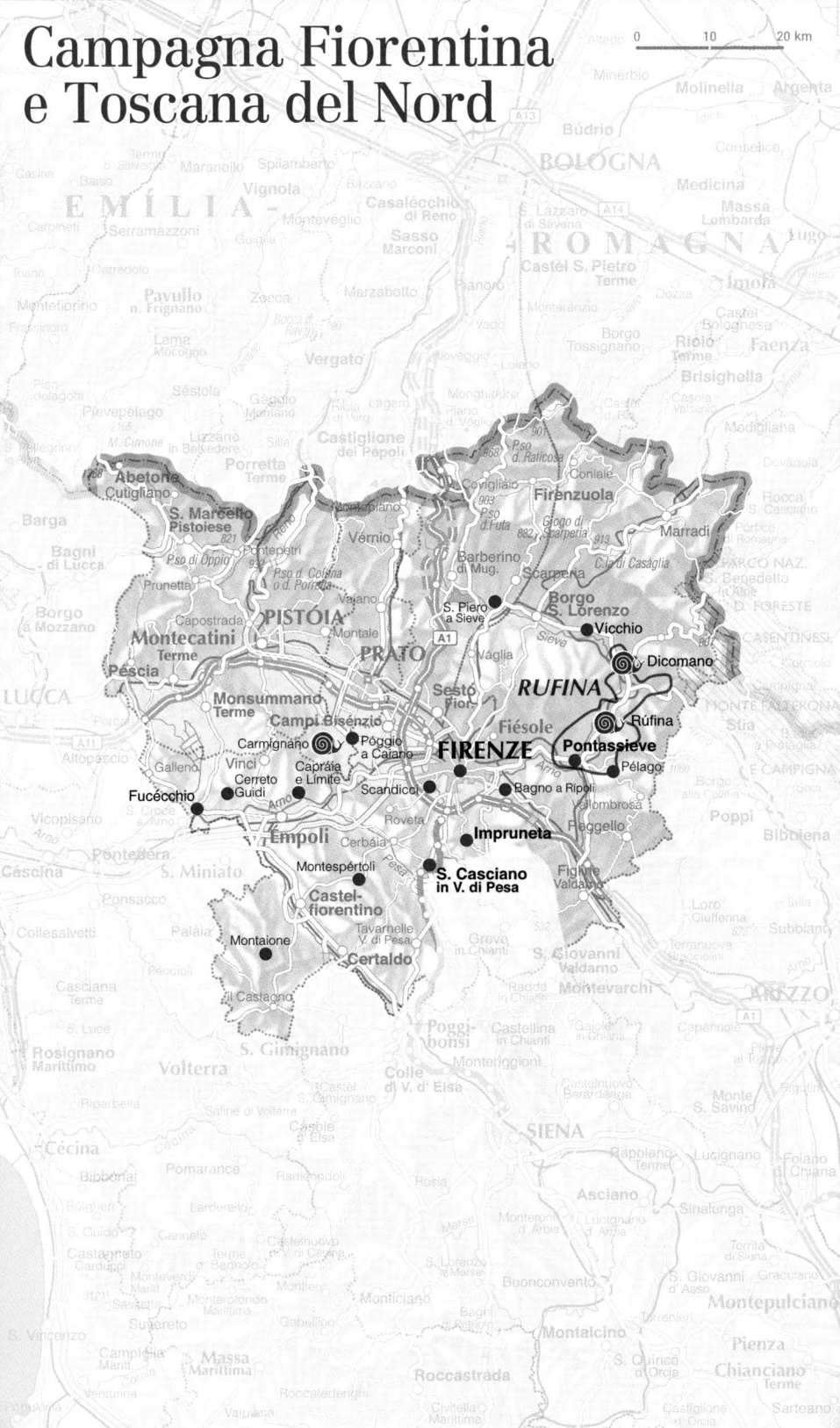

Campagna Fiorentina e Toscana del Nord

CARMIGNANO (PO)

Fattoria di Bacchereto 🐌
Terre a Mano
Via Fontemorana, 179
tel. 055 8717191
terreamano@gmail.com

---

8 ha - 23,000 bt

❝ A model company that combines biodynamics with the production of clean, good, typical, long-lasting wines. What more can you ask? ❞

PEOPLE - Fattoria di Bacchereto, active since 1920, is surrounded by the woods of Montalbano. Managed with great passion by Rossella Bencini Tesi, it functions as a veritable guardian of the land. Rossella is helped by cellarman and enologist Marco Vannucci and consultant agronomist Adriano Zago.

VINEYARDS - The slightly sloping vineyards are situated at altitudes of 350-500 meters on gravelly *alberese* soil and are Guyot- and spurred cordon-trained. The grapes are harvested by hand in various stages and undergo final selection on arrival at the cellar. The company does not prune the vines, but bends them sideways, supports them with poles and binds them with willow twigs.

WINES - The essential, functional cellar houses cement, stainless steel and wooden casks and vinification is carried out manually vineyard by vineyard with fermentation of the grapes on their skins. **Sassocarlo 2010** (○ trebbiano, malvasia; 3,000 bt) is produced in casks with frequent *bâtonnages*. Its intense aromas are accompanied by mineral and spicy notes and the palate is complex and rich. **Vin Santo di Carmignano 2001** (◉ 1,500 bt) was a big surprise for us. Made with grapes dried until December, it releases aromas of fig and dried and tropical fruits. The palate is juicy and elegant, enriched by notes of apricot, licorice and cinnamon.

slow wine CARMIGNANO TERRE A MANO **2009** (● 18,000 bt) A *vin de terroir* with intense scents of fruit and peppers that linger over an elegant, very pleasant palate.

CARMIGNANO (PO)

Tenuta di Capezzana
Via Capezzana, 100
tel. 055 8706005
www.capezzana.it
capezzana@capezzana.it

---

105 ha - 500,000 bt

PEOPLE - After 57 years at the helm of this over 100-year-old estate, Ugo Contini Bonacossi passed away this spring, just before we were due to go to there. We still remember his pledge to raise the profile of the fantastic Carmignano terroir and the way he performed with patience and class. Now the reins have been taken over by his children Benedetta, Beatrice, Vittorio and Filippo, who manage the various sectors of the company helped, in turn, by their own children.

VINEYARDS - The vineyards are managed by Vittorio, who is adamant that organic methods are the only way to produce great terroir-rooted wines. The many parcels combine to create a breathtaking landscape but are, logistically speaking, hard to work and present the skilled staff with many a headache. The marvelously located Trefiano vineyard, the cru below the historic villa, is particularly beautiful.

WINES - **Carmignano Villa di Trefiano Ris. 2008** (● 18,500 bt) stands out for its elegance with intriguing earthy notes, very fine tannins and a lingering finish. The first-rate **Carmignano Villa di Capezzana 2008** (● 64,500 bt) has a floral bouquet with dynamic, elegant structure. The balsamic, silky **Ghiaie della Furba 2008** (● cabernet sauvignon, merlot, syrah; 17,000 bt) is less terroir-rooted. **Trebbiano 2009** (○ 5,000 bt) epitomizes the grape wonderfully with citron nuances on a long, well-structured palate.

slow wine CARMIGNANO VIN SANTO RIS. **2006** (○ 7,000 bt) A masterpiece! A feast of dried and candied fruit supported by perfect acid thrust. Traditional and very long indeed.

FERTILIZERS green manure	FERTILIZERS green manure
PLANT PROTECTION copper and sulphur	PLANT PROTECTION copper and sulphur
WEED CONTROL mechanical	WEED CONTROL mechanical
YEASTS native	YEASTS native
GRAPES 100% estate-grown	GRAPES 100% estate-grown
CERTIFICATION biodynamic	CERTIFICATION converting to organics

Frascole

Località Frascole, 27 A
tel. 055 8386340
www.frascole.it
frascole@frascole.it

Colognole

Via del Palagio, 15
tel. 055 8319870
www.colognole.it
info@colognole.it

16 ha - 50,000 bt

27 ha - 110,000 bt

" The range Frascole presented this year was of the highest level. Wines that speak a language of their own, the fruit of good, old-fashioned farming but also projected into the future "

PEOPLE - Elisa Santoni has been cultivating the vineyard in the Cavaliere district for some years now, but it was only in 1992, the year she married Enrico Lippi, that she bought Frascole and the story of the winery began. With the consultancy of the former Ornellaia enologist Staderini, Elisa tends the vineyards. Enrico decided to devote himself to the company full-time in 1996.

VINEYARDS - Situated at an altitude of 400 meters, the vineyards surround the house and extend into two separate plots further north, both well ventilated. Most parcels are limited in size and often grow different grape varieties. Sangiovese grapes occupy the best vineyards, but there is also no lack of canaiolo, colorino, trebbiano, merlot and now also pinot nero.

WINES - Attention to detail is the watchword of the essential cellar, where since 2009 the grapes are fermented in small batches to achieve the best results. Witness, for example, **Chianti Rufina 2010** (● 30,000 bt), a wine with a floral, mineral bouquet and a fine, elegant palate with mineral, flinty notes. The traditional **Bitornino 2010** (● sangiovese, colorino, canaiolo, trebbiano; 15,000 bt) is an effective blend of numerous varieties. Last but not least, **Vin Santo del Chianti Rufina 2003** (● 1,100 bt), has exceptionally clear-cut aromas of dried fruit and licorice.

slow wine | CHIANTI RUFINA RIS. 2009 (● 6,000 bt) Heady aromas of ripe fruit followed by an extremely attractive fresh, mineral tone on the palate with faintly perceptible tannins. A little gem of a wine!

PEOPLE - A few kilometers out of the village of Rufina in the Forlì direction, you come to the turn-off for Colognole. The uphill dirt road leads to the villa that serves as the company's headquarters. Here the air you breathe and the landscape all round come as a surprise. Colognole is a historic company run by a family now in its fifth generation. Today it is run by Mario and Cesare, sons of Contessa Gabriella Spalletti Trivelli, who began to revamp it a few years ago.

VINEYARDS - The company boasts two wine estates: one at Poggio Reale, near the village of Rufina at an altitude of 230 meters, another higher up at Colognole, at an altitude of 500 meters, where a syrah vineyard is planted on mainly pebbly soil. The aim is to put the potential of international grapes to the test in a zone traditionally given over to sangiovese. The influence of the nearby Tuscan-Emilian Apennines ensures a good night-to-day temperature swing.

WINES - Chianti Rufina wines develop slowly. Our tasting began with **Chianti Rufina 2009** (● 60,000 bt), which has a nose rich in ripe fruits and a juicy body — a perfect Everyday Wine. **Chianti Rufina Ris. 2007** (● 45,000 bt) has elegant notes, a palate that is still developing and fine tannins. **Le Lastre 2009** (● sangiovese, syrah, merlot; 7,000 bt), named for the vineyard of origin, has a bouquet with notes of fruit and a palate with outstanding freshness and lingering flavor. It was a pleasure to taste the limited-edition Collezione Colognole 2004, made with grapes from the oldest vineyard and aged three years in barrels and three years in the bottle. "This label," explains Cesare, who joined us for the tasting, "helps us understand how the wine evolves in the course of time. As far as we're concerned, the result is excellent!"

FERTILIZERS manure pellets, green manure	FERTILIZERS organic-mineral
PLANT PROTECTION copper and sulphur	PLANT PROTECTION organic
WEED CONTROL mechanical	WEED CONTROL mechanical
YEASTS native	YEASTS selected
GRAPES 100% estate-grown	GRAPES 100% estate-grown
CERTIFICATION organic	CERTIFICATION none

RUFINA (FI)

Fattoria Selvapiana

Località Selvapiana, 43
tel. 055 8369848
www.selvapiana.it
selvapiana@tin.it

RUFINA (FI)

Podere Il Balzo

Via del Poggiolo, 12
tel. 055 8397556
podereilbalzo@alice.it

60 ha - 240,000 bt   **10% discount**

6 ha - 5,000 bt   **10% discount**

❝ Located in an area wrongly regarded as marginal on the Tuscan viticultural map, the company is an institution in the history of Italian enology. Federico stresses the historical importance of Selvapiana, and his wines, all sheer class, reassert the absolute nobility of Rufina ❞

PEOPLE - Federico Giuntini represents the fifth generation of the family at the helm of Fattoria Selvapiana. Consistent quality, respect for the land and lucid productive vision are the key features of this pillar of Tuscan winemaking history.

VINEYARDS - This year saw the completion of the program embarked upon in 2002 to renew the vineyard and the cellar. In the last few years, Federico has been looking around for new vineyards, such as Masseto, which he bought to improve Chianti Rufina. He tends the Bucerchiale, Fornace and other vineyards with the same goal in mind. The clay, medium-texture, pebbly soil leaves a unique mark on the grapes of Selvapiana.

WINES - Chianti Rufina Bucerchiale Ris. 2009 (● 30,000 bt) has still to develop fully. It will still take some time, but for the moment it expresses a deep but undefined nose and a palate marked by ripeness. **Chianti Rufina 2010** (● 200,000 bt) is approachable, pleasurable and paradigmatic of the typology. The interesting **Fornace 2009** (● cabernet sauvignon e franc, merlot; 4,000 bt) has enfolding, elegant flavor. Worth tasting is **Syrah 2009** (● 2,500 bt) a new entry. **Vin Santo del Chianti Rufina 2004** (○ 6,000 bt) has ethereal, enthralling aromas and a concentrated palate supported by a streak of vibrant acidity.

PEOPLE - The Podere Il Balzo winery may be tiny, but it's worth keeping an eye on. Paolo Ponticelli manages not only the vineyard and the cellar but the entire farm, including chestnut pole-making work in the woods. He's helped by his sister Irene on the administration side and his mum Roberta Bongi in the kitchen. After selling wine unbottled for years, the farm released its first bottle in 2006. It was Federico Giuntini of Selvapiana who convinced his buddy Paolo to take the big step.

VINEYARDS - June is dedicated to green pruning, July to thinning out. The soil between the vine rows, planted halfway up the hillside, are fertilized with green manure every other year. In one part of the property are the vines planted Paolo's grandfather in the 1970s: hence canaiolo, malvasia rossa, ciliegiolo, malvasia bianca and trebbiano. The farm also grows olives, renting some of the trees. It's not infrequent for roe deer and wild boar to cause damage to the vines.

WINES - Podere Il Balzo currently makes just one wine, but that won't be for long. **Chianti Rufina Podere Il Balzo 2009** (5,000 bt) has intense aromas rich in forest fruits and notes of cherry. Full-bodied with a leisurely palate and a burst of moreish freshness, it's an excellent Everyday Wine. The 2006 vintage, the first produced, wasn't in the guide but was a pleasure and a surprise to taste. It has a well-developed bouquet with red fruit and spices, enfolding, silky flavor and well-crafted tannins. On our tour of the cellar we stopped in front of the barrel in which the Riserva, due to be released in 2013, is resting. When Paolo asked us to taste the freshly drawn wine, we naturally accepted. The bouquet is virtually ready, while the palate is still developing but already has an identity of its own. You're sure to hear more about this wine in the future.

FERTILIZERS organic-mineral, green manure	FERTILIZERS green manure
PLANT PROTECTION copper and sulphur	PLANT PROTECTION copper and sulphur
WEED CONTROL mechanical	WEED CONTROL mechanical
YEASTS native	YEASTS native
GRAPES 100% estate-grown	GRAPES 100% estate-grown
CERTIFICATION converting to organics	CERTIFICATION none

Chianti Classico

Castello della Paneretta €

Strada della Paneretta, 35
tel. 055 8059003
www.paneretta.it
paneretta@paneretta.it

22 ha - 105,000 bt · **10% discount**

PEOPLE - In an ideal map of Tuscan wine-growing areas, the Monsanto road at Barberino Val d'Elsa could be a prestigious grand cru. Castello della Paneretta, which stands in the district, has always played a leading role in the history of Chianti. The Albisetti family bought the company in the mid 1980s and today Enrico Albisetti manages its roughly 300 hectares in an agricultural and architectural environment of considerable worth.

VINEYARDS - Enrico took us on a tour of the vineyards. We were impressed by the Barbiano Galestri property, planted in February , 2012. The area is entirely covered by surface slabs of purplish *galestro* marl and the sound of our footsteps was an unreal echo of cobbles being trodden upon down the ages. *Galestro* marl is common in all the vineyards, including Torre a Destra, the one the wine of the same name comes from. Only sangiovese and colorino grapes are grown.

WINES - The wines are still aged in the castle's historic wine cellars. "Working here," says Enrico, "gives you a great sense of respect for the terroir, which we want to capture and convey in our wines." **Chianti Cl. Torre a Destra Ris. 2007** (● 6,000 bt), which ages in French oak casks, is a complex wine with slow progression but confident depth. Aged exclusively in large barrels, the typical, racy **Chianti Cl. 2009** (● 60,000 bt) is pleasant and more approachable. **Chianti Cl. Ris. 2008** (● 20,000 bt) was as good as ever with nice fruity aromas and a full, vertical body.

> **slow wine** **TERRINE 2006** (● sangiovese; 11,000 bt) With its splendid blossomy tones, an elegiaic, moving wine of great class. A hymn to sangiovese.

FERTILIZERS natural manure, compost
PLANT PROTECTION copper and sulphur
WEED CONTROL mechanical
YEASTS selected
GRAPES 100% estate-grown
CERTIFICATION none

Castello di Monsanto

Via Monsanto, 8
tel. 055 8059000
www.castellodimonsanto.it
monsanto@castellodimonsanto.it

70 ha - 400,000 bt

PEOPLE - This company has been producing wine for half a century. You can trace its history walking among the piles of bottles of its historic reserve, scattered along the passageways in its splendid underground cellar, conserved with commendable foresight by owner Fabrizio Bianchi, now increasingly abetted by his daughter Laura. When everything got underway in 1962, Fabrizio had the vision to put his money on quality without compromise and to believe in a single vineyard, Poggio, the first Chianti Classico cru.

VINEYARDS - Andrea Giovannini oversees and coordinates production from vineyard to cellar. It was he who took us round the estate, made up of various vineyards on partly tufaceous and Pliocene soils, rich in *galestro* marl. They are, on average, over 20 years old and are progressively renewed. The most outstanding is Poggio, which has a 360° aspect and was recently enlarged with spectacular recovery work on the stone terraces.

WINES - "Poggio always comes to the fore" is Fabrizio Bianchi's motto. A splendid vertical tasting of Chianti Cl. Il Poggio Ris. (not produced in 2008), organized for the company's 50th anniversary, confirmed its sense of place and longevity. It concluded with **Chianti Cl. Cinquantenario Ris. 2008** (● 15,000 bt), made mostly with grapes from the historic cru, whose typical characteristics come out in the wine's youthful impetuosity. The austere **Chianti Cl. Ris. 2009** (● 130,000 bt) is still restrained by the power of the matière. **Chianti Cl. 2010** (● 40,000 bt) is more floral and subtle. **Chardonnay Fabrizio Bianchi 2010** (○ 15,000 bt) is balanced, while the racy **Chianti Monrosso 2010** (● 80,000 bt) proves how good the cellar's base wines can be. It's a perfect Everday Wine. **Rosato Fabrizio Bianchi 2010** (◉ sangiovese; 6,000 bt), finally, is fruity.

FERTILIZERS organic-mineral, green manure
PLANT PROTECTION chemical, copper and sulphur
WEED CONTROL mechanical
YEASTS selected
GRAPES 100% estate-grown
CERTIFICATION none

Isole e Olena

Località Isole, 1
tel. 055 8072763
isolena@tin.it

50 ha - 200,000 bt

66 After almost 40 harvests, Paolo De Marchi has reached the objective he set himself: wines with a sense of place and respect for the environment. He has done so by experimenting with new sangiovese clones and travelling round the world to sell enthusiasts bottles from this corner of paradise 99

PEOPLE - Paolo De Marchi has achieved an incredible goal. Namely, he manages to produce a relatively high number of bottles and labels with a strong sense of artisanship and place.

VINEYARDS - "My dream was to make wines with native and international grapes, always with separate vinification. Which is why I've tried to understand which soils are most suitable for each variety. My sole hope is that my wines manage to express not only the grape they are made from, but also the place they come from," says Paolo, as we walk through his lovely vineyard at an altitude of over 400 meters. What a view! Immersed in the greenery, it embraces the village of Olena and the towers of San Gimignano beyond.

WINES - Chianti Cl. 2010 (● 137.000 bt) is a splendid example of a sangiovese wine: edgy, sanguine and juicy. **Cepparello 2009** (● sangiovese; 38.000 bt) is emblematic. An aromatic *vin de terroir*, lip-smacking, intense and long, it's likely one of the best versions we've ever tasted A Great Wine. Elegant and complex, **Cabernet Sauvignon 2006** (● 4,000 bt) is a great Bordeaux in the heart of Chianti. The excellent **Syrah 2007** (● 5,000 bt) is peppery and perfumed with a balanced bouquet. **Chardonnay 2011** (○ 15,000 bt) is tangy and fresh. Not to be missed is **Vin Santo del Chianti Cl. 2004** (○ 15,000 bt).

FERTILIZERS organic-mineral, natural manure, compost
PLANT PROTECTION copper and sulphur
WEED CONTROL mechanical
YEASTS selected
GRAPES 100% estate-grown
CERTIFICATION none

Fattoria Rodano

Località Rodano, 84
tel. 0577 743107
www.fattoriarodano.it
rodano@chianticlassico.com

34 ha - 120,000 bt

66 We'd like to remind the few wine lovers who are still unacquainted with this cellar that Rodano can be defined as the essence of a kind of unfussy Chianti Classico that lets its bottles speak for themselves 99

PEOPLE - It's difficult to talk about Rodano, largely because almost everything has already been said about the company and the Pozzesi family, and it's easy to lapse into rhetoric. Enrico Pozzesi, who is very much bound to the Chianti tradition, takes care of the land and the cellar.

VINEYARDS - Vineyards are managed with organic methods and are cordon- and Guyot-trained according to clones and health of the grapes. They are situated partly on slight slopes round the cellar and are turfed and cover-cropped. Vines are planted with a density of about 5,000 plants per hectare and the soil composition varies from clayey to gravelly. Besides the classic sangiovese, canaiolo and colorino grapes, cabernet and merlot are also grown.

WINES - Enrico wants bottles of character. For him, Rodano wines made with the sangiovese grape have to age for a long time in large oak barrels, and if this causes initial reduction, so be it. The important thing is important to ensure sense of place and longevity. The history of Enrico's wines vouches for his productive philosophy, with wonderful old vintages and unique flavor that makes them stand out among thousands of others. Aged in large barrels, **Chianti Cl. 2007** (● 70,000 bt) has intriguing fragrances of flowers and tobacco and notes of soil, followed by a fresh, lean, leisurely palate with silky, perfectly extracted tannins. **Poggialupi 2011** (● sangiovese, merlot), made with the youngest sangiovese grapes, has a nicely intense, fragrant bouquet and a fresh, tangy palate.

FERTILIZERS green manure
PLANT PROTECTION copper and sulphur
WEED CONTROL mechanical
YEASTS native
GRAPES 100% estate-grown
CERTIFICATION organic

CASTELLINA IN CHIANTI (SI)

Tenuta di Bibbiano €

Località Bibbiano, 76
tel. 0577 743065
www.tenutadibibbiano.it
info@tenutadibibbiano.com

25 ha - 100,000 bt

PEOPLE - The Marroccheschi Marzi family's Bibbiano estate has existed since 1865. The present owners, Tommaso and Federico, are following in the footsteps of their father, who began bottling wine in 1969. The sales manager is Elisa Bacci, the cellar manager Davide Biagiotti, while Stefano Porcinai has been charged with the agronomic side of the business since 1999. In 2003 Porcinai also began to oversee work in the cellar, assisted at the time by the late Giulio Gambelli.

VINEYARDS - The vineyards, some of which at low density, are split into two parcels and encircle the owners' villa. The Capannino vineyard, situated to the southwest was replanted with sangiovese grosso grapes following modern criteria in 2009. Three hectares of the Montornello, which has a northwest exposure, were replanted with sangiovese grapes in 2012. It is here that the Marroccheschi Marzi will concentrate its investment to complete its vineyard improvement plans.

WINES - Elegant, soft and drinkable, the wines epitomize their terroir. The outstanding **Chianti Cl. Montornello 2010** (● 20,000 bt) offers aromas of cherry and red fruits and a sweet, well-rounded palate. Especially worthy of note is **Vinsanto del Chianti Cl. San Lorenzo a Bibbiano 2001** (○ trebbiano, malvasia; 1,500 bt) with its brilliant golden color and hints of almond and brown sugar. Rhe Riserva won't be rrelaesded this year since th vineyard was replanted in 2009 with clones selected by Gambelli.

slow wine | CHIANTI CL. BIBBIANO 2010 (● 40,000 bt) A bouquet of morello cherry with a refreshing, balanced palate and tangy drinkability. The fruit of clean agriculture at a very reasonable price indeed.

FERTILIZERS organic-mineral, manure pellets, green manure
PLANT PROTECTION copper and sulphur
WEED CONTROL mechanical
YEASTS native
GRAPES 100% estate-grown
CERTIFICATION converting to organics

CASTELLINA IN CHIANTI (SI)

Villa Pomona €

Località Pomona, 39
Strada Chiantigiana S.R. 222
tel. 0577 740930
www.fattoriapomona.it
villapomona@virgilio.it

4.5 ha - 13,000 bt

PEOPLE - The "Strada Chiantigiana" throws up one breathtaking landscape after another. At number 39, in the Pomona district, near Castellina, lives winemaker Monica Raspi. Ten years ago, Monica gave up her veterinary practice to take over the farm left to her by her father. She and her husband Enrico Selvi thus began to pick up the ropes of winemaking and in a short time she not only allowed the winery to survive, but also turned it into one of Tuscany's most exciting.

VINEYARDS - The oldest vineyard, planted about 30 years ago, is just down from the farmhouse in a great winegrowing area. It is perfectly located on a well-ventilated ridge with mostly *alberese* soils. In view of the optimal vegetation conditions, Monica decided to embark upon the road of organic agriculture, and the company received certification last year. "You only have to be in the vineyards," she told us. "We're small and the organic approach makes us more conscious of the work we do."

WINES - We first came across the wines of Villa Pomona three years ago and we reckon consistent quality is one of the company's chief characteristics. **Chianti Cl. Ris 2009** (● 4,000 bt) comes from the oldest vineyards and is a sumptuous interpretation of the vintage which, generally speaking, conjured up most excitement in the base wines. The intact, contrasting nose leads into an impressive, dynamic taste profile, rich in fruit. **Villa Pomona 2010** (● sangiovese, cabernet sauvignon; 1,000 bt) was pleasant but a little over-alcoholic.

slow wine | CHIANTI CL. 2010 (● 8,000 bt) Aged in large Slavonian oak barrels, a wine with full-blooded, very fine, floral aromas and a palate that starts unobtrusively but follows through impetuously with acid and structure to spare. Plus the price is truly fantastic.

FERTILIZERS natural manure, green manure
PLANT PROTECTION copper and sulphur
WEED CONTROL mechanical
YEASTS native
GRAPES 100% estate-grown
CERTIFICATION organic

Fattoria di Fèlsina

Via del Chianti, 101
tel. 0577 355117
www.felsina.it
info@felsina.it

75 ha - 500,000 bt

66 The company is a virtuous system in which ancestral peasant wisdom lives on in harmony with modern agricultural knowhow. The driving force behind what is one of Italy's top wine cellars is the philosophy of striking a balance between agriculture and people and the environment 99

PEOPLE - The new generation at Fèlsina, cousins Caterina Mazzocolin and Giovanni Poggiali are confidently continuing the journey embarked upon 50 years ago.

VINEYARDS - Caterina took us to see the vineyards. "Ours is a borderland. We have one foot in Chianti Classico and the other in the Siena hills," she says. For any enthusiast the view of the Rancia vineyard is a memorable emotion. The vineyards are managed using organic methods with the consultancy of Ellis Topini. Fèlsina's sangiovese grapes are the fruit of study of the cellar's ampelographic pool, partly carried out in collaboration with elderly viticulturists.

WINES - Fèlsina's wines convey classicism with textbook naturalness of expression. This year the internecine struggle between Fontalloro and Rancia saw **Fontalloro 2009** (● sangiovese; 33.000 bt) come out on top in a photo finish. Made with grapes from three parcels, the wine ages 18 months in barriques. It has a well-rounded, blossomy nose and a palate of splendid progression. It goes without saying that it's a Great Wine. The excellent **Chianti Cl. Rancia Ris. 2009** (● 40,000 bt) is austere, vegetal and full of flavor. Aged in Slavonian oak barrels for about a year, **Chianti Cl. 2010** (● 200,000 bt) is also a very pleasant drink. **Maestro Raro 2009** (● cabernet sauvignon; 6,000 bt) comes from the small Rancia vineyard. Aged for about a year in barriques, it has all the character of a Chianti plus plenty of depth.

FERTILIZERS biodynamic preparations, green manure, humus
PLANT PROTECTION copper and sulphur
WEED CONTROL mechanical
YEASTS native
GRAPES 100% estate-grown
CERTIFICATION none

Badia a Coltibuono

Località Badia a Coltibuono
tel. 0577 746110
www.coltibuono.com
info@coltibuono.com

70 ha - 250,000 bt

66 The company is highly sensitive towards biodiversity. It has made numerous massal selections from old grape varieties found bedded in the vineyards. It is seeking to reduce copper-based treatments and to stimulate the immune defense systems of its vines. The wines are a faithful mirror of their terroir 99

PEOPLE - Roberto Stucchi Prinetti and his sister Emanuela welcomed us to the company. Their courtyard is a hectic place with cellermen busy racking bottles, tourists attending the cookery course and clients arriving at the restaurant. You receive an impression of great vitality. Organic agriculture conducted with seriousness and rigor is something that Roberto champions adamantly.

VINEYARDS - "We've been certified organic since 2000," says Roberto, "but we haven't used chemicals for 20 years." The winery also defends the landscape. Proof of the fact is its fight against a power cable that would cause huge damage to the surrounding area.

WINES - The splendid aging cellar is situated beneath the original winery buildings. The wines of Badia a Coltibuono have a reassuring style based on respect for the grapes and an enological technique that is never over the top. **Chianti Cl. Ris. 2008** (● 40,000 bt) ages for two years in oak barrels of various sizes. It's a complex wine with aromas of ripe fruit and licorice and a layered palate that promises to develop well. **Chianti Cl. Cultus Boni 2008** (● 12,000 bt) is more concentrated with a horizontal taste profile that makes for immediate enjoyability.

slow wine **CHIANTI CL. 2010** (● 200,000 bt) Aged in large wooden barrels, an example of expressive naturalness. The tempting flowery bouquet reappears on the palate, juicy with a richly acid backbone. A model of authenticity.

FERTILIZERS natural manure, compost, green manure
PLANT PROTECTION copper and sulphur, organic
WEED CONTROL mechanical
YEASTS native
GRAPES 100% estate-grown
CERTIFICATION organic

Riecine

Località Riecine
tel. 0577 749098
www.riecine.it
info@riecine.com

11 ha - 50,000 bt

66 Sean O'Callaghan, a winemaker in love with Chianti Classico and its vineyards, is the brains behind this company. He displays tremendous sensitivity from vine rows to barrels, and the results are there for all to see in his wines 99

PEOPLE - It's been a year of great innovation at Riecine. On January 1 2012, the company was taken over by a group of nine international investors. Won over by the commendable work carried out to date, they have left the management in the hands of Sean O'Callaghan, the soul of the estate, and his team, which counts on the collaboration of Ilda Roci. Plans are now in place for a new cellar and the acquisition of vineyards to optimize production.

VINEYARDS - The vineyards, protected by woodland, stand in quite a high position at an average altitude of 450 meters. The oldest, planted in 1971, is situated in front of the cellar, the others fan out over the surrounding areas. They are cultivated organically and, for the most part, trained with the Guyot (pruned low down using a technique perfected by Sean), bush vine and cordon systems.

WINES - To heighten the complexity of each single vineyard, grapes are vinified in separate tubs for a very high number of fermentations. Subsequent assemblage and long aging add life to wines that privilege fruit, freshness and sense of place. The pleasant **Rosé 2011** (☉ sangiovese; 3,000 bt) is fruity, floral, fresh and clean. Bad weather meant that Riserva and Gioia weren't produced in 2008, but we did have the pleasure of having another taste of Gioia 2007, which now, a year on, is revealing all its huge potential.

| slow wine | **CHIANTI CL. 2009** (● 38,000 bt) Fruity, mineral and balsamic notes, well-developed, fresh palate, ultra-fine tannins — a perfect example of the winery's style. |

FERTILIZERS compost, biodynamic preparations, green manure
PLANT PROTECTION copper and sulphur
WEED CONTROL mechanical
YEASTS native
GRAPES 100% estate-grown
CERTIFICATION organic

Rocca di Castagnoli

Località Castagnoli
tel. 0577 731004
www.roccadicastagnoli.com
info@roccadicastagnoli.com

87 ha - 400,000 bt

PEOPLE - Rocca di Castagnoli was formed in 1981. In 2003, the owner, the lawyer Calogero Calì, gave the job of managing the company to Rolando Bernacchini, who has since enhanced its potential. The same is true of all the other companies on the group: from Castello di San Sano and Tenuta di Capraia in the Chianti zone to Poggio Maestrin in the Maremma, to Poggio Graffetta in Sicily. The staff is completed by enologist Daniele Pagni, agronomist Giacomo Fanetti and, in the cellar, Diego Radaelli.

VINEYARDS - The various companies' terroirs, situated at an altitude of 450-550 and covering a vast area, were chosen on the basis of their exposures, with grape varieties being planted on the slopes best suited to their specific characteristics. A peculiarity of Castagnoli is its bush-trained sangiovese grapes: five hectares with a density of 9,000 plants per hectare. In the course of the year, new vineyards were replanted with colorino and pugnitello, as well as malvasia and trebbiano for Vin Santo.

WINES - The group's companies produced a number of excellent labels. **Chianti Cl. Capraia Ris. 2009** (● 30,000) is elegant and earthy with rich fruit and sweet tannins. **Chianti Cl. Poggio A' Frati 2009** (● 30,000 bt) is darker, tannic and tight — the soul of Chianti! We were impressed by **Buriano 2008** (● cabernet; 7,000 bt) is laid-back and clean. **Castello di San Sano Borro al Fumo 2008** (● sangiovese, malvasia lunga del Chianti; 7,500 bt), made partly with white grapes, is sapid, soft and sumptuous. One of the best reds of the year, hence a Great Wine. Redolent of red fruit, the plush **Chianti Cl. Rocca di Castagnoli 2010** (● 250,000 bt) has a strong sense of place. **Morellino di Scansano Spiaggiole 2010** (● 60,000 bt) exudes delectable aromas.

FERTILIZERS organic-mineral, natural manure
PLANT PROTECTION copper and sulphur
WEED CONTROL chemical, mechanical
YEASTS selected
GRAPES 100% estate-grown
CERTIFICATION none

GREVE IN CHIANTI (FI)

I Fabbri €

Località Lamole
Via Casale, 52
tel. 055 2345719
www.agricolaifabbri.it
info@agricolaifabbri.it

10 ha - 35,000 bt	**10% discount**

PEOPLE - The climb to I Fabbri is a metaphorical journey through the history of Chianti Classico. The thick woodland and the old terraced vineyards guard over an agriculture that stands as an example to learn from. Susanna Grassi, whose family, records show, has been living in Lamole since 1690, returned to run the company in the year 2000. She has adjusted her rhythm to those of the surrounding environment and become one of its most faithful interpreters.

VINEYARDS - In May we toured the country's vineyards setting out from the splendid terraces near the cellar. They are planted on sandstone soil in a southwest exposure at an altitude of 550 meters in a landscape in which the borders between agriculture and art history are blurred. Higher up at an altitude of 630 meters are the vineyards of Terrato Alto and La Sala, planted with sangiovese grosso di Lamole. After progressively moving towards sustainability, I Fabbri is now happily converting to organics.

WINES - The grapes of Lamole have peculiar characteristics forged by an environment unique for altitude, temperature swings and viticultural tradition. And it's an environment which the company's wines epitomize perfectly. In the cellar Susanna goes along with the character of the vintage without interfering overmuch. **Chianti Cl. Terre di Lamole 2010** (● 12,000 bt) has sweet fruit, splendid linearity of flavor and a mouthfeel rich in contrasts and juice. Aged in stainless steel tanks, **Chianti Cl. Lamole 2010** (● 6,000 bt) is a pleasant quaff, coaxing out cut-glass florality on a crisp, flavorful palate. **Chianti Cl. Olinto 2010** (● 6,000 bt) has notes of forest fruit and enfolding, taut juiciness. It's a very good Everyday Wine indeed. **Doccio 2010** (● merlot; 1,300 bt) has a deep bouquet and typically Chianti-style taste profile.

FERTILIZERS	green manure
PLANT PROTECTION	copper and sulphur
WEED CONTROL	mechanical
YEASTS	native
GRAPES	100% estate-grown
CERTIFICATION	converting to organics

PANZANO IN CHIANTI (FI)

Castello dei Rampolla

Via Case Sparse, 22
tel. 055 852001
castellodeirampolla.cast@tin.it

30 ha - 80,000 bt	

❝ Maurizia Di Napoli Rampolla borrows the words of her brother Luca, who runs the company with her, to define their approach to winemaking. She calls it "light agriculture". The word "light" refers to human impact on the land. She also stresses the importance of in-depth knowledge of the vines, which are accompanied, almost pampered, through every stage of their vegetative cycle ❞

PEOPLE - The brother and sister partnership receives vital help from Marcus von der Planitz, an enologist-cum-cellarman who came in from Germany in the late 1990s.

VINEYARDS - The winery has been adopting a biodynamic approach for 18 years. Luca spoke to us about common sense, the importance of understanding the land and treating it with respect. The vineyards form a single plot of about 30 hectares round the farm. Most have a southern exposure and some portions were planted as long ago as 1978. We saw sangiovese grapes and a few grapes of French origin planted by Maurizia and Luca's father Alceo Di Napoli, who was convinced that bedding them in the Chianti zone would yield excellent results. He was right!

WINES - Convinced of the importance of forging links with the land, the Di Napolis and Marcus have decided to vinify a monovarietal Sangiovese in earthenware jars made in Impruneta, without added sulfur. The result is **Sangiovese 2010** (● 1,000 bt), which has a heady fragrance of flowers and fruit and a note of strawberry. It's a fresh, tangy wine with a soft finish. The excellent, well-formed **Chianti Cl. 2010** (● 17,000 bt) has intact fruit and fine tannins. **Sammarco 2008** (● cabernet sauvignon, merlot, sangiovese; 13,000 bt) is as full-blooded as ever, spacious and beautifully balanced. No less convincing is **d'Alceo 2008** (● cabernet, petit verdot; 12.000 bt) with its soft palate and very long finish.

FERTILIZERS	biodynamic preparations
PLANT PROTECTION	copper and sulphur, organic
WEED CONTROL	mechanical
YEASTS	native
GRAPES	100% estate-grown
CERTIFICATION	none

Fontodi

Via San Leolino, 89
tel. 055 852005
www.fontodi.com
fontodi@fontodi.com

80 ha - 300,000 bt

66 Giovanni Manetti's professionalism comes out in every word he says to describe the development of winemaking in Panzano in Chianti. Clean agriculture equals exciting wines with a sense of place 99

PEOPLE - Fontodi started life in the 1960s as a specialized wine company. Since then it has grown progressively, not only in terms of the area of its vineyards, but also as a complex farm in which every activity, from livestock breeding to cereal growing, contributes to wine production.

VINEYARDS - Walking through the vineyards with Manetti is an exciting experience. Here each single vine is tended individually. The manure comes from the farm's *Chianina* cattle and is composted with the vine shoots and grape debris. During our visit, the barley tinged the vine rows with gold, creating the competition necessary for the vegetative balance of the vines. The Fontodi vineyards form a single plot at the heart of Panzano's celebrated Conca d'Oro district.

WINES - "The wine made adopting this type of agriculture transcends the concept of quality and develops an indissoluble bond with its place of origin," says Giovanni. Proof of the fact is **Flaccianello della Pieve 2009** (● sangiovese; 60,000 bt) made from a rigorous selection of perfectly ripe grapes. The wine matures for two years in new barriques, has a deep nose and a perfectly extracted taste profile. **Chianti Cl. Vigna del Sorbo Ris. 2009** (● 20,000 bt) comes from a single vineyard. Two years in barriques, half of which new, make it a wine rich in spice and fruit with a concentrated, hefty body. **Chianti Cl. 2009** (● 170,000 bt) ages for two years in 20-hectoliter barrels. It encapsulates all the character of Chianti, with flowery, full-bodied notes and a dynamic palate.

FERTILIZERS natural manure, green manure
PLANT PROTECTION copper and sulphur
WEED CONTROL mechanical
YEASTS native
GRAPES 100% estate-grown
CERTIFICATION organic

Il Palagio

Località Il Palagio
Via Case Sparse, 38
tel. 055 852175
www.aziendaagricolailpalagio.com
info@aziendaagricolailpalagio.com

7.5 ha - 28,000 bt   10% discount

PEOPLE - Via Case Sparse in Panzano is a sort of grand cru within the denomination. At number 38 is Il Palagio, a small but important winery at the heart of the Conca d'oro district. Monia Piccini is carrying on her father's good work with Chianti Classico, seen not only as a wine, but also as a place of culture and belonging. Now Monia's husband Franco Guarducci has also joined the company, ensuring consistency and quality.

VINEYARDS - The vineyards exploit one of the best positions for sangiovese grapes. Round the company grow the oldest vines on *galestro* marl and clay. Other vineyards are to be found in the classic Tuscan landscape of San Martino in Cecione, a spectacular natural amphitheater of *galestro* marl, *alberese* limestone and clay. Conversion to organic methods is now complete and Franco is always ready to intervene at every stage of work in the field.

WINES - Il Palagio's wines have distinctive, recognizable features. Which is music to the ears of Franco, who is keen for them to evoke the character and identity of the land. Since he joined the company, he has carried out painstaking research in each parcel of vineyard to identify the best grapes and reserve them differentiated treatment in the cellar. His preference goes to large wooden barrels and long macerations on the skins. Monia preferred to leave Chianti Cl. Ris. 2009 in the bottle for another year, so we'll taste it next time round. **Chianti Cl. 2010** (● 18,000 bt), aged in 30-hectoliter barrels, is full-blooded with a very strong sense of place. The pleasant **Torgentile 2008** (● sangiovese, merlot; 2,000 bt) is juicy with a fruity bouquet.

FERTILIZERS natural manure, green manure
PLANT PROTECTION copper and sulphur
WEED CONTROL mechanical
YEASTS native
GRAPES 100% estate-grown
CERTIFICATION organic

Le Cinciole

Via Case Sparse, 83
tel. 055 852636
www.lecinciole.it
info@lecinciole.it

12 ha - 40,000 bt | **10% discount**

66 What fantastic wines! This year they impressed us with their energy, cleanness, sense of place and value for money. The full deal! 99

PEOPLE - Le Cinciole is a dream come true for Luca Orsini and Valeria Viganò, who moved to Panzano in Chianti in 1991. Immersed in the world of wine, Luca pulled out all his talent as a maker. His gift emerged after a handful of harvests with very local, typical wines.

VINEYARDS - The main vineyards are situated close to the cellar, northwest of Panzano. The vine rows, which were standing in grass when we visited, hide clayey soil rich in pebbles. Luca took us to see the latest vineyards to be planted in the Conca d'Oro district: three plots with great potential covering a total area of four hectares. His agronomic approach is shared by Ruggero Mazzilli. "We're becoming a model of sustainable viticulture," says Luca proudly.

WINES - The most important fermentations are the ones performed in open barriques. These "micro-vinifications" heighten the diversities that exist between the company's vineyards. **Chianti Cl. Petresco Ris. 2008** (● 4,000 bt) is made from a selection of the best sangiovese grapes available. It's a very complex wine, austere and packed with acidity, from a vintage that is still hard to judge. **Cinciorosso 2010** (● sangiovese, cabernet sauvignon, syrah, merlot; 8,300 bt;) is beautifully aromatic and **Rosato 2011** (◉ sangiovese; 1,000 bt) is fragrant and tangy.

> **slow wine** CHIANTI CL. 2009 (● 25,000 bt) Fermented in cement tanks and aged in 20-hectoliter barrels, a moving wine for goodness and sense of place.

FERTILIZERS natural manure, green manure
PLANT PROTECTION copper and sulphur
WEED CONTROL mechanical
YEASTS native
GRAPES 100% estate-grown
CERTIFICATION organic

Monte Bernardi

Via Chiantigiana
tel. 055 852400
www.montebernardi.com
mb@montebernardi.com

15 ha - 42,000 bt

66 Biodynamics, traditional vinification, serious relations with neighbors, perfect integration in the social fabric of this stupendous corner of Tuscany — in Panzano, the Schmeltzer brothers have created a model winery 99

PEOPLE - As one young winemaker in Panzano in Chianti told us, "My father adores Michael. He's one of the producers who still takes an interest in Chianti Classico's difficult past. He wants to find out about the lives of the sharecroppers". It was this tremendous passion for Chianti Classico that brought Michael Schmeltzer to Panzano in 2003.

VINEYARDS - Michael oversees the production and transport of the grapes with the dynamism typical of cosmopolitan winemakers. But when the conversation turns to Panzano, he becomes a monovarietal fanatic. His top vineyard is Saetta, where very old sangiovese vines grow on hard stone, the rest of the vines growing on mainly marly soil. The company practices natural viticulture and takes great care over the products it uses in the vineyards.

WINES - In the vineyard everything is done slowly and aging is long. His desire to extract complexity induces Michael to work by reduction, designing wines that initially may be reluctant to let themselves go. **Chianti Cl. Ris. 2009** (● 6,000 bt) is surly at the outset, but we caught a glimpse of its potential in its earthy, deep nose and complex taste profile full of noble tannins. **Chianti Cl. Retromarcia 2010** (● 30,000 bt) ages in barriques and second-hand casks. Its nose is almost mature and its palate expressive, albeit not as well-defined as in other vintages. **Tzingana 2009** (● merlot, cabernet sauvignon e franc; petit verdot; 2,000 bt) ages in barriques — a Bordeaux blend for a wine that exudes a strong sense of place.

FERTILIZERS natural manure, green manure
PLANT PROTECTION copper and sulphur
WEED CONTROL mechanical
YEASTS native
GRAPES 5% bought in
CERTIFICATION organic

POGGIBONSI (SI)

Fattoria Ormanni

Località Ormanni
tel. 0577 937212
www.ormanni.it
info@ormanni.it

RADDA IN CHIANTI (SI)

Caparsa

S.C. Caparsa, 47
tel. 0577 738174
www.caparsa.it
caparsa@caparsa.it

68 ha - 65,000 bt | **10% discount**

PEOPLE - The estate, named for the ancient Florentine patrician family cited by Dante in The Divine Comdey, is owned by Paolo Brini Batacchi and capably managed by Rocco Giorgio, helped in the cellar by Roberto Ciani with the consultancy of agronomist Ruggero Mazzilli and enologist Paolo Salvi. The renowned master taster Giulio "Bicchierino" Gambelli used to pop in here on his professional rounds, and his knowhow is certainly impressed in the wines it produces.

VINEYARDS - The company is near Poggibonsi at the side of the winding road that climbs past cypresses, Romanesque churches and hillside vineyards to Castellina in Chianti. Its own vineyards grow on harsh terrain furrowed by a steep canal that marks the administrative boundary with Barberino Val d'Elsa and gives its name to the precious grapes grown for Riserva. Among the cordon-trained and spur-pruned vineyards is an old plot still trained using an unusual bush system.

WINES - The cellar was built round the original building, hewn out of the sandstone rock under the owners' villa. Fermentations take place in stainless steel, aging in large barrels or barriques, then in vitrified cement tanks. **Chianti Cl. 2009** (● 40,000 bt) is fruity, balanced and rich in flavor. The well crafted **Julius 2007** (● sangiovese, merlot, syrah; 3,000 bt), a tribute to the abovementioned master taster is fruity and pleasantly acid. **Chianti 2010** (● 20,000 bt) is refreshing and tannic.

slow wine | **CHIANTI CL. BORRO DEL DIAVOLO RIS. 2008** (● 10,000 bt) Made with wines from the most characteristic vineyard, a wine with distinct Chianti-style aromas and a long, vibrant, lingering palate with deft tannins. Considering vintage and quality, the price is perfect.

FERTILIZERS green manure
PLANT PROTECTION chemical, copper and sulphur
WEED CONTROL mechanical
YEASTS native
GRAPES 100% estate-grown
CERTIFICATION none

12 ha - 20,000 bt | **10% discount**

66 Caparsa is an unspoilt corner of the Chianti Classico zone whose true essence Paolo Cianferoni and his family capture, unfussily, in their wines 99

PEOPLE - Even before we tasted the wines and saw the vineyards, we only had to look into Paolo's eyes and listen to him talking to realize that we weren't wrong. In him live the tangible soul of the wine and the land. Caparsa was one of the first wine companies in Chianti to practice organic agriculture and Paolo is justly proud of the fact.

VINEYARDS - "Blessed be the vineyards to the northeast" was the title of one post on Paolo's blog. The fact is that Caparsa has benefited from the rise in temperature, which ensures that the grapes ripen optimally. A meteo station now sends the weather news to Paolo's mobile directly from the vineyard. Which is why Paolo was on the phone al the time, like a teenager with his girlfriend. "It's vital if you used organic methods, especially if you need to step in quickly," he says.

WINES - The Caparsa cellar is worth the visit on its own. It's a labyrinth of cement tanks and large wood barrels in which time has coated everything, new and used, with a patina of charm. "Either you do things for the sake of doing them or you take care of every detail, which is what you do to make a good wine." Cianferoni bottles only the stuff he reckons to be worthy of the honor. The rest he sells unbottled. Usually impenetrable at first, **Chianti Cl. Doccio a Matteo Ris. 2008** (● 7,900 bt) plays an overture of spices and fruit preserved in alcohol. Slightly clenched by the tannins, the body subsequently develops well.

slow wine | **CHIANTI CL. CAPARSINO RIS. 2008** (● 5,300 bt) The initial impact is blossomy with balsamic aromas and impressive depth. A long-lingering wine with an authentic sense of place.

FERTILIZERS green manure
PLANT PROTECTION copper and sulphur
WEED CONTROL mechanical
YEASTS native
GRAPES 100% estate-grown
CERTIFICATION organic

Monteraponi

Località Monteraponi
tel. 055 352601
www.monteraponi.it
mail@monteraponi.it

10 ha - 28,000 bt · 10% discount

PEOPLE - A leading player in the true Chianti revolution, crowned by wines with a real sense of place, over the last few years Monteraponi has asserted itself at the top of the denomination. The role the company's vineyards have had in this rapid rise is indisputable. As is that of Michele Braganti, who began by putting his ear to the ground in Radda and has since, with great personality, become one of its most sensitive interpreters.

VINEYARDS - "I don't have any special merits, I'm just lucky to have these vineyards," says Michele. Lucky or not, this young producer has had the ability to recognize the different aptitudes of the properties at his disposal. He has singled out two crus that originate two distinct Chianti Classicos: Campitello, at an altitude of 420 meters, and Baron Ugo, a spectacular vineyard at 550 meters, where the oldest vines grow. A phytodepuration plant has been installed for the biological treatment of waste water.

WINES - Tasting from the barrel gives an idea of the different souls of the sangiovese grape in Radda. Campitello is floral and classical, Baron Ugo full-blooded and ferrous. The wines are fermented in cement tanks with native yeasts. **Chianti Cl. 2010** (● 25,000 bt) is paradigmatic for the typology: it has a forthright, flowery nose, a palate of impeccable identity and spectacular juice and tannins. Merlot, which Michele calls a "juvenile error", is the grape that goes into **lugèro 2009** (● 1,300 bt). The wine is aged in wood, but the grape fails to repress the power of the terroir. The result is full-blooded and vertical.

> **slow wine** **CHIANTI CL. IL CAMPITELLO RIS. 2009** (● 4,000 bt) Aged in large wooden barrels, this is a special version made partly with grapes from the Baron Ugo vineyard. A wine of massive depth, it offers violets with hints of iodine on the nose and a juicy palate rich in complexity.

FERTILIZERS green manure
PLANT PROTECTION copper and sulphur
WEED CONTROL mechanical
YEASTS native
GRAPES 100% estate-grown
CERTIFICATION organic

Montevertine

Località Montevertine
tel. 0577 738009
www.montevertine.it
info@montevertine.it

16 ha - 85,000 bt

66 It's hard to come across purer land-rootedness than that of the wines of Montevertine. The result of meticulous, clean farming work, they echo, loud and clear, the voice of the hills they come from 99

PEOPLE - Martino Manetti is a worthy heir to his father Sergio, whose work he carries on on the farm founded in 1971. Martino follows and coordinates every stage in the winemaking process with enologist Paolo Salvi in the cellar and Bruno Bini and agronomist Ruggero Mazzilli in the vineyard.

VINEYARDS - The vineyards are all situated near the main farm buildings on the slopes of Montevertine, the same today as they were in the great Sergio's time. Martino has added his own personal touch and, though, contrary to expectations (for reasons of certification), he has decided not to convert the company to organics, the rigor with which he grows his healthy, fine quality grapes is impeccable.

WINES - The wines produced in the cellar at Montevertine extract the quintessence of the sangiovese grape and foster the legend that cloaks the estate. **Pergole Torte 2009** (● sangiovese; 25,000 bt) always stands out for its pleasantly spicy aromatic complexity and its length in the mouth, adorned by wonderfully balanced tannins. There are no other words left to describe what, for us, naturally enough, is a Great Wine. **Pian del Ciampolo 2010** (● sangiovese, colorino, canaiolo; 22,000 bt) is young, fresh and drinkable with straighforward notes of fruit and flowers.

> **slow wine** **MONTEVERTINE 2009** (● sangiovese, colorino, canaiolo; 26,000 bt) Zesty and juicy, lip-smacking and leisurely with deft spicy notes. A wine that conjures up its place of origin with freshness and elegance.

FERTILIZERS natural manure, compost, green manure
PLANT PROTECTION copper and sulphur
WEED CONTROL mechanical
YEASTS native
GRAPES 100% estate-grown
CERTIFICATION none

Val delle Corti

Località La Croce
Case Sparse Val delle Corti, 144
tel. 0577 738215
www.valdellecorti.it
info@valdellecorti.it

7 ha - 30,000 bt | **10% discount**

66 A cellar we're ready to wager on: reds that tell the story of the land, a vineyard and a farming world in a modern key 99

PEOPLE - It was quite an experience to chat to Roberto Bianchi under the pergola in front of his house. Especially when he told us the story of something that happened after the death of his father Giorgio in 1999. "One night, it was the third year I'd been cover cropping, I went out onto the terrace and saw a tide of fireflies over the vineyard. It was then I realized the difference between living earth and dead earth. It was a signal and it induced me to continue down the road I'd chosen to follow."

VINEYARDS - "Mine is a small company," says Roberto. "I have four hectares with an eastern exposure surrounded by a barrier of green woods which, in turn, surround my house. My vineyard is almost 40 years old and, though the density of vines is low, the grapes are truly fantastic. I also rent three hectares on the other side of the wood. Indulging a desire I had as a youngster, I work 7,000 square meters of merlot grapes as well. I hope that isn't a sin!"

WINES - Presenting his wines for tasting, Roberto explained that Chianti Cl. Ris. 2009 won't be released because it fails to capture the soul of the local area. No way would he wish to disappoint his customers, he confided. **Campino 2011** (● 8.000 bt) has all the edgy leanness of the sangiovese grape and is cheap at the price. Fruity, full-bodied and tangy, **Rosè 2011** (☉ sangiovese 2,500 bt) has more color and is just as enjoyable.

> slow wine **Chianti Cl. 2009** (● 20,000 bt) An excellent value-for-money wine with fruity, flowery scents and an incredible taste profile. Typicality and juice — fantastic!

FERTILIZERS manure pellets, green manure
PLANT PROTECTION copper and sulphur, organic
WEED CONTROL mechanical
YEASTS native
GRAPES 100% estate-grown
CERTIFICATION converting to organics

Corzano e Paterno

Frazione San Pancrazio
Via Paterno, 8
tel. 055 8248179
www.corzanoepaterno.it
info@corzanoepaterno.it

17 ha - 80,000 bt | **10% discount**

66 The agriculture practiced at Corzano is the fruit of a modern vision which sees viticulture not as the sole resource, but as one of the many that combine to enrich the land 99

PEOPLE - The experienced agronomist Aljoscha Goldshmidt runs the farm's wine-making (it also produces wonderful Pecorino cheese and elegant monovarietal olive oil, as well as offering an agriturismo facility) with a firm hand. For a few years his cousin, the young enologist Arianna Gelpke, has effectively taken over a growing number of responsibilities in the cellar, thus allowing Aljoscha to take care of the sales side.

VINEYARDS - The vineyards surround Corzano, increasingly the heart of the enterprise after the opening of a farm shop 2011. They are mostly halfway up the hill, but can be very step here and there. A third of them are over 20 years old. The petit manseng grape was recently introduced to add freshness and acidity to the white wines. A lot of excellent work is being performed in the vineyards, where pruning is intelligent and barley and mustard seeds are sown periodically to invigorate the roots of the vines.

WINES - The new cellar boasts a sophisticated bottling line, steel tanks and French wooden casks. The top wine is again the dark spicy **Corzano 2009** (● sangiovese, cabernet, merlot; 6,000 bt), still young and a mite stiff but with well-developed aromas and fine texture. **Chianti I 3 Borri Ris. 2009** (● 5,800 bt) has freshness, lingering aromas and soft tannins. **Passito di Corzano** (○ trebbiano, malvasia; 2,000 bt) is amber in color with lingering aromas of dried fruit. Fresh and pleasant, racy and sharp, **Corzanello 2011** (○ trebbiano, malvasia, chardonnay, petit manseng; 20,000 bt) is as convincing as ever. The splendid **Chianti Terre di Corzano 2010** (● 28,000 bt) is an excellent Everyday Wine.

FERTILIZERS natural manure
PLANT PROTECTION copper and sulphur
WEED CONTROL mechanical
YEASTS selected, native
GRAPES 100% estate-grown
CERTIFICATION none

Nobili terre del Sud

BUCINE (AR)

Podere Il Carnasciale

Località Mercatale Valdarno
tel. 0559 911142

CORTONA (AR)

Stefano Amerighi

Poggiobello di Farneta
tel. 0575 648340
info@stefanoamerighi.it

3.5 ha - 3,200 bt

PEOPLE - Small in size — just 3.5 hectares of vines — this family business near Mercatale Valdarno has been run with determination by owner Bettina Ragosky and her son Moritz since 1986. Since 2002 Peter Schilling, an accomplished, extrovert enologist, has been working full-time on the production side, dividing his time between vineyard and wine cellar. The external consultants are agronomist Remigio Bordini and enologist Vittorio Fiore.

VINEYARDS - The only grape cultivated is caberlot, a natural hybrid of cabernet franc and merlot, discovered in the early 1960s in a vineyard in the Euganean Hills. The history and destiny of this company's vineyards depend on care for this unique grape. There are four holdings: one, the oldest, situated near the town, is densely planted with bush-trained vines; the others lie on different terrains, chosen for their specific characteristics, and are cordon-trained and spur-pruned at lower density.

WINES - The highly original wine reflects the company's decision to go for elegance, minerality and a certain, though never over-the-top, potency. The present wine cellar is small, simple and essential, but a new one is now being built. The grapes are picked from late September to mid October and ferment briefly in stainless steel. They are vinified separately by vineyard and punched down manually twice a day. The wines age in new barriques for 22 months and, after the assemblage of the best batches, are bottled without filtering. **Caberlot 2009** (● 3,200 magnum) is a wine of great body and texture, elegant and deep-reaching. It has dynamism and energy, rich and fine tannins and an aromatic profile with marked herbaceous spices, balsamic, rich in fruit, well-developed and long — a Great Wine.

8.5 ha - 13,000 bt | **10% discount**

❝ Passion, courage and a pinch of recklessness — these are the qualities that have allowed youngster Stefano Amerighi to crown his dream of turning from wine lover into winemaker ❞

PEOPLE - Over the last ten years, helped by his father and with the consultancy of enologist Federico Staderini and agronomist Adriano Zago, Stefano has become a benchmark producer for lovers of Syrah in the Cortona area and beyond.

VINEYARDS - Stefano's story is not that of a rich kid who's been given a toy to play with. No, everything he has achieved he has done so with in-depth study, following his passion for biodynamics and constantly consulting top experts in the sector. He has positioned his vineyards in an area of clay-silt soil at Poggiobello di Farneta, where the vines are cordons trained, both mono- and bilateral, as well as increasingly in *candelabra*-shape.

WINES - The functional cellar is almost totally underground and fits beautifully into the landscape. Here the biodynamic approach comes easily and permeates the entire productive philosophy. It is rounded off by minimal, non-invasive vinification practices, implemented by Stefano with loving, "paternal" care. This was our first tasting of **Cortona Syrah Apice 2008** (● 1,000 bt), named for the area of origin of the grapes — the highest on the estate — the result of French mass selections. We liked it a lot. Balsamic and full-bodied, it is deep and caressing with polished tannins.

> **slow wine** **CORTONA SYRAH 2009** (● 12,000 bt) A superlative wine in which tannins, ripe fruit and pepper blend in a warm, leisurely embrace.

FERTILIZERS natural manure, compost
PLANT PROTECTION copper and sulphur
WEED CONTROL mechanical
YEASTS native
GRAPES 100% estate-grown
CERTIFICATION none

FERTILIZERS biodynamic preparations, green manure
PLANT PROTECTION copper and sulphur, organic
WEED CONTROL mechanical
YEASTS native
GRAPES 100% estate-grown
CERTIFICATION biodynamic, organic

MONTALCINO (SI)
Baricci

Località Colombaio di Montosoli, 13
tel. 0577 848109
baricci1955@libero.it

5 ha - 30,000 bt

66 The wines mirror the souls of the men who make them. They represent all the best qualities of the Tuscan character: rough but kind, stubborn but easygoing and, above all, genuine 99

PEOPLE - It was 1955 when, as a young sharecropper, Nello Baricci took the big step and bought the Colombaio di Montosoli property. He convinced himself of the potential of the vines and, after a few years, began to specialize in wine production. One of the founders of the Consortium (he still proudly conserves his membership card "number one"), he is still very fond of his vineyards. The company is now run by his daughter Graziella and his grandsons Francesco and Federico with the consultancy of Paolo Vagaggini, but Nello knows it's in good hands.

VINEYARDS - The secret of the success of these wines resides in the unsurpassable terroir: five hectares of sangiovese grapes situated on the north side of the hill of Montalcino, with a south-southeastern exposure on soil of marine origin, rich in marl. The youngest part was planted in 2001, the oldest in 1988, the rest in the mid-1990s. Vegetative equilibrium is respected to the full, simply without recourse to chemicals. In other words, nature enjoys all the space it needs.

WINES - The excellent **Rosso di Montalcino 2010** (● 18,000 bt) is, without a doubt, one of the best labels of the denomination. It's a wine that never disappoints, a wine that's authentic, a wine that combines fresh fruit with silky, flavorsome tannins.

slow wine BRUNELLO DI MONTALCINO **2007** (● 12,000 bt) Taut, linear and charismatic, a great, elegant, multi-faceted red that captures the mood of soil and scrub. After initial shyness, it turns into a roller coaster with a very long finish.

FERTILIZERS	manure pellets
PLANT PROTECTION	copper and sulphur
WEED CONTROL	mechanical
YEASTS	selected
GRAPES	100% estate-grown
CERTIFICATION	none

MONTALCINO (SI)
Biondi Santi Tenuta Greppo

Località Villa Greppo, 183
tel. 0577 848087
www.biondisanti.it
biondisanti@biondisanti.it

25 ha - 80,000 bt

PEOPLE - Franco Biondi Santi, "Il Dottore" as he's respectfully called in the cellar, is now over 90 years of age but he's still on top form, as forthright, blunt and charismatic as ever — like his wines! Biondi Santi is the quintessence of Brunello, built with love, passion and extreme attention to detail. One of the main creators of the wine's fame worldwide, the company is still run with a steady hand by "Il Dottore" and continues to be a pillar of the denomination.

VINEYARDS - The cellar is situated on the Montalcino-Castelnuovo dell'Abate road and 17 of its 25 hectares are situated around it in the Greppo district. Some of the vines here are over 30 years old, others are younger. Most of the vineyards have a south-southeastern exposure and the soil is rich in *galestro* marl. In the others, about eight hectares in the Pieri and Pievecchia districts, the soil also contains clay and tufa.

WINES - Biondi Santi's wines are not only terroir-rooted, they are Tradition itself. Only large barrels, some dating from the late 19th century, are used to age the wine and give it its characteristic longevity. The difference between the different wines comes from the vines, the age of which establishes the type of wine that will be produced. Rosso di Montalcino 2009, made with grapes from the youngest vineyards, wasn't ready for tasting, so we didn't review it. The heftily structured Brunello di Montalcino 2007 (● 77,000 bt) is a wine that opens slowly, releasing full, deep fruit, well-knit spices and a log, juicy palate. A Great Wine if ever there was one! And what can we say about **Brunello di Montalcino Ris. 2006** (● 11,000 bt)? It's nuanced and iridescent, intense with aromas of fruit that blend with tertiary notes in a solid. Harmonious embrace.

FERTILIZERS	organic-mineral
PLANT PROTECTION	chemical, copper and sulphur
WEED CONTROL	mechanical
YEASTS	native
GRAPES	100% estate-grown
CERTIFICATION	none

Brunelli
Le Chiuse di Sotto

Località Podernovone
tel. 0577 849337
www.giannibrunelli.it
laura.brunelli@giannibrunelli.it

6.5 ha - 35,000 bt | 10% discount

PEOPLE - We were welcomed by Maria Laura Vacca who, since the premature death of her husband Gianni Brunelli has managed this small winery with energy and enthusiasm. You only have to see the way she tends her own kitchen garden to see how fond she is of the local area. During our visit, she was engaged in the tough task of tidying up the surrounding woodland, which she sees as being part and parcel of the life of the winery.

VINEYARDS - Maria Laura relies upon the help of trusted collaborators and the consultancy of Paolo Vagaggini. The vineyards are situated in two different zones: four and a half hectares sit in the spectacular natural amphitheater of Podernovone at an altitude of about 300 meters against the backdrop of Monte Amiata; another two are to be found at Le Chiuse Di Sotto, on the north face of the mountain, where the soil is fresher and water more abundant, all of which translates into excellent grapes even in warm, very dry years.

WINES - "Every vintage has characteristics of its own, and you have to help nature along as much as possible," says Maria Laura. It's almost as if she feels obliged to justify the fact that they can differ from year to year. But we for our part feel obliged to add that they always manage to interpret to perfection the character of the sangiovese grosso grape. Brunello di Montalcino Ris. 2006 (● 4,000 bt) wasn't good, it was very good. Pervasive, complex with precise aromatic nuances, earthy, full-blooded, vertical, beautifully colored, long … in short, a Great Wine! **Brunello di Montalcino 2007** (● 13,500 bt), which comes from a more problematic vintage, has warmer, ethereal notes, nicely contrasting flavors and juicy tannins. **Rosso di Montalcino 2010** (● 13,500 bt) has a tempting bouquet of cherries and rich spices and is reactive and tangy on the palate. The 2008 vintage of Amor Costante wasn't produced.

FERTILIZERS manure pellets, green manure
PLANT PROTECTION copper and sulphur
WEED CONTROL mechanical
YEASTS native
GRAPES 100% estate-grown
CERTIFICATION none

Caprili   (€)

Località Podere Caprili, 268
tel. 0577 848566
www.caprili.it
info@caprili.it

16 ha - 80,000 bt

PEOPLE - The Santa Restituta district is famous for the big names in Montalcino winemaking. It's easy to forget that in the same soil under the same sun grow the vines of the Bartolommei families, who bought back the Podere Caprili plot in 1965 when they were still working as sharecroppers — a story that's more peasant epic than business adventure. With admirable common sense the Bartolommei brothers, sons of founder Alfio, have made a name for themselves with wines of great personality, quality and sense of place.

VINEYARDS - The spectacular vineyard planted by Alfio Bartolommei the same year he bought the land bears the wonderful name of Madre. From vines here, some ungrafted, clones are obtained for new vineyards, one of which was recently ploughed, but was yet to be bedded when we made our visit. The density of 4,000 vines per hectare gives breathing space to the sangiovese grapes.

WINES - Vinification is classic with grape selection in the field, spontaneous fermentations and aging in large Slavonian oak barrels. **Brunello di Montalcino 2007** (● 30,000 bt) is aged for 36 months in the barrels of the Riserva and exudes warmth and intensity with fruity aromas and a leisurely palate with fine tannins. **Rosso di Montalcino 2010** (● 75,000 bt), aged for about six months in wooden casks, offers crunchy fruit and an approachable palate.

| slow wine | BRUNELLO DI MONTALCINO RIS. 2006 (● 11,000 bt) The fruit of four years' aging in wood, a wine with wonderfully intact aromas with fragrant flowery tones. The palate is austere with natural concentration, prolonged by plenty of acid thrust. A label that will teach a lot to anyone who wants to find out more about Brunello as it should be. |

FERTILIZERS natural manure
PLANT PROTECTION copper and sulphur
WEED CONTROL mechanical
YEASTS native
GRAPES 100% estate-grown
CERTIFICATION none

MONTALCINO (SI)

Fattoi

Località Santa Restituta
Podere Capanna, 101
tel. 0577 848613
www.fattoi.it
info@fattoi.it

9 ha - 50,000 bt

66 Fattoi adopts a simple, linear approach to vinification, without too much technology and with common sense interventions in the vineyard. The result is gutsy, genuine, expressive sangiovese di Montalcino wines 99

PEOPLE - The Fattoi family is totally involved in wine production and farming. Theirs is the forthright peasant spirit in the noblest sense of the term. Ofelio, who bought the property in 1965 — he bottled his first Brunello in 1979 — still takes an active part in the running of the company, his sons Leonardo and Lamberto see to the production side, and Lucia, Leonardo's daughter, is in charge of public relations.

VINEYARDS - The air you breathe visiting the company is "fresh" thanks to the personality of the people — in a figurative sense and in a literal one too. Open, well-ventilated and luminous vineyards with soils rich in marl, its position couldn't be better, and the same applies to the southwest exposure of the immaculately kept vineyards.

WINES - **Brunello di Montalcino Ris. 2006** (● 4,500 bt) has developing aromas of citrus fruits and spices with notes of blood. The noble, taut body develops vertically and closes with tangy tannins. **Rosso di Montalcino 2010** (● 20,000 bt) is satisfying and succulent in the mouth with crunchy fruit. It has racy progression and assertive acidity.

> **slow wine** **BRUNELLO DI MONTALCINO 2007** (● 22,000 bt) Earthy, sappy, dense with sweet, flavorsome tannins, long and lingering, super-dynamic — undoubtedly one of the best Brunellos of the vintage.

FERTILIZERS organic-mineral
PLANT PROTECTION chemical, copper and sulphur
WEED CONTROL mechanical
YEASTS selected, native
GRAPES 100% estate-grown
CERTIFICATION none

MONTALCINO (SI)

Il Paradiso di Manfredi

Via Canalicchio, 305
tel. 0577 848478
www.ilparadisodimanfredi.com
info@ilparadisodimanfredi.com

2.25 ha - 9,500 bt

66 Florio Guerrini runs Il Paradiso with all the spontaneity of someone who realizes he is part of a harmonious, balanced whole of which wine is the wondrous final expression 99

PEOPLE - With disarming naturalness, Florio says he learned the winemaking profession from his father-in-law Manfredi Martini, who bought the property in 1950. "I stole it with my eyes," he says. His wife Rosella Martini and their daughters Silvia and Gioia help him tend this fairy-tale place.

VINEYARDS - The vineyards nestle on seven terraces round the property. "Every one is different," explains Florio, stressing the key concept of the individuality of every parcel and every vine. His daughter Silvia, who took us round, showed us the fossils in the soil that add extraordinary natural minerality to the wines. The vineyards stand to the north of Montalcino at an altitude of 340-370 meters and have always been managed using organic methods.

WINES - Biodiversity is important. "Pollen from the trees serves to nourish the native yeasts," explains Florio. His wines speak of the different harvests, the rhythm of the seasons and the terroir with total naturalness. As Florio puts it, "They shape themselves, develop themselves and balance themselves". The bright **Brunello di Montalcino 2007** (● 7,000 bt) is a thrill to drink. It has earthy aromas of humus, damp soil and undergrowth with wonderful vertical progression and vibrant, gutsy grip. With its intriguing aromas of iodine, succulence, tanginess and masterfully crafted tannins, **Brunello di Montalcino Ris. 2006** (● 1,200 bt) is a class act. A Great Wine! **Rosso di Montalcino 2010** (● 2,500 bt) is fruity, earthy and mineral.

FERTILIZERS none
PLANT PROTECTION copper and sulphur
WEED CONTROL mechanical
YEASTS native
GRAPES 100% estate-grown
CERTIFICATION none

MONTALCINO (SI)
La Cerbaiola - Salvioni

Piazza Cavour, 19
tel. 0577 848499
aziendasalvioni@libero.it

4 ha - 15,000 bt

PEOPLE - Giulio Salvioni, a member of one of the oldest families in Montalcino, has been producing fine wines for almost 30 years. Given the limited number of his vineyards, he is able to monitor every stage in the production process carefully. He is aided in his work by his wife Mirella Civitelli and his sons David and Alessia. His infectious energy has helped raise the international profile of a terroir rich in potential and allure.

VINEYARDS - The company's four hectares of vineyards are situated in the Cerbaiona district and combine to form a single southeast facing plot planted entirely with sangiovese grapes. Giulio spoke to us of all the efforts he and others have put in over the years to select and analyze the best clones with the aim of improving quality. Though yields are never fantastic anyway, the grape bunches are thinned drastically and average output rarely exceeds 30 quintals per hectare.

WINES - All the company's vineyards are registered as Brunello. This means that in fortunate years it can decide not to produce Rosso and allocate all the grapes to the more prized wine. Thus, for the very promising 2010 vintage, Rosso wasn't presented. "I don't want to repeat the error I made in 2004," says Giulio with the air of someone who's learned a lesson. So we had to "make do" with a taste of **Brunello di Montalcino 2007** (● 10,100 bt). It's a wine that struts its stuff as soon as you bring it close to your nose. It has deep, dynamic aromas of brambles and red berries enhanced by deft balsamic hints. The palate is vertical, very juicy and richly textured. It's a sangiovese of great character.

FERTILIZERS	organic-mineral
PLANT PROTECTION	copper and sulphur
WEED CONTROL	mechanical
YEASTS	native
GRAPES	100% estate-grown
CERTIFICATION	none

MONTALCINO (SI)
Le Chiuse

Località Pullera, 228
tel. 055 597052
www.aziendaagricolalechiuse.it
info@lechiuse.com

7 ha - 25,000 bt   `10% discount`

❝ No loudmouthing here. Just measured, attentive organic management for fragrant, typical, traditional wines in which the last word is left to sangiovese … and sangiovese alone ❞

PEOPLE - At Le Chiuse they're sticklers for transitivity: which, in their case, means the handing down of passion for vines and wonderful wines. In the course of our annual visit, we were received by Simonetta Valiani and her son Lorenzo Magnelli, who impressed us with his competence and maturity. Here the management is, very obviously, all in the family.

VINEYARDS - We made our tour of the vineyards with Lorenzo. They are situated at an altitude of 300 meters and surround the totally restored winery farmhouse in the northern part of the denomination. Conversion to organics started in 2000 and the first wine produced with organic grapes was released in 2005. The vineyards have been gradually replanted with the clone derived from 70-year-old mother vines with a density of 5,500 plants per hectare.

WINES - In the tasting room, Lorenzo served us a really promising experimental sangiovese spumante. But it was Simonetta Valiani who really got us going when she said, "My uncle (Franco Biondi Santi) always says that while you're tasting a wine, you have to watch it with your eyes; if they close it means it's not interesting". On the palate, **Brunello di Montalcino Ris. 2006** (● 3,000 bt) brings out all the body, fullness and tannins of a wine with great aging potential. **Brunello di Montalcino 2007** (● 10,300 bt) has bashful aromas, but also rigorous, warm, lip-smacking flavor and excellent length. **Rosso di Montalcino 2010** (● 8,000 bt) is subtly fresh and vibrant, while **Q Rosé 2010** (◉ 1,200 bt) is deliciously thirst-quenching.

FERTILIZERS	manure pellets, green manure
PLANT PROTECTION	copper and sulphur
WEED CONTROL	mechanical
YEASTS	native
GRAPES	100% estate-grown
CERTIFICATION	organic

MONTALCINO (SI)

Le Ragnaie

Loc. Le Ragnaie
tel. 0577 848639
www.leragnaie.com
info@leragnaie.com

MONTALCINO (SI)

Pietroso

Podere Pietroso, 257
tel. 0577 848573
www.pietroso.it
info@pietroso.it

14 ha - 45,000 bt   **10% discount**

5.5 ha - 40,000 bt   **10% discount**

PEOPLE - Le Ragnaie is now something of an institution in Montalcino. Much of the credit obviously belongs to the vineyards themselves, but it's also important to mention the astonishing winemaking talent of the young owner Riccardo Campinoti. "I've got a very precise idea about Sangiovese based on vertical acidity and lightness of flavor. The high altitude of my vineyards is fundamental in this respect."

VINEYARDS - When he speaks of altitude, Riccardo is referring to Passo del Lume Spento, the highest point of the denomination. "I find it incredible that at one time ripening grapes was a problem here," he says. This is where his oldest vineyard, planted in 1968, is situated, from which he obtains one of his two crus. The other comes from the 8,000-square-meter Fornace vineyard, near Castelnuovo dell'Abate. The company also owns a few important vine rows in the area of the old onyx quarry and a vineyard in the Pietroso district.

WINES - In the cellar they use cement vats for fermentation and large barrels for aging. **Brunello di Montalcino VV 2007** (● 2,000 bt) is made with grapes from the old vineyards round the cellar and oozes class. It is well-defined and floral on the nose, dynamic, deep and linear on the palate. It's one of Montalcino's greatest wines and we rated it the best of the bunch. In short, a Great Wine. **Brunello di Montalcino Fornace 2007** (● 3,300 bt), from the southern side of the denomination, is warmer and more mature. Excellent too is **Brunello di Montalcino 2007** (● 13,000 bt), blossomy and spicy with hints of quinine, sapid, fine and splendidly harmonious. **Rosso di Montalcino 2010** (● 22,000 bt) is floral and juicy and calls out to be drunk. We couldn't leave, finally, without tasting **Chianti Colli Senesi 2010** (● 7,000 bt), super-juicy and packed with aging potential.

PEOPLE - A trip to the company Gianni Pignattai runs with his son Andrea and wife Cecilia Brandini, who works as sales manager, is like taking a breath of fresh air. Partly on account of the warm welcome they give you, partly for the wild beauty of the place, bought in 1970 by Domenico Berni, Gianni's grandfather and his first teacher in the art of winemaking, from vineyard to cellar. Since 1992 Gianni has managed the estate independently with the help of enologist Alessandro Dondi.

VINEYARDS - The company's four hectares, all given over to sangiovese, are divided into three plots. The first, around the house and the cellar, is terraced and grows on well-draining, pebbly soil. The second is at Fornello in the Canalicchi zone. The third is on the hilltop looking onto the abbey of Sant'Antimo. The company recently bought a new parcel of land at Villa Montosoli, with 70-year-old vines mainly of sangiovese and other traditional grapes.

WINES - In the pretty little cellar under the house, the grapes from the three vineyards are vinified separately and, prior to bottling, reassembled in variable proportions to bring out the specific components of the three crus. We look forward with some trepidation to the wine produced at Montosoli, which will rest in barrels for another year. At first the beautifully crafted **Brunello di Montalcino 2007** (● 17,000 bt) develops a bouquet of flowers, then spices and minerality kick in to support ripe fruit. The palate is clean, soft and elegant with sumptuous tannins, freshness and tanginess that make you beg for more. Also top-level is **Rosso di Montalcino 2010** (● 17,000 bt), young but well-balanced, at once pervasive, soft and rich in flavor.

FERTILIZERS natural manure, green manure	FERTILIZERS none
PLANT PROTECTION copper and sulphur	PLANT PROTECTION copper and sulphur
WEED CONTROL mechanical	WEED CONTROL mechanical
YEASTS native	YEASTS native
GRAPES 100% estate-grown	GRAPES 20% bought in
CERTIFICATION organic	CERTIFICATION none

MONTALCINO (SI)

Podere Salicutti

Località Podere Salicutti, 174
tel. 0577 847003
www.poderesalicutti.it
leanza@poderesalicutti.it

MONTALCINO (SI)

Poggio di Sotto

Frazione Castelnuovo dell'Abate
Località Poggio di Sotto
tel. 0577 835502
www.poggiodisotto.com
palmucci@poggiodisotto.com

---

4 ha - 15,000 bt   **10% discount**

PEOPLE - The company, set up by Francesco Leanza in 1944, enjoys a truly breathtaking setting. From the terrace over the wine cellar it's possible to admire a truly gorgeous vista: a broad valley scattered with vineyards and Monte Amiata looming in the background. Francesco, who describes himself as a self-taught winemaker, is a meticulous perfectionist who works with the deepest respect for nature and follows its rhythms. He has always adopted the criteria of organic agriculture.

VINEYARDS - The vineyards encircle the farmhouse and are divided into three plots: Piaggione, lower down with a southern exposure, which produces the grapes for Brunello; Sorgente, to the southwest, where the grapes for Rosso come from; and Teatro, to the southeast, where cabernet grapes are grown. The soils are mainly composed of *galestro* marl with infiltrations of clay and sand. The main grape is sangiovese, which is cordon-trained, save for a recent replanting which is Guyot-trained. Viticultural practices are very traditional and in no way invasive.

WINES - The wines are vinified very simply to express the biodiversity of each single vineyard. They are aged in large barrels to respect the original fruit. Each year the grapes for winemaking are carefully selected in the vineyard. This is the only way to achieve wines such as **Brunello di Montalcino Piaggione 2007** (● 8,000 bt), which offers complex aromas of soil, fruit and fresh meat in sequence, followed by a soft, sapid, agreeable palate. It's a Great Wine. Enjoyable too was **Rosso di Montalcino 2007** (● 2,600 bt) from the Sorgente vineyard, warm, spicy and tangy with nice acidity on the finish. **Dopoteatro 2009** (● cabernet sauvignon, canaiolo; 1,300 bt) has typically varietal fresh, vegetal aromas of green pepper and cherry and a dry, mineral palate.

10 ha - 35,000 bt

PEOPLE - "If I'd failed to buy Poggio di Sotto, I woudn't have bought any other company in Montalcino," confided Claudio Tipa, the new owner of Poggio di Sotto and other wineries in the Montecucco area and in Bolgheri. A great enthusiast, he told us he used to adore the wines of Palmucci and admired the old owner. He was also at pains to stress that "the new ownership won't alter the style of the company wines in any way".

VINEYARDS - The vineyards, optimally located to make the most of the varietal finesse of sangiovese, will continue to be managed by winemaker Vali Grigore, who picked up great professional expertise under the previous owner. Methods will continue to be organic and the land will be worked according to the rhythms and schedules established by the old owners without altering the delicate equilibria achieved through many years of sacrifice and experience.

WINES - In the cellar Giulio Gambelli's rich legacy has been gathered by the talented Luca Marrone, under the expert supervision of Federico Staderini. Together they assess the nuances of taste that guide their choice of the barrels to allocate to Rosso/Brunello di Montalcino, and the style is identical to that of the past. The excellent **Brunello di Montalcino Ris. 2006** (● 3,500 bt) has a floral bouquet against a background note of tar, a palate impregnated with freshness and juice, and a tangy, sweet finish — a Great Wine. **Brunello di Montalcino 2007** (● 18,000 bt) shows the signs of the warm vintage with an ethereal bouquet and warm tones. The palate is subtle, rich in flavor and nicely complex. Very good too was **Rosso di Montalcino 2009** (● 13,500 bt) has a fruity, fragrant bouquet and a palate packed with lively, subtle, continuous freshness.

FERTILIZERS natural manure
PLANT PROTECTION copper and sulphur
WEED CONTROL mechanical
YEASTS native
GRAPES 100% estate-grown
CERTIFICATION organic

FERTILIZERS manure pellets, green manure
PLANT PROTECTION copper and sulphur
WEED CONTROL mechanical
YEASTS native
GRAPES 100% estate-grown
CERTIFICATION organic

Stella di Campalto

Frazione Castelnuovo dell'Abate
Località Podere San Giuseppe
tel. 0577 835754
www.stelladicampalto.com
info@stelladicampalto.com

6.5 ha - 27,500 bt

PEOPLE - As a young woman in 1992, Stella di Campalto didn't think she would become a winemaker and the Podere San Giuseppe farm served solely to produce oil for self-consumption. In 1997 she began to become aware of the enological potential of this side of Montalcino and started plowing her first vineyard. Since she released her first wines in 2001, Stella has proved to be a talented producer and an excellent interpreter of the sangiovese grape.

VINEYARDS - The aptitude for natural viticulture has been transmitted from place to person as if by osmosis. It's not hard to see that strolling round the vineyards with Stella. In this unspoiled environment, protected by woodland, a sentiment of mutual respect emerges spontaneously. The agronomic management limits intervention to a minimum and protection of the environment is one of the producer's main objectives. In 2002 she received biodynamic certification.

WINES - In the cellar too, Stella has completed a veritable training course and her wines increasingly epitomize her philosophy. The cellar is structured on three levels. After stemming, the grapes drop into small 10-15-liter Allier oak tubs. Larger tubs were bought in order to reduce the use of wood during aging. With the 2007 vintage, wood sensations are hazier and the wine has greater naturalness of expression. **Rosso di Montalcino 2009** (● 13,500 bt) has a floral, earthy matrix with a palate whose juicy body is supported by acid weight. The fantastic Brunello di Montalcino 2007 (● 14,000 bt) offers minerals and red fruits combined with taut, generous, racy, vibrant flavor. It's a Great Wine.

FERTILIZERS biodynamic preparations, green manure
PLANT PROTECTION copper and sulphur
WEED CONTROL mechanical
YEASTS native
GRAPES 100% estate-grown
CERTIFICATION biodynamic, organic

Terre Nere

Frazione Castelnuovo dell'Abate
tel. 0577 373316
www.terreneremontalcino.com
terrenere1@virgilio.it

10 ha - 70,000 bt   **10% discount**

PEOPLE - Pasquale Vallone is the owner of this company, which came into being in 1997, and he runs it enthusiastically with the help of the whole family. His brother Gaetano works in the cellar, his wife Pierina and kids Francesa and Federico manage sales. Pasquale told us he'd spent his life doing other jobs but that he hails from the countryside and has never forgotten the lessons and values his father taught him, which can be summed up in two words: "Peasant honesty".

VINEYARDS - The 10 hectares of vines stand in a lovely setting in a southeast location in the Castelnuovo dell'Abate zone. The soil is very dark (hence the name of the company which literally means "Black Lands") with traces of clay and limestone here and there. Pasquale, who manages the vineyards firsthand, says it's thanks to the wind if he manages to work among the vine rows even when it's boiling hot. He points out the woods and the watercourses in the valleys and says they're important in froming great aromas in the wines.

WINES - We rate the wines of Terre Nere, produced with grapes from one of the best growing areas in Montalcino, pretty highly. **Brunello di Montalcino 2007** (● 13,000 bt) has good grip and richness of flavor. The **Brunello di Montalcino Sel. 2007** (● 5,000 bt) selection has spacious aromas and a long finish with a good acidic structure and, above all, great harmony and balance. We also liked **Rosso di Montalcino 2009** (● 7,000 bt) is simpler with approachable aromas and a nice feel in the mouth.

> **slow wine** **BRUNELLO DI MONTALCINO RIS. 2006** (● 5,000 bt) Earthy and compact with delightfully heady aromas of undergrowth. It stands out for its richness of flavor on the palate and well-crafted tannins. Don't underestimate its terroir-rootedness and staggering price either.

FERTILIZERS manure pellets
PLANT PROTECTION copper and sulphur
WEED CONTROL mechanical
YEASTS selected
GRAPES 100% estate-grown
CERTIFICATION none

Tiezzi

Località Soccorso
tel. 0577 848187
www.tiezzivini.it
tiezzie@tiscali.it

5.5 ha - 22,000 bt **10% discount**

PEOPLE - A conversation with Enzo Tiezzi, who began working at Col d'Orica in 1959 when he was nicknamed "Il Citto", is a total immersion in the history of the local area. Enzo has devoted his whole life to viticulture and has always believed in sangiovese and its expressive potential. Which is why he set up a winery all of his own in the 1980s. A former president of the local wine consortium he can be considered one of the fathers of Rosso di Montalcino, whose birth he fought for with passion.

VINEYARDS - The cellar is in Podere Soccorso district, directly below the Santuario della Madonna del Soccorso, near the old 13th-century walls of Montalcino. The vineyards are magnificently bush-trained and are the ones whose grapes that went into the first label of Brunello in 1870. Cigaleta and Cerrino, the company's other two vineyards, are to the northeast, about three kilometers from the town at an altitude of about 350 meters.

WINES - Enzo believes in tradition and is adamant that vines have to speak of the terroir they come from. He prefers to use large wooden tubs for fermenting and oak casks for aging. **Rosso di Montalcino 2010** (● 7,000 bt) is amazingly fragrant with enfolding fruit and a juicy mouthfeel. **Brunello di Montalcino 2007** (● 7,500 bt) expresses a strong sense of place. Its impact is severe and earthy but it gradually comes out of its shell with a flavorful palate and splendid acidity.

> **slow wine** BRUNELLO DI MONTALCINO VIGNA SOCCORSO RIS. 2006 (● 5,300 bt) An imposing wine with fine, sweet spices with pleasant ripe fruit seeping through. The palate is nicely meaty, warm and soft with a commendably clean finish.

FERTILIZERS	organic-mineral
PLANT PROTECTION	copper and sulphur
WEED CONTROL	chemical, mechanical
YEASTS	native
GRAPES	100% estate-grown
CERTIFICATION	none

Boscarelli

Frazione Cervognano
Via di Montenero, 28
tel. 0578 767277
www.poderiboscarelli.com
info@poderiboscarelli.com

14 ha - 100,000 bt

❝ The company's pride and joy is the Vigna del Nocio vineyard from which the De Ferraris produce a rich, potent, long-living wine with a strong sense of place. A concentrate of the qualities we approve of ❞

PEOPLE - "The first vineyards were planted in the 1960s," explained Luca De Ferrari as we strolled through the countryside opposite the property. "My grandfather was a believer in Montepulciano." Luca runs the company with his brother Nicolò and his mother Paola Corradi, but it was his grandfather Egidio Corradi who singled out this magnificent winegrowing land in the Cervognano district. It was thus that, in 1962, he acquired the Boscarelli estate and gave rise to one of the most renowned wine companies in the environs.

VINEYARDS - Cervognano is a well-ventilated area but is also warm, a factor that optimizes grape ripening. The vines are planted with a density of 6-7,000 per hectare. This makes the plants compete against each other, the roots reaching down deep to ensure greater acidity.

WINES - When he presented us his wines, Luca explained that he has changed his approach slightly and now limits the use of oak in the ageing process. **Nobile di Montepulciano Nocio dei Boscarelli 2008** (● 4,500 bt) has a mature nose of cherries supported by nice acidity. It's a succulent, powerful wine in which the tannins are still pretty evident. Exemplary and dynamic, **Nobile di Montepulciano Ris. 2007** (● 10,000 bt) is potent, elegant, juicy and long — a Great Wine. **Nobile di Montepulciano 2009** (● 43,000 bt) is earthy and spacious. **Rosso di Montepulciano Prugnolo 2010** (● 15,000 bt) is well made and pleasurable with aromas of strawberry and blossom and a fresh, fragrant bouquet. Just as supple but simpler is **De Ferrari 2011** (● sangiovese, merlot; 18,000 bt).

FERTILIZERS	natural manure, green manure
PLANT PROTECTION	chemical, copper and sulphur
WEED CONTROL	chemical, mechanical
YEASTS	native
GRAPES	100% estate-grown
CERTIFICATION	none

Dei

Villa Martiena
tel. 0578 716878
www.cantinedei.com
info@cantinedei.com

55 ha - 210,000 bt · **10% discount**

PEOPLE - The company is managed today by Caterina Dei, but it was her grandfather Alibrando who had the brainwave of planting the first vineyard in Bossona, one of the best winemaking zones in the entire Montepulciano area. Since then more have been planted, giving rise to the company that now boasts 55 hectares in all and, over the years, has testified through its wines to the potential and greatness of this extraordinary terroir.

VINEYARDS - The Bossona vineyard, a south-facing natural amphitheater with tufaceous soil rich in fossils, is a truly magical place. It is situated at an altitude of 370-400 meters in a zone with constant ventilation. The other vineyards are at Martiena, where the cellar is situated, La Piaggia and La Ciarliana. The soils vary according to area and great efforts are made in the vineyards and the cellar to ensure that their different characteristics are expressed in the wines.

WINES - The impressively racy **Rosso di Montepulciano 2010** (● 90,000 bt) kicks off with magnificent fruit and follows through with a fragrant palate. It's a perfect Everyday Wine. **Nobile di Montepulciano 2009** (● 90,000 bt) is a mature wine with great flesh and an enfolding, tannic finish. **Nobile di Montepulciano Ris. Bossona 2008** (● 18,000 bt) is more contained and elegant with notes of soil and cherries and plenty of depth and dynamism. **Sancta Catharina 2009** (● sangiovese, syrah, cabernet sauvignon, petit verdot; 5,000 bt) has sweet, spicy nuances; herbaceous on the nose, it has a soft, balanced palate. Sweet but in no way cloying, **Vin Santo di Montepulciano 2005** (○ malvasia, grechetto, trebbiano; 1,200 bt) has a pleasant finish redolent of almond paste.

FERTILIZERS	organic-mineral, manure pellets
PLANT PROTECTION	copper and sulphur
WEED CONTROL	mechanical
YEASTS	selected
GRAPES	100% estate-grown
CERTIFICATION	none

Poderi Sanguineto I e II

Frazione Acquaviva
Via Sanguineto, 2/4
tel. 0578 767782
www.sanguineto.com
sanguineto@tin.it

3.7 ha - 30,000 bt · **10% discount**

❝ What a pleasure it was to meet two winemakers as volcanic as Dora Forsoni and Patrizia Brogi! Traditional, eco-friendly agriculture, typical wines and honest prices are their hallmarks ❞

PEOPLE - Patrizia states bluntly that, "I'm in charge of the commercial side of this small, little known company. We are neither organic nor biodynamic, we just try to make good wine". The company's first bottled wine went on sale in 1997.

VINEYARDS - We were looking out over the vineyard, planted in 1963, a single 3.7-hectare property not far from the company. Dora started rattling off pearls of farming wisdom filled with good old-fashioned common sense. Then she turned to the vineyard and said, "Keep me poor and I'll make you rich". She stressed how it is important to monitor the vines closely and avoid pruning them. "From old vines you get good wine," she concluded, "Just as you can make good broth with an old hen."

WINES - The wines are aged in Slavonian oak barrels of various sizes. Dora and Patrizia take their quality grapes to the cellar, then let the wine follow its natural course. The excellent **Nobile di Montepulciano 2009** (● 6,300 bt) is fruity, soft, racy and long. **Rosso di Montepulciano 2010** (● 13,000 bt) has deep aromas and a balanced palate. Worth tasting is **Bianco 2011** (○ malvasia bianca e verde, biancone; 5,500 bt).

> **slow wine** NOBILE DI MONTEPULCIANO RIS. 2007 (● 4,000 bt) The palate is admirably fresh and silky, the finish tangy, aristocratic and long — a superb version of the wine.

FERTILIZERS	none
PLANT PROTECTION	chemical, copper and sulphur
WEED CONTROL	mechanical
YEASTS	native
GRAPES	100% estate-grown
CERTIFICATION	none

SAN GIMIGNANO (SI)

Il Colombaio di Santa Chiara €

Località il Colombaio, 10 C
tel. 0577 942004
www.colombaiosantachiara.it
info@colombaiosantachiara.it

11 ha - 80,000 bt | **10% discount**

PEOPLE - In the 1980s, Mario Logi bought the first portions of the property, now managed by his sons Alessio (vineyards and cellar), Giampiero (sales) and Stefano (administration) —though dad always has the last word! The cellar is housed in the old vicarage in the small village of San Donato, while the farmhouse and agriturismo facility are in Santa Chiara. The vineyards and olive groves are to be found at both. Nicola Berti and Paolo Caciorgna collaborate as consultant enologists.

VINEYARDS - The vineyards span out over four adjacent zones on mostly tufaceous soil at an altitude of about 350 meters. The oldest vineyard is about 35 years old and successive plantings date from 2002. Most vines are Guyot-trained or cordon-trained and spur-pruned. The vineyards are managed using organic methods, with no chemical weed control, only mechanical soil working under the vine rows. By the end of the year the present cellar will be moved to allow modernization and extension work.

WINES - The common denominator of the wines is pleasurable plushness and a strong sense of place. The fantastic **Vernaccia di San Gimignano Selvabianca 2011** (O 40,000 bt) has delicious citrusy notes and a dynamic, acid, soft palate. In view of its affordable price, this is our Everyday Wine. **Vernaccia di San Gimignano Albereta Ris. 2010** (O 5,000 bt) is fine, balanced and velvety. With its heady scents and neat finish, **Chianti Colli Senesi Campale 2011** (● sangiovese, merlot; 11,000 bt) proves that in San Gimignano they can make great wines too.

slow wine | VERNACCIA DI SAN GIMIGNANO CAMPO DELLA PIEVE **2010** (O 4,000 bt) A truly persuasive white whose full flavor is set off by a typical, land-rooted tangy, lingering finish.

FERTILIZERS manure pellets, green manure
PLANT PROTECTION copper and sulphur
WEED CONTROL mechanical
YEASTS selected, native
GRAPES 100% estate-grown
CERTIFICATION organic

SAN GIMIGNANO (SI)

Montenidoli

Località Montenidoli
tel. 0577 941565
www.montenidoli.com
montenidoli@valdelsa.net

24 ha - 90,000 bt

❝ What an energetic winemaker Elisabetta Fagiuoli is! Every time we go to see her she amazes us with her charisma and her in-depth technical knowhow, the result of years spent "listening" to the land and talking to her French *vigneron* friends ❞

PEOPLE - This year Elisabetta sprung a surprise on us. She reckoned her wines were too young and didn't want us to taste them. "The character of my wines comes out and conquers you in the long term," she explained.

VINEYARDS - There's nothing formal about a trip to Montenidoli. Elisabetta decides what you're going to do. Instead of taking us to her vineyards, such as Templare and Primo Sole, the highest in San Gimignano, she laid on a premiere tasting of a red wine made with sangiovese grapes from the Primo Sole vineyard. Not that the surprises ended there. In fact, she also served us an excellent deep red wine made with colorino grapes from another cask. Two treats in one go, exclusively for us!

WINES - Elisabetta Fagiuoli produces original wines full of sincere expressiveness, fruit of a genuine viticulture mindful of environmental equilibrium. **Templare 2008** (O vernaccia, trebbiano, malvasia; 6,000 bt) is splendid with a succulent palate, balance and richness of flavor. Excellent too is **Vernaccia di San Gimignano Fiore 2010** (O 12,700 bt), packed with vibrant personality. **Canaiuolo 2011** (☉ 6,000 bt) is delicious, one of the finest rosés in all Tuscany. **Chianti Colli Senesi Garrulo 2010** (● 11,000 bt) is a supple quaffing wine, while the tonic **Chianti Colli Senesi Montenidoli 2008** (● 3,000 bt), finally, works to perfection.

slow wine | VERNACCIA DI SAN GIMIGNANO CARATO **2008** (O 7,000 bt) A wine of great character, its mineral flavor leaving a long trail of tanginess and freshness.

FERTILIZERS green manure
PLANT PROTECTION copper and sulphur
WEED CONTROL mechanical
YEASTS native
GRAPES 100% estate-grown
CERTIFICATION organic

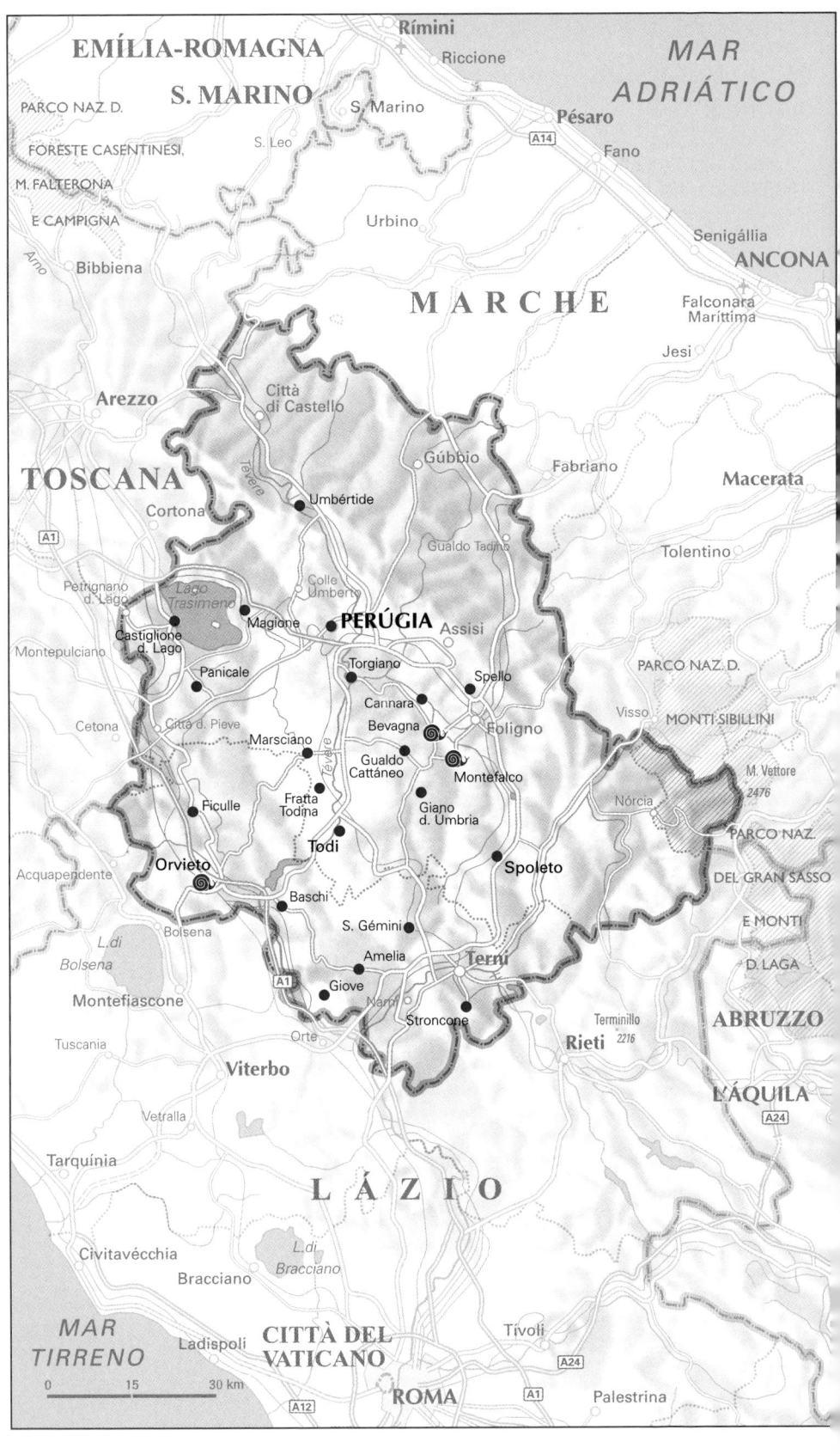

UMBRIA

Umbria is an important region for Italian agriculture in general, and a veritable laboratory for winemaking in particular, one of the most active in the country. Up-and-coming wineries, investment in large companies, historic estates that have made Umbrian wines famous the world over — these elements all combine to create the rich mosaic of labels, disparate commercial situations and different agronomic approaches that, once again this year, we have sought to analyze in this guide. In the first two editions we lamented a certain lull in production and style, but this time round we are pleased to report that things are changing.

All this is due to a multiplicity of factors, and we believe it is true to say that, with our constant presence in the various terroirs, we too have helped to give the situation a shake. Having said that, the bulk of the work has been carried out by the viticulturists themselves, who are now more conscious of the job they are doing, operating not only for themselves but also for the region as a whole. This is why we have awarded a Snail to Tabarrini of Montefalco, for example. Here the talented Giampaolo not only produces great *vins de terroir*, but also does his best to affirm Sagrantino and Umbrian viticulture nationally and internationally. "They're uprooting sagrantino to plant trebbiano," joked Francesco Antano in the cellar.

Trebbiano spoletino is attracting a lot of interest from producers and Antano's quip words hit where it hurts. Too much planting was done in the 1990s and we wouldn't like to see the same error repeated. Good news came from the province of Terni, where the classic makers of Orvieto are always a guarantee of quality. Vinified with respect for its expressive fragrance, the ciliegiolo grape could also become an excellence for the region.

Adanti

Località Vocabolo Arquata
tel. 0742 360435
www.cantineadanti.com
info@cantineadanti.com

30 ha - 150,000 bt	10% discount

66 Two of the distinctive features of this wine company are its hospitality and openness to the outside world. Its superb wines are an expression of the land by which they are nurtured and which they, in turn, nurture 99

PEOPLE - The enthusiasm and passion of Daniele Palini, chief of the cellar owned by the Adanti family, ensure continuity to the excellent work carried out over the years by his father, tailor-cum-cellarman Alvaro, a legend in his own right and one of the finest interpreters of the sagrantino grape.

VINEYARDS - The Arquata terroir needs no introductions. In the course of time it has become one of the most important for the sagrantino grape. Most of the winery's vineyards, some of which over 40 years old, have their roots in these clay hills. For some years, Daniele has cultivated another single vineyard, Colcimino, where the soil is different.

WINES - Daniele is more reflective and measured than his father. But the two share one thing in common; namely a fine palate and the ability to interpret the grapes from the different vineyards to achieve increasingly elegant wines. Made with the best grapes from Colcimino, **Sagrantino di Montefalco Il Domenico 2007** (● 5,000 bt) is complex, profound and vertical. A wine well worth waiting for. **Montefalco Rosso Ris. 2008** (● 6,000 bt) is elegant and dynamic with a juicy palate. **Montefalco Rosso 2008** (● 80,000 bt) puts the onus on fruit, but it is not without complexity and supporting acidity.

slow wine **SAGRANTINO DI MONTEFALCO 2007** (● 25,000 bt) A wine with a whistle-clean, floral bouquet and a harmonious palate with perfectly integrated tannins. Aged in large oak barrels, a splendid expression of its terroir.

FERTILIZERS natural manure	
PLANT PROTECTION chemical, copper and sulphur	
WEED CONTROL chemical, mechanical	
YEASTS selected	
GRAPES 100% estate-grown	
CERTIFICATION none	

Fattoria Colleallodole

Vocabolo Colle Allodole, 228
tel. 0742 361897
www.fattoriacolleallodole.it
info@fattoriacolleallodole.com

12 ha - 80,000 bt	10% discount

66 Francesco Antano is not only a winemaker, but also an artist and an interpreter. He accompanies his efforts to express his philosophy with a touch of folly and constant dedication 99

PEOPLE - Since the 1960s Fattoria Colleallodole, founded by Milziade Antano and now managed by his son Francesco, has been following the local enological tradition. Over the years it has increasingly placed the onus on quality.

VINEYARDS - Climbing up to Fattoria Colleallodole from Bevagna, you can see the winery's vineyards, all excellently located, cordon-trained and spur-pruned, naturally fertilized and cultivated manually in all the phases of their life-cycle. Extreme care for the vineyard and grape selection ensure added value to the cellar's wines.

WINES - All Francesco's personality and flair come out in the cellar, where the wines express character and great aging capacity. The excellent **Montefalco Rosso Ris. 2008** (● sangiovese, sagrantino, merlot, cabernet; 2,700 bt), has complex structure with great intensity and lingering flavor. **Bianco di Milziade 2011** (○ miscellaneous white grapes; 4.500 bt) has good acidity and aroma. **Sagrantino di Montefalco Passito 2009** (● 2,400 bt), finally, has a balanced, palate with soft tannins and texture.

slow wine **SAGRANTINO DI MONTEFALCO COLLEALLODOLE 2008** (● 1,300 bt) Splendid spicy notes pervade the nose, softness, elegance and intensity fill the palate. A thrilling, authentic expression of the sagrantino grape.

FERTILIZERS green manure	
PLANT PROTECTION copper and sulphur	
WEED CONTROL mechanical	
YEASTS native	
GRAPES 100% estate-grown	
CERTIFICATION none	

Omero Moretti €

Via San Sabino, 19
tel. 0742 90433
www.morettiomero.it
info@morettiomero.it

11 ha - 45,000 bt `10% discount`

PEOPLE - Omero Moretti planted his vines in 1997, even though his family has always made wine true to the peasant tradition. They were already making it when the present cellar was being built and Omero was still breeding pigs and growing olives — oil being a great passion of his, as he freely admits. The family still plays a key role in the winery where the contribution of enologist Tiziano Vistalli is also invaluable.

VINEYARDS - From the vineyards it is possible to admire the village of Montefalco. Here the native grechetto and sagrantino grapes grow on mixed soil, though this year Omero Moretti is also banking a lot on the first wines from a new ciliegiolo vineyard. To his credit, since 1991 he has managed the vineyard using organic methods.

WINES - The style of Omero Moretti's wines reflects their maker's simplicity and skill. Cellar operations aim solely to enhance the work of the vineyard — no more, no less. **Grechetto 2011** (○ 13,000) is a simple, refreshing wine with a great sense of place. **Nessuno 2011** (○ grechetto, malvasia; 7,000 bt) is the aromatic version, soft and flowery thanks to the addition of malvasia. **Montefalco Rosso 2009** (● sangiovese, merlot, sagrantino; 15,000 bt) has marked red fruit with deft balsamic notes; the alcohol and right tannic structure make it a wine of great equilibrium.

> **slow wine** **SAGRANTINO DI MONTEFALCO 2008** (● 9,000 bt) With its garnet-red color and complex tertiary aromas and elegant tannins, a label that expresses all the character of the grape. A master class in wine making.

FERTILIZERS natural manure, compost
PLANT PROTECTION copper and sulphur
WEED CONTROL mechanical
YEASTS selected
GRAPES 100% estate-grown
CERTIFICATION organic

Antonelli San Marco

Località San Marco
tel. 0742 379158
www.antonellisanmarco.it
info@antonellisanmarco.it

45 ha - 300,000 bt `10% discount`

❝ Filippo Antonelli always keeps a careful eye on the future, interpreting modern times while preserving the charm of the past. Which is why his cellar is one of the finest expressions of the Umbrian winemaking tradition ❞

PEOPLE - Filippo, whose family has been living in Montefalco since 1881, took over the management of the winery in 1986. The cellar is situated in the area of San Marco, already cited in medieval documents for the quality of its winemaking. The company staff is formed by enologist Massimiliano Caburazzi, cellarman Sandro Bertoni and agronomist Alessio Moretti.

VINEYARDS - The vineyards occupy 45 hectares of the total area of the company's land on rolling hills at an average altitude of 350 meters. The soil is clayey, rich in limestone, organic substances and microbiological activity, an effect of the intelligent conversion to organics decided upon some years ago.

WINES - Painstaking work in the vineyard and careful vinification in the cellar make for bottles of consistent quality, both for the young, fresh, easy-drinking wines and for the more important ones. **Montefalco Rosso 2009** (● sangiovese, sagrantino, merlot; 120,000 bt) is pleasant to drink and balanced with discreet tannins. **Contrario 2009** (● sagrantino; 26,000 bt) is aged in stainless steel and represents an interesting experiment with the variety. It manages to bring out all the grape's fruity character without interfering with the tannins.

> **slow wine** **TREBBIANO SPOLETINO 2010** (○ 13,000 bt) Aged 50% in stainless steel, 25% in tonneau and 25% in barriques, a wine of great character and complexity that captures all the freshness of the grape. Drink it now if you wish, but it's also built to last.

FERTILIZERS compost, green manure
PLANT PROTECTION copper and sulphur
WEED CONTROL mechanical
YEASTS native
GRAPES 5% bought in
CERTIFICATION organic

MONTEFALCO (PG)
Paolo Bea

Località Cerrete, 8
tel. 0742 378128
www.paolobea.com
info@paolobea.com

11 ha - 55,000 bt

66 Paolo Bea defended and promoted the wine of Montefalco as a natural expression of a centuries-old culture that transcends fashions and interests other than those handed down by past generations. Nothing has changed with his son Giampaolo, who has projected the company's wines into the contemporary era without losing a smidgeon of their identity 99

PEOPLE - In Montefalco the Bea family has represented good farming and, by virtue of their history, the very essence of the area, ever since the 16th century.

VINEYARDS - The vineyard management handed down by the Bea family for generations brings out real traces of terroir. A question not so much of the discovery of the suitability of the land for winegrowing, but rather an innate awareness, typical of peasant wisdom, of the right places to do the job. The vineyards are scattered round the Montefalco countryside: organic vineyard management is a simple consequence of the work of every day.

WINES - Giampiero doesn't like intervening in the cellar. He likes the grapes to be picked at the right moment, then allowed to evolve until they have what it takes to make quality wine. **Arboreus 2009** (○ trebbiano spoletino; 5,550 bt), fermented with the skins and aged slowly on its yeasts, is balsamic and mineral on the nose and complex on the palate. **Sanvalentino 2007** (● sangiovese, montepulciano, sagrantino; 22,500 bt) has character; made with grapes from a single vineyard, it has aromas of red berries with a juicy, austere palate. **Rosso de Veo 2006** (● 14,000 bt), an enjoyable wine made with grapes from the youngest sagrantino vineyards, has intact aromas with balsamic notes.

FERTILIZERS compost, green manure
PLANT PROTECTION copper and sulphur, organic
WEED CONTROL mechanical
YEASTS native
GRAPES 5% bought in
CERTIFICATION organic

MONTEFALCO (PG)
Perticaia

Località Casale
tel. 0742 379014
www.perticaia.it
guidoguardigli@libero.it

15 ha - 100,000 bt   **10% discount**

PEOPLE - Guido Guardigli was actually born in Romagna, but he only goes home at Christmas. In Umbria, he's the heart and soul of the Perticaia winery — an important tessera in the Montefalco winemaking mosaic — which he set up about ten years ago. One of the great connoisseurs of the local area, Guardigli is helped in the cellar by the talented in-house enologist Alessandro Meniconi, consultant Emiliano Falsini and agronomist Stefano Dini.

VINEYARDS - The vineyards are situated in the southern part of the denomination zone and encircle the cellar where a monumental old plough — locally known as a *perticaia* in the old days — is on display. Most of the 15 hectares or so are planted with sagrantino. The slightly sloping terrain drains well and contains many traces of clay and pebbles. Albeit not organic, Perticaia adopts sustainable methods.

WINES - Trebbiano Spoletino 2011 (○ 20,000 bt) has a rich suite of aromas with a fine, elegant, fragrant, deep palate and good overall harmony, which lived up to our expectations re the grape. Aged in stainless steel tanks, it's a good Everyday Wine. The decent **Montefalco Rosso Ris. 2008** (● sangiovese, colorino, sagrantino; 4,700 bt), aged in wooden casks for about two years, has a balsamic nose, delicious fruit and satisfying flavor. Insofar as it reflects the owner's style — blunt, rigorous and level-headed — the fascinating **Sagrantino di Montefalco 2007** (● 25,000 bt) is the company's most representative wine. Aged first in barriques, then in stainless steel tanks, then for at least a year in the bottle, it has deep balsamic notes on the nose and a palate that is well-rounded and succulent but never intrusive.

FERTILIZERS organic-mineral
PLANT PROTECTION chemical, copper and sulphur
WEED CONTROL mechanical
YEASTS selected
GRAPES 10% bought in
CERTIFICATION none

MONTEFALCO (PG)

Tabarrini

Frazione Turrita
tel. 0742 379351
www.tabarrini.com
info@tabarrini.com

16 ha - 70,000 bt `10% discount`

66 A profound respect for the land, explosive energy and a uniquely friendly disposition — these are the qualities of Giampaolo Tabarrini and his wines 99

PEOPLE - Giampaolo cultivates the land with passion and respect for the farming passion picked up from his family. His trusted collaborators are Stefano Dini, an agronomist, and the enologist Emiliano Falsini.

VINEYARDS - The property is divided into various plots. Thanks to experimentation and constant research, Giampaolo has managed to exploit the different nature of the soils to the full. This is particularly true of the three main sagrantino vineyards, in which the soil and climate conditions vary greatly.

WINES - Tabarrini wines are a happy marriage between tradition and innovation. **Montefalco Rosso Colle Grimaldesco 2009** (● sangiovese, sagrantino, barbera; 18,000 bt) is mature with notes of fruit and elegant, lingering tannins. **Sagrantino di Montefalco Colle Grimaldesco 2008** (● 15,000 bt) has intense fruit and sweet spices and is the softest expression of the various crus. **Sagrantino di Montefalco Colle alle Macchie 2006** (● 15,000 bt) is the traditional version and makes no attempt to hide the texture of its tannins. **Sagrantino di Montefalco Campo alla Cerqua 2008** (● 3,400 bt), a perfect synthesis of the two, is an elegant, refined Great Wine, already alluring despite its youth.

> slow wine | **ADARMANDO 2010** (○ 14,500 bt) Made with the juicy trebbiano spoletino grapes from a vineyard over 50 years old, a wine born of tradition. A heady bouquet and a flavorsome, deep and lingering palate — an awesome performance!

FERTILIZERS natural manure, green manure
PLANT PROTECTION copper and sulphur
WEED CONTROL mechanical
YEASTS native
GRAPES 100% estate-grown
CERTIFICATION converting to organics

ORVIETO (TR)

Palazzone

Località Rocca Ripesena, 68
tel. 0763 344921
www.palazzone.com
info@palazzone.com

24 ha - 140,000 bt `10% discount`

66 In some senses, Giovanni Dubini is the last winemaker left to hold high the name of a prestigious denomination now on the wane — too large to ensure diffuse quality and too small to become a brand with an international reputation 99

PEOPLE - Palazzone, named for the huge 14th-century palace that towers halfway up its hill, was taken over by Angelo Dubini in the late 1960s. Now it's run by his sons Giovanni, the production manager, and Ludovico.

VINEYARDS - The vineyards, some of which very old, are clustered over the hillsides round the cellar. The grapes on all the plots are harvested and vinified separately. The methods used are regulated by old-fashioned common sense and veer on the organic.

WINES - Palazzone's wines shun easy softness, maintaining an austere timbre based on straightforward expressiveness, lively freshness and fine minerality. **Grechetto Grek 2011** (○ 6,000 bt) is fresh and fragrant with a taut, fruity, tangy, lingering finish. Even better is the pleasantly drinkable **Orvieto Cl. Sup. Terre Vineate** 2011 (○ 50,000 bt), which manages to combine immediacy and complexity — a great Everyday Wine. **Ultima Spiaggia 2011** (○ viognier; 4,000 bt) is packed with fruit and endowed with a nicely fresh finish.

> slow wine | **ORVIETO CL. SUP. CAMPO DEL GUARDIANO 2010** (○ 8,000 bt) Fine, rich, deep with a lip-smacking, dry finish, this wine of great elegance and longevity is made with a selection of grapes — mainly procanico — from the old vineyard above the cellar plus the pick of the best batches of grechetto.

FERTILIZERS organic-mineral, natural manure, green manure
PLANT PROTECTION chemical, copper and sulphur
WEED CONTROL mechanical
YEASTS selected
GRAPES 100% estate-grown
CERTIFICATION none

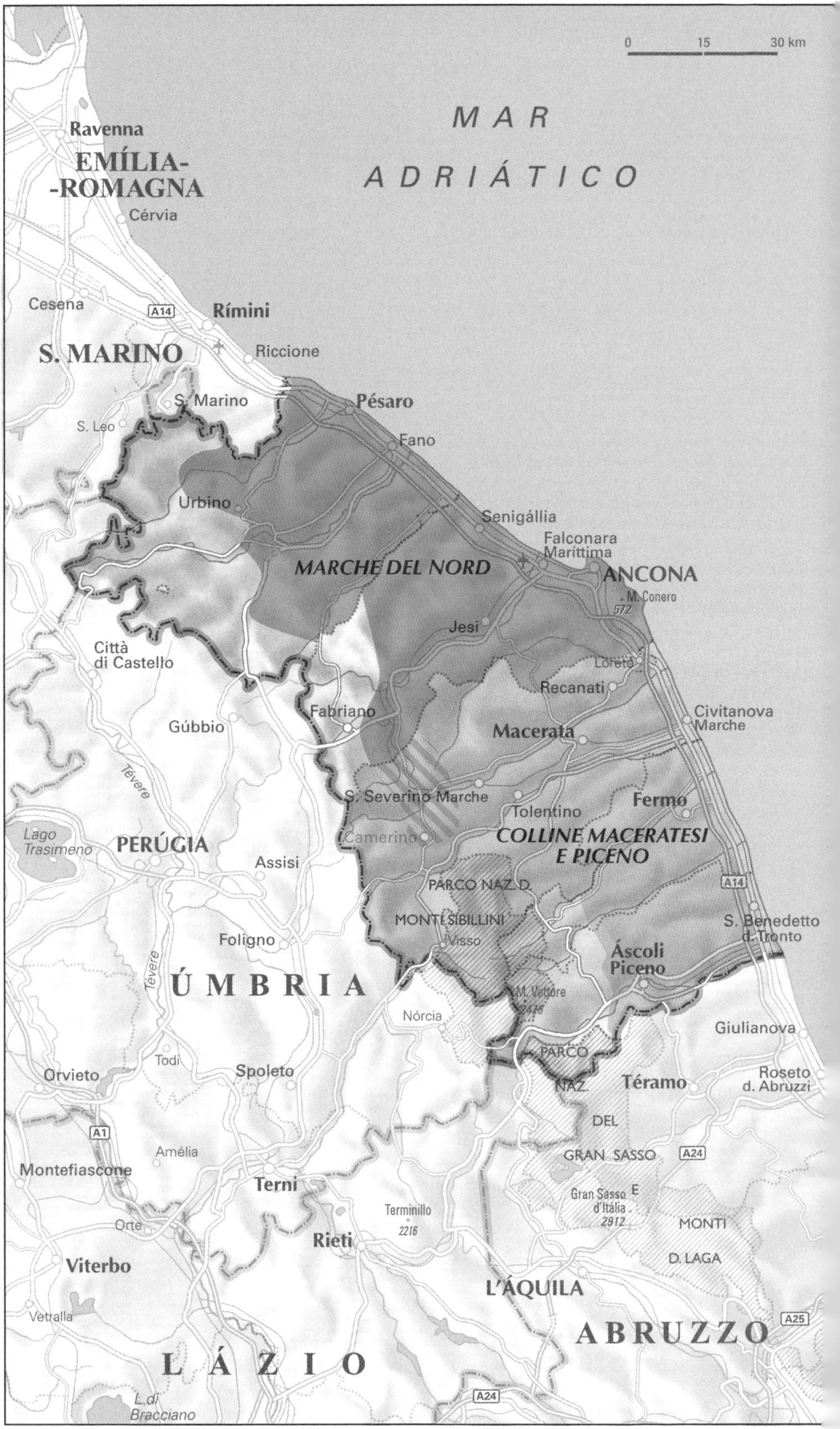
0
15
30 km
MAR
ADRIÁTICO
Ravenna
EMÍLIA-
-ROMAGNA
Cérvia
Cesena
A14
Rímini
S. MARINO
Riccione
S. Marino
Pésaro
S. Leo
Fano
Urbino
Senigállia
Falconara
Maríttima
MARCHE DEL NORD
ANCONA
M. Conero
572
Jesi
Città
di Castello
Loreto
Recanati
Fabriano
Civitanova
Marche
Gúbbio
Macerata
Tévere
S. Severino Marche
Fermo
Tolentino
Lago
Trasimeno
PERÚGIA
Camerino
COLLINE MACERATESI
E PICENO
Assisi
PARCO NAZ. D.
A14
MONTI SIBILLINI
S. Benedetto
d. Tronto
Foligno
Visso
Áscoli
Piceno
Tévere
ÚMBRIA
M. Vettore
2476
Nórcia
Giulianova
PARCO
Todi
Orvieto
Spoleto
Roseto
d. Abruzzi
NAZ.
Téramo
DEL
A1
GRAN SASSO
A24
Amélia
Montefiascone
Terni
Gran Sasso
d'Itália
2912
E
Terminillo
2216
Orte
MONTI
Rieti
D. LAGA
Viterbo
L'ÁQUILA
Vetralla
A25
ABRUZZO
LÁZIO
A24
L. di
Bracciano

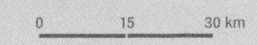

MARCHE

The Marche wine scene is growing all the time, and many small wineries have sprung up in the provinces of Pesaro-Urbino and Ascoli Piceno. In some cases entrepreneurs have taken up viticulture as a hobby or to diversify their business, in others cooperative closedowns have driven viticulturists to vinify and bottle their wine on their own. Here's hoping that their lack of commercial experience does not hinder them on the way. Another thing we noted during our cellar visits was a constant increase in eco-sustainable agricultural practices. Many wineries are converting to organics or limiting chemical weeding and plant protection treatments, at least in vintages in which the weather is favorable. The last point worth stressing is the constant increase in the number of young people who are investing in viticulture for their future, often taking over their parents' wineries. This is a commendable development, especially when backed by good planning and clear ideas.

With the 2009 vintage, Verdicchio dei Castelli di Jesi Riserva and Verdicchio di Matelica Riserva are entitled to use the new DOCG, though as far as the 2009 harvest is concerned the decision to do so was discretionary, which is why in the guide you'll find both DOC and DOCG Riserva wines. As usual in cases like this, we only hope this won't confuse consumers. In the province of Ascoli Piceno, as of 2011 the Rosso (with a minimum 85 per cent montepulciano grapes), Pecorino and Passerina typologies are entitled to use the Offida DOCG. But with the Falerio Pecorino Doc to fall back on, confusion could again be created among consumers.

Moving on to analysis of recent growing years, the 2011 vintage was characterized by warm, stable weather until August, when very high temperatures speeded up the ripening of the grapes and reduced their acidity. The 2010 vintage exhibited freshness, richness of flavor and very tonic, fragrant aromas which promise excellent bottle aging. The 2009 vintage, finally, saw weeks of warm weather followed by weeks of rain, especially heavy in the southern part of the region.

snails 🐌

199	COLLESTEFANO
200	PIEVALTA
201	FATTORIA LA MONACESCA
201	FATTORIA SAN LORENZO
203	BUCCI
203	FATTORIA CORONCINO
206	OASI DEGLI ANGELI
207	AURORA
207	FATTORIA DEZI

bottles 🍾

197	MORODER
197	ANDREA FELICI
198	GIOACCHINO GAROFOLI
199	VALLEROSA BONCI
200	VALTURIO
202	UMANI RONCHI
205	VELENOSI

coins €

198	TENUTA DELL'UGOLINO
202	MAROTTI CAMPI
205	TENUTA DE ANGELIS

Marche del Nord

0   10   20 km

MAR ADRIÁTICO

EMÍLIA-
Cesenático
Bellária
Viserba

RÍMINI
ROMAGNA
Riccione
Cattólica

S. MARINO

PÉSARO

Fano

Macerata
Féltria

Torrette di Fano
Marotta
Cesano

Sasso-
corvaro
Urbino
Fossombrone

Senigállia
LACRIMA DI
MORRO D'ALBA

S. Ángelo
in Vado
Urbánia

Cartoceto
Calcinelli
Piagge
Mondávio
Barchi
Corinaldo

Ostra Vétere Ostra
Morro
d'Alba
Chiaravalle
Falconara Maritt.
ANCONA
ROSSO
CONERO

S. Lorenzo
in Campo
Pérgola
Bárbara
Serra de' Conti
Montecarotto
Arcévia

Belvedere
Ostrense
Póggio
S. Marcello
Jesi

Camerano
Sirolo
Numana

Cagli

VERDICCHIO DEI
CASTELLI DI JESI

Castelplánio
Maiolati Spontini
Serra
S. Quírico
Cupramontana
Apiro

S. Páolo di Jesi
Stáffolo
Cíngoli

Ósimo
Castelfidardo
Loreto
Porto Recanati
Recanati

Fabriano

VERDICCHIO
DI MATÉLICA

Gúbbio
Umbértide

Matélica

Macerata

Castelraimondo
Pióraco
Camerino
Múccia

Tolentino
FERMO

PERÚGIA
Assisi
Nocera
Umbra
Spello

Montegiórgio
S. Ginésio
Samano
Monterubbiano

Foligno
Bevagna
Montefalco
Trevi

Amándola
Ripatransone

ÚMBRIA
Nórcia

ÁSCOLI
PICENO
Offida

Spoleto
Cáscia

ABRUZZO
TÉRAMO

ANCONA

Moroder

Via Montacuto, 112
tel. 071 898232
www.moroder-vini.it
info@moroder-vini.it

28 ha - 140,000 bt   `10% discount`

PEOPLE - It was in the 1960s that Alessandro Moroder, then a young man, decided to leave Rome to go and work the land owned by his father's family in the Conero area. After planting his first vineyards, he learned the secrets of the art of winemaking and gradually developed what has since become the best known trademark in the area. Today he is carrying on all the good work with customary humility, refinement and intelligence. In recent years the cellar has been expertly managed by Roberto Cantori.

VINEYARDS - Most of the vineyards fan out round the cellar, situated inland from the Conero peninsula, just a kilometer as the crow flies from the sea. Another two are situated near Varano and Candia. The oldest plantings are over 40 years old; they are the ones that produce the best grapes, the ones that go into Dorico. Since 2011 all the impeccably kept vineyards have been managed using certified organic methods.

WINES - Moroder teases out all the character of the montepulciano grape, exalting their aromas and structure without over-extraction. **Rosso Conero Moroder 2009** (● 50,000 bt) is once more an excellent Everyday Wine. Its sweet fruit is in no way cloying and makes for a dynamic, rich, tonic and supple palate. The fragrant **Rosso Conero Aiòn 2010** (● 30,000 bt) has less volume, but is just as rich in flavor. **Ankon 2009** (● montepulciano, merlot, cabernet; 3,000 bt) smacks of the Mediterranean and impresses with its robust palate. **Elleno 2011** (○ malvasia; 6,000 bt) is taut, citrusy with a bright and breezy mouthfeel.

| slow wine | **CONERO DORICO RIS. 2008** (● 15,000 bt) A textbook example of elegant vinification of the montepulciano grape. Well-crafted without being over-structured, it melds the fleshiness of the fruit with an edgy, sober, by no means heavy taste profile. |

FERTILIZERS natural manure, green manure
PLANT PROTECTION copper and sulphur
WEED CONTROL mechanical
YEASTS selected
GRAPES 100% estate-grown
CERTIFICATION organic

APIRO (MC)

Andrea Felici

Frazione Sant'Isidoro
tel. 0733 611431
www.andreafelici.it
leo@andreafelici.it

6 ha - 35,000 bt   `10% discount`

PEOPLE - Leo Felici is a young man with very clear ideas about the future and the quality of his Verdicchio. Just six years ago he gave up his job as a sommelier in the world of haute cuisine to go back to the house in the country where he was born to carry on the family business and make his dream — to produce a top quality Verdicchio — come true. Strictly organic agriculture and careful vinification — with the support of Aroldo Belelli — are his secrets when it comes to making the most of the cold Apiro terroir.

VINEYARDS - The vineyard is the domain of Leo's father Andrea. The company owns four hectares in the stupendous setting of the San Francesco district, surrounded by woodland at an altitude of 400 meters in the shadow of Mount San Vicino. Here the 50-year-old vineyard provided the grafts for plantings in 2007. The rest of the vineyards are rented at Ca' di Chiocco, near Cupra, at an altitude of 600 meters. In the field all the work is carried out by hand, the soil is fertilized with natural manure and heavy snowfalls prevent water stress.

WINES - The wines have a very clean style. "The less I do to them, the happier I am," says Leo. His aim is to preserve freshness and aroma with vinification by reduction and aging in steel without malolactic fermentation. We were expecting Leo to elevate the company to high levels and now he has done so at last with two excellent wines. **Verdicchio dei Castelli di Jesi Cl. Sup. Andrea Felici 2011** (○ 30,000 bt) is acid-crisp, tonic and balanced — a very good Everyday Wine indeed.

| slow wine | **CASTELLI DI JESI VERDICCHIO RIS. CL. IL CANTICO DELLA FIGURA 2009** (○ 5,000 bt) A deep, savory wine with stylish structure. The bouquet oscillates between peaches and blossom, aniseed and vegetal tones with a pronounced mineral matrix. A taut, dry, dynamic Verdicchio that honors typology and terroir. |

FERTILIZERS natural manure, green manure
PLANT PROTECTION copper and sulphur
WEED CONTROL mechanical
YEASTS selected, native
GRAPES 100% estate-grown
CERTIFICATION organic

CASTELFIDARDO (AN)

Gioacchino Garofoli 🍷

Località Villa Musone
Via Marx, 123
tel. 071 7820162
www.garofolivini.it
mail@garofolivini.it

50 ha - 2,000,000 bt · **10% discount**

PEOPLE - The historic Garofoli company was formed in 1901 and turned into a success story by his grandson Carlo in the 1980s. A mixture of small enterprise artisanship and industrial organization, it is a guarantee of quality for the local area. Its force lies in its vineyards, all situated in optimal zones for the denominations and in its fiduciary rapport with grape growers. Carlo is helped in the cellar by his daughter Beatrice and in the management of the business by his brother Gianfranco and other relatives.

VINEYARDS - The vinification of grapes from bordering vineyards takes place in the cellar at Montecarotto. The company's own 15 hectares of vines are situated in a single plot that extends through a gentle valley with sandy soil of marine origin. The red grapes grow on two properties: at Paterno, where the soil is warm and compact, and inland from the Conero peninsula, where the montepulciano grape releases finesse and elegance thanks to the stony, calcareous terrain.

WINES - It's in the tough years that you note the hand of Carlo. In the warm 2011 he and Beatrice showed off **Verdicchio dei Castelli di Jesi Cl. Sup. Macrina 2011** (○ 130,000 bt), a symbol of the completeness of Verdicchio. An excellent Everyday Wine, it has tonic, vibrant, aromatic finesse, fullness, balance and length. In **Verdicchio dei Castelli di Jesi Cl. Sup. Podium 2010** (○ 55,000 bt), the cool vintage favors refined, complex aromas that extend dynamically over a balanced, sapid, lingering palate. What a Great Wine! **M. Cl. Brut Ris. 2007** (○ 11,000 bt) is taut and tangy. Very good too is **Conero La Selezione G. Garofoli Ris. 2007** (● 2,700 bt), a solid Montepulciano that combines structure, potency and well-knit tannins. **Rosso Conero Piancarda 2009** (● 120,000 bt) is pulpy, fruity and enjoyable.

FERTILIZERS organic-mineral, mineral, manure pellets, natural manure, green manure
PLANT PROTECTION chemical, copper and sulphur
WEED CONTROL chemical, mechanical
YEASTS selected
GRAPES 50% bought in, wine bought in
CERTIFICATION none

CASTELPLANIO (AN)

Tenuta dell'Ugolino €

Località Macine
Via Copparoni, 32
tel. 071 812569
www.tenutaugolino.it
cantina@tenutaugolino.it

6.5 ha - 33,000 bt

PEOPLE - Andrea Petrini, who named the winery for his maternal grandfather, has run the place for many years with the collaboration of Aroldo Bellelli, who has driven and guided him to evident improvements in quality. All to the great satisfaction of Andrea's dad, Costantino, who bought the property in the 1980s in order to return to life on the farm after working for years in the oil industry. The company bottled its first wine, made with grapes from the single hectare of vines it owned at the time, in 1993.

VINEYARDS - The cool, ventilated microclimate and healthy 13-year-old vineyards allow Andrea to limit plant protection interventions. The two parcels of verdicchio with southerly exposure at an altitude of about 200 meters are situated in a narrow natural valley round the cellar itself. The Balluccio vineyard is trained on mixed, rich and fertile soil with a clone that makes the harvested grapes exceptionally green. The other vines grow on the hillside opposite, where the climate is very cool and the soil loose.

WINES - Andrea Petrini passed the test with flying colors once again, interpreting the variety effectively to create great drinkability and complexity. The value for money of both labels is an added value not to be sneezed at. **Verdicchio dei Castelli di Jesi Cl. 2011** (○ 24,500 bt) has heady scents of fruit and flowers, a cut-glass, zippy palate and a long, leisurely finish.

> slow wine **VERDICCHIO DEI CASTELLI DI JESI CL. SUP. VIGNETO DEL BALLUCCIO 2011** (○ 8,500 bt) An elegant, complete version of the wine in which distinct varietal notes intermingle within a dynamic, complex suite of aromas. The palate is measured, taut and balanced and, despite the apparent glyceric attack, not without follow-through, saltiness and depth.

FERTILIZERS manure pellets
PLANT PROTECTION chemical, copper and sulphur
WEED CONTROL chemical, mechanical
YEASTS selected
GRAPES 100% estate-grown
CERTIFICATION none

Collestefano

Frazione Rustano
Località Colle Stefano, 3
tel. 0737 640439
www.collestefano.com
info@collestefano.com

17 ha - 85,000 bt

66 "Our efficiency depends on the earth and nature. Given the wholesomeness of the grapes and the correctness of work in the cellar, the wine just has to be good." Endowed with unique strength and energy and very attached to the place of his birth, Fabio really believes in these values 99

PEOPLE - The winery's new home in Collestefano is a modern, functional facility, built with passion but also no shortage of worry and sacrifice. "I designed the cellar," says Fabio, "thinking about what I'm doing today. I believe in Verdicchio and I'm not planning any changes, so I made what already existed more functional. Mine is a family enterprise, and if it were to grow we'd lose our sense of artisanship."

VINEYARDS - The secret of Collestefano is its vineyards, all 17 hectares of them, old and recent, built from mass selections and located in a ventilated, cool position. The rest is achieved thanks to soils rich in gravel and limestone and kept alive by organic, non-invasive treatments. "If the grape is good and tasty, it'll give a good wine," says Fabio.

WINES - "Since I'm not obsessed with results, I accept what comes from nature and the vintage. If, at the end of the season, people like my wine, then I'm happy." That's how Fabio described his work in the hot, difficult year of 2011. **Verdicchio di Matelica Collestefano 2011** (O 85,000 bt) lacks its customary depth. Though it has greater fruity sweetness, its aromas are as clear-cut as ever. The palate is juicy without some of its usual acidity, but it flows evenly into a precious saline finish. **Rosa di Elena 2011** (⊙ 4,000 bt), made with sangiovese and cabernet grapes, is as impeccable as ever, graceful, deft and fine.

FERTILIZERS	manure pellets, natural manure, green manure
PLANT PROTECTION	copper and sulphur
WEED CONTROL	mechanical
YEASTS	selected
GRAPES	15% bought in
CERTIFICATION	organic

Vallerosa Bonci

Via Torre 15/17
tel. 0731 789129
www.vallerosa-bonci.com
info@vallerosa-bonci.com

32 ha - 250,000 bt   **10% discount**

PEOPLE - A tight bond links this family to Verdicchio and a town that is one of the symbols of the Castelli district. This year marked the 50th anniversary of their business. It was 1962 in fact that the Bonci brothers began to sell their wine. The modern history of the winery is tied to the figure of Giuseppe who extended the vineyards in the 1970s and began to vinify his own grapes, making the family label a local institution.

VINEYARDS - The added value of Bonci wines is in its vineyards: 32 hectares on the best slopes of Cupra, with old vines that ensure consistent production. The heart of the company is at San Michele, a, 20-year-old property in a sunny area with a southeast exposure and deep clay and limestone soil. Further north on very fresh terrains in the Pietrone district, in another property of ten hectares with 169 different clones, work on promoting the verdicchio grape is being carried out.

WINES - The Boncis can always bank on their San Michele vineyard, which turns out impeccable, deep, robust wine every year that goes by. **Verdicchio dei Castelli di Jesi Cl. Sup. Manciano 2011** (O 10,000 bt), the fruit of a fortunate vintage, has a pleasantly soft style with non-cloying tropical aromas. The scented, soft **Verdicchio dei Castelli di Jesi Cl. Viatorre 2011** (O 100,000 bt). **Verdicchio dei Castelli di Jesi M. Cl. 2008** (O 6,000 bt) has soft fizziness, cakeshop, yeasty and dried fruit aromas.

> **slow wine** VERDICCHIO DEI CASTELLI DI JESI CL. SUP. SAN MICHELE 2010 (O 30,000 bt) A crush of varietal aromas, fruit and aniseed that play the same score in harmony. The palate is assertive and robust, but also refined, soft and full of racy flavor. A benchmark for the right bank of the River Esino.

FERTILIZERS	organic-mineral
PLANT PROTECTION	chemical, copper and sulphur
WEED CONTROL	chemical, mechanical
YEASTS	selected
GRAPES	100% estate-grown
CERTIFICATION	none

MACERATA FELTRIA (PU)

Valturio

Via dei Pelasgi, 10
tel. 0722 728049
www.valturio.com
valturio@valturio.com

MAIOLATI SPONTINI (AN)

Pievalta

Via Monteschiavo, 18
tel. 0731 780375
www.baronepizzini.it
pievalta@baronepizzini.it

10 ha - 40,000 bt	10% discount

PEOPLE - Up where no one had ever thought of planting vines, that's where Adriano Galli threw down the gauntlet. It was at the start of the new century that he and his wife Isabella bought their house in Macerata Feltria. Soon after they acquired two abandoned properties of 55 hectares and planted their first vines to create the Valturio vineyard and improve a wild, uncontaminated terrain previously covered with bushes, shrubs and grass. The gamble has paid off. Today all is harmonious and even a balm for the eye.

VINEYARDS - The vineyards cover an area of 10 hectares out of a total of 55 and are planted on calcareous, sandy soils. They are the result of salvage work on the land, the terraces and the steepest slopes. Despite the harshness of the terrain, the company is now putting its money on exclusively mechanical soil management as opposed to chemical weeding. The well-ventilated, chilly climate prevents diseases and molds, favoring copper- and sulfur-based interventions instead.

WINES - The wines have an enviable identity conspicuous for its fruit, vividness and measured, never over-the-top body. **Chiù 2010** (● merlot, cabernet, alicante; 4,000 bt) suffered the adverse effects of a cool vintage. Hence a wine of lower-than-average potency, though it does retain its crispy palate. The bouquet is fleshy and tempting with spices accentuating its complexity. Very good indeed was **Solco 2010** (● incrocio Rigotti; 5,000 bt) offering a blend of small red berries and tobacco, which enfolds the palate and, flows through into a cut-glass finish.

> **slow wine** **VALTURIO 2010** (● 23,000 bt) A wine made with the high-altitude sangiovese grapes that epitomize the terroir. The palate is lively with polished tannins and enviable complexity. The fruit never loses the grip that makes the wine elegant.

27 ha - 120,000 bt	10% discount

66 Years of study, doubt and sacrifice have made Alessandro grow up. After his conversion to organics in 2005, the step towards biodynamics was a short one. Pievalta is the fruit of the sustainable work carried out to make sincere wines that ooze terroir 99

PEOPLE - Pievalta, Barone Pizzini's Marche winery, has shown a strong belief in Alessandro Fenino, a young Milanese enologist "on loan" from Franciacorta. After arriving in Maiolati in 2002, Fenino took up the tough challenge of working with a grape variety about which he knew little or nothing. This up-and-coming company is now an institution for the Castelli di Jesi.

VINEYARDS - The company owns 27 hectares of which five at Follonica di San Paolo and 22 at Moie in front of the cellar, with thickened vines from the 1970s and modern, dense plantings. "I manage the vineyards using biodynamic methods," says Alessandro, "because I want to give life to the soil, and life gives balance." The vine rows are sowed with legumes and fertilized with green and cow horn manure to produce organic substance.

WINES - Pievalta is back with wines of great personality, rich in salt and acidity to support them. **Verdicchio dei Castelli di Jesi Cl. Sup. Dominè 2011** (○ 14,000 bt) is deft with acidy, tangy oomph. **Verdicchio dei Castelli di Jesi Cl. Sup. Pievalta 2011** (○ 90,000 bt), fruity, juicy and taut, and **M. Cl. Extra Brut Perlugo** (○ verdicchio; 20,000 bt), fine, zesty and creamy, are both very good indeed.

> **slow wine** **VERDICCHIO DEI CASTELLI DI JESI CL. SAN PAOLO RIS. 2009** (○ 11,000 bt) A dashing, taut and pleasantly austere version of the wine. The profile on the nose is complex and nuanced, the palate is dynamic, rigorous and very racy. Aromas and structure are emblematic of the right bank of the Esino.

FERTILIZERS none
PLANT PROTECTION copper and sulphur
WEED CONTROL mechanical
YEASTS selected
GRAPES 100% estate-grown
CERTIFICATION converting to organics

FERTILIZERS manure pellets, natural manure, biodynamic preparations, green manure
PLANT PROTECTION copper and sulphur
WEED CONTROL mechanical
YEASTS selected, native
GRAPES 100% estate-grown
CERTIFICATION biodynamic, organic

Fattoria La Monacesca

Contrada Monacesca
tel. 0733 812602
www.monacesca.it
info@monacesca.it

---

27 ha - 180,000 bt

❝ Tradition, terroir, variety. These are the values of Monacesca which, without changing style, has developed its Verdicchio with historic clones to bring out all the structure and character the cold Valle Camertina gives its grapes ❞

PEOPLE - The Cifolas are a pillar in the history of Verdicchio di Matelica. Casimiro bought the farm, then abandoned, in 1966 and his son Aldo joined the business in the early 1980s after completing his agricultural studies. It was he who introduced grape selection in the vineyard and prolonged maturation on the lees to exalt the cold local terroir.

VINEYARDS - The vineyards are situated on the lovely hillsides round the farm at an altitude of 400 meters against the backdrop of the Monti Sibillini. The four-hectare vineyard planted in 1971 is no longer productive, but Aldo has renovated the others by reproducing the clones of the mother vineyard with grafting in the field.

WINES - The years go by but the Cifola style — aimed at enhancing the substance and rigor of the grape variety — never changes. **Verdicchio di Matelica La Monacesca 2011** (○ 150,000 bt) is a masterpiece of drinkability. It oozes energy and has a structured, fresh, tangy palate. Also excellent is **Camerte 2009** (● 15,000 bt), an essay in structure and suppleness without asperity.

> **slow wine** VERDICCHIO DI MATELICA MIRUM RIS. **2010** (○ 15,000 bt) A benchmark of the Camerino version of the grape. Rich and dynamic, it has a deep, creamy but never too heavy a palate. Assertive tanginess animates the wine and gives it balance. The nose is a concerto of aromas fused with harmony. This one of the best offerings of recent years. So store it in the cellar and forget about it!

FERTILIZERS mineral
PLANT PROTECTION chemical, copper and sulphur
WEED CONTROL mechanical
YEASTS selected
GRAPES 100% estate-grown
CERTIFICATION none

Fattoria San Lorenzo

Via San Lorenzo, 6
tel. 0731 89656
www.fattoriasanlorenzo.com
info@fattoriasanlorenzo.com

---

35 ha - 100,000 bt

❝ "To establish when to harvest the grapes, I taste them, I don't analyze them," says Natalino. The wines speak for themselves. They make you wait, then they explode with terroir ❞

PEOPLE - Natalino Crognaletti has the appearance and the innate wisdom of the winemaker. To think that until 1999 he was an electronics technician! But even then he used to help his father Gino to make Verdicchio for selling unbottled. His commitment has been progressive and aimed at quality. Today his Verdicchio is an institution in the area.

VINEYARDS - "My father was an artist in the vineyards," recalls Natalino proudly, "and the vineyards are his precious legacy." The one called Vigna delle Oche, near the farm in a ventilated area at an altitude of 350 meters, is a fantastic property of seven plots of 38,10 square meters, each planted with 17 verdicchio clones selected by Gino, recently regrafted in a five-hectare vineyard too. The winery also owns an 80-year-old montepulciano vineyard in Ostra.

WINES - Freedom of expression and richness are the hallmarks of Natalino's wines, never overrefined but all possessing the unmistakable features of the verdicchio grape variety. **Verdicchio dei Castelli di Jesi Cl. Sup. Le Oche 2010** (○ 20,000 bt) has a balanced, tonic mid-palate and a tangy and racy finish redolent of aniseed, fennel and fruit. **Verdicchio dei Castelli di Jesi Di Gino 2011** (○ 25,000 bt) is a lip-smacking Everyday Wine: it gives peach, aniseed and almond on the nose and has a measured, tonic, salty body. The soft, pervasive **Verdicchio dei Castelli di Jesi Cl. Campo delle Oche Ris. 2009** (○ 10,000 bt) is potent and alcoholic with a finish animated by a hint of salinity. **Solleone 2007** (● montepulciano; 3,000 bt) is a mature wine and **Rosso Piceno Di Gino 2010** (● 18.000 bt) is also noteworthy .

FERTILIZERS natural manure, compost, biodynamic preparations, green manure
PLANT PROTECTION copper and sulphur
WEED CONTROL mechanical
YEASTS native
GRAPES 100% estate-grown
CERTIFICATION organic

MORRO D'ALBA (AN)

Marotti Campi €

Via Sant'Amico, 14
tel. 0731 618027
www.marotticampi.it
wine@marotticampi.net

OSIMO (AN)

Umani Ronchi

Via Adriatica, 12
tel. 071 7108019
www.umanironchi.it
wine@umanironchi.it

56 ha - 206,000 bt	10% discount

PEOPLE - After graduating, Lorenzo Marotti Campi intended to dabble briefly in winemaking before finding the right job. Today he is still working for the company, travelling round the world to talk about the local area and tell the over-100-year history of his family, which has been farming and making wine since 1860, though the Marotti Campi brand only came into being to promote their grapes through bottling.

VINEYARDS - The company's 56 hectares of vineyards, with vines of other 30 years and recent, modern plantings, are subdivided into different adjacent plots in the Sant'Amico di Morro d'Alba district. From a 20-year-old vineyard with a southwest exposure near the 19th-century farmhouse that serves as the company's headquarters, comes Verdicchio Salmariano, while another vineyard in the prime of life in the Sant'Amico district yields the grapes for Orgiolo. Ivano Belardinelli is in charge of the agronomic management.

WINES - It is impressive how Marotti Campi gets every vintage right, interpreting the character of the grapes in exemplary fashion. **Lacrima di Morro d'Alba Sup. Orgiolo 2010 (●** 26,000 bt) is as reliable as ever, though more pronounced, with spiciness well integrated with fruit. The palate is contained, succulent, solid and nicely long. This year's labels were also good. **Lacrima di Morro d'Alba Rubico 2011 (●** 50,000 bt) is crisp and supple, while **Verdicchio dei Castelli di Jesi Cl. Sup. Luzano 2011** (○ 60,000 bt) is refreshing and enjoyable without being banal.

> **slow wine** VERDICCHIO DEI CASTELLI DI JESI CL. SALMARIANO RIS. 2009 (○ 26,000 bt) What is striking about this wine is its elegance. It's a concentrate of finesse, dynamism and complexity, oozing floral aromas, aniseed and fruit peppered with lively minerality. The palate is plump and juicy with an intriguing salty finish.

FERTILIZERS organic-mineral
PLANT PROTECTION chemical, copper and sulphur
WEED CONTROL chemical, mechanical
YEASTS selected
GRAPES 100% estate-grown
CERTIFICATION none

230 ha - 2,800,000 bt	10% discount

PEOPLE - Umani Ronchi is a large company with the same attention to detail as a single winemaker. Formed in1957, it has taken the generational turnover into its stride. It is guided today with vision and dynamism by Michele Bernetti, who has picked a team of young, motivated collaborators. He is a manager whose pragmatic spirit embraces innovation. In the cellar he can count on the consultancy of Beppe Caviola and the young enologist Giacomo Mattioli, while Luigi Piersanti is overseeing the vineyards.

VINEYARDS - The feather in the company's hat is the 21-hectare verdicchio property at Busche di Montecarotto, where 40-year-old vineyards yield the grapes for the selection of the same name. From the vineyard at Cupramontana, planted in 1993, come the grapes for Plenio. In the Conero area and round the company headquarters grow the red grape vines, of varying ages and densities, on soils turfed to compensate for the excess of active limestone, fertilized with manure in the fall and all carefully and respectfully managed.

WINES - Local origin and international caliber are the main traits of a precise, undemonstrative style that aims at elegance. Deep and dynamic, *Verdicchio dei Castelli di Jesi Cl. Sup. Vecchie Vigne 2010* (○ 15,500 bt) is a Great Wine with a seductively taut palate, a layered, sapid finish and complex fruity and floral aromas. Another wonderful wine is **Castelli di Jesi Verdicchio Ris. Cl. Plenio 2009** (○ 25,000 bt), soft, spacious and flavorful with well-blended fruit and oaky tones. **Conero Cumaro Ris. 2009 (●** 53,000 bt) has a full-bodied, solid, enveloping structure in which the fruit is just one element in a well-developed suite of aromas. **Pelago 2009 (●** montepulciano, cabernet, merlot; 24,500 bt) is a fine-polished mixture of red fruits of great charm and elegance. **Rosso Conero San Lorenzo 2010 (●** 70,000 bt) is stylish and succulent.

FERTILIZERS natural manure
PLANT PROTECTION chemical, copper and sulphur, organic
WEED CONTROL chemical, mechanical
YEASTS selected, native
GRAPES 20% bought in
CERTIFICATION none

Bucci

Località Pongelli
Via Cona, 30
tel. 071 964179
www.villabucci.com
bucciwines@villabucci.com

31 ha - 120,000 bt   **10% discount**

66 At Bucci everything seems simple and spontaneous — a perfect marriage of people, grapes and land. The great elegance of the company's wines is the result of straightforward, sustainable methods in which human intervention is kept to a bare minimum 99

PEOPLE - The years go by, new cellars spring up and the wine scene changes at an incredible pace, but Bucci is always Bucci, with an inimitable terroir-rooted style. Here they love wine and, more generally, agriculture as the central activities of human life, which would otherwise be empty without them. Theirs is a mission and they'll never abandon it.

VINEYARDS - Gabriele Tanfani is Ampelio Bucci's right-hand … farmer! For years he has been running the company with consummate skill, the result of experience acquired in the field. At Villa Bucci they observe the soil and the vines and employ organic methods. Sparse plantings from massal selections, spontaneous grassing, green manure cropping — these are the secrets behind the balance of the limestone soils.

WINES - You can see Ampelio's management style in the wines, which are measured, refined and leisurely. The pure, racy **Verdicchio dei Castelli di Jesi Cl. Villa Bucci Ris. 2009** (○ 12,000 bt) is a clear-cut example. Juicy with plenty of bite, it tempts the palate with its customary progression. The bouquet is sinuous and refined, typical of the variety. A truly Great Wine. Excellent too is **Verdicchio dei Castelli di Jesi Cl. Sup. Bucci 2010** (○ 70,000 bt), dry, tonic and lip-smacking with subdued mineral aromas. **Rosso Piceno Villa Bucci 2008** (● 3,000 bt) is a smooth, crisp red with no hint of heaviness. **Rosso Piceno Pongelli 2009** (● 13,000 bt) is simpler and fruitier.

FERTILIZERS manure pellets, biodynamic preparations, green manure, none
PLANT PROTECTION copper and sulphur, organic
WEED CONTROL mechanical
YEASTS selected, native
GRAPES 100% estate-grown
CERTIFICATION organic

Fattoria Coroncino

Contrada Coroncino, 7
S.P.35 Km. 5,5
tel. 0731 779494
www.coroncino.it
info@coroncino.it

11.5 ha - 55,000 bt

66 Lucio is a winemaker who produces unpredictable wines of admirable coherence and unmistakable style. He believes we should "take what nature gives us" 99

PEOPLE - Lucio Canestrari is "a winemaker out of necessity and a philosopher by nature", yet he has played a key role in the history of Verdicchio. He was only a young man when, in 1980, he left Rome with his wife Rosella for Staffolo and a new life project. At first he produced only unbottled wine, but in 1986 he released his first bottle and never looked back.

VINEYARDS - Lucio is a careful observer of the zone. He has recovered many small vineyards, so his property is broken up into small parcels. Everything began at the two-hectare vineyard of Spescia, planted in 1979, with a massal selection for another 3.5 hectare vineyard in the same district and the two-hectare vineyard at Cerrete, planted in 1991. Herbs, woodland, biodiversity — this is the habitat the vines grow in. Lucio has adopted mechanical weed control for the last 40 years and has reduced the use of copper to a minimum.

WINES - "I take what comes from nature". For Lucio every vintage is different, as is every wine he makes. The reliable **Verdicchio dei Castelli di Jesi Cl. Sup. Il Coroncino 2010** (○ 32,000 bt) is rich and caressing with a pleasant contrast between softness and tanginess. The aromas typical of the grape shine through with great charisma. The excellent **Verdicchio dei Castelli di Jesi Cl. Sup. Gaiospino 2009** (○ 7,000 bt) is soft and even, the creaminess from the oak being animated by a lip-smacking finish. **Verdicchio dei Castelli di Jesi Passito Bambulè 2010** (○ 2.980 bt) is a wine packed with passion, its bouquet ranging from dried fruits to flower blossom, its palate fresh and full of flavor. **Verdicchio dei Castelli di Jesi Passito Orocacio 2010** (○ 336 bt) is denser with mature aromas.

FERTILIZERS biodynamic preparations, none
PLANT PROTECTION copper and sulphur, organic
WEED CONTROL mechanical
YEASTS selected, native
GRAPES 100% estate-grown
CERTIFICATION none

Colline Maceratesi e Piceno

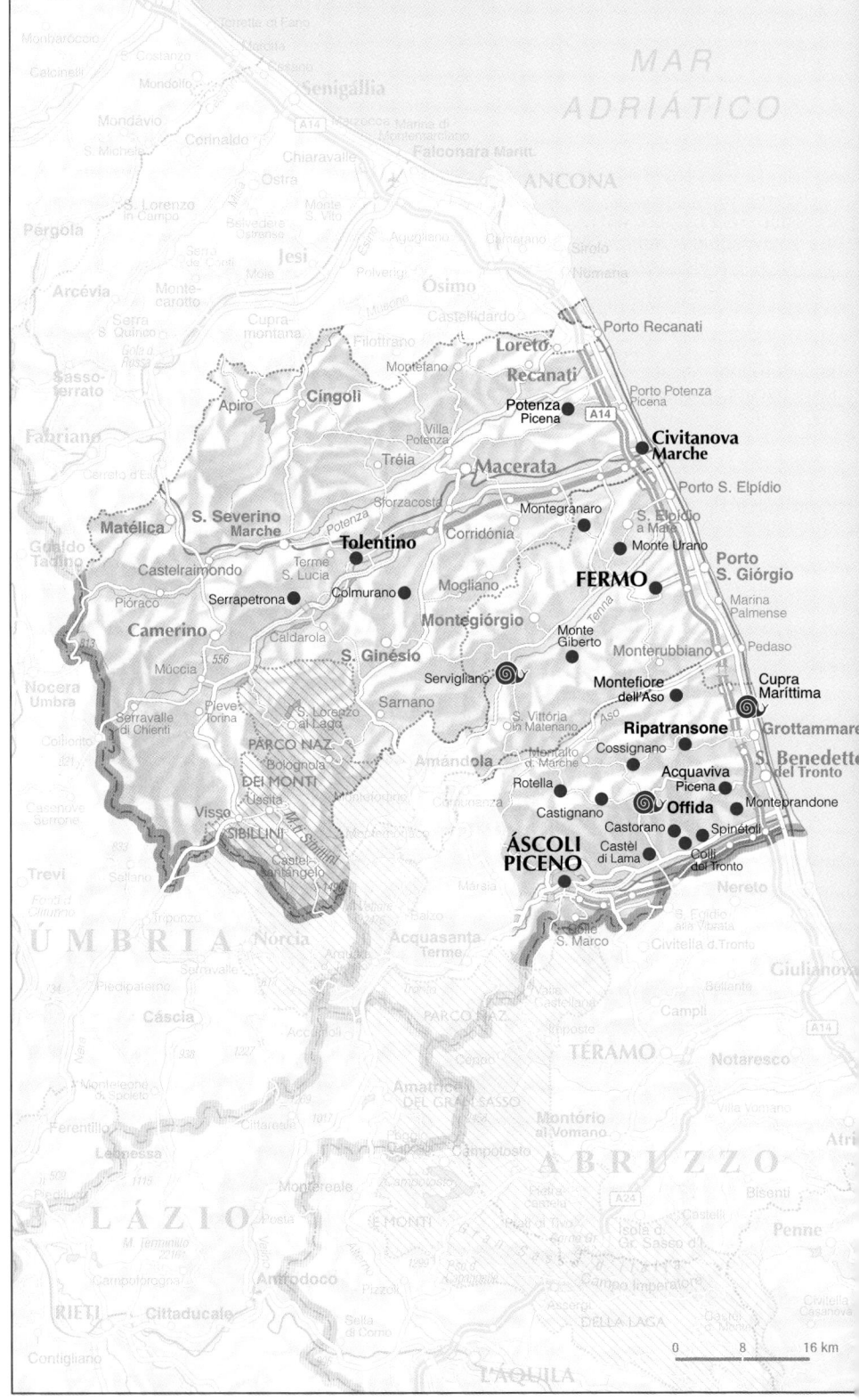

Velenosi

Via dei Biancospini, 11
tel. 0736 341218
www.velenosivini.com
info@velenosivini.com

Tenuta De Angelis

Via San Francesco, 10
tel. 0736 87429
www.tenutadeangelis.it
info@tenutadeangelis.it

140 ha - 2,000,000 bt   `10% discount`

50 ha - 500,000 bt   `10% discount`

PEOPLE - Angela Velenosi never stops for a minute. Year by year, she has attacked the market with impeccable labels that combine stylistic modernity and varietal consistency. Her bottles, which encapsulate passion, entrepreneurial spirit and sense of place, never disappoint. Collaborators and consultants also do their impeccable bit with dedication and devotion. Angela, a bulldozer in constant pursuit of perfection, does the rest with *savoir faire*, infectious enthusiasm and guts.

VINEYARDS - With 140 hectares of vines at her disposal, she can select grapes and choose the best times to harvest with rigor and care. The main properties, in which native and international grapes grow side by side, are situated at Castorano, Castel di Lama and Ascoli Piceno. Turfing, cover cropping and mechanical under-vine mowing are practiced in the vineyards, while the plants undergo short pruning with wide barriers. Good ventilation in all properties helps to keep treatments to a minimum.

WINES - Wines that impress for their stylistic perfection and varietal symmetry — a vintage to write home about. **Rosso Piceno Sup. Roggio del Filare 2008** (● 45,000 bt) combines a refinedly dynamic bouquet and a fleshy palate in a perfect compromise between structure and suppleness. **Rosso Piceno Sup. Brecciarolo 2009** (● 450,000 bt) is an Everyday Wine impeccable for the uniformity of its drinkability, mouthfeel and personality. The two pecorino wines are outstanding: **Offida Pecorino Villa Angela 2011** (○ 60,000 bt), streamlined and dynamic, oozes minerality and energy, its super-elegant finish making it a Great Wine; the oak in **Offida Pecorino Réve 2010** (○ 20,000 bt) brings out solar, clear-cut, fruity aromas, amplified by a soft, well-balanced, zesty palate. **Offida Rosso Ludi 2008** (● 40,000 bt) is deft and nimble and the rest of the range is on a par.

PEOPLE - De Angelis is the emblem of the evolution of the local winemaking tradition. Since the 1950s, Alighiero De Angelis had bought grapes and made wine. which he sold unbottled in tanks. In 1985 the company moved from Cossignano to Castel di Lama, where Alighiero's son-in-law Quinto Fausti gradually began to acquire vineyards. In the early 1990s, he enlarged the cellar and vinified in larger quantities. It was thus that he embarked on the road to bottling, which now predominates.

VINEYARDS - The main property, which covers an area of 40 hectares, was bought in the 1990s. It is situated in Offida, in an open, sunny valley. White grapes are grown in the lower part, native and international red grapes in the upper, warmer part. The land is simply mowed and turfed. The other vineyards are situated near the company in Castel di Lama. All the company's properties are now managed using organic methods.

WINES - Coherent style, reliability, consistent quality and fair pricing — these are the values of the wines Quinto Fausti produces in abundance for every market sector. **Anghelos 2009** (● 25,000 bt) is a blend of montepulciano, sangiovese and cabernet. The palate is assertive, crisp and tempting, nicely balanced with well-knit tannins. The impeccable **Rosso Piceno Sup. 2009** (● 150,000 bt;) is an Everyday Wine that owes its flavor to the crunchiness of the fruit. The palate is racy, supple and clear-cut with light, enhancing spiciness. **Rosso Piceno 2011** (● 120,000 bt) is juicy and fragrant. Moving on to the whites, in **Offida Pecorino 2011** (○ 30,000 bt) the very sweet fruit is refreshed by citrusy notes, a rich palate and an attractively tangy finish. The fruity **Offida Passerina 2011** (○ 13,000 bt) is supple and simple.

FERTILIZERS natural manure, green manure	
PLANT PROTECTION chemical, copper and sulphur	
WEED CONTROL mechanical	
YEASTS selected, native	
GRAPES 40% bought in, wine bought in	
CERTIFICATION none	

FERTILIZERS manure pellets	
PLANT PROTECTION copper and sulphur	
WEED CONTROL mechanical	
YEASTS selected	
GRAPES 100% estate-grown	
CERTIFICATION organic	

CASTIGNANO (AP)

Tenuta Spinelli

Via Lago, 2
tel. 0736 821489 - 334 9135914
simonespinelli@tiscali.it

CUPRA MARITTIMA (AP)

Oasi degli Angeli

Contrada Sant'Egidio, 50
tel. 0735 778569
www.kurni.it
info@kurni.it

---

4 ha - 20,000 bt   **10% discount**

PEOPLE - After his excellent debut last year, Simone Spinelli has performed well again. A wine enthusiast ever since studying at hotel management school, he began working at his family's agriturismo. Then, in 2006, he decided to cultivate four hectares of land that belong to his mother with pecorino grapes. He had his mind set on making a *vin de terroir* with a personal touch. He was right: the terroir gives structure and flavor to the wines and Simone's own non-nonsense character goes well with their straightforward, uncompromising style.

VINEYARDS - The pecorino vineyard, at an altitude of over 500 meters below Monte dell'Ascensione, really is gorgeous. The northeast exposure, the cool breezes that blow down from the mountain and sharp daytime temperature swings produce ideal conditions for rich-flavored, intensely aromatic wines. The dark, pebbly soil hinders mechanical work — so sometimes chemical weed control is necessary — but it does allow the vines to delve deep in search of air and water.

WINES - Only stainless steel is used to tease out the acidity, salinity and aroma. This is how Simone allows his wines to express the terroir and their varietal profile. The excellent Offida Pecorino Artemisia 2011 (○ 14,000 bt) is a good Everyday Wine to which the vintage has given sweet aromas of tropical fruit and flowers. On the palate it lacks the perky acidity of the previous year, but, despite softness and volume, it slides away evenly and racily. **Eden 2011** (○ 4.000 bt), produced with bought-in passerina grapes, has less depth, but offers sweet aromas of fruit and a juicy, cut-glass palate. A new entry this year is **M. Cl. Méroe 2009** (○ 1,500 bt), a taut, personality-packed Pecorino with a fine perlage, even though the fruit is still somewhat overwhelmed by hints of crusty bread.

10 ha - 7,500 bt

" "The treatments I use," says Marco, "are alternative, because we spend our lives in the vineyards and we don't like breathing in chemicals and the like. Balance reigns there and interventions with natural products are the best way of preserving it" "

PEOPLE - The agriturismo facility, the livestock, the vineyard —ways of showing one's love for the small Valle di Sant'Egidio, more than once threatened by destructive building projects that Marco and the small local community have always fought against. With the family vineyards, Marco and Eleonora have simply followed the advice of the father of the former and the uncle of the latter, proceeding to do what had always been done in the past. The result is Kurni.

VINEYARDS - Ten hectares of small terraced vineyards are situated in unspoiled woodland up to an altitude of 400 meters, with a density of 13,000-22,000 plants per hectare. Here the white soil is sandy and pebbly. "It's a viticulture for idiots," says Marco, "with bush-training with one-spur and tuft-tied vines". For 50 years the vineyards have been managed plant by plant with supporting poles.

WINES - An unmistakable version of Montepulciano in which the fruit is exalted to create complexity and bewitch with a thousand nuances. With **Kurni 2010** (● 7,000 bt), Marco has created a perfect amalgam of flesh, aromatic herbs, oaky tones and sweetness on the palate, mitigated by measured body and well-knit, elegant tannins. Its consequent depth and balance make it a Great Wine. **Kupra 2009** (● 500 bt) is the fruit of the recovery of a clone of the grenache grape, known here as bordò. It offers a unique suite of aromas, including lavender, spices and crisp fruit. The palate is inviting and the well-knit tannins entrancing.

FERTILIZERS organic-mineral, mineral	FERTILIZERS none
PLANT PROTECTION chemical, copper and sulphur	PLANT PROTECTION organic
WEED CONTROL chemical, mechanical	WEED CONTROL mechanical
YEASTS selected	YEASTS native
GRAPES 10% bought in	GRAPES 100% estate-grown
CERTIFICATION none	CERTIFICATION none

Aurora

Località Santa Maria in Carro
Contrada Ciafone, 98
tel. 0736 810007
www.viniaurora.it
enrico@viniaurora.it

9.5 ha - 50,000 bt   **10% discount**

❝ Every activity is performed simply with the health of the soil and the wine in mind. Aurora is proof that sustainability and wines of personality really can go hand in hand. ❞

PEOPLE - "At first there were only a few vine rows, the idea of making wine never crossed our minds. It was only at Lorenzo's place that they made wine. We thought in terms of a farm with lots of crops and fruit." This is how Federico recalls the origins of Aurora, conceived for subsistence reasons and little else. More than an agriturismo and cellar, Aurora is a hospitable farmhouse where brotherhood and conviviality are essential values.

VINEYARDS - When they started producing wine at Aurora, they did so with native grape varieties. They were excited by the acidity of the grapes and the results of their first attempts at vinification. Following the advice of Guido Cocci Grifoni, they began to plant pecorino. Aurora has been using organic methods since it was set up in the 1980s. The soil is fertilized with green manure to produce humus and never plowed. The resulting thick canopy is never pruned. Today the company has converted to biodynamics.

WINES - Aurora speaks of the flavor of the grapes and the soil with a style that is never overrefined. Offida Pecorino Fiobbo 2010 (○ 8,000 bt) releases aromas of ripe fruit that expand on the palate with freshness and plenty of juice... a wonderful Everyday Wine. The excellent **Rosso Piceno Sup. 2010** (● 12,000 bt) stands out for its fruity fragrance and the character it builds from its young tannins.

> **slow wine** BARRICADIERO 2010 (● 4,000 bt) The emblem of Montepulciano expressed without austerity or over-extraction. It offers juicy crisp fruit with an energy-packed, robust palate and close-knit tannins that add depth and dynamism. The progression is overwhelming.

FERTILIZERS	biodynamic preparations, green manure
PLANT PROTECTION	copper and sulphur, organic
WEED CONTROL	mechanical
YEASTS	native
GRAPES	100% estate-grown
CERTIFICATION	organic

Fattoria Dezi

Contrada Fontemaggio, 14
tel. 0734 710090
fattoriadezi@hotmail.com

15 ha - 50,000 bt   **10% discount**

❝ The Snail symbol is a recognition of the passionate work with which Dezi has raised the profile of its local area and grape varieties with wines of great personality. Without stooping to compromises or following fashions ❞

PEOPLE - Dezi: a family, a terroir and a passion. Romolo and Remo yesterday, Davide and Stefano today — the productive continuity of a family that has been working for almost 40 years. Servigliano and Contrada Fontemaggio are an example of a terroir in which land conserves its value. Passion leads the brothers to seek quality by leaving their wines all the time it takes to mature.

VINEYARDS - They began with 2.5 hectares, they now have 15. The Dezi family vineyards have grown in size little by little. Careful work has allowed them to save old sangiovese and montepulciano vineyards and draw on them for new plantings. They keep the soil balanced with manure and cover cropping, prune prudently and limit other interventions to a bare minimum.

WINES - The Dezi brothers love rich, fleshy grapes and enjoy transforming them into wines of great extraction. **Regina del Bosco 2009** (● 6,000 bt) is a humoral Montepulciano of great fruity, spicy intensity. The palate is rich and smooth but supple with well-knit tannins accentuating its depth. The aromas of **Solo 2010** (● sangiovese; 6,000 bt) come out slowly with mature notes of soil and spices. It is fleshy, hematic and rustic with a solid, warm palate. Tonic, juicy, dynamic and incisive, **Dezio 2010** (● montepulciano, sangiovese; 20,000 bt) is as authoritative as it ever was. In whites such as **Le Solagne 2010** (○ verdicchio, malvasia; 10,000 bt), we admired the crispness and balance. **Servigliano P 2010** (○ 3,000 bt) is a soft, slightly alcoholic Pecorino.

FERTILIZERS	manure pellets, natural manure, green manure
PLANT PROTECTION	chemical, copper and sulphur
WEED CONTROL	chemical, mechanical
YEASTS	native
GRAPES	100% estate-grown
CERTIFICATION	none

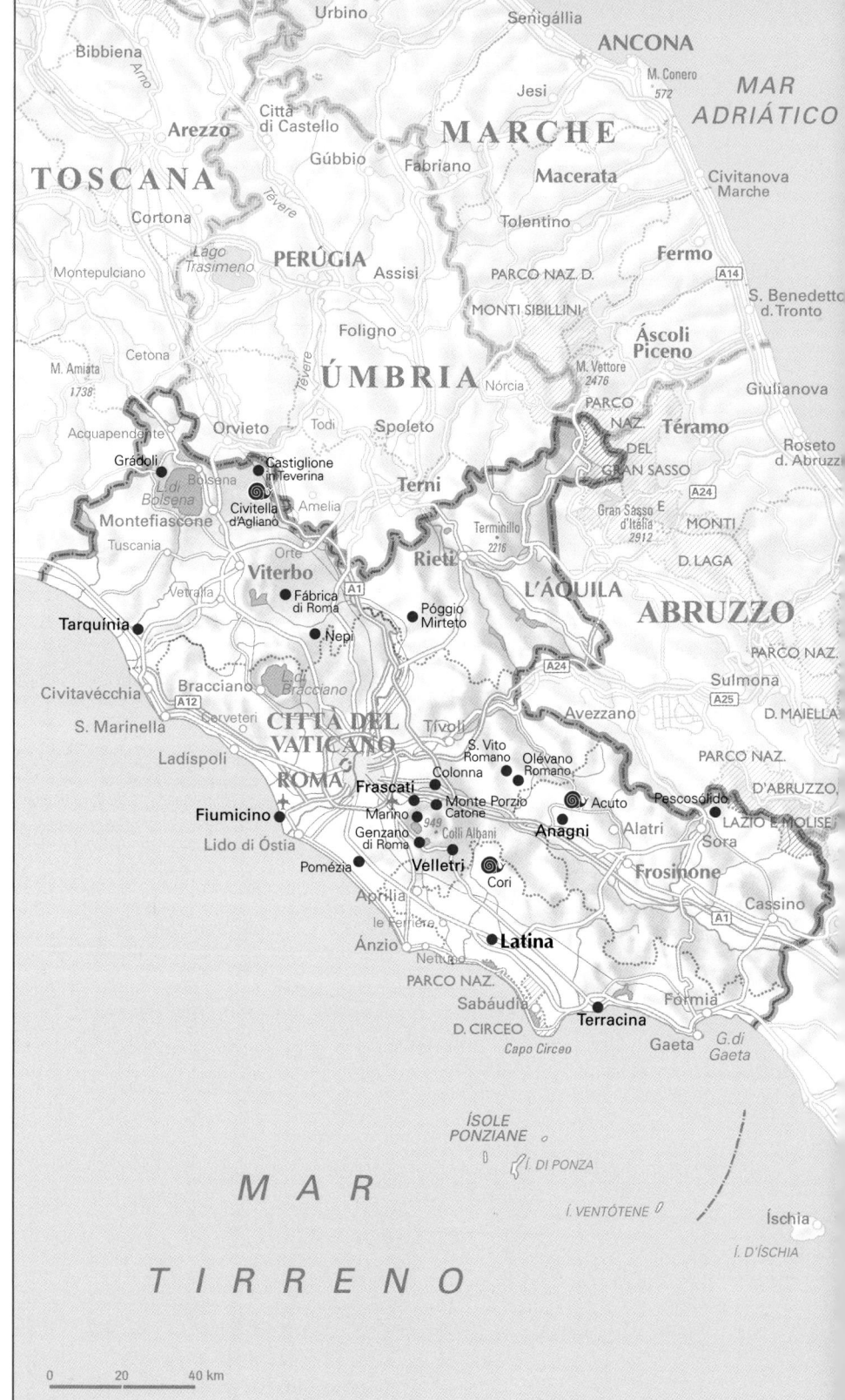

LAZIO

In Lazio, though the past year was a substantially positive one, if we assess it in a wider context, it demands profounder reflection.

A total of 1,205,117 hectoliters of wine produced from 26,549 hectares signifies a 4.4 per cent decrease with respect to the previous year. But this is a mere trifle compared with the results of the General Agricultural Census on the performance of the wine sector in the first decade of the millennium published by Istat, the Italian National Statistical Institute, which show that the number of wine companies in Lazio has decreased by 70.5 per cent with respect to 2000, while the hectares planted with vines has dropped by 45,7 per cent. No other region recorded such a decrease — or rather collapse. Not even 2011 served to turn the situation round. Last year, as elsewhere, the whites were static, a little "stiff" and lacking in complexity, while in the reds the balance between flesh and dynamism wasn't always all that stable.

Albeit different one from another, the Cesaneses (Piglio, Affile and Olevano Romano) performed well, while the Frascatis suffered in many cases from the high temperatures. From next year the only producer still remaining will leave the historic Marino denomination on account of unsolved grievances. Luckily, we had the chance to taste the best of Cori, now a reliable denomination.

Last year was one of transition for Moscato di Terracina, while in the north of the region the many TGIs made from aleatico and grechetto hit the spot more than the classic Est!Est!!Est!!!, Coste di Tarquinia and Cerveteri. The overall picture was thus reasonably satisfactory, but a lot of work has still to be done.

snails

210	CASALE DELLA IORIA
210	SERGIO MOTTURA
211	MARCO CARPINETI

bottles

211	L'OLIVELLA

ACUTO (FR)

Casale della Ioria

Località Agnani
Strada Provinciale 118 Anagni-Paliano km. 4,200
tel. 0775 56031
www.casaledellaioria.com
info@casaledellaioria.com

38 ha - 60,000 bt `10% discount`

❝ If cesanese — especially the Affile typology — is one of Italy's noblest grapes today, it's thanks to Paolo Perinelli, who likes grappling with and taming difficult grapes. Respecting their characteristics, of course ❞

PEOPLE - Paolo Perinelli works in the vineyards with agronomist Lorenzo Costantini, and in the cellar, with great sensitivity, with the help of the expert Roberto Mazzer.

VINEYARDS - The vineyards are situated at an altitude of 330-400 meters and are Guyot- and spur-trained. The soil is partly volcanic and partly made up of sub-acid clay. Only copper and sulfur are used to treat the grapes. Apart from cesanese, the star of the company's vineyards, other grapes grown are merlot, cabernet, grechetto and the local passerina. Worthy of mention is the recovery of a selection of old clones of olivella, a variety in danger of extinction.

WINES - **Passerina 2011** (○ 8,000 bt) is dynamic on the palate. **Olivella 2011** (● 4,000 bt) is fruity with just the right tartness and perky but not overaggressive tannins. Then comes an army of reds. **Cesanese del Piglio Camponovo 2010** (● 15,000 bt), made with grapes from a seven-year-old vineyard and aged in stainless steel vats, has nuances of sour and black cherries. **Cesanese del Piglio Sup. Torre del Piano Ris. 2010** (● 5,000 bt) comes from a vineyard of almost 40 years and is aged in casks for eight months. It exudes class, texture and depth — in short, it's a jewel.

> **slow wine** CESANESE DEL PIGLIO SUP. TENUTA DELLA IORIA 2010 (● 35,000 bt) A wine made with grapes from a 30-year-old vineyard and aged six months in large barrels. It is rich and charming with well dosed oak. Price, complexity and strong sense of place make it a perfect Slow Wine.

FERTILIZERS	manure pellets, green manure
PLANT PROTECTION	copper and sulphur
WEED CONTROL	mechanical
YEASTS	selected
GRAPES	100% estate-grown
CERTIFICATION	none

CIVITELLA D'AGLIANO (VT)

Sergio Mottura

Via Poggio della Costa, 1
tel. 0761 914533
www.motturasergio.it
vini@motturasergio.it

36 ha - 95,000 bt `10% discount`

❝ A cellar of granitic consistency that is now an institution. It interprets the unique terroir — gently rolling hills and soil ideal for complex, long-lasting white wines — and the grechetto grape with consummate mastery ❞

PEOPLE - Sergio Mottura welcomed us to his beautiful house in the center of Civitella d'Agliano and told us his life story. He also stressed the importance of training young winemakers.

VINEYARDS - The vineyards surround the hills of Civitella D'Agliano. The company is certified organic and the vines are Guyot- and spur-trained. Some of the vines, especially the pinot nero, come from a nurseryman in Jura, a friend of Sergio's. The company's care for the environment is constant. You can see this in its use of advanced technology, such as the atomizer, a tool that cuts product waste.

WINES - **M. Cl. Sergio Mottura 2006** (○ chardonnay; 6,600 bt) is now ready for drinking. After five years on yeasts, it offers aromas of honey and bread crusts. With its blossomy notes, **Orvieto Tragugnano 2011** (○ 15,000 bt) has an attractive palate and good acidity — a pleasure to drink. **Latour a Civitella 2010** (○ grechetto; 13,000 bt) is complex with very pleasant aromas and an extra-long, nicely mineral palate. It's one of Central Italy's great whites, hence a Great Wine too.

> **slow wine** POGGIO DELLA COSTA 2011 (○ grechetto; 30,000 bt) There are no adjectives left to describe this wine! It would be almost offensive to call it Latour's younger brother. The aromas are very forthright with notes of tropical fruit, while the palate, which possesses just the right acidity, is racy, intense and leisurely with great structure.

FERTILIZERS	none
PLANT PROTECTION	copper and sulphur
WEED CONTROL	mechanical
YEASTS	selected
GRAPES	100% estate-grown
CERTIFICATION	organic

Marco Carpineti

S.P. Velletri-Anzio, km 14,300
tel. 06 9679860
www.marcocarpineti.com
info@marcocarpineti.com

54 ha - 220,000 bt

❝ You couldn't get slower! Without ever going over the top, Marco Carpineti has recovered native grapes and, embracing organics, teased the best out of them in the cellar with care and rigor. The results are there for all to see — in the glass ❞

PEOPLE - Thanks to painstaking selection in the vineyard, carried out with the fundamental help of enologists Emiliano Rossi and Francesco Silvi, Marco Carpineti has created a model winery. Also indispensable is the help of his son, Paolo, an economics graduate.

VINEYARDS - Everything rotates round three properties: San Pietro, red soil and tufa, planted with greco, bellone, montepulciano, nero buono and a small portion of cesanese; Capolemole, with some vine rows over 70 years old, where arciprete, the local name of bellone, is king; and, last but not least, Campanile, where the soil is pebbly, given over to nero buono.

WINES - **Brut M. Cl. 2009** (○ bellone; 12,000 bt) rests for two years on yeasts and it stands out for its drinkability and finesse. **Capolemole Bianco 2011** (○ bellone, greco; 35,000 bt) is arguably the wine's best vintage to date. It's fresh and juicy, mineral and crisp. The best red is the solid, fruity **Dithyrambus 2008** (● nero buono, montepulciano; 4,000 bt), aged in casks for two years. A new entry this year is **Apolide 2007** (● nero buono; 3,000 bt), at its first vintage, warm and mature, only ever so slightly out of kilter. **Ludum 2009** (○ bellone; 4,000 bt) rounds off the range on a sweet note: a taste of honey with vague hints of peach jam and a fine palate.

> **slow wine** **MORO 2010** (○ greco moro; 16,000 bt) Spacious, creamy, tangy, fine, elegant… On the whole Italian wine scene it's hard to find a label with a stronger sense of place and complexity at this price.

FERTILIZERS none	
PLANT PROTECTION copper and sulphur	
WEED CONTROL mechanical	
YEASTS selected, native	
GRAPES 100% estate-grown	
CERTIFICATION organic	

L'Olivella

Via Colle Pisano, 5
tel. 06 9424527
www.racemo.it
info@racemo.it

30 ha - 88,000 bt

PEOPLE - The Violo family winery is situated in Notarnicola, in an area that has attracted visitors, for study or for pleasure, in every era. Here innovation has been a specialty of the house ever since the early 1980s, when traditional grape varieties were replanted, and 1988, when the company converted to organic methods. More recently a farm holiday facility has been added and a modern cellar built nearby.

VINEYARDS - From the vineyards, the view of this beautiful area, just a few kilometers outside Rome, is truly breathtaking. Granite rock over volcanic soil adds a wealth of minerals to the wines, enhancing their complexity and aromatic profile. Temperature swings and constant ventilation also do their bit. The Guyot-trained vineyards produce an average of 90 quintals of grapes per hectare.

WINES - We were fascinated by the pronounced fruit of the monovarietal **Bombino 2011** (○ 4,000 bt). Intriguing too was **Tre Grome Passito** (○ malvasia puntinata, malvasia rossa, bellone; 1,800 bt), fermented in acacia barriques, which seduces with its color before winning you over with its well-articulated fruity aromas, good supporting acidity on the palate and consummate elegance and complexity. We also recommend **Frascati Sup. Racemo 2011** (○ 32,000 bt), an institution among Lazio's whites, and **Racemo Rosso 2008** (● sangiovese, cesanese; 4,000 bt), a level-headed take on two terroir-rooted grape varieties.

FERTILIZERS green manure	
PLANT PROTECTION copper and sulphur	
WEED CONTROL mechanical	
YEASTS selected	
GRAPES 100% estate-grown	
CERTIFICATION organic	

ABRUZZO AND MOLISE

The number of Abruzzo and Molise wineries has increased, proof of ongoing improvements in quality in the two regions. Abruzzo is familiar to the popular imagination for its production of Montepulciano, but the march forward of native white grapes, such as trebbiano, pecorino, passerina and cococciola — partly determined by a shift in demand away from reds towards whites —has redefined the ampelographic map of the region. Hence another impressive performance by white wines. Abruzzo has all it takes to achieve freshness, elegance and longevity in its wines, especially in higher areas, such as those round Ofena and Capestrano, all increasingly geared to excellence. The other face of Abruzzo is that of its wine cooperatives, which have rewarded the labor of a great many growers over the last 30 years. Probably on account of unsuccessful sales policies, the same cooperatives are suffering a period of economic difficulty that is progressively driving members to abandon their vineyards.
Worth mentioning is the growing trend towards care for the salubriousness of the soil and non-invasive enological practices in the cellar. This approach has been followed by the larger wine companies and, above all, by up-and-coming small-scale producers. Another interesting phenomenon is the replacement of traditional pergola vine training with the spurred cordon and Guyot systems.
In Molise they have decided to gamble heavily on the native tintilia grape, which is producing great results in terms both of quality and of market success, locally and also further afield.
The vintages tasted revealed the complexity and breadth of wine production in the two regions. Last year the torrid end-of-summer heat created problems, especially among the whites, in some cases reducing aroma and freshness. Not surprisingly, the most interesting results came from cellars that left their whites the right time to evolve properly. It was a good vintage instead for Cerasuolo d'Abruzzo, which had intense aromas and freshness without losing structure and concentration. The story is more complicated for Montepulciano d'Abruzzo, often richly extracted and aged in wood casks; results vary according to vintage and production zone. Generally speaking, 2007 and 2008 yielded very good wines indeed. Last but not least, the passito version of moscatello di Castiglione is producing commendable results.

snails 🐌

215 TORRE DEI BEATI
215 VALENTINI
216 CATALDI MADONNA
216 PRAESIDIUM
219 EMIDIO PEPE

bottles 🍾

214 SAN LORENZO
217 MASCIARELLI
218 FEUDO ANTICO

coins €

214 COLLEFRISIO
217 CANTINA FRENTANA
219 TENUTA TERRAVIVA

CASTILENTI (TE)

San Lorenzo

Contrada Plavignano, 2
tel. 0861 999325
www.sanlorenzovini.com
info@sanlorenzovini.com

FRISA (CH)

Collefrisio

Località Piane di Maggio
tel. 085 9039074
www.collefrisio.it
info@collefrisio.it

---

150 ha - 800,000 bt   **10% discount**

36 ha - 350,000 bt

PEOPLE - This attractive, reliable winery is owned by the Barbone and Galasso families and run by the young brothers Gianluca and Fabrizio Galasso, who manage the technical and sales side with dynamism and professionalism, their uncle Gianfranco Barbone, who tends the vines with great expertise and the accomplished enologist Riccardo Brighigna, who directs cellar operations.

VINEYARDS - A hundred hectares of vines form a single plot that stretches over three consecutive ridges round Castilenti. Another 40 hectares are at Loreto Aprutino and another property still is situated in the Teramo area. All the vines in the new vineyards, where montepulciano prevails over white grapes, were taken from the company's oldest rows. Sound vineyard management and efficient mechanization limit the use of chemicals on the soil.

WINES - Precise execution, well-defined character and easy drinking — these are the features that characterize all San Lorenzo wines. The pick of the bunch was **Montepulciano d'Abruzzo Colline Teramane Escol 2008** (● 200,000 bt), a wine with a heavyweight structure yet perfectly balanced, polished and dynamic on the palate. The quaffable **Montepulciano d'Abruzzo Antares 2009** (● 200,000 bt) is soft and endowed with nice fruity depth. **Montepulciano d'Abruzzo Colline Teramane Oinos 2009** (● 200,000 bt) is more rounded and sweeter as a result of aging in oak. We were intrigued by the version of **Trebbiano d'Abruzzo Casabianca 2011** (○ 100,000 bt). Produced with spontaneous fermentation without the addition of yeasts, it offers a broader, more complex suite of aromas and an enjoyable flavorful palate. **Pecorino Il Pecorino 2011** (● 60,000 bt) has finely vegetal aromas with a spacious, rich, complex palate.

PEOPLE - Antonio Patricelli, Amedeo De Luca and Katiuscia Di Ciano, the company's owners, are advocates of a one-step-at-a-time approach. With the completion of work on the cellar's reception area, they have now concluded the project they undertook with great foresight about a decade ago. The wines are improving in quality all the time and output is increasing. In the cellar the company relies on the precious consultancy of enologist Romeo Taraborelli.

VINEYARDS - The vineyards are managed using organic methods. They are split into three distinct zones and are pergola-trained, save for a few hectares of cordon-trained and spur-pruned montepulciano vines on the Morrecine estate. The pecorino grapes come mainly from old vineyards on the clay and ferrous soil in the countryside round Giuliano Teatino. The montepulciano grapes on the Frisa estate, where the soil is light, calcareous and pebbly, give elegant, aromatic wines, those from Giuliano Teatino full-bodied, beautifully colored wines.

WINES - The wines of Collefrisio are elegant, technically impeccable and commendably well-priced. **Trebbiano d'Abruzzo Zero 2011** (○ 60,000 bt) shows off exuberant fruity notes and pleasing saltiness. **Pecorino 2011** (○ 53,000 bt) veers towards citrusy, balsamic notes with lively supporting acidity. **Cerasuolo d'Abruzzo 2011** (◉ 20,000 bt) is extraordinarily drinkable, but has complex aromas and flavors as well. **Montepulciano d'Abruzzo Morrecine 2010** (● 13,000 bt) brings out all the character of the grape with notes of red fruit and spices, good acid and tannic follow-through and a pleasingly spicy finish. **Montepulciano d'Abruzzo Uno 2009** (● 60,000 bt) has a mature bouquet of blackberries, a tannic palate and a spicy finish.

FERTILIZERS organic-mineral, manure pellets, green manure
PLANT PROTECTION copper and sulphur
WEED CONTROL mechanical
YEASTS selected, native
GRAPES 100% estate-grown
CERTIFICATION none

FERTILIZERS organic-mineral, natural manure
PLANT PROTECTION copper and sulphur
WEED CONTROL mechanical
YEASTS selected
GRAPES 100% estate-grown
CERTIFICATION organic

LORETO APRUTINO (PE)

Torre dei Beati

Contrada Poggioragone, 56
tel. 333 3832344
www.torredeibeati.it
info@torredeibeati.it

17 ha - 100,000 bt

66 More than a winery, Torre dei Beati is a life project, a dream come true for the Adriana Galasso and Fausto Albanesi husband-and-wife team. With measured, level-headed determination, they have built up a company that produces good wine using the most sustainable viticultural techniques 99

PEOPLE - Having completed its first harvest in 2000, Adriana and Fausto's company is relatively young, but the couple run it with the utmost competence. She follows work in the countryside full-time, he divides his time between his job as an architect and management of the cellar.

VINEYARDS - The vineyards that encircle the cellar grow on flat land or on gentle slopes, where the soil tends to be sandy and clayey. They are managed using organic methods. The 40-year-old montepulciano vineyard is pergola-trained, while the pecorino vineyard is Guyot-trained.

WINES - We were impressed by the care devoted to the harvest. The grapes are picked in stages, with priority being given to properly ripe bunches. Further selection is carried out in the cellar. Pleasant and approachable, **Pecorino Giocheremo con i Fiori 2011** (○ 25,000 bt) has juicy fruit and intriguing mineral notes. **Cerasuolo d'Abruzzo Rosa-ae 2011** (⊙ 25,000 bt) is fruity and tangy. Elegant in its simplicity, the excellent **Montepulciano d'Abruzzo 2010** (● 40,000 bt) has typical fruity aromas, while **Montepulciano d'Abruzzo Mazzamurello 2009** (● 5,000 bt) is more powerful and exuberant.

> **slow wine** **MONTEPULCIANO D'ABRUZZO COCCIAPAZZA 2009** (● 7,000 bt) A Montepulciano of extraordinary force and an outstanding taste profile. It has a powerful extractive style with fantastic acidity and tannins, plus perfectly dosed wood.

FERTILIZERS natural manure
PLANT PROTECTION copper and sulphur
WEED CONTROL mechanical
YEASTS selected
GRAPES 100% estate-grown
CERTIFICATION organic

LORETO APRUTINO (PE)

Valentini

Via del Baio, 2
tel. 085 8291138

66 ha - 35,000 bt

66 It's getting harder and harder to introduce Valentini. We'd prefer to avoid using the word "legend" and rhetorical talk about outstanding farsightedness and uncompromising productive style. Let's just say that this family has given and will continue to give a lot — to their land and to wine lovers alike 99

PEOPLE - Since 2006, the year of his father Edoardo's death, Francesco Paolo Valentini has managed the company with his wife Elena and son Gabriele.

VINEYARDS - The vineyards are dominated by the region's two principal grapes, montepulciano and trebbiano. They cover an area of 30 hectares and are split up mainly between the holdings on Colle Mantello and Colle Cavaliere, where they were planted 40 or so years ago. Another large property is situated in the Castelluccio district. The vineyards are managed with great respect for the environment thanks to Valentini's in-depth knowledge of his vines and agricultural practices.

WINES - Valentini's wines are recognizable and memorable. As the two labels presented this year demonstrate.

> **slow wine** **CERASUOLO D'ABRUZZO 2011** (⊙ 9,000 bt) A thrilling bouquet of fruit backed by notes of spice and coffee. The compact palate has a nice follow-through with supporting acidity and a pleasant spicy finish.
> **slow wine** **TREBBIANO D'ABRUZZO 2007** (○ 23,000 bt) In the wake of 2008 and 2009, at last a wine from a warm vintage — and it's been well worth waiting for. It takes next to no time to savor the mineral, balsamic notes, accompanied by notes of freshly mown grass and fruit, in the glass. The palate displays character and texture enhanced by perky minerality and a wonderful fruity encore.

FERTILIZERS none
PLANT PROTECTION copper and sulphur
WEED CONTROL mechanical
YEASTS native
GRAPES 100% estate-grown
CERTIFICATION none

Cataldi Madonna

Località Piano
tel. 0862 954252
www.cataldimadonna.it
cataldimadonna@virgilio.it

27.4 ha - 240,000 bt   **10% discount**

66 Though he divides his time between his job as a philosophy teacher and winemaking, Luigi Cataldi has raised the profile of a previously forgotten terroir, now unanimously regarded as one of the best in the region for vine growing 99

PEOPLE - You sense a laid-back, collaborative atmosphere at this historic Abruzzo company, where Luigi is helped by his daughter Giulia and enologists Raffaele Orlandini and Lorenzo Landi.

VINEYARDS - Most of the vineyards are situated near the cellar on a flat expanse of land at the bottom of a picturesque hollow, at an altitude of 350 meters. In 2004 two montepulciano vineyards — Picolle and Campo Galliano — were planted not far away on sandy, gravelly limestone soil of the Gran Sasso National Park. The first pecorino grapes were planted in 1990 from a massal selection at the company.

WINES - The wines of Cataldi Madonna owe their peculiarity to the sandy soil and sharp temperature swings. A good example is **Pecorino Giulia 2011** (○ 37,000 bt), which is aromatic, nicely acid and cellarable. The traditional **Cerasuolo d'Abruzzo Piè delle Vigne 2010** (◉ 3.000 bt) is complex, profound and racy. **Montepulciano d'Abruzzo Malandrino 2010** (● 12,000 bt) combines aromatic complexity with drinkability. **Montepulciano d'Abruzzo Tonì 2009** (● 3,000 bt) is well-structured, impeccably balanced and built to last with well-knit, well-rounded tannins.

slow wine **PECORINO 2010** (○ 3,500 bt) This celebrated flagship wine — which possesses the wherewithal to improve with time — impresses for its fine, complex aromatic bouquet ranging from Mediterranean scrub to tropical fruit. The palate is taut and digs deep, very deep.

FERTILIZERS organic-mineral, natural manure
PLANT PROTECTION chemical, copper and sulphur
WEED CONTROL mechanical
YEASTS selected
GRAPES 100% estate-grown
CERTIFICATION none

Praesidium

Via Nazzareno Giovannucci, 24
tel. 0864 45103
info@vinipraesidium.it

5 ha - 25,000 bt

66 The story of Enzo Pasquale and his son Ottaviano is a simple one of simplicity and success. Like that of their company. It tells of an old-fashioned agriculture that speaks a modern language of environmental sustainability and bonds with the land 99

PEOPLE - Prezza is a small town in the Valle Peligna, one of the most God-forsaken districts in the whole of the Abruzzo region, but also one of the best for winemaking. Here Enzo, who has named the winery for Prezza's Roman name, has always trained his montepulciano grapes with the vertical trellis system.

VINEYARDS - "If you work naturally, you've got to let the roots feed themselves," explained Ottaviano when we visited his small family vineyards, now being converted to organics. Hence his reduction of treatments to a bare minimum and preference for manual labor, with hoes being used to grub weeds from under the vine rows. The soil is low in minerals and montepulciano, the only grape grown here, has very low natural yields.

WINES - Praesidium's wines are stern in character, like the area they come from. Unfussy and traditional in style, they are dark-colored, packed with minerality and predisposed for aging. **Montepulciano d'Abruzzo 2007** (● 15,000 bt) displays all these characteristics, reticently at first, then with great confidence, ripe fruit, spices and a faint hint of herbs ushering in an elegant, energy-filled palate. Richly extracted with heady scents of fruit, **Cerasuolo d'Abruzzo Sup. 2011** (◉ 6,000 bt) is full of structure and beautifully fresh drinkability. Worth a mention, finally, is Ratafià, a typical Abruzzo liqueur made of sour cherries and Montepulciano wine.

FERTILIZERS natural manure, none
PLANT PROTECTION copper and sulphur
WEED CONTROL mechanical
YEASTS native
GRAPES 100% estate-grown
CERTIFICATION converting to organics

ROCCA SAN GIOVANNI (CH)

Cantina Frentana €

Via Perazza, 32
tel. 0872 60152
www.cantinafrentana.it
info@cantinafrentana.it

SAN MARTINO SULLA MARRUCINA (CH)

Masciarelli

Via Gamberale, 1
tel. 0871 85241
www.masciarelli.it
info@masciarelli.it

600 ha - 680,000 bt   **10% discount**

420 ha - 2,500,000 bt   **10% discount**

PEOPLE - Frentana is one of the few Abruzzo cooperatives to deliberately put its money on quality wines and competitive prices. Its professional management — president Carlo Romanelli, sales manager Felice Di Biase and enologist Gianni Pasquale — are conscious of their responsibilities towards their more than 500 members.

VINEYARDS - A wine cooperative's vineyards usually can't all be supervised by the cooperative itself. But here, with 60 viticulturists adhering to the Quality Project, they are controlled and tended regularly and a company agronomist follows all the members personally and visits them constantly. A couple of years ago the cooperative made a further step forward by starting to manage some plots (25 hectares so far) directly, half of which using organic methods.

WINES - Thanks to vinification respectful of the character of the land, Frentana's wines are endowed with freshness and quaffability. **Cococciola Costa del Mulino 2011** (O cococciola, pecorino; 18,000 bt) is a real pleasure to drink. It has vegetal and fresh fruity aromas with a tangy, acid vein that ensures fragrance and drinkability — a worthy Everyday Wine. **Montepulciano d'Abruzzo Costa del Mulino 2010** (● 20,000 bt) banks on red fruit and a balanced, well-sustained palate. **Montepulciano d'Abruzzo Panarda 2009** (● 8,000 bt) is plusher.

> **slow wine** PECORINO DONNA GRETA 2010 (O 12,000) Vinification in steel tanks with native yeasts and maceration on the skins have produced a wine with a forthright, varietal nose, which alternates citrusy notes with a herbaceous, mineral streak.

PEOPLE - Despite its lightning, dizzy growth — set up in 1981, by the late Gianni Masciarelli, it now boasts 70 employees — and the accolades of consumers and critics alike, thanks to Marina Cvetic, Gianni's widow, the spirit and enthusiasm at the winery are still as strong as they ever were. Talking to Marina and sales manager Rocco Cipollone, you note a passion and respect for the terroir that you would normally associate with a small family winery.

VINEYARDS - The company's 420 hectares fan out over all four provinces of the Abruzzo region on wine hills with varying soil and climate conditions. At San Martino sulla Marrucina the vineyards are Guyot-trained and densely planted. In other districts they are trained using the rod-and-spur and traditional *tendone* systems. The company has two ancillary vinification facilities at Ancarano (Teramo) and Re Martello (Pescara).

WINES - The wines we tasted are complex, elegant and reliable with a strong sense of place. **Trebbiano d'Abruzzo Castello di Semivicoli 2010** (O 12,000 bt) is once again an elegant, mineral wine, rich in fruit, extremely pleasant and drinkable. We also liked **Cerasuolo d'Abruzzo Villa Gemma 2011** (⊙ 70,000 bt), fruity, freshy and full-bodied. **Montepulciano d'Abruzzo 2010** (● 1,200,000 bt) has a fruity nose, a linear palate and good acid-tannic texture. It proves that quality is possible even with high outputs and thoroughly deserves to be an Everyday Wine. Fruity notes, herby hints and a fresh, tannic palate characterize **Montepulciano d'Abruzzo Marina Cvetic 2009** (● 400,000 bt), while **Castello di Semivicoli Rosso 2010** (● montepulciano, merlot, cabernet sauvignon; 20,000 bt) has superlative mouthfeel, juicy fruit and lively tannins.

FERTILIZERS organic-mineral, manure pellets
PLANT PROTECTION chemical, copper and sulphur, organic
WEED CONTROL chemical, mechanical
YEASTS selected
GRAPES 100% estate-grown
CERTIFICATION organic for some vineyards

FERTILIZERS organic-mineral, natural manure,
PLANT PROTECTION copper and sulphur, organic
WEED CONTROL mechanical
YEASTS selected, native
GRAPES 100% estate-grown
CERTIFICATION none

SANT'OMERO (TE)

Valori

Via Torquato al Salinello, 8
tel. 086 188461
vinivalori@tin.it

TOLLO (CH)

Feudo Antico

Via Perruna, 35
tel. 0871 969128
www.feudoantico.it
info@feudoantico.it

---

20 ha - 80,000 bt

PEOPLE - "I'm happy because I have the chance to do what I actually enjoy in life: farming and winemaking." Luigi Valori is a good-natured, cheerful person who has been doing these jobs since 1997. Today he has an almost symbiotic rapport with the land, to which he devotes the best part of himself and from which he finds it hard to pull himself away.

VINEYARDS - Valori firmly believes that the best wines come from vineyards "cultivated to the limit". The aim of this extreme philosophy is to achieve the best possible natural expression of the vine and the fruit. In his vineyards, divided between the hills of Sant'Omero and, in part, Controguerra, the terrains are sandy and lean. The vineyards are densely planted and stand in grass to create competition among the vines.

WINES - The wines are richly extracted but eminently drinkable and fruitily fragrant. This is true especially of the reds, the feather in the winery's cap. **Montepulciano d'Abruzzo 2011** (● 50,000 bt), a selection that was released late, has fleshy, crisp fruit and enjoyably drinkable. Deservedly an Everyday Wine. Aged for a year in barriques, **Merlot Inkiostro 2008** (● 3,000 bt) is more international in style with an assertive, no-nonsense character and exhibits nice roundness with lots of black berries and spices. Simple and approachable, **Trebbiano d'Abruzzo 2011** (○ 8,000 bt) has fresh and intriguing citrus notes.

---

14 ha - 85,000 bt

PEOPLE - It hasn't taken long for Feudo Antico, which debuted on the market with his wines in 2009, to carve out a niche for itself. The project got underway with the institution of the Tullum DOC, one of the smallest in Italy, and can now bank on about 20 viticulturists, all members of Tollo's two great wine cooperatives, Cantina Tollo and Cantina Coltivatori Diretti. Feudo Antico is run by Andrea Di Fabio, assisted by enologist Riccardo Brighigna and agronomist Antonio Sitti.

VINEYARDS - Feudo Antico's wines are made exclusively with Tollo grapes and the single typologies belong to specific zones on the ampelographic map. At the end of the year a zoning project, coordinated by Attilio Scienza and researchers from the University of Milan, was embarked upon to make an in-depth study of the characteristics of the terroir.

WINES - In the cellar, the winery is reviving old practices such as short maceration of the skins and fermentation at controlled temperatures for the whites and vinification in cement for the reds. We found **Rosato 2011** (◉ montepulciano; 5,000 bt) very interesting. Complex and very pleasant, it offers balsamic, spicy notes and elegant mineral flavor. We were also won over by **Tullum Bianco 2011** (○ trebbiano, passerina; 5,000 bt), which will be vinified in future using only native yeasts and no filtering prior to bottling (the same technique used for the rosé). It has a fresh bouquet of fruit and flowers and a taut palate with a herbaceous finish. The new entry, **Tullum Passito Rosso 2009** (● montepulciano; 3.000 bt; 28 €), is enchanting and complex. **Tullum Pecorino 2011** (○ 25,000 bt) is a pleasant quaff, while **Tullum Passerina 2011** (○ 13,000 bt) is fresh and convincing.

FERTILIZERS organic-mineral, natural manure, humus
PLANT PROTECTION copper and sulphur, organic
WEED CONTROL mechanical
YEASTS selected
GRAPES 100% estate-grown
CERTIFICATION none

FERTILIZERS organic-mineral, manure pellets
PLANT PROTECTION copper and sulphur
WEED CONTROL mechanical
YEASTS selected
GRAPES 100% estate-grown
CERTIFICATION none

TORANO NUOVO (TE)
Emidio Pepe

Via Chiesi, 10
tel. 086 1856493
www.emidiopepe.com
info@emidiopepe.com

TORTORETO (TE)
Tenuta Terraviva
€

Via del Lago. 19
tel. 0861 786056
www.tenutaterraviva.it
info@tenutaterraviva.it

---

17 ha - 70,000 bt

6 ha - 20,000 bt

66 Emidio Pepe — now aided by his daughters Sofia and Daniela — is one of the last repositories of almost forgotten farming skills. He manages his vineyards using biodynamic principles to strengthen symbiosis with the soil. Pepe is ultimately a humble but magnificently accomplished farmer 99

PEOPLE - Emidio attends to the land, Sofia to the cellar and external relations, Daniela to the administration. The wine has always been managed in a somewhat original manner, some being bottled and released for sale immediately, the rest left to age in the quaint cellar. Years, sometimes decades, on, the old bottles are uncorked, hand-decanted, recorked and sold.

VINEYARDS - The various holdings, all situated a few kilometers from the cellar, have now been joined by three new hectares. Emidio only starts touching the soil when he "senses" the moment has come to do so. The vineyard management, traditionally organic, has now been certified biodynamic.

WINES - The white grapes are pressed by foot and ferment in cement tanks. The montepulciano grapes are stemmed by hand, pressed by foot, transferred to buckets by hand and piled into the barrels with the pressed wine. **Rosato 2011** (◉ montepulciano; 8,000 bt) has crisp fruit, fleshiness and a dynamic taste profile. The excellent **Pecorino 2010** (○ 6,000 bt) is the first wine to be made with grapes from a vineyard bedded a few years ago. Vinified traditionally, it's a wine of great complexity with a deep, very mineral bouquet and perky acidity. **Trebbiano d'Abruzzo 2010** (○ 30,000 bt) is initially bashful, but soon pulls out its customary bold character, full of texture and fine minerality.

PEOPLE - The entrepreneurial empathy that exists between Pietro Topi and Martino Taraschi was born when the two met to decide whether to uproot an old trebbiano vineyard or not. It was thus that in 2006 an offshoot of the Collebello farm gave rise to the Tenuta Terraviva project whose aim was to produce terroir-dedicated wines at reasonable prices, reducing technology and chemistry to a bare minimum both in the vineyard and in the cellar. The winery's consultant enologist is Claudia Galterio.

VINEYARDS - The old pergola-trained trebbiano vineyard is still in place, of course. Together with the company's other vines, cordon-trained and spur-pruneded, it continues to yield excellent fruits. Part of the merit has to go to the enviable position of the wide valley — with calcareous-clay soil — in which they are situated, between the Adriatic, breezes from which lower the heat by day, and the Gran Sasso, which brings cool air by night. The vineyards are managed using organic methods.

WINES - This year the winery failed to produce Pecorino Ekwo, deeming below standard the quality of the harvested grapes. The well-crafted, beefy **Cerasuolo d'Abruzzo Giusi 2011** (◉ 2,000 bt), made using the drawing-off technique, is fruity with intriguing minerality. **Solorosso 2010** (● sangiovese; 2,000 bt) has a full, fragrant bouquet of red fruit and leisurely drinkability. **Trebbiano d'Abruzzo Mario's 38 2010** (○ 6,000 bt) is the fruit of ten days of fermentation on the skins in large wooden barrels and subsequent aging, again in wood, for eight months. The wine displays aromatic complexity, minerality and a taste profile that ranges from blossom to white fruit with hints of spice.

FERTILIZERS natural manure, biodynamic preparations, green manure
PLANT PROTECTION copper and sulphur
WEED CONTROL mechanical
YEASTS native
GRAPES 100% estate-grown
CERTIFICATION biodynamic, organic

FERTILIZERS organic-mineral, humus
PLANT PROTECTION copper and sulphur
WEED CONTROL mechanical
YEASTS native
GRAPES 100% estate-grown
CERTIFICATION organic

ABRUZZO

Chieti

Lanciano

MAR ADRIÁTICO

PARCO

NAZ.

Sulmona

2793 la Maiella

D. MAIELLA

Vasto

Bomba

Térmoli

ÍSOLE TRÉMITI

PARCO NAZ.

D. GARGANO

S. Giovanni

Rotondo

1055

PARCO NAZ.

D'ABRUZZO,

Pescolanciano

MOLISE

S. Severo

Manfredónia

LAZIO E MOLISE

2247

M.ti della

Meta

Isérnia

CAMPOBASSO

Fóggia

LÁZIO

Cassino

Lucera

PÚGLIA

Gallúccio

Caianello

Sessa

Aurunca

G. di

Gaeta

Célloie

Carínola

Vitulázio

Falciano

del Mássico

Cápua

Guárdia

Sanframondi

Castelvénere

Castél

Campagnano

Castél

Paupisi

Casalduni

Ponte

Torrecuso

Frasso

Telesino

Calazzo

S. Ágata de' Goti

Benevento

Cerignola

A16

IRPINIA

Melfi

S. Ángelo

d. Lombardi

S. Maria

Cápua Vétere

Casérta

PARCO NAZ.

D.VESUVIO

Avellino

BASILICATA

Quarto

Pozzuoli

Bácoli

Vesúvio

1281

NÁPOLI

Trecase

Terzigno

Boscotrecase

S. Giuseppe Vesuviano

POTENZA

Forío

Í. D'ÍSCHIA

Ischia

Castellammare

di Stábia

Tramonti

Pimonte

Sorrento

Furore

Amalfi

Vietri

sul Mare

Salerno

S. Cipriano

Picentino

Montecorvino

Rovella

Éboli

Battipaglia

PARCO NAZ

Í. DI CAPRI

G. di

Salerno

S. Ángelo

a Fasanella

PARCO

DELL'APPENNINC

LUCANC

Sala

Consilina

A3

Agrópoli

Prignano

Cilento

NAZ. D. CILENTO

Stio

VAL D'AGR

Castellabate

Torchiara

Vallo

di Lucania

VALLO DI DIANO

LAGONEGRES

Sapri

MAR

Palinuro

Capo Palinuro

Camerota

G. di

Policastro

TIRRENO

0   15   30 km

CAMPANIA

The 2011 vintage was marked by an unexpectedly long heatwave in the second half of August, but Campania came out of it well. Whites continued to exhibit the character traits they have developed over the last few years: namely "unabashed" acid thrust, richness of flavor and erasure of cloying exotic and sweet notes. The various winemaking areas thus hit the spot and, in the case of Fiano di Avellino, promise to develop well.

Piedirosso, a historic wine of Naples and Benevento, made great leaps forward, as did Coda di Volpe, at last geared towards easy drinkability and aromatic elegance. Campanian wine production registered a 7.6 per cent decrease in 2011 for a total of just over 1.7 million hectoliters. Unfortunately, about three quarters of the total are table wines, a trend which has stood still for at least five years, despite the fame now achieved by the three Irpinian DOCGs — Fiano, Taurasi and Greco — and the general reorganization of the DOCs in the province of Benevento (where they occupy 10,500 hectares of the total 29,000 hectares planted with vines). Speaking of which, Falanghina del Sannio DOC and Aglianico del Taburno Rosato made memorable debuts.

More and more surprises are appearing from the Vesuvius and Campi Flegrei area, whereas the province of Caserta would appear to be going through the phase of stylistic indecision common to other zones of the South. The province of Salerno area proves once more to be a niche area with great quality potential, especially on the Costiera Amalfitana and the Cilento district.

Irpinia remains the cutting-edge of the region. Now, besides Greco and Fiano, Taurasi (and Aglianico in general) exhibits a common identity, even allowing for a certain diversity of interpretation.

BOSCOTRECASE (NA)

Sorrentino

Via Casciello, 5
tel. 081 8584963
www.sorrentinovini.com
info@sorrentinovini.com

25 ha - 230,000 bt — **10% discount**

66 The Sorrentino estate is a sort of oasis: tidy vine rows, organic agriculture, the sea a stone's throw away, Vesuvius in the background. Then there are the wines, the fruit of careful experiments with native grapes. We were totally impressed 99

PEOPLE - If you aren't familiar with these areas, arriving at the Sorrentino vineyards will come as something of a trauma. Al around, houses, houses and more houses in an urban sprawl with few equals. Which is why when you eventually reach the peace and quiet inside the estate, you'll appreciate the scenic effect all the more.

VINEYARDS - Paolo Sorrentino, father of enologist Benny, is the agricultural brains behind the cellar. Over the years he has bought a good number of vineyards, bringing them together in a single plot. Since 2003 he has used organic methods. From the top of the main property, known as Fruscio, it's possible to see the ruins of Pompei in the distance. The soil is volcanic and contains lapilli. Interesting projects are underway to recover old local grape varieties and centuries-old vines.

WINES - Sorrentino's bottles aren't made to amaze, but simply to evoke a sense of place at competitive prices. **Piedirosso Versacrum 2011** (● 10,000 bt) is fruity and perfumed, almost spicy, with a tangy, flavorsome finish. It's a perfect Everyday Wine. With its fresh nose of apricots and long finish, **Coda di Volpe Natì 2010** (○ 10,000 bt) is intriguing too. **Catalò 2010** (● catalanesca; 10,000 bt) is more ambitious, but it's still stiff and very balsamic and will take time to develop. We were suitably impressed by **Vesuvio Lacryma Christi Rosso Vigna Lapillo 2010** (● piedirosso, aglianico; 15,000 bt), which offers notes of cherry and pine, but **Vesuvio Lacryma Christi Bianco Vigna Lapillo 2011** (○ falanghina, caprettone; 15,000 bt) seemed slightly below par.

FERTILIZERS organic-mineral, natural manure, green manure
PLANT PROTECTION copper and sulphur
WEED CONTROL mechanical
YEASTS selected, native
GRAPES 100% estate-grown
CERTIFICATION organic

CASTELLABATE (SA)

Maffini

Località Cenito
tel. 0974.966345
www.luigimaffini.it
info@luigimaffini.it

11 ha - 100,000 bt

PEOPLE - The winery came into being in 1974, when Luigi's parents made the first harvest. After graduating in agriculture, Luigi Maffini specialized in enology in Portici, near Naples. There he met his wife, Raffaella Gallo, who has been working with him ever since. Their first labels hit the market in 1995. It was when Professor Luigi Moio subsequently joined the winery that the "Cilento revolution" got underway. Luigi and Raffaella then built a house in Giungano near properties purchased in 2002. Afterwards came a brand-new wine cellar.

VINEYARDS - The oldest vineyard in Castellabate was replanted in 1993: it consists of 1.5 hectares of aglianico vines, whose grapes go into Cenito, and 2.3 hectares of fiano with plants 40 years old. The new seven-hectare vineyard in Giungano, at an altitude of 300-350 meters, is also planted with fiano and aglianico. The soil composition— sandier in Castellabate, rich in gravel and clay at Giungano — is typical of the Cilento area.

WINES - Denazzano 2011 (◉ aglianico; 5,000 bt) is a rosé vinified like a white wine: it's rich in fruit, sapid, pleasant and very, very fresh on account of the early vintage. **Kratos 2011** (○ fiano; 40,000 bt) has notes of white-fleshed fruit and well-balanced acidity with a full-flavored, pleasing finish. **Kleos 2010** (● aglianico; 35,000 bt) is a well-crafted red, drinkable and relatively soft. **Cilento Cenito 2007** (● aglianico; 5,000 bt) has fine notes of ripe fruit supported by sweet spices and hints of toast. In the mouth it's zesty, dry and lubricious.

> **slow wine** CILENTO PIETRAINCATENATA 2010 (○ fiano; 8,000 bt) Aromas of sweet spices set off by a tangy, fresh palate. It's very rare to find a white so generous, so complex. A wine to wait for.

FERTILIZERS natural manure, green manure
PLANT PROTECTION copper and sulphur, organic
WEED CONTROL mechanical
YEASTS selected
GRAPES 20% bought in
CERTIFICATION converting to organics

CASTELLABATE (SA)

San Giovanni

Località Punto Tresino
Parco Nazionale del Cilento
tel. 0974 965136
www.agricolasangiovanni.it
info@agricolasangiovanni.it

4 ha - 20,000 bt

" "Kalòs kai agathòs," the ancient Greeks used to say. It means, "Beautiful and good". Never has a definition been more fitting in the wine world. For this farm is one of the most spectacular in Italy: excellent wines and clean agriculture "

PEOPLE - The winery is situated on a small gulf in the Cilento National Park. Ida Budetta and Mario Corrado have made sacrifices for 13 years to turn it into a paradise on earth.

VINEYARDS - A portion of the four-hectare vineyard looks directly onto the sea and some of the vine rows are just a few meters from the waves. The oldest vines are about 30 years old. A second property sits higher up behind the cellar at an altitude of about 70 meters. Here voracious wild boars are a real danger and, at harvest time, Mario sleeps in a tent among the vine rows to protect the grapes from their forays. The whole estate is embraced by Mediterranean scrub.

WINES - These are very enjoyable wines with a strong sense of place, a natural expression of the grapes they are made from. Hence beauty and goodness. The cellar is overseen by the young Irpinian enologist Michele D'Argenio. **Cilento Aglianico Castellabate 2011** (● 5,000 bt) is salty with a scent of maritime pines and refreshing sweet tannins. Aged solely in stainless steel tanks, **Fiano 2011** (○ 10,000 bt) is as intriguing as it was last year. Tart with notes of thyme and lovely fruity flesh, it's a perfect Everyday Wine. **Fiano Tresinus 2011** (○ 3,500 bt), a selection from the oldest vineyard, has more potent aromas, hints of citrus fruit and alluring tanginess. Thanks to the improved use of wood, **Cilento Aglianico Maroccia 2009** (● 2.000 bt), works better year by year.

FERTILIZERS	natural manure
PLANT PROTECTION	copper and sulphur
WEED CONTROL	mechanical
YEASTS	selected
GRAPES	100% estate-grown
CERTIFICATION	organic

CASTELVENERE (BN)

Antica Masseria Venditti

Via Sannitica, 120/122
tel. 0824 940306
www.venditti.it
masseria@venditti.it

11 ha - 75,000 bt   `10% discount`

" A model cellar that prides itself on its organic agriculture. Not for commercial but for cultural reasons, seeing how the Vendittis were among the first in Italy to adopt the approach in the 1980s "

PEOPLE - Nicola Venditti is an accomplished farmer. One merits worth highlighting is the precision and meticulousness of his work in the field and in the cellar. He is helped by his family, his wife Lorenza and his children Andrea and Serena.

VINEYARDS - Nicola manages numerous parcels, a fact that doesn't make his job easy. The vineyards are all situated near Castelvenere, probably the town with the highest concentration of winemaking in the region. All the vine rows have been converted to the hanging-curtain training system, which involves cutting the vigor and productivity of the vines to adapt them to the very rich soil.

WINES - "Wood never entered my cellar and never will, if you except the beams of the roof," is a concept Nicola likes repeating. Hence his wines stand out for their approachability and simple drinkability. With its explosion of blossom on the nose and salty palate, **Sannio Barbera Barbetta 2009** (● 9,000 bt) was a real discovery. Give it a try: remember that Barbera from the Sannio area has nothing in common with the Piedmontese version. It's a racy Everyday Wine. **Sannio Bianco 2011** (○ grieco di Castelvenere, cerreto; 15,000 bt) is fresh, pleasant and flavorsome. **Falanghina del Sannio Vandari 2011** (○ 15,000 bt) is tangy and quaffable. **Sannio Bacalat 2011** (○ falanghina, grieco di Castelvenere, cerreto; 2,500 bt) is warmer and powerful. The rigorous **Sannio Aglianico Marraioli 2009** (● 8,000 bt) conjures up a strong sense of place. **Solopaca Bosco Caldaia 2008** (● aglianico, piedirosso; 4,000 bt) is made with grapes from an old vineyard.

FERTILIZERS	organic-mineral, green manure
PLANT PROTECTION	copper and sulphur
WEED CONTROL	mechanical
YEASTS	selected, native
GRAPES	100% estate-grown
CERTIFICATION	organic

PONTE (BN)

Nifo Sarrapochiello €

Via Piana
tel. 0824 876450
www.nifo.eu
l.nifo@libero.it

12 ha - 70,000 bt

PEOPLE - The more the years go by the better Lorenzo Nifo gets to know this rural area on the west bank of the River Calore. And the more time passes the harder he finds it to suppress the "peasant" genuineness he has inherited from his folks, Erasmo and Rosa. He now has about 15 grape harvests under his belt and his marriage to Mariangela has anchored him even more to the land of his birth.

VINEYARDS - The vineyards are a sight for sore eyes at any time of the year. Guyot-trained behind the cellar, they climb up to a considerable height. Nestling on the hillside, under the sun for most of the day, the one tended by Erasmo is as pretty as a picture. The clayey-pebbly soil, indispensable for quality grapes, makes the view all the more evocative.

WINES - The falanghina grape goes into three different wines. **Falanghina del Sannio Taburno 2011** (○ 15,000 bt) is floral and fruity, elegant and tangy. **Sannio Falanghina Alenta 2010** (○ 4,000 bt) releases all the potential of the grape, the late harvest boosting its power without diminishing freshness. The sweet version, **Passito Sarriano** (○ 2,500 bt) also brings out all the grape's qualities. The interesting **Sannio Fiano 2011** (○ 2,700 bt) is generous on the nose and smooth and even on the palate. **Aglianico del Taburno Rosato Marosa 2011** (◉ 3,500 bt) is a fruity red.

---

slow wine **AGLIANICO DEL TABURNO D'ERASMO RIS. 2006** (● 3,500 bt) We have to confess that we tasted the wine blind with the Taurasis! Not only did it cut a good figure, it also put its noble Irpinian cousins to the test. Tangy, juicy, deep and packed with character, it epitomizes its terroir perfectly.

FERTILIZERS natural manure, green manure
PLANT PROTECTION copper and sulphur
WEED CONTROL mechanical
YEASTS selected
GRAPES 100% estate-grown
CERTIFICATION organic

POZZUOLI (NA)

Contrada Salandra ◎

Via Tre Piccioni, 40
tel. 0815265258
www.dolciqualita.com
dolciqualita@libero.it

4.5 ha - 15,000 bt   **10% discount**

❝ We were struck by the efforts Giuseppe Fortunato and his wife Sandra Castaldo have made to withstand the onslaught of cement in this corner of the Campi Flegrei. They have achieved their success by making excellent, personality-packed wines ❞

PEOPLE - In the 1990s the Fortunato husband-and-wife team were beekeepers. It was only going to Montalcino in Tuscany in search of honey that they discovered the magical world of wine. It was this eye-opener that drove Giovanni to give up his engineering job and recover his family's vine rows.

VINEYARDS - From the company headquarters it is possible to enjoy a view of the Tyrrhenian Sea which, just a few kilometres away, makes its influence felt. The oldest vines grow near the cellar, while a new vineyard has been planted at a higher altitude further from the sea. A third property, finally, is situated at an altitude of a few hundred meters and is home to almost 200 families of bees. The soil is volcanic with a high percentage of sand. Albeit not certified, the methods used to manage the vineyards are organic.

WINES - We look forward to the moment in which the new plantings start to yield their fruits. In the meantime, we tasted only two wines, both simple but genuine, a direct expression of this fragile terroir of sea, woodland, volcanic soil and native varieties. The brilliant **Campi Flegrei Falanghina 2010** (○ 8,500 bt) is a white wine with a strong Mediterranean spirit with volcanic, sulfurous notes. Tangy and dry on the palate, it is made to go with food. Hence a perfect Everyday Wine. Given its quality and adherence to the characteristics of the grape, the intriguing **Campi Flegrei Piedirosso 2010** (● 6,800 bt) can now be considered a classic. It is un-tannic, moreish and racy. Served at 14°C, it's sure to please.

FERTILIZERS natural manure, green manure
PLANT PROTECTION copper and sulphur
WEED CONTROL mechanical
YEASTS selected
GRAPES 100% estate-grown
CERTIFICATION none

Montevetrano

Località Nido
Via Montevetrano, 3
tel. 089 882285
www.montevetrano.it
info@montevetrano.it

6 ha - 30,000 bt · 10% discount

PEOPLE - A visit to Montevetrano is always a big event. Every time we go there Silvia adds a new piece to the mosaic of her celebrated winery. Twenty years have gone by since she released her first label, but she, Silvia — stubborn and kind, intelligent and always ready to capture the latest novelties in the wine world — never changes. Her companions on this adventure of hers are Mimì La Rocca and Riccardo Cotarella.

VINEYARDS - It was Domenico, nicknamed Mimì, who took us on a tour of the vineyards, which are split into two holdings only a few hundred meters one from the other, in the magnificent hills just a kilometer or two from the Gulf of Salerno. The vineyards are surrounded by woodland and managed using virtually organic methods. The soil is of volcanic origin, the vines are over 20 years old and most of the plots nestle on small terraces. Last but not least, more and more aglianico grapes are being grown.

WINES - "I reckon that today we need lighter wines, much more suited to our frantic way of living." That's what Silvia told us, and it seems to us that the style of her "new" Montevetrano is going precisely in that direction. The label is the stuff of legend — in 1994 Robert Parker dubbed it the "Sassicaia del Sud" — though our impression is that it has lost a bit of weight over the last two years. Montevetrano 2010 (● aglianico, cabernet, merlot; 30,000 bt) has measured sweet fruit on the nose and on the palate. It's rich but not opulent, powerful but not top-heavy. Its aromas are redolent of cherries and the palate possesses all the refreshing acidity needed to support its imposing structure. It is still aged barriques, but the wood is functional to the pursuit of longevity. A Great Wine that ennobles Campanian enology.

FERTILIZERS organic-mineral	
PLANT PROTECTION chemical, copper and sulphur	
WEED CONTROL mechanical	
YEASTS selected	
GRAPES 100% estate-grown	
CERTIFICATION none	

Giuseppe Apicella

Frazione Capitignano
Via Castello Santa Maria, 1
tel. 089 856209
www.giuseppeapicella.it
info@giuseppeapicella.it

8 ha - 50,000 bt · 10% discount

❝ Given the environmental conditions — steep, inaccessible vineyards — and unfavorable social conditions, making wine at Tramonti is no easy matter. The Apicellas soldier on with their work regaling us with excellent bottles from century-old vines ❞

PEOPLE - Apicella is a historic trademark on the Costiera Amalfitana, its first labels dating back to 1977. Today the company is managed by Giuseppe and his children Fiorina and Prisco, who graduated in enology in Turin ten years ago.

VINEYARDS - The vineyards form a natural amphitheater in the Valle di Tramonti, with the mountains in the background and the sea in front. The environment is wild and harsh with small pocket-handkerchief plots and chestnut woods. The Apicella train their old vineyards with the traditional *pergola amalfitana* system. A number of vines grow on their own roots. The real jewel is the vineyard known as 'A Scippata, where the plants, which look more like trees than vines, grow on a system of terraces that has few equals in Italy.

WINES - Apicella's bottles do not aspire to opulence and potency, but rather to subtlety, sense of place and a capacity to capture the spirit of the grapes that go into their making. The pleasant **Costa d'Amalfi Tramonti Rosso 2009** (● aglianico, piedirosso, tintore; 16,000 bt) has aromas reminiscent of ripe cherries while the palate shows soft, sweet tannins. We have chosen the very competitively priced Piedirosso 2011 (● 4,000 bt) as an Everyday Wine. **Costa d'Amalfi Tramonti Bianco Colle di Santa Marina 2011** (○ 4,000 bt) is an ambitious wine that needs time to mature. **Costa d'Amalfi Tramonti Bianco 2011** (○ falanghina, biancolella; 16,000 bt) is flavorsome, floral and fresh, while **Costa d'Amalfi Tramonti Rosato 2011** (◉ 4,000 bt) is a pleasant quaff.

FERTILIZERS organic-mineral	
PLANT PROTECTION chemical, copper and sulphur	
WEED CONTROL mechanical	
YEASTS selected	
GRAPES 10% bought in	
CERTIFICATION none	

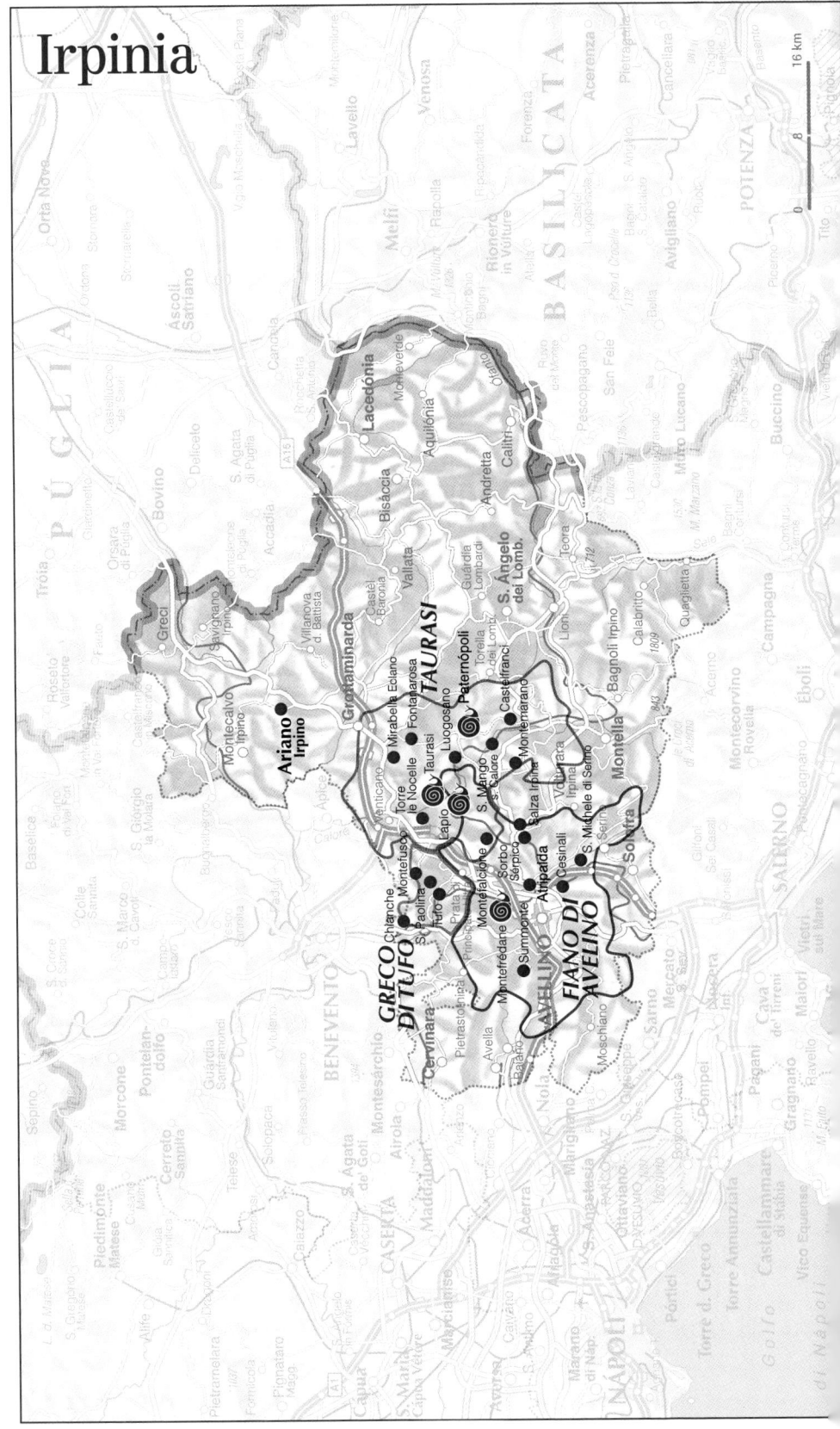
Irpinia

Colli di Lapio

Via Arianiello
tel. 0825 982184
www.collidilapio.it
info@collidilapio.it

Pietracupa

Contrada Vadiaperti, 17
tel. 0825 607418
pietracupa@email.it

---

6 ha - 50,000 bt

" Simple, careful aging of the wines in steel, coherent, painstaking work in the vineyard and a serious sales policy — in other words, the form and substance of a company we have always followed and admired "

PEOPLE - The company run by Clelia Romano with the support of her children Carmela and Federico, is celebrating the birth of granddaughter ... Clelia! It's also presenting a new Fiano, born of friendship with the enologist Angelo Pizzi.

VINEYARDS - The Arianello district is a hill between two rivers, constantly refreshed by the winds of the Terminio massif. The clay-limestone soil, preserved by modest, self-sustenance agriculture, and sharp swings in temperature are the secrets of the success of Lapio's white wines.

WINES - Clelia offers us a top-notch range of wines. **Greco di Tufo 2011** (○ 4,000 bt) has the mineral notes typical of the San Paolo di Tufo zone, where the company buys its grapes. It has acid verve, plenty of body and full-blooded flavor. **Donna Chiara Irpinia Campi Taurasini 2010** (● aglianico; 4,000 bt) is redolent of munchy red berries with a super-zesty palate, refreshing and long. **Taurasi Vigna Andrea 2008** (● 4,000 bt) confirms the quality of the grapes bought in from Venticano. It is fresh, juicy, long and full-bodied with an acidity that promises long life.

> **slow wine** **FIANO DI AVELLINO 2011** (○ 38,000 bt) Luscious and rich in fruit with hints of sage and thyme, a wine that reflects the vintage right from its bouquet. The palate starts racily before following through into a pleasant, long-lasting finish. A wine with a brilliant nose-mouth balance, sense of place and charisma.

7.5 ha - 45,000 bt

PEOPLE - The best you could do, dear reader, would be to visit Pietracupa, Villa Diamante and Vadiaperti all on the same day. They are each only a few meters from the other and the respective owners are very friendly and collaborate intelligently. Jokingly paraphrasing Sergio Leone, we like to call them the Tough, the Intellectual and the Wise. The Tough is Sabino Loffredo, a man of a few, clear words. Like him, his wines are direct and precisely "focused", without pointless superstructures.

VINEYARDS - The vineyards, the clay soil, the plantings and the microclimate of the hill of Montefredane are all concentrated in the Fiano. The Greco is produced with grapes from the vineyards rented at Santa Paolina, an area particularly suitable for the variety. Conventional agronomic methods are used, with the maker's sureness of touch and personality coming through first in the field, then in the bottle.

WINES - We'll never tire of repeating that if a wine superstar exists in Campania, then it's Sabino Loffredo. His wines are a one-man show. This year the prize goes to a sumptuous version of **Greco di Tufo 2011** (○ 16,000 bt). Uber-mineral on the nose with hints of flint, pear and apple, it has a vertical, edgy, acid, deep palate. A racy Great Wine. Exceptional too is **Fiano di Avellino 2011** (○ 16,000 bt), buttery and oaky on the nose with a gutsy, zesty palate. **Cupo 2010** (○ fiano; 4.500 bt), finally, has fantastic flesh and structure with entrancing balsamic notes. This is a wine released exclusively in great vintages whose aging capacity we have often put to the test by retasting old bottles.

FERTILIZERS green manure	FERTILIZERS natural manure, green manure
PLANT PROTECTION copper and sulphur	PLANT PROTECTION chemical, copper and sulphur
WEED CONTROL mechanical	WEED CONTROL mechanical
YEASTS selected	YEASTS selected
GRAPES 10% bought in	GRAPES 100% estate-grown
CERTIFICATION none	CERTIFICATION none

MONTEFREDANE (AV)
Vadiaperti

Contrada Vadiaperti
tel. 0825 607270
www.vadiaperti.it
info@vadiaperti.it

MONTEFREDANE (AV)
Villa Diamante

Via Toppole, 16
tel. 0825 670014
www.villadiamante.eu
villadiamante1996@gmail.com

---

10 ha - 80,000 bt

4 ha - 10,000 bt   `10% discount`

---

66 Spending a few hours at Vadiaperti is tantamount to attending a lecture on agriculture and enology. Here the viticulture is precise and punctilious, fruit of a modern vision of the farming profession 99

PEOPLE - Raffaele Troisi is the "wise man" of the Tre di Montefredane triangle (Villa Diamante, Pietracupa and Vadiaperti). Since 1998, the year his father died, he has shown great maturity and rare agricultural sensitivity.

VINEYARDS - Raffaele works with passion and an analytic eye. His care for his vineyards is influenced by his training as a chemist and any use of systemic products to prevent attacks from parasites is always the consequence of a well-pondered decision. The vineyards fan out over steep terrains. Meticulous zoning of the vineyards serves to exalt in the glass all the subtle nuances that microclimate, soil and exposure conjure up during grape ripening.

WINES - Don't miss the chance to savor the old Vadiaperti vintages, all emblematic of the evolution that the white wines of this area are capable of. **Coda di Volpe 2011** (O 10,000 bt) is a *vin de terroir* with all the distinctive features of the grape. **Fiano di Avellino 2011** (O 28,000 bt) has a fine nose and a gorgeous body. **Greco di Tufo 2011** (O 31,000 bt) is varietal on the nose with a potent bouquet. **Fiano di Avellino Aipierti 2010** (O 3,000 bt) impressed us with its geometric balance. **Greco di Tufo Tornante** 2010 (O 3,000 bt) is fresh and powerful.

> slow wine **CODA DI VOLPE TORAMA 2011** (O 2,500 bt). A wine made with selected grapes, balanced on the nose with tremendous attack and finish. For people like us who believe in the potential of the grape, this is a bottle to be treasured.

PEOPLE - If you're using this book intelligently, not only as a wine guide but also as a travel guide, then don't miss the chance to visit the Montefredane Three: Pietracupa, Villa Diamante and Vadiaperti. In a Sergio Leone movie they'd be called The Tough, the Intellectual and the Wise. The three are different yet complementary and a whistle-stop tour of their wineries is more educational than a treatise on enology. The intellectual is Antoine Gaita, a hard-bitten, cultured winemaker on a passionate quest for the meaning of the term *vin de terroir*.

VINEYARDS - OK, so what is a *vin de terroir*? One of the many possible answers is to be found in wines made with passion by producers such as Antoine, who eschews "easy" labels and leaves no detail to chance. The fiano vineyards are on the hill of Montefredane, at an altitude of 400 meters and enjoy sharp temperature swings. They are managed using organic methods and vertical trellis systems. The grapes for Taurasi are bought in from the Paternopoli district.

WINES - In Gaita's wines, the terroir shines through in space —the hill of Montefredane, the Paternopoli zone, the clay soil, the microclimates — but also in time, in a mental exercise made up of choices pondered year after year in a dialectic rapport with natural phenomena. **Fiano di Avellino Vigna della Congregazione 2010** (O 6,000 bt) is fine on the nose with typical notes and a hint of minerality that turns into perfectly balanced acidity, flavor and body. It's a wine that will express all its distinctive features to the full in the years to come, a hymn to the terroir and, deservedly, a Great Wine. **Taurasi Pater Nobilis 2007** (● 4,000 bt) has an elegant bouquet with delectable hints of forest fruits. The palate has a youthfulness that is sure to develop well.

FERTILIZERS organic-mineral	FERTILIZERS green manure
PLANT PROTECTION chemical, copper and sulphur	PLANT PROTECTION copper and sulphur
WEED CONTROL mechanical	WEED CONTROL mechanical
YEASTS selected	YEASTS selected
GRAPES 30% bought in	GRAPES 3% bought in
CERTIFICATION none	CERTIFICATION organic

Luigi Tecce

Via Trinità, 6
tel. 0827 71375
lteccel@libero.it

4 ha - 7,500 bt

❝ Luigi Tecce is deeply sensitive towards the world of farming. The vineyards are his natural habitat. It was there that he revived his family's winemaking tradition through careful study of the techniques of the past ❞

PEOPLE - Though the company only came into being in 2005, Luigi Tecce had been planning the aglianico of his dreams for years. The results have exceeded all expectations.

VINEYARDS - The old family vineyards are split into small holdings at Paternopoli, one of the best areas for Taurasi, thanks not only to the altitude, which ranges from 500 to 600 meters, but also to their south-facing exposure, which allows the grapes to ripen perfectly. Constant ventilation makes for healthy grapes and the limestone soil rich in volcanic ash adds finesse to the wines.

WINES - During our visit Luigi treated us to all the wines he has ever made! From the first experiment in 2000, to the 2003, to the 2006 which, to cite the one and only Muhammad Ali, "flies like a butterfly and stings like a bee". The common denominator of Tecce's wines is precisely their capacity to live on without fear. Like all the great legends.

slow wine TAURASI POLIPHEMO **2008** (● 4,800 bt) Aged in large chestnut barrels, a stylish label full of freshness and silky tannins with a bouquet of cherries and Alpine mint. A hymn to the terroir of Irpinia.

slow wine CAMPI TAURASINI AGLIANICO SATYRICON **2009** (● 2,500 bt) This was our first taste of the magnificent "younger brother" of Poliphemo, made with grapes from the younger vines in cordon and spur-pruned vineyards. It's hard to find a wine with aromas like these at a better price.

FERTILIZERS green manure
PLANT PROTECTION copper and sulphur
WEED CONTROL mechanical
YEASTS native
GRAPES 100% estate-grown
CERTIFICATION none

Villa Raiano

Località Cerreto
Via Bosco Satrano, 1
tel. 0825 495663
www.villaraiano.com
info@villaraiano.com

20 ha - 250,000 bt

PEOPLE - The team that guides this company — now with a new, functional cellar — is increasingly tight-knit and confident about what it can do. Agronomist Sabino Basso, his brother Simone and their brother-in-law Paolo Sibillo deserve a round of applause. The modernity of the cellar is counterbalanced by a return to a traditional style for white and red wines and the pursuit of sustainable agricultural and vinification practices— especially since the arrival of Fortunato Sebastiano.

VINEYARDS - The main vineyards — 10 hectares of aglianico planted at an altitude of 500 meters on marly, clay soil rich in organic substances and gravel — are in Castelfranci. Another four hectares are in the greco area of Montefusco, higher up at an altitude of 600 metrers where the soil is a mixture of silt, sand and clay. Three hectares of fiano grapes grow on the hill of Montefredane and another three are also planted with fiano round the cellar itself.

WINES - Refreshing, subtle, pleasantly citrusy without superfluous sweetness, **Fiano di Avellino 2011** (○ 50,000 bt) came through the tasting with flying colors. We were so impressed we decided to name it a Great Wine. The two crus aged with lees contact were elegant and rich in vibrant acidity. Made with grapes from Montefredane **Fiano di Avellino Alimata 2011** (○ 3,000 bt) is redolent of flowers and Mediterranean maquis. **Fiano di Avellino Ventidue 2011** (○ 3,000 bt), made with grapes grown at Lapio, is fruitier with hints of pear enhanced by an oaky follow-through. Citrusy, long and dry, **Greco di Tufo Marotta 2011** (○ 3,000 bt) has full body well supported by acidity. The refreshing **Aglianico 2011** (● 60,000 bt) has a pleasant nose of red fruit. **Taurasi Raiano 2008** (● 15,000 bt), the only wine aged in oak, is very rounded in the mouth.

FERTILIZERS natural manure, green manure
PLANT PROTECTION copper and sulphur, organic
WEED CONTROL mechanical
YEASTS selected
GRAPES 15% bought in
CERTIFICATION converting to organics

Feudi di San Gregorio

Località Cerza Grossa
tel. 0825 986611
www.feudi.it
feudi@feudi.it

250 ha - 3,800,000 bt

PEOPLE - The duo formed by Pierpaolo Sirch and Antonio Capaldo, respectively CEO and president of Feudi, treated us to a magnificent tour of the estate. Since 2009 they have been at the helm of a company that has grown exponentially over the last 15 years. Their dedication and energy justify high hopes for the future of a wine cellar that, with 400 growers at its disposal and 60 employees, places the onus on teamwork.

VINEYARDS - Feudi works in three main areas: the one close to the canteen where it grows 40 hectares of fiano vines, now being converted to organics (the first label complete with official certification was produced in 2012); Taurasi, where the aglianico vineyards enjoy excellent exposures; and, last but not least, Cutizzi, a rugged vineyard snatched from the volcanic rock, the most important greco cru.

WINES - The presentation of Feudi's wines was two-sided. We were totally impressed by the whites, a little less by the reds, which have something of an old-fashioned structure. At the forefront was the magnificent **Fiano di Avellino Pietracalda 2011** (○ 30,000 bt) with its aromas of meadow flowers and deep, creamy, mineral palate. It won us over and it deserves to be a Great Wine. Just a rung below was **Greco di Tufo Cutizzi 2011** (○ 40,000 bt), naturally acid and vibrant with a dry, edgy finish. **Greco di Tufo 2011** (○ 900,000 bt) is a state-of-the art bestseller (just note the number of bottles produced). Of the reds our preference went to **Taurasi 2008** (● 60,000 bt), which has a bouquet of graphite and cherry. The modern **Irpinia Serpico 2008** (● aglianico; 15,000 bt) has aromas of toast. **Taurasi Piano di Montevergine Ris. 2007** (● 12,000 bt) is tight and still has to find the right balance.

| FERTILIZERS natural manure, green manure |
| PLANT PROTECTION chemical, copper and sulphur |
| WEED CONTROL chemical, mechanical |
| YEASTS selected |
| GRAPES 50% bought in |
| CERTIFICATION none |

Ciro Picariello   Ⓔ

Località Acqua della Festa
Via Marroni
tel. 0825 702516
www.ciropicariello.com
info@ciropicariello.com

7 ha - 50,000 bt   **10% discount**

PEOPLE - Ciro Picariello was working as a surveyor when his wife Rita Guerriero inherited a small vineyard. Ciro, deciding to set out on a new life, bought other vineyards and devoted himself to viticulture. His style is simple and effective: fermentation and aging in steel tanks, care and attention in the vineyard and an extra year in the cellar for wines before release. Success hasn't changed Ciro, who is now busy restructuring the cellar.

VINEYARDS - The company's vineyards are situated in Montefredane — three hectares of clay and marl soil at an altitude of 550 meters — and Summonte — four hectares of clay soil rich in gravel covered by a stratum of volcanic residue at an altitude of about 600 meters. In both cases the climate is harsh in winter and cool in summer with sharp temperature swings between day and night.

WINES - **Irpinia Fiano 2011** (○ 10,000 bt) is a tremendous white, an explosion of pear on the nose and in the mouth, very tangy, long and fresh, the embodiment of an exceptionally favorable vintage. Made from grapes bought in from Prata, **Greco di Tufo 2011** (○ 6,000 bt) has a very refreshing, sulfureous nose. The classic method **Brut Contadino** (○ 3,000 bt) made with fiano grapes, is fresh, citrusy and mineral — an excellent debut! **Irpinia Aglianico Zi Felicella 2010** (● 5,000 bt) has a forthright, approachable palate.

> **slow wine** **FIANO DI AVELLINO 2010** (○ 15,000 bt) The bouquet is long, pleasant and complex with a slightly smoky follow-up and a whiff of mushrooms. The palate is fresh and dynamic and echoes the bouquet. The finish is racy, slightly almondy. A serious full-bodied white for drinking with food made with a well-judged blend of grapes from Montefredane and Summonte. A wine that has taken just a few years to become a great classic.

| FERTILIZERS green manure |
| PLANT PROTECTION copper and sulphur |
| WEED CONTROL mechanical |
| YEASTS selected |
| GRAPES 10% bought in |
| CERTIFICATION none |

TAURASI (AV)

Antonio Caggiano

Contrada Sala
tel. 0827 74723
www.cantinecaggiano.it
info@cantinecaggiano.it

28 ha - 150,000 bt

66 Antonio Caggiano is the very soul of Taurasi, and we owe the relaunch of this noble red to his intelligence and perseverance. He is also at the forefront in the promotion of the single vineyards. In short, he's an institution 99

PEOPLE - 1994 saw the release of Taurasi Macchia dei Goti, born of the meeting in France between Antonio Caggiano and youngster Luigi Moio, who returned to Italy from Bordeaux at the older man's insistence. The cellar-museum was completed in 2011.

VINEYARDS - The vineyards are all situated at Taurasi. Macchia dei Goti is a six-hectare vineyard overlooking the River Calore at an altitude of 300 meters with a south-western exposure. The density of the vines is high with 5,000 cordon and spur-trained plants per hectare. The other old vineyard is Salae Domini, over 25 years old. Thanks to the favorable local climate, the harvest takes place from the end of October to the first 10 days of November.

WINES - The excellent **Irpinia Campi Taurasini Salae Domini 2009** (● aglianico; 8,000 bt) has a complex nose with aromas of forest fruits, balsamic undertones and a thousand other nuances. In the mouth, distinctive freshness balances the alcohol. The wonderful **Taurasi Vigna Macchia dei Goti 2008** (● aglianico; 13,000 bt) offers red berries preserved in alcohol and deep notes of undergrowth. The bouquet is soft with good supporting acid and a velvety texture. Nicely long too, this is one of the finest red wines in Campania, hence a Great Wine. **Greco di Tufo Devon 2011** (○ 23,000 bt) is a pleasant wine with definite apricot on the nose and a long, sweetish palate. **Irpinia Aglianico Taurì 2011** (● 35,000 bt) exudes scents of red fruit and spices with well-crafted tannins. **Fiano di Avellino Béchar 2011** (○ 25,000 bt) is a decent wine too.

FERTILIZERS	organic-mineral, natural manure, green manure
PLANT PROTECTION	chemical, copper and sulphur
WEED CONTROL	mechanical
YEASTS	selected
GRAPES	35% bought in
CERTIFICATION	none

TAURASI (AV)

Contrade di Taurasi

Via Municipio, 39
tel. 0827 74483
www.contradeditaurasi.it
info@cantinelonardo.it

5 ha - 20,000 bt   **10% discount**

66 This is a company that has invested intelligently and farsightedly in clean agriculture and in the promotion of its crus and grapes in danger of extinction such as grecomusc' 99

PEOPLE - The last vintage marked a turnaround for Contrade di Taurasi, thanks to the commitment of the Lonardo family and Professor Giancarlo Moschetti. The first two crus from Taurasi were released on the market after long preparatory work on native yeasts and the terrains.

VINEYARDS - Two and a half hectares are at Case d'Alte, the district in which the cellar is situated, at an altitude of about 400 meters on loose volcanic soil. Another hectare and a half is located slightly further down at Macchia dei Goti, towards the River Calore. A hectare is at Coste, at an altitude of 320 meters on clay and limestone soil. The vineyards are managed using organic methods and the vines are trained using the *starseto taurasino* and vertical trellis systems. All grow aglianico, while the grecomusc' comes from Mirabella and Bonito.

WINES - **Grecomusc' 2010** (○ roviello bianco; 2,500 bt) has all the character of the great white wines of Irpinia. It offers aromas of citrus fruits, pear, sage, spices and Mediterranean scrub. The awesome bouquet is well supported by acidity. **Aglianico 2009** (● 8,000 bt) has traditional style with length and definite aging potential. This year the spectacular, didactic Taurasi 2007 crus made their debut. **Taurasi Coste 2007** (● 1,300 bt) is well supported by freshness. It's very long but still slightly reticent on the nose.

> **slow wine** **TAURASI VIGNE D'ALTO 2007** (● 1,300 bt) A label of unique character which brings out the qualities of this noble wine to the full. Scented, complex, intriguing, rich and drinkable, it's a hymn to its terroir.

FERTILIZERS	none
PLANT PROTECTION	copper and sulphur
WEED CONTROL	mechanical
YEASTS	native
GRAPES	100% estate-grown
CERTIFICATION	converting to organics

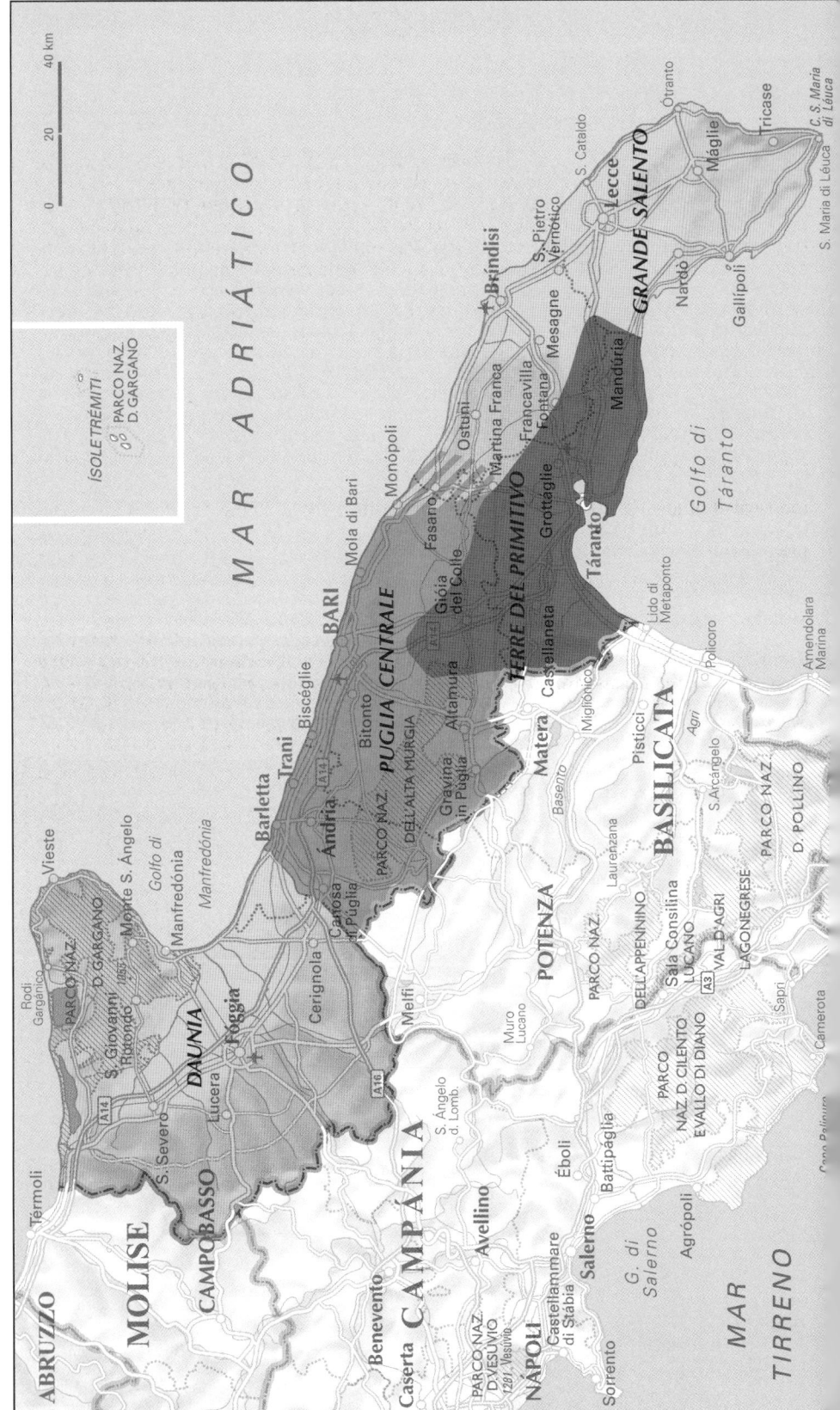

PUGLIA

Even in vast, variegated Puglia, the 2011 vintage was marked by a drastic fall in production — 24.1 per cent lower than last year — but the region still came third in the Italy league table (source: Istat). Reds and rosés enjoyed clear predominance and, for the first time ever, DOP and TGI wines accounted for more than half the total (56 per cent), a record that warrants satisfaction. The Salento is again the top area for both quantity and quality thanks to its high- standard viticulture. Reds made with the negroamaro grape are full of Mediterranean warmth and capable of maturing for many years. Though their main admirers are mostly abroad, they are now very much back in the national limelight. In recent years Primitivo has enjoyed growing success in Italy too, thanks to the new styles developed alongside the traditional ones at Manduria and subsequently at Gioia del Colle. Even on the Adriatic coast of the Salentine Peninsula, between Brindisi and Lecce, the grape is giving life to bigger and bigger wines. Further north, between Bari and Foggia, driven on by the monovarietal vinifications of the mid-1990s, work continues on developing the identity of the uva di Troia grape. Quality-wise, the rosé and sweet wines reached peaks of quality everywhere, while the ever improving whites are exhibiting a personality all of their own as a result of the revival of local grape varieties. Another positive signal is the proliferation of collaborations between wine companies and public and private research institutes. The prices even of top wines are still very reasonable, especially compared to those in other regions.

Vintages tasted
If the white and rosé wines are vintage, the region's reds are released in "ready-to-drink" and cellarable versions after three to five years and even more. Many producers hold back the release times of their most prized reserves, and rightly so. Given the specific characteristics of the different zones, it's impossible to give the various vintages single definitions. Generally speaking, after two excellent years — 2007 and 2008 — 2009 proved very difficult, especially in the Salento. Albeit unevenly, the 2010 vintage delivered first-rate wines, while 2011 is very promising indeed, as the improved rate of return on production costs has already suggested.

snails 🐌

235	GIANCARLO CECI
236	I PÀSTINI
237	PAOLO PETRILLI
240	AGRICOLE VALLONE
244	POLVANERA
244	GIANFRANCO FINO
245	ATTANASIO

bottles 🍾

236	ALBERTO LONGO TERRAVECCHIA
239	AZIENDA MONACI
240	L'ASTORE MASSERIA
241	FRANCESCO CANDIDO
243	CHIAROMONTE
245	MORELLA

coins €

235	CEFALICCHIO
239	ROSA DEL GOLFO
243	PLANTAMURA

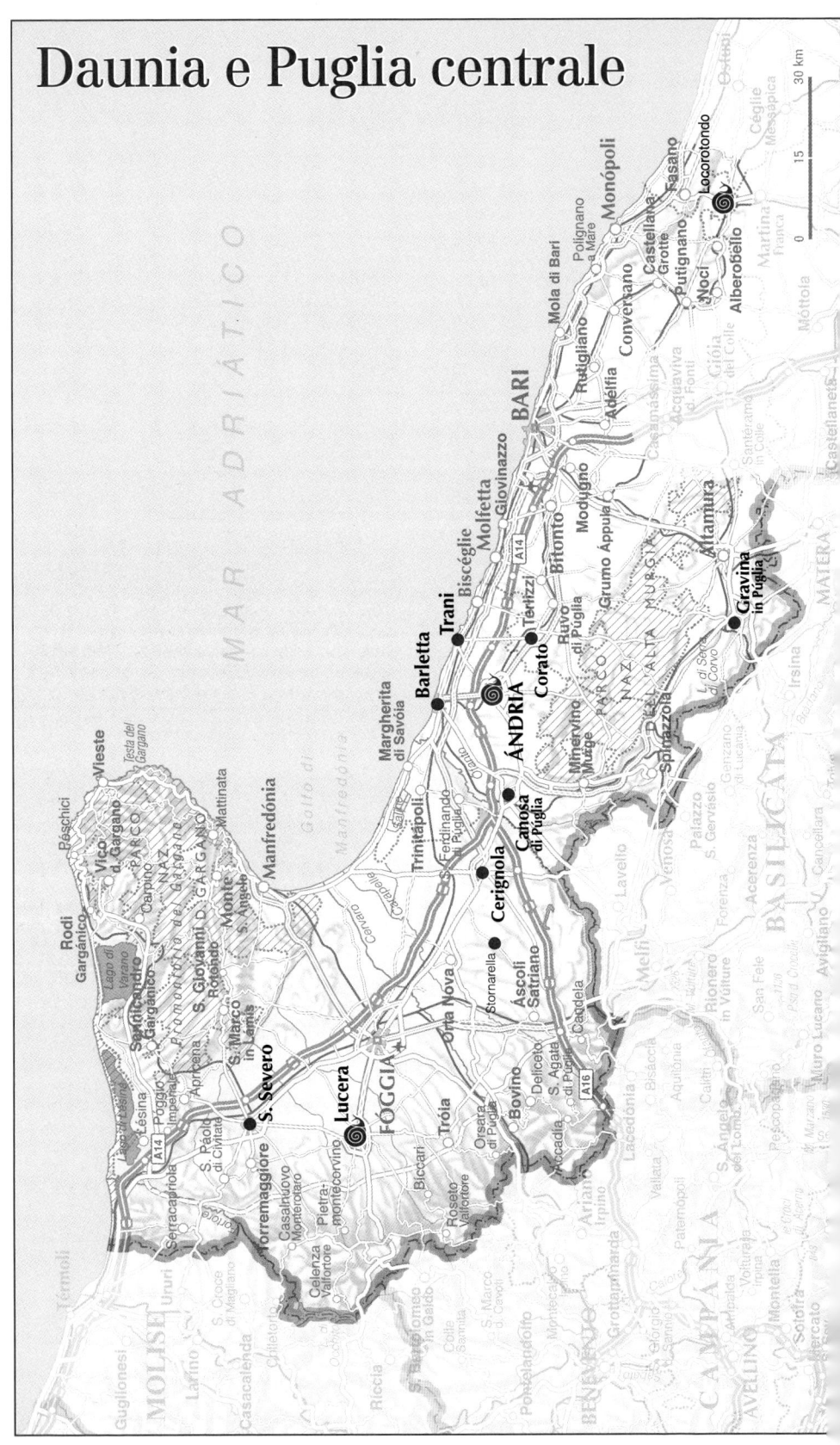

Daunia e Puglia centrale

ANDRIA (BA)

Giancarlo Ceci

Contrada Sant'Agostino
tel. 0883 565220
www.agrinatura.net
info@agrinatura.net

70 ha - 500,000 bt   **10% discount**

" Ever since 1988, when he graduated and took over the famly farm, Giancarlo Ceci has devoted his life to natural wine production "

PEOPLE - Wine production is a relatively recent addition to the farm's activities, and the consultant enologist Lorenzo Landi is charged with following it step by step. The modern cellar, which has been generating its own energy for some time now, is managed by the brilliant young enologist Sebastiano Matarazzo. Tommaso Sagaramella takes painstaking care of work in the vineyard.

VINEYARDS - Giancarlo Ceci's farm covered an area of 350 hectares of which 70 given over to winegrowing. In 2011 it converted from its traditional organic methods to biodynamics: hence cover cropping, the use of preparations made from discards from the processing of the farm's vegetables and limited treatments to avoid devitalizing the soil. All this, plus a well-ventilated position and limestone, gravelly terrains ensure healthy wines with mineral aromas.

WINES - All the wines stand out for their elegance and balance. We were impressed by **Castel del Monte Felice Ceci 2009** (● uva di Troia; 6,000 bt) made with a selection of grapes from the San Nicola vineyard. It is well-developed and august with clearcut but fine tannins. **Castel del Monte Parco Grande 2011** (● 23,000 bt) is a blend of uva di Troia, aglianico and montepulciano, full-bodied with plenty of fruit, complex and long on the palate, with a very strong sense of place. **Castel del Monte Parco Marano 2010** (● 40,000 bt) is aged in wood casks and has alluring aromas, good structure and a long, tonic finish. **Castel del Monte Bombino Bianco 2011** (○ 20,000 bt) is fresh and tangy with notes of iodine. The seductive **Moscato di Trani Dolce Rosalia 2011** (○ 1,000 bt) is beautifully balanced.

FERTILIZERS compost, biodynamic preparations, green manure
PLANT PROTECTION copper and sulphur
WEED CONTROL mechanical
YEASTS selected
GRAPES 100% estate-grown
CERTIFICATION biodynamic, organic

CANOSA DI PUGLIA (BAT)

Cefalicchio

Contrada Cefalicchio
tel. 0883 642123
www.cefalicchio.it
info@cefalicchio.it

27 ha - 100,000 bt

PEOPLE - The Rossi family has been living in the Canosa area since the 17th century and practicing viticulture since 1870. Today the work is shared out between Fabrizio, the vineyard and cellar manager, and Nicola and Fili, sales and external relations managers. Advocates of biodynamics, which they have been practicing since 1992, the three are assisted by enologist Pasquale Pastore, whose job it is to preserve the fruits of the earth in the cellar. The impeccable welcome merits a mention apart.

VINEYARDS - The main body of the vineyard — on a surfaced marine plate composed of mixed soils — surrounds an elegant country house and restaurant, which uses the produce of the kitchen garden, olive grove and orchard in its kitchens. The woodland and the use of 20 horses for manure ensure animal and vegetable biodiversity and combine to form the ecosystem prescribed by the principles of biodynamics.

WINES - The wines of Cefalicchio reflect the terroir with limited use of sulfites and the use of native yeasts selected in collaboration with Isvea. The thoroughbred **Rosso Canosa Romanico Ris. 2008** (● 13,000 bt) shows off fruit and spices and big tannins, as well as great aging potential. Moving on to the whites, the best of the bunch by a whisker is Castel del Monte Bombino Bianco Lefkò 2011 (○ 5,000 bt), delicate and elegant, with flowery tones and good complexity — a fine Everyday Wine. **Jalal 2011** (○ moscato bianco; 7,000 bt) is as good as ever with pronounced minerality and length. Both interesting and competitive are the two new wines produced without added sulfites: **Cefalicchio Rosso 2011** (● uva di Troia, montepulciano; 6,000 bt) and **Cefalicchio Rosato 2011** (● montepulciano; 6,000 bt). Last but not least, **Castel del Monte Nero di Troia Ponte della Lama 2011** (● 8,000 bt) is well-crafted.

FERTILIZERS compost, biodynamic preparations, green manure
PLANT PROTECTION copper and sulphur
WEED CONTROL mechanical
YEASTS native
GRAPES 100% estate-grown
CERTIFICATION biodynamic

LOCOROTONDO (BA)

I Pàstini

Via Italo Balbo, 22/24
tel. 080 4313309
www.ipastini.it
Info@ipastini.it

12 ha - 100,000 bt — **10% discount**

❝ Lino Carparelli is the heart and soul of this winery. After numerous and important experiences as an enologist, about 15 years ago he decided to restore impulse to the grapes of his native Valle d'Itria. The project has been a resounding success ❞

PEOPLE - On his own and with the help of old farmers, Lino sourced the material necessary for the plantings and launched the experiments that allowed him to consolidate his production, especially of whites, surprising in a region as sunny as Puglia.

VINEYARDS - The explanation for this apparent contradiction is the position of his vineyard on limestone soil at an altitude of 350 meters with a north-south exposure and constant ventilation, and the ripening of the grapes at the start of October, which makes it possible to benefits from temperature swings in September. The company isn't certified but it takes almost obsessive care of the soil and the vines to achieve very healthy grapes in the vineyard.

WINES - Traditional white wines that revive the splendors of Locorotondo in the 1980s. We witnessed their unexpected longevity for ourselves in a vertical of every vintage (2003-2011) of Rampone. Only native yeasts are used for the fresh, tangy, flowery **Rampone 2011** (○ minutolo; 20,000 bt) which, as the years go by, is taking on almost riesling-like elegant, mineral tones. An experiment of maceration on the skins for four days was attempted for **Cupa 2011** (○ bianco di Alessano; 12,000 bt), a wine of tannic tones and great complexity. The fresh and mineral **Locorotondo Antico 2011** (○ verdeca, bianco di Alessano, minutolo; 10,000 bt) is filled with great tradition. **Faraone 2011** (○ verdeca; 20.000 bt) is smoky and citrusy with light acidity. **Elogio alla Lentezza 2006** (● aleatico; 6,000 bt), whose name translates as "In Praise of Slowness", is a delicate sweet wine.

FERTILIZERS	organic-mineral
PLANT PROTECTION	copper and sulphur
WEED CONTROL	chemical, mechanical
YEASTS	selected, native
GRAPES	100% estate-grown
CERTIFICATION	none

LUCERA (FG)

Alberto Longo Terravecchia

Contrada Padulecchia
S.P. Lucera-Pietramontecorvino, km 4
tel. 0881 539057
www.albertolongo.it
info@albertolongo.it

35 ha - 130,000 bt

PEOPLE - At his modern, efficient company, Alberto Longo's collaborators include his volcanic dad Giovanni and his seraphic mum Adele. But he can also rely on a competent, consolidated staff consisting of Antonio Quaranta, the vineyard manager, Michele Di Gregorio and Roberto Cardillo, the cellar managers, plus external consultants such as Enzo Corazzina, an agronomist, and Graziana Grassini, an enologist. At the moment, Alberto is involved in research on native yeasts with Professor Spano of the University of Foggia.

VINEYARDS - The vineyards are situated on relatively flat land and are divided into two properties: one at the Fattoria Cavalli farm, here the soil is more calcareous, the other at the Masseria Celentano farm where it is sandier. Both enjoy good ventilation and temperature swings thanks to the proximity of the sea and the uplands of the Gargano peninsula. The vines are cordon spurtrained and have contained yields. The grapes are divided between native and international varieties.

WINES - The company's wines, which exhibit all the mineral characteristics of the soils, are modern in style and generally balanced and clean-cut. This year's champion bottle was **Cacc'e Mmitte di Lucera 2010** (● 33,000 bt), well-balanced, long and spicy with vegetal undertones — an Everyday Wine. Excellent too was **Le Cruste 2010** (● nero di Troia; 10,000 bt), with its bouquet of black berries and sweet spices, supported by elegant tannins. The admirable **Le Fossette 2011** (○ falanghina; 21,000 bt) has flowery, fruity tones and richness of flavor with supporting acidity. The most ambitious wine of all, the spicy **4.7.7 2009** (● syrah; 10,000 bt), rests in casks for 14 months. The two wines made with negroamaro grapes, **Capotosto 2010** (● 15,000 bt) and **Donnadele 2011** (⊙ 10,000 bt) are both well-crafted.

FERTILIZERS	organic-mineral
PLANT PROTECTION	copper and sulphur
WEED CONTROL	chemical, mechanical
YEASTS	selected
GRAPES	100% estate-grown
CERTIFICATION	none

LUCERA (FG)

Paolo Petrilli

Località Motta Caropresa
tel. 0881 523982
lamotticella@libero.it

SAN SEVERO (FG)

d'Araprì

Via Zannotti, 30
tel. 088 2227643
www.darapri.it
info@darapri.it

11 ha - 19,000 bt

12 ha - 80,000 bt   `10% discount`

" After tomatoes, Paolo Petrilli now applies his single-minded character to the production of wine. His secret is rigorously close control of the entire production chain "

PEOPLE - Paolo is helped in his work by agronomist Filippo Giannone, enologist Andrea Boaretti and cellar manager Giuseppe Sirena.

VINEYARDS - The vineyard consists of a single plot of 11 hectares on a slight slope at an altitude of 300 meters near the small town of Lucera. The soil is mostly limestone and is very pale in color. Here proximity of the Gargano peninsula favors considerable temperature swings. Cordon-trained and spur-pruned, the grape varieties are either native or have grown locally for a long time. Over the last few years zoning work has made it possible to single out the best portions of the vineyard.

WINES - This year Petrilli had an interesting surprise up his sleeve, selecting one of the 12 Guerro casks to produce the fine, elegant **Nero di Troia 2010** (● 250 bt), a wine of great personality and character, different from **Guerro 2010** (● uva di Troia; 2,800 bt), beautifully balanced and long with potent, elegant tannins. Excellent wines too are **Cacc'e Mmitte di Lucera Agramante 2010** (● 7,500 bt), which has a clear-cut, elegant nose, great freshness and equilibrium, and **Cacc'e Mmitte di Lucera Ferraù 2010** (● 1,800 bt), enfolding and elegant, very long with silky tannins. Another exciting new entry is the warm, sweetly spicy, full-bodied **Montepulciano 2010** (● 250 bt). **Fortuita 2010** (● varie uve rosse; 4,500 bt) is more structured and complex.

PEOPLE - "Let's hope that our children are driven by the same enthusiasm and passion that we were way back in 1979, and that they put their money on the terroir and the local white bombino grape refermented with the "classic method". That's what Ulrico Priore said when he welcomed us. Ulrico is one of the co-founders — the others are Girolamo D'Amico and Louis Rapini — of this splendid, now well-consolidated company, a feather in the cap of the winemaking not only of the Capitanata area but also of the entire region.

VINEYARDS - The vineyards, located in the countryside round San Severo, are vertical-trellised and enjoy a favorable microclimate, which protects against frost, and good ventilation, which helps preserve the grapes from disease. The clay-limestone soil, which gives the slightly sloping terrains their typical yellow-gray color, is never fertilized. The small walled vineyard in San Severo is ready to yield its first fruits.

WINES - In compliance with the "Ethical Charter of D'Araprì Spumantes", the wines are a blend of artisanship and sound production style, which allows them to enjoy good health for years. We had proof of this when we tasted the 2000 Brut Rosé, which has a distinctly recognizable style. Paradigmatic for the category is the flowery **M. Cl. Pas Dosé** (○ bombino bianco, pinot nero; 12,000 bt). Also as good as ever was **M. Cl. Brut Rosé** (◉ montepulciano, pinot nero; 15,000 bt), which has an attractive onion-peel color. **M. Cl. Brut** (○ bombino bianco, pinot nero; 25.000 bt) is well-styled and drinkable.

slow wine **M. Cl. Gran Cuvée XXI Secolo 2007** (○ pinot nero, bombino bianco, montepulciano; 10,000 bt) An exceptional vintage selection with complex aromas of dried fruit, sweet spices and yeasts with a sharp, tangy palate and lingering length.

FERTILIZERS none
PLANT PROTECTION copper and sulphur
WEED CONTROL mechanical
YEASTS selected
GRAPES 100% estate-grown
CERTIFICATION organic

FERTILIZERS none
PLANT PROTECTION copper and sulphur
WEED CONTROL mechanical
YEASTS selected
GRAPES 100% estate-grown
CERTIFICATION none

Grande Salento

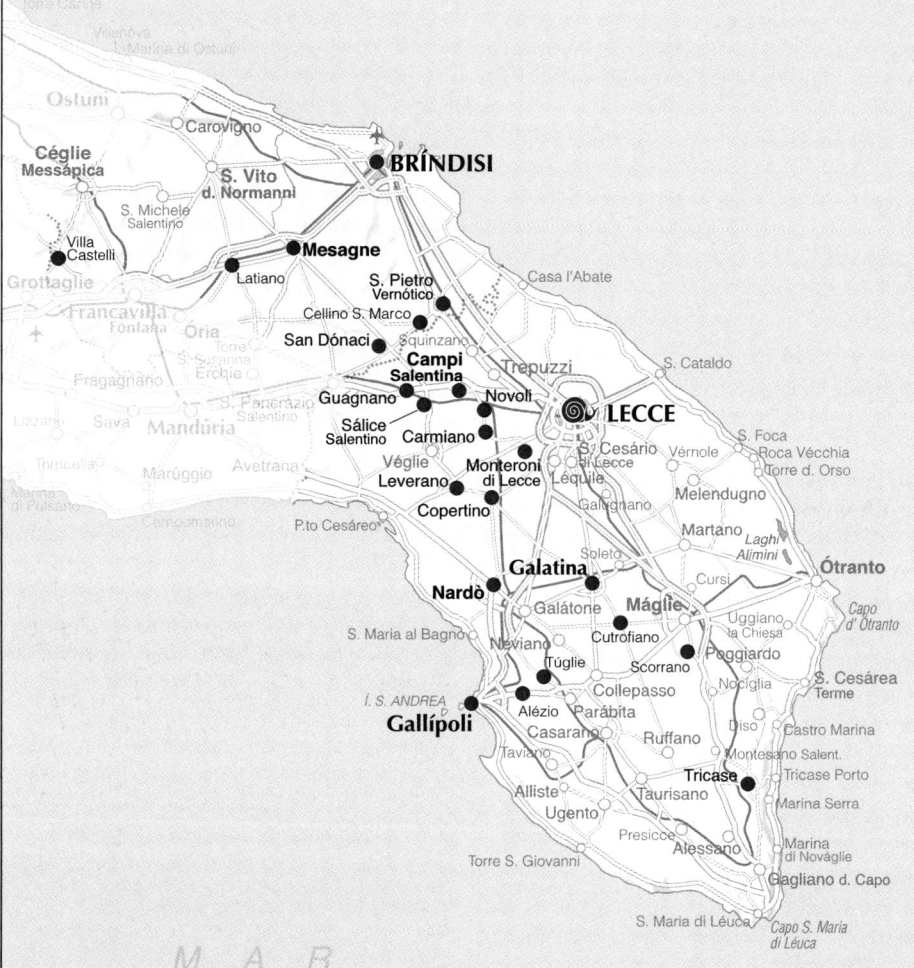

MAR ADRIÁTICO

Torre Canne
Villanóva
Marina di Ostuni

Ostuni
Ceglie
Messápica
S. Michele
Salentino
Carovigno
S. Vito
d. Normanni
BRÍNDISI
Casa l'Abate

Villa
Castelli
Grottaglie
Francavilla
Fontana
Oria
Torre
S. Susanna
Erchie
S. Pancrázio
Salentino
Fragagnano
Mandúria
Latiano
Mesagne
S. Pietro
Vernótico
Cellino S. Marco
San Dónaci
Squinzano
Campi
Salentina
Guagnano
Novoli
Sálice
Salentino
Carmiano
Véglie
Monteroni
di Lecce
Trepuzzi
S. Cataldo
LECCE
S. Cesário
di Lecce
Vérnole
S. Foca
Roca Vécchia
Torre d. Orso
Léquile
Galugnano
Melendugno
Lizzano
Sava
Tonnicella
Marúggio
Avetrana
Leverano
Copertino
Marina
di Pulsano
Campomarino
P.to Cesáreo
Galatina
Nardò
Galátone
Martano
Laghi
Alimini
Soleto
Cursi
Ótranto
Capo
d' Ótranto
S. Maria al Bagno
Naviano
Túglie
Máglie
Cutrofiano
Scorrano
Uggiano
la Chiesa
Nocíglia
S. Cesárea
Terme
Í. S. ANDREA
Gallípoli
Alézio
Parábita
Casarano
Taviano
Collepasso
Ruffano
Diso
Montesano Salent.
Castro Marina
Tricase
Tricase Porto
Marina Serra
Alliste
Ugento
Taurisano
Presicce
Alessano
Marina
di Nováglie
Torre S. Giovanni
S. Maria di Léuca
Gagliano d. Capo
Capo S. Maria
di Léuca

MAR

IÓNIO

0   10   20 km

Rosa del Golfo €

Via Garibaldi, 56
tel. 0833 281045
www.rosadelgolfo.com
calo@rosadelgolfo.com

---

40 ha - 300,000 bt

PEOPLE - The company came into being about two centuries ago but it only named itself for its top, now internationally famous wine, Rosa del Golfo, in 1988. It has always been owned by the Calò family and is currently managed by the dynamic, affable Damiano, the last of the dynasty. He is helped in the cellar by enologist Angelo Solci. The company offices are in Albizzate (Varese), the productive headquarters in Alezio (Lecce).

VINEYARDS - The vineyards are situated in communes in the province of Lecce, such as Alezio, Parabita, Sannicola and Salice Salentino. Not all are owned by the company, but the grapes that are bought in are all monitored directly during their growth process. An interesting recent acquisition was that of a plot with an old bush-trained vineyard from which the grapes for the finest wines used to be bought.

WINES - Rosé wines have always been important for Rosa del Golfo. We tasted three different versions: **Rosa del Golfo 2011** (☉ negroamaro, malvasia; 115,000 bt), elegant and delicate with fruity, tangy notes; **Vigna Mazzì 2011** (☉ negroamaro, malvasia; 8,000 bt), spicy, fruity and leisurely after brief aging in oak barrels; and, finally, the soft and refreshing **M. Cl. Brut Rosé** (☉ negroamaro, chardonnay; 10,000 bt). The company's other wines are no less impressive. They include the every agreeable **Scaliere 2010** (● negromaro; 40,000), **Portulano 2009** (● negroamaro, malvasia; 20,000 bt), which have warm, spicy notes redolent of fruit preserved in alcohol, and the balanced, lingering **Quarantale 2008** (● negroamaro, primitivo, malvasia; 5,000 bt).

Azienda Monaci

Località Tenuta Monaci
tel. 0832 947512
www.aziendamonaci.com
vini@aziendamonaci.com

---

36 ha - 220,000 bt   `10% discount`

PEOPLE - Formed in 1995, Azienda Monaci is the crowning achievement of Severino Garofano. As enologist at the most important wineries on the Salentine Peninsula, he has been instrumental in asserting negroamaro as one of the grapes with the greatest potential in all the South of Italy. One of Severino's merits is that he has left increasing latitude to his son Stefano, who oversees the cellar, and daughter Renata, the sales manager.

VINEYARDS - The company owns 16 hectares of vines and rents about 20, all supervised by agronomist Antonio Protezione. Spurred cordon — proudly described by Severino as "propped-up-bush" — is the prevalent training system. The use of pesticides and other plant protection products is used to a bare minimum and the soil is fertilized with green manure from fava beans.

WINES - Azienda Monaci identifies increasingly with the negroamaro grape, which stars in all its wines. It has also had the courage to abandon chardonnay, hence the production of white wine. **Girofle 2011** (☉ 30,000 bt), a traditional Salentine rosé, pulls out all the characteristics of the negroamaro grape and once again comes through with flying colors. **Copertino Eloquenzia 2009** (● 100,000 bt) is elegant, well-structured and soft, while malvasia nera makes **I Censi 2008** (● 30,000 bt) pleasantly fruity.

> **slow wine** **LE BRACI 2006** (● 10,000 bt) Severino's belief in the huge potential of negroamaro is borne out by this wine. Produced with grapes dried on the vine, it is a perfect synthesis of complexity, elegance, thick flesh, well-knit tannins and total pleasure.

FERTILIZERS organic-mineral	FERTILIZERS green manure
PLANT PROTECTION copper and sulphur	PLANT PROTECTION copper and sulphur
WEED CONTROL chemical, mechanical	WEED CONTROL mechanical
YEASTS selected	YEASTS selected
GRAPES 100% estate-grown	GRAPES 50% bought in
CERTIFICATION none	CERTIFICATION none

CUTROFIANO (LE)
L'Astore Masseria

Località L'Astore
Via Giuseppe di Vittorio, 1
tel. 0836 542020
www.lastoremasseria.it
info@lastoremasseria.it

LECCE
Agricole Vallone
Via XXV Luglio, 7
tel. 0832 308041
www.agricolevallone.it
info@agricolevallone.it

---

24 ha - 90,000 bt   `10% discount`

161 ha - 420,000 bt

PEOPLE - Achille Benegiamo's main job used to be in medicine, but his great love of the land drove him to invest in his family's farm. He was also spurred on by the passion of his son Paolo, who now runs this, one of the most exciting new wineries on the Salentine scene, with his brothers Stefano and Luca. Pietro Mandorino is charged with the agronomic management, while Cosimo Cataldi attends to communication.

VINEYARDS - Almost all the international grapes that the winery began with have been replaced over the years by native ones, grafted onto pre-existing vines. All this involved a not inconsiderable cost — and a sacrifice — but it served to exploit the roots of the plants, endowing the grapes now used for vinification with great quality, despite their being so young.

WINES - As proof of the effectiveness of the work carried out to date, the average quality of the wines is improving all the time. The well-crafted **Filimei 2010** (● negroamaro; 12,000 bt) is very pleasant and approachable thanks to the fragrance of its fruit. We also liked **Massaro Rosa 2011** (☉ negroamaro; 5,000 bt), rich in fruit and flowery, and the savory **Krita 2011** (○ malvasia bianca; 10,000 bt). We closed with the spicy **Jema 2010** (● primitivo; 12,000 bt) and the austere, elegant **L'Astore 2009** (● aglianico; 7,000 bt).

> **slow wine** **ALBERELLI DI NEGROAMARO 2008** (● 3,500 bt) It was a thrill to taste this well-structured, elegant and ever so long wine, made with late-harvest grapes from a single parcel of bush-trained vineyard planted in 1947. Only a few thousand numbered bottles were produced.

66 History, tradition and personality — these are the distinctive features of this prestigious company, which managed to stick to healthy tradition and wise viticulture at a moment in time when the world around it was moving in different directions 99

PEOPLE - The company is run by sisters Vittoria and Maria Teresa Vallone, who have always charged the managerial side to the specialist Donato Lazzari. The staff are all local and the enologist is Grazia Grassini.

VINEYARDS - The company's vineyards are divided into a number of plots, all in the province of Brindisi: to the south, the seven hectares of Tenuta Caragnuli near San Pancrazio Salentino, where negroamaro vines almost 70 years old grow, and the larger Vigna Flaminio, near the city itself; to the north, Tenuta Serranova, whose young vineyards, surrounded by dry-stone walls, look onto the nature reserve of Torre Guaceto. Management is not organic but very respectful of the environment.

WINES - Vallone has a responsible style, which is why this year there are no Graticciaia and Vigna Castello, both still aging. In the meantime, two other classics performed well: **Salice Salentino Vereto Ris. 2008** (● 6,000 bt) is spicy and soft, while **Brindisi Rosso Vigna Flaminio Ris. 2008** (● 6,000 bt) is more austere, gutsy and fruity. Lots of bottles of the full-bodied **Salice Salentino Vereto 2010** (● 150,000 bt) have been released at a very reasonable price. **Fiano Tenuta Serranova 2011** (○ fiano; 3,000 bt) convinces with its finesse and rigor. **Corte Valesio 2011** (○ sauvignon, chardonnay; 40,000 bt) is fresh and enjoyable.

> **slow wine** **BRINDISI ROSATO VIGNA FLAMINIO 2011** (☉ 15,000 bt) A classic rosé from the great Salento tradition. Exemplary for its typicality, freshness and crisp drinkability.

FERTILIZERS compost, green manure	FERTILIZERS green manure
PLANT PROTECTION copper and sulphur, organic	PLANT PROTECTION copper and sulphur
WEED CONTROL mechanical	WEED CONTROL chemical, mechanical
YEASTS native	YEASTS selected
GRAPES 100% estate-grown	GRAPES 100% estate-grown
CERTIFICATION organic	CERTIFICATION none

Castello Monaci

Contrada Monaci
tel. 0831 665700
www.castellomonaci.it
castello.monaci@giv.it

150 ha - 2,000,000 bt

PEOPLE - Castello Monaci is controlled by the large Gruppo Italiano Vini, but is still rooted to its terroir thanks to the presence and passion of its Salentine owners, the Seracca-Memmo family, whose Vitantonio still oversees the vineyards. The winery is managed by Andrea Lonardi, experienced despite his youth, while Sergio Leonardo supervises the cellar. Luigi Seracca, also young, is the marketing manager.

VINEYARDS - Castello Monaci's many hectares are split up into two main properties: one in Torchiarolo, a few kilometers from the sea in the province of Brindisi, the other in the countryside round Salice Salentino, where the company is based. Under Andrea Lonardi's management, the company continues to promote exclusively native grapes, such as verdeca.

WINES - The company's wines are characterized by freshness and pleasurability. The cream of the crop is undoubtedly Negroamaro Maru 2011 (● 120,000 bt), which offers beautifully enjoyable fruit without perverting the distinctive traits of the negroamaro grape — it's an excellent Everyday Wine. Then comes **Malvasia Nera Medos 2011** (● 24,000 bt), fruity and fresh with plush tannins. Albeit rich in flavor and strong in structure, the two flagship wines — **Salice Salentino Aiace Ris. 2009** (● 15,00 bt) and the austere **Primitivo Artas 2010** (● 22,000 bt) — are nonetheless enjoyably drinkable, both tonic, plush and wonderfully harmonious. **Rosato Kreos 2011** (⊙ negroamaro; 70,000 bt) is tangy and refreshing, walking the wire between the minerality of its marine notes and the rotundity of the fruit.

Francesco Candido

Via Diaz, 46
tel. 0831 635674
www.candidowines.it
candido@candidowines.it

140 ha - 1,800,000 bt

PEOPLE - Alessandro Candido is sure his company's current approach, based on, among other things, the conversion to organic methods and research on yeasts, represents the future of winemaking. His undisputed experience and skill — witness the institutional positions he has held and holds — make him one of Puglia's agricultural experts. He is backed by a large team of collaborators, including the agronomist Emanuele De Milito and the enologist Donato Lanati.

VINEYARDS - The vineyards, situated between the provinces of Brindisi and Lecce, are trained with the bush and spurred cordon systems. Some are up to 50 years old and rest on different soils, from rich clay to dry limestone. They haven't been fertilized for years and local grape varieties grow side by side with experimental, non-native cultivars.

WINES - The Candido style translates into modern elegance in every label. A top performer is the fleshy, sensual **Cassio Dione 2006** (● negroamaro, primitivo; 10,500 bt), while **Salice Salentino Rosato Le Pozzelle 2011** (⊙ 75,000 bt) adds extra luster to the Salentine rosé tradition. The flowery **Tenuta Marini 2011** (○ fiano; 18,000 bt) has reached accomplished levels of expression. The velvety but rigorous **Immensum 2008** (● negroamaro, cabernet sauvignon; 15,000 bt) and the fruity, tangy **Salice Salentino Bianco Portafalsa 2011** (○ 18,000 bt), are both well-crafted wines.

> **slow wine** **DUCA D'ARAGONA 2006** (● negroamaro, montepulciano; 65,000 bt) A historic label for Salentine winemaking and a perfect synthesis between modernity and tradition. An aristocratic, very stylish wine, beautifully drinkable after five years' aging.

FERTILIZERS manure pellets	FERTILIZERS none
PLANT PROTECTION copper and sulphur	PLANT PROTECTION copper and sulphur
WEED CONTROL mechanical	WEED CONTROL mechanical
YEASTS selected, native	YEASTS selected
GRAPES 5% bought in, wine bought in	GRAPES 40% bought in
CERTIFICATION none	CERTIFICATION converting to organics

Terre del Primitivo

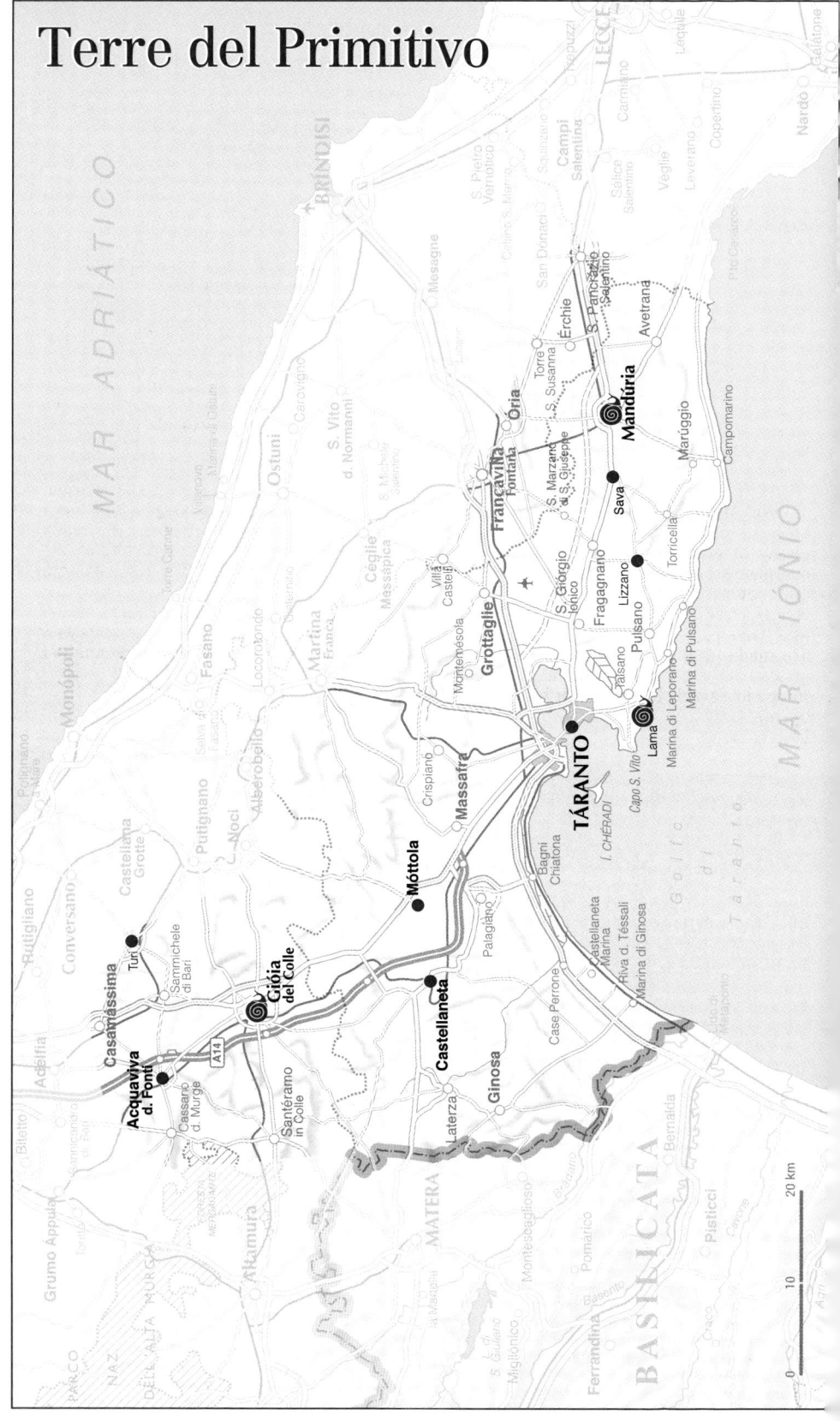

Chiaromonte

Strada Vicinale dell'Annunziata
tel. 080 758575
www.vinichiaromonte.com
nicola.chiaromonte@tin.it

---

25 ha - 60,000 bt

PEOPLE - Nicola Chiaromonte, enologist and heir to his family's winemaking tradition, has been running the company in businesslike fashion for more than ten years: inspired by his mother's precious advice, his vision is one of a gradual increase in output. The project to recover the old headquarters in the old center of Acquaviva is proceeding to plan. In the cellar we couldn't help but notice a functional photovoltaic plant, there to supply the company's energy requirement.

VINEYARDS - The vineyards are well ventilated and planted on calcareous soil with plenty of gravel, hence well drained. No complementary irrigation is practiced and only natural manure is used. Primitivo accounts for 80% of the grapes grown, aleatico and fiano for the rest. The oldest vineyards are made up of primitivo vines of no fewer than 50 years old, and are hand-worked manually, largely by the owner himself. Biodynamic practices are currently being experimented with.

WINES - The owner's enterprising character is mirrored in that of his wine, all reliable and full of personality. First rate as ever — so much so that we've elected it as a Great Wine —Primitivo Gioia del Colle Chiaromonte Ris. 2009 (● 2,400 bt), is opulent and assertive and sure to last. **Primitivo Gioia del Colle Muro Sant'Angelo Contrada Barbatto 2009** (● 7,000 bt), the company's other beautifully textured selection, is tannic with just the right tannins and very fine aromas. Albeit less challenging, **Primitivo Gioia del Colle Muro Sant'Angelo 2009** (● 10,000 bt) is very good just the same. Two big surprises are the new **Rubedo 2010** (● primitivo; 6.000 bt), full-bodied with a sweet finish, and the white **Kimìa 2011** (○ fiano minutolo; 7,000), fresh and perfumed. **Elè 2010** (● primitivo; 25,000 bt) is, once again, a pleasure to drink.

FERTILIZERS	natural manure
PLANT PROTECTION	copper and sulphur
WEED CONTROL	mechanical
YEASTS	selected, native
GRAPES	100% estate-grown
CERTIFICATION	organic

Plantamura

€

Via Santa Candida, 1
tel. 080 3430044
www.viniplantamura.it
info@viniplantamura.it

---

8 ha - 50,000 bt

PEOPLE - Plantamura is a small family cellar that is growing year by year thanks to the dedication of Mariangela Plantamura and her husband Vincenzo Maggialetti, who oversee cellar and vineyards personally. Despite recent extensions, the company still has an artisan feel about it and, in the cellar, still uses an old-fashioned wood press. The enologist is Fabrizio Tomas, the agronomist Stefano Borsa.

VINEYARDS - The company's three vineyards cover a total area of just over four hectares and are eight to 12 years old and are situated at an altitude of about 360 meters. The clay-calcareous soil with groundwater that nourishes the soil in dry years. The vines are cordon spur-trained, bush-trained in the older vineyards. As of this year the company is currently replanting another 20-year-old, four-hectare vineyard.

WINES - This year we are reviewing only two of the company's three wines. **Gioia del Colle Primitivo Etichetta Rossa 2010** (● primitivo; 20,000 bt), aged for 12 months in steel tanks and made with grapes from the vineyards in the Rosati and Parco Largo districts, exhibits hints of fruit, enjoyable tannins and a sinuous finish. Gioia del Colle Primitivo Etichetta Nera 2010 (● primitivo; 20,000 bt) is superlative, a Great Wine if ever there was one. Half the liquid mass is left in second- and third-hand barriques for about six months, hence the resulting spicy, fruity aromas. The palate is warm, voluptuous and pleasurable. Next year Primitivo Riserva Etichetta Bianca will also be released.

FERTILIZERS	manure pellets
PLANT PROTECTION	copper and sulphur
WEED CONTROL	mechanical
YEASTS	selected
GRAPES	20% bought in
CERTIFICATION	organic

GIOIA DEL COLLE (BA)

Polvanera

Contrada Marchesana, 601
tel. 080 758900
www.cantinepolvanera.com
info@cantinepolvanera.it

LAMA (TA)

Gianfranco Fino

Via Fior di Salvia, 8
tel. 099 7773970
www.gianfrancofino.it
gianfrancofino@libero.it

---

40 ha - 200,000 bt

9.5 ha - 18,000 bt   `10% discount`

---

66 The agronomic and enological competence and human qualities of Filippo Cassano explain the rapid progress and success of this wine company, refounded in 2003 following the recovery of old primitivo vineyards, and managed using organic methods 99

PEOPLE - Going to see Filippo Cassano in his cellar, hewn out of the rock amid the splendid vineyards, is always a thrill.

VINEYARDS - Some of the vineyards surround the cellar in the Marchesana district, always a prolific primitivo growing area, between Gioia del Colle and Acquaviva delle Fonti. Cordon-trained and spur-pruned, the vineyard planted 12 years ago sinks its roots in the limestone through a thin stratum of lean soil. The top wines come from vineyards over 60 year's old.

WINES - Polvanera's style is unmistakable: fruity, fresh, potent but drinkable wines. All the wines display a strong sense of place and are aged exclusively in stainless steel. **Gioia del Colle Primitivo 16 2009** (● 13,000 bt) is balsamic and mineral, deep and seductive. The young Gioia del Colle Primitivo 14 2009 (● 50,000 bt) is fresh and fruity, an excellent Everyday Wine. The brilliant **Minutolo 2011** (○ fiano minutolo; 50,000 bt) is aromatic with balanced flavor and structure. Impressive too are the two rosés: **M. Cl. 2011** (◉ 20,000 bt), a lively, enjoyable brut made with primitive racemes, and **Rosato 2011** (◉ 20,000 bt), made with aleatico, primitivo and aglianico grapes.

> slow wine GIOIA DEL COLLE PRIMITIVO **17 2009** (● 13,000 bt) A wine that has been a model of consistency over the years. This version displays standout fruity scents, aromatic complexity and elegant balsamic and mineral notes with a long, velvety finish.

FERTILIZERS none
PLANT PROTECTION copper and sulphur
WEED CONTROL mechanical
YEASTS selected
GRAPES 100% estate-grown
CERTIFICATION organic

66 Gianfranco Fino's adventure in winemaking got underway fewer than ten years ago when he bought an old bush-trained vineyard. Since then it has progressed by leaps and bounds and is now a standout phenomenon in the sector in Puglia 99

PEOPLE - The impressive string of accolades the company has received in the course of its brief history renders merit to the painstaking work in the vineyard and cellar of Gianfranco and his wife Simona Natale, an irreplaceable collaborator. Worth mentioning is their purchase of new, larger offices in Sava.

VINEYARDS - After the purchase of its first vineyard, 80 years old, the company bought new properties with small and old primitivo and negroamaro vines, all scattered round the area between Manduria and Sava. In collaboration with research institutes, the company has also planted new vineyards at incredibly high densities and with the use of different biotypes. The vines are bedded in red soil with white rock outcrops.

WINES - Once again this year we are unable to review Negroamaro Jo since the 2010 vintage was limited to a few thousand bottles which sold out quickly, whereas the 2009 failed to come up to expectations and, commendably, not released. Primitivo di Manduria Es 2010 (● 15,000 bt) is once more very successful, combining typical power and structure with a taste and aromatic profile of elegance, drinkability and just the right tannins. These qualities and freshness anticipate the wine's great longevity. The broad spectrum of aromas spans from fruit to spices, which once more reveals masterful use of oak. An unquestionably Great Wine.

FERTILIZERS none
PLANT PROTECTION copper and sulphur
WEED CONTROL mechanical
YEASTS selected
GRAPES 100% estate-grown
CERTIFICATION none

MANDURIA (TA)

Attanasio

Via per Oria, 13
tel. 099 9737121
www.primitivo-attanasio.com
info@primitivo-attanasio.com

7.2 ha - 14,000 bt

❝ Luca Attanasio is proceeding on his journey through the world of wine with determination and exemplary maturity. Proof of the fact is his natural vineyard management based on manual work and his deft enological touch ❞

PEOPLE - Over the last year, two important events have marked Luca's life: the tenth anniversary of bottling and his wedding. He relies on the precious advice of Bruno Garofano in the cellar and Alfredo Tocchini in the vineyard.

VINEYARDS - The small vineyards are situated on various sites round Manduria, some on red, pebbly soil, others on richer black soil rich in clay. The vines are all bush-trained true to consolidated local tradition and are at least 40-50 years old. This year Luca extended his property with the acquisition of another small plot of old vines in the Colonna district.

WINES - We'll never tire of defining the style of these bottles as "classic modernity": meaning traditional vinification, medium maceration on the skins, aging in wooden casks for dry wines. Looking forward to the new version of the passito, we were impressed by the brilliant dry version of **Primitivo di Manduria 2009** (● 13,000 bt), finer and more elegant than previously, but as alcoholic as ever with velvety tannins well balanced by a freshness that makes for a complex mouthfeel, despite a certain opulence.

slow wine PRIMITIVO DI MANDURIA DOLCE NATURALE **2008** (● 1,000 bt) A wine at the top of an often inexplicably neglected typology. It offers a generous suite of aromas, incredible structural richness and perfect balance between sugars and acidity.

MANDURIA (TA)

Morella

Via San Pietro, 65
tel. 099 9791482
www.morellavini.com
azag.morella@libero.it

---

15 ha - 20,500 bt   10% discount

PEOPLE - Attracted by all the old bush-trained vines scattered round the area — though without snubbing the cordon spurred system — more than ten years ago, Lisa Gilbee of Australia and Gaetano Morella of Barletta decided to invest in and dedicate all their time to the terroir of Manduria. Their adventure has forged on since then and this year they plan to build a new 15-hectare estate following the criteria of biodynamics.

VINEYARDS - The owners feel that all the bush-trained vines should be saved and guarded jealously. In the meantime, they are on the lookout for new opportunities. Their vineyards are situated at the center of one of the best winegrowing areas in the area. They have an average age of 50 years and are worked by the skilled hands of Gaetano, who follows biodynamic principles, though without applying for certification.

WINES - The tiny cellar is reminiscent of some of those you see in France. Of the wines up for tasting we recommend **Primitivo Old Wines 2009** (● 3,000 bt), which has notes of bramble and cherry with balanced, enfolding tannins, and **Primitivo La Signora 2009** (● 3,000 bt), potent and nicely warm. Mezzogiorno 2011 (○ fiano; 2,500 bt) is an agreeable, lightly aromatic white. The two blends — **Primitivo Malbek 2009** (● 7,000 bt) and **Primitivo Negroamaro 2009** (● 5,000 bt) exhibit, respectively, enjoyable hints of undergrowth enhanced by the use of barriques, and notes of brambles and red fruit balanced by French oak from the barrel.

FERTILIZERS green manure
PLANT PROTECTION copper and sulphur
WEED CONTROL mechanical
YEASTS selected
GRAPES 100% estate-grown
CERTIFICATION none

FERTILIZERS biodynamic preparations, green manure
PLANT PROTECTION copper and sulphur, organic
WEED CONTROL mechanical
YEASTS native
GRAPES 100% estate-grown
CERTIFICATION none

BASILICATA

A small region with a great history: unspoiled woodland, the castles of Frederick II, sheer sea cliffs, villages in which time seems to have stood still and Mount Vulture, one of the cradles of Southern Italian viticulture. This is Basilicata, a magnificent land but incredibly without a voice in and excluded from the Italian wine revolution, even though it did play a leading role in the past. It is here in fact that aglianico, a star of the first magnitude in the national grape firmament and the very base of regional wine-making, was born.

In 2010 production — 125 hectoliters — dropped by 13 per cent with respect to the previous year, much more than anywhere else in Italy. The area planted with vines fell by 2 per cent in 2010 and the figure now stands at 4,455 hectares. Yet one light shines through in all this darkness and it's a bright one: we refer to the DOC and TGI shares of total production, respectively 16.5 per cent and 12.8 per cent against 11.8 per cent and 11 per cent in 2005.

Another surprising new phenomenon is the growth of white wines, whose share of total production shot up from 17 per cent to 35 per cent in just one year. It's a positive signal only in part insofar as it also reflects the hard time Aglianico is going through on the market.

So there's no hiding from the fact that the region's winegrowing is experiencing arguably the worst period in its recent history, paying the price of rash stylistic decisions (the use of wood has yet to be totally assimilated), lack of self-confidence and an unstrategic commercial vision, symbolized by the confusion between DOC and DOCG. It's in this context that the baton is being passed over to a number — still, alas, small — of producers firmly convinced of the need to deliver high quality and wines of great character. The signs that emerged from our tastings were encouraging in this regard — a breath of fresh air for the future of winemaking in the "green lung" of the Italian South.

 **snails**

248 ELENA FUCCI

 **bottles**

248 MUSTO CARMELITANO

coins €

249 GRIFALCO DELLA LUCANIA

BARILE (PZ)

Elena Fucci

Contrada Solagna del Titolo
tel. 0972 770736
www.elenafuccivini.com
info@elenafuccivini.com

MASCHITO (PZ)

Musto Carmelitano

Via Nenni, 23
tel. 0972 33312
www.mustocarmelitano.it
info@mustocarmelitano.it

6 ha - 17,000 bt

4 ha - 20,000 bt   **10% discount**

66 Elena Fucci's is quite a story. Just 30, she's regarded as one of the best wine producers in the South of Italy. Tenacious and competent, she has revolutionized a denomination with a single label 99

PEOPLE - We were accompanied on our visit by Elena and her father Salvatore Fucci, who helped her produce her first Aglianico in 2000. At the ripe old age of 86, Elena's grandfather Generoso still works in the vineyard too.

VINEYARDS - The main building is surrounded by tidily arranged vine rows. The present cellar is somewhat cramped, but in 2013 a new, larger one will be added. The property stands on volcanic soil whose strata augment the complexity of the wines, at an altitude of 600 meters above sea level. The vines differ in age. One of the vineyards was planted in the 1950s and five spectacular new terraces were added in 1996.

WINES - 2010 was a cool year with abundant spring rain. The grapes were harvested on November 3, then macerated and fermented for ten days in steel tanks. **Aglianico del Vulture Titolo 2010** (● 16,000 bt) rests for one year in barriques, then for another in the bottle. The bouquet has scents of morello cherries and the palate has a potent and juicy overture, followed by astonishing depth. The lingering finish is packed with sweet tannins. We enjoyed the wine's uncomplicated straightforwardness. No numbing sweetness and or immoderate alcohol here. If the expression weren't too hackneyed, the wine's supreme elegance might tempt us to describe it as a "feminine" take on Aglianico. During our visit, we tasted the 2009 vintage. Its blatant, harsh tannins suggest it is less ready than the 2010. But it'll certainly be worth waiting for.

PEOPLE - The company set up by Francesco Carmelitano and his uncle Giuseppe Musto has just celebrated 60 years in the business. At the outset they simply sold their grapes and unbottled wine, but with the new generation came a step forward in quality. The winery as it is now came into being in 2007, also the year of the first harvest with wine in bottles with labels. Thanks to the family's experience and the skill of enologist Fortunato Sebastiano, the company produces traditional wines of great character and a recognizable sense of place.

VINEYARDS - The oldest vineyard, situated at Pian del Moro at an altitude of 600 meters, dates back almost 90 years. It consists of an hectare of clay soil planted with high- and bush-trained aglianico vines. At a lower altitude in the Serre district, high-trained vineyards stretch over about two hectares. One portion was planted almost half a century ago, the other 25 years ago. The third vineyard is situated in the Varnavà district.

WINES - **Maschitano Bianco 2011** (○ moscato; 1,500 bt) is a wonderfully charismatic wine with a scented nose and a dry, salty palate. A wine in the same mold is **Maschitano Rosato 2011** (◉ aglianico; 2,000 bt), a full-bodied wine, thirst-quenching, long and enjoyable. Both are vinified and aged in cement vats, whereas **Maschitano Rosso 2010** (● 8,000 bt), a drinkable, well-crafted aglianico, is aged in steel only. **Aglianico del Vulture Pian del Moro 2010** (● 4,000 bt) is made with grapes from the oldest vineyard. Aged in old casks, its fruit integrates perfectly with the wood.

> **slow wine** **AGLIANICO DEL VULTURE SERRA DEL PRETE 2010** (● 8,000 bt) Aged in wood and cement, an essential wine that's more earthy than fruity. Tangy, very fresh and long, it has a satisfying, clean finish. It won us over with its capacity to evoke Lucania and its very reasonable price.

FERTILIZERS green manure	FERTILIZERS natural manure, green manure
PLANT PROTECTION copper and sulphur	PLANT PROTECTION copper and sulphur
WEED CONTROL mechanical	WEED CONTROL mechanical
YEASTS selected	YEASTS selected
GRAPES 100% estate-grown	GRAPES 100% estate-grown
CERTIFICATION none	CERTIFICATION organic

RIONERO IN VULTURE (PZ)

Cantine del Notaio
Via Roma, 159
tel. 0972 723689
www.cantinedelnotaio.it
info@cantinedelnotaio.it

VENOSA (PZ)

Grifalco della Lucania €
Località Pian di Camera
tel. 0972 31002
www.grifalco.com
grifalcodellalucania@email.it

30 ha - 230,000 bt	10% discount

14 ha - 70,000 bt	10% discount

PEOPLE - In the late 1990s, Gerardo Giuratrabocchetti and Luigi Moio were the leading lights in what can be considered a veritable renaissance in Vulture winemaking, turning out bottles with a modern, elegant style backed by a dynamic commercial approach and a corporate image in step with the times. They've come a long way since then. The old cellars in the center of Rionero now welcome many visitors and a large, functional new facility was built recently at Ripacandida.

VINEYARDS - Gerardo, son of a notary public, used to work in livestock breeding and farming. The knowledge he picked up helped him in his choice of properties, scattered about between Ginestra, Maschito, Barile, Ripacandida and Rionero. The vineyards grow on black volcanic soil at altitudes of 350-500 meters, are well drained and have variable exposures. The management was certified organic right from the outset, but Gerardo, never content, has now moved on to biodynamics, again properly certified.

WINES - L'Atto 2010 (● aglianico; 85,000 bt) is a fantastic wine that also happens to offer good value for money: it has well integrated fruit and wood, a leisurely but spacious mouthfeel and a clean, fresh finish. An Everyday Wine not to be missed. **Aglianico del Vulture Il Repertorio 2009** (● 20,000 bt) is once again traditional in style, tangy with oaky nuance. **Aglianico del Vulture La Firma 2009** (● 25,000 bt) has a fruity nose and *matière* well supported by acidity. **Aglianico del Vulture Il Sigillo 2009** (● 25,000 bt), made with drying grapes, denotes sweetness balanced by balsamic notes and silky tannins. Cherries and violets are to the fore in **Rogito 2010** (◉ aglianico; 15,000 bt), a rosé matured in wood. Last but not least, the passito **Autentica 2009** (○ moscato, malvasia; 6,000 bt) is supremely elegant.

PEOPLE - Grifalco derives its name of two birds: the gryphon, symbol of Montepulciano, where the Piccin family, the owners, comes from, and the falcon, symbol of Mount Vulture. This is truly a family affair: Fabrizio is the agronomist and enologist, his wife Cecilia Naldoni is the sales manager, and their son Lorenzo, an enology student, lends his dad a hand. The enterprise is administered by the ever-present Maria Madio.

VINEYARDS - About 10 years ago, the Piccins bought five hectares of land in the Pian di Camera district near Venosa and built a modern cellar on it with an underground bottle and barrel cellar. They also own hillside properties, all at an altitude of around 500 meters: seven and a half hectares with vines 15-60 years old in the San Martino di Maschito district and one and a half hectares with vines 50-60 years old at Ginestra. All the terrains are volcanic and part of the Aglianico del Vulture DOCG.

WINES - The company produces only Aglianico and, overall, its bottles are elegant and enjoyable. Bosco del Falco and Damaschito, from the oldest vineyards of Maschito and Ginestra, are produced only in very good years. **Aglianico del Vulture Bosco del Falco 2007** (● 4,500 bt) has excellent aromas of undergrowth and truffle and a juicy, fruity mouth. **Aglianico del Vulture Damaschito 2008** (● 5,000 bt) has delicate scents of aromatic herbs and along, opulent palate. Succulent and exhilarating in the mouth, the excellent Aglianico del Vulture Grifalco 2010 (● 20,000 bt) is again of a very high standard — a true Everyday Wine. **Aglianico del Vulture Gricos 2010** (● 35,000 bt) has reasonable length.

FERTILIZERS natural manure, compost, green manure	FERTILIZERS natural manure, green manure
PLANT PROTECTION copper and sulphur	PLANT PROTECTION copper and sulphur
WEED CONTROL mechanical	WEED CONTROL mechanical
YEASTS selected	YEASTS native
GRAPES 30% bought in	GRAPES 100% estate-grown
CERTIFICATION organic, biodynamic	CERTIFICATION organic

CALABRIA

In the old days they used to speak about Calabria in the plural — "Le Calabrie", the Calabrias. Maybe this is the key to understanding this stupendous region where it only takes 30 minutes — or a rapid change of perspective or view — to move from mountains to sea, or from one sea to another.

The region's different winemaking areas are following different logics. 2010 recorded a drop in production from 400,000 hectoliters to 323,000 hectoliters (-17%). This statistic is affected by the province of Crotone, meaning Cirò. Here we believe that, with the change in the production discipline to allow for the use of international grapes, a wrong answer has been given to the problem. Interpreted in the traditional manner, in fact, the gaglioppo grape produced some of the most pleasant surprises for this edition of the guide. A small group of producers are showing that they really believe in this approach and we are obviously supporting them. Another new trend was the increased production of white wines, which now account for 17 per cent of the total with respect to 11 per cent five years ago. DOC and TGI wines still represent only a tiny portion, respectively of 17 per cent and 11 per cent.

The most dynamic province was again Cosenza, also the one to produce most wine, which ranges from the magliocco-based reds and the whites of the Pollino and the Sila — increasingly complex and mineral — to the fantastic moscato of Saracena, which scored once more with its most representative cellars.

In conclusion, a couple of notes on style. Some producers still seem enamored of the idea of feisty, sweet, invasive wood. Yet it's now clear to anyone that, when they dispense with this diehard cliché, Calabrian wines hold fantastic surprises in store for enthusiasts, expressing great character and sense of place. It's our hope that the wineries that are banking on elegance and balance will set the trend in future.

CIRÒ MARINA (KR)

Sergio Arcuri

Via Roma Vico III, 3
tel. 0962 31723
www.vinicirosergioarcuri.it
info@vinicirosergioarcuri.it

CIRÒ MARINA (KR)

'A Vita

S.S. 106, km 279,800
tel. 0962 31044
www.avitavini.it
avita.info@gmail.com

3.75 ha - 10,000 bt

PEOPLE - The Arcuri family has grown gaglioppo in Cirò since 1880, when they used to transport the grapes on donkey- or mule-back. In 1973 Giuseppe set up a cellar to vinify his own grapes and sell unbottled wine. The turnaround came in 2009, when his sons Sergio and Francesco decided to begin bottling. Cement tanks, vinification techniques with reduced environmental impact, consciously healthy production — these are the cornerstones of this up-and-coming cellar.

VINEYARDS - The well-ventilated vineyard is situated at an altitude of about 100 meters and managed directly by Giuseppe and his sons using organic methods. Two hectares are bush-trained with yields of 70 quintals or slightly less. The vines are all old, some planted in 1945, others in 1980. The rest of the property, cordon-trained and spur-pruned, dates from 2005. The soil is composed of clay, silt and red earth.

WINES - Cirò Rosso Cl. Sup. Aris 2009 (● 7,500 bt) is made with grapes from the old-bush trained vines. After fermentation, it ages first in stainless steel tanks for a year and a half, then in the bottle for three months. The non-concentrated style makes for a simple, fresh, very elegant palate with prevalent notes of fruit and earthiness and a long, clean finish that leaves a pleasant tanginess in the mouth. You can tell from our description that we liked the label! For us it's a good Everyday Wine. The enjoyable rosé **Il Marinetto 2011** (⊙ gaglioppo; 2,500 bt), made with early-harvested grapes from the younger vineyard, is bereft of cloying sweetness; it is instead essential and would go well with seafood and vegetable dishes. The two wines are deceptively simple, but actually epitomize all the ancient, consolidated tradition of the Cirò terroir.

---

8 ha - 15,000 bt

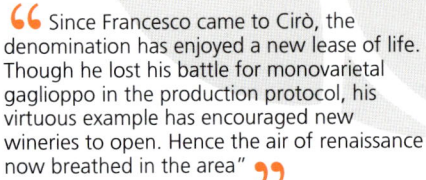

❝ Since Francesco came to Cirò, the denomination has enjoyed a new lease of life. Though he lost his battle for monovarietal gaglioppo in the production protocol, his virtuous example has encouraged new wineries to open. Hence the air of renaissance now breathed in the area" ❞

PEOPLE - Francesco De Franco is a doctor twice over, in Architecture and in Enology. The second degree, the one that corresponds to his real vocation in life, came in handy when he took over the family vineyards, to which he added new properties in 2004.

VINEYARDS - The estate is made up of four distinct vineyards. Halfway up the hillside at Sant'Anastasia two south-facing hectares of clayey-chalky soil are planted with gaglioppo. The four-hectare vineyard in the Muzzunetto district faces north at an altitude of 50-100 meters. The two are situated on either side of the Lipuda valley, where vines have always thrived. To complete the picture, half a hectare of land is given over to greco bianco at Frassà and just over one hectare at Fego, down by the sea.

WINES - Cirò Rosso Cl. Sup. 'A Vita 2010 (● 8,000 bt) is again a joy to drink. The bouquet is rich in fruit, the palate fresh, lingering and tangy. With its bouquet of Mediterranean scrub, **Cirò Rosso Cl. Sup. 'A Vita Ris. 2008** (● 6,000 bt), presented as a Riserva since the first harvest, puts one in mind of traditional gaglioppo.

> **slow wine** **Rosso 2009** (● 3,500 bt) This new blend of magliocco (30%) and gaglioppo (70%) was produced at the Fego vineyard. We liked it a lot. It has fresh cherry, beautiful smoky notes and a lingering, generous palate with a pronounced finish. It verges on perfection!

FERTILIZERS green manure
PLANT PROTECTION copper and sulphur
WEED CONTROL mechanical
YEASTS native
GRAPES 100% estate-grown
CERTIFICATION organic

FERTILIZERS green manure
PLANT PROTECTION copper and sulphur
WEED CONTROL mechanical
YEASTS native
GRAPES 100% estate-grown
CERTIFICATION organic

CIRÒ MARINA (KR)

Cote di Franze

Località Piana di Franze
tel. 392 6911606 - 348 5614031
www.cotedifranze.it
info@cotedifranze.it

CIRÒ MARINA (KR)

Librandi

Contrada San Gennaro
S.S. 106
tel. 0962 31518
www.librandi.it
librandi@librandi.it

---

9 ha - 13,500 bt   **10% discount**

232 ha - 2,700,000 bt

PEOPLE - Brothers Francesco and Vincenzo Scilanga are proud of the history of their family, whose winemaking activities were first documented in the 18th century. They stress how with their ongoing projects — including the building of a new cellar among the vineyards — they are carrying on from the past. Their aim is to defend a simple, traditional style, bush-training and the potential of the gaglioppo and greco bianco grapes.

VINEYARDS - The vineyards are mostly concentrated in the wind-beaten district of Piana di Franze, inland from Cirò Marina. Other lots are at Cutura and Piciara. Of the nine hectares, planted between 1958 and 1980, a couple are still bush-trained Cirò-style with the typical Greek planting pattern. The rest are cordon-trained and spur-pruned. The soil consists of clay and sand in Franze, of silt at Cutura and Piciara.

WINES - Cirò Rosso Cl. Sup. 2010 (● 7,500 bt) is made with grapes grown in the three areas mentioned above and matured only in stainless steel tanks. It's an unextracted, drinkable red with a bouquet of red fruit and a tangy, refreshing palate, a wine that goes against the trend that brought about a change in the production discipline — an excellent Everyday Wine. We were favorably surprised by **Cirò Bianco 2011** (○ greco; 2,500 bt) with its distinct notes of broom and a freshness and tanginess on a par with those of the Rosso. The company range also includes a Rosato, but it wasn't produced in 2011.

6️6️ In an area in which winegrowing is a complicated business, the Librandi cellar shines like a beacon. Its message is that with hefty investment in clonal research it is possible to work the land the right way and produce wines of character 9️9️

PEOPLE - One generation has virtually handed the baton over to another at this Cirò flagship winery, set up by brothers Antonio and Nicodemo Librandi. If the trademark is still forging ahead, it's partly thanks to the hard work of Davide De Santis in the vineyard and Donato Lanati's organization of production.

VINEYARDS - Librandi owns two main properties: the original Strongoli vineyard, where international grape varieties prevail, and the Rosaneti vineyard in Rocca di Neto, where clonal research is being carried out. The company has always invested a lot in research and is currently monitoring the behavior of selected clones of the gaglioppo, magliocco and pecorello grapes as well as studies on dozens of native Calabrian grapes.

WINES - **Melissa Asylia 2011** (○ greco; 60,000 bt) is a beautifully fresh white that goes well with food. **Efeso 2011** (○ mantonico; 12,000 bt), aged effectively in both wood and steel, is rich in fruit on the nose with a dynamic palate. Cirò Rosso 2011 (● 300,000 bt) also has a blossomy, fruity bouquet. It may be a value-for-money base label, but we liked it so much we decided to name it as an Everyday Wine. The elegant **Cirò Duca San Felice Ris. 2010** (● 120,000 bt) is redolent of red fruit with balsamic and ashy notes. In the mouth it's vibrant, tangy and muscular. The balanced, rich, complex **Magno Megonio 2010** (● magliocco; 30,000 bt) is an explosion of fruit, while **Gravello 2010** (● gaglioppo, cabernet; 70,000 bt) is an enjoyable tipple.

FERTILIZERS green manure
PLANT PROTECTION copper and sulphur
WEED CONTROL mechanical
YEASTS selected
GRAPES 100% estate-grown
CERTIFICATION organic

FERTILIZERS organic-mineral, green manure
PLANT PROTECTION chemical, copper and sulphur
WEED CONTROL mechanical
YEASTS selected
GRAPES 30% bought in
CERTIFICATION none

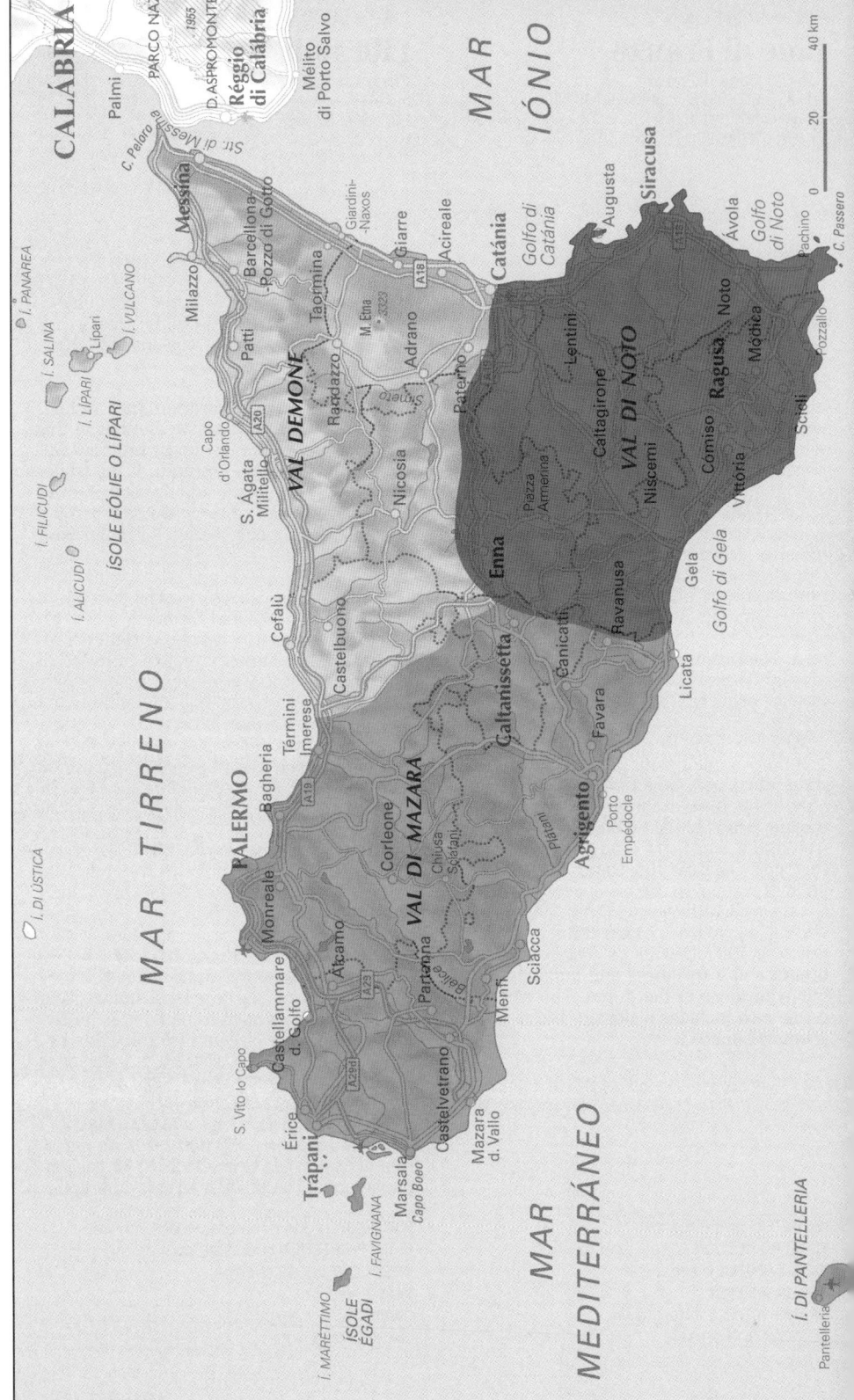

CALÁBRIA

PARCO NAZ.
1965
D. ASPROMONTE
Réggio
di Calábria
Palmi
Mélito
di Porto Salvo

C. Peloro
Str. di Messina

MAR
IÓNIO

MAR TIRRENO

I. DI ÚSTICA

I. PANAREA
I. SALINA
Lípari
I. VULCANO
I. LÍPARI
I. FILICUDI
ISOLE EÓLIE O LÍPARI
I. ALICUDI

Messina
Barcellona
Pozza di Gotto
Giardini-
Naxos
Giarre
Acireale
Milazzo
Patti
Taormina
M. Etna
3323
Catánia
Golfo di
Catánia
Augusta
Siracusa
Ávola
Golfo
di Noto
Pachino
C. Passero

Capo
d'Orlando
S. Ágata
Militello
Randazzo
Adrano
Paterno
Simeto
Lentini
Noto
Múdica
Ragusa
Scicli
Pozzallo

VAL DEMONE
Nicosia
Piazza
Armerina
Caltagirone
Comiso
Vittória
VAL DI NOTO
Niscemi

Cefalú
Castelbuono
Enna
Ravanusa
Gela
Golfo di Gela

MAR
TIRRENO

Términi
Imerese
Bagheria
Caltanissetta
Canicattì
Licata

PALERMO
Monreale
Favara
Porto
Empédocle
Agrigento

Castellammare
d. Golfo
Altamo
Corleone
Chiusa
Sclafani
Partanna
Bèlice
Plátani
VAL DI MAZARA

S. Vito lo Capo
Érice
Trápani
Castelvetrano
Menfi
Sciacca

Marsala
Capo Boeo
Mazara
d. Vallo

I. FAVIGNANA
I. MARETTIMO
ISOLE
ÉGADI

MAR
MEDITERRÁNEO

Í. DI PANTELLERIA
Pantelleria

0   20   40 km

SICILY

A land of incomparable beauty and profound contradictions, Sicily is arguably the most dynamic of all Italian winemaking regions. Yet the situation isn't all rosy. Let's begin by looking at the figures.

Sicily is the fourth Italian region for wine production — the first for area planted with vines — and represents 10 per cent of the national total, but is showing a downward trend and accounts for only 4 per cent in terms of value. This negative statistic is not only relative but also absolute, since the decrease is more pronounced than in any other region. Meaning lots of wine sold at very low prices, the consequences of which are all too predicable. In the last ten years, 10 per cent of the island's vines have been lost and the sight of the abandoned vineyards is a depressing one. It's not easy to identify the root causes of this situation. To remedy the fact that its DOC wines constituted only 4 per cent of the total, a Sicilia DOC has entered into force, the effects of which will become evident, we believe, from next year onwards. On paper, this decision could bring about a series of advantages, but it also risks leveling out the differences between the various winemaking areas which, with the exception of Etna, have yet to be fully blazoned.

These are the causes for concern. Fortunately, we are also seeing a constant and rapid improvement in the quality of the wines of a region that produced some of the best labels tasted in 2012. An interesting point, in our opinion, is the lack of specialization in reds or whites. Both categories achieve peaks of excellence but neither prevails over the other. The contest is not confined to Etna alone. Certain Nero d'Avola wines are superlative as are others from the the high, inland zones of the Val di Mazara. The general picture is thus exciting and also very original. The pages that follow speak of a Sicily different from the stereotype too often portrayed over the last few years by shortsighted wine critics.

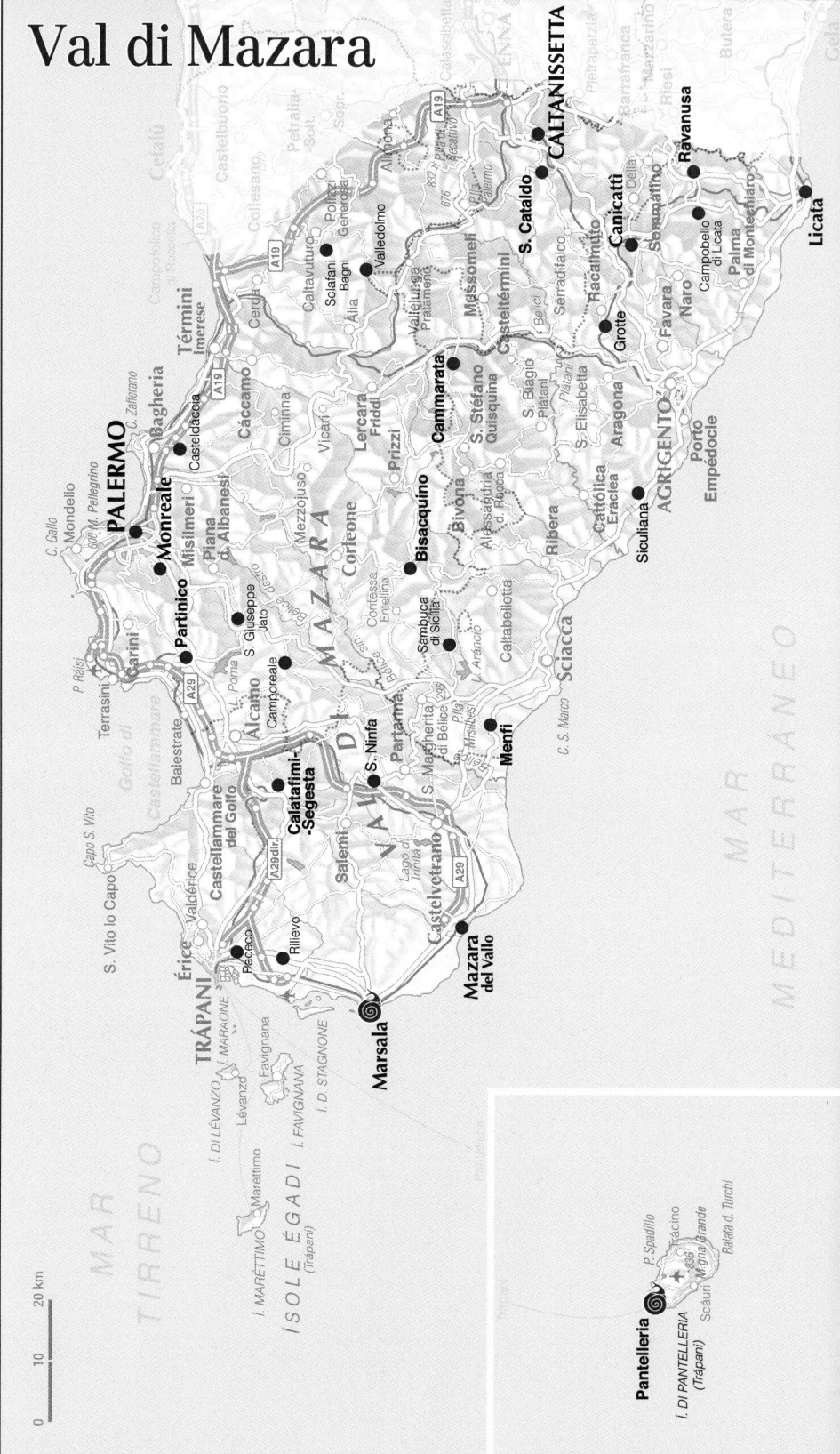

Val di Mazara

CAMPOREALE (PA)

Valdibella €

Via Belvedere, 91
tel. 0924 582021
www.valdibella.com
info@valdibella.com

---

38 ha - 70,000 bt **10% discount**

PEOPLE - Over the years, a scheme organized by the Salesians for laudable social purposes — to offer concrete job prospects to minors on probation — has turned into a wine cooperative with consistently high standards of quality. The brains behind its success are consultant agronomist Massimiliano Solano and the talented young enologist Salvatore Zuppardo, who relies on the external consultancy of Vincenzo Drago. The cooperative now has ten members.

VINEYARDS - The first thing to point out is that the cooperative's 38 hectares of vineyards — on clay soil rich in iron — are all managed using organic methods. Grapes from 34 hectares currently go into the wines. The vineyards are divided into eight parcels of land in the communes of Camporeale and Monleale. Worthy of separate mention as far as the promotion of biodiversity is concerned is the decision to plant woods and leave some of the land fallow.

WINES - The company style is aimed at preserving the rich aromas and nutritional elements naturally created by the vineyard in its wines. The wines are subtle but not lean, deep and complex and hugely drinkable. Three vines are made with the catarratto grapes. They are: **Isolano 2011** (○ catarratto; 3,300 bt), vinified with native yeasts, alluring and juicy; **Munir 2011** (○ catarratto; 18,000 bt) is lemony and full of cocky elegance; **Ninfa 2011** (○ catarratto; 6,000), without added sulfites, has personality and character, richness of flavor and a "marine" finish. Juicy **Ariddu 2011** (○ grillo; 6,000) has a rich, refreshing dynamic palate. **Kerasos 2011** (● nero d'Avola; 18,000 bt) is deep and enjoyable with a rich texture — a perfect Everyday Wine. **Acamante 2011** (● perricone; 3,300 bt) has a simple character that exudes *joie da vivre* and a pleasing, complete palate.

FERTILIZERS green manure
PLANT PROTECTION copper and sulphur
WEED CONTROL mechanical
YEASTS native
GRAPES 100% estate-grown
CERTIFICATION organic

CANICATTÌ (AG)

Viticultori Associati Canicattì €

Contrada Aquilata
tel. 092 2829371
www.viticultoriassociati.it
info@viticultoriassociati.it

1,000 ha - 800,000 bt

PEOPLE - A great cooperative that works: quality wines with a sense of place and good value for money. Formed in 1985, it now boasts more than 500 members. At the helm is Giovanni Greco, while the capable Salvatore Messina manages sales. The cellar is supervised by the enologist Angelo Molito with the backing of external consultant Tonino Guzzo. In its wines the cooperative seeks to raise the profile of its terroir.

VINEYARDS - All the members are helped to grow quality grapes, hence to ensure quality wines. The vineyards spread out over the hills inland from Agrigento. They grow traditional Sicilian white grapes such a grillo, catarratto and inzolia — plus some fiano — and black grapes such as nero d'Avola, nerello mascalese and nerello cappuccino — plus very high quality syrah.

WINES - This wine cooperative's true forte is the nero d'Avola grape which it vinifies in various ways, all geared to stylistic precision and drinkability. The most structured label is **Aynat 2009** (● 10,000 bt), an explosion of red fruit with balsamic notes and attractive spiciness. The very reasonably priced **Centuno 2010** (● nero d'Avola; 40,000 bt) has assertive juice, texture and saltiness and makes a very good Everyday Wine. **Nero d'Avola Aquilae 2010** (● 120,000 bt) relies more on spiciness. The latter two wines are both perfect for everyday drinking. Another red we recommend is **Calìo 2010** (● nerello cappuccio, nero d'Avola; 20,000 bt). Moving on to whites, **Filèno 2011** (○ grillo; 20,000 bt) is very flowery, while **Catarratto Aquilae 2011** (○ 40,000 bt) is varietal, citrusy and tangy.

FERTILIZERS organic-mineral
PLANT PROTECTION chemical, copper and sulphur
WEED CONTROL chemical, mechanical
YEASTS selected
GRAPES 100% estate-grown
CERTIFICATION none

Barraco

Contrada Fontanelle, 252
tel. 329 2073935
www.vinibarraco.it
vinibarraco@libero.it

8 ha - 21,000 bt

PEOPLE - Nino Barraco has a view of wine all of his own. His singular interpretation is based on his personal dialogue with the vines and the earth, which he respects and enhances according to the tradition handed down to him by his father. Free fermentations, long macerations and unorthodox cellar operations are the distinctive features of the work of this interpreter of the land and the grapes of this corner of Sicily.

VINEYARDS - Nino manages eight hectares of vineyards round Marsala with respect for the ecosystem. Albeit without certifications, Nino follows the principles of organic agriculture. Some vineyards are at sea level, where they feel the influence of the salt air. The grillo grapes, for example, are trained at Manicalunga on sand and red earth just meters from the coast. The other grapes grow in the Badessa, Paolini and Marausa districts.

WINES - Barraco's wines take time and arouse curiosity. **Zibibbo 2010** (○ 4,200 bt) has a definite varietal feel and a fresh, pleasant palate. **Catarratto 2010** (○ 3,000 bt) has a bouquet with salty, mineral nuances and a complex, savory palate. **Pignatello 2010** (● 2,500 bt), made with a grape better known as perricone, has plenty of fruit and expresses itself with great intensity. **Nero d'Avola 2010** (● 4,400 bt) is slightly introvert but reveals all its many varietal nuances with the right aeration, plus good juice and tannic structure. The intense **Milocca 2006** (● nero d'Avola; 3,000 bt) is made with late-harvested grapes.

slow wine	**GRILLO 2010** (○ 3,000 bt) Nino's exemplary personal take on this common Trapani grape. Brief fermentative maceration has given the wine complexity, character and length.

FERTILIZERS natural manure
PLANT PROTECTION copper and sulphur
WEED CONTROL mechanical
YEASTS native
GRAPES 30% bought in
CERTIFICATION none

Marco De Bartoli

Contrada Fornaia Samperi, 292
tel. 0923 962093
www.marcodebartoli.com
info@marcodebartoli.com

20 ha - 90,000 bt

❝ In partnership with his brother Sebastiano and sister Giuseppina, Renato De Bartoli continues to plow the broad furrow left by his father with a steady hand. And it is with the same skill as his father that he continues to concentrate production round the grillo grape, adding an authoritativeness all of his own to the job ❞

PEOPLE - As the sense of void left by the death of Marco fades to melancholic memory, the presence of his children at the cellar is increasingly reassuring.

VINEYARDS - Bukkuram and Samperi, respectively on Pantelleria and at Marsala, are the two vineyards in which De Bartoli's triumphal masterpieces come into being. They are ideal for the zibibbo and grillo grapes, but there is no shortage either of international varieties, such as syrah and merlot.

WINES - This year's wines are worthy of a standing ovation. The beautifully crafted **Grappoli del Grillo 2011** (○ 13,000 bt) is juicy, rich, unctuous and complex. The deep, citric **Pietra Nera 2011** (○ zibibbo; 12,000 bt) evokes the volcanic origin of the soil of Pantelleria. Personality, freshness and character are the distinctive features of **Passito di Pantelleria Bukkuram 2008** (8,000 bt). **Marsala Sup. Oro Vigna La Miccia** (○ 7,000 bt) is proud and self-confident, while **Vecchio Samperi Solera Trentennale** (○ 999 bt) is a rarity we cannot afford not to mention.

slow wine	**VECCHIO SAMPERI VENTENNALE** (○ 6,000 bt) We unanimously announce this, masterfully produced using the Soleras method, to be one of the most exciting wines tasted this year.
slow wine	**MARSALA SUP. RIS. 1987** (○ 1,000 bt) A monumental almost moving wine, a triumph of elegance, in which aromas of tobacco and dried figs are followed by a sweet palate and refreshing acidity.

FERTILIZERS none
PLANT PROTECTION copper and sulphur
WEED CONTROL mechanical
YEASTS native
GRAPES 100% estate-grown
CERTIFICATION none

MARSALA (TP)

Donnafugata

Via Sebastiano Lipari, 18
tel. 0923 724200
www.donnafugata.it info@donnafugata.it

MARSALA (TP)

Terzavia

Via Bruzzesi, 28
tel. 335 7725238
www.terzaviavino.com
debartolirenato@gmail.com

---

260 ha - 2,300,000 bt

0 ha - 13,000 bt

PEOPLE - It only takes a few important words to describe the Donnafugata brand: passion, competence, professionalism and communication. These were the qualities Giacomo Rallo was banking on in the 1980s when he embarked on the adventure with his wife Gabriella Anca. Today the team also fields their dynamic sons José and Antonio, adapting to the size of the business without straying from the chosen path.

VINEYARDS - The vineyards stretch out over seven different districts in the great winegrowing area of Contessa Entellina, in which the family has always believed and invested — so much so that it's now a DOC. The rest are on Pantelleria in a zone given over to the zibibbo grape, recently the subject of successful enological experiments.

WINES - The Rallo family range is, as always, reliable, precise and up to the mark. **Contessa Entellina Vigna di Gabri 25° Anniversario 2011** (O inzolia, catarratto, chardonnay, sauvignon; 60,000 bt) strikes just the right balance between aroma and acidity. Similar in style but simpler is **Damarino 2011** (O inzolia, catarratto, grecanico; 140,000 bt), while **Lighea 2011** (O zibibbo; 160,000 bt) stands out for its aromatic attack. Moving on to reds, we liked **Sherazade 2011** (● nero d'Avola; 100,000 bt), a wine that coaxes out all the grape's typicity. **Contessa Entellina Mille e una Notte 2008** (● 45,000 bt), is a richly extracted, extremely potent nero d'Avola.

PEOPLE - Renato De Bartoli runs Terzavia in Marsala in parallel with his family's historic winery. His aim and ambition are to raise the profile of the local terroir — more precisely, that of Samperi — with naturally-inspired still wines of straightforward, uncompromising character.

VINEYARDS - Renato buys grapes in from trusted growers and cultivates some himself. The family company also owns historic parcels of land growing old catarratto vines, among others, at an altitude of 500 meters. Renato is pledged to promoting a viticulture with low impact on the environment.

WINES - The style of the wines concentrates on character and expressive finesse. **M. Cl. Brut Nature Terzavia 2009** (● grillo; 6,000 bt) originates from a base wine made from an almost obsessive selection of the finest grapes. Aged for 16 months on yeasts, its forceful character and acid structure make it a first-rate label. **Nero d'Avola 2010** (● 3.000 bt) is pervasive, rich and varietal. An exciting cuvée of various vintages of grillo since 2006, it is still waiting to reach its right level of aging — and also for a name.

slow wine | **LUCIDO 2011** (O catarratto lucido; 3,500 bt) Common sense in liquid form! That's a good definition for this thrilling wine, an amalgam of character, terroir, personality and virtuous agriculture.

slow wine | **PASSITO DI PANTELLERIA BEN RYÉ 2010** (O 80,000 bt) A wine which encapsulates all the experience and professional expertise of Donnafugata. A label with such a strong sense of place and such a special, unique project deserve this recognition.

FERTILIZERS natural manure, compost, green manure
PLANT PROTECTION chemical, copper and sulphur
WEED CONTROL mechanical
YEASTS selected
GRAPES 100% estate-grown
CERTIFICATION none

FERTILIZERS natural manure, green manure
PLANT PROTECTION copper and sulphur
WEED CONTROL mechanical
YEASTS native
GRAPES 100% bought in
CERTIFICATION none

Planeta

Contrada Dispensa
tel. 091 327965
www.planeta.it
planeta@planeta.it

370 ha - 2,000,000 bt

PEOPLE - As in the fairytale of Peter Pan, Alessio, Santi and Francesca Planeta — at the helm since 1995 — believed in Neverland. Now that, with curiosity and perseverance, they've come through the test with flying colors, they've gone back to their origins — as in Barrie's story. And thanks to their unceasing discovery of the authenticity of the island's single terroirs, Sicily has become Everland!

VINEYARDS - Starting out from Sambuca, 93 hectares of vineyard on the shores of Lake Lago Arancio, in 1985 Planeta began to systematically buy other important properties: Menfi (161 hectares), Vittoria (34 hectares), Noto (51 hectares), Castiglione di Sicilia sull'Etna (16 hectares) and Capo Milazzo. The aim has been to raise the profile of the terroir and promote native grapes, especially the most unknown and unusual.

WINES - The range of wines tasted was very good indeed. Here are our impressions from east to west. The engrossing varietal **Noto Nero d'Avola Santa Cecilia 2009** (● 50,000 bt) pleasantly expresses the richness and marine essence of the terroir. Elegance and flavor sum up the identity of **Passito di Noto 2010** (○ 24,000 bt). Fourteen months on yeasts have added richness, consistency and minerality to **M. Cl. Brut 2010** (○ carricante; 10,000 bt), a label made with grapes grown on Etna. **Cerasuolo di Vittoria Cl. Dorilli 2010** (● 12.000 bt) is mild, notably expressive and drinkable — for us it's a Great Wine. **Alastro 2011** (○ grecanico; 80.000 bt) is introvert and pleasurable, while **Maroccoli 2009** (● syrah; 65,000 bt) is rich, spicy and balsamic.

Ferrandes

Contrada Tracino Kamma
Via del Fante, 8
tel. 0923 915475
www.passitodipantelleriaferrandes.com
dsferrandes@meditel.it

2 ha - 6,000 bt   **10% discount**

❝ His cellar is like a wedding cake, a doll's house even. The difference is that this is no game for Salvatore. Albeit in a carefree, lighthearted manner, he knows his whole life, present, past and future, is contained in his small wine tanks ❞

PEOPLE - Salvatore Ferrandes, or in praise of slowness. There is nothing frantic in the way Salvatore goes about things and his activities follow the rhythm of the seasons. With one eye on the sky and another on the sea, he is always ready to grasp the signs which, on Pantelleria, demand emergency interventions. Obliged by the urgency of the situation to defend his vineyard, only in moments like this does Salvatore go against his own nature.

VINEYARDS - Salvatore has inherited two hectares of vineyards from his father. The vine rows are situated at altitudes of 200-450 meters above sea level and tending methods are certified organic. The vines are bush-trained in the lava hollows.

WINES - Salvatore's big passion is drying grapes, an art for which he has a real talent and which every year (the cellar has now around 45 under its belt) provides new pointers for vinification. His passito (first released in 2000) is an exciting discovery every year that goes by.

> **slow wine** **PASSITO DI PANTELLERIA 2008** (○ zibibbo; 6,000 bt) Tasting this wine is like making a tour of the island. Notes of wild Mediterranean herbs, sun-dried peach and apricot, dates and almonds run off the nose like rosary beads. The palate is timid with rigorous flavors, a clever synthesis of raisins and the aroma sensed on the nose. Mineral and, in bursts, complex and tactile, the wine suddenly becomes friendly, pleasant and incredibly long.

FERTILIZERS organic-mineral, green manure	FERTILIZERS manure pellets
PLANT PROTECTION chemical, copper and sulphur	PLANT PROTECTION copper and sulphur
WEED CONTROL chemical, mechanical	WEED CONTROL mechanical
YEASTS selected	YEASTS native
GRAPES 100% estate-grown	GRAPES 100% estate-grown
CERTIFICATION none	CERTIFICATION organic

SCLAFANI BAGNI (PA)
Tasca d'Almerita
Contrada Regaleali
tel. 091 6459711
www.tascadalmerita.it
info@tascadalmerita.it

VALLEDOLMO (PA)
Castellucci Miano €
Via Sicilia, 1
tel. 0921 542385
www.castelluccimiano.it
info@castelluccimiano.it

427 ha - 2,860,000 bt

130 ha - 135,000 bt   `10% discount`

PEOPLE - This monumental Sicilian company owns five estates with which it has always sought to raise the profile of island winegrowing. The brains behind the project are the brothers Alberto and Giuseppe, ever keen to exalt the many nuances of their "continent" of which they are, without rhetoric, among the best interpreters.

VINEYARDS - Complexity is the concept best suited to describing the vineyards of Tasca d'Almerita. You get tangible proof of that when you visit the historic family estate of Regaleali. On this closed-cycle farm agricultural models that conserve biodiversity and the beauty of the landscape live side by side — all with the scientific support of the SOStain project, a sustainability program shared with other enterprises.

WINES - Five distinct terroirs provide the base for wines that epitomize Sicily's diversity. The Tenuta Whitaker estate on the island of Mozia yields **Grillo di Mozia 2011** (○ 40,000 bt), richly textured with salty notes. Regaleali produces the beautifully balanced **Nozze d'Oro 2011** (○ inzolia, sauvignon; 65,000 bt) and the historic **Chardonnay 2010** (○ 40,000 bt), again a Great Wine, versatile with a superb tannic structure, one of the best takes on the grape around. Also worthy of mention is the juicy. deep **Contea di Scafani Rosso del Conte 2008** (● nero d'Avola, perricone; 35,000 bt). Etna fever has also infected Tascas who use their Castiglione di Sicilia holdings to produce **Tascante Ghiaia Nera 2010** (● nerello mascalese; 25,000 bt), a very successful label indeed. **M. Cl. Extra Brut Almerita 2007** (○ chardonnay; 5,000 bt) is enjoyable.

PEOPLE - President Antonino Piazza, sales manager Piero Buffa and agronomist and enologist Tonino Guzzo are the brains behind this rave and ambitious project for the promotion and recovery of the vine heritage of Valledolmo, a town whose true wealth has always been agriculture. The initiative is putting its money on the land itself in order to drive away the specter of the abandonment of the vineyards and offer new prospects to two traditional grape varieties: catarratto and perricone.

VINEYARDS - The local mountain viticulture is a "heroic" enterprise. The vineyards, often mere pocket-handkerchiefs of land, are situated at altitudes of 700 to 1,050 meters and are, on average, about 50 years old. They are managed with old-fashioned common sense by 80 growers (and stakeholders in the company) on soils of great viticultural potential. The main crus are Miano, Castelucci, Schiarazzi, Cifiliana and Acqua del Corvo.

WINES - Finesse, minerality and character are the main traits of the company's wines, all fresh and built to last. **Miano 2011** (○ catarratto; 25,000 bt) epitomizes the varietals of the Valledolmo biotype (small-berried catarratto) on the nose, which leads into a juicy, citrusy palate. **PerricOne 2009** (● perricone; 16,000 bt) is deep and exceptionally drinkable. **Maravita 2008** (● perricone; 6,500 bt) is structured and complex, but still young. **La Masa 2010** (○ inzolia; 6,000 bt), made with partly botrytized grapes.

`slow wine` SHIARÀ 2010 (○ catarratto; 13,000 bt) Selected from the oldest vineyards at the highest altitudes, elegant, iodated, vertical and deeply mineral. A label that speaks of an alternative Sicily.

FERTILIZERS organic-mineral
PLANT PROTECTION chemical, copper and sulphur
WEED CONTROL chemical, mechanical
YEASTS selected
GRAPES 20% bought in
CERTIFICATION none

FERTILIZERS organic-mineral, natural manure
PLANT PROTECTION copper and sulphur
WEED CONTROL mechanical
YEASTS selected
GRAPES 100% estate-grown
CERTIFICATION none

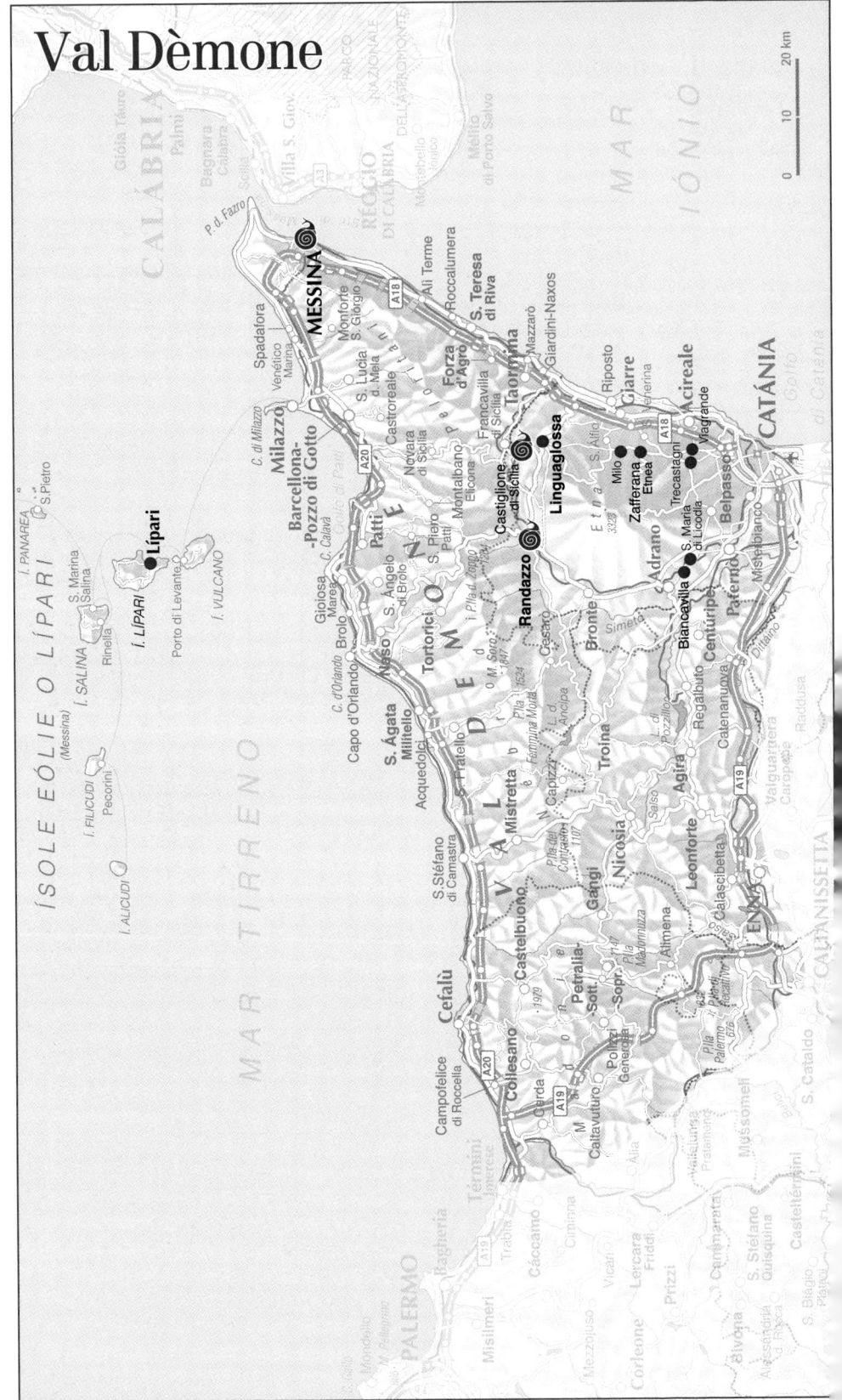

Val Dèmone

Graci

Contrada Arcuria Passopisciaro
tel. 095 7016773
www.graci.eu
info@graci.eu

18 ha - 25,000 bt **10% discount**

66 Alberto, in his early thirties, is one of the leading players in the Etna wine renaissance and, above all, an emblem of the younger generation's return to agriculture. He is assisted in his work by his friendly sister Elena, also very young 99

PEOPLE - The affinity between Etna and Alberto Aiello Graci can be moving. You grasp as much climbing with him up to his splendid vineyards at an altitude of 1,000 meters or chatting with him about agriculture, the landscape and local culture over a glass of wine.

VINEYARDS - It's impossible to understand the Etna phenomenon without spending a few hours among the vineyards. Which is what we did, guided by Alberto, clambering up and down among lava flows and torn roads, from the Arcuria holdings at 600 meters, near the family farmhouse, to those of Barbibecchi at 1,000 meters. Without following any particular protocol, the agronomic approach couldn't be more virtuous.

WINES - Graci's convincing style aims at crisp, precise wines with an emphasis on freshness and drinkability. The arrival this year of Graci's friend and consultant Emiliano Falsini is sure to add impetus to the company without affecting the personality of Alberto's wines. The excellent **Etna Bianco Quota 600 2010** (○ 1,800 bt) is a wine with a good suite of aromas and floral sensations. It's a pleasure to drink and has good aging potential. **Etna Rosso Quota 600 2010** (● 8,000 bt) is a tangible example of Etna elegance. Hugely intense, fine and complex with light tannic texture and a thrilling finish. Commendable too are the base versions, the excellent value-for-money **Etna Rosso 2010** (● 24,000 bt), and the nicely salty **Etna Bianco 2011** (○ 10,000 bt).

FERTILIZERS natural manure
PLANT PROTECTION copper and sulphur
WEED CONTROL mechanical
YEASTS native
GRAPES 100% estate-grown
CERTIFICATION none

I Custodi
delle vigne dell'Etna

Contrada Moganazzi
tel. 393 1898430
www.icustodi.it
info@icustodi.it

11 ha - 21,000 bt

PEOPLE - This was a brilliant debut name for this new name on the Etna wine scene. Created by Mario Paoluzi, encouraged by the I Vigneri consortium, I Custodi delle vigne dell'Etna ("The Keepers of the vineyards of Etna" — the name says all) is well-rooted in the local area and is working to preserve its traditions with respect for the people who work there. It is, in short, a model for the promotion of agriculture in this exciting corner of Sicilian winemaking.

VINEYARDS - Everything starts in the vineyards. This may appear a rhetorical, hackneyed affirmation, but it corresponds to the truth among the vineyards of I Custodi. The vines, some of which 250 years old — or so they say — are spread over the east and north sides of Etna in the Nave, Puntalazzo, Moganazzi and Cosentino districts at an altitude of 600-1,200 meters, all in total harmony with nature. Here the old dry-stone walls have been painstakingly preserved.

WINES - After just two harvests, the immense wealth of the vineyards and Mario's clear ideas combined with Salvo Foti's sure hand and recognizable personal style have regaled us with wines of enormous elegance. This is the case of **Etna Rosso Aetneus 2007** (● 19,000 bt), enhanced by a smidgeon of alicante, virtually inevitable in pre-phylloxera vines over 100 years old. The end-result is a wine that is at once complex and rich, potent and fine — and how could it be otherwise? A test passed with flying colors.

> **slow wine** **ANTE 2010** (○ carricante, minnella, greganico; 5,200 bt) Made with a selection of grapes about 40 years old harvested on the north side of the volcano at an altitude of 800-1,200 meters. It's a wine that embodies all the complexity and depth of the Etna terroir. It's already enjoyable, but will certainly improve if you forget it in the cellar. It has a bouquet of hazelnuts, pronounced tanginess and edgy, agreeable acidity.

FERTILIZERS natural manure
PLANT PROTECTION copper and sulphur
WEED CONTROL mechanical
YEASTS native
GRAPES 100% estate-grown
CERTIFICATION converting to organics

Passopisciaro

Via Santo Spirito
tel. 0578 267110
www.passopisciaro.com
info@passopisciaro.com

---

26 ha - 65,000 bt

PEOPLE - You only have to talk to local viticulturists to realize the esteem the celebrated Tuscan producer Andrea Franchetti has managed to earn himself here. His arrival on the slopes of Etna in the year 2000 and his hugely expressive wines have combined to speed up the renaissance throughout the area. Proof of the fact is the successful annual Le Contrade dell'Etna event, attended by producers, journalists and enthusiasts.

VINEYARDS - First comes Etna. Then come brains, those of Franchetti, who, in his efforts to interpret the terroir, has brought in innovations such as high-density planting and grapes uncommon in the area, such as cesanese, petit verdot and chardonnay. Notwithstanding the difficulties the area and the neglect thereof are capable of generating — witness the tragic fire in the summer of 2012 — Franchetti does his job with scrupulous care and great professional skill.

WINES - Sciaronuova, Rampante, Porcaria, Chiappemacine, Guardiola: these names, which correspond to some of the area's best winegrowing districts (this year mentioned on the labels only by their initials), tell you just how much Andrea wants to bring the specificities of the terroir to the foreground. His wines are an impeccable class act worthy of acclaim. **Contrada C 2010** (● 2,700 bt), elegant with distinct notes of pepper, is a symphony of spiciness and a Great Wine. **Contrada R 2010** (● 2,000 bt) is characterized by better-defined fruit. **Contrada P 2010** (● 2,700 bt) is full of finesse like a great pinot noir, while **Contrada S 2010** (● 2,000 bt) has a pleasantly spicy vein. Also exemplary is the base wine **Passopisciaro 2010** (● 30,000 bt) and **Guardiola 2011** (○ chardonnay; 16,000 bt) is very agreeable too.

FERTILIZERS none
PLANT PROTECTION copper and sulphur
WEED CONTROL mechanical
YEASTS selected
GRAPES 100% estate-grown
CERTIFICATION none

Girolamo Russo

Frazione Passopisciaro
Via Regina Margherita, 78
tel. 0942 983142
www.girolamorusso.it
info@girolamorusso.it

---

15 ha - 15,000 bt   **10% discount**

❝ Giuseppe Russo deserves a prize … for humility. It is by no means rhetorical to describe him as the leader of the Etna viticultural renaissance, a role he is proud of, albeit playing it with modesty and always ready to collaborate with his colleague friends ❞

PEOPLE - Peasant roots can't be erased. After his father's death, this is the concept that drove Giuseppe Russo to review his work in the countryside. His mission is to add value to the long tradition of his family, which has lived and worked on the slopes of Etna for generations.

VINEYARDS - San Lorenzo, Feudo, Feudo di Mezzo, Calderara Sottana: four districts on the north side of Etna, which testify to the diversity of the soil there. Even as he continues the work of his father, very sensitive to environmental sustainability in his own right, Giuseppe has embarked on the road of total respect for naturalness and has already received organic certification.

WINES - The teamwork between Giuseppe and his enologist friend Emiliano Falsini has given rise to essential labels of great character and personality. **Etna Rosso 'A Rina 2010** (● 18,000 bt) is a textbook wine made with a selection of grapes from different districts. The grapes for **Etna Rosso San Lorenzo 2010** (● 4,500 bt) come from vineyards that are 60-100 years old. The wine is profound and supported by balanced alcohol content. Made from the bunches of carricante grapes scattered round the old vineyards, **Nerina 2011** (● 2,000 bt), dedicated to Giuseppe's mother, is a pleasure to drink.

> **slow wine** **ETNA ROSSO FEUDO 2010** (● 3,500 bt) Sense of place, texture, drinkability, sincerity and immediacy — these are the characteristics that make this label a testimonial of Etna winemaking and a faithful mirror of the soul of its maker.

FERTILIZERS manure pellets
PLANT PROTECTION copper and sulphur
WEED CONTROL mechanical
YEASTS selected, native
GRAPES 100% estate-grown
CERTIFICATION organic

CASTIGLIONE DI SICILIA (CT)

Tenuta di Fessina

Località Contrada Rovittello
Via Nazionale
tel. 0571 55284
silviamaestrelli@tenutadifessina.com

LIPARI (ME)

Tenuta di Castellaro

Via Caolino
tel. 035 233337
www.tenutadicastellaro.it
info@comarkspa.it

---

16 ha - 55,000 bt

PEOPLE - Visiting the slopes of Etna and their extraordinary patrimony of old vineyards, framed by spectacular volcanic terrain, you understand rightaway why so many wine producers and technicians have flocked here from the rest of Italy. For Federico Curtaz, a consultant agronomist of international fame, and Silvia Maestrelli, the famous Tuscan winemaker, it was love at first sight and now, respectfully and with professional skill, they make great wine here.

VINEYARDS - Federico's competence is visible in the vineyards, which he manages mindful of the Etna tradition, bringing out the complexity and balance of the old vineyards — some of which planted more than 100 years ago — that fan out over lava flows of different eras. He adopts a rational agronomic approach based on common sense and decades of experience. Outside the Etna zone, the company also owns small vineyards in the province of Trapani and near Noto.

WINES - Silvia and Federico's range has grown over the years and now spans from the classic wines of Etna to the new labels produced elsewhere. We found that every one was exceptionally clean and drinkable with a strong sense of place. **Etna Rosso Il Musmeci 2009** (● 10,000 bt) is the result of a vintage that, locally, was judged unfavorable. Immaculate work in vineyard and cellar has given it fragrance, subtlety, depth and delicious juiciness. Etna Bianco A' Puddara 2010 (○ 3,500 bt) is outstanding again, combining aromatic complexity with extraordinary minerality. An exceptional testimonial of the potential of Etna, it is, naturally enough, a Great Wine. **Laeneo 2011** (● nerello cappuccio; 3,500 bt) is rich in fruit and a tad husky. **Nakone 2011** (○ chardonnay; 10,000 bt) is potent and stylish.

7.5 ha - 20,000 bt

PEOPLE - It was love at first sight — and how could it have been otherwise? — that drove the Bergamo businessman Massimo Lentsch to embark upon this wonderful adventure of his on the island of Lipari. Spurred on by the I Vigneri consortium under Salvo Foti, his company has become a symbol of the island's wine renaissance with bottles of great finesse that embody the seriousness of the owners and the potential of this unique terroir.

VINEYARDS - The numerous propeeties chosen by Massimo and I Vigneri include Cappero, Castellaro, Maggiore, Lisca, Caolino and Gelso, where they have bedded malvasia, carricante, corinto, nero d'Avola, and local grape vines bush-trained at a density of over 9,000 per hectare. Vineyard management follows the I Vigneri ground rules and places the onus on total respect for the environment.

WINES - The winery is a sight for sore eyes. Tourists and enthusiasts are hereby invited to come for a stroll. Here you'll find not only a new model of agriculture, but also a veritable wine cathedral in which bottles of great elegance are produced. **Nero Ossidiana 2010** (● corinto, nero d'Avola; 6,500 bt) is a masterpiece, courtesy of Salvo Foti, with fine notes of earth and suprising saltiness.

> **slow wine** **BIANCO POMICE 2010** (○ malvasia, carricante; 11,000 bt) A symphony for the nose with distinct mineral aromas followed up by a balanced palate in which sweetness, depth, character and drinkability all play a part. A truly monumental wine, tangible proof of a highly original approach to viticulture. A white with typically Mediterranean notes, but also edgy northern-style acidity.

FERTILIZERS none	FERTILIZERS natural manure
PLANT PROTECTION chemical, copper and sulphur	PLANT PROTECTION copper and sulphur
WEED CONTROL mechanical	WEED CONTROL mechanical
YEASTS selected	YEASTS native
GRAPES 5% bought in	GRAPES 100% estate-grown
CERTIFICATION none	CERTIFICATION none

MESSINA

Palari

Contrada Barnia
Località Santo Stefano Briga
tel. 090 630194
www.palari.it
info@palari.it

7 ha - 30,000 bt

66 Salvatore and Giampiero Geraci are on a mission to offer us thrilling wines in a fragile, delicate area 99

PEOPLE - Getting to the Geraci's 18th-century villa is an exciting and, in some respects, scary experience. Indifferent to the incessant spillover of the urban sprawl all around, the family is gradually restoring this building of magnificent artistic beauty.

VINEYARDS - "Quantity is not what we're about," are the wise words of Giampiero, the operational arm of the Geraci brothers and guardian of the precious, extreme terraced vineyards in the hills behind Messina. Visiting them is something of an enterprise but also a moral duty and, of course, a pleasure. The vineyards overlook the sea and are a symbol of a type of agriculture that is unconventional and, in a sense, moving.

WINES - Salvatore Geraci guided us on a voyage of discovery of his wines, which for some years now have given this tiny and unusual corner of Sicily due international visibility. It is partly thanks to the steady hand of a technician of the caliber of Donato Lanati that this year we were able to taste the wines of the 2010 vintage. **Faro Palari 2010** (● nerello mascalese, nerello cappuccio, nocera; 12,000 bt) is as interesting as ever. Particularly thrilling is its capacity to be an outstandingly narrative wine, recounting its terroir while maintaining freshness, drinkability, warmth and power. It's a label that passes the test of time too, as our tastings of a 2004 and a 2001 proved. **Rosso del Soprano 2010** (● 12,000 bt), supported by deep texture and lively juice, is no less impressive.

RANDAZZO (CT)

I Vigneri

Largo Signore Pietà, 17
tel. 0933 982942
www.ivigneri.it
info@ivigneri.it

2 ha - 7,000 bt

66 The Snail symbol is a well deserved reward for a man who had the foresight to create a well-knit group of people to trigger a grassroots revolution 99

PEOPLE - The spiritual guide of I Vigneti has a name and a surname: Salvo Foti. With him at the helm of an innovative consortium are a group of friends and a mule called Gino. Their declared mission is to save the distinctive features of Etna and surrounds by encouraging new generations of winegrowers.

VINEYARDS - The winery has a number of objectives, one of them extremely ambitious: saving and protecting the bush-training culture and the immense landscape of centuries-old vineyards. Wherever it works, the group promotes a productive philosophy of total harmony with history and nature. You can see this visiting the vineyards, from the first to the last, all rich in biodiversity and characterized by vegetative harmony.

WINES - The technical experience of Salvo Foti, consultant to a number of major Italian wineries, has culminated in the I Vigneti consortium project. Salvo's style is precise and uncompromising. From his hands come wines of notable personality which exalt Etna and its land in all their nuances. This year he treated us to the only label he deemed ready: **Vinujancu 2011** (○ riesling, grecanico, minnella; 1,500 bt), a well thought out blend of varieties, in which the celebrated German variety, planted ungrafted in a vineyard at an altitude of 1,200 meters near Bronte, stands out. It's inevitably a complex, profound wine with a promising future ahead of it.

FERTILIZERS natural manure	FERTILIZERS natural manure
PLANT PROTECTION copper and sulphur	PLANT PROTECTION copper and sulphur
WEED CONTROL mechanical	WEED CONTROL mechanical
YEASTS selected	YEASTS native
GRAPES 100% estate-grown	GRAPES 100% estate-grown
CERTIFICATION none	CERTIFICATION none

Tenuta delle Terre Nere

Contrada Calderara
tel. 095 924002
www.marcdegrazia.com
tenutaterrenere@tiscali.it

25 ha - 150,000 bt   **10% discount**

" Marco's vocation for the vineyards of Etna turns to devotion in his meticulous efforts to squeeze the specificity out of every single district in the area" "

PEOPLE - It was love at first sight between Etna and Marco De Grazia, a top international distributor of great Italian wines and a consultant enologist. Which is why he moved to the area to make wines from its grapes. Not only for himself but also as the charismatic leader of a cohort of small winemaker friends.

VINEYARDS - The key to understanding the winery Marco runs in collaboration with Calogero Statella is diversity. As you move from the dusty volcanic sand of Santo Spirito to the rock of Moganazzi, from pre-phylloxera vines to new high-trained plantings all managed organically, a tour of their vineyards is a feast for the eyes.

WINES - The courageous decision to differentiate each district was a strategic and fortunate one. The result is wines of great expressive power, so conspicuously multifaceted as to render simplistic any attempt to classify them in order of goodness. The Great Wine recognition goes to Etna Rosso Guardiola 2010 (● 8,000 bt), a "monster" of elegance. **Etna Rosso Feudo di Mezzo 2010** (● 3,500 bt), **Etna Rosso Calderara 2010** (● 3,800 bt) and **Etna Rosso Santo Spirito 2010** (● 7.000 bt) are pieces in a glittering mosaic. Worthy of a special note of merit is **Etna Rosso Pre Fillossera Vigna Don Peppino 2010** (● 2,500 bt), made with grapes from a monumental vineyard. Besides offering good value for money, even the base wine **Etna Rosso 2011** (● 90,000 bt) is excellent, as are the two whites, born to exalt the potential of the carricante grape in the area.

FERTILIZERS natural manure, green manure	
PLANT PROTECTION copper and sulphur	
WEED CONTROL mechanical	
YEASTS selected	
GRAPES 30% bought in	
CERTIFICATION organic	

Vini Biondi

Corso Sicilia, 20
tel. 095 7633933
www.vinibiondi.it
c.biondi@vinibiondi.it

7.5 ha - 20,000 bt

PEOPLE - He doesn't lack passion for his native land. On the contrary, Ciro Biondi is a vigneron with a love of extreme vineyards, which he tends with meticulous care and proudly shows off to tourists or any one else who appears interested. For some years now, his work has been facilitated by the help of his friendly nephew Manfredi. The winery is situated in the Trecastagni, on the south side of Etna, in the Catania direction.

VINEYARDS - Chianta, one of the most beautiful vineyards we've ever visited on Etna, is a monumental construction of rows of terraced stones, just outside the village of Trecastagni at an altitude of about 700 meters. Here secular vines alternate with new ones. Also impressive is the vineyard on Monte Ilice, in which the influence of the sea combines with the unique volcanic terrains. The vineyards are managed using virtuous agronomic methods.

WINES - Seriousness and personality are two words to describe Ciro and his wines. These are labels that leave a mark. True, they may not be immediately approachable, but after adequate aging, they are capable of being truly thrilling. This isn't the first time the decision has been taken to wait before releasing the wines, but this is a sign of professionalism. In the meantime, the only wine presented this year is a wonderful calling card for Etna winemaking.

slow wine **ETNA ROSSO OUTIS 2008** (● 14,000 bt) A wine that thrills for its depth and its capacity to recount the unique terroir of which it's an icon. The result of a selection from all the vineyards, it suavely reflects the character of its maker. Reminiscent of a Burgundy, it is very pale, almost rosé, in color with notes of pepper that conquer the nose. The finish is so deep and juicy it almost sends a shiver down your spine.	

FERTILIZERS green manure	
PLANT PROTECTION copper and sulphur	
WEED CONTROL mechanical	
YEASTS selected	
GRAPES 100% estate-grown	
CERTIFICATION none	

Val di Noto

MAR IÓNIO

MAR MEDITERRÁNEO

Golfo di Catánia

Golfo di Gela

CATÁNIA

SIRACUSA

Acireale

Belpasso

Paternò

Centuripe

Leonforte

Agira

ENNA

Valguarnera

Caropepe

Piazza Armerina

Aidone

Barrafranca

Mazzarino

Riesi

Butera

Gela

Licata

CALTANISSETTA

Mussomeli

S. Cataldo

Canicattì

Naro

Palma di Montechiaro

AGRIGENTO

Favara

Aragona

Porto Empedocle

S. Biágio Plátani

S. Stefano Quisquina

Castelfermini

Cammarata

Raddusa

Ramacca

Mineo

Grammichele

Caltagirone

Niscemi

Vizzini

Militello in Val di Catánia

Scordia

Lentini

Francofonte

Sortino

Buccheri

Palazzolo Acréide

Floridia

Solarino

Melilli

Augusta

Avola

Noto

Pachino

Ispica

Scicli

Módica

RAGUSA

Cómiso

Vittória

Chiaramonte Gulfi

Acate

CERASUOLO DI VITTORIA

Marina di Ragusa

Pozzallo

Capo Passero

Portopalo di C. Passero

0   10   20 km

Gianfranco Daino

Via Croce del Vicario, 115
tel. 0933 58226 - 335 5243345
www.vinidaino.it
info@vinidaino.it

3 ha - 13,000 bt   `10% discount`

PEOPLE - A solid friendship binds the owner of this splendid winery, Gianfranco Daino, to Salvo Foti, the brains behind the I Vigneri consortium. Since they first met a few years ago, they have given life to this new project to raise awareness of viticulture in the Calatino district round the town of Caltagirone in the province of Catania, one of the most attractive in Sicily. Gianfranco manages the enterprise with great confidence and respect for tradition.

VINEYARDS - Secular cork trees, holm oaks, wild fauna, including numerous bird species — in a word, biodiversity. This is the natural and environmental context, a stone's throw from the Orientata del Bosco Nature Reserve at San Pietro, at an altitude of more than 400 meters, in which Gianfranco works. It is here that, encouraged by I Vigneri, he cultivates three native Sicilian grapes —nero d'Avola, frappato e alicante — bush-trained at a density of 9,000 vines per hectare. The agronomic approach is totally natural.

WINES - Just one wine actually. Gianfranco and his friend Salvo concentrate all their efforts on a single label that aspires to evoke a sense of place and express the balance of the three native grapes. They do the job without going over the top in the cellar, promoting an enological approach which, true to the style of I Vigneri, limits intervention to a minimum to preserve the true character of the Calatino terroir.

> **slow wine** **SUBER 2010** (● nero d'Avola, frappato, alicante; 13,000 bt) The red soil on which the three grapes grow comes out in this personality-packed, potent, profound wine. In this emblem of a popular viticultural renaissance, the roles of Gianfranco and Salvo fuse to give a new clean face to Sicilian winemaking.

FERTILIZERS natural manure
PLANT PROTECTION copper and sulphur
WEED CONTROL mechanical
YEASTS native
GRAPES 100% estate-grown
CERTIFICATION none

Gulfi

Contrada Patrìa
tel. 0932 921654
www.gulfi.it
info@gulfi.it

75 ha - 280,000 bt   `10% discount`

PEOPLE - In the second half of the 1990s, Vito Catania, a successful northern Italian businessman, made a dream came true when he revived the activity of his family, winemakers for three generations. In the countryside round Chiaramonte he established a cellar with the aim of practicing a viticulture respectful of the environment. His decision to sign up an enologist of the caliber of Salvo Foti, a great believer in bush-training and non-invasive vinification, has proved the right one, helping determine the company's success. The farmhouse comprises an inn and a restaurant.

VINEYARDS - The cellar is situated in one of the most beautiful landscapes in the Ragusa area in the Cerasuolo di Vittoria district beneath the town of Chiaramonte Gulfi in the Val Canzeria. The vines are bush-trained in all the terroirs, despite huge differences in soil and climate. The vineyards are at least 40 years old, some more than 100.

WINES - Once again this year the wines gave us a great sense of reliability during our tastings, and it was an arduous enterprise to exclude four of the ten labels presented. We rated highly two of the four Pachino crus, each with a base of nero d'Avola: **Nero SanLorè 2008** (● 6,000 bt) and **NeroBufaleffj 2008** (● 6,000 bt), both elegant and refined, sure to improve in the course of time. Another two takes on nero d'Avola are **RossoJbleo 2011** (● 40,000 bt), juicy with a tangy finish, made with grapes from the Licodia Eubea vineyard, and **NeroJbleo 2009** (● 110,000 bt), spicier and more mouthfilling, made with grapes from a vineyard in the Val Canzeria. **Valcanzjria 2011**(○ chardonnay, carricante) has floral notes and lovely richness of flavor.

> **slow wine** **CERASUOLO DI VITTORIA 2011** (● 20,000 bt) Once again a monumental, wonderfully drinkable wine, the undisputed champion of a terroir with huge potential.

FERTILIZERS manure pellets, green manure
PLANT PROTECTION copper and sulphur
WEED CONTROL mechanical
YEASTS selected
GRAPES 100% estate-grown
CERTIFICATION organic

Poggio di Bortolone €

Frazione Roccazzo
Contrada Bortolone, 19
tel. 0932 921161
www.poggiodibortolone.it
info@poggiodibortolone.it

15 ha - 70,000 bt · **10% discount**

PEOPLE - For four generations now the Cosenza family has dedicated itself to wine- and olive-growing. Modernization of the company began under Ignazio in 1980, the year in which the company bottled its first Cerasuolo label. For some time now, Ignazio has been assisted in the management by his son Pierluigi, a graduate in agronomy who has picked up lots of experience in the vineyard and in the cellar working with enologist Nino Di Marco.

VINEYARDS - The company vineyards, encircled by secular olive trees of rare beauty, are managed with respect for the environment without the use of chemical or synthetic treatments. The grapes cultivated are nero d'Avola and frappato, classics in this corner of Sicily, together with a few international varieties. The soil is typical of the countryside of Chiaramonte Gulfi, hence calcareous with traces of sand and pebbles.

WINES - A welcome new entry in the range was **Frappato 2010** (● 8,000 bt), which has a bouquet of red berries with mineral notes and an assertive, extremely enjoyable palate. As impeccable as ever, Cerasuolo di Vittoria Cl. Poggio di Bortolone 2009 (● 15,000 bt) is typical and ultra-elegant. In view of the price, for us it's an excellent Everyday Wine. We were also intrigued by **Petitverdò 2008** (● petit verdot; 5,000 bt) with its mineral, animal notes and tannic, salty, leisurely palate. **Addamanera 2010** (● cabernet sauvignon, syrah; 15,000 bt) is fruity with pleasantly refreshing flavor. **Pigi 2007** (● 6,000 bt), made with the same international grapes and well aged, relies on good acidity and sweetness.

Marabino

Contrada Buonivini
tel. 335 5284101
www.marabino.it
info@marabino.it

27 ha - 135,000 bt

PEOPLE - The company is run with commitment and passion by Pierpaolo Messina, son of a well-known Siracusa businessman who formed the Marabino farming enterprise about ten years ago. The project was geared to environmental sustainability right from the outset, as demonstrated by the recent shift to biodynamics. It relies on the critical and professional support of enologist Salvatore Marino and agronomist Luca Gentile.

VINEYARDS - You reach the Buonivini district, near Noto, from the Rosolini-Pachino provincial highway. It's here that the farm buildings and almost all the vineyards are situated — the rest are in the Baroni district — alongside olive groves, orchards and green meadows with hedges and flowers, proof of the company's pledge to protect biodiversity. Near the cellar are some of the oldest vines — planted over 40 years ago, all bush-trained — of grapes locally known as pachinese or impupato.

WINES - Production is almost entirely centered round monovarietal wines. One such is the value-for-money Noto Nero d'Avola 2010 (● 80,000 bt), which has aromas of licorice and carobs with powerful structure, just the right acidity and enjoyable drinkability. It's an excellent Everyday Wine. We were also attracted by **Eloro Pachino Archimede Ris. 2009** (● nero d'Avola; 15,000 bt), which combines ripe fruit with faint hints of oak on the nose and follows up with a spacious, juicy palate. With its bouquet of aromatic herbs, its great structure and richness of flavor, **Eureka 2011** (○ chardonnay; 23,000 bt) confirms the positive impression we received from the previous vintage. **Eloro Rosato Rosa Nera 2011** (◉ nero d'Avola; 6,000 bt) has hints of fruit and forthright tannins.

FERTILIZERS mineral, natural manure
PLANT PROTECTION copper and sulphur
WEED CONTROL mechanical
YEASTS native
GRAPES 100% estate-grown
CERTIFICATION none

FERTILIZERS biodynamic preparations, green manure
PLANT PROTECTION copper and sulphur
WEED CONTROL mechanical
YEASTS native
GRAPES 100% estate-grown
CERTIFICATION organic

Cos

S.P. 3 Acate-Chiaramonte, Km. 14,500
tel. 0932 876145
www.cosvittoria.it
info@cosvittoria.it

30 ha - 190,000 bt   **10% discount**

66 Terroir, biodynamics, passion, reliability — just some of the many words we could use to describe this Vittoria winery, a leader in the cerasuolo renaissance 99

PEOPLE - The Cos farm was founded in 1980 by three young friends, Giambattista Cilia, Cirino Strano and Giusto Occhipinti. Since then it has made giant steps forward and is now one of the best established wineries in Vittoria. The enologist is Jaques Mell.

VINEYARDS - The vineyards are managed naturally and pragmatically using biodynamic methods that respect the land. All over 20 years old, they are spread around the heart of cerasuolo, between Acate and Vittoria, in the Bastonaca and Fontane districts. A perfectly restored 19th-century farmhouse accommodates not only the cellar but also vacation accommodation. The company generates its own energy with a photovoltaic plant.

WINES - Cos wines are full of character. The decision to use glazed cement tanks and, increasingly, amphorae shows just how much they are seeking to exalt personality and style here. **Pithos Rosso 2010** (● nero d'Avola, frappato; 25,000 bt) is a gusty, fragrant, well-crafted wine. **Frappato 2011** (● 38,000 bt) is typical and juicy, while **Nero di Lupo 2010** (● nero d'Avola; 16,000 bt) is more on the rustic side. With its lingering, spicy notes, **Contrada 2007** (● 5,000 bt) is made with nero d'Avola grapes from vines that are more than 50 years old. **Maldafrica 2008** (● cabernet, merlot; 10,000 bt) does the grapes it's made from proud.

> **slow wine** CERASUOLO DI VITTORIA CL. 2009 (● 70,000 bt) A stalwart of the terroir. With its determined character, this label provides tangible proof of the elegance of this distinguished Sicilian denomination.

FERTILIZERS biodynamic preparations
PLANT PROTECTION copper and sulphur
WEED CONTROL mechanical
YEASTS native
GRAPES 100% estate-grown
CERTIFICATION organic

Arianna Occhipinti

Contrada Fossa di Lupo
SP68 Vittoria-Pedalino km 5,4
tel. 339 7383580
www.agricolaocchipinti.it
info@agricolaocchipinti.it

18 ha - 100,000 bt

66 All the accolades and awards for her great results over just a few years make Arianna Occhipinti a force to be reckoned with on the Italian wine scene, no longer just another hopeful. Well deserved congratulations to her and her combative approach! 99

PEOPLE - A graduate in viticulture and enology, Arianna monitors vineyard, cellar and the marketing of her winery, plus the terroir of Cerasuolo and Vittoria, of which she is an active supporter and exemplary promoter.

VINEYARDS - The winery recently extended its estate with the acquisition of new nero d'Avola and frappato vineyards in the Bombolieri district, a prolongation of Fossa di Lupo, Arianna's oldest holding. All the vineyards, including one given over to frappato over 50 years old, are cultivated with respect for the ecosystem and the landscape with techniques based on the principles of biodynamic agriculture.

WINES - A well assembled range, starting with the excellent **SP 68 2011** (● frappato, nero d'Avola; 50,000 bt), which combines drinkability, juice and softness. A fantastic Everyday Wine. Not that **Frappato 2010** (● 15.000 bt) has anything to envy it. Yet again it offers an interesting interpretation of the wine, combining typical fruity fragrance with the sensations released as a result of well-pondered aging in wood and pleasing aromatic length. The distinctive features of **Cerasuolo di Vittoria Cl. Grotte Alte 2006** (● 4,000 bt), which we tasted again after suitable aging in the bottle, are a complex, round nose and a suitably tart palate. Excellent too is **SP 68 2011** (○ moscato di Alessandria, albanello; 20,000 bt) with its sensations of spices and herbs and a sensational mineral note on the palate. **Siccagno 2009** (● nero d'Avola; 15,000 bt) is fruity with just the right measure of tannins.

FERTILIZERS biodynamic preparations, green manure
PLANT PROTECTION copper and sulphur
WEED CONTROL mechanical
YEASTS native
GRAPES 100% estate-grown
CERTIFICATION organic

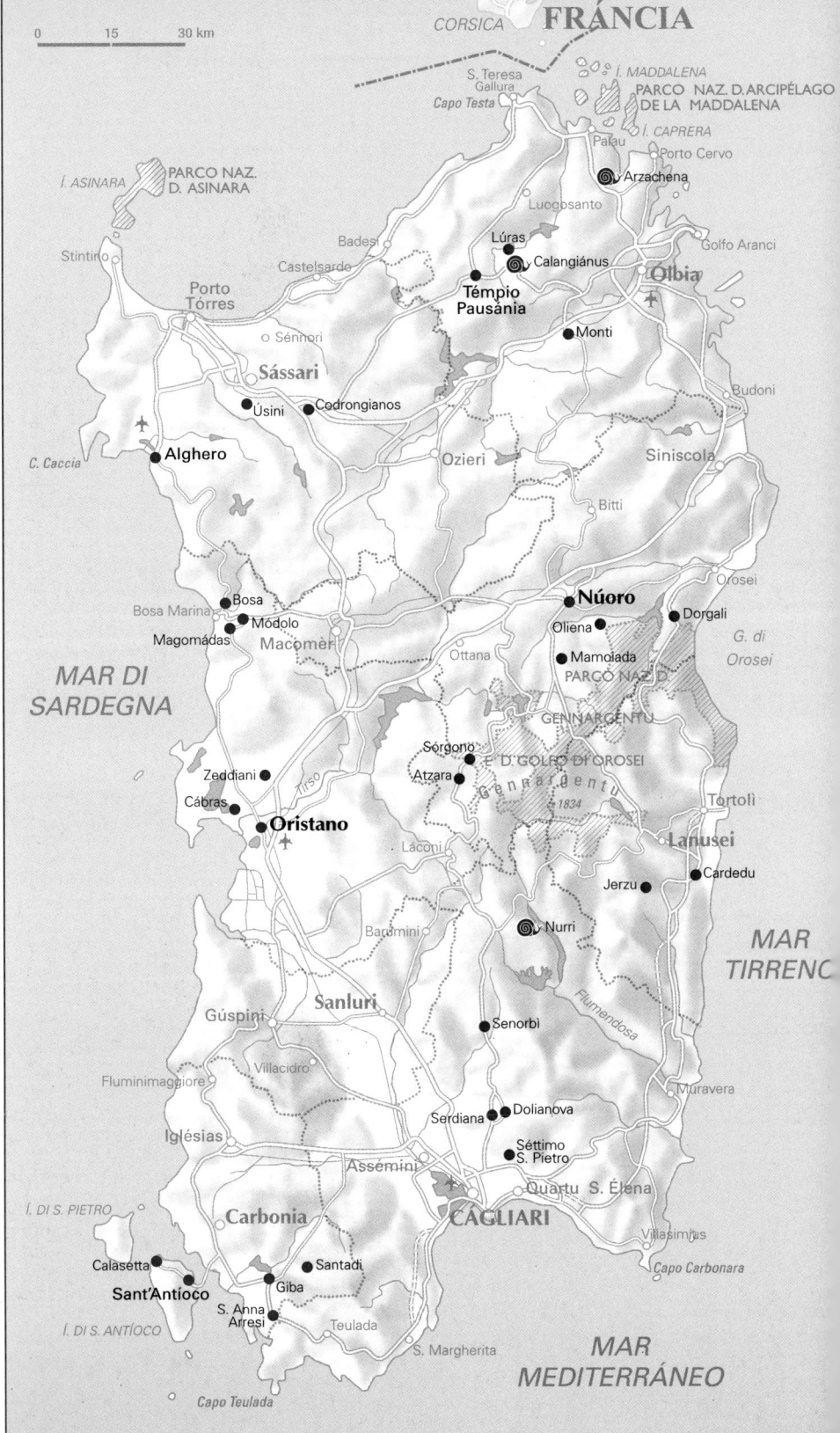

SARDINIA

As an island Sardinia boasts huge and unique climatic, geographical and geological wealth and complexity, not to mention great biodiversity with numerous traditional varieties, many of which native. A combination of all these factors plus historical and cultural specificities determines the identity of Sardinian winemaking and represent its true forte.

The main grape varieties in northern Sardinia are vermentino, which is used to make elegant wines of absolute excellence in Gallura, where the microclimate is particularly favorable, and the native torbato and cagnulari. The central zone produces magnificent versions of Malvasia di Bosa and Vernaccia di Oristano, as well as Bovale, on the west coast, the warm Mandrolisai, made with cannonau, muristellu and monica in the zone of the same name, and deep Cannonaus, the best of which are produced in the province of Nuoro and the Ogliastra district. In the south, in the province of Cagliari, they make hugely juicy reds, including Cannonau and Monica, but also fleshy whites such as Vermentino, Nuragus, Moscato and Nasco. The warm earth and sand of the Sulcis district yield wines of considerable structure and the wonderful Carignano del Sulcis.

The 2011 vintage was good, with a somewhat harsh, wet winter being followed by a pleasant, favorable spring in which the vines vegetated well. The summer was characterized by increased northwest ventilation and a drop in temperature with abundant rainfall protecting the vines from water stress. In the first ten days in August the weather returned to the standard pattern and the climate was ideal. The downy mildew attacks that had destroyed whole areas of Campidano and Sulcis in 2010 failed to return and odd cases of powdery mildew among the most sensitive varieties were well controlled by growers. The rise in temperature in the second half of August helped the grapes to ripen, bringing the harvest forward slightly and adding concentration and aroma to the wines. Sweet and sipping wines were the ones that benefited most. Production, finally, increased by 15 per cent with respect to 2010.

snails 🐌

bottles 🍾

Capichera

S.S. Arzachena-Sant'Antonio, km 4
tel. 078 980612
www.capichera.it
info@capichera.it

50 ha - 250,000 bt

66 Capichera's wines are packed with personality and very typical. The vineyards are cultivated with almost obsessive care and respect for the natural environment. The use of chemical substances is limited and, where necessary, clearly motivated by Fabrizio Ragnedda 99

PEOPLE - At the helm the charismatic Fabrizio Ragnedda, who takes care of the vineyards and the cellar, is flanked by his brothers Alberto and Mario and his sister Giovannella. Mario's son Emanuele is the sales manager.

VINEYARDS - The vineyards are beautifully tended with tidy, well-ordered vine rows. The amazing thing about the ones that surround the cellar itself is that the soil ground they grow on is virtually all granite, and using machinery under the rows would risk causing runoffs. The oldest vine rows are in the Capichera district, where the company bottled its first labels.

WINES - The 2011 vintage has yielded very potent, rich wines. With **Vermentino di Gallura Vigna'ngena 2011** (○ 50,000 bt), Fabrizio Ragnedda has produced a minor masterpiece. Extraordinarily complex aromas, richness and power, a deep, hefty and refreshingly acid bouquet for a truly Great Wine. **Capichera Classico 2010** (○ vermentino; 70,000 bt) is a rich and powerful wine with oaky, buttery after-aromas from maturation in wood, suitable for long aging. As is the magnificent **Santigaini 2008** (○ vermentino; 1,200 bt), spicy, balsamic and deep. **Viormennay 2011** (○ vermentino; 25,000 bt) is fresh and drinkable. **Assajé 2009** (● carignano; 20,000 bt) has character, fruity sweetness and depth.

FERTILIZERS	green manure
PLANT PROTECTION	chemical, copper and sulphur, organic
WEED CONTROL	chemical, mechanical
YEASTS	selected
GRAPES	5% bought in
CERTIFICATION	none

Orlando Tondini

Località San Leonardo
tel. 079 661359
www.cantinatondini.it
cantinatondini@tiscali.it

22 ha - 70,000 bt   `10% discount`

66 Antonio and Orlando's productive philosophy limits intervention and technology to a minimum. The two prefer to devote time to work in the vineyard. They reckon that, in an area as generous as theirs, careful tending of the vines is right way to come up with wines of the highest standard 99

PEOPLE - Orlando Tondini founded the company in 1991. He now runs it with the help of his family, especially his son Antonio, a graduate in enology, who collaborates in the cellar and the vineyard with great passion.

VINEYARDS - The vineyards surround the cellar on a sunlit hilltop at an altitude of about 300 meters. The soils are a breakdown of granitic rock rich in pebbles. Ventilation is constant and temperature swings are sharp — more than 20°C between day and night — conditions ideal for giving the grapes the characteristics that make Vermentino di Gallura a unique wine. Fourteen hectares of land are given over to the vermentino grape, though cannonau, nebbiolo, sangiovese and moscato are also grown.

WINES - **Cannonau di Sardegna Taroni 2010** (● cannonau, nebbiolo, sangiovese; 9,000 bt) is juicy and fruity, while the more structured **Siddaju 2009** (● nebbiolo, cannonau, carignano; 3,000 bt) is well-knit, balsamic and potent. **Lajcheddu 2010** (○ moscato; 4,500 bt), made from grapes dried on the vine, is aromatic, fresh and mineral and evokes a convincing sense of place.

> **slow wine** VERMENTINO DI GALLURA SUP. KARAGNANJ **2011** (○ 51,000 bt) A great wine from a great winemaking area. Its complex profile on the nose aromas span from aromatic herbs to fine, elegant fruitiness and the palate is fleshy, warm and distinctly mineral.

FERTILIZERS	none
PLANT PROTECTION	chemical, copper and sulphur
WEED CONTROL	mechanical
YEASTS	selected
GRAPES	100% estate-grown
CERTIFICATION	none

NUORO

Giuseppe Gabbas

Via Trieste, 59
tel. 0784 33745
www.gabbas.it
ggabbas@tiscali.it

NURRI (CA)

Panevino

Via Trento, 61
tel. 348 8241060
mancagfranco@tiscali.it

---

20 ha - 70,000 bt	**10% discount**

PEOPLE - Giuseppe Gabbas is one of the winegrowers who can be credited with raising the profile of the cannonau grape and the terroir where he works — the commune of Oliena in the Barbagia area, at an altitude of about 350 meters. It's here that the cellar is situated in the Lillovè district, which gave its name to the first wine to be bottled in 1994. Giuseppe is helped by his nephew Francesco and enologist Lorenzo Landi.

VINEYARDS - Gabbas owns 15 of his total 20 hectares and rents the other five. Besides cannonau, he also grows small amounts of other grapes such as muristellu, pascale di Cagliari, vermentino, syrah, merlot and sangiovese. The vineyards encircle the cellar on steep slopes, where there are breakdowns of granitic rock and sharp day-to-night temperature swings.

WINES - To meet market demand, this year the cellar produced **Vermentino di Sardegna Manzanile 2011** (○ 1,000 bt), which is warm in the mouth and endowed with plenty of freshness and minerality. **Cannonau di Sardegna Lillovè 2010** (● 30,000 bt) has a rich, enfolding palate and an extremely pleasant, long, elegant finish in which all the varietal aromas return — a perfect Everyday Wine. Concentrated and powerful, **Cannonau di Sardegna Arbore Ris. 2009** (● 4,000 bt) is made with grapes from the oldest vineyards and ferments on the skins for 30 days. The sweet **Avra 2008** (● cannonau; 4,000 bt) offers morello cherries and spices.

> **slow wine** CANNONAU DI SARDEGNA DULE RIS. 2009 (● 20,000 bt) Rich, spicy aromas and a well-rounded, balsamic, exceptionally elegant finish — a wine with an outstanding sense of place and a very reasonable price.

---

6 ha - 12,500 bt

“ Gianfranco compares wine to painting: the grapes are the colors and he is the artist. He wants to depict his world and interpret what the wines have to offer. Which is why, for him, intervening in the vineyard and the cellar with chemicals means interfering with nature and, worse still, not understanding a thing about wine ”

PEOPLE - Coming to Nurri and spending an afternoon with Gianfranco Manca and Elena Gallo is a revitalizing experience. Gianfranco is a true winemaker who tends his vines one by one, observing them with the eyes of someone keen to understand them and interpret them his own way.

VINEYARDS - Gianfranco's properties are situated in the lovely countryside round Nurri, some on steep land at an altitude of 700 meters. This year a new cannonau and alicante planting was harvested for the first time and the grapes from a vineyard rescued from explanting by the Manca family last year were also vinified.

WINES - The wines are always different, amazing and exciting precisely because they are unlike anything else you are used to tasting. This year one wine — the fragrant **Billukè 2011** (○ vernaccia, vermentino, trebbiano; 1,500 bt) — developed bubbles: hence well-knit, compact fizziness and no dégorgement or filtration. **Tanca li Canti 2011** (● cannonau, alicante; 1,000 bt) has scents of fruit, pleasurable flavor and gaminess. **U.V.A. 2010** (● cannonau, uve locali; 4,000 bt) has scents of red berries and good tannins. **Piccadè 2011** (● carignano, monica; 4,000 bt) has pleasant initial softness and a robust finish. **Alvas 2010** (○ vernaccia, nuragus, malvasia, semidano, nasco; 1,200 bt) combines oxidated notes with nice acidity and pleasant aromas. **Girotondo 2010** (○ girò, moscato; 800 bt) is a sipping wine.

FERTILIZERS	organic-mineral, natural manure
PLANT PROTECTION	chemical, copper and sulphur
WEED CONTROL	mechanical
YEASTS	selected
GRAPES	100% estate-grown
CERTIFICATION	none

FERTILIZERS	none
PLANT PROTECTION	copper and sulphur
WEED CONTROL	mechanical
YEASTS	native
GRAPES	100% estate-grown
CERTIFICATION	none

SANTADI (CI)

Agricola Punica

Località Barrua
tel. 0781 941012
www.agripunica.it
info@agripunica.it

65 ha - 250,000 bt

PEOPLE - The joint venture between Cantina di Santadi and Tenuta San Guido in Tuscany has given rise to Agricola Punica, a cellar that seeks to add expressiveness to a combination of the native carignano variety and international grapes such as cabernet and merlot. Here the soil, climate and grapes are conducive to the production of great reds. The CEO is Antonello Pilloni, the president Niccolò Incisa della Rocchetta, the agronomist Gianni Poeta and the enologist Umberto Trombelli, who grew up at the court of the one and only Giacomo Tachis.

VINEYARDS - Two properties combine to form the company's 65-hectare vineyard (it rents another 115 hectares): Barrùa near Santadi (22 hectares) and Narcao (43 hectares). Carignano accounts for 60% of production, while 13 hectares are given over to cabernet sauvignon e franc, and three hectares to syrah. The vines are high-trained with more Guyot than spurred cordon. The altitude ranges between 16 and 140 meters.

WINES - Production is geared to the overseas market and the style is deliberately international. It is aimed at discerning drinkers and banks on the quality of the wine in the bottle, which have fascinating sensory characteristics and offer an alternative take on the carignano grape (until recently Carignano del Sulcis was a much sought after as a blending wine for the French market). Climate and terroir make these wines unique. **Barrua 2009** (● carignano, cabernet sauvignon, merlot; 100,000 bt) is warm and deep and offers flavors and aromas ranging from cherry to tobacco to coffee. We rate this as a truly Great Wine. The headily scented **Montessu 2010** (● carignano, cabernet sauvignon e franc, merlot, syrah; 150,000 bt) is well-rounded and spicy.

SANTADI (CI)

Cantina Santadi

Via Cagliari, 78
tel. 0781 950127
www.cantinadisantadi.it
cantinadisantadi@cantinadisantadi.it

600 ha - 1,500,000 bt

PEOPLE - Presidente Antonello Pilloni and director Raffaele Cani are the pillars of one of the most active, thriving wine cooperatives in Sardinia. Adopting a system of meritocracy, the enterprise provides an income for about 200 members. Another positive result has been a generational turnover that goes against the general trend in the Sulcis area. Here children tend to take over the reins of their families' wine companies. The agronomist is Gianni Poeta, the enologist Umberto Trombelli.

VINEYARDS - Of a total of 600 hectares, 120 are situated in the valleys of Porto Pino and are planted with carignano vines, on their own roots, low bush-trained and three-spur short-pruned. It's a joy for the the eyes and the spirit to see the new plantings: small portions of cane, chosen from the best vines, which peep out of the sand facing the sea with just two gems. The members' vineyards are located in eight communes, from sea level to an altitude of 300 meters.

WINES - All the wines rest in cement tanks, the first of which were built in the 1960s. A standout white was the fresh, tangy **Nuragus di Cagliari Pedraia 2011** (○ 50,000 bt) a nice take on the awkward nuragus grape. It's a perfect Everyday Wine. **Vermentino di Sardegna Cala Silente 2011** (○ 120,000 bt) is rich, as befits any good wine of the South. The carignano-based reds stand out for their drinkability. One such is **Carignano del Sulcis Grotta Rossa 2010** (● 380,000 bt), which has nice acidity. The velvety **Carignano del Sulcis Rocca Rubia 2009** (● 400,000 bt) is a crescendo of fine aromas. The international-style **Carignano del Sulcis Terre Brune 2008** (● 90,000 bt) is beefy, heady and vibrant. The sweet **Latinia 2007** (○ nasco; 18,000 bt) caresses the nose and palate.

FERTILIZERS organic-mineral, manure pellets, natural manure	FERTILIZERS organic-mineral, manure pellets
PLANT PROTECTION chemical, copper and sulphur	PLANT PROTECTION chemical, copper and sulphur
WEED CONTROL chemical, mechanical	WEED CONTROL chemical, mechanical
YEASTS selected	YEASTS selected, native
GRAPES 100% estate-grown	GRAPES 100% estate-grown
CERTIFICATION none	CERTIFICATION none

SETTIMO SAN PIETRO (CA)

Ferruccio Deiana

Via Gialeto, 7
tel. 070 767960
www.ferrucciodeiana.it
deiana.ferruccio@tiscali.it

USINI (SS)

Chessa

Via San Giorgio
tel. 328 3747069
www.cantinechessa.it
info@cantinechessa.it

95 ha - 200,000 bt

12 ha - 40,000 bt — 10% discount

PEOPLE - Charismatic Ferruccio Deiana, a smooth, reliable operator blessed with enviable energy, is the heart and soul of this company which he built up in the 1990s around his family's vineyards. The present cellar dates from 1995. He is helped on the administrative side by his wife Maria Grazia Perra and by his son Dario, who is following in his father's footsteps by studying enology. The consultant enologist is Riccardo Cotarella, the agronomist Carlo Pisu.

VINEYARDS - Ferruccio in person took us round the company's two vast properties at Settimo San Pietro (38 hectares to which another 15) and Serdiana (42 hectares). The first is situated at an altitude of 120 meters in a well-ventilated area with medium-texture and granite terrains, the second on more calcareous soil in the Sibiola and Staniu Saliu areas.

WINES - This year, alas, the new vintages of some wines of the superior line — always top-notch in the past — were not released. Which is why we had a second tasting of the excellent Ajana 2008 and Pluminus 2009. Vermentino di Sardegna Arvali 2011 (O 55,000 bt) appeals for its nicely herby bouquet and richness of flavor. It's a perfect Everyday Wine. **Vermentino di Sardegna Donnikalia 2011** (O 90,000 bt) has aromas of tropical fruit. Of the wines from the higher, older vineyards, the most outstanding is the red **Monica di Sardegna Karel 2010** (● 85,000 bt), which has delicious fruit. **Cannonau di Sardegna Sileno 2009** (● 90,000 bt) and **Cannonau di Sardegna Sileno Ris. 2008** (● 15,000 bt) are supported by good structure. The first is softer, the second has a tannic finish. The super-scented, sweet **Oirad 2010** (O 7,000 bt) is a blend of nasco, malvasia and moscato grapes.

PEOPLE - Giovanna Chessa comes from a family of viticulturists and has followed in his father Luigi's footsteps. Rightly so, judging by the results. His is a young company — it produced its first bottle in 2005 — but, thanks to painstaking work in the vineyard and cellar, it has asserted itself successfully in a matter of just a few years.

VINEYARDS - The company's 12 hectares are situated on limestone and clay soils. The first is to be found in the beautiful, sunny property of Sant'Andria (seven hectares at an altitude of 280 meters, a hectare of which is 45 years old and low bush-trained), ideal for moscato and vermentino. Most of the cagnulari vines grow on the clayier soils and are high-trained.

WINES - We were bowled over by this fantastic range of wines with their sense of place and amazing character and flavor. From the Sant'Andria vineyard comes a Great Wine — **Kentàles 2010** (O moscato; 2,500 bt). The grapes are hand-picked and selected and dried in the vineyard. Beautifully scented and leisurely on the palate, it owes its extraordinary drinkability to its freshness. **Vermentino di Sardegna Mattàriga 2011** (O 18,000 bt) strikes a remarkable balance between texture and freshness. Moving on to the reds, **Cagnulari 2010** (● cagnulari; 18,000 bt) impresses for its stylish bouquet of aromatic herbs and poise. **Lugherra 2010** (● cannonau, cagnulari; 2,600 bt) has a very spicy, fruity bouquet with a warm palate and varietal finish.

FERTILIZERS none	FERTILIZERS organic-mineral
PLANT PROTECTION chemical, copper and sulphur	PLANT PROTECTION chemical, copper and sulphur
WEED CONTROL mechanical	WEED CONTROL mechanical
YEASTS selected, native	YEASTS selected
GRAPES 100% estate-grown	GRAPES 100% estate-grown
CERTIFICATION none	CERTIFICATION none

INDEX of the wineries

INDEX of places

TASTING notes